2000
America's
Top-Rated Cities:
A Statistical Handbook

Volume 4: Eastern Region

Grey House
Publishing

LAKEVILLE, CT 06039

PUBLISHER: Leslie Mackenzie
EDITOR: David Garoogian
EDITORIAL DIRECTOR: Laura Mars
EDITORIAL ASSISTANT: Robin Williams
PRODUCTION MANAGER: Timothy Cushman
MARKET RESEARCH: Jessica Moody
GRAPHIC DESIGNER: Deb Fletcher

Grey House Publishing, Inc.
Pocket Knife Square
Lakeville, CT 06039
860.435.0868
FAX 860.435.6613
http://www.greyhouse.com

While every effort has been made to ensure the reliability of the information presented in this publication, Grey House Publishing neither guarantees the accuracy of the data contained herein nor assumes any responsibility for errors, omissions or discrepancies. Grey House accepts no payment for listing; inclusion in the publication of any organization, agency, institution, publication, service or individual does not imply endorsement of the editors or publisher.

Errors brought to the attention of the publisher and verified to the satisfaction of the publisher will be corrected in future editions.

First edition published 1992
Seventh edition published 1999

Printed in the USA

Library of Congress Cataloging in Publication Data available

4-Volume Set	ISBN 1-891482-50-5
Volume 1	ISBN 1-891482-51-3
Volume 2	ISBN 1-891482-52-1
Volume 3	ISBN 1-891482-53-X
Volume 4	**ISBN 1-891482-54-8**

Table of Contents

Akron, Ohio

Baltimore, Maryland

Boston, Massachusetts

Charlotte, North Carolina

Cincinnati, Ohio

Cleveland, Ohio

Greensboro, North Carolina

Lexington, Kentucky

Louisville, Kentucky

Manchester, New Hampshire

New York, New York

Norfolk, Virginia

Philadelphia, Pennsylvania

Pittsburgh, Pennsylvania

Providence, Rhode Island

Raleigh, North Carolina

Richmond, Virginia

Rochester, New York

Washington, DC

Introduction

Welcome to *America's Top-Rated Cities, A Statistical Handbook, 2000,* a current and concise statistical profile of 76 cities that have received high marks for their business and living environment. This 7th edition of *ATRC*, previously published by Universal Reference Publications, incorporates information from hundreds of resources into one, easy-to-use format. It combines magazine rankings (*Money, Fortune, Entrepreneur, Sales & Marketing Management, Working Woman*, etc.) latest Federal, state and local statistics, published newspaper and magazine reports, and web site data to fill more than 60 charts and tables for each city.

Each of the four volumes is approximately 400 pages, and comprises a different region of the country – Southern, Western, Central and Eastern, and each region includes 19 cities, all with populations over 100,000.

Every year, our editors review hundreds of sources to develop the list of top cities in each region, invariably dropping some and adding others. This year's edition has 17 new cities not included last year – five Southern (**Birmingham, Chattanooga, Columbia, Jackson, Memphis**), five Eastern (**Akron, Louisville, Manchester, Providence, Rochester**), four Central (**Gary, Lansing, Omaha, Wichita**), and three Western (**Albuquerque, Reno, Spokane**). Plus, the cities from last year that made this year's cut have been revised and refreshed with new and updated data.

Within each volume, city chapters are arranged alphabetically, and each is divided into two sections: Business Environment and Living Environment. Each chapter begins with a background about the city, and narrative comments about changes in its environmental, political, or employment atmosphere that occurred in the past year. You'll learn, for example, that Las Vegas is cleaning up its image, how Chicago's mayor – an avid cyclist – supports his fellow riders, and the Y2K-ready measures the cities are taking.

There is data on cost of living, finances, taxes, population, employment and earnings, commercial real estate, education, major employers, media, crime, climate, professional sports teams and more. In most cases, you'll find comparisons between Metropolitan Statistical Areas (MSA) and U.S. census figures.

In addition to the comprehensive chapters, each volume contains four appendices: **Appendix A, Comparative Statistics:** City by city comparison of more than 50 categories that gives not just an overview of the city, but a broad profile of each geographic region of the country.

Appendix B, Metropolitan Statistical Areas (MSA): Includes the counties (and in some cases, state) that combine to form each city's MSA – an official designation used to define the area in terms of population, finance, economy, etc.

Appendix C, Chambers of Commerce and Economic Development Organizations: Includes address, phone numbers and fax numbers of these additional resources to help the readers to get further, more detailed information on each city.

Appendix D, State Departments of Labor and Employment: Another source of additional, more specific economic and employment data for each city, with address and phone numbers for easy access.

As in all previous editions, the material provided by public and private agencies and organizations was supplemented by numerous library sources and Internet sites. The editors thank everyone who responded to our requests for information, especially the Chambers of Commerce, Economic Development Organizations and Labor Market Information groups.

America's Top-Rated Cities is designed for a wide range of readers: private individuals considering relocating a residence or business; professionals considering expanding their business or changing careers; corporations considering relocation, opening up additional offices or creating new divisions; government agencies; general and market researchers; real estate consultants; human resource personnel; urban planners; investors; and urban government students.

Grey House Publishing has also acquired from Universal Reference Publications the following titles: *America's Top-Rated Smaller Cities, Health & Environment in America's Top-Rated Cities* and *Crime in America's Top-Rated Cities*, developed in the spirit of offering a series of comprehensive statistical reference books about America's top cities. Grey House is revising and updating each of these and will offer the *Smaller Cities* and *Crime* titles in the Spring of 2000, and *Environment* in the Fall of that year.

As always, we welcome your comments and suggestions for continuous improvement.

Akron, Ohio

Background

A variety of Native American tribes, including the Chippewa, Delaware, and Erie, inhabited Northeast Ohio. White settlers began to arrive in the early nineteenth century. General Simon Perkins searched the area for a suitable town site along the planned Ohio and Erie Canal. He and Paul Williams found a site on a ridge, and named the former Akron, after the Greek word akros, which means high point.

Workers completed the canal up to Akron in 1827, and five years later the entire waterway was finished, connecting the Cuyahoga River to the Ohio. In 1840, the Pennsylvania and Ohio Canal opened in Akron, giving the city easier access to Pittsburgh. Being at the hub of two canals made Akron a center of commerce and industry for the area. An early source of wealth came from exploiting local deposits of clay. As might be expected, the building of canal boats was of importance. In 1863, in the midst of the Civil War, a German immigrant, Ferdinand Schumacher, using waterpower from the canal, set up a gristmill, and the city soon became known for the production of cereal.

But Akron's claim to fame would be rubber production. This began in 1870 when Benjamin F. Goodrich moved his New York rubber plant to the Buckeye State, the first such facility west of the Allegheny Mountains. Other rubber manufacturers followed in the next few years: Goodyear, Firestone, and General Tire. Akron quickly earned the sobriquet of Rubber Capital of the World. The invention of the automobile and its subsequent popularity, made Akron prosperous as it produced the rubber wheels for the vehicles. In the 1930s, Goodyear began building blimps for the Navy, and the company still maintains a small fleet.

At the present time, the city's rubber factories no longer produce tires for cars and trucks. Rubber production is still important, however, and much research regarding rubber takes place in Akron. The Akron industries are now much more diverse and include nuclear power, chemicals, plastics, metals and metalworking, aerospace, construction, and automotive.

Akron is also an important center in research and development of polymers and four-fifths of all such research is done in the area. Leading the way is the Institute of Polymer Science of the University of Akron. Four hundred companies here are involved in the polymer industry, including the Edison Polymer Innovation Corporation.

The citizens of Akron engage in efforts to better their city. For instance, the Downtown Akron Partnership is an organization whose aim is to revitalize the city's core. The city government, in the late 1990s, devised a project, Imagine.Akron 2025, to improve its ability to serve its citizens.

Lake Erie, just forty miles to the north, has a tremendous effect on Akron's climate. Lake effect snows can dump nearly fifty inches of snow in the area during the winter months, much of it during short but intense storms. Rainfall tends to be around thirty-six inches a year. Winter temperatures range from the teens to the forties. Summers tend to be moderate, with temperatures ranging from the fifties to the eighties, often with high humidity.

General Rankings and Evaluative Comments

- Akron was ranked #3 out of 24 mid-sized, midwestern metropolitan areas in *Money's* 1998 survey of "The Best Places to Live in America." The survey was conducted by first contacting 512 representative households nationwide and asking them to rank 37 quality-of-life factors on a scale of 1 to 10. Next, a demographic profile was compiled on the 300 largest metropolitan statistical areas in the U.S. The numbers were crunched together to arrive at an overall ranking (things Americans consider most important, like clean air and water, low crime and good schools, received extra weight). Unlike previous years, the 1998 rankings were broken down by region (northeast, midwest, south, west) and population size (100,000 to 249,999; 250,000 to 999,999; 1 million plus). The city had a nationwide ranking of #231 out of 300 in 1997 and #284 out of 300 in 1996. *Money, July 1998; Money, July 1997; Money, September 1996*

- *Ladies Home Journal* ranked America's 200 largest cities based on the qualities women care about most. Akron ranked #170 out of 200. Criteria: low crime rate, well-paying jobs, quality health and child care, good public schools, the presence of women in government, size of the gender wage gap, number of sexual-harassment and discrimination complaints filed, unemployment and divorce rates, commute times, population density, number of houses of worship, parks and cultural offerings, number of women's health specialists, how well a community's women cared for themselves, complexion kindness index based on UV radiation levels, odds of finding affordable fashions, rental rates for romance movies, champagne sales and other matters of the heart. *Ladies Home Journal, November 1998*

- Zero Population Growth ranked 229 cities in terms of children's health, safety, and economic well-being. Akron was ranked #64 out of 112 independent cities (cities with populations greater than 100,000 which were neither Major Cities nor Suburbs/Outer Cities) and was given a grade of C. Criteria: total population, percent of population under 18 years of age, household language, percent population change, percent of births to teens, infant mortality rate, percent of low birth weights, dropout rate, enrollment in preprimary school, violent and property crime rates, unemployment rate, percent of children in poverty, percent of owner occupied units, number of bad air days, percent of public transportation commuters, and average travel time to work. *Zero Population Growth, Children's Environmental Index, Fall 1999*

- Reliastar Financial Corp. ranked the 125 largest metropolitan areas according to the general financial security of residents. Akron was ranked #52 (tie) out of 125 with a score of 3.2. The score indicates the percentage a metropolitan area is above or below the metropolitan norm. A metro area with a score of 10.6 is 10.6% above the metro average. Criteria: Earnings and Wealth Potential (household income, education, net assets, cost of living); Safety Net (health insurance, retirement savings, life insurance, income support programs); Personal Threats (unemployment rate, low-income households, crime rate); Community Economic Vitality (cost of community services, job quality, job creation, housing costs). *Reliastar Financial Corp., "The Best Cities to Earn and Save Money," 1999 Edition*

Business Environment

STATE ECONOMY

State Economic Profile

"Ohio's expansion has started to decelerate. OH is expected to lag the nation in growth for some time. The slowdown in employment growth is concentrated in the manufacturing sector and outside of OH's larger metro areas. OH's weak demographic trends will constrain job growth and the housing market.

OH manufacturing shed about 7,000 jobs in 1998. A large share of these losses were in the Cleveland and Columbus areas, while Cincinnati managed to add a small number of manufacturing jobs. Job growth in the services sectors, particularly business, financial and health services, has helped to offset a slowdown in manufacturing in these urban areas. Bank merger and acquisition activity has resulted in jobs being shifted from rural and smaller areas to the larger metropolitan areas.

While OH's rural areas have suffered from a declining employment base, economic activity has also been shifting from the northern part of the state toward the middle and south. Last year's employment growth for Cincinnati was 2.5%, compared to only 1.6% for Columbus and 1.6% for Cleveland. Population growth has followed a similar pattern, although the state as a whole is among one of the weakest in the nation, losing a considerable number of younger households.

Ohio's housing market had a strong 1998, with sales up 8.6% and single family permits up 3.2%. Price appreciation was just below the nation and will likely remain modest given the increase in construction. Both construction and sales should contract in 1999 and 2000. Prices are likely to rise the most in Cincinnati, where construction has been modest and job growth strongest." *National Association of Realtors, Economic Profiles: The Fifty States and the District of Columbia, http://nar.realtor.com/databank/profiles.htm*

IMPORTS/EXPORTS

Total Export Sales

Area	1994 ($000)	1995 ($000)	1996 ($000)	1997 ($000)	% Chg. 1994-97	% Chg. 1996-97
MSA[1]	1,606,289	1,931,665	2,260,275	2,353,272	46.5	4.1
U.S.	512,415,609	583,030,524	622,827,063	687,597,999	34.2	10.4

Note: (1) Metropolitan Statistical Area - see Appendix A for areas included
Source: U.S. Department of Commerce, International Trade Association, Metropolitan Area Exports: An Export Performance Report on Over 250 U.S. Cities, November 10, 1998

CITY FINANCES

City Government Finances

Component	FY92 ($000)	FY92 (per capita $)
Revenue	225,593	1,017.84
Expenditure	231,949	1,046.52
Debt Outstanding	152,321	687.25
Cash & Securities	66,180	298.60

Source: U.S. Bureau of the Census, City Government Finances: 1991-92

City Government Revenue by Source

Source	FY92 ($000)	FY92 (per capita $)	FY92 (%)
From Federal Government	22,076	99.60	9.8
From State Governments	17,739	80.04	7.9
From Local Governments	736	3.32	0.3
Property Taxes	18,245	82.32	8.1
General Sales Taxes	0	0.00	0.0
Selective Sales Taxes	0	0.00	0.0
Income Taxes	70,715	319.06	31.3
Current Charges	46,276	208.79	20.5
Utility/Liquor Store	25,414	114.66	11.3
Employee Retirement[1]	0	0.00	0.0
Other	24,392	110.05	10.8

Note: (1) Excludes "city contributions," classified as "nonrevenue," intragovernmental transfers.
Source: U.S. Bureau of the Census, City Government Finances: 1991-92

City Government Expenditures by Function

Function	FY92 ($000)	FY92 (per capita $)	FY92 (%)
Educational Services	0	0.00	0.0
Employee Retirement[1]	0	0.00	0.0
Environment/Housing	74,200	334.78	32.0
Government Administration	17,295	78.03	7.5
Interest on General Debt	9,606	43.34	4.1
Public Safety	52,447	236.63	22.6
Social Services	7,309	32.98	3.2
Transportation	24,981	112.71	10.8
Utility/Liquor Store	32,398	146.18	14.0
Other	13,713	61.87	5.9

Note: (1) Payments to beneficiaries including withdrawal of contributions.
Source: U.S. Bureau of the Census, City Government Finances: 1991-92

Municipal Bond Ratings

Area	Moody's	S & P
Akron	A2	n/a

Note: n/a not available; n/r not rated
Source: Moody's Bond Record, 6/99

POPULATION

Population Growth

Area	1980	1990	% Chg. 1980-90	July 1998 Estimate	% Chg. 1990-98
City	237,177	223,019	-6.0	215,712	-3.3
MSA[1]	660,328	657,575	-0.4	687,664	4.6
U.S.	226,545,805	248,765,170	9.8	270,299,000	8.7

Note: (1) Metropolitan Statistical Area - see Appendix A for areas included;
July 1998 MSA population estimate was calculated by the editors
Source: 1980/1990 Census of Housing and Population, Summary Tape File 3C;
Census Bureau Population Estimates 1998

Population Characteristics

Race	City 1980 Population	%	City 1990 Population	%	% Chg. 1980-90	MSA[1] 1990 Population	%
White	182,664	77.0	164,868	73.9	-9.7	584,196	88.8
Black	52,634	22.2	54,395	24.4	3.3	64,736	9.8
Amer Indian/Esk/Aleut	333	0.1	614	0.3	84.4	1,462	0.2
Asian/Pacific Islander	1,072	0.5	2,550	1.1	137.9	6,052	0.9
Other	474	0.2	592	0.3	24.9	1,129	0.2
Hispanic Origin[2]	1,172	0.5	1,503	0.7	28.2	3,844	0.6

Note: (1) Metropolitan Statistical Area - see Appendix A for areas included;
(2) people of Hispanic origin can be of any race
Source: 1980/1990 Census of Housing and Population, Summary Tape File 3C

Ancestry

Area	German	Irish	English	Italian	U.S.	French	Polish	Dutch
City	28.1	16.0	11.7	6.8	5.3	2.6	2.7	2.3
MSA[1]	35.0	18.8	15.5	8.6	4.6	3.1	4.7	2.9
U.S.	23.3	15.6	13.1	5.9	5.3	4.2	3.8	2.5

Note: Figures are percentages and include persons that reported multiple ancestry (eg. if a person
reported being Irish and Italian, they were included in both columns); (1) Metropolitan Statistical Area -
see Appendix A for areas included
Source: 1990 Census of Population and Housing, Summary Tape File 3C

Age

Area	Median Age (Years)	Age Distribution (%) Under 5	Under 18	18-24	25-44	45-64	65+	80+
City	32.5	7.5	24.5	12.1	31.6	16.9	14.8	3.4
MSA[1]	33.4	6.9	24.5	11.6	31.9	19.2	12.8	2.7
U.S.	32.9	7.3	25.6	10.5	32.6	18.7	12.5	2.8

Note: (1) Metropolitan Statistical Area - see Appendix A for areas included
Source: 1990 Census of Population and Housing, Summary Tape File 3C

Male/Female Ratio

Area	Number of males per 100 females (all ages)	Number of males per 100 females (18 years old+)
City	88.7	84.7
MSA[1]	92.4	88.8
U.S.	95.0	91.9

Note: (1) Metropolitan Statistical Area - see Appendix A for areas included
Source: 1990 Census of Population, General Population Characteristics

INCOME

Per Capita/Median/Average Income

Area	Per Capita ($)	Median Household ($)	Average Household ($)
City	12,015	22,279	29,376
MSA[1]	13,997	29,280	36,513
U.S.	14,420	30,056	38,453

Note: All figures are for 1989; (1) Metropolitan Statistical Area - see Appendix A for areas included
Source: 1990 Census of Population and Housing, Summary Tape File 3C

Household Income Distribution by Race

Income ($)	City (%)					U.S. (%)				
	Total	White	Black	Other	Hisp.[1]	Total	White	Black	Other	Hisp.[1]
Less than 5,000	10.2	7.2	20.0	19.0	12.3	6.2	4.8	15.2	8.6	8.8
5,000 - 9,999	13.3	11.9	17.9	19.3	17.4	9.3	8.6	14.2	9.9	11.1
10,000 - 14,999	10.7	10.9	10.0	7.5	8.2	8.8	8.5	11.0	9.8	11.0
15,000 - 24,999	20.8	21.6	18.2	17.8	11.9	17.5	17.3	18.9	18.5	20.5
25,000 - 34,999	16.8	17.8	13.6	14.8	23.6	15.8	16.1	14.2	15.4	16.4
35,000 - 49,999	14.7	15.7	11.5	10.6	11.9	17.9	18.6	13.3	16.1	16.0
50,000 - 74,999	8.9	9.6	6.9	5.7	9.0	15.0	15.8	9.3	13.4	11.1
75,000 - 99,999	2.5	2.8	1.5	1.8	5.6	5.1	5.5	2.6	4.7	3.1
100,000+	2.0	2.4	0.5	3.6	0.0	4.4	4.8	1.3	3.7	1.9

Note: All figures are for 1989; (1) people of Hispanic origin can be of any race
Source: 1990 Census of Population and Housing, Summary Tape File 3C

Effective Buying Income

Area	Per Capita ($)	Median Household ($)	Average Household ($)
City	14,488	27,173	35,222
MSA[1]	17,264	34,762	44,532
U.S.	16,803	34,536	45,243

Note: Data as of 1/1/99; (1) Metropolitan Statistical Area - see Appendix A for areas included
Source: Standard Rate & Data Service, Newspaper Advertising Source, 9/99

Effective Household Buying Income Distribution

Area	% of Households Earning						
	$10,000 -$19,999	$20,000 -$34,999	$35,000 -$49,999	$50,000 -$74,999	$75,000 -$99,000	$100,000 -$124,999	$125,000 and up
City	19.3	25.4	16.9	13.9	3.8	1.3	1.4
MSA[1]	15.5	22.9	18.6	19.4	7.0	2.3	2.3
U.S.	16.0	22.6	18.2	18.9	7.2	2.4	2.7

Note: Data as of 1/1/99; (1) Metropolitan Statistical Area - see Appendix A for areas included
Source: Standard Rate & Data Service, Newspaper Advertising Source, 9/99

Poverty Rates by Race and Age

Area	Total (%)	By Race (%)				By Age (%)		
		White	Black	Other	Hisp.[2]	Under 5 years old	Under 18 years old	65 years and over
City	20.5	15.0	36.0	35.3	25.7	35.6	31.2	11.4
MSA[1]	12.1	9.5	34.2	23.0	15.6	20.1	17.1	8.7
U.S.	13.1	9.8	29.5	23.1	25.3	20.1	18.3	12.8

Note: Figures show the percent of people living below the poverty line in 1989. The average poverty threshold was $12,674 for a family of four in 1989; (1) Metropolitan Statistical Area - see Appendix A for areas included; (2) people of Hispanic origin can be of any race
Source: 1990 Census of Population and Housing, Summary Tape File 3C

EMPLOYMENT

Labor Force and Employment

Area	Civilian Labor Force			Workers Employed		
	Jun. 1998	Jun. 1999	% Chg.	Jun. 1998	Jun. 1999	% Chg.
City	110,736	115,170	4.0	104,318	108,318	3.8
MSA[1]	354,940	369,193	4.0	340,651	353,716	3.8
U.S.	138,798,000	140,666,000	1.3	132,265,000	134,395,000	1.6

Note: Data is not seasonally adjusted and covers workers 16 years of age and older;
(1) Metropolitan Statistical Area - see Appendix A for areas included
Source: Bureau of Labor Statistics, http://stats.bls.gov

Unemployment Rate

Area	1998						1999					
	Jul.	Aug.	Sep.	Oct.	Nov.	Dec.	Jan.	Feb.	Mar.	Apr.	May.	Jun.
City	5.1	4.8	5.4	5.1	5.4	5.2	6.7	6.6	6.1	5.6	5.0	5.9
MSA[1]	3.7	3.4	3.7	3.6	3.8	3.6	4.8	4.7	4.4	4.0	3.5	4.2
U.S.	4.7	4.5	4.4	4.2	4.1	4.0	4.8	4.7	4.4	4.1	4.0	4.5

Note: Data is not seasonally adjusted and covers workers 16 years of age and older; all figures are percentages; (1) Metropolitan Statistical Area - see Appendix A for areas included
Source: Bureau of Labor Statistics, http://stats.bls.gov

Employment by Industry

Sector	MSA[1]		U.S.
	Number of Employees	Percent of Total	Percent of Total
Services	92,700	28.2	30.4
Retail Trade	62,200	18.9	17.7
Government	44,600	13.6	15.6
Manufacturing	64,100	19.5	14.3
Finance/Insurance/Real Estate	13,600	4.1	5.9
Wholesale Trade	20,600	6.3	5.4
Transportation/Public Utilities	15,200	4.6	5.3
Construction	15,000	4.6	5.0
Mining	500	0.2	0.4

Note: Figures cover non-farm employment as of 6/99 and are not seasonally adjusted;
(1) Metropolitan Statistical Area - see Appendix A for areas included
Source: Bureau of Labor Statistics, http://stats.bls.gov

Employment by Occupation

Occupation Category	City (%)	MSA[1] (%)	U.S. (%)
White Collar	54.8	57.7	58.1
Executive/Admin./Management	9.7	12.1	12.3
Professional	11.4	13.7	14.1
Technical & Related Support	4.1	4.0	3.7
Sales	11.8	12.1	11.8
Administrative Support/Clerical	17.7	15.9	16.3
Blue Collar	27.4	27.6	26.2
Precision Production/Craft/Repair	10.6	11.7	11.3
Machine Operators/Assem./Insp.	8.9	7.9	6.8
Transportation/Material Movers	3.8	4.0	4.1
Cleaners/Helpers/Laborers	4.1	4.0	3.9
Services	17.0	13.6	13.2
Farming/Forestry/Fishing	0.8	1.0	2.5

Note: Figures cover employed persons 16 years old and over;
(1) Metropolitan Statistical Area - see Appendix A for areas included
Source: 1990 Census of Population and Housing, Summary Tape File 3C

Occupational Employment Projections: 1996 - 2006

Occupations Expected to Have the Largest Job Growth (ranked by numerical growth)	Fast-Growing Occupations[1] (ranked by percent growth)
1. Cashiers	1. Systems analysts
2. Salespersons, retail	2. Occupational therapy assistants
3. Systems analysts	3. Desktop publishers
4. General managers & top executives	4. Paralegals
5. Truck drivers, light	5. Physical therapy assistants and aides
6. Registered nurses	6. Medical assistants
7. Food preparation workers	7. Personal and home care aides
8. Nursing aides/orderlies/attendants	8. Home health aides
9. Home health aides	9. Physical therapists
10. Marketing & sales, supervisors	10. Occupational therapists

Note: Projections cover Ohio; (1) Excludes occupations with total job growth less than 300
Source: U.S. Department of Labor, Employment and Training Administration, America's Labor Market Information System (ALMIS)

TAXES

Major State and Local Tax Rates

State Corp. Income (%)	State Personal Income (%)	Residential Property (effective rate per $100)	Sales & Use		State Gasoline (cents/ gallon)	State Cigarette (cents/ pack)
			State (%)	Local (%)		
5.1 - 8.5[a]	0.673 - 6.799	n/a	5.0	0.75	22.0	24.0

Note: Personal/corporate income, sales, gasoline and cigarette tax rates as of January 1999. Property tax rates as of 1997; (a) Or 4.0 mils times the value of the taxpayer's issued and outstanding share of stock ($150K max). An additional litter tax is imposed equal to 0.11% on the first $50,000 of taxable income, 0.22% on income over $50,000; or 0.14 mills on net worth
Source: Federation of Tax Administrators, www.taxadmin.org; Washington D.C. Department of Finance and Revenue, Tax Rates and Tax Burdens in the District of Columbia: A Nationwide Comparison, July 1998; Chamber of Commerce, 1999

Total Taxes Per Capita and as a Percent of Income

Area	Per Capita Income ($)	Per Capita Taxes ($)			Percent of Income (%)		
		Total	Federal	State/ Local	Total	Federal	State/ Local
Ohio	26,684	9,354	6,322	3,033	35.1	23.7	11.4
U.S.	27,876	9,881	6,690	3,191	35.4	24.0	11.4

Note: Figures are for 1998
Source: Tax Foundation, www.taxfoundation.org

COMMERCIAL REAL ESTATE

Industrial Market

Location	Total Space (sq. ft.)	Vacant Space (sq. ft.)	Vac. Rate (%)	Under Constr. (sq. ft.)	Net Absorp. (sq. ft.)	Gross Lease ($/sq.ft./yr.)
Central City	24,800,000	660,635	2.7	450,000	74,598	2.25-5.25
Suburban	26,400,000	702,505	2.7	1,200,000	1,654,888	2.25-5.50

Note: Data as of 10/98 and covers Akron; n/a not available
Source: Society of Industrial and Office Realtors, 1999 Comparative Statistics of Industrial and Office Real Estate Markets

"The forces of globalization and securitization must enter into the local market outlook for 1999. Capital goods exporting is expected to be very slow in the coming year, particularly in the face of the Asian crisis. Markets like Akron, which are important producers of capital goods components (as indicated by the 60 percent share of inventory dedicated to manufacturing), will find their demand levels affected. The curious flatness of industrial property prices, in the face of tight occupancy, in part reflects the behavior of the REITs, which have not looked upon Akron as a market with investor appeal on Wall Street. More positively, little is happening on the supply side to suggest emerging imbalances in 1999. Financing for speculative construction is just about nonexistent. The SIOR reporters anticipate

250,000 sq. ft. of construction for the year—dependent upon a 51 percent pre-lease commitment." *Society of Industrial and Office Realtors, 1999 Comparative Statistics of Industrial and Office Real Estate Markets*

COMMERCIAL UTILITIES

Typical Monthly Electric Bills

Area	Commercial Service ($/month)		Industrial Service ($/month)	
	12 kW demand 1,500 kWh	100 kW demand 30,000 kWh	1,000 kW demand 400,000 kWh	20,000 kW demand 10,000,000 kWh
City	256	3,202	32,614	455,832
U.S.	150	2,174	23,995	508,569

Note: Based on rates in effect January 1, 1999
Source: Edison Electric Institute, Typical Residential, Commercial and Industrial Bills, Winter 1999

TRANSPORTATION

Transportation Statistics

Average minutes to work	18.8
Interstate highways	I-76; I-77
Bus lines	
In-city	Metropolitan Regional TA
Inter-city	2
Passenger air service	
Airport	Akron Fulton Muni.; Akron-Canton & Cleveland Hopkins Int'l.
Airlines	10
Aircraft departures	n/a
Enplaned passengers	n/a
Rail service	No Amtrak Service
Motor freight carriers	146
Major waterways/ports	None

Source: Editor & Publisher Market Guide, 1999; FAA Airport Activity Statistics, 1997; Amtrak National Time Table, Northeast Timetable, Spring/Summer 1999; 1990 Census of Population and Housing, STF 3C; Chamber of Commerce/Economic Development 1999; Jane's Urban Transport Systems 1999-2000

Means of Transportation to Work

Area	Car/Truck/Van		Public Transportation			Bicycle	Walked	Other Means	Worked at Home
	Drove Alone	Car-pooled	Bus	Subway	Railroad				
City	78.8	11.9	3.2	0.0	0.0	0.1	3.5	0.7	1.8
MSA[1]	83.1	9.6	1.5	0.0	0.0	0.1	3.1	0.6	2.0
U.S.	73.2	13.4	3.0	1.5	0.5	0.4	3.9	1.2	3.0

Note: Figures shown are percentages and only include workers 16 years old and over;
(1) Metropolitan Statistical Area - see Appendix A for areas included
Source: 1990 Census of Population and Housing, Summary Tape File 3C

BUSINESSES

Major Business Headquarters

Company Name	1999 Rankings	
	Fortune 500	Forbes 500
FirstEnergy	280	-
Goodyear Tire	130	-

Note: Companies listed are located in the city; dashes indicate no ranking
Fortune 500: Companies that produce a 10-K are ranked 1 to 500 based on 1998 revenue
Forbes 500: Private companies are ranked 1 to 500 based on 1997 revenue
Source: Forbes, November 30, 1998; Fortune, April 26, 1999

HOTELS & MOTELS

Hotels/Motels

Area	Hotels/ Motels	Rooms	Luxury-Level Hotels/Motels		Average Minimum Rates ($)		
			♦♦♦♦	♦♦♦♦♦	♦♦	♦♦♦	♦♦♦♦
City	19	2,165	0	0	59	90	n/a
Airport	2	281	0	0	n/a	n/a	n/a
Total	21	2,446	0	0	n/a	n/a	n/a

Note: n/a not available; classifications range from one diamond (budget properties with basic amenities) to five diamond (luxury properties with the finest service, rooms and facilities).
Source: OAG, Business Travel Planner, Winter 1998-99

CONVENTION CENTERS

Major Convention Centers

Center Name	Meeting Rooms	Exhibit Space (sq. ft.)
John S. Knight Center	18	n/a

Note: n/a not available
Source: Trade Shows Worldwide, 1998; Meetings & Conventions, 4/15/99; Sucessful Meetings, 3/31/98

Living Environment

COST OF LIVING

Cost of Living Index

Composite Index	Groceries	Housing	Utilities	Trans-portation	Health Care	Misc. Goods/ Services
96.7	101.3	88.3	119.2	101.9	98.9	94.2

Note: U.S. = 100
Source: ACCRA, Cost of Living Index, 3rd Quarter 1998

HOUSING

Median Home Prices and Housing Affordability

Area	Median Price[2] 1st Qtr. 1999 ($)	HOI[3] 1st Qtr. 1999	Afford-ability Rank[4]
MSA[1]	105,000	74.8	93
U.S.	134,000	69.6	–

Note: (1) Metropolitan Statistical Area - see Appendix A for areas included; (2) U.S. figures calculated from the sales of 524,324 new and existing homes in 181 markets; (3) Housing Opportunity Index - percent of homes sold that were within the reach of the median income household at the prevailing mortgage interest rate; (4) Rank is from 1-181 with 1 being most affordable
Source: National Association of Home Builders, Housing Opportunity Index, 1st Quarter 1999

Median Home Price Projection

It is projected that the median price of existing single-family homes in the metro area will decrease by -1.0% in 1999. Nationwide, home prices are projected to increase 3.8%.
Kiplinger's Personal Finance Magazine, January 1999

Average New Home Price

Area	Price ($)
City	120,000
U.S.	138,988

Note: Figures are based on a new home with 1,800 sq. ft. of living area on an 8,000 sq. ft. lot.
Source: ACCRA, Cost of Living Index, 3rd Quarter 1998

Average Apartment Rent

Area	Rent ($/mth)
City	563
U.S.	586

Note: Figures are based on an unfurnished two bedroom, 1-1/2 or 2 bath apartment, approximately 950 sq. ft. in size, excluding all utilities except water
Source: ACCRA, Cost of Living Index, 3rd Quarter 1998

RESIDENTIAL UTILITIES

Average Residential Utility Costs

Area	All Electric ($/mth)	Part Electric ($/mth)	Other Energy ($/mth)	Phone ($/mth)
City	–	77.66	43.45	22.45
U.S.	103.76	55.93	43.48	19.86

Source: ACCRA, Cost of Living Index, 3rd Quarter 1998

HEALTH CARE

Average Health Care Costs

Area	Hospital ($/day)	Doctor ($/visit)	Dentist ($/visit)
City	523.60	46.00	58.00
U.S.	405.11	50.96	63.88

Note: Hospital—based on a semi-private room; Doctor—based on a general practitioner's routine exam of an established patient; Dentist—based on adult teeth cleaning and periodic oral exam.
Source: ACCRA, Cost of Living Index, 3rd Quarter 1998

Distribution of Office-Based Physicians

Area	Family/Gen. Practitioners	Specialists		
		Medical	Surgical	Other
MSA[1]	128	318	269	268

Note: Data as of 12/31/97; (1) Metropolitan Statistical Area - see Appendix A for areas included
Source: American Medical Assn., Physician Characteristics & Distribution in the U.S., 1999

Hospitals

Akron has 2 general medical and surgical hospitals, 1 rehabilitation, 1 children's general. *AHA Guide to the Healthcare Field, 1998-99*

According to *U.S. News and World Report,* Akron has 1 of the best hospitals in the U.S.: **Summa Health System**, noted for cardiology, neurology, orthopedics, pulmonology. *U.S. News Online, "America's Best Hospitals," 10th Edition, www.usnews.com*

EDUCATION

Public School District Statistics

District Name	Num. Sch.	Enroll.	Classroom Teachers	Pupils per Teacher	Minority Pupils (%)	Current Exp.[1] ($/pupil)
Akron City SD	63	32,361	2,372	13.6	n/a	n/a
Coventry Local SD	7	2,628	148	17.8	n/a	n/a
Manchester Local SD	3	1,494	71	21.0	n/a	n/a
Northeast OH Network Educ Tec	n/a	n/a	n/a	n/a	n/a	n/a
Springfield Local SD	8	3,476	206	16.9	n/a	n/a

Note: Data covers the 1997-1998 school year unless otherwise noted; (1) Data covers fiscal year 1996; SD = School District; ISD = Independent School District; n/a not available
Source: National Center for Education Statistics, Common Core of Data Public Education Agency Universe 1997-98; National Center for Education Statistics, Characteristics of the 100 Largest Public Elementary and Secondary School Districts in the United States: 1997-98, July 1999

Educational Quality

School District	Education Quotient[1]	Graduate Outcome[2]	Community Index[3]	Resource Index[4]
Akron City	76.0	67.0	90.0	90.0

Note: Nearly 1,000 secondary school districts were rated in terms of educational quality. The scores range from a low of 50 to a high of 150; (1) Average of the Graduate Outcome, Community and Resource indexes; (2) Based on graduation rates and college board scores (SAT/ACT); (3) Based on the surrounding community's average level of education and the area's average income level; (4) Based on teacher salaries, per-pupil expenditures and student-teacher ratios.
Source: Expansion Management, Ratings Issue, 1998

Educational Attainment by Race

Area	High School Graduate (%)					Bachelor's Degree (%)				
	Total	White	Black	Other	Hisp.[2]	Total	White	Black	Other	Hisp.[2]
City	72.9	74.9	65.3	71.5	77.5	14.9	16.6	7.0	36.1	18.8
MSA[1]	78.5	79.6	66.8	80.2	82.7	19.3	20.0	8.5	44.4	23.6
U.S.	75.2	77.9	63.1	60.4	49.8	20.3	21.5	11.4	19.4	9.2

Note: Figures shown cover persons 25 years old and over; (1) Metropolitan Statistical Area - see Appendix A for areas included; (2) people of Hispanic origin can be of any race
Source: 1990 Census of Population and Housing, Summary Tape File 3C

School Enrollment by Type

Area	Preprimary Public Enrollment	%	Preprimary Private Enrollment	%	Elementary/High School Public Enrollment	%	Elementary/High School Private Enrollment	%
City	2,292	61.2	1,452	38.8	31,965	88.9	3,982	11.1
MSA[1]	7,419	57.9	5,400	42.1	97,708	89.9	11,025	10.1
U.S.	2,679,029	59.5	1,824,256	40.5	38,379,689	90.2	4,187,099	9.8

Note: Figures shown cover persons 3 years old and over;
(1) Metropolitan Statistical Area - see Appendix A for areas included
Source: 1990 Census of Population and Housing, Summary Tape File 3C

School Enrollment by Race

Area	Preprimary (%) White	Black	Other	Hisp.[1]	Elementary/High School (%) White	Black	Other	Hisp.[1]
City	72.7	24.9	2.4	1.7	62.6	35.1	2.3	1.0
MSA[2]	88.8	9.2	2.0	0.9	84.3	13.9	1.8	0.9
U.S.	80.4	12.5	7.1	7.8	74.1	15.6	10.3	12.5

Note: Figures shown cover persons 3 years old and over; (1) people of Hispanic origin can be of any race; (2) Metropolitan Statistical Area - see Appendix A for areas included
Source: 1990 Census of Population and Housing, Summary Tape File 3C

Classroom Teacher Salaries in Public Schools

District	B.A. Degree Min. ($)	Rank[1]	M.A. Degree Max. ($)	Rank[1]	Maximum Max. ($)	Rank[1]
Akron	24,529	75	45,726	48	48,086	64
Average	26,980	-	46,065	-	51,435	-

Note: Salaries are for 1997-1998; (1) Rank ranges from 1 to 100
Source: American Federation of Teachers, Survey & Analysis of Salary Trends, 1998

Higher Education

Two-Year Colleges Public	Private	Four-Year Colleges Public	Private	Medical Schools	Law Schools	Voc/Tech
0	1	1	0	0	1	10

Source: College Blue Book, Occupational Education, 1997; Medical School Admission Requirements, 1999-2000; Peterson's Guide to Two-Year Colleges, 1999; Peterson's Guide to Four-Year Colleges, 2000; Barron's Guide to Law Schools, 1999

MAJOR EMPLOYERS

Major Employers

Goodyear Tire & Rubber
First Merit Bank
Cleveland Electric Illuminating Co.
Sterling Jewelers
Aircraft Braking Systems Corp.
Akron General Medical Center
Children's Hospital Medical Center of Akron
Firstenergy Corp.
Roadway Express
Beacon Journal Publishing Co..

Note: Companies listed are located in the city
Source: Dun's Business Rankings, 1999; Ward's Business Directory, 1998

PUBLIC SAFETY

Crime Rate

Area	All Crimes	Violent Crimes Murder	Forcible Rape	Robbery	Aggrav. Assault	Property Crimes Burglary	Larceny -Theft	Motor Vehicle Theft
City	7,168.3	6.3	86.9	363.2	593.8	1,283.5	3,924.3	910.4
Suburbs[1]	3,254.4	2.0	25.7	48.7	126.3	522.1	2,338.5	191.2
MSA[2]	4,548.6	3.4	45.9	152.7	280.9	773.9	2,862.9	429.0
U.S.	5,086.6	7.4	36.3	201.9	390.9	944.8	2,979.7	525.6

Note: Crime rate is the number of crimes per 100,000 pop.; (1) defined as all areas within the MSA but located outside the central city; (2) Metropolitan Statistical Area - see Appendix A for areas incl.
Source: FBI Uniform Crime Reports, 1996

RECREATION

Culture and Recreation

Museums	Symphony Orchestras	Opera Companies	Dance Companies	Professional Theatres	Zoos	Pro Sports Teams
3	2	0	1	1	1	0

Source: International Directory of the Performing Arts, 1997; Official Museum Directory, 1999; Stern's Performing Arts Directory, 1997; USA Today Four Sport Stadium Guide, 1997; Chamber of Commerce/Economic Development, 1999

Library System

The Akron-Summit County Public Library has 17 branches, holdings of 1,087,517 volumes, and a budget of $20,221,546 (1997). *American Library Directory, 1998-1999*

MEDIA

Newspapers

Name	Type	Freq.	Distribution	Circulation
The Akron Beacon Journal	General	7x/wk	Local	146,477
Akron Legal News	n/a	5x/wk	Local	1,000

Note: Includes newspapers with circulations of 1,000 or more located in the city; n/a not available
Source: Burrelle's Media Directory, 1999 Edition

Television Stations

Name	Ch.	Affiliation	Type	Owner

No stations listed.

Note: Stations included broadcast in the Akron metro area; n/a not available
Source: Burrelle's Media Directory, 1999 Edition

AM Radio Stations

Call Letters	Freq. (kHz)	Target Audience	Station Format	Music Format
WHLO	640	Religious	M/S/T	Christian
WTOU	1350	General	M	Urban Contemporary
WHK	1420	General	N/T	n/a
WAKR	1590	General	M/N/S	Adult Contemporary

Note: Stations included broadcast in the Akron metro area; n/a not available
Target Audience: A=Asian; B=Black; C=Christian; E=Ethnic; F=French; G=General; H=Hispanic; M=Men; N=Native American; R=Religious; S=Senior Citizen; W=Women; Y=Young Adult; Z=Children
Station Format: E=Educational; M=Music; N=News; S=Sports; T=Talk
Source: Burrelle's Media Directory, 1999 Edition

FM Radio Stations

Call Letters	Freq. (mHz)	Target Audience	Station Format	Music Format
WZIP	88.1	General	M/N/S	R&B/Urban Contemporary
WKSU	89.7	General	M/N	Classical/MOR
WAPS	91.3	General	M	AOR/Jazz
WQMX	94.9	General	M	Country
WKDD	96.5	General	M	Adult Contemporary
WONE	97.5	General	M	AOR/Classic Rock
WHK	98.1	Religious	T	n/a

Note: Stations included broadcast in the Akron metro area; n/a not available
Station Format: E=Educational; M=Music; N=News; S=Sports; T=Talk
Target Audience: A=Asian; B=Black; C=Christian; E=Ethnic; F=French; G=General; H=Hispanic; M=Men; N=Native American; R=Religious; S=Senior Citizen; W=Women; Y=Young Adult; Z=Children
Music Format: AOR=Album Oriented Rock; MOR=Middle-of-the-Road
Source: Burrelle's Media Directory, 1999 Edition

CLIMATE

Average and Extreme Temperatures

Temperature	Jan	Feb	Mar	Apr	May	Jun	Jul	Aug	Sep	Oct	Nov	Dec	Yr.
Extreme High (°F)	70	68	81	88	92	100	101	98	99	86	80	76	101
Average High (°F)	33	36	46	59	70	79	82	81	74	62	49	37	59
Average Temp. (°F)	26	28	37	49	59	68	72	71	64	53	42	31	50
Average Low (°F)	18	20	28	38	48	57	61	60	53	43	33	23	40
Extreme Low (°F)	-24	-13	-3	10	24	32	43	41	32	20	-1	-16	-24

Note: Figures cover the years 1948-1990
Source: National Climatic Data Center, International Station Meteorological Climate Summary, 3/95

Average Precipitation/Snowfall/Humidity

Precip./Humidity	Jan	Feb	Mar	Apr	May	Jun	Jul	Aug	Sep	Oct	Nov	Dec	Yr.
Avg. Precip. (in.)	2.6	2.3	3.2	3.3	3.7	3.4	4.0	3.2	3.1	2.3	2.8	2.8	36.7
Avg. Snowfall (in.)	11	9	9	3	Tr	0	0	0	0	1	5	10	47
Avg. Rel. Hum. 7am (%)	80	80	79	77	77	80	83	87	87	84	80	80	81
Avg. Rel. Hum. 4pm (%)	68	65	59	53	53	54	54	55	56	56	64	70	59

Note: Figures cover the years 1948-1990; Tr = Trace amounts (<0.05 in. of rain; <0.5 in. of snow)
Source: National Climatic Data Center, International Station Meteorological Climate Summary, 3/95

Weather Conditions

Temperature			Daytime Sky			Precipitation		
5°F & below	32°F & below	90°F & above	Clear	Partly cloudy	Cloudy	0.01 inch or more precip.	0.1 inch or more snow/ice	Thunder-storms
12	129	8	67	134	164	153	48	38

Note: Figures are average number of days per year and covers the years 1948-1990
Source: National Climatic Data Center, International Station Meteorological Climate Summary, 3/95

AIR & WATER QUALITY

Maximum Pollutant Concentrations

	Particulate Matter (ug/m³)	Carbon Monoxide (ppm)	Sulfur Dioxide (ppm)	Nitrogen Dioxide (ppm)	Ozone (ppm)	Lead (ug/m³)
MSA[1] Level	63	3	0.072	n/a	0.11	0.04
NAAQS[2]	150	9	0.140	0.053	0.12	1.50
Met NAAQS?	Yes	Yes	Yes	n/a	Yes	Yes

Note: (1) Metropolitan Statistical Area - see Appendix A for areas included; (2) National Ambient Air Quality Standards; ppm = parts per million; ug/m³ = micrograms per cubic meter; n/a not available
Source: EPA, National Air Quality and Emissions Trends Report, 1997

Pollutant Standards Index

In the Akron MSA (see Appendix A for areas included), the Pollutant Standards Index (PSI) exceeded 100 on 6 days in 1997. A PSI value greater than 100 indicates that air quality would be in the unhealthful range on that day. *EPA, National Air Quality and Emissions Trends Report, 1997*

Drinking Water

Water System Name	Pop. Served	Primary Water Source Type	Number of Violations in 1998	Type of Violation/ Contaminants
City of Akron	308,720	Surface	55	(1)

Note: Data as of July 10, 1999; (1) System failed to conduct initial or repeat sampling, or to accurately report an analytical result for 55 specific contaminants.
Source: EPA, Office of Ground Water and Drinking Water, Safe Drinking Water Information System

Akron tap water is alkaline, soft.
Editor & Publisher Market Guide, 1999

Baltimore, Maryland

Background

No one industry dominates Baltimore. But many industries have one thing in common: Baltimore's port and facilities. These facilities provide companies in the city's municipal area access to domestic and international markets. Baltimore's port is the 15th largest by volume in the United States. It also has the advantage of being 150 miles closer to the Midwest than other eastern U.S. port cities. With its easily accessible harbor, reached via a 42-foot deep main canal from Chesapeake Bay, and its renowned stable work force, Baltimore is truly an economy based upon maritime trade.

The city was founded in 1729 and named for the Barons Baltimore, who established the colony of Maryland in the early 17th century.

Since Baltimore's founding, much of its history has revolved around its maritime presence. In 1812, composer Francis Scott Key wrote *The Star Spangled Banner*, while watching an unsuccessful bombardment of the city by the British, from a warship. During World War I, the city's economy prospered due to a need for ships and other industrial products.

There remains a wealth of history, however, that is not related to its ships or the sea. Baltimore is the site of the first Roman Catholic Cathedral in the country, the Basilica of the Assumption of the Blessed Virgin Mary, which was designed by Benjamin H. Latrobe. The first telegraph line in the United States occurred in Baltimore. Among the city's more famous institutions are Johns Hopkins University, the Peabody Conservatory of Music and the Maryland Institute College of Art.

Despite the urban decay experienced during the 1950s, 60s, and 70s, reconstruction of many of its old areas, such as Inner Harbor, and the construction of new complexes, such as the Charles Center, are bringing people back to Baltimore.

The Baltimore waterfront area is being redeveloped into a retail and entertainment district. The historic power plant complex located in the heart of the Inner Harbor is undergoing massive renovation and the first two anchor tenants, Hard Rock Cafe and Barnes & Noble, which both opened this past year, represent the kind of national presence not usually evidenced along the downtown waterfront redevelopment district.

As part of its 200th birthday celebration, Baltimore earmarked $500 million to fund more projects: Port Discovery, a Disney-designed children's museum, recently opened; the Inner Harbor is home to the Orioles at Camden Park; just to the south, a new stadium for the National Football League Ravens just opened.

The region is subject to frequent changes in weather, although the mountains to the west, and the bay and ocean to the east produce a more equable climate compared with other locations farther inland at the same latitude.

In the summer, the area is under the influence of the high pressure system commonly known as the "Bermuda High" which brings warm, humid air. In general, the humidity tends to be high year round. In winter, snow is frequently mixed with rain and sleet, but seldom remains on the ground for more than a few days. Rainfall distribution is rather uniform throughout the year, but the summer and early fall receives the most precipitation. Hurricanes and severe thunderstorms are confined to summer and fall as well, but rarely have hurricanes caused widespread damage.

General Rankings and Evaluative Comments

- Baltimore was ranked #6 out of 15 large, northeastern metropolitan areas in *Money's* 1998 survey of "The Best Places to Live in America." The survey was conducted by first contacting 512 representative households nationwide and asking them to rank 37 quality-of-life factors on a scale of 1 to 10. Next, a demographic profile was compiled on the 300 largest metropolitan statistical areas in the U.S. The numbers were crunched together to arrive at an overall ranking (things Americans consider most important, like clean air and water, low crime and good schools, received extra weight). Unlike previous years, the 1998 rankings were broken down by region (northeast, midwest, south, west) and population size (100,000 to 249,999; 250,000 to 999,999; 1 million plus). The city had a nationwide ranking of #156 out of 300 in 1997 and #91 out of 300 in 1996. *Money, July 1998; Money, July 1997; Money, September 1996*

- *Ladies Home Journal* ranked America's 200 largest cities based on the qualities women care about most. Baltimore ranked #140 out of 200. Criteria: low crime rate, well-paying jobs, quality health and child care, good public schools, the presence of women in government, size of the gender wage gap, number of sexual-harassment and discrimination complaints filed, unemployment and divorce rates, commute times, population density, number of houses of worship, parks and cultural offerings, number of women's health specialists, how well a community's women cared for themselves, complexion kindness index based on UV radiation levels, odds of finding affordable fashions, rental rates for romance movies, champagne sales and other matters of the heart. Ladies Home Journal, November 1998

- Zero Population Growth ranked 229 cities in terms of children's health, safety, and economic well-being. Baltimore was ranked #25 out of 25 major cities (main city in a metro area with population of greater than 2 million) and was given a grade of F. Criteria: total population, percent of population under 18 years of age, household language, percent population change, percent of births to teens, infant mortality rate, percent of low birth weights, dropout rate, enrollment in preprimary school, violent and property crime rates, unemployment rate, percent of children in poverty, percent of owner occupied units, number of bad air days, percent of public transportation commuters, and average travel time to work. *Zero Population Growth, Children's Environmental Index, Fall 1999*

- Baltimore was ranked #35 out of 59 metro areas in *The Regional Economist's* "Rational Livability Ranking of 59 Large Metro Areas." The rankings were based on the metro area's total population change over the period 1990-97 divided by the number of people moving in from elsewhere in the United States (net domestic in-migration). *St. Louis Federal Reserve Bank of St. Louis, The Regional Economist, April 1999*

- Baltimore appeared on *Travel & Leisure's* list of the world's 100 best cities. It was ranked #36 in the U.S. and #99 in the world. Criteria: activities/attractions, culture/arts, people, restaurants/food, and value. *Travel & Leisure, 1998 World's Best Awards*

- Baltimore was selected by *Yahoo! Internet Life* as one of "America's Most Wired Cities & Towns." The city ranked #20 out of 50. Criteria: home and work net use, domain density, hosts per capita, directory density and content quality. *Yahoo! Internet Life, March 1999*

- Cognetics studied 273 metro areas in the United States, ranking them by entrepreneurial activity. Baltimore was ranked #37 out of the 50 largest metro areas. Criteria: Significant Starts (firms started in the last 10 years that still employ at least 5 people) and Young Growers (percent of firms 10 years old or less that grew significantly during the last 4 years). *Cognetics, "Entrepreneurial Hot Spots: The Best Places in America to Start and Grow a Company," 1998*

- Baltimore was selected as one of the "Best American Cities to Start a Business" by *Point of View* magazine. Criteria: coolness, quality-of-life, and business concerns. The city was ranked #70 out of 75. *Point of View, November 1998*

■ Reliastar Financial Corp. ranked the 125 largest metropolitan areas according to the general
financial security of residents. Baltimore was ranked #61 out of 125 with a score of 2.3. The
score indicates the percentage a metropolitan area is above or below the metropolitan norm.
A metro area with a score of 10.6 is 10.6% above the metro average. Criteria: Earnings and
Wealth Potential (household income, education, net assets, cost of living); Safety Net (health
insurance, retirement savings, life insurance, income support programs); Personal Threats
(unemployment rate, low-income households, crime rate); Community Economic Vitality
(cost of community services, job quality, job creation, housing costs).
Reliastar Financial Corp., "The Best Cities to Earn and Save Money," 1999 Edition

Business Environment

STATE ECONOMY

State Economic Profile

"Maryland's economy has trailed the nation for most of this decade. A heavy reliance on federal spending left MD vulnerable to cutbacks in the federal budget. With federal spending and employment in MD stabilizing, and with a growing service sector, MD's growth should converge on the nation's over the next few years.

Military spending made up almost 5% of GSP in 1997. Federal jobs constitute twice the share of MD's employment than they do nationally. In addition many of MD's private companies depend heavily upon federal contracting. Clearly MD's economy is tied to federal spending. Although budget cuts seemed to run their course, and there remains the prospect of renewed defense spending, federal dollars will not provide the level of job growth in MD that it did in the past.

MD's economy is driven by two geographic areas, Baltimore and suburban Washington. Baltimore's job growth continues to be about half the state average, with a continuing contraction in its manufacturing base. Baltimore's population loss has come down from its earlier levels, although the city still cannot attract skilled workers. Suburban DC has performed slightly better as high-tech and biotech jobs created along I-270 have offset some losses in defense contracting.

Price appreciation has been very weak in most of MD, with some exception in the DC suburbs. Sales have been robust, however, as has permit activity, which increased 21% in 1998.

The MD outlook remains one of moderate growth converging on to the national rate. A continued federal budget surplus could result in increased federal spending, a potential upside to MD's job outlook." *National Association of Realtors, Economic Profiles: The Fifty States and the District of Columbia, http://nar.realtor.com/databank/profiles.htm*

IMPORTS/EXPORTS

Total Export Sales

Area	1994 ($000)	1995 ($000)	1996 ($000)	1997 ($000)	% Chg. 1994-97	% Chg. 1996-97
MSA[1]	1,868,968	2,209,168	2,110,417	2,171,305	16.2	2.9
U.S.	512,415,609	583,030,524	622,827,063	687,597,999	34.2	10.4

Note: (1) Metropolitan Statistical Area - see Appendix A for areas included
Source: U.S. Department of Commerce, International Trade Association, Metropolitan Area Exports: An Export Performance Report on Over 250 U.S. Cities, November 10, 1998

CITY FINANCES

City Government Finances

Component	FY94 ($000)	FY94 (per capita $)
Revenue	2,135,033	3,036.64
Expenditure	1,728,616	2,458.60
Debt Outstanding	1,232,157	1,752.49
Cash & Securities	2,231,273	3,173.52

Source: U.S. Bureau of the Census, City Government Finances: 1993-94

City Government Revenue by Source

Source	FY94 ($000)	FY94 (per capita $)	FY94 (%)
From Federal Government	57,575	81.89	2.7
From State Governments	833,052	1,184.84	39.0
From Local Governments	47,721	67.87	2.2
Property Taxes	483,428	687.58	22.6
General Sales Taxes	0	0.00	0.0
Selective Sales Taxes	46,281	65.83	2.2
Income Taxes	125,858	179.01	5.9
Current Charges	103,920	147.80	4.9
Utility/Liquor Store	60,312	85.78	2.8
Employee Retirement[1]	220,003	312.91	10.3
Other	156,883	223.13	7.3

Note: (1) Excludes "city contributions," classified as "nonrevenue," intragovernmental transfers.
Source: U.S. Bureau of the Census, City Government Finances: 1993-94

City Government Expenditures by Function

Function	FY94 ($000)	FY94 (per capita $)	FY94 (%)
Educational Services	616,590	876.97	35.7
Employee Retirement[1]	108,608	154.47	6.3
Environment/Housing	269,309	383.04	15.6
Government Administration	102,340	145.56	5.9
Interest on General Debt	82,648	117.55	4.8
Public Safety	256,080	364.22	14.8
Social Services	67,451	95.94	3.9
Transportation	93,650	133.20	5.4
Utility/Liquor Store	59,595	84.76	3.4
Other	72,345	102.90	4.2

Note: (1) Payments to beneficiaries including withdrawal of contributions.
Source: U.S. Bureau of the Census, City Government Finances: 1993-94

Municipal Bond Ratings

Area	Moody's	S & P
Baltimore	A1	n/a

Note: n/a not available; n/r not rated
Source: Moody's Bond Record, 6/99

POPULATION

Population Growth

Area	1980	1990	% Chg. 1980-90	July 1998 Estimate	% Chg. 1990-98
City	786,775	736,014	-6.5	645,593	-12.3
MSA[1]	2,199,531	2,382,172	8.3	2,504,766	5.1
U.S.	226,545,805	248,765,170	9.8	270,299,000	8.7

Note: (1) Metropolitan Statistical Area - see Appendix A for areas included;
July 1998 MSA population estimate was calculated by the editors
Source: 1980/1990 Census of Housing and Population, Summary Tape File 3C;
Census Bureau Population Estimates 1998

Population Characteristics

Race	City 1980 Population	%	City 1990 Population	%	% Chg. 1980-90	MSA[1] 1990 Population	%
White	346,692	44.1	287,933	39.1	-16.9	1,710,510	71.8
Black	430,934	54.8	435,619	59.2	1.1	615,218	25.8
Amer Indian/Esk/Aleut	2,170	0.3	2,373	0.3	9.4	6,653	0.3
Asian/Pacific Islander	4,898	0.6	7,982	1.1	63.0	41,870	1.8
Other	2,081	0.3	2,107	0.3	1.2	7,921	0.3
Hispanic Origin[2]	7,638	1.0	6,997	1.0	-8.4	28,538	1.2

Note: (1) Metropolitan Statistical Area - see Appendix A for areas included;
(2) people of Hispanic origin can be of any race
Source: 1980/1990 Census of Housing and Population, Summary Tape File 3C

Ancestry

Area	German	Irish	English	Italian	U.S.	French	Polish	Dutch
City	13.9	9.3	5.4	3.5	2.6	1.2	3.9	0.8
MSA[1]	28.5	17.2	13.2	6.1	3.3	2.5	5.5	1.6
U.S.	23.3	15.6	13.1	5.9	5.3	4.2	3.8	2.5

Note: Figures are percentages and include persons that reported multiple ancestry (eg. if a person reported being Irish and Italian, they were included in both columns); (1) Metropolitan Statistical Area - see Appendix A for areas included
Source: 1990 Census of Population and Housing, Summary Tape File 3C

Age

Area	Median Age (Years)	Age Distribution (%) Under 5	Under 18	18-24	25-44	45-64	65+	80+
City	32.5	7.7	24.5	11.1	32.9	17.9	13.7	3.0
MSA[1]	33.3	7.4	24.2	10.2	34.6	19.4	11.7	2.4
U.S.	32.9	7.3	25.6	10.5	32.6	18.7	12.5	2.8

Note: (1) Metropolitan Statistical Area - see Appendix A for areas included
Source: 1990 Census of Population and Housing, Summary Tape File 3C

Male/Female Ratio

Area	Number of males per 100 females (all ages)	Number of males per 100 females (18 years old+)
City	87.7	83.1
MSA[1]	93.5	90.2
U.S.	95.0	91.9

Note: (1) Metropolitan Statistical Area - see Appendix A for areas included
Source: 1990 Census of Population, General Population Characteristics

INCOME

Per Capita/Median/Average Income

Area	Per Capita ($)	Median Household ($)	Average Household ($)
City	11,994	24,045	31,415
MSA[1]	16,596	36,550	44,405
U.S.	14,420	30,056	38,453

Note: All figures are for 1989; (1) Metropolitan Statistical Area - see Appendix A for areas included
Source: 1990 Census of Population and Housing, Summary Tape File 3C

Household Income Distribution by Race

Income ($)	City (%)					U.S. (%)				
	Total	White	Black	Other	Hisp.[1]	Total	White	Black	Other	Hisp.[1]
Less than 5,000	11.7	6.9	15.8	16.0	13.7	6.2	4.8	15.2	8.6	8.8
5,000 - 9,999	11.6	10.4	12.6	11.3	7.5	9.3	8.6	14.2	9.9	11.1
10,000 - 14,999	9.5	9.1	9.9	8.3	11.0	8.8	8.5	11.0	9.8	11.0
15,000 - 24,999	18.7	18.0	19.3	16.3	16.9	17.5	17.3	18.9	18.5	20.5
25,000 - 34,999	15.7	16.4	15.1	16.2	16.0	15.8	16.1	14.2	15.4	16.4
35,000 - 49,999	15.9	17.3	14.6	14.7	19.0	17.9	18.6	13.3	16.1	16.0
50,000 - 74,999	11.3	13.6	9.3	12.2	11.3	15.0	15.8	9.3	13.4	11.1
75,000 - 99,999	3.2	4.1	2.3	3.0	2.5	5.1	5.5	2.6	4.7	3.1
100,000+	2.4	4.2	0.9	2.0	2.1	4.4	4.8	1.3	3.7	1.9

Note: All figures are for 1989; (1) people of Hispanic origin can be of any race
Source: 1990 Census of Population and Housing, Summary Tape File 3C

Effective Buying Income

Area	Per Capita ($)	Median Household ($)	Average Household ($)
City	13,022	26,878	34,728
MSA[1]	18,025	40,160	48,394
U.S.	16,803	34,536	45,243

Note: Data as of 1/1/99; (1) Metropolitan Statistical Area - see Appendix A for areas included
Source: Standard Rate & Data Service, Newspaper Advertising Source, 9/99

Effective Household Buying Income Distribution

Area	% of Households Earning						
	$10,000 -$19,999	$20,000 -$34,999	$35,000 -$49,999	$50,000 -$74,999	$75,000 -$99,000	$100,000 -$124,999	$125,000 and up
City	18.4	23.8	16.8	14.4	4.2	1.2	1.4
MSA[1]	12.4	21.0	20.0	23.0	8.9	2.7	2.6
U.S.	16.0	22.6	18.2	18.9	7.2	2.4	2.7

Note: Data as of 1/1/99; (1) Metropolitan Statistical Area - see Appendix A for areas included
Source: Standard Rate & Data Service, Newspaper Advertising Source, 9/99

Poverty Rates by Race and Age

Area	Total (%)	By Race (%)				By Age (%)		
		White	Black	Other	Hisp.[2]	Under 5 years old	Under 18 years old	65 years and over
City	21.9	12.6	27.9	25.2	21.5	34.3	32.5	19.3
MSA[1]	10.1	5.4	23.2	10.8	11.5	15.3	14.4	11.6
U.S.	13.1	9.8	29.5	23.1	25.3	20.1	18.3	12.8

Note: Figures show the percent of people living below the poverty line in 1989. The average poverty threshold was $12,674 for a family of four in 1989; (1) Metropolitan Statistical Area - see Appendix A for areas included; (2) people of Hispanic origin can be of any race
Source: 1990 Census of Population and Housing, Summary Tape File 3C

EMPLOYMENT

Labor Force and Employment

Area	Civilian Labor Force			Workers Employed		
	Jun. 1998	Jun. 1999	% Chg.	Jun. 1998	Jun. 1999	% Chg.
City	307,395	312,138	1.5	276,940	286,254	3.4
MSA[1]	1,308,390	1,336,571	2.2	1,233,127	1,274,601	3.4
U.S.	138,798,000	140,666,000	1.3	132,265,000	134,395,000	1.6

Note: Data is not seasonally adjusted and covers workers 16 years of age and older;
(1) Metropolitan Statistical Area - see Appendix A for areas included
Source: Bureau of Labor Statistics, http://stats.bls.gov

Unemployment Rate

Area	1998						1999					
	Jul.	Aug.	Sep.	Oct.	Nov.	Dec.	Jan.	Feb.	Mar.	Apr.	May.	Jun.
City	10.3	9.7	8.6	8.3	7.9	6.8	7.2	7.6	6.8	6.9	7.6	8.3
MSA[1]	5.7	5.3	4.9	4.6	4.5	3.9	4.3	4.6	4.0	3.9	4.2	4.6
U.S.	4.7	4.5	4.4	4.2	4.1	4.0	4.8	4.7	4.4	4.1	4.0	4.5

Note: Data is not seasonally adjusted and covers workers 16 years of age and older; all figures are percentages; (1) Metropolitan Statistical Area - see Appendix A for areas included
Source: Bureau of Labor Statistics, http://stats.bls.gov

Employment by Industry

Sector	MSA[1]		U.S.
	Number of Employees	Percent of Total	Percent of Total
Services	420,300	34.6	30.4
Retail Trade	208,900	17.2	17.7
Government	219,000	18.0	15.6
Manufacturing	100,000	8.2	14.3
Finance/Insurance/Real Estate	75,900	6.2	5.9
Wholesale Trade	65,000	5.4	5.4
Transportation/Public Utilities	59,500	4.9	5.3
Construction	65,800	5.4	5.0
Mining	400	<0.1	0.4

Note: Figures cover non-farm employment as of 6/99 and are not seasonally adjusted;
(1) Metropolitan Statistical Area - see Appendix A for areas included
Source: Bureau of Labor Statistics, http://stats.bls.gov

Employment by Occupation

Occupation Category	City (%)	MSA[1] (%)	U.S. (%)
White Collar	56.1	64.5	58.1
Executive/Admin./Management	10.0	14.8	12.3
Professional	13.3	15.8	14.1
Technical & Related Support	4.2	4.4	3.7
Sales	8.8	11.5	11.8
Administrative Support/Clerical	19.8	17.8	16.3
Blue Collar	24.9	22.1	26.2
Precision Production/Craft/Repair	9.3	10.7	11.3
Machine Operators/Assem./Insp.	6.4	4.3	6.8
Transportation/Material Movers	4.7	3.9	4.1
Cleaners/Helpers/Laborers	4.6	3.3	3.9
Services	18.3	12.4	13.2
Farming/Forestry/Fishing	0.7	1.0	2.5

Note: Figures cover employed persons 16 years old and over;
(1) Metropolitan Statistical Area - see Appendix A for areas included
Source: 1990 Census of Population and Housing, Summary Tape File 3C

Occupational Employment Projections: 1996 - 2006

Occupations Expected to Have the Largest Job Growth (ranked by numerical growth)	Fast-Growing Occupations[1] (ranked by percent growth)
1. Salespersons, retail	1. Desktop publishers
2. Systems analysts	2. Computer engineers
3. General managers & top executives	3. Systems analysts
4. Cashiers	4. Database administrators
5. Janitors/cleaners/maids, ex. priv. hshld.	5. Personal and home care aides
6. Database administrators	6. Emergency medical technicians
7. Truck drivers, light	7. Adjustment clerks
8. Clerical supervisors	8. Respiratory therapists
9. Marketing & sales, supervisors	9. Child care workers, private household
10. Computer engineers	10. Manicurists

Note: Projections cover Maryland; (1) Excludes occupations with total job growth less than 300
Source: U.S. Department of Labor, Employment and Training Administration, America's Labor Market Information System (ALMIS)

TAXES

Major State and Local Tax Rates

State Corp. Income (%)	State Personal Income (%)	Residential Property (effective rate per $100)	Sales & Use State (%)	Sales & Use Local (%)	State Gasoline (cents/ gallon)	State Cigarette (cents/ pack)
7.0	2.0 - 4.85	2.42	5.0	None	23.5	36.0

Note: Personal/corporate income, sales, gasoline and cigarette tax rates as of January 1999. Property tax rates as of 1997.
Source: Federation of Tax Administrators, www.taxadmin.org; Washington D.C. Department of Finance and Revenue, Tax Rates and Tax Burdens in the District of Columbia: A Nationwide Comparison, July 1998; Chamber of Commerce, 1999

Total Taxes Per Capita and as a Percent of Income

Area	Per Capita Income ($)	Per Capita Taxes ($) Total	Per Capita Taxes ($) Federal	Per Capita Taxes ($) State/ Local	Percent of Income (%) Total	Percent of Income (%) Federal	Percent of Income (%) State/ Local
Maryland	30,954	10,895	7,454	3,441	35.2	24.1	11.1
U.S.	27,876	9,881	6,690	3,191	35.4	24.0	11.4

Note: Figures are for 1998
Source: Tax Foundation, www.taxfoundation.org

Estimated Tax Burden

Area	State Income	Local Income	Property	Sales	Total
Baltimore	2,850	1,710	3,250	488	8,298

Note: The numbers are estimates of taxes paid by a married couple with two children and annual earnings of $75,000. Sales tax estimates assume they spend average amounts on food, clothing, household goods and gasoline. Property tax estimates assume they live in a $250,000 home.
Source: Kiplinger's Personal Finance Magazine, October 1998

COMMERCIAL
REAL ESTATE

Office Market

Class/ Location	Total Space (sq. ft.)	Vacant Space (sq. ft.)	Vac. Rate (%)	Under Constr. (sq. ft.)	Net Absorp. (sq. ft.)	Rental Rates ($/sq.ft./yr.)
Class A						
CBD	8,026,649	857,145	10.7	0	132,399	15.00-29.00
Outside CBD	12,788,591	1,336,690	10.5	450,000	125,082	14.00-21.00
Class B						
CBD	5,835,394	1,395,435	23.9	0	325,083	9.00-16.00
Outside CBD	12,349,856	969,843	7.9	0	-337,879	13.50-17.00

Note: Data as of 10/98 and covers Baltimore; CBD = Central Business District; n/a not available;
Source: Society of Industrial and Office Realtors, 1999 Comparative Statistics of Industrial and Office Real Estate Markets

"The local economy has been growing for five years now, and our SIOR reporter expects this trend to persist in 1999. Strong leasing activity is anticipated, which will drive rental rates even higher. As a result, developers' interest in new projects should be renewed. In the suburbs, almost 800,000 sq. ft. of office construction is planned. Investment trends are already starting to reshape the market. Pension funds and insurers have been swapping properties for REIT shares, and the trusts have been buying both properties and local companies. Thus, properties long controlled by local interests are now in the hands of national players. Even so, plenty of financing is available through conventional channels, including commercial banks and the insurance companies. The outlook for 1999 is quite positive." *Society of Industrial and Office Realtors, 1999 Comparative Statistics of Industrial and Office Real Estate Markets*

Industrial Market

Location	Total Space (sq. ft.)	Vacant Space (sq. ft.)	Vac. Rate (%)	Under Constr. (sq. ft.)	Net Absorp. (sq. ft.)	Gross Lease ($/sq.ft./yr.)
Central City	37,850,000	6,500,000	17.2	100,000	2,400,000	3.00-5.00
Suburban	108,900,000	9,600,000	8.8	1,160,000	5,200,000	3.00-8.00

Note: Data as of 10/98 and covers Baltimore; n/a not available
Source: Society of Industrial and Office Realtors, 1999 Comparative Statistics of Industrial and Office Real Estate Markets

"The forecast for 1999 is cautious but still upbeat. This market is expected to hold its own even if the situation in the Far East and continued Wall Street volatility clouds the economic horizon. There is high demand for small industrial space in an era of downsizing, especially as entrepreneurs look for new niches. Development may see a lull, especially in the speculative construction arena, but Baltimore will still see a number of big box deliveries. The southern part of the market is preferred for bulk space, especially along the I-95 corridor toward Washington. The northern area captures more of the demand for traditional distribution facilities and flex space. With 150 bio-technology companies, Baltimore sees a significant 20 percent of its industrial absorption captured by High Tech/R&D facilities." *Society of Industrial and Office Realtors, 1999 Comparative Statistics of Industrial and Office Real Estate Markets*

Retail Market

Shopping Center Inventory (sq. ft.)	Shopping Center Construction (sq. ft.)	Construction as a Percent of Inventory (%)	Torto Wheaton Rent Index[1] ($/sq. ft.)
47,132,000	0	0.0	13.01

Note: Data as of 1997 and covers the Metropolitan Statistical Area - see Appendix A for areas included; (1) Index is based on a model that predicts what the average rent should be for leases with certain characteristics, in certain locations during certain years.
Source: National Association of Realtors, 1997-1998 Market Conditions Report

"Baltimore's retail sector has stagnated over the past few years. The area's retail rent index has remained in the $13.00 per square foot range, which is slightly lower than the South's average of $13.79 per square foot. One major reason is a decline in new residents to the area due to the loss of high-paying defense-related and banking jobs. Population growth has declined to 0.4% per year over the past two years. Weak income growth, ranking near the bottom nationally, will continue to hinder the prospect of any new retail developments in the near future." *National Association of Realtors, 1997-1998 Market Conditions Report*

COMMERCIAL UTILITIES

Typical Monthly Electric Bills

Area	Commercial Service ($/month)		Industrial Service ($/month)	
	12 kW demand 1,500 kWh	100 kW demand 30,000 kWh	1,000 kW demand 400,000 kWh	20,000 kW demand 10,000,000 kWh
City	113	2,171	23,538	349,976
U.S.	150	2,174	23,995	508,569

Note: Based on rates in effect January 1, 1999
Source: Edison Electric Institute, Typical Residential, Commercial and Industrial Bills, Winter 1999

TRANSPORTATION

Transportation Statistics

Average minutes to work	26.0
Interstate highways	I-70; I-83; I-95; I-97
Bus lines	
In-city	Maryland MTA, 811 vehicles
Inter-city	7
Passenger air service	
Airport	Baltimore-Washington International
Airlines	14
Aircraft departures	73,917 (1996)
Enplaned passengers	5,907,010 (1996)
Rail service	Amtrak; Metro/Light Rail
Motor freight carriers	160
Major waterways/ports	Chesapeake Bay; Port of Baltimore

Source: Editor & Publisher Market Guide, 1999; FAA Airport Activity Statistics, 1997; Amtrak National Time Table, Northeast Timetable, Spring/Summer 1999; 1990 Census of Population and Housing, STF 3C; Chamber of Commerce/Economic Development 1999; Jane's Urban Transport Systems 1999-2000

Means of Transportation to Work

Area	Car/Truck/Van		Public Transportation			Bicycle	Walked	Other Means	Worked at Home
	Drove Alone	Car-pooled	Bus	Subway	Railroad				
City	50.9	16.8	19.3	1.6	0.4	0.2	7.4	1.7	1.6
MSA[1]	70.9	14.2	6.2	0.8	0.3	0.2	4.0	1.1	2.3
U.S.	73.2	13.4	3.0	1.5	0.5	0.4	3.9	1.2	3.0

Note: Figures shown are percentages and only include workers 16 years old and over;
(1) Metropolitan Statistical Area - see Appendix A for areas included
Source: 1990 Census of Population and Housing, Summary Tape File 3C

BUSINESSES

Major Business Headquarters

Company Name	1999 Rankings	
	Fortune 500	Forbes 500
Baltimore Gas & Electric	439	-
Sunbelt Beverage	-	295
Whiting-Turner Contracting	-	188

Note: Companies listed are located in the city; dashes indicate no ranking
Fortune 500: Companies that produce a 10-K are ranked 1 to 500 based on 1998 revenue
Forbes 500: Private companies are ranked 1 to 500 based on 1997 revenue
Source: Forbes, November 30, 1998; Fortune, April 26, 1999

Fast-Growing Businesses

According to *Fortune*, Baltimore is home to one of America's 100 fastest-growing companies: Sylvan Learning Systems. Companies were ranked based on earnings-per-share growth, revenue growth and total return over the previous three years. Criteria for inclusion: public companies with sales of least $50 million. Companies that lost money in the most recent quarter, or ended in the red for the past four quarters as a whole, were not eligible. Limited partnerships and REITs were also not considered. *Fortune, "America's Fastest-Growing Companies," 1999*

Women-Owned Firms: Number, Employment and Sales

Area	Number of Firms	Employ-ment	Sales ($000)	Rank[2]
MSA[1]	84,300	163,100	23,539,200	29

Note: (1) Metropolitan Statistical Area - see Appendix A for areas included;
(2) Calculated on an averaging of the number of businesses, employment and sales
Source: The National Foundation for Women Business Owners, 1999 Facts on Women-Owned Businesses: Trends in the Top 50 Metropolitan Areas

Women-Owned Firms: Growth

Area	% change from 1992 to 1999			Rank[2]
	Number of Firms	Employ-ment	Sales	
MSA[1]	44.0	61.2	95.5	43

Note: (1) Metropolitan Statistical Area - see Appendix A for areas included; (2) Calculated on an averaging of the percent growth of number of businesses, employment and sales
Source: The National Foundation for Women Business Owners, 1999 Facts on Women-Owned Businesses: Trends in the Top 50 Metropolitan Areas

Minority Business Opportunity

Baltimore is home to two companies which are on the Black Enterprise Industrial/Service 100 list (largest based on gross sales): Stop Shop Save Food Markets (supermarkets); Super Pride Markets (supermarkets) . Criteria: operational in previous calendar year, at least 51% black-owned and manufactures/owns the product it sells or provides industrial or consumer services. Brokerages, real estate firms and firms that provide professional services are not eligible. *Black Enterprise, www.blackenterprise.com*

HOTELS & MOTELS

Hotels/Motels

Area	Hotels/ Motels	Rooms	Luxury-Level Hotels/Motels		Average Minimum Rates ($)		
			♦♦♦♦	♦♦♦♦♦	♦♦	♦♦♦	♦♦♦♦
City	38	6,393	1	0	72	129	255
Airport	23	2,912	0	0	n/a	n/a	n/a
Suburbs	37	4,682	0	0	n/a	n/a	n/a
Total	98	13,987	1	0	n/a	n/a	n/a

Note: n/a not available; classifications range from one diamond (budget properties with basic amenities) to five diamond (luxury properties with the finest service, rooms and facilities).
Source: OAG, Business Travel Planner, Winter 1998-99

CONVENTION CENTERS

Major Convention Centers

Center Name	Meeting Rooms	Exhibit Space (sq. ft.)
Baltimore Convention Center	34	194,984
Hyatt Regency Baltimore	20	19,849
Omni Inner Harbor Hotel Baltimore	25	20,600
Stouffer-Harbor Place	n/a	18,606
The Conference Center at Sheppard Pratt	5	n/a
USF&G Mount Washington Conference Center	12	n/a

Note: n/a not available
Source: Trade Shows Worldwide, 1998; Meetings & Conventions, 4/15/99;
Sucessful Meetings, 3/31/98

Living Environment

COST OF LIVING

Cost of Living Index

Composite Index	Groceries	Housing	Utilities	Trans-portation	Health Care	Misc. Goods/ Services
95.3	94.8	93.5	118.6	102.2	91.9	89.9

Note: U.S. = 100
Source: ACCRA, Cost of Living Index, 1st Quarter 1999

HOUSING

Median Home Prices and Housing Affordability

Area	Median Price[2] 1st Qtr. 1999 ($)	HOI[3] 1st Qtr. 1999	Afford-ability Rank[4]
MSA[1]	125,000	79.6	60
U.S.	134,000	69.6	–

Note: (1) Metropolitan Statistical Area - see Appendix A for areas included; (2) U.S. figures calculated from the sales of 524,324 new and existing homes in 181 markets; (3) Housing Opportunity Index - percent of homes sold that were within the reach of the median income household at the prevailing mortgage interest rate; (4) Rank is from 1-181 with 1 being most affordable
Source: National Association of Home Builders, Housing Opportunity Index, 1st Quarter 1999

Median Home Price Projection

It is projected that the median price of existing single-family homes in the metro area will increase by 3.3% in 1999. Nationwide, home prices are projected to increase 3.8%.
Kiplinger's Personal Finance Magazine, January 1999

Average New Home Price

Area	Price ($)
City	134,896
U.S.	142,735

Note: Figures are based on a new home with 1,800 sq. ft. of living area on an 8,000 sq. ft. lot.
Source: ACCRA, Cost of Living Index, 1st Quarter 1999

Average Apartment Rent

Area	Rent ($/mth)
City	534
U.S.	601

Note: Figures are based on an unfurnished two bedroom, 1-1/2 or 2 bath apartment, approximately 950 sq. ft. in size, excluding all utilities except water
Source: ACCRA, Cost of Living Index, 1st Quarter 1999

RESIDENTIAL UTILITIES

Average Residential Utility Costs

Area	All Electric ($/mth)	Part Electric ($/mth)	Other Energy ($/mth)	Phone ($/mth)
City	–	64.54	54.30	22.01
U.S.	100.02	55.73	43.33	19.71

Source: ACCRA, Cost of Living Index, 1st Quarter 1999

HEALTH CARE

Average Health Care Costs

Area	Hospital ($/day)	Doctor ($/visit)	Dentist ($/visit)
City	551.00	45.40	52.50
U.S.	430.43	52.45	66.35

Note: Hospital—based on a semi-private room; Doctor—based on a general practitioner's routine exam of an established patient; Dentist—based on adult teeth cleaning and periodic oral exam.
Source: ACCRA, Cost of Living Index, 1st Quarter 1999

Distribution of Office-Based Physicians

| Area | Family/Gen. Practitioners | Specialists | | |
		Medical	Surgical	Other
MSA[1]	402	2,286	1,567	1,633

Note: Data as of 12/31/97; (1) Metropolitan Statistical Area - see Appendix A for areas included
Source: American Medical Assn., Physician Characteristics & Distribution in the U.S., 1999

Hospitals

Baltimore has 1 general medical and surgical hospital, 3 psychiatric, 1 rehabilitation, 1 orthopedic, 1 chronic disease, 1 other specialty, 2 children's other specialty. *AHA Guide to the Healthcare Field, 1998-99*

According to *U.S. News and World Report,* Baltimore has 5 of the best hospitals in the U.S.: **Johns Hopkins Hospital**, noted for cancer, cardiology, endocrinology, gastroenterology, geriatrics, gynecology, neurology, ophthalmology, orthopedics, otolaryngology, pediatrics, psychiatry, rehabilitation, rheumatology, urology; **Sheppard and Enoch Pratt Hospital**, noted for psychiatry; **Greater Baltimore Medical Center**, noted for cancer; **Johns Hopkins Bayview Medical Center**, noted for endocrinology; **Sinai Hospital of Baltimore**, noted for endocrinology, geriatrics. *U.S. News Online, "America's Best Hospitals," 10th Edition, www.usnews.com*

EDUCATION

Public School District Statistics

District Name	Num. Sch.	Enroll.	Classroom Teachers	Pupils per Teacher	Minority Pupils (%)	Current Exp.[1] ($/pupil)
Baltimore City Pub Sch System	182	107,416	5,833	18.4	87.2	6,370

Note: Data covers the 1997-1998 school year unless otherwise noted; (1) Data covers fiscal year 1996; SD = School District; ISD = Independent School District; n/a not available
Source: National Center for Education Statistics, Common Core of Data Public Education Agency Universe 1997-98; National Center for Education Statistics, Characteristics of the 100 Largest Public Elementary and Secondary School Districts in the United States: 1997-98, July 1999

Educational Quality

School District	Education Quotient[1]	Graduate Outcome[2]	Community Index[3]	Resource Index[4]
Baltimore City	n/a	n/a	n/a	n/a

Note: Nearly 1,000 secondary school districts were rated in terms of educational quality. The scores range from a low of 50 to a high of 150; (1) Average of the Graduate Outcome, Community and Resource indexes; (2) Based on graduation rates and college board scores (SAT/ACT); (3) Based on the surrounding community's average level of education and the area's average income level; (4) Based on teacher salaries, per-pupil expenditures and student-teacher ratios.
Source: Expansion Management, Ratings Issue, 1998

Educational Attainment by Race

| Area | High School Graduate (%) | | | | | Bachelor's Degree (%) | | | | |
	Total	White	Black	Other	Hisp.[2]	Total	White	Black	Other	Hisp.[2]
City	60.7	64.4	57.3	72.5	66.7	15.5	23.5	8.6	32.7	25.3
MSA[1]	74.7	78.2	63.0	80.4	79.7	23.1	26.2	12.0	39.5	30.6
U.S.	75.2	77.9	63.1	60.4	49.8	20.3	21.5	11.4	19.4	9.2

Note: Figures shown cover persons 25 years old and over; (1) Metropolitan Statistical Area - see Appendix A for areas included; (2) people of Hispanic origin can be of any race
Source: 1990 Census of Population and Housing, Summary Tape File 3C

School Enrollment by Type

Area	Preprimary				Elementary/High School			
	Public		Private		Public		Private	
	Enrollment	%	Enrollment	%	Enrollment	%	Enrollment	%
City	7,935	67.4	3,830	32.6	102,104	85.5	17,364	14.5
MSA[1]	25,147	55.8	19,929	44.2	320,507	86.2	51,108	13.8
U.S.	2,679,029	59.5	1,824,256	40.5	38,379,689	90.2	4,187,099	9.8

Note: Figures shown cover persons 3 years old and over;
(1) Metropolitan Statistical Area - see Appendix A for areas included
Source: 1990 Census of Population and Housing, Summary Tape File 3C

School Enrollment by Race

Area	Preprimary (%)				Elementary/High School (%)			
	White	Black	Other	Hisp.[1]	White	Black	Other	Hisp.[1]
City	34.8	63.7	1.4	1.4	26.1	72.4	1.5	1.1
MSA[2]	73.5	24.2	2.4	1.6	64.4	32.6	3.0	1.5
U.S.	80.4	12.5	7.1	7.8	74.1	15.6	10.3	12.5

Note: Figures shown cover persons 3 years old and over; (1) people of Hispanic origin can be of any
race; (2) Metropolitan Statistical Area - see Appendix A for areas included
Source: 1990 Census of Population and Housing, Summary Tape File 3C

Classroom Teacher Salaries in Public Schools

District	B.A. Degree		M.A. Degree		Maximum	
	Min. ($)	Rank[1]	Max. ($)	Rank[1]	Max. ($)	Rank[1]
Baltimore	25,184	63	48,920	27	51,908	41
Average	26,980	-	46,065	-	51,435	-

Note: Salaries are for 1997-1998; (1) Rank ranges from 1 to 100
Source: American Federation of Teachers, Survey & Analysis of Salary Trends, 1998

Higher Education

Two-Year Colleges		Four-Year Colleges		Medical Schools	Law Schools	Voc/Tech
Public	Private	Public	Private			
3	1	4	8	3	2	23

Source: College Blue Book, Occupational Education, 1997; Medical School Admission Requirements,
1999-2000; Peterson's Guide to Two-Year Colleges, 1999; Peterson's Guide to Four-Year Colleges,
2000; Barron's Guide to Law Schools, 1999

MAJOR EMPLOYERS

Major Employers

Baltimore Gas & Electric	Baltimore Sun
Bell-Atlantic Maryland	Greater Baltimore Medical Center
Johns Hopkins Bayview Medical Center	Johns Hopkins Hospital
Sinai Hospital of Baltimore	Petscape Pet Products
University of Maryland Medical System	Mercy Medical Center

Note: Companies listed are located in the city
Source: Dun's Business Rankings, 1999; Ward's Business Directory, 1998

PUBLIC SAFETY

Crime Rate

Area	All Crimes	Violent Crimes				Property Crimes		
		Murder	Forcible Rape	Robbery	Aggrav. Assault	Burglary	Larceny -Theft	Motor Vehicle Theft
City	10,783.3	43.4	66.7	1,199.2	1,111.1	1,772.5	5,363.2	1,227.2
Suburbs[1]	4,927.5	2.5	26.5	199.0	397.6	834.8	3,053.7	413.5
MSA[2]	6,609.0	14.2	38.1	486.2	602.5	1,104.1	3,716.9	647.1
U.S.	4,922.7	6.8	35.9	186.1	382.0	919.6	2,886.5	505.8

Note: Crime rate is the number of crimes per 100,000 pop.; (1) defined as all areas within the MSA but
located outside the central city; (2) Metropolitan Statistical Area - see Appendix A for areas incl.
Source: FBI Uniform Crime Reports, 1997

RECREATION

Culture and Recreation

Museums	Symphony Orchestras	Opera Companies	Dance Companies	Professional Theatres	Zoos	Pro Sports Teams
25	4	1	3	3	1	2

Source: International Directory of the Performing Arts, 1997; Official Museum Directory, 1999; Stern's Performing Arts Directory, 1997; USA Today Four Sport Stadium Guide, 1997; Chamber of Commerce/Economic Development, 1999

Library System

The Enoch Pratt Free Library has 26 branches, holdings of 2,412,009 volumes, and a budget of $22,505,449 (1997-1998). *American Library Directory, 1998-1999*

MEDIA

Newspapers

Name	Type	Freq.	Distribution	Circulation
Baltimore Messenger	General	1x/wk	Local	15,738
The Baltimore Press	n/a	6x/wk	Area	15,000
Baltimore Times	General	1x/wk	Local	32,000
Catonsville Times	General	1x/wk	Local	15,748
Daily Record	n/a	6x/wk	State	18,000
East Baltimore Guide	General	1x/wk	Local	40,000
The Enterprise	General	1x/wk	Local	30,000
Every Wednesday	Black	1x/wk	Area	40,000
Northeast Times Reporter	General	1x/wk	Local	17,223
Owings Mills Times	General	1x/wk	Local	34,000
The Perry Hall & Parkville Avenue	General	1x/wk	Local	40,000
Rooster Community Newspaper	General	2x/mo	Local	70,000
The Sun	General	7x/wk	Area	320,986
Towson Times	General	1x/wk	Local	38,261

Note: Includes newspapers with circulations of 10,000 or more located in the city; n/a not available
Source: Burrelle's Media Directory, 1999 Edition

Television Stations

Name	Ch.	Affiliation	Type	Owner
WMAR	n/a	ABCT	Commercial	Scripps Howard Broadcasting
WBAL	11	NBCT	Commercial	Hearst-Argyle Broadcasting
WJZ	13	CBST	Commercial	Westinghouse Broadcasting Company
WUTB	24	n/a	Commercial	United Television Inc.
WBFF	45	FBC	Commercial	Sinclair Communications Inc.
WNUV	54	WB	Commercial	Glencairn Communications
WMPB	67	PBS	Public	State of Maryland

Note: Stations included broadcast in the Baltimore metro area; n/a not available
Source: Burrelle's Media Directory, 1999 Edition

AM Radio Stations

Call Letters	Freq. (kHz)	Target Audience	Station Format	Music Format
WCAO	600	General	M/N/S/T	Christian
WCBM	680	General	T	n/a
WBMD	750	General	M	Christian
WAMD	970	General	M/N/S	Oldies
WOL	1010	General	N/T	n/a
WBAL	1090	General	N/S/T	n/a
WITH	1230	General	M/N/T	Christian
WWLG	1360	General	M	Adult Standards
WWIN	1400	General	M	Christian
WKDB	1570	General	S/T	n/a

Note: Stations included broadcast in the Baltimore metro area; n/a not available
Target Audience: A=Asian; B=Black; C=Christian; E=Ethnic; F=French; G=General; H=Hispanic;
M=Men; N=Native American; R=Religious; S=Senior Citizen; W=Women; Y=Young Adult; Z=Children
Station Format: E=Educational; M=Music; N=News; S=Sports; T=Talk
Source: Burrelle's Media Directory, 1999 Edition

FM Radio Stations

Call Letters	Freq. (mHz)	Target Audience	Station Format	Music Format
WJHU	88.1	General	M/N/T	Jazz
WEAA	88.9	Black	M/N/S/T	Adult Contemporary/Jazz/Oldies/ R&B/Urban Contemporary
WBJC	91.5	General	M/N	Classical
WERQ	92.3	Black	M/N/S	Urban Contemporary
WPOC	93.1	General	M/N/S	Country
WRBS	95.1	Religious	M/N/S	Christian
WWIN	95.9	General	M	Urban Contemporary
WIYY	97.9	General	M	AOR
WLIF	101.9	General	M	Adult Contemporary
WOCT	104.3	General	M/N/T	Classic Rock
WWMX	106.5	General	M/N/S	Adult Contemporary

Note: Stations included broadcast in the Baltimore metro area
Station Format: E=Educational; M=Music; N=News; S=Sports; T=Talk
Target Audience: A=Asian; B=Black; C=Christian; E=Ethnic; F=French; G=General; H=Hispanic;
M=Men; N=Native American; R=Religious; S=Senior Citizen; W=Women; Y=Young Adult; Z=Children
Music Format: AOR=Album Oriented Rock; MOR=Middle-of-the-Road
Source: Burrelle's Media Directory, 1999 Edition

CLIMATE

Average and Extreme Temperatures

Temperature	Jan	Feb	Mar	Apr	May	Jun	Jul	Aug	Sep	Oct	Nov	Dec	Yr.
Extreme High (°F)	75	79	87	94	98	100	104	105	100	92	86	77	105
Average High (°F)	41	44	53	65	74	83	87	85	79	68	56	45	65
Average Temp. (°F)	33	36	44	54	64	73	77	76	69	57	47	37	56
Average Low (°F)	24	26	34	43	53	62	67	66	58	46	37	28	45
Extreme Low (°F)	-7	-3	6	20	32	40	50	45	35	25	13	0	-7

Note: Figures cover the years 1950-1990
Source: National Climatic Data Center, International Station Meteorological Climate Summary, 3/95

Average Precipitation/Snowfall/Humidity

Precip./Humidity	Jan	Feb	Mar	Apr	May	Jun	Jul	Aug	Sep	Oct	Nov	Dec	Yr.
Avg. Precip. (in.)	2.9	3.0	3.5	3.3	3.7	3.7	3.9	4.2	3.4	3.0	3.2	3.3	41.2
Avg. Snowfall (in.)	6	7	4	Tr	Tr	0	0	0	0	Tr	1	4	21
Avg. Rel. Hum. 7am (%)	72	71	71	71	77	79	80	83	85	83	78	74	77
Avg. Rel. Hum. 4pm (%)	56	53	48	47	52	53	53	55	55	54	55	57	53

Note: Figures cover the years 1950-1990; Tr = Trace amounts (<0.05 in. of rain; <0.5 in. of snow)
Source: National Climatic Data Center, International Station Meteorological Climate Summary, 3/95

Weather Conditions

Temperature			Daytime Sky			Precipitation		
10°F & below	32°F & below	90°F & above	Clear	Partly cloudy	Cloudy	0.01 inch or more precip.	0.1 inch or more snow/ice	Thunder-storms
6	97	31	91	143	131	113	13	27

Note: Figures are average number of days per year and covers the years 1950-1990
Source: National Climatic Data Center, International Station Meteorological Climate Summary, 3/95

AIR & WATER QUALITY

Maximum Pollutant Concentrations

	Particulate Matter (ug/m³)	Carbon Monoxide (ppm)	Sulfur Dioxide (ppm)	Nitrogen Dioxide (ppm)	Ozone (ppm)	Lead (ug/m³)
MSA[1] Level	63	5	0.026	0.026	0.16	0.01
NAAQS[2]	150	9	0.140	0.053	0.12	1.50
Met NAAQS?	Yes	Yes	Yes	Yes	No	Yes

Note: (1) Metropolitan Statistical Area - see Appendix A for areas included; (2) National Ambient Air Quality Standards; ppm = parts per million; ug/m3 = micrograms per cubic meter; n/a not available
Source: EPA, National Air Quality and Emissions Trends Report, 1997

Pollutant Standards Index

In the Baltimore MSA (see Appendix A for areas included), the Pollutant Standards Index (PSI) exceeded 100 on 30 days in 1997. A PSI value greater than 100 indicates that air quality would be in the unhealthful range on that day. *EPA, National Air Quality and Emissions Trends Report, 1997*

Drinking Water

Water System Name	Pop. Served	Primary Water Source Type	Number of Violations in 1998	Type of Violation/ Contaminants
Baltimore City	1,600,000	Surface	None	None

Note: Data as of July 10, 1999
Source: EPA, Office of Ground Water and Drinking Water, Safe Drinking Water Information System

Baltimore tap water is alkaline, very soft and fluoridated.
Editor & Publisher Market Guide, 1999

Boston, Massachusetts

Background

Who would think that Boston, a city founded upon the Puritan principles of hard work, plain living, sobriety, and unyielding religious conviction would be known for such a radical act throwing tea overboard from a ship?

The answer lies in the wealth upon which Boston grew: ship trading. Because Boston sea captains reaped more profits than the English in molasses from the West Indies, mahogany from Honduras, and slaves from Guinea, jealous England decided to impose additional taxes upon her colonial subjects. The unpopular Stamp Tax and Molasses Tax aroused resentment among Boston citizens against its mother country. In defiance against additional taxes, Samuel Adams led the Sons of Liberty to throw a precious cargo of tea, so dear to the English, overboard. Events catapulted, resulting in the shot "heard 'round the world" in Concord, and the American Revolution began.

After the Revolution, Boston continued to grow into the Yankee capital that it is today. "Boston Brahmins" (a reference to the highest social caste in India) such as Isabella Stewart Gardiner, brought artistic cache to the city. Thinkers, such as Louisa May Alcott, Ralph Waldo Emerson, and Henry David Thoreau contributed significant ideas to the classrooms of many Liberal Arts schools; indeed, Boston is now home to more than 50 institutions of higher learning.

As the largest city in New England, Boston has been recognized not only as a leading educational, cultural, and medical center but also as an area for high technology and electronics research.

The new ballpark proposed by the Boston Red Sox would generate dramatic increases in economic activity and job creation, according to an independent report that was recently made public by the Greater Boston Chamber of Commerce and the Greater Boston Convention & Visitors Bureau.

Boston's weather is influenced by three factors: latitude, placing it in the path of both tropical and polar air masses; proximity to several low pressure storm tracks, causing fluctuating weather conditions; east-coast ocean location, creating a moderating influence on temperature extremes.

Hot summer afternoons are relieved by sea breezes. In winter the severity of cold waves is often reduced by the proximity of the relatively warm ocean.

General Rankings and Evaluative Comments

- Boston was ranked #2 out of 15 large, northeastern metropolitan areas in *Money's* 1998 survey of "The Best Places to Live in America." The survey was conducted by first contacting 512 representative households nationwide and asking them to rank 37 quality-of-life factors on a scale of 1 to 10. Next, a demographic profile was compiled on the 300 largest metropolitan statistical areas in the U.S. The numbers were crunched together to arrive at an overall ranking (things Americans consider most important, like clean air and water, low crime and good schools, received extra weight). Unlike previous years, the 1998 rankings were broken down by region (northeast, midwest, south, west) and population size (100,000 to 249,999; 250,000 to 999,999; 1 million plus). The city had a nationwide ranking of #23 out of 300 in 1997 and #69 out of 300 in 1996. *Money, July 1998; Money, July 1997; Money, September 1996*

- *Ladies Home Journal* ranked America's 200 largest cities based on the qualities women care about most. Boston ranked #104 out of 200. Criteria: low crime rate, well-paying jobs, quality health and child care, good public schools, the presence of women in government, size of the gender wage gap, number of sexual-harassment and discrimination complaints filed, unemployment and divorce rates, commute times, population density, number of houses of worship, parks and cultural offerings, number of women's health specialists, how well a community's women cared for themselves, complexion kindness index based on UV radiation levels, odds of finding affordable fashions, rental rates for romance movies, champagne sales and other matters of the heart. *Ladies Home Journal, November 1998*

- Boston was selected as one of the 10 healthiest cities for women by *American Health*. It was ranked #3 out of America's 120 most populous metro areas. Criteria: number and quality of doctors and hospitals, quality of women's health centers, number of recreational opportunities, rate of violent crimes, cleanliness of air and water, percentage of women-owned businesses, and the number of family-friendly employers.

  "The city has banned smoking in restaurants (due to Federal legislation), and nearly 10% of its residents carpool to work." *American Health, 1998*

- Zero Population Growth ranked 229 cities in terms of children's health, safety, and economic well-being. Boston was ranked #9 out of 25 major cities (main city in a metro area with population of greater than 2 million) and was given a grade of C+. Criteria: total population, percent of population under 18 years of age, household language, percent population change, percent of births to teens, infant mortality rate, percent of low birth weights, dropout rate, enrollment in preprimary school, violent and property crime rates, unemployment rate, percent of children in poverty, percent of owner occupied units, number of bad air days, percent of public transportation commuters, and average travel time to work. *Zero Population Growth, Children's Environmental Index, Fall 1999*

- Boston was ranked #44 out of 59 metro areas in *The Regional Economist's* "Rational Livability Ranking of 59 Large Metro Areas." The rankings were based on the metro area's total population change over the period 1990-97 divided by the number of people moving in from elsewhere in the United States (net domestic in-migration). *St. Louis Federal Reserve Bank of St. Louis, The Regional Economist, April 1999*

- Boston appeared on *Travel & Leisure's* list of the world's 100 best cities. It was ranked #9 in the U.S. and #20 in the world. Criteria: activities/attractions, culture/arts, people, restaurants/food, and value. *Travel & Leisure, 1998 World's Best Awards*

- *Conde Nast Traveler* polled 37,293 readers for travel satisfaction. Cities were ranked based on the following criteria: people/friendliness, environment/ambiance, cultural enrichment, restaurants and fun/energy. Boston appeared in the top 25, ranking number 7, with an overall rating of 72.1 out of 100. *Conde Nast Traveler, Readers' Choice Poll 1998*

- Boston was selected by *Yahoo! Internet Life* as one of "America's Most Wired Cities & Towns." The city ranked #5 out of 50. Criteria: home and work net use, domain density, hosts per capita, directory density and content quality. *Yahoo! Internet Life, March 1999*

- Cognetics studied 273 metro areas in the United States, ranking them by entrepreneurial activity. Boston was ranked #36 out of the 50 largest metro areas. Criteria: Significant Starts (firms started in the last 10 years that still employ at least 5 people) and Young Growers (percent of firms 10 years old or less that grew significantly during the last 4 years). *Cognetics, "Entrepreneurial Hot Spots: The Best Places in America to Start and Grow a Company," 1998*

- Boston was included among *Entrepreneur* magazine's listing of the "20 Best Cities for Small Business." It was ranked #3 among northeastern metro areas. Criteria: entrepreneurial activity, small-business growth, economic growth, and risk of failure. Entrepreneur, October 1999

- Boston was selected as one of the "Best American Cities to Start a Business" by *Point of View* magazine. Criteria: coolness, quality-of-life, and business concerns. The city was ranked #11 out of 75. *Point of View, November 1998*

- Boston appeared on *Sales & Marketing Management's* list of the "20 Hottest Cities for Selling." Rank: #8 out of 20. *S&MM* editors looked at Metropolitan Statistical Areas with populations of more than 150,000. The areas were ranked based on population increases, retail sales increases, effective buying income, increase in both residential and commercial building permits issued, unemployment rates, job growth, mix of industries, tax rates, number of corporate relocations, and the number of new corporations. *Sales & Marketing Management, April 1999*

- *Computerworld* selected the best markets for IT job seekers based on their annual salary, skills, and hiring surveys. Boston ranked #1 out of 10. *Computerworld, January 11, 1999*

- Reliastar Financial Corp. ranked the 125 largest metropolitan areas according to the general financial security of residents. Boston was ranked #48 out of 125 with a score of 3.8. The score indicates the percentage a metropolitan area is above or below the metropolitan norm. A metro area with a score of 10.6 is 10.6% above the metro average. Criteria: Earnings and Wealth Potential (household income, education, net assets, cost of living); Safety Net (health insurance, retirement savings, life insurance, income support programs); Personal Threats (unemployment rate, low-income households, crime rate); Community Economic Vitality (cost of community services, job quality, job creation, housing costs). *Reliastar Financial Corp., "The Best Cities to Earn and Save Money," 1999 Edition*

Business Environment

STATE ECONOMY

State Economic Profile

"After some recent years of pretty impressive performance, the Massachusetts economy should maintain steady, but slower growth in 1999-2001. MA's biggest constraint on continued growth is its shortage of skilled workers. While its loss of residents is no longer a problem, it still cannot attract enough skilled workers to fuel its economy.

After several years of above-trend economic growth, MA's housing markets heated up in 1998. For the first year in almost a decade, home price appreciation outpaced the nation, with much of the gains centered around Boston. Sales were record highs. After strong homebuilding activity in 1998, permit activity has slowed. Single-family permits were up only 6% in 1998, well below the national. The real burst has been in multifamily permit activity, which increased 37% in 1998. This restraint on single-family housing should result in pretty strong price appreciation in 1999.

MA's economy is being driven by its high-tech industry and services. About two-thirds of job creation came from the services sector, while the construction sector also witnessed an almost 8% increase in employment. The 2% decline in manufacturing employment masked the job growth occurring in biotech and software. The real job declines have come in computer/semiconductor, textile and machinery. While much of this decline is due to weak exports, heavy manufacturing in MA is not likely to rebound in the near term.

MA's weaknesses have been more than outbalanced by strong job growth in other, often high-paying, sectors. Poor demographics, tight labor markets and strict building constraints will slow MA's economy from its recent pace." *National Association of Realtors, Economic Profiles: The Fifty States and the District of Columbia, http://nar.realtor.com/databank/profiles.htm*

IMPORTS/EXPORTS

Total Export Sales

Area	1994 ($000)	1995 ($000)	1996 ($000)	1997 ($000)	% Chg. 1994-97	% Chg. 1996-97
MSA[1]	7,095,349	7,902,660	8,715,804	9,570,608	34.9	9.8
U.S.	512,415,609	583,030,524	622,827,063	687,597,999	34.2	10.4

Note: (1) Metropolitan Statistical Area - see Appendix A for areas included
Source: U.S. Department of Commerce, International Trade Association, Metropolitan Area Exports: An Export Performance Report on Over 250 U.S. Cities, November 10, 1998

CITY FINANCES

City Government Finances

Component	FY94 ($000)	FY94 (per capita $)
Revenue	2,048,866	3,704.14
Expenditure	1,927,067	3,483.94
Debt Outstanding	1,115,253	2,016.27
Cash & Securities	2,009,932	3,633.76

Source: U.S. Bureau of the Census, City Government Finances: 1993-94

City Government Revenue by Source

Source	FY94 ($000)	FY94 (per capita $)	FY94 (%)
From Federal Government	56,173	101.56	2.7
From State Governments	753,445	1,362.15	36.8
From Local Governments	2,360	4.27	0.1
Property Taxes	654,945	1,184.07	32.0
General Sales Taxes	0	0.00	0.0
Selective Sales Taxes	27,486	49.69	1.3
Income Taxes	0	0.00	0.0
Current Charges	215,595	389.77	10.5
Utility/Liquor Store	88,635	160.24	4.3
Employee Retirement[1]	155,692	281.48	7.6
Other	94,535	170.91	4.6

Note: (1) Excludes "city contributions," classified as "nonrevenue," intragovernmental transfers.
Source: U.S. Bureau of the Census, City Government Finances: 1993-94

City Government Expenditures by Function

Function	FY94 ($000)	FY94 (per capita $)	FY94 (%)
Educational Services	509,205	920.59	26.4
Employee Retirement[1]	190,606	344.60	9.9
Environment/Housing	215,673	389.92	11.2
Government Administration	51,962	93.94	2.7
Interest on General Debt	51,730	93.52	2.7
Public Safety	294,926	533.20	15.3
Social Services	319,299	577.26	16.6
Transportation	64,422	116.47	3.3
Utility/Liquor Store	54,043	97.70	2.8
Other	175,201	316.75	9.1

Note: (1) Payments to beneficiaries including withdrawal of contributions.
Source: U.S. Bureau of the Census, City Government Finances: 1993-94

Municipal Bond Ratings

Area	Moody's	S & P
Boston	Aa3	n/a

Note: n/a not available; n/r not rated
Source: Moody's Bond Record, 6/99

POPULATION

Population Growth

Area	1980	1990	% Chg. 1980-90	July 1998 Estimate	% Chg. 1990-98
City	562,994	574,283	2.0	555,447	-3.3
MSA[1]	2,805,911	2,870,650	2.3	3,274,844	14.1
U.S.	226,545,805	248,765,170	9.8	270,299,000	8.7

Note: (1) Metropolitan Statistical Area - see Appendix A for areas included;
July 1998 MSA population estimate was calculated by the editors
Source: 1980/1990 Census of Housing and Population, Summary Tape File 3C;
Census Bureau Population Estimates 1998

Population Characteristics

Race	City 1980 Population	%	City 1990 Population	%	% Chg. 1980-90	MSA[1] 1990 Population	%
White	396,635	70.5	361,513	63.0	-8.9	2,503,373	87.2
Black	126,438	22.5	146,695	25.5	16.0	208,075	7.2
Amer Indian/Esk/Aleut	1,455	0.3	1,865	0.3	28.2	5,245	0.2
Asian/Pacific Islander	16,298	2.9	30,457	5.3	86.9	94,285	3.3
Other	22,168	3.9	33,753	5.9	52.3	59,672	2.1
Hispanic Origin[2]	36,068	6.4	59,692	10.4	65.5	122,999	4.3

Note: (1) Metropolitan Statistical Area - see Appendix A for areas included;
(2) people of Hispanic origin can be of any race
Source: 1980/1990 Census of Housing and Population, Summary Tape File 3C

Ancestry

Area	German	Irish	English	Italian	U.S.	French	Polish	Dutch
City	5.9	22.4	6.7	10.5	1.8	2.8	3.0	0.6
MSA[1]	8.5	29.0	14.1	16.9	2.7	5.6	4.0	0.9
U.S.	23.3	15.6	13.1	5.9	5.3	4.2	3.8	2.5

Note: Figures are percentages and include persons that reported multiple ancestry (eg. if a person reported being Irish and Italian, they were included in both columns); (1) Metropolitan Statistical Area - see Appendix A for areas included
Source: 1990 Census of Population and Housing, Summary Tape File 3C

Age

Area	Median Age (Years)	Under 5	Under 18	18-24	25-44	45-64	65+	80+
City	30.2	6.2	19.1	17.3	36.8	15.3	11.5	2.9
MSA[1]	33.3	6.4	20.8	12.4	35.1	18.9	12.9	3.1
U.S.	32.9	7.3	25.6	10.5	32.6	18.7	12.5	2.8

Note: (1) Metropolitan Statistical Area - see Appendix A for areas included
Source: 1990 Census of Population and Housing, Summary Tape File 3C

Male/Female Ratio

Area	Number of males per 100 females (all ages)	Number of males per 100 females (18 years old+)
City	91.4	90.3
MSA[1]	92.0	89.2
U.S.	95.0	91.9

Note: (1) Metropolitan Statistical Area - see Appendix A for areas included
Source: 1990 Census of Population, General Population Characteristics

INCOME

Per Capita/Median/Average Income

Area	Per Capita ($)	Median Household ($)	Average Household ($)
City	15,581	29,180	37,907
MSA[1]	19,288	40,491	50,478
U.S.	14,420	30,056	38,453

Note: All figures are for 1989; (1) Metropolitan Statistical Area - see Appendix A for areas included
Source: 1990 Census of Population and Housing, Summary Tape File 3C

Household Income Distribution by Race

Income ($)	City (%)					U.S. (%)				
	Total	White	Black	Other	Hisp.[1]	Total	White	Black	Other	Hisp.[1]
Less than 5,000	8.0	6.3	10.5	15.3	12.6	6.2	4.8	15.2	8.6	8.8
5,000 - 9,999	12.5	11.3	15.1	15.2	17.1	9.3	8.6	14.2	9.9	11.1
10,000 - 14,999	7.4	7.2	7.5	8.3	9.7	8.8	8.5	11.0	9.8	11.0
15,000 - 24,999	15.8	14.6	18.7	18.6	20.2	17.5	17.3	18.9	18.5	20.5
25,000 - 34,999	14.6	14.5	14.9	13.9	14.0	15.8	16.1	14.2	15.4	16.4
35,000 - 49,999	16.2	17.0	15.0	13.3	13.4	17.9	18.6	13.3	16.1	16.0
50,000 - 74,999	15.3	16.6	13.0	10.7	9.1	15.0	15.8	9.3	13.4	11.1
75,000 - 99,999	5.4	6.4	3.3	2.8	2.4	5.1	5.5	2.6	4.7	3.1
100,000+	4.8	6.1	1.9	1.8	1.4	4.4	4.8	1.3	3.7	1.9

Note: All figures are for 1989; (1) people of Hispanic origin can be of any race
Source: 1990 Census of Population and Housing, Summary Tape File 3C

Effective Buying Income

Area	Per Capita ($)	Median Household ($)	Average Household ($)
City	18,614	36,460	47,456
MSA[1]	19,850	43,852	52,960
U.S.	16,803	34,536	45,243

Note: Data as of 1/1/99; (1) Metropolitan Statistical Area - see Appendix A for areas included
Source: Standard Rate & Data Service, Newspaper Advertising Source, 9/99

Effective Household Buying Income Distribution

Area	% of Households Earning						
	$10,000 -$19,999	$20,000 -$34,999	$35,000 -$49,999	$50,000 -$74,999	$75,000 -$99,000	$100,000 -$124,999	$125,000 and up
City	14.8	19.3	16.3	19.2	9.1	3.6	3.5
MSA[1]	11.9	17.9	17.8	23.8	11.0	4.0	3.8
U.S.	16.0	22.6	18.2	18.9	7.2	2.4	2.7

Note: Data as of 1/1/99; (1) Metropolitan Statistical Area - see Appendix A for areas included
Source: Standard Rate & Data Service, Newspaper Advertising Source, 9/99

Poverty Rates by Race and Age

Area	Total (%)	By Race (%)				By Age (%)		
		White	Black	Other	Hisp.[2]	Under 5 years old	Under 18 years old	65 years and over
City	18.7	13.9	24.2	32.0	33.9	27.9	28.3	15.3
MSA[1]	8.3	6.3	21.7	23.4	28.4	12.1	11.5	9.2
U.S.	13.1	9.8	29.5	23.1	25.3	20.1	18.3	12.8

Note: Figures show the percent of people living below the poverty line in 1989. The average poverty threshold was $12,674 for a family of four in 1989; (1) Metropolitan Statistical Area - see Appendix A for areas included; (2) people of Hispanic origin can be of any race
Source: 1990 Census of Population and Housing, Summary Tape File 3C

EMPLOYMENT

Labor Force and Employment

Area	Civilian Labor Force			Workers Employed		
	Jun. 1998	Jun. 1999	% Chg.	Jun. 1998	Jun. 1999	% Chg.
City	302,404	302,266	-0.0	290,922	292,119	0.4
MSA[1]	1,834,847	1,837,503	0.1	1,780,127	1,787,579	0.4
U.S.	138,798,000	140,666,000	1.3	132,265,000	134,395,000	1.6

Note: Data is not seasonally adjusted and covers workers 16 years of age and older;
(1) Metropolitan Statistical Area - see Appendix A for areas included
Source: Bureau of Labor Statistics, http://stats.bls.gov

Unemployment Rate

Area	1998						1999					
	Jul.	Aug.	Sep.	Oct.	Nov.	Dec.	Jan.	Feb.	Mar.	Apr.	May.	Jun.
City	3.6	3.4	3.8	3.0	2.7	2.6	3.4	2.9	3.0	2.7	3.0	3.4
MSA[1]	2.7	2.6	3.0	2.4	2.3	2.2	3.0	2.6	2.7	2.3	2.5	2.7
U.S.	4.7	4.5	4.4	4.2	4.1	4.0	4.8	4.7	4.4	4.1	4.0	4.5

Note: Data is not seasonally adjusted and covers workers 16 years of age and older; all figures are percentages; (1) Metropolitan Statistical Area - see Appendix A for areas included
Source: Bureau of Labor Statistics, http://stats.bls.gov

Employment by Industry

Sector	MSA[1]		U.S.
	Number of Employees	Percent of Total	Percent of Total
Services	784,400	39.4	30.4
Retail Trade	314,300	15.8	17.7
Government	239,200	12.0	15.6
Manufacturing	217,100	10.9	14.3
Finance/Insurance/Real Estate	168,200	8.4	5.9
Wholesale Trade	113,500	5.7	5.4
Transportation/Public Utilities	87,600	4.4	5.3
Construction	68,300	3.4	5.0
Mining	400	<0.1	0.4

Note: Figures cover non-farm employment as of 6/99 and are not seasonally adjusted; (1) Metropolitan Statistical Area - see Appendix A for areas included
Source: Bureau of Labor Statistics, http://stats.bls.gov

Employment by Occupation

Occupation Category	City (%)	MSA[1] (%)	U.S. (%)
White Collar	66.2	70.2	58.1
Executive/Admin./Management	14.5	16.6	12.3
Professional	18.2	19.6	14.1
Technical & Related Support	4.4	4.5	3.7
Sales	9.4	11.4	11.8
Administrative Support/Clerical	19.7	18.1	16.3
Blue Collar	16.0	16.9	26.2
Precision Production/Craft/Repair	6.4	8.2	11.3
Machine Operators/Assem./Insp.	4.1	3.7	6.8
Transportation/Material Movers	2.8	2.5	4.1
Cleaners/Helpers/Laborers	2.7	2.5	3.9
Services	17.3	12.2	13.2
Farming/Forestry/Fishing	0.4	0.7	2.5

Note: Figures cover employed persons 16 years old and over; (1) Metropolitan Statistical Area - see Appendix A for areas included
Source: 1990 Census of Population and Housing, Summary Tape File 3C

Occupational Employment Projections: 1996 - 2006

Occupations Expected to Have the Largest Job Growth (ranked by numerical growth)	Fast-Growing Occupations[1] (ranked by percent growth)
1. Systems analysts	1. Computer engineers
2. General managers & top executives	2. Personal and home care aides
3. Computer engineers	3. Home health aides
4. Home health aides	4. Paralegals
5. Registered nurses	5. Physical therapy assistants and aides
6. Cashiers	6. Medical assistants
7. Nursing aides/orderlies/attendants	7. Physical therapists
8. Database administrators	8. Desktop publishers
9. Salespersons, retail	9. Human services workers
10. Engineering/science/computer sys. mgrs.	10. Occupational therapists

Note: Projections cover Massachusetts; (1) Excludes occupations with total job growth less than 300
Source: U.S. Department of Labor, Employment and Training Administration, America's Labor Market Information System (ALMIS)

TAXES

Major State and Local Tax Rates

State Corp. Income (%)	State Personal Income (%)	Residential Property (effective rate per $100)	Sales & Use State (%)	Sales & Use Local (%)	State Gasoline (cents/ gallon)	State Cigarette (cents/ pack)
9.5[a]	5.95	1.35	5.0	None	21.0	76.0

Note: Personal/corporate income, sales, gasoline and cigarette tax rates as of January 1999.
Property tax rates as of 1997; (a) Rate includes a 14% surtax, as does the following: an additional tax of $7.00 per $1,000 on taxable tangible property (or net worth allocable to state for intangible property corporations). Minimum tax is $456
Source: Federation of Tax Administrators, www.taxadmin.org; Washington D.C. Department of Finance and Revenue, Tax Rates and Tax Burdens in the District of Columbia: A Nationwide Comparison, July 1998; Chamber of Commerce, 1999

Total Taxes Per Capita and as a Percent of Income

Area	Per Capita Income ($)	Per Capita Taxes ($) Total	Per Capita Taxes ($) Federal	Per Capita Taxes ($) State/ Local	Percent of Income (%) Total	Percent of Income (%) Federal	Percent of Income (%) State/ Local
Massachusetts	34,469	12,654	8,728	3,926	36.7	25.3	11.4
U.S.	27,876	9,881	6,690	3,191	35.4	24.0	11.4

Note: Figures are for 1998
Source: Tax Foundation, www.taxfoundation.org

Estimated Tax Burden

Area	State Income	Local Income	Property	Sales	Total
Boston	3,912	0	3,250	488	7,650

Note: The numbers are estimates of taxes paid by a married couple with two children and annual earnings of $75,000. Sales tax estimates assume they spend average amounts on food, clothing, household goods and gasoline. Property tax estimates assume they live in a $250,000 home.
Source: Kiplinger's Personal Finance Magazine, October 1998

COMMERCIAL REAL ESTATE

Office Market

Class/ Location	Total Space (sq. ft.)	Vacant Space (sq. ft.)	Vac. Rate (%)	Under Constr. (sq. ft.)	Net Absorp. (sq. ft.)	Rental Rates ($/sq.ft./yr.)
Class A						
CBD	35,367,157	899,291	2.5	586,421	128,026	28.00-60.00
Outside CBD	62,334,993	4,394,942	7.1	4,767,274	566,952	23.00-35.00
Class B						
CBD	3,862,099	156,006	4.0	0	117,005	16.00-38.00
Outside CBD	5,290,279	573,160	10.8	0	89,152	14.00-29.00

Note: Data as of 10/98 and covers Boston; CBD = Central Business District; n/a not available;
Source: Society of Industrial and Office Realtors, 1999 Comparative Statistics of Industrial and Office Real Estate Markets

"Between 1999 and 2003, Boston's major office districts—the Financial area, the Seaport, and the Back Bay—will see nearly seven million sq. ft. of new development, if projects announced move through the pipeline. To date, though, the specter of aggressive speculative development has not haunted the market. That's good, because there is a reasonable concern that absorption could slow in 1999, although part of the reason is a paucity of attractive new space. To put things in perspective, all that new space merely represents a 1.3 percent annual increase in inventory over the next five years. Boston's job base grew 2.9 percent in 1998. It is not excessively optimistic to anticipate another year of rental rate increases before the curve starts to flatten." *Society of Industrial and Office Realtors, 1999 Comparative Statistics of Industrial and Office Real Estate Markets*

Industrial Market

Location	Total Space (sq. ft.)	Vacant Space (sq. ft.)	Vac. Rate (%)	Under Constr. (sq. ft.)	Net Absorp. (sq. ft.)	Net Lease ($/sq.ft./yr.)
Central City	n/a	n/a	n/a	n/a	n/a	n/a
Suburban	85,251,250	5,225,740	6.1	340,652	1,676,057	4.25-6.00

Note: Data as of 10/98 and covers Boston; n/a not available
Source: Society of Industrial and Office Realtors, 1999 Comparative Statistics of Industrial and Office Real Estate Markets

"The area's economy looks strong going into 1999, with unemployment hovering in the 3.5 percent range. Global disturbances triggered by the Asian crisis, however, will likely affect local companies, especially those in the manufacturing and high-tech sectors. Many firms have already experienced a drop-off in exports. Raytheon and Compaq/Digital Equipment, two companies important in this market, have announced layoffs and plant closings. Sales prices and lease prices may have seen their peaks in 1998. Downsizing could increase vacancies next year. Tightening in the capital markets will make financing harder to come by. On a positive note, this scenario should keep a lid on new construction, helping supply stay in balance with demand. This could be a year of stasis for a market which has seen a remarkable recovery over the course of the decade." *Society of Industrial and Office Realtors, 1999 Comparative Statistics of Industrial and Office Real Estate Markets*

Retail Market

Shopping Center Inventory (sq. ft.)	Shopping Center Construction (sq. ft.)	Construction as a Percent of Inventory (%)	Torto Wheaton Rent Index[1] ($/sq. ft.)
61,005,000	1,036,000	1.7	15.18

Note: Data as of 1997 and covers the Metropolitan Statistical Area - see Appendix A for areas included; (1) Index is based on a model that predicts what the average rent should be for leases with certain characteristics, in certain locations during certain years.
Source: National Association of Realtors, 1997-1998 Market Conditions Report

"Since 1992, the Boston retail rent index has improved 35% and is higher than the Northeast average of $14.30 per square foot. The area has benefitted from a net influx of new residents and an unemployment rate that has fallen below 4.5%. The strong economy has provided small retailers the opportunity to move to better locations or open new space. Shopping centers are becoming an increasingly attractive investment because intense competition for office space has investors looking for alternatives. Rents in the Boston area are expected to rise above 5% per year through the year 2000." *National Association of Realtors, 1997-1998 Market Conditions Report*

COMMERCIAL UTILITIES

Typical Monthly Electric Bills

Area	Commercial Service ($/month)		Industrial Service ($/month)	
	12 kW demand 1,500 kWh	100 kW demand 30,000 kWh	1,000 kW demand 400,000 kWh	20,000 kW demand 10,000,000 kWh
City	272	4,319	43,910	742,985
U.S.	150	2,174	23,995	508,569

Note: Based on rates in effect January 1, 1999
Source: Edison Electric Institute, Typical Residential, Commercial and Industrial Bills, Winter 1999

TRANSPORTATION

Transportation Statistics

Average minutes to work	24.9
Interstate highways	I-90; I-93; I-95
Bus lines	
In-city	Massachusetts Bay TA, 980 vehicles
Inter-city	12
Passenger air service	
Airport	Logan International
Airlines	37
Aircraft departures	135,865 (1996)
Enplaned passengers	10,653,062 (1996)
Rail service	Amtrak; Metro/Light Rail
Motor freight carriers	500+
Major waterways/ports	Boston Harbor; Port of Boston

Source: Editor & Publisher Market Guide, 1999; FAA Airport Activity Statistics, 1997; Amtrak National Time Table, Northeast Timetable, Spring/Summer 1999; 1990 Census of Population and Housing, STF 3C; Chamber of Commerce/Economic Development 1999; Jane's Urban Transport Systems 1999-2000

Means of Transportation to Work

Area	Car/Truck/Van		Public Transportation			Bicycle	Walked	Other Means	Worked at Home
	Drove Alone	Car-pooled	Bus	Subway	Railroad				
City	40.1	10.5	13.6	13.2	1.0	0.9	14.0	4.5	2.2
MSA[1]	65.8	9.8	5.4	5.9	1.4	0.5	6.5	2.0	2.6
U.S.	73.2	13.4	3.0	1.5	0.5	0.4	3.9	1.2	3.0

Note: Figures shown are percentages and only include workers 16 years old and over;
(1) Metropolitan Statistical Area - see Appendix A for areas included
Source: 1990 Census of Population and Housing, Summary Tape File 3C

BUSINESSES

Major Business Headquarters

Company Name	1999 Rankings	
	Fortune 500	Forbes 500
BankBoston Corp.	218	-
Boston Consulting Group	-	349
Connell Limited Partnership	-	155
Fidelity Investments	-	21
Fleet Financial Group	161	-
Gillette	159	-
International Data Group	-	73
John Hancock Mutual Life	179	-
Liberty Mutual Group	124	-
State Street Corp.	366	-
Unicco Service Company	-	404

Note: Companies listed are located in the city; dashes indicate no ranking
Fortune 500: Companies that produce a 10-K are ranked 1 to 500 based on 1998 revenue
Forbes 500: Private companies are ranked 1 to 500 based on 1997 revenue
Source: Forbes, November 30, 1998; Fortune, April 26, 1999

Best Companies to Work For

Beth Israel Deaconess Medical Center and Hill Holliday Connors Cosmopulos (advertising), headquartered in Boston, are among the " 100 Best Companies for Working Mothers." Criteria: fair wages, opportunities for women to advance, support for child care, flexible work schedules, family-friendly benefits, and work/life supports. *Working Mother, October 1998*

Keane, Inc. (professional services/consulting), Cabot Corp. (chemicals), John Hancock Mutual Life Insurance Co. (financial services), BankBoston Corp. (banking) and Fleet Financial Group (banking), headquartered in Boston, are among the " 100 Best Places to Work in IS." Criteria: compensation, turnover and training. *Computerworld, May 25, 1998*

Fast-Growing Businesses

According to *Inc.*, Boston is home to one of America's 100 fastest-growing private companies: Counsell Group. Criteria for inclusion: must be an independent, privately-held, U.S. corporation, proprietorship or partnership; sales of at least $200,000 in 1995; five-year operating/sales history; increase in 1999 sales over 1998 sales; holding companies, regulated banks, and utilities were excluded. *Inc. 500, 1999*

According to *Fortune*, Boston is home to one of America's 100 fastest-growing companies: Keane. Companies were ranked based on earnings-per-share growth, revenue growth and total return over the previous three years. Criteria for inclusion: public companies with sales of least $50 million. Companies that lost money in the most recent quarter, or ended in the red for the past four quarters as a whole, were not eligible. Limited partnerships and REITs were also not considered. *Fortune, "America's Fastest-Growing Companies," 1999*

According to Deloitte & Touche LLP, Boston is home to one of America's 100 fastest-growing high-technology companies: Invention Machine Corp.. Companies are ranked by percentage growth in revenue over a five-year period. Criteria for inclusion: must be a U.S. company developing and/or providing technology products or services; company must have been in business for five years with 1993 revenues of at least $50,000. *Deloitte & Touche LLP, November 17, 1998*

Women-Owned Firms: Number, Employment and Sales

Area	Number of Firms	Employ-ment	Sales ($000)	Rank[2]
MSA[1]	125,900	257,600	36,459,300	18

Note: (1) Metropolitan Statistical Area - see Appendix A for areas included;
(2) Calculated on an averaging of the number of businesses, employment and sales
Source: The National Foundation for Women Business Owners, 1999 Facts on Women-Owned Businesses: Trends in the Top 50 Metropolitan Areas

Women-Owned Firms: Growth

Area	% change from 1992 to 1999			Rank[2]
	Number of Firms	Employ-ment	Sales	
MSA[1]	34.3	42.2	54.2	50

Note: (1) Metropolitan Statistical Area - see Appendix A for areas included; (2) Calculated on an averaging of the percent growth of number of businesses, employment and sales
Source: The National Foundation for Women Business Owners, 1999 Facts on Women-Owned Businesses: Trends in the Top 50 Metropolitan Areas

Minority Business Opportunity

Boston is home to one company which is on the Black Enterprise Industrial/Service 100 list (largest based on gross sales): Grimes Oil Co. Inc. (petroleum products distributor) . Criteria: operational in previous calendar year, at least 51% black-owned and manufactures/owns the product it sells or provides industrial or consumer services. Brokerages, real estate firms and firms that provide professional services are not eligible. *Black Enterprise, www.blackenterprise.com*

Small Business Opportunity

According to *Forbes*, Boston is home to one of America's 200 best small companies: Tech-Ops Sevcon. Criteria: companies included must be publicly traded since November 1997 with a stock price of at least $5 per share and an average daily float of 1,000 shares. The company's latest 12-month sales must be between $5 and $350 million, return on equity (ROE) must be a minimum of 12% for both the past 5 years and the most recent four quarters, and five-year sales and EPS growth must average at least 10%. Companies with declining sales or earnings during the past year were dropped as well as businesses with debt/equity ratios over 1.25. Companies with negative operating cash flow in each of the past two years were also excluded. *Forbes, November 2, 1998*

HOTELS & MOTELS

Hotels/Motels

Area	Hotels/Motels	Rooms	Luxury-Level Hotels/Motels		Average Minimum Rates ($)		
			♦♦♦♦	♦♦♦♦♦	♦♦	♦♦♦	♦♦♦♦
City	37	11,220	3	1	100	229	296
Airport	4	1,314	0	0	n/a	n/a	n/a
Suburbs	95	14,703	0	0	n/a	n/a	n/a
Total	136	27,237	3	1	n/a	n/a	n/a

Note: n/a not available; classifications range from one diamond (budget properties with basic amenities) to five diamond (luxury properties with the finest service, rooms and facilities).
Source: OAG, Business Travel Planner, Winter 1998-99

Boston is home to two of the top 100 hotels in the world according to *Travel & Leisure*: Four Seasons (#30) and Ritz-Carlton (#58) . Criteria: value, rooms/ambience, location, facilities/activities and service. *Travel & Leisure, 1998 World's Best Awards, Best Hotels and Resorts*

CONVENTION CENTERS

Major Convention Centers

Center Name	Meeting Rooms	Exhibit Space (sq. ft.)
Bayside Expo Center	17	240,000
Boston Garden	n/a	n/a
Boston Park Plaza Castle Expo & Conference Center	35	17,280
Exec. Conf. Ctr. at the World Trade Center of Boston	24	120,000
John B. Hynes Veterans Memorial Convention Center	38	193,000
John Hancock Conference Center	12	n/a
The Exec. Ctr. at the Sheraton Boston Hotel & Towers	10	1,276
World Trade Center-Boston	24	120,000

Note: n/a not available
Source: Trade Shows Worldwide, 1998; Meetings & Conventions, 4/15/99;
Sucessful Meetings, 3/31/98

Living Environment

COST OF LIVING

Cost of Living Index

Composite Index	Groceries	Housing	Utilities	Trans- portation	Health Care	Misc. Goods/ Services
136.6	112.9	182.3	141.6	116.5	134.0	114.7

Note: U.S. = 100; Figures are for the Metropolitan Statistical Area - see Appendix A for areas included
Source: ACCRA, Cost of Living Index, 1st Quarter 1999

HOUSING

Median Home Prices and Housing Affordability

Area	Median Price[2] 1st Qtr. 1999 ($)	HOI[3] 1st Qtr. 1999	Afford- ability Rank[4]
MSA[1]	170,000	66.7	133
U.S.	134,000	69.6	–

Note: (1) Metropolitan Statistical Area - see Appendix A for areas included; (2) U.S. figures calculated from the sales of 524,324 new and existing homes in 181 markets; (3) Housing Opportunity Index - percent of homes sold that were within the reach of the median income household at the prevailing mortgage interest rate; (4) Rank is from 1-181 with 1 being most affordable
Source: National Association of Home Builders, Housing Opportunity Index, 1st Quarter 1999

Median Home Price Projection

It is projected that the median price of existing single-family homes in the metro area will increase by 3.5% in 1999. Nationwide, home prices are projected to increase 3.8%.
Kiplinger's Personal Finance Magazine, January 1999

Average New Home Price

Area	Price ($)
MSA[1]	249,550
U.S.	142,735

Note: Figures are based on a new home with 1,800 sq. ft. of living area on an 8,000 sq. ft. lot; (1) Metropolitan Statistical Area - see Appendix A for areas included
Source: ACCRA, Cost of Living Index, 1st Quarter 1999

Average Apartment Rent

Area	Rent ($/mth)
MSA[1]	1,246
U.S.	601

Note: Figures are based on an unfurnished two bedroom, 1-1/2 or 2 bath apartment, approximately 950 sq. ft. in size, excluding all utilities except water; (1) Metropolitan Statistical Area - see Appendix A for areas included
Source: ACCRA, Cost of Living Index, 1st Quarter 1999

RESIDENTIAL UTILITIES

Average Residential Utility Costs

Area	All Electric ($/mth)	Part Electric ($/mth)	Other Energy ($/mth)	Phone ($/mth)
MSA[1]	–	79.14	65.30	23.03
U.S.	100.02	55.73	43.33	19.71

Note: (1) (1) Metropolitan Statistical Area - see Appendix A for areas included
Source: ACCRA, Cost of Living Index, 1st Quarter 1999

HEALTH CARE

Average Health Care Costs

Area	Hospital ($/day)	Doctor ($/visit)	Dentist ($/visit)
MSA[1]	694.00	74.50	79.20
U.S.	430.43	52.45	66.35

Note: Hospital—based on a semi-private room; Doctor—based on a general practitioner's routine exam of an established patient; Dentist—based on adult teeth cleaning and periodic oral exam; (1) Metropolitan Statistical Area - see Appendix A for areas included
Source: ACCRA, Cost of Living Index, 1st Quarter 1999

Distribution of Office-Based Physicians

Area	Family/Gen. Practitioners	Specialists		
		Medical	Surgical	Other
Metro Area[1]	487	4,439	2,350	3,395

Note: Data as of December 31, 1997; (1) Essex, Middlesex, Norfolk, Plymouth and Suffolk Counties
Source: American Medical Assn., Physician Characteristics & Distribution in the U.S., 1999

Hospitals

Boston has 1 general medical and surgical hospital, 2 psychiatric, 1 eye, ear, nose and throat, 1 rehabilitation, 4 other specialty, 1 children's general, 1 children's chronic disease, 1 children's other specialty. *AHA Guide to the Healthcare Field, 1998-99*

According to *U.S. News and World Report,* Boston has 8 of the best hospitals in the U.S.: **Massachusetts General Hospital**, noted for cancer, cardiology, endocrinology, gastroenterology, geriatrics, gynecology, neurology, ophthalmology, orthopedics, pediatrics, psychiatry, pulmonology, rheumatology, urology; **Brigham & Women's Hospital**, noted for cancer, cardiology, endocrinology, gastroenterology, geriatrics, gynecology, neurology, orthopedics, otolaryngology, pulmonology, rheumatology, urology; **Beth Israel Deaconess Medical Center**, noted for cardiology, endocrinology, gastroenterology, geriatrics, gynecology, neurology, otolaryngology, pulmonology, urology; **New England Medical Center**, noted for cardiology, geriatrics, gynecology, rheumatology; **Spaulding Rehabilitation Hospital**, noted for rehabilitation; **Children's Hospital**, noted for pediatrics; **Massachusetts Eye & Ear Infirmary**, noted for ophthalmology, otolaryngology; **Boston Medical Center**, noted for cardiology, geriatrics, pulmonology, rheumatology. *U.S. News Online, "America's Best Hospitals," 10th Edition, www.usnews.com*

EDUCATION

Public School District Statistics

District Name	Num. Sch.	Enroll.	Classroom Teachers	Pupils per Teacher	Minority Pupils (%)	Current Exp.[1] ($/pupil)
Academy of Pacific Rim	1	100	n/a	n/a	n/a	n/a
Boston School District	127	63,762	n/a	n/a	83.8	9,126
Boston University	1	n/a	n/a	n/a	n/a	n/a
City On A Hill	1	146	n/a	n/a	n/a	n/a
Renaissance Charter Sch	1	1,077	n/a	n/a	n/a	n/a

Note: Data covers the 1997-1998 school year unless otherwise noted; (1) Data covers fiscal year 1996; SD = School District; ISD = Independent School District; n/a not available
Source: National Center for Education Statistics, Common Core of Data Public Education Agency Universe 1997-98; National Center for Education Statistics, Characteristics of the 100 Largest Public Elementary and Secondary School Districts in the United States: 1997-98, July 1999

Educational Quality

School District	Education Quotient[1]	Graduate Outcome[2]	Community Index[3]	Resource Index[4]
Boston SD	79.0	54.0	69.0	131.0

Note: Nearly 1,000 secondary school districts were rated in terms of educational quality. The scores range from a low of 50 to a high of 150; (1) Average of the Graduate Outcome, Community and Resource indexes; (2) Based on graduation rates and college board scores (SAT/ACT); (3) Based on the surrounding community's average level of education and the area's average income level; (4) Based on teacher salaries, per-pupil expenditures and student-teacher ratios.
Source: Expansion Management, Ratings Issue, 1998

Educational Attainment by Race

Area	High School Graduate (%)					Bachelor's Degree (%)				
	Total	White	Black	Other	Hisp.[2]	Total	White	Black	Other	Hisp.[2]
City	75.7	81.5	66.7	55.8	52.8	30.0	36.7	14.0	20.3	13.9
MSA[1]	83.7	85.4	70.7	68.0	58.8	33.1	34.1	17.9	33.9	18.2
U.S.	75.2	77.9	63.1	60.4	49.8	20.3	21.5	11.4	19.4	9.2

Note: Figures shown cover persons 25 years old and over; (1) Metropolitan Statistical Area - see Appendix A for areas included; (2) people of Hispanic origin can be of any race
Source: 1990 Census of Population and Housing, Summary Tape File 3C

School Enrollment by Type

Area	Preprimary				Elementary/High School			
	Public		Private		Public		Private	
	Enrollment	%	Enrollment	%	Enrollment	%	Enrollment	%
City	3,504	56.5	2,698	43.5	58,244	77.2	17,231	22.8
MSA[1]	27,026	49.3	27,803	50.7	331,757	85.6	55,619	14.4
U.S.	2,679,029	59.5	1,824,256	40.5	38,379,689	90.2	4,187,099	9.8

Note: Figures shown cover persons 3 years old and over;
(1) Metropolitan Statistical Area - see Appendix A for areas included
Source: 1990 Census of Population and Housing, Summary Tape File 3C

School Enrollment by Race

Area	Preprimary (%)				Elementary/High School (%)			
	White	Black	Other	Hisp.[1]	White	Black	Other	Hisp.[1]
City	50.0	37.8	12.2	11.7	39.1	42.1	18.8	17.4
MSA[2]	88.2	6.8	5.1	3.7	80.9	11.0	8.2	6.6
U.S.	80.4	12.5	7.1	7.8	74.1	15.6	10.3	12.5

Note: Figures shown cover persons 3 years old and over; (1) people of Hispanic origin can be of any race; (2) Metropolitan Statistical Area - see Appendix A for areas included
Source: 1990 Census of Population and Housing, Summary Tape File 3C

Classroom Teacher Salaries in Public Schools

District	B.A. Degree		M.A. Degree		Maximum	
	Min. ($)	Rank[1]	Max. ($)	Rank[1]	Max. ($)	Rank[1]
Boston	32,001	5	51,712	12	57,545	12
Average	26,980	-	46,065	-	51,435	-

Note: Salaries are for 1997-1998; (1) Rank ranges from 1 to 100
Source: American Federation of Teachers, Survey & Analysis of Salary Trends, 1998

Higher Education

Two-Year Colleges		Four-Year Colleges		Medical Schools	Law Schools	Voc/Tech
Public	Private	Public	Private			
1	8	2	18	3	6	20

Source: College Blue Book, Occupational Education, 1997; Medical School Admission Requirements, 1999-2000; Peterson's Guide to Two-Year Colleges, 1999; Peterson's Guide to Four-Year Colleges, 2000; Barron's Guide to Law Schools, 1999

MAJOR EMPLOYERS

Major Employers

BankBoston Corp.	Beth Israel Deaconess Medical Center
Brigham & Women's Hospital	Frontier Health Care
Globe Newspaper Co.	John Hancock Mutual Life Insurance
Liberty Mutual Fire Insurance	FMR Corp. (investment advice)
New England Medical Center	Stone & Webster Engineering

Note: Companies listed are located in the city
Source: Dun's Business Rankings, 1999; Ward's Business Directory, 1998

PUBLIC SAFETY

Crime Rate

Area	All Crimes	Violent Crimes				Property Crimes		
		Murder	Forcible Rape	Robbery	Aggrav. Assault	Burglary	Larceny -Theft	Motor Vehicle Theft
City	6,817.4	7.7	63.1	491.5	858.5	774.9	3,228.7	1,392.9
Suburbs[1]	2,801.3	1.3	16.6	58.1	295.7	489.4	1,618.5	321.7
MSA[2]	3,445.9	2.3	24.1	127.6	386.1	535.2	1,876.9	493.6
U.S.	4,922.7	6.8	35.9	186.1	382.0	919.6	2,886.5	505.8

Note: Crime rate is the number of crimes per 100,000 pop.; (1) defined as all areas within the MSA but located outside the central city; (2) Metropolitan Statistical Area - see Appendix A for areas incl.
Source: FBI Uniform Crime Reports, 1997

RECREATION

Culture and Recreation

Museums	Symphony Orchestras	Opera Companies	Dance Companies	Professional Theatres	Zoos	Pro Sports Teams
15	3	3	6	5	1	4

Source: International Directory of the Performing Arts, 1997; Official Museum Directory, 1999; Stern's Performing Arts Directory, 1997; USA Today Four Sport Stadium Guide, 1997; Chamber of Commerce/Economic Development, 1999

Library System

The Boston Public Library has 26 branches and holdings of 6,319,206 volumes. *American Library Directory, 1998-1999*

MEDIA

AM Radio Stations

Call Letters	Freq. (kHz)	Target Audience	Station Format	Music Format
WECB	640	General	M/N/S/T	Alternative/Classic Rock/Urban Contemporary
WTBU	640	General	M/N/S	Alternative/Classic Rock/R&B/Urban Contemporary
WRKO	680	General	T	n/a
WEEI	850	General	S	n/a
WBPS	890	H/M	M/N/S/T	Christian/Latin/R&B/Urban Contemporary
WROL	950	General	M/T	Christian
WBZ	1030	General	M/N/S/T	n/a
WILD	1090	Black	M/N/S	Urban Contemporary
WRNI	1290	General	n/a	n/a
WXKS	1430	General	M/N/T	Adult Standards/Big Band/Oldies
WNTN	1550	General	M/T	MOR
WUNR	1600	G/H	M/N/S/T	Latin

Note: Stations included broadcast in the Boston metro area; n/a not available
Target Audience: A=Asian; B=Black; C=Christian; E=Ethnic; F=French; G=General; H=Hispanic; M=Men; N=Native American; R=Religious; S=Senior Citizen; W=Women; Y=Young Adult; Z=Children
Station Format: E=Educational; M=Music; N=News; S=Sports; T=Talk
Music Format: AOR=Album Oriented Rock; MOR=Middle-of-the-Road
Source: Burrelle's Media Directory, 1999 Edition

FM Radio Stations

Call Letters	Freq. (mHz)	Target Audience	Station Format	Music Format
WERS	88.9	General	M/N/S	n/a
WGBH	89.7	General	E/M/N	Classical/Jazz
WBUR	90.9	General	M/N/S/T	Jazz
WFPB	91.9	B/G	M/N	Alternative/Urban Contemporary
WBPR	91.9	B/G	M/N	Alternative/Country
WUMB	91.9	Z/G	E/M/T	Big Band/Jazz/MOR
WBOS	92.9	General	M/N/T	Adult Top 40/Classic Rock
WEGO	93.7	General	M/N/T	Classic Rock/R&B
WSJZ	96.9	General	M/N	Jazz
WBMX	98.5	General	M	Adult Contemporary
WKLB	99.5	General	M/N	Country
WZLX	100.7	General	M/N/S	Classic Rock
WODS	103.3	General	M	Oldies
WBCN	104.1	Men	M/S/T	Alternative
WRBB	104.9	General	M/N/S/T	Alternative/Classic Rock/Jazz/Latin/ R&B/Urban Contemporary
WROR	105.7	General	M	Oldies
WMJX	106.7	G/W	M/N/T	Adult Contemporary

Note: Stations included broadcast in the Boston metro area; n/a not available
Station Format: E=Educational; M=Music; N=News; S=Sports; T=Talk
Target Audience: A=Asian; B=Black; C=Christian; E=Ethnic; F=French; G=General; H=Hispanic; M=Men; N=Native American; R=Religious; S=Senior Citizen; W=Women; Y=Young Adult; Z=Children
Music Format: AOR=Album Oriented Rock; MOR=Middle-of-the-Road
Source: Burrelle's Media Directory, 1999 Edition

Newspapers

Name	Type	Freq.	Distribution	Circulation
Boston Chinese News	Asian	1x/wk	Regional	10,000
Boston Globe	General	7x/wk	Regional	466,000
The Boston Herald	General	7x/wk	Regional	285,335
The Christian Science Monitor	General	5x/wk	U.S.	87,257
The Daily Free Press	n/a	5x/wk	Camp/Comm	12,000
East Boston Times-Free Press	General	1x/wk	Local	15,500
El Mundo	Hispanic	1x/wk	Local	35,000
The Episcopal Times	Religious	8x/yr	Regional	40,000
In News Weekly	n/a	1x/wk	U.S.	21,000
Post-Gazette	n/a	1x/wk	Local	15,900

Note: Includes newspapers with circulations of 10,000 or more located in the city; n/a not available
Source: Burrelle's Media Directory, 1999 Edition

Television Stations

Name	Ch.	Affiliation	Type	Owner
WGBH	n/a	PBS	Public	WGBH Educational Foundation
WBZ	n/a	CBST	Commercial	Westinghouse Broadcasting Company
WCVB	n/a	ABCT	Commercial	Hearst Corporation
WHDH	n/a	NBCT	Commercial	WHDH-TV
WCEA	19	n/a	Commercial	WCEA-TV
WNBU	21	n/a	Commercial	BUCI Television
WSBK	38	n/a	Commercial	UPN
WGBX	44	PBS	Public	WGBH Educational Foundation
WLVI	56	WB	Commercial	Tribune Broadcasting Company
WZBU	58	n/a	Commercial	BUCI Television
WMFP	62	n/a	Commercial	Shop at Home Inc.
WABU	68	n/a	Commercial	BUCI Television

Note: Stations included broadcast in the Boston metro area; n/a not available
Source: Burrelle's Media Directory, 1999 Edition

CLIMATE

Average and Extreme Temperatures

Temperature	Jan	Feb	Mar	Apr	May	Jun	Jul	Aug	Sep	Oct	Nov	Dec	Yr.
Extreme High (°F)	72	70	85	94	95	100	102	102	100	90	83	73	102
Average High (°F)	36	38	46	56	67	76	82	80	73	63	52	41	59
Average Temp. (°F)	30	31	39	48	58	68	74	72	65	55	45	34	52
Average Low (°F)	22	23	31	40	50	59	65	64	57	47	38	27	44
Extreme Low (°F)	-12	-4	1	16	34	45	50	47	37	28	15	-7	-12

Note: Figures cover the years 1945-1990
Source: National Climatic Data Center, International Station Meteorological Climate Summary, 3/95

Average Precipitation/Snowfall/Humidity

Precip./Humidity	Jan	Feb	Mar	Apr	May	Jun	Jul	Aug	Sep	Oct	Nov	Dec	Yr.
Avg. Precip. (in.)	3.8	3.6	3.8	3.7	3.5	3.1	2.9	3.6	3.1	3.3	4.4	4.1	42.9
Avg. Snowfall (in.)	12	12	8	1	Tr	0	0	0	0	Tr	1	8	41
Avg. Rel. Hum. 7am (%)	68	68	69	68	71	72	73	76	79	77	74	70	72
Avg. Rel. Hum. 4pm (%)	58	57	56	56	58	58	58	61	61	59	61	60	59

Note: Figures cover the years 1945-1990; Tr = Trace amounts (<0.05 in. of rain; <0.5 in. of snow)
Source: National Climatic Data Center, International Station Meteorological Climate Summary, 3/95

Weather Conditions

Temperature			Daytime Sky			Precipitation		
5°F & below	32°F & below	90°F & above	Clear	Partly cloudy	Cloudy	0.01 inch or more precip.	0.1 inch or more snow/ice	Thunder-storms
4	97	12	88	127	150	253	48	18

Note: Figures are average number of days per year and covers the years 1945-1990
Source: National Climatic Data Center, International Station Meteorological Climate Summary, 3/95

AIR & WATER QUALITY

Maximum Pollutant Concentrations

	Particulate Matter (ug/m³)	Carbon Monoxide (ppm)	Sulfur Dioxide (ppm)	Nitrogen Dioxide (ppm)	Ozone (ppm)	Lead (ug/m³)
MSA[1] Level	59	5	0.049	0.030	0.12	n/a
NAAQS[2]	150	9	0.140	0.053	0.12	1.50
Met NAAQS?	Yes	Yes	Yes	Yes	Yes	n/a

Note: (1) Metropolitan Statistical Area - see Appendix A for areas included; (2) National Ambient Air Quality Standards; ppm = parts per million; ug/m³ = micrograms per cubic meter; n/a not available
Source: EPA, National Air Quality and Emissions Trends Report, 1997

Pollutant Standards Index

In the Boston MSA (see Appendix A for areas included), the Pollutant Standards Index (PSI) exceeded 100 on 10 days in 1997. A PSI value greater than 100 indicates that air quality would be in the unhealthful range on that day. *EPA, National Air Quality and Emissions Trends Report, 1997*

Drinking Water

Water System Name	Pop. Served	Primary Water Source Type	Number of Violations in 1998	Type of Violation/ Contaminants
Boston Water & Sewer Commiss.	574,283	Purchased surface	None	None

Note: Data as of July 10, 1999
Source: EPA, Office of Ground Water and Drinking Water, Safe Drinking Water Information System

The Metropolitan Water District (combined sources, Quabbin Reservoir and Wachusett Reservoir) supplies municipal Boston and the ABC City Zone. Water is soft and slightly acid. *Editor & Publisher Market Guide, 1999*

Charlotte, North Carolina

Background

Charlotte's relationship with England began amiably enough. Settled by Scotch-Irish and German migrants from Pennsylvania, New Jersey, and Virginia in 1750, the area was named in honor of Charlotte Sophia of Mecklenburg-Strelitz, Queen to England's King George III. The county in which Charlotte lies was named for Queen Charlotte Sophia's Duchy of Mecklenburg.

Trouble started in 1775, however, when the citizens of Charlotte signed the Mecklenburg Resolves, a document invalidating the power of the King and the English Parliament over their lives. The British General, Lord Cornwallis, found subduing these treasoners so difficult, that he called Charlotte a "Hornet's Nest of Rebellion."

Today, a better behaved Charlotte is the largest metropolitan area in the Carolinas. More than one million residents make their living from a variety of jobs in retailing, distribution, manufacturing, and finance. The city is the center of a booming banking industry, and now the financial capital of the South and the third largest banking center in the United States. Its role as the nucleus of the Carolinas crescent, an industrial arc extending from Raleigh, North Carolina to Greenville, South Carolina adds to its prosperity as well.

Charlotte is one of North Carolina's economic "hot spots" with growth predicted at 19 percent by the year 2005. The city and the metro area had more than $1 billion in investments by new and expanding firms and created more than 13,000 new jobs. Charlotte has also become a major call center operator, with 15 centers employing more than 3,000 people. Bell South, EDS, Vanguard, and First Data all plan to either expand or open call center operations in the Charlotte area. *Site Selection, July/July 1997*

Charlotte is located in the Piedmont of the Carolinas, a transitional area of rolling country between the mountains to the west and the Coastal Plain to the east.

The city enjoys a moderate climate, characterized by cool winters and warm summers. Winter weather is changeable, with occasional cold periods, but extreme cold is rare. Snow is infrequent. Summer afternoon temperatures range in the low 90s. Rainfall is generally evenly distributed throughout the year. Hurricanes that strike the Carolina coast can produce heavy rain, but seldom cause dangerous winds.

General Rankings and Evaluative Comments

■ Charlotte was ranked #12 out of 19 large, southern metropolitan areas in *Money's* 1998 survey of "The Best Places to Live in America." The survey was conducted by first contacting 512 representative households nationwide and asking them to rank 37 quality-of-life factors on a scale of 1 to 10. Next, a demographic profile was compiled on the 300 largest metropolitan statistical areas in the U.S. The numbers were crunched together to arrive at an overall ranking (things Americans consider most important, like clean air and water, low crime and good schools, received extra weight). Unlike previous years, the 1998 rankings were broken down by region (northeast, midwest, south, west) and population size (100,000 to 249,999; 250,000 to 999,999; 1 million plus). The city had a nationwide ranking of #113 out of 300 in 1997 and #84 out of 300 in 1996. *Money, July 1998; Money, July 1997; Money, September 1996*

■ *Ladies Home Journal* ranked America's 200 largest cities based on the qualities women care about most. Charlotte ranked #118 out of 200. Criteria: low crime rate, well-paying jobs, quality health and child care, good public schools, the presence of women in government, size of the gender wage gap, number of sexual-harassment and discrimination complaints filed, unemployment and divorce rates, commute times, population density, number of houses of worship, parks and cultural offerings, number of women's health specialists, how well a community's women cared for themselves, complexion kindness index based on UV radiation levels, odds of finding affordable fashions, rental rates for romance movies, champagne sales and other matters of the heart. *Ladies Home Journal, November 1998*

■ Zero Population Growth ranked 229 cities in terms of children's health, safety, and economic well-being. Charlotte was ranked #42 out of 112 independent cities (cities with populations greater than 100,000 which were neither Major Cities nor Suburbs/Outer Cities) and was given a grade of C+. Criteria: total population, percent of population under 18 years of age, household language, percent population change, percent of births to teens, infant mortality rate, percent of low birth weights, dropout rate, enrollment in preprimary school, violent and property crime rates, unemployment rate, percent of children in poverty, percent of owner occupied units, number of bad air days, percent of public transportation commuters, and average travel time to work. *ZPG, Children's Environmental Index, Fall 1999*

■ Charlotte was ranked #10 out of 59 metro areas in *The Regional Economist's* "Rational Livability Ranking of 59 Large Metro Areas." The rankings were based on the metro area's total population change over the period 1990-97 divided by the number of people moving in from elsewhere in the United States (net domestic in-migration). *St. Louis Federal Reserve Bank of St. Louis, The Regional Economist, April 1999*

■ Charlotte was selected by *Yahoo! Internet Life* as one of "America's Most Wired Cities & Towns." The city ranked #50 out of 50. Criteria: home and work net use, domain density, hosts per capita, directory density and content quality. *Yahoo! Internet Life, March 1999*

■ Cognetics studied 273 metro areas in the United States, ranking them by entrepreneurial activity. Charlotte was ranked #9 out of the 50 largest metro areas. Criteria: Significant Starts (firms started in the last 10 years that still employ at least 5 people) and Young Growers (percent of firms 10 years old or less that grew significantly during the last 4 years). *Cognetics, "Entrepreneurial Hot Spots: The Best Places in America to Start and Grow a Company," 1998*

■ Charlotte was included among *Entrepreneur* magazine's listing of the "20 Best Cities for Small Business." It was ranked #18 among large metro areas. Criteria: entrepreneurial activity, small-business growth, economic growth, and risk of failure. *Entrepreneur, Oct. 1999*

■ Charlotte was selected as one of the "Best American Cities to Start a Business" by *Point of View* magazine. Criteria: coolness, quality-of-life, and business concerns. The city was ranked #32 out of 75. *Point of View, November 1998*

■ Reliastar Financial Corp. ranked the 125 largest metropolitan areas according to the general financial security of residents. Charlotte was ranked #14 (tie) out of 125 with a score of 9.8. The score indicates the percentage a metropolitan area is above or below the metropolitan norm. A metro area with a score of 10.6 is 10.6% above the metro average. Criteria: Earnings and Wealth Potential (household income, education, net assets, cost of living); Safety Net (health insurance, retirement savings, life insurance, income support programs); Personal Threats (unemployment rate, low-income households, crime rate); Community Economic Vitality (cost of community services, job quality, job creation, housing costs). *Reliastar Financial Corp., "The Best Cities to Earn and Save Money," 1999 Edition*

Business Environment

STATE ECONOMY

State Economic Profile

"In spite of declines in textiles and apparels, North Carolina has seen impressive job growth in the last few years. As NC continues to diversify its economy away from its traditional manufacturing base and toward its newer high-tech and financial services sectors, job growth will outpace the nation for a number of years to come, albeit at a slightly slower rate than those seen in 1997 and 1998.

Raleigh-Durham has been and will continue to be one of NC's growth engines. High-tech firms in the Research Triangle Park have expanded employment considerably. Cisco Systems, for one, is planning to expand its operations, adding as many as 4,000 jobs over the next three years. Raleigh's housing market has more than doubled in size during the 1990s. Price appreciation has been strong, although homes still remain affordable. 1999 should be another hot year for sales and new construction in Raleigh-Durham.

NC's other hot spot has been Charlotte. While many parts of the country have been hurt by consolidation in the financial services industry, many of these jobs have made their way to Charlotte. As this wave of consolidation has slowed, so has job growth in Charlotte, reflected in its 0.6% job growth rate in 1998, far below that of previous years. Continued restructuring in NC's textiles, apparel and furniture industries will slow job growth in the Charlotte area.

The outlook for NC, while a slowdown from its recent pace, is still one of impressive job growth, far outpacing the nation. With its business friendly atmosphere and the decision of Federal Express to locate its Mid-Atlantic hub here, NC will likely attract more corporate relocations. Its affordable housing markets and overall high quality of life will also attract residents, helping fuel job growth." *National Association of Realtors, Economic Profiles: The Fifty States and the District of Columbia, http://nar.realtor.com/databank/profiles.htm*

IMPORTS/EXPORTS

Total Export Sales

Area	1994 ($000)	1995 ($000)	1996 ($000)	1997 ($000)	% Chg. 1994-97	% Chg. 1996-97
MSA[1]	1,782,827	2,087,970	2,291,296	2,588,757	45.2	13.0
U.S.	512,415,609	583,030,524	622,827,063	687,597,999	34.2	10.4

Note: (1) Metropolitan Statistical Area - see Appendix A for areas included
Source: U.S. Department of Commerce, International Trade Association, Metropolitan Area Exports: An Export Performance Report on Over 250 U.S. Cities, November 10, 1998

CITY FINANCES

City Government Finances

Component	FY92 ($000)	FY92 (per capita $)
Revenue	472,749	1,115.22
Expenditure	566,347	1,336.02
Debt Outstanding	999,281	2,357.32
Cash & Securities	677,473	1,598.17

Source: U.S. Bureau of the Census, City Government Finances: 1991-92

City Government Revenue by Source

Source	FY92 ($000)	FY92 (per capita $)	FY92 (%)
From Federal Government	21,692	51.17	4.6
From State Governments	49,503	116.78	10.5
From Local Governments	39,337	92.80	8.3
Property Taxes	140,111	330.52	29.6
General Sales Taxes	0	0.00	0.0
Selective Sales Taxes	12,172	28.71	2.6
Income Taxes	0	0.00	0.0
Current Charges	103,874	245.04	22.0
Utility/Liquor Store	34,061	80.35	7.2
Employee Retirement[1]	11,111	26.21	2.4
Other	60,888	143.64	12.9

Note: (1) Excludes "city contributions," classified as "nonrevenue," intragovernmental transfers.
Source: U.S. Bureau of the Census, City Government Finances: 1991-92

City Government Expenditures by Function

Function	FY92 ($000)	FY92 (per capita $)	FY92 (%)
Educational Services	0	0.00	0.0
Employee Retirement[1]	5,137	12.12	0.9
Environment/Housing	174,711	412.15	30.8
Government Administration	19,778	46.66	3.5
Interest on General Debt	59,676	140.78	10.5
Public Safety	77,006	181.66	13.6
Social Services	3,513	8.29	0.6
Transportation	97,761	230.62	17.3
Utility/Liquor Store	61,140	144.23	10.8
Other	67,625	159.53	11.9

Note: (1) Payments to beneficiaries including withdrawal of contributions.
Source: U.S. Bureau of the Census, City Government Finances: 1991-92

Municipal Bond Ratings

Area	Moody's	S & P
Charlotte	Aaa	n/a

Note: n/a not available; n/r not rated
Source: Moody's Bond Record, 6/99

POPULATION

Population Growth

Area	1980	1990	% Chg. 1980-90	July 1998 Estimate	% Chg. 1990-98
City	314,447	396,003	25.9	504,637	27.4
MSA[1]	971,391	1,162,093	19.6	1,374,044	18.2
U.S.	226,545,805	248,765,170	9.8	270,299,000	8.7

Note: (1) Metropolitan Statistical Area - see Appendix A for areas included;
July 1998 MSA population estimate was calculated by the editors
Source: 1980/1990 Census of Housing and Population, Summary Tape File 3C;
Census Bureau Population Estimates 1998

Population Characteristics

Race	City				% Chg. 1980-90	MSA[1]	
	1980		1990			1990	
	Population	%	Population	%		Population	%
White	212,293	67.5	259,710	65.6	22.3	911,871	78.5
Black	97,896	31.1	126,128	31.9	28.8	231,450	19.9
Amer Indian/Esk/Aleut	1,162	0.4	1,529	0.4	31.6	4,692	0.4
Asian/Pacific Islander	2,393	0.8	6,686	1.7	179.4	10,762	0.9
Other	703	0.2	1,950	0.5	177.4	3,318	0.3
Hispanic Origin[2]	3,418	1.1	5,261	1.3	53.9	9,817	0.8

Note: (1) Metropolitan Statistical Area - see Appendix A for areas included;
(2) people of Hispanic origin can be of any race
Source: 1980/1990 Census of Housing and Population, Summary Tape File 3C

Ancestry

Area	German	Irish	English	Italian	U.S.	French	Polish	Dutch
City	17.0	11.8	14.3	2.4	5.7	2.6	1.4	2.0
MSA[1]	22.1	14.0	12.8	1.9	9.4	2.2	1.1	2.7
U.S.	23.3	15.6	13.1	5.9	5.3	4.2	3.8	2.5

Note: Figures are percentages and include persons that reported multiple ancestry (eg. if a person
reported being Irish and Italian, they were included in both columns); (1) Metropolitan Statistical Area -
see Appendix A for areas included
Source: 1990 Census of Population and Housing, Summary Tape File 3C

Age

Area	Median Age (Years)	Age Distribution (%)						
		Under 5	Under 18	18-24	25-44	45-64	65+	80+
City	32.0	7.5	24.3	10.6	37.3	18.0	9.8	2.0
MSA[1]	32.7	7.2	24.8	10.9	34.2	19.3	10.9	2.2
U.S.	32.9	7.3	25.6	10.5	32.6	18.7	12.5	2.8

Note: (1) Metropolitan Statistical Area - see Appendix A for areas included
Source: 1990 Census of Population and Housing, Summary Tape File 3C

Male/Female Ratio

Area	Number of males per 100 females (all ages)	Number of males per 100 females (18 years old+)
City	90.2	86.7
MSA[1]	93.0	89.8
U.S.	95.0	91.9

Note: (1) Metropolitan Statistical Area - see Appendix A for areas included
Source: 1990 Census of Population, General Population Characteristics

INCOME

Per Capita/Median/Average Income

Area	Per Capita ($)	Median Household ($)	Average Household ($)
City	16,793	31,873	41,578
MSA[1]	14,611	31,125	38,214
U.S.	14,420	30,056	38,453

Note: All figures are for 1989; (1) Metropolitan Statistical Area - see Appendix A for areas included
Source: 1990 Census of Population and Housing, Summary Tape File 3C

Household Income Distribution by Race

Income ($)	City (%)					U.S. (%)				
	Total	White	Black	Other	Hisp.[1]	Total	White	Black	Other	Hisp.[1]
Less than 5,000	5.5	2.8	12.3	4.3	5.1	6.2	4.8	15.2	8.6	8.8
5,000 - 9,999	6.7	5.3	10.3	4.9	2.9	9.3	8.6	14.2	9.9	11.1
10,000 - 14,999	7.5	6.0	11.2	7.4	7.0	8.8	8.5	11.0	9.8	11.0
15,000 - 24,999	18.0	16.3	22.2	21.9	25.0	17.5	17.3	18.9	18.5	20.5
25,000 - 34,999	17.2	17.0	17.5	19.2	21.7	15.8	16.1	14.2	15.4	16.4
35,000 - 49,999	18.8	20.1	15.4	20.1	18.6	17.9	18.6	13.3	16.1	16.0
50,000 - 74,999	15.7	18.6	8.6	16.2	14.2	15.0	15.8	9.3	13.4	11.1
75,000 - 99,999	5.6	7.2	1.7	4.0	2.7	5.1	5.5	2.6	4.7	3.1
100,000+	5.1	6.8	0.9	2.1	2.8	4.4	4.8	1.3	3.7	1.9

Note: All figures are for 1989; (1) people of Hispanic origin can be of any race
Source: 1990 Census of Population and Housing, Summary Tape File 3C

Effective Buying Income

Area	Per Capita ($)	Median Household ($)	Average Household ($)
City	20,063	39,155	49,348
MSA[1]	17,835	36,772	46,411
U.S.	16,803	34,536	45,243

Note: Data as of 1/1/99; (1) Metropolitan Statistical Area - see Appendix A for areas included
Source: Standard Rate & Data Service, Newspaper Advertising Source, 9/99

Effective Household Buying Income Distribution

Area	% of Households Earning						
	$10,000 -$19,999	$20,000 -$34,999	$35,000 -$49,999	$50,000 -$74,999	$75,000 -$99,000	$100,000 -$124,999	$125,000 and up
City	12.5	22.9	18.8	21.0	8.8	3.4	3.6
MSA[1]	14.4	23.1	19.4	20.7	7.7	2.4	2.3
U.S.	16.0	22.6	18.2	18.9	7.2	2.4	2.7

Note: Data as of 1/1/99; (1) Metropolitan Statistical Area - see Appendix A for areas included
Source: Standard Rate & Data Service, Newspaper Advertising Source, 9/99

Poverty Rates by Race and Age

Area	Total (%)	By Race (%)				By Age (%)		
		White	Black	Other	Hisp.[2]	Under 5 years old	Under 18 years old	65 years and over
City	10.8	5.1	22.5	12.2	9.9	18.4	16.0	13.8
MSA[1]	9.6	6.2	22.9	11.6	11.1	14.3	12.9	15.2
U.S.	13.1	9.8	29.5	23.1	25.3	20.1	18.3	12.8

Note: Figures show the percent of people living below the poverty line in 1989. The average poverty
threshold was $12,674 for a family of four in 1989; (1) Metropolitan Statistical Area - see Appendix A
for areas included; (2) people of Hispanic origin can be of any race
Source: 1990 Census of Population and Housing, Summary Tape File 3C

EMPLOYMENT

Labor Force and Employment

Area	Civilian Labor Force			Workers Employed		
	Jun. 1998	Jun. 1999	% Chg.	Jun. 1998	Jun. 1999	% Chg.
City	270,372	275,617	1.9	262,695	269,672	2.7
MSA[1]	752,534	766,779	1.9	729,609	747,580	2.5
U.S.	138,798,000	140,666,000	1.3	132,265,000	134,395,000	1.6

Note: Data is not seasonally adjusted and covers workers 16 years of age and older;
(1) Metropolitan Statistical Area - see Appendix A for areas included
Source: Bureau of Labor Statistics, http://stats.bls.gov

Unemployment Rate

Area	1998						1999					
	Jul.	Aug.	Sep.	Oct.	Nov.	Dec.	Jan.	Feb.	Mar.	Apr.	May.	Jun.
City	2.7	2.6	2.4	2.3	2.2	1.8	2.3	2.2	2.0	1.7	2.0	2.2
MSA[1]	3.0	2.9	2.6	2.5	2.3	2.0	2.5	2.6	2.2	2.0	2.4	2.5
U.S.	4.7	4.5	4.4	4.2	4.1	4.0	4.8	4.7	4.4	4.1	4.0	4.5

Note: Data is not seasonally adjusted and covers workers 16 years of age and older; all figures are percentages; (1) Metropolitan Statistical Area - see Appendix A for areas included
Source: Bureau of Labor Statistics, http://stats.bls.gov

Employment by Industry

Sector	MSA[1]		U.S.
	Number of Employees	Percent of Total	Percent of Total
Services	214,600	27.0	30.4
Retail Trade	128,700	16.2	17.7
Government	88,400	11.1	15.6
Manufacturing	139,900	17.6	14.3
Finance/Insurance/Real Estate	65,500	8.2	5.9
Wholesale Trade	57,200	7.2	5.4
Transportation/Public Utilities	49,900	6.3	5.3
Construction	n/a	n/a	5.0
Mining	n/a	n/a	0.4

Note: Figures cover non-farm employment as of 6/99 and are not seasonally adjusted;
(1) Metropolitan Statistical Area - see Appendix A for areas included; n/a not available
Source: Bureau of Labor Statistics, http://stats.bls.gov

Employment by Occupation

Occupation Category	City (%)	MSA[1] (%)	U.S. (%)
White Collar	65.3	55.6	58.1
Executive/Admin./Management	15.0	12.1	12.3
Professional	13.7	11.4	14.1
Technical & Related Support	3.7	3.4	3.7
Sales	15.0	12.8	11.8
Administrative Support/Clerical	17.8	15.9	16.3
Blue Collar	22.0	32.4	26.2
Precision Production/Craft/Repair	8.8	12.7	11.3
Machine Operators/Assem./Insp.	5.6	11.0	6.8
Transportation/Material Movers	3.6	4.0	4.1
Cleaners/Helpers/Laborers	4.0	4.6	3.9
Services	11.9	10.7	13.2
Farming/Forestry/Fishing	0.9	1.3	2.5

Note: Figures cover employed persons 16 years old and over;
(1) Metropolitan Statistical Area - see Appendix A for areas included
Source: 1990 Census of Population and Housing, Summary Tape File 3C

Occupational Employment Projections: 1996 - 2006

Occupations Expected to Have the Largest Job Growth (ranked by numerical growth)	Fast-Growing Occupations[1] (ranked by percent growth)
1. Cashiers	1. Occupational therapy assistants
2. Registered nurses	2. Computer engineers
3. General managers & top executives	3. Database administrators
4. Nursing aides/orderlies/attendants	4. Systems analysts
5. Salespersons, retail	5. Physical therapy assistants and aides
6. Child care workers, private household	6. Physical therapists
7. Food service workers	7. Occupational therapists
8. Marketing & sales, supervisors	8. Home health aides
9. Janitors/cleaners/maids, ex. priv. hshld.	9. Desktop publishers
10. Truck drivers, light	10. Respiratory therapists

Note: Projections cover North Carolina; (1) Excludes occupations with total job growth less than 300
Source: U.S. Department of Labor, Employment and Training Administration, America's Labor Market Information System (ALMIS)

TAXES

Major State and Local Tax Rates

| State Corp. Income (%) | State Personal Income (%) | Residential Property (effective rate per $100) | Sales & Use | | State Gasoline (cents/ gallon) | State Cigarette (cents/ pack) |
			State (%)	Local (%)		
7.0	6.0 - 7.75	1.08	4.0	2.0	21.6	5.0

Note: Personal/corporate income, sales, gasoline and cigarette tax rates as of January 1999. Property tax rates as of 1997.
Source: Federation of Tax Administrators, www.taxadmin.org; Washington D.C. Department of Finance and Revenue, Tax Rates and Tax Burdens in the District of Columbia: A Nationwide Comparison, July 1998; Chamber of Commerce, 1999

Total Taxes Per Capita and as a Percent of Income

| Area | Per Capita Income ($) | Per Capita Taxes ($) | | | Percent of Income (%) | | |
		Total	Federal	State/ Local	Total	Federal	State/ Local
North Carolina	25,480	8,669	5,924	2,745	34.0	23.3	10.8
U.S.	27,876	9,881	6,690	3,191	35.4	24.0	11.4

Note: Figures are for 1998
Source: Tax Foundation, www.taxfoundation.org

Estimated Tax Burden

Area	State Income	Local Income	Property	Sales	Total
Charlotte	3,498	0	3,250	897	7,645

Note: The numbers are estimates of taxes paid by a married couple with two children and annual earnings of $75,000. Sales tax estimates assume they spend average amounts on food, clothing, household goods and gasoline. Property tax estimates assume they live in a $250,000 home.
Source: Kiplinger's Personal Finance Magazine, October 1998

**COMMERCIAL
REAL ESTATE**

Office Market

Class/ Location	Total Space (sq. ft.)	Vacant Space (sq. ft.)	Vac. Rate (%)	Under Constr. (sq. ft.)	Net Absorp. (sq. ft.)	Rental Rates ($/sq.ft./yr.)
Class A						
CBD	6,668,870	120,000	1.8	1,509,800	733,115	22.00-28.00
Outside CBD	9,671,639	950,000	9.8	1,036,700	880,141	16.50-23.00
Class B						
CBD	3,379,574	180,000	5.3	21,500	-31,198	15.00-23.50
Outside CBD	4,821,268	360,000	7.5	268,600	138,863	13.00-18.00

Note: Data as of 10/98 and covers Charlotte; CBD = Central Business District; n/a not available;
Source: Society of Industrial and Office Realtors, 1999 Comparative Statistics of Industrial and Office Real Estate Markets

"Charlotte's overall office vacancy rate of 6.6 percent is one of the nation's lowest, attracting major institutional investors and developers. There is some concern about overbuilding, although demand has kept pace with supply. New construction is occurring throughout the market in a balanced pattern. Development is heavily concentrated in the downtown and I-771 southwest sub-markets. Of the 2.8 million sq. ft. of multi-tenant space under construction, approximately 40 percent is pre-leased. Proposed space in Charlotte totals 2.9 million sq. ft. Local economic development officials are continuing to pursue space for expanding and relocating tenants. Strong levels of population and employment growth are projected for the MSA. With new space coming on line, the market will continue to grow at a healthy pace." *Society of Industrial and Office Realtors, 1999 Comparative Statistics of Industrial and Office Real Estate Markets*

Industrial Market

Location	Total Space (sq. ft.)	Vacant Space (sq. ft.)	Vac. Rate (%)	Under Constr. (sq. ft.)	Net Absorp. (sq. ft.)	Gross Lease ($/sq.ft./yr.)
Central City	3,475,861	267,641	7.7	0	144,573	n/a
Suburban	17,300,000	2,525,800	14.6	530,000	1,219,200	3.50-5.00

Note: Data as of 10/98 and covers Charlotte; n/a not available
Source: Society of Industrial and Office Realtors, 1999 Comparative Statistics of Industrial and Office Real Estate Markets

"Setting the tone for the New South, 1999 should mark North Carolina's eighth consecutive year of economic expansion, albeit at a slower pace than in 1998. With the future in mind, the Charlotte Chamber of Commerce is producing a strategic plan for the community's economic development, looking ahead at the new technologies that will impact the local economy. The community will be doing all that is possible to ensure that businesses are competitive, that new jobs are being generated, and that living standards are increasing for all the residents. With 530,000 sq. ft. currently under construction and 730,000 sq. ft. proposed, construction projects will probably push the vacancy rates slightly down as current levels of absorption surpasses construction levels, in the judgment of SIOR's reporter." *Society of Industrial and Office Realtors, 1999 Comparative Statistics of Industrial and Office Real Estate Markets*

Retail Market

Shopping Center Inventory (sq. ft.)	Shopping Center Construction (sq. ft.)	Construction as a Percent of Inventory (%)	Torto Wheaton Rent Index[1] ($/sq. ft.)
27,498,000	782,000	2.8	10.61

Note: Data as of 1997 and covers the Metropolitan Statistical Area - see Appendix A for areas included; (1) Index is based on a model that predicts what the average rent should be for leases with certain characteristics, in certain locations during certain years.
Source: National Association of Realtors, 1997-1998 Market Conditions Report

"The retail rent index in Charlotte has leveled off at around $10.50 [per sq. ft.] as demand has caught up with some very ambitious building in recent years. The Charlotte economy has been

outperforming the nation in nearly every category. Employment and population growth have been among the strongest in the nation, and average annual wages have grown over 5.0% per year compared to 3.7% nationally. However, developers realize that Charlotte's growth won't continue forever. New construction is expected to diminish over the next few years."
National Association of Realtors, 1997-1998 Market Conditions Report

COMMERCIAL UTILITIES

Typical Monthly Electric Bills

Area	Commercial Service ($/month)		Industrial Service ($/month)	
	12 kW demand 1,500 kWh	100 kW demand 30,000 kWh	1,000 kW demand 400,000 kWh	20,000 kW demand 10,000,000 kWh
City	150	1,814	20,801	295,548
U.S.	150	2,174	23,995	508,569

Note: Based on rates in effect January 1, 1999
Source: Edison Electric Institute, Typical Residential, Commercial and Industrial Bills, Winter 1999

TRANSPORTATION

Transportation Statistics

Average minutes to work	21.5
Interstate highways	I-77; I-85
Bus lines	
In-city	Charlotte Transit, 161 vehicles
Inter-city	2
Passenger air service	
Airport	Charlotte-Douglas International
Airlines	14
Aircraft departures	136,330 (1996)
Enplaned passengers	10,007,754 (1996)
Rail service	Amtrak
Motor freight carriers	294
Major waterways/ports	None

Source: Editor & Publisher Market Guide, 1999; FAA Airport Activity Statistics, 1997; Amtrak National Time Table, Northeast Timetable, Spring/Summer 1999; 1990 Census of Population and Housing, STF 3C; Chamber of Commerce/Economic Development 1999; Jane's Urban Transport Systems 1999-2000

Means of Transportation to Work

Area	Car/Truck/Van		Public Transportation			Bicycle	Walked	Other Means	Worked at Home
	Drove Alone	Car-pooled	Bus	Subway	Railroad				
City	77.2	12.9	4.3	0.0	0.0	0.2	2.2	1.0	2.2
MSA[1]	78.8	14.5	1.7	0.0	0.0	0.1	2.1	1.0	1.9
U.S.	73.2	13.4	3.0	1.5	0.5	0.4	3.9	1.2	3.0

Note: Figures shown are percentages and only include workers 16 years old and over;
(1) Metropolitan Statistical Area - see Appendix A for areas included
Source: 1990 Census of Population and Housing, Summary Tape File 3C

BUSINESSES

Major Business Headquarters

Company Name	1999 Rankings	
	Fortune 500	Forbes 500
Baker & Taylor	-	244
BankAmerica Corp.	11	-
Belk Stores Services	-	64
Duke Energy	81	-
First Union	56	-
GS Industries	-	274
Hendrick Automotive Group	-	57
Nucor	374	-

Note: Companies listed are located in the city; dashes indicate no ranking
Fortune 500: Companies that produce a 10-K are ranked 1 to 500 based on 1998 revenue
Forbes 500: Private companies are ranked 1 to 500 based on 1997 revenue
Source: Forbes, November 30, 1998; Fortune, April 26, 1999

Best Companies to Work For

First Union Corp. and NationsBank, headquartered in Charlotte, are among the "100 Best Companies for Working Mothers." Criteria: fair wages, opportunities for women to advance, support for child care, flexible work schedules, family-friendly benefits, and work/life supports. *Working Mother, October 1998*

Fast-Growing Businesses

According to Deloitte & Touche LLP, Charlotte is home to one of America's 100 fastest-growing high-technology companies: Advanced Technology Systems. Companies are ranked by percentage growth in revenue over a five-year period. Criteria for inclusion: must be a U.S. company developing and/or providing technology products or services; company must have been in business for five years with 1993 revenues of at least $50,000. *Deloitte & Touche LLP, November 17, 1998*

Women-Owned Firms: Number, Employment and Sales

Area	Number of Firms	Employ-ment	Sales ($000)	Rank[2]
MSA[1]	42,200	140,000	19,161,200	40

Note: (1) Metropolitan Statistical Area - see Appendix A for areas included;
(2) Calculated on an averaging of the number of businesses, employment and sales
Source: The National Foundation for Women Business Owners, 1999 Facts on Women-Owned Businesses: Trends in the Top 50 Metropolitan Areas

Women-Owned Firms: Growth

Area	% change from 1992 to 1999			Rank[2]
	Number of Firms	Employ-ment	Sales	
MSA[1]	51.5	134.6	160.0	11

Note: (1) Metropolitan Statistical Area - see Appendix A for areas included; (2) Calculated on an averaging of the percent growth of number of businesses, employment and sales
Source: The National Foundation for Women Business Owners, 1999 Facts on Women-Owned Businesses: Trends in the Top 50 Metropolitan Areas

Minority Business Opportunity

Charlotte is home to two companies which are on the Black Enterprise Auto Dealer 100 list (largest based on gross sales): S & J Enterprises (Ford, Lincoln-Mercury); Hubbard Investments LLC (Dodge, Chevrolet, Isuzu) . Criteria: 1) operational in previous calendar year; 2) at least 51% black-owned. *Black Enterprise, www.blackenterprise.com*

Charlotte is home to one company which is on the Hispanic Business Fastest-Growing 100 list (greatest sales growth from 1994 to 1998): Zapata Engineering (full engineering svcs.).
Hispanic Business, July/August 1999

HOTELS & MOTELS

Hotels/Motels

Area	Hotels/Motels	Rooms	Luxury-Level Hotels/Motels		Average Minimum Rates ($)		
			♦♦♦♦	♦♦♦♦♦	♦♦	♦♦♦	♦♦♦♦
City	71	9,496	1	0	68	114	200
Airport	8	1,077	0	0	n/a	n/a	n/a
Suburbs	25	2,160	0	0	n/a	n/a	n/a
Total	104	12,733	1	0	n/a	n/a	n/a

Note: n/a not available; classifications range from one diamond (budget properties with basic amenities) to five diamond (luxury properties with the finest service, rooms and facilities).
Source: OAG, Business Travel Planner, Winter 1998-99

CONVENTION CENTERS

Major Convention Centers

Center Name	Meeting Rooms	Exhibit Space (sq. ft.)
Adam's Mark Hotel-Charlotte	31	52,000
Charlotte Convention Center	46	412,500
Charlotte Merchandise Mart	1	224,000
New Charlotte Convention Center	46	412,500

Source: Trade Shows Worldwide, 1998; Meetings & Conventions, 4/15/99; Sucessful Meetings, 3/31/98

Living Environment

COST OF LIVING

Cost of Living Index

Composite Index	Groceries	Housing	Utilities	Trans-portation	Health Care	Misc. Goods/ Services
101.1	102.2	101.0	97.3	100.2	92.7	103.0

Note: U.S. = 100
Source: ACCRA, Cost of Living Index, 1st Quarter 1999

HOUSING

Median Home Prices and Housing Affordability

Area	Median Price[2] 1st Qtr. 1999 ($)	HOI[3] 1st Qtr. 1999	Afford-ability Rank[4]
MSA[1]	142,000	68.8	122
U.S.	134,000	69.6	–

Note: (1) Metropolitan Statistical Area - see Appendix A for areas included; (2) U.S. figures calculated from the sales of 524,324 new and existing homes in 181 markets; (3) Housing Opportunity Index - percent of homes sold that were within the reach of the median income household at the prevailing mortgage interest rate; (4) Rank is from 1-181 with 1 being most affordable
Source: National Association of Home Builders, Housing Opportunity Index, 1st Quarter 1999

Median Home Price Projection

It is projected that the median price of existing single-family homes in the metro area will increase by 3.6% in 1999. Nationwide, home prices are projected to increase 3.8%.
Kiplinger's Personal Finance Magazine, January 1999

Average New Home Price

Area	Price ($)
City	148,500
U.S.	142,735

Note: Figures are based on a new home with 1,800 sq. ft. of living area on an 8,000 sq. ft. lot.
Source: ACCRA, Cost of Living Index, 1st Quarter 1999

Average Apartment Rent

Area	Rent ($/mth)
City	548
U.S.	601

Note: Figures are based on an unfurnished two bedroom, 1-1/2 or 2 bath apartment, approximately 950 sq. ft. in size, excluding all utilities except water
Source: ACCRA, Cost of Living Index, 1st Quarter 1999

RESIDENTIAL UTILITIES

Average Residential Utility Costs

Area	All Electric ($/mth)	Part Electric ($/mth)	Other Energy ($/mth)	Phone ($/mth)
City	97.99	–	–	17.51
U.S.	100.02	55.73	43.33	19.71

Source: ACCRA, Cost of Living Index, 1st Quarter 1999

HEALTH CARE

Average Health Care Costs

Area	Hospital ($/day)	Doctor ($/visit)	Dentist ($/visit)
City	396.67	53.00	56.80
U.S.	430.43	52.45	66.35

Note: Hospital—based on a semi-private room; Doctor—based on a general practitioner's routine exam of an established patient; Dentist—based on adult teeth cleaning and periodic oral exam.
Source: ACCRA, Cost of Living Index, 1st Quarter 1999

Distribution of Office-Based Physicians

| Area | Family/Gen. Practitioners | Specialists | | |
		Medical	Surgical	Other
MSA[1]	282	711	657	516

Note: Data as of 12/31/97; (1) Metropolitan Statistical Area - see Appendix A for areas included
Source: American Medical Assn., Physician Characteristics & Distribution in the U.S., 1999

Hospitals

Charlotte has 4 general medical and surgical hospitals, 1 psychiatric, 1 eye, ear, nose and throat, 1 rehabilitation, 1 orthopedic, 1 alcoholism and other chemical dependency. *AHA Guide to the Healthcare Field, 1998-99*

EDUCATION

Public School District Statistics

District Name	Num. Sch.	Enroll.	Classroom Teachers	Pupils per Teacher	Minority Pupils (%)	Current Exp.[1] ($/pupil)
Charlotte-Mecklenburg Schools	130	95,795	6,147	15.6	49.0	5,093
Community Charter School	1	76	n/a	n/a	n/a	n/a

Note: Data covers the 1997-1998 school year unless otherwise noted; (1) Data covers fiscal year 1996; SD = School District; ISD = Independent School District; n/a not available
Source: National Center for Education Statistics, Common Core of Data Public Education Agency Universe 1997-98; National Center for Education Statistics, Characteristics of the 100 Largest Public Elementary and Secondary School Districts in the United States: 1997-98, July 1999

Educational Quality

School District	Education Quotient[1]	Graduate Outcome[2]	Community Index[3]	Resource Index[4]
Charlotte-Mecklenburg	82.0	85.0	129.0	68.0

Note: Nearly 1,000 secondary school districts were rated in terms of educational quality. The scores range from a low of 50 to a high of 150; (1) Average of the Graduate Outcome, Community and Resource indexes; (2) Based on graduation rates and college board scores (SAT/ACT); (3) Based on the surrounding community's average level of education and the area's average income level; (4) Based on teacher salaries, per-pupil expenditures and student-teacher ratios.
Source: Expansion Management, Ratings Issue, 1998

Educational Attainment by Race

| Area | High School Graduate (%) | | | | | Bachelor's Degree (%) | | | | |
	Total	White	Black	Other	Hisp.[2]	Total	White	Black	Other	Hisp.[2]
City	81.0	86.9	66.5	71.9	73.2	28.4	34.5	12.5	27.7	21.9
MSA[1]	72.5	74.8	61.7	68.7	69.5	19.6	21.4	10.5	24.5	19.9
U.S.	75.2	77.9	63.1	60.4	49.8	20.3	21.5	11.4	19.4	9.2

Note: Figures shown cover persons 25 years old and over; (1) Metropolitan Statistical Area - see Appendix A for areas included; (2) people of Hispanic origin can be of any race
Source: 1990 Census of Population and Housing, Summary Tape File 3C

School Enrollment by Type

| Area | Preprimary | | | | Elementary/High School | | | |
| | Public | | Private | | Public | | Private | |
	Enrollment	%	Enrollment	%	Enrollment	%	Enrollment	%
City	4,071	53.5	3,540	46.5	55,638	89.3	6,640	10.7
MSA[1]	10,978	56.1	8,605	43.9	176,791	92.7	13,957	7.3
U.S.	2,679,029	59.5	1,824,256	40.5	38,379,689	90.2	4,187,099	9.8

Note: Figures shown cover persons 3 years old and over;
(1) Metropolitan Statistical Area - see Appendix A for areas included
Source: 1990 Census of Population and Housing, Summary Tape File 3C

School Enrollment by Race

Area	Preprimary (%)				Elementary/High School (%)			
	White	Black	Other	Hisp.[1]	White	Black	Other	Hisp.[1]
City	67.5	30.4	2.0	1.3	53.0	43.8	3.2	1.4
MSA[2]	78.5	19.9	1.6	0.8	71.2	26.7	2.0	1.0
U.S.	80.4	12.5	7.1	7.8	74.1	15.6	10.3	12.5

Note: Figures shown cover persons 3 years old and over; (1) people of Hispanic origin can be of any race; (2) Metropolitan Statistical Area - see Appendix A for areas included
Source: 1990 Census of Population and Housing, Summary Tape File 3C

Classroom Teacher Salaries in Public Schools

District	B.A. Degree		M.A. Degree		Maximum	
	Min. ($)	Rank[1]	Max. ($)	Rank[1]	Max. ($)	Rank[1]
Charlotte	24,533	74	48,776	28	51,306	44
Average	26,980	-	46,065	-	51,435	-

Note: Salaries are for 1997-1998; (1) Rank ranges from 1 to 100
Source: American Federation of Teachers, Survey & Analysis of Salary Trends, 1998

Higher Education

Two-Year Colleges		Four-Year Colleges		Medical Schools	Law Schools	Voc/ Tech
Public	Private	Public	Private			
1	1	1	3	0	0	15

Source: College Blue Book, Occupational Education, 1997; Medical School Admission Requirements, 1999-2000; Peterson's Guide to Two-Year Colleges, 1999; Peterson's Guide to Four-Year Colleges, 2000; Barron's Guide to Law Schools, 1999

MAJOR EMPLOYERS

Major Employers

BankAmerica Corp.	Charlotte Mecklenburg Hospital Authority
Duke Energy Corp.	Royal Indemnity Co.
First Union National Bank	Lance Inc. (cookies & crackers)
Presbyterian Hospital	NationsBank Corp.
Marketing Associates International	Philipp Holzmann USA (construction)

Note: Companies listed are located in the city
Source: Dun's Business Rankings, 1999; Ward's Business Directory, 1998

PUBLIC SAFETY

Crime Rate

Area	All Crimes	Violent Crimes				Property Crimes		
		Murder	Forcible Rape	Robbery	Aggrav. Assault	Burglary	Larceny -Theft	Motor Vehicle Theft
City	9,409.9	10.5	61.4	483.3	1,075.6	1,852.8	5,146.2	780.1
Suburbs[1]	4,949.9	8.4	28.5	120.6	432.6	1,131.4	3,011.4	217.0
MSA[2]	6,847.8	9.3	42.5	274.9	706.2	1,438.4	3,919.8	456.6
U.S.	4,922.7	6.8	35.9	186.1	382.0	919.6	2,886.5	505.8

Note: Crime rate is the number of crimes per 100,000 pop.; (1) defined as all areas within the MSA but located outside the central city; (2) Metropolitan Statistical Area - see Appendix A for areas incl.
Source: FBI Uniform Crime Reports, 1997

RECREATION

Culture and Recreation

Museums	Symphony Orchestras	Opera Companies	Dance Companies	Professional Theatres	Zoos	Pro Sports Teams
5	1	1	2	3	0	2

Source: International Directory of the Performing Arts, 1997; Official Museum Directory, 1999; Stern's Performing Arts Directory, 1997; USA Today Four Sport Stadium Guide, 1997; Chamber of Commerce/Economic Development, 1999

Library System

The Public Library of Charlotte & Mecklenburg County has 21 branches, holdings of 1,407,602 volumes, and a budget of $16,611,328 (1996-1997). *American Library Directory, 1998-1999*

MEDIA

Newspapers

Name	Type	Freq.	Distribution	Circulation
The Catholic News Herald	Religious	1x/wk	Local	40,000
The Charlotte Observer	n/a	7x/wk	Area	236,579
Charlotte Post	Black	1x/wk	Area	11,847

Note: Includes newspapers with circulations of 1,000 or more located in the city; n/a not available
Source: Burrelle's Media Directory, 1999 Edition

Television Stations

Name	Ch.	Affiliation	Type	Owner
KMID	n/a	ABCT	Commercial	Gocom Communications
WBTV	n/a	CBST	Commercial	Jefferson-Pilot Communications Company
WSOC	n/a	ABCT	Commercial	Cox Enterprises Inc.
WCCB	18	FBC	Commercial	Bahakel Communications Inc.
WFXZ	35	n/a	n/a	Gocom Communications
WCNC	36	NBCT	Commercial	A.H. Belo Corporation
WTVI	42	n/a	Public	Charlotte-Mecklenburg Public Broadcasting Auth.
WJZY	46	UPN	Commercial	Capitol Broadcasting Company Inc.
WFVT	55	WB	Commercial	n/a

Note: Stations included broadcast in the Charlotte metro area; n/a not available
Source: Burrelle's Media Directory, 1999 Edition

AM Radio Stations

Call Letters	Freq. (kHz)	Target Audience	Station Format	Music Format
WFNZ	610	General	N/S/T	n/a
WYFQ	930	Religious	N/T	n/a
WNOW	1030	Religious	T	n/a
WBT	1110	General	N/S/T	n/a
WAVO	1150	n/a	T	n/a
WHVN	1240	General	E/M/N/T	Christian/Gospel
WGAS	1420	General	M	Christian
WGFY	1480	General	E/M	n/a
WOGR	1540	Religious	M/N	Adult Contemporary/Christian

Note: Stations included broadcast in the Charlotte metro area; n/a not available
Target Audience: A=Asian; B=Black; C=Christian; E=Ethnic; F=French; G=General; H=Hispanic; M=Men; N=Native American; R=Religious; S=Senior Citizen; W=Women; Y=Young Adult; Z=Children
Station Format: E=Educational; M=Music; N=News; S=Sports; T=Talk
Source: Burrelle's Media Directory, 1999 Edition

FM Radio Stations

Call Letters	Freq. (mHz)	Target Audience	Station Format	Music Format
WDAV	89.9	General	M	Classical
WFHE	90.3	n/a	M/N/T	Jazz
WFAE	90.7	General	E/M/N/T	Jazz
WCCJ	92.7	n/a	n/a	n/a
WNKS	95.1	Y	M/N/T	Top 40
WXRC	95.7	General	M/N/S	Classic Rock
WWMG	96.1	General	M/N/S/T	Oldies
WKKT	96.9	General	M/N/S	Country
WPEG	97.9	General	M	Urban Contemporary
WBT	99.3	n/a	N/S/T	n/a
WRFX	99.7	General	M/N/S	Classic Rock
WLYT	102.9	General	M	Adult Contemporary
WSOC	103.7	General	M/N/S	Country
WSSS	104.7	General	M	Oldies
WNMX	106.1	General	M	Adult Standards
WEND	106.5	General	M/N/T	Modern Rock
WLNK	107.9	General	M	Adult Contemporary

Note: Stations included broadcast in the Charlotte metro area; n/a not available
Station Format: E=Educational; M=Music; N=News; S=Sports; T=Talk
Target Audience: A=Asian; B=Black; C=Christian; E=Ethnic; F=French; G=General; H=Hispanic;
M=Men; N=Native American; R=Religious; S=Senior Citizen; W=Women; Y=Young Adult; Z=Children
Source: Burrelle's Media Directory, 1999 Edition

CLIMATE

Average and Extreme Temperatures

Temperature	Jan	Feb	Mar	Apr	May	Jun	Jul	Aug	Sep	Oct	Nov	Dec	Yr.
Extreme High (°F)	78	81	86	93	97	103	103	103	104	98	85	77	104
Average High (°F)	51	54	62	72	80	86	89	88	82	72	62	53	71
Average Temp. (°F)	41	44	51	61	69	76	79	78	72	61	51	43	61
Average Low (°F)	31	33	40	48	57	65	69	68	62	50	40	33	50
Extreme Low (°F)	-5	5	4	25	32	45	53	53	39	24	11	2	-5

Note: Figures cover the years 1948-1990
Source: National Climatic Data Center, International Station Meteorological Climate Summary, 3/95

Average Precipitation/Snowfall/Humidity

Precip./Humidity	Jan	Feb	Mar	Apr	May	Jun	Jul	Aug	Sep	Oct	Nov	Dec	Yr.
Avg. Precip. (in.)	3.6	3.8	4.5	3.0	3.7	3.4	3.9	3.9	3.4	3.2	3.1	3.4	42.8
Avg. Snowfall (in.)	2	2	1	Tr	0	0	0	0	0	0	Tr	1	6
Avg. Rel. Hum. 7am (%)	78	77	78	78	82	83	86	89	89	87	83	79	82
Avg. Rel. Hum. 4pm (%)	53	49	46	43	49	51	54	55	54	50	50	54	51

Note: Figures cover the years 1948-1990; Tr = Trace amounts (<0.05 in. of rain; <0.5 in. of snow)
Source: National Climatic Data Center, International Station Meteorological Climate Summary, 3/95

Weather Conditions

Temperature			Daytime Sky			Precipitation		
10°F & below	32°F & below	90°F & above	Clear	Partly cloudy	Cloudy	0.01 inch or more precip.	0.1 inch or more snow/ice	Thunder-storms
1	65	44	98	142	125	113	3	41

Note: Figures are average number of days per year and covers the years 1948-1990
Source: National Climatic Data Center, International Station Meteorological Climate Summary, 3/95

AIR & WATER QUALITY

Maximum Pollutant Concentrations

	Particulate Matter (ug/m^3)	Carbon Monoxide (ppm)	Sulfur Dioxide (ppm)	Nitrogen Dioxide (ppm)	Ozone (ppm)	Lead (ug/m^3)
MSA[1] Level	61	6	0.016	0.018	0.13	0.01
NAAQS[2]	150	9	0.140	0.053	0.12	1.50
Met NAAQS?	Yes	Yes	Yes	Yes	No	Yes

Note: (1) Metropolitan Statistical Area - see Appendix A for areas included; (2) National Ambient Air Quality Standards; ppm = parts per million; ug/m^3 = micrograms per cubic meter; n/a not available
Source: EPA, National Air Quality and Emissions Trends Report, 1997

Pollutant Standards Index

In the Charlotte MSA (see Appendix A for areas included), the Pollutant Standards Index (PSI) exceeded 100 on 31 days in 1997. A PSI value greater than 100 indicates that air quality would be in the unhealthful range on that day. *EPA, National Air Quality and Emissions Trends Report, 1997*

Drinking Water

Water System Name	Pop. Served	Primary Water Source Type	Number of Violations in 1998	Type of Violation/ Contaminants
Charlotte-Mecklenburg Utility	413,500	Surface	None	None

Note: Data as of July 10, 1999
Source: EPA, Office of Ground Water and Drinking Water, Safe Drinking Water Information System

Charlotte tap water is alkaline, very soft and fluoridated.
Editor & Publisher Market Guide, 1999

Cincinnati, Ohio

Background

The fashion in which Cincinnati derived its name runs like a group of gallant gentlemen paying excessive praise to long ago elders. After the American Revolution, former Continental Army soldiers formed a fraternal organization called the Society of Cincinnati, alluding to the Roman General Lucius Quinctius Cincinnatus. In 1790 General Arthur St. Clair, a member of that society, and the first governor of the Northwest Territory, felt that this lovely city overlooking the Ohio River could only be called Cincinnati. As if that were not enough, he had to pay homage to fellow fraternal member, Alexander Hamilton. St. Clair named the county, in which Cincinnati lies, after him.

Since its incorporation as a city in 1819, the Miami and Erie Canals have played great roles in Cincinnati's economic growth. Because of these waterways, farmers had the transportation necessary to sell their produce in town. From there, businesses would process the farmers' wares such as corn, pigs, and wheat into products such as whiskey, pork, and flour. Incidentally, the South which was Cincinnati's greatest market for pork, made the city's loyalties difficult to declare during the Civil War. However, Cincinnati finally decided where its sympathies lay, when its political climate made it a major station of the underground railroad, as well as the haven where Harriet Beecher Stowe could write her classic, *Uncle Tom's Cabin.*

In a move to attract overseas tourist dollars, Cincinnati has joined forces with Louisville (KY) and Indianapolis (IN) to market the three city triangle area as a package to foreign tourists from Britain, France, Germany, and later Japan. Cincinnati itself gets at least 200,000 foreign tourists a year and nearly 4 million total tourists annually, with the visitors spending over $2 billion in 1996. What makes this three city experiment unique is that it is the first three-city, three-state partnership aimed solely at European tourists. *New York Times, 7/4/97*

Today, the city is home to the University of Cincinnati and Xavier University, and its centralized location has attracted numerous Fortune 500 corporate headquarters.

Cincinnati experiences a rather wide range of temperatures from winter to summer. Summers are warm and quite humid, with the temperature reaching 100 degrees or more in one out of three years. Winters are moderately cold with numerous periods of extensive cloudiness.

General Rankings and Evaluative Comments

- Cincinnati was ranked #5 out of 11 large, midwestern metropolitan areas in *Money's* 1998 survey of "The Best Places to Live in America." The survey was conducted by first contacting 512 representative households nationwide and asking them to rank 37 quality-of-life factors on a scale of 1 to 10. Next, a demographic profile was compiled on the 300 largest metropolitan statistical areas in the U.S. The numbers were crunched together to arrive at an overall ranking (things Americans consider most important, like clean air and water, low crime and good schools, received extra weight). Unlike previous years, the 1998 rankings were broken down by region (northeast, midwest, south, west) and population size (100,000 to 249,999; 250,000 to 999,999; 1 million plus). The city had a nationwide ranking of #194 out of 300 in 1997 and #257 out of 300 in 1996. *Money, July 1998; Money, July 1997; Money, September 1996*

- *Ladies Home Journal* ranked America's 200 largest cities based on the qualities women care about most. Cincinnati ranked #25 out of 200. Criteria: low crime rate, well-paying jobs, quality health and child care, good public schools, the presence of women in government, size of the gender wage gap, number of sexual-harassment and discrimination complaints filed, unemployment and divorce rates, commute times, population density, number of houses of worship, parks and cultural offerings, number of women's health specialists, how well a community's women cared for themselves, complexion kindness index based on UV radiation levels, odds of finding affordable fashions, rental rates for romance movies, champagne sales and other matters of the heart. *Ladies Home Journal, November 1998*

- Zero Population Growth ranked 229 cities in terms of children's health, safety, and economic well-being. Cincinnati was ranked #98 out of 112 independent cities (cities with populations greater than 100,000 which were neither Major Cities nor Suburbs/Outer Cities) and was given a grade of D. Criteria: total population, percent of population under 18 years of age, household language, percent population change, percent of births to teens, infant mortality rate, percent of low birth weights, dropout rate, enrollment in preprimary school, violent and property crime rates, unemployment rate, percent of children in poverty, percent of owner occupied units, number of bad air days, percent of public transportation commuters, and average travel time to work. *Zero Population Growth, Children's Environmental Index, Fall 1999*

- Cincinnati was ranked #16 out of 59 metro areas in *The Regional Economist's* "Rational Livability Ranking of 59 Large Metro Areas." The rankings were based on the metro area's total population change over the period 1990-97 divided by the number of people moving in from elsewhere in the United States (net domestic in-migration). *St. Louis Federal Reserve Bank of St. Louis, The Regional Economist, April 1999*

- Cincinnati was selected by *Yahoo! Internet Life* as one of "America's Most Wired Cities & Towns." The city ranked #23 out of 50. Criteria: home and work net use, domain density, hosts per capita, directory density and content quality. *Yahoo! Internet Life, March 1999*

- Cognetics studied 273 metro areas in the United States, ranking them by entrepreneurial activity. Cincinnati was ranked #24 out of the 50 largest metro areas. Criteria: Significant Starts (firms started in the last 10 years that still employ at least 5 people) and Young Growers (percent of firms 10 years old or less that grew significantly during the last 4 years). *Cognetics, "Entrepreneurial Hot Spots: The Best Places in America to Start and Grow a Company," 1998*

- Cincinnati was included among *Entrepreneur* magazine's listing of the "20 Best Cities for Small Business." It was ranked #16 among large metro areas and #4 among central metro areas. Criteria: entrepreneurial activity, small-business growth, economic growth, and risk of failure. *Entrepreneur, October 1999*

- Cincinnati was selected as one of the "Best American Cities to Start a Business" by *Point of View* magazine. Criteria: coolness, quality-of-life, and business concerns. The city was ranked #46 out of 75. *Point of View, November 1998*

■ Cincinnati appeared on *Sales & Marketing Management's* list of the "20 Hottest Cities for Selling." Rank: #10 out of 20. *S&MM* editors looked at Metropolitan Statistical Areas with populations of more than 150,000. The areas were ranked based on population increases, retail sales increases, effective buying income, increase in both residential and commercial building permits issued, unemployment rates, job growth, mix of industries, tax rates, number of corporate relocations, and the number of new corporations.
Sales & Marketing Management, April 1999

■ Reliastar Financial Corp. ranked the 125 largest metropolitan areas according to the general financial security of residents. Cincinnati was ranked #41 out of 125 with a score of 5.1. The score indicates the percentage a metropolitan area is above or below the metropolitan norm. A metro area with a score of 10.6 is 10.6% above the metro average. Criteria: Earnings and Wealth Potential (household income, education, net assets, cost of living); Safety Net (health insurance, retirement savings, life insurance, income support programs); Personal Threats (unemployment rate, low-income households, crime rate); Community Economic Vitality (cost of community services, job quality, job creation, housing costs).
Reliastar Financial Corp., "The Best Cities to Earn and Save Money," 1999 Edition

Business Environment

STATE ECONOMY

State Economic Profile

"Ohio's expansion has started to decelerate. OH is expected to lag the nation in growth for some time. The slowdown in employment growth is concentrated in the manufacturing sector and outside of OH's larger metro areas. OH's weak demographic trends will constrain job growth and the housing market.

OH manufacturing shed about 7,000 jobs in 1998. A large share of these losses were in the Cleveland and Columbus areas, while Cincinnati managed to add a small number of manufacturing jobs. Job growth in the services sectors, particularly business, financial and health services, has helped to offset a slowdown in manufacturing in these urban areas. Bank merger and acquisition activity has resulted in jobs being shifted from rural and smaller areas to the larger metropolitan areas.

While OH's rural areas have suffered from a declining employment base, economic activity has also been shifting from the northern part of the state toward the middle and south. Last year's employment growth for Cincinnati was 2.5%, compared to only 1.6% for Columbus and 1.6% for Cleveland. Population growth has followed a similar pattern, although the state as a whole is among one of the weakest in the nation, losing a considerable number of younger households.

Ohio's housing market had a strong 1998, with sales up 8.6% and single family permits up 3.2%. Price appreciation was just below the nation and will likely remain modest given the increase in construction. Both construction and sales should contract in 1999 and 2000. Prices are likely to rise the most in Cincinnati, where construction has been modest and job growth strongest." *National Association of Realtors, Economic Profiles: The Fifty States and the District of Columbia, http://nar.realtor.com/databank/profiles.htm*

IMPORTS/EXPORTS

Total Export Sales

Area	1994 ($000)	1995 ($000)	1996 ($000)	1997 ($000)	% Chg. 1994-97	% Chg. 1996-97
MSA[1]	4,056,506	4,256,653	4,784,140	5,674,148	39.9	18.6
U.S.	512,415,609	583,030,524	622,827,063	687,597,999	34.2	10.4

Note: (1) Metropolitan Statistical Area - see Appendix A for areas included
Source: U.S. Department of Commerce, International Trade Association, Metropolitan Area Exports: An Export Performance Report on Over 250 U.S. Cities, November 10, 1998

CITY FINANCES

City Government Finances

Component	FY92 ($000)	FY92 (per capita $)
Revenue	675,058	1,873.15
Expenditure	659,385	1,829.66
Debt Outstanding	259,517	720.11
Cash & Securities	1,358,049	3,768.32

Source: U.S. Bureau of the Census, City Government Finances: 1991-92

City Government Revenue by Source

Source	FY92 ($000)	FY92 (per capita $)	FY92 (%)
From Federal Government	26,948	74.78	4.0
From State Governments	50,132	139.11	7.4
From Local Governments	18,636	51.71	2.8
Property Taxes	43,195	119.86	6.4
General Sales Taxes	0	0.00	0.0
Selective Sales Taxes	4,040	11.21	0.6
Income Taxes	175,002	485.60	25.9
Current Charges	116,948	324.51	17.3
Utility/Liquor Store	64,154	178.01	9.5
Employee Retirement[1]	87,809	243.65	13.0
Other	88,194	244.72	13.1

Note: (1) Excludes "city contributions," classified as "nonrevenue," intragovernmental transfers.
Source: U.S. Bureau of the Census, City Government Finances: 1991-92

City Government Expenditures by Function

Function	FY92 ($000)	FY92 (per capita $)	FY92 (%)
Educational Services	0	0.00	0.0
Employee Retirement[1]	53,156	147.50	8.1
Environment/Housing	211,662	587.32	32.1
Government Administration	32,066	88.98	4.9
Interest on General Debt	12,526	34.76	1.9
Public Safety	121,152	336.17	18.4
Social Services	32,368	89.81	4.9
Transportation	74,925	207.90	11.4
Utility/Liquor Store	80,747	224.06	12.2
Other	40,783	113.16	6.2

Note: (1) Payments to beneficiaries including withdrawal of contributions.
Source: U.S. Bureau of the Census, City Government Finances: 1991-92

Municipal Bond Ratings

Area	Moody's	S & P
Cincinnati	Aa1	n/a

Note: n/a not available; n/r not rated
Source: Moody's Bond Record, 6/99

POPULATION

Population Growth

Area	1980	1990	% Chg. 1980-90	July 1998 Estimate	% Chg. 1990-98
City	385,457	364,040	-5.6	336,400	-7.6
MSA[1]	1,401,491	1,452,645	3.6	1,621,106	11.6
U.S.	226,545,805	248,765,170	9.8	270,299,000	8.7

Note: (1) Metropolitan Statistical Area - see Appendix A for areas included;
July 1998 MSA population estimate was calculated by the editors
Source: 1980/1990 Census of Housing and Population, Summary Tape File 3C;
Census Bureau Population Estimates 1998

Population Characteristics

Race	City 1980 Population	%	City 1990 Population	%	% Chg. 1980-90	MSA[1] 1990 Population	%
White	251,332	65.2	220,207	60.5	-12.4	1,246,669	85.8
Black	130,490	33.9	138,110	37.9	5.8	190,029	13.1
Amer Indian/Esk/Aleut	567	0.1	592	0.2	4.4	2,258	0.2
Asian/Pacific Islander	2,332	0.6	4,184	1.1	79.4	11,362	0.8
Other	736	0.2	947	0.3	28.7	2,327	0.2
Hispanic Origin[2]	2,988	0.8	2,319	0.6	-22.4	7,579	0.5

Note: (1) Metropolitan Statistical Area - see Appendix A for areas included;
(2) people of Hispanic origin can be of any race
Source: 1980/1990 Census of Housing and Population, Summary Tape File 3C

Ancestry

Area	German	Irish	English	Italian	U.S.	French	Polish	Dutch
City	30.7	14.7	8.5	3.3	3.3	2.3	1.2	1.4
MSA[1]	44.2	20.3	13.8	3.7	4.7	3.3	1.3	2.3
U.S.	23.3	15.6	13.1	5.9	5.3	4.2	3.8	2.5

Note: Figures are percentages and include persons that reported multiple ancestry (eg. if a person reported being Irish and Italian, they were included in both columns); (1) Metropolitan Statistical Area - see Appendix A for areas included
Source: 1990 Census of Population and Housing, Summary Tape File 3C

Age

Area	Median Age (Years)	Under 5	Under 18	18-24	25-44	45-64	65+	80+
City	30.8	8.4	25.0	12.8	32.6	15.7	13.9	3.7
MSA[1]	32.4	7.9	26.8	10.1	32.6	18.4	12.0	2.8
U.S.	32.9	7.3	25.6	10.5	32.6	18.7	12.5	2.8

Note: (1) Metropolitan Statistical Area - see Appendix A for areas included
Source: 1990 Census of Population and Housing, Summary Tape File 3C

Male/Female Ratio

Area	Number of males per 100 females (all ages)	Number of males per 100 females (18 years old+)
City	87.2	81.7
MSA[1]	92.1	87.8
U.S.	95.0	91.9

Note: (1) Metropolitan Statistical Area - see Appendix A for areas included
Source: 1990 Census of Population, General Population Characteristics

INCOME

Per Capita/Median/Average Income

Area	Per Capita ($)	Median Household ($)	Average Household ($)
City	12,547	21,006	29,010
MSA[1]	14,610	30,691	38,344
U.S.	14,420	30,056	38,453

Note: All figures are for 1989; (1) Metropolitan Statistical Area - see Appendix A for areas included
Source: 1990 Census of Population and Housing, Summary Tape File 3C

Household Income Distribution by Race

Income ($)	City (%)					U.S. (%)				
	Total	White	Black	Other	Hisp.[1]	Total	White	Black	Other	Hisp.[1]
Less than 5,000	13.5	7.2	25.0	14.3	19.1	6.2	4.8	15.2	8.6	8.8
5,000 - 9,999	13.6	11.3	17.6	14.5	14.1	9.3	8.6	14.2	9.9	11.1
10,000 - 14,999	10.7	10.3	11.3	15.9	10.0	8.8	8.5	11.0	9.8	11.0
15,000 - 24,999	19.3	20.1	18.1	16.5	14.4	17.5	17.3	18.9	18.5	20.5
25,000 - 34,999	14.7	16.2	12.0	13.0	20.4	15.8	16.1	14.2	15.4	16.4
35,000 - 49,999	14.1	16.6	9.5	11.8	11.2	17.9	18.6	13.3	16.1	16.0
50,000 - 74,999	8.8	11.0	5.0	7.6	7.5	15.0	15.8	9.3	13.4	11.1
75,000 - 99,999	2.7	3.5	1.1	2.7	2.0	5.1	5.5	2.6	4.7	3.1
100,000+	2.6	3.8	0.4	3.6	1.3	4.4	4.8	1.3	3.7	1.9

Note: All figures are for 1989; (1) people of Hispanic origin can be of any race
Source: 1990 Census of Population and Housing, Summary Tape File 3C

Effective Buying Income

Area	Per Capita ($)	Median Household ($)	Average Household ($)
City	15,477	26,169	35,902
MSA[1]	17,989	36,959	47,155
U.S.	16,803	34,536	45,243

Note: Data as of 1/1/99; (1) Metropolitan Statistical Area - see Appendix A for areas included
Source: Standard Rate & Data Service, Newspaper Advertising Source, 9/99

Effective Household Buying Income Distribution

Area	% of Households Earning						
	$10,000 -$19,999	$20,000 -$34,999	$35,000 -$49,999	$50,000 -$74,999	$75,000 -$99,000	$100,000 -$124,999	$125,000 and up
City	20.0	22.9	15.3	13.7	4.7	1.6	2.1
MSA[1]	14.3	21.6	18.6	20.5	8.1	2.6	2.7
U.S.	16.0	22.6	18.2	18.9	7.2	2.4	2.7

Note: Data as of 1/1/99; (1) Metropolitan Statistical Area - see Appendix A for areas included
Source: Standard Rate & Data Service, Newspaper Advertising Source, 9/99

Poverty Rates by Race and Age

Area	Total (%)	By Race (%)				By Age (%)		
		White	Black	Other	Hisp.[2]	Under 5 years old	Under 18 years old	65 years and over
City	24.3	14.7	39.4	24.8	29.7	42.0	37.4	17.3
MSA[1]	11.4	8.0	34.0	14.1	18.3	19.4	16.4	11.0
U.S.	13.1	9.8	29.5	23.1	25.3	20.1	18.3	12.8

Note: Figures show the percent of people living below the poverty line in 1989. The average poverty threshold was $12,674 for a family of four in 1989; (1) Metropolitan Statistical Area - see Appendix A for areas included; (2) people of Hispanic origin can be of any race
Source: 1990 Census of Population and Housing, Summary Tape File 3C

EMPLOYMENT

Labor Force and Employment

Area	Civilian Labor Force			Workers Employed		
	Jun. 1998	Jun. 1999	% Chg.	Jun. 1998	Jun. 1999	% Chg.
City	175,852	184,751	5.1	166,085	174,713	5.2
MSA[1]	846,760	885,339	4.6	814,672	852,921	4.7
U.S.	138,798,000	140,666,000	1.3	132,265,000	134,395,000	1.6

Note: Data is not seasonally adjusted and covers workers 16 years of age and older; (1) Metropolitan Statistical Area - see Appendix A for areas included
Source: Bureau of Labor Statistics, http://stats.bls.gov

Unemployment Rate

Area	1998						1999					
	Jul.	Aug.	Sep.	Oct.	Nov.	Dec.	Jan.	Feb.	Mar.	Apr.	May.	Jun.
City	4.2	5.0	5.4	5.1	4.9	4.3	4.8	4.7	4.3	4.5	4.4	5.4
MSA[1]	3.1	3.3	3.5	3.4	3.2	2.9	3.7	3.5	3.1	3.0	2.9	3.7
U.S.	4.7	4.5	4.4	4.2	4.1	4.0	4.8	4.7	4.4	4.1	4.0	4.5

Note: Data is not seasonally adjusted and covers workers 16 years of age and older; all figures are percentages; (1) Metropolitan Statistical Area - see Appendix A for areas included
Source: Bureau of Labor Statistics, http://stats.bls.gov

Employment by Industry

Sector	MSA[1]		U.S.
	Number of Employees	Percent of Total	Percent of Total
Services	272,000	30.4	30.4
Retail Trade	167,600	18.8	17.7
Government	104,100	11.6	15.6
Manufacturing	143,600	16.1	14.3
Finance/Insurance/Real Estate	56,900	6.4	5.9
Wholesale Trade	59,700	6.7	5.4
Transportation/Public Utilities	47,600	5.3	5.3
Construction	41,400	4.6	5.0
Mining	700	0.1	0.4

Note: Figures cover non-farm employment as of 6/99 and are not seasonally adjusted;
(1) Metropolitan Statistical Area - see Appendix A for areas included
Source: Bureau of Labor Statistics, http://stats.bls.gov

Employment by Occupation

Occupation Category	City (%)	MSA[1] (%)	U.S. (%)
White Collar	61.7	61.4	58.1
Executive/Admin./Management	11.7	13.2	12.3
Professional	17.6	14.5	14.1
Technical & Related Support	4.3	4.1	3.7
Sales	10.5	12.1	11.8
Administrative Support/Clerical	17.7	17.5	16.3
Blue Collar	20.9	25.1	26.2
Precision Production/Craft/Repair	7.8	10.6	11.3
Machine Operators/Assem./Insp.	6.2	6.7	6.8
Transportation/Material Movers	3.0	3.7	4.1
Cleaners/Helpers/Laborers	3.9	4.0	3.9
Services	16.6	12.6	13.2
Farming/Forestry/Fishing	0.7	1.0	2.5

Note: Figures cover employed persons 16 years old and over;
(1) Metropolitan Statistical Area - see Appendix A for areas included
Source: 1990 Census of Population and Housing, Summary Tape File 3C

Occupational Employment Projections: 1996 - 2006

Occupations Expected to Have the Largest Job Growth (ranked by numerical growth)	Fast-Growing Occupations[1] (ranked by percent growth)
1. Cashiers	1. Systems analysts
2. Salespersons, retail	2. Occupational therapy assistants
3. Systems analysts	3. Desktop publishers
4. General managers & top executives	4. Paralegals
5. Truck drivers, light	5. Physical therapy assistants and aides
6. Registered nurses	6. Medical assistants
7. Food preparation workers	7. Personal and home care aides
8. Nursing aides/orderlies/attendants	8. Home health aides
9. Home health aides	9. Physical therapists
10. Marketing & sales, supervisors	10. Occupational therapists

Note: Projections cover Ohio; (1) Excludes occupations with total job growth less than 300
Source: U.S. Department of Labor, Employment and Training Administration, America's Labor Market Information System (ALMIS)

TAXES

Major State and Local Tax Rates

State Corp. Income (%)	State Personal Income (%)	Residential Property (effective rate per $100)	Sales & Use State (%)	Sales & Use Local (%)	State Gasoline (cents/gallon)	State Cigarette (cents/pack)
5.1 - 8.5[a]	0.673 - 6.799	n/a	5.0	1.0	22.0	24.0

Note: Personal/corporate income, sales, gasoline and cigarette tax rates as of January 1999. Property tax rates as of 1997; (a) Or 4.0 mils times the value of the taxpayer's issued and outstanding share of stock ($150K max). An additional litter tax is imposed equal to 0.11% on the first $50,000 of taxable income, 0.22% on income over $50,000; or 0.14 mills on net worth
Source: Federation of Tax Administrators, www.taxadmin.org; Washington D.C. Department of Finance and Revenue, Tax Rates and Tax Burdens in the District of Columbia: A Nationwide Comparison, July 1998; Chamber of Commerce, 1999

Total Taxes Per Capita and as a Percent of Income

Area	Per Capita Income ($)	Per Capita Taxes ($) Total	Per Capita Taxes ($) Federal	Per Capita Taxes ($) State/Local	Percent of Income (%) Total	Percent of Income (%) Federal	Percent of Income (%) State/Local
Ohio	26,684	9,354	6,322	3,033	35.1	23.7	11.4
U.S.	27,876	9,881	6,690	3,191	35.4	24.0	11.4

Note: Figures are for 1998
Source: Tax Foundation, www.taxfoundation.org

COMMERCIAL REAL ESTATE

Office Market

Class/Location	Total Space (sq. ft.)	Vacant Space (sq. ft.)	Vac. Rate (%)	Under Constr. (sq. ft.)	Net Absorp. (sq. ft.)	Rental Rates ($/sq.ft./yr.)
Class A						
CBD	6,785,950	151,369	2.2	0	301,696	16.85-25.90
Outside CBD	6,619,622	426,580	6.4	520,000	178,638	13.00-23.00
Class B						
CBD	5,652,228	676,548	12.0	0	211,563	10.35-19.25
Outside CBD	13,226,157	1,577,207	11.9	0	3,850,005	6.00-16.00

Note: Data as of 10/98 and covers Cincinnati; CBD = Central Business District; n/a not available;
Source: Society of Industrial and Office Realtors, 1999 Comparative Statistics of Industrial and Office Real Estate Markets

"Where as some other Midwest markets may anticipate weaker 1999 economies due to weakening exports, Cincinnati should see little, if any, negative effects because it is the home of consumer goods firms that are little affected by the Asian crisis. Our SIOR observers call for a stable market in the coming year, even with new construction now rising. Two former corporate headquarters are being renovated, adding 350,000 square feet to inventory. Several other buildings are under construction, and more are planned. There are some fears of an overbuilding episode. There is room for upward movement in CBD office pricing, which our reporters suggest may rise in the six to 10 percent range. Suburban properties now seem fully priced." *Society of Industrial and Office Realtors, 1999 Comparative Statistics of Industrial and Office Real Estate Markets*

Industrial Market

Location	Total Space (sq. ft.)	Vacant Space (sq. ft.)	Vac. Rate (%)	Under Constr. (sq. ft.)	Net Absorp. (sq. ft.)	Net Lease ($/sq.ft./yr.)
Central City	78,700,000	550,000	0.7	0	300,000	3.75-5.15
Suburban	122,100,000	6,950,000	5.7	1,540,000	5,650,000	2.90-6.00

Note: Data as of 10/98 and covers Cincinnati; n/a not available
Source: Society of Industrial and Office Realtors, 1999 Comparative Statistics of Industrial and Office Real Estate Markets

"Cincinnati's industrial market should fare well in 1999, perhaps better than many other cities in the industrial Midwest. There is relatively little exposure to Asian export difficulties, although some companies are negatively affected by depressed energy prices. There may be some risks on the supply side, as developers are excited by current market conditions. New speculative construction will be seen both in the vicinity of the airport and north of Cincinnati at the Union Centre interchange of I-75 SIOR's reporters estimate as much as two million sq. ft. of speculative construction coming during the next 12 months. Hundreds of acres of former farmland have recently been opened for development in the north-central sector of the market as well. This should make for a very competitive year among the builders, and keep most of the pricing parameters flat into 1999."

Society of Industrial and Office Realtors, 1999 Comparative Statistics of Industrial and Office Real Estate Markets

Retail Market

Shopping Center Inventory (sq. ft.)	Shopping Center Construction (sq. ft.)	Construction as a Percent of Inventory (%)	Torto Wheaton Rent Index[1] ($/sq. ft.)
28,415,000	560,000	2.0	12.40

Note: Data as of 1997 and covers the Metropolitan Statistical Area - see Appendix A for areas included; (1) Index is based on a model that predicts what the average rent should be for leases with certain characteristics, in certain locations during certain years.
Source: National Association of Realtors, 1997-1998 Market Conditions Report

"After declining for three consecutive years, Cincinnati's retail rent index rebounded in 1995, and has inched higher over the past two years. Retail rents currently stand slightly below the Midwest average of $12.27. Sluggish population growth and mild personal income gains have restrained the retail sector. Nonetheless, unprecedented levels of planning and development by city officials and business leaders have aided the area's economy. The city recently attempted to lure Nordstrom to the downtown area, and the Fountain Place development managed to keep Lazarus and Saks from moving to the suburbs. Solid levels of absorption should push retail rents higher over the next few years." *National Association of Realtors, 1997-1998 Market Conditions Report*

COMMERCIAL UTILITIES

Typical Monthly Electric Bills

Area	Commercial Service ($/month)		Industrial Service ($/month)	
	12 kW demand 1,500 kWh	100 kW demand 30,000 kWh	1,000 kW demand 400,000 kWh	20,000 kW demand 10,000,000 kWh
City	145	2,163	23,501	361,166
U.S.	150	2,174	23,995	508,569

Note: Based on rates in effect January 1, 1999
Source: Edison Electric Institute, Typical Residential, Commercial and Industrial Bills, Winter 1999

TRANSPORTATION

Transportation Statistics

Average minutes to work	21.1
Interstate highways	I-71; I-74; I-75
Bus lines	
In-city	SW Ohio Regional TA, 429 vehicles
Inter-city	3
Passenger air service	
Airport	Cincinnati-Northern Kentucky International Airport
Airlines	8
Aircraft departures	99,285 (1996)
Enplaned passengers	7,299,565 (1996)
Rail service	Amtrak
Motor freight carriers	85
Major waterways/ports	Ohio River; Port of Cincinnati

Source: Editor & Publisher Market Guide, 1999; FAA Airport Activity Statistics, 1997; Amtrak National Time Table, Northeast Timetable, Spring/Summer 1999; 1990 Census of Population and Housing, STF 3C; Chamber of Commerce/Economic Development 1999; Jane's Urban Transport Systems 1999-2000

Means of Transportation to Work

Area	Car/Truck/Van		Public Transportation			Bicycle	Walked	Other Means	Worked at Home
	Drove Alone	Car-pooled	Bus	Subway	Railroad				
City	67.4	12.6	10.9	0.0	0.0	0.2	5.9	0.9	2.0
MSA[1]	78.6	11.6	4.1	0.0	0.0	0.1	2.8	0.7	2.1
U.S.	73.2	13.4	3.0	1.5	0.5	0.4	3.9	1.2	3.0

Note: Figures shown are percentages and only include workers 16 years old and over; (1) Metropolitan Statistical Area - see Appendix A for areas included
Source: 1990 Census of Population and Housing, Summary Tape File 3C

BUSINESSES

Major Business Headquarters

Company Name	1999 Rankings	
	Fortune 500	Forbes 500
American Financial Group	381	-
Cinergy	279	-
Federated Dept. Stores	95	-
Kroger	36	-
Procter & Gamble	17	-

Note: Companies listed are located in the city; dashes indicate no ranking
Fortune 500: Companies that produce a 10-K are ranked 1 to 500 based on 1998 revenue
Forbes 500: Private companies are ranked 1 to 500 based on 1997 revenue
Source: Forbes, November 30, 1998; Fortune, April 26, 1999

Best Companies to Work For

Ohio National Financial Services and Lenscrafters (eyeglasses), headquartered in Cincinnati, are among the "100 Best Companies to Work for in America." Criteria: trust in management, pride in work/company, camaraderie, company responses to the Hewitt People Practices Inventory, and employee responses to their Great Place to Work survey. The companies also had to be at least 10 years old and have a minimum of 500 employees. *Fortune, January 11, 1999*

Cinergy Corp. (utility) and Procter & Gamble, headquartered in Cincinnati, are among the "100 Best Companies for Working Mothers." Criteria: fair wages, opportunities for women to advance, support for child care, flexible work schedules, family-friendly benefits, and work/life supports. *Working Mother, October 1998*

Cincinnati Financial Corp. (insurance), headquartered in Cincinnati, is among the "100 Best Places to Work in IS." Criteria: compensation, turnover and training. *Computerworld, May 25, 1998*

Procter & Gamble, headquartered in Cincinnati, is among the top public firms for executive women. Criteria: number of female directors, women in senior management positions and the ratio of female managers to female employees. *Working Women, September 1998*

Women-Owned Firms: Number, Employment and Sales

Area	Number of Firms	Employment	Sales ($000)	Rank[2]
MSA[1]	51,100	128,400	19,485,000	39

Note: (1) Metropolitan Statistical Area - see Appendix A for areas included;
(2) Calculated on an averaging of the number of businesses, employment and sales
Source: The National Foundation for Women Business Owners, 1999 Facts on Women-Owned Businesses: Trends in the Top 50 Metropolitan Areas

Women-Owned Firms: Growth

Area	% change from 1992 to 1999			Rank[2]
	Number of Firms	Employment	Sales	
MSA[1]	45.0	75.0	137.7	33

Note: (1) Metropolitan Statistical Area - see Appendix A for areas included; (2) Calculated on an averaging of the percent growth of number of businesses, employment and sales
Source: The National Foundation for Women Business Owners, 1999 Facts on Women-Owned Businesses: Trends in the Top 50 Metropolitan Areas

Minority Business Opportunity

Cincinnati is home to one company which is on the Black Enterprise Auto Dealer 100 list (largest based on gross sales): Kemper Dodge Inc. (Dodge cars and trucks) . Criteria: 1) operational in previous calendar year; 2) at least 51% black-owned. *Black Enterprise, www.blackenterprise.com*

One of the 500 largest Hispanic-owned companies in the U.S. are located in Cincinnati. *Hispanic Business, June 1999*

Small Business Opportunity

According to *Forbes*, Cincinnati is home to one of America's 200 best small companies: LSI Industries. Criteria: companies included must be publicly traded since November 1997 with a stock price of at least $5 per share and an average daily float of 1,000 shares. The company's latest 12-month sales must be between $5 and $350 million, return on equity (ROE) must be a minimum of 12% for both the past 5 years and the most recent four quarters, and five-year sales and EPS growth must average at least 10%. Companies with declining sales or earnings during the past year were dropped as well as businesses with debt/equity ratios over 1.25. Companies with negative operating cash flow in each of the past two years were also excluded. *Forbes, November 2, 1998*

HOTELS & MOTELS

Hotels/Motels

Area	Hotels/ Motels	Rooms	Luxury-Level Hotels/Motels		Average Minimum Rates ($)		
			♦♦♦♦	♦♦♦♦♦	♦♦	♦♦♦	♦♦♦♦
City	32	6,337	1	0	52	107	172
Airport	17	2,101	0	0	n/a	n/a	n/a
Suburbs	57	8,213	0	0	n/a	n/a	n/a
Total	106	16,651	1	0	n/a	n/a	n/a

Note: n/a not available; classifications range from one diamond (budget properties with basic amenities) to five diamond (luxury properties with the finest service, rooms and facilities).
Source: OAG, Business Travel Planner, Winter 1998-99

CONVENTION CENTERS

Major Convention Centers

Center Name	Meeting Rooms	Exhibit Space (sq. ft.)
Cincinnati Convention-Exposition Center	41	162,000
Cincinnati Gardens Arena and Exhibition Center	n/a	53,000

Note: n/a not available
Source: Trade Shows Worldwide, 1998; Meetings & Conventions, 4/15/99;
Sucessful Meetings, 3/31/98

Living Environment

COST OF LIVING

Cost of Living Index

Composite Index	Groceries	Housing	Utilities	Trans-portation	Health Care	Misc. Goods/ Services
98.7	94.4	98.1	109.3	102.1	92.1	98.6

Note: U.S. = 100
Source: ACCRA, Cost of Living Index, 1st Quarter 1999

HOUSING

Median Home Prices and Housing Affordability

Area	Median Price[2] 1st Qtr. 1999 ($)	HOI[3] 1st Qtr. 1999	Afford-ability Rank[4]
MSA[1]	112,000	80.4	53
U.S.	134,000	69.6	–

Note: (1) Metropolitan Statistical Area - see Appendix A for areas included; (2) U.S. figures calculated from the sales of 524,324 new and existing homes in 181 markets; (3) Housing Opportunity Index - percent of homes sold that were within the reach of the median income household at the prevailing mortgage interest rate; (4) Rank is from 1-181 with 1 being most affordable
Source: National Association of Home Builders, Housing Opportunity Index, 1st Quarter 1999

Median Home Price Projection

It is projected that the median price of existing single-family homes in the metro area will increase by 1.2% in 1999. Nationwide, home prices are projected to increase 3.8%.
Kiplinger's Personal Finance Magazine, January 1999

Average New Home Price

Area	Price ($)
City	139,847
U.S.	142,735

Note: Figures are based on a new home with 1,800 sq. ft. of living area on an 8,000 sq. ft. lot.
Source: ACCRA, Cost of Living Index, 1st Quarter 1999

Average Apartment Rent

Area	Rent ($/mth)
City	647
U.S.	601

Note: Figures are based on an unfurnished two bedroom, 1-1/2 or 2 bath apartment, approximately 950 sq. ft. in size, excluding all utilities except water
Source: ACCRA, Cost of Living Index, 1st Quarter 1999

RESIDENTIAL UTILITIES

Average Residential Utility Costs

Area	All Electric ($/mth)	Part Electric ($/mth)	Other Energy ($/mth)	Phone ($/mth)
City	–	63.97	44.13	22.13
U.S.	100.02	55.73	43.33	19.71

Source: ACCRA, Cost of Living Index, 1st Quarter 1999

HEALTH CARE

Average Health Care Costs

Area	Hospital ($/day)	Doctor ($/visit)	Dentist ($/visit)
City	409.80	48.80	58.40
U.S.	430.43	52.45	66.35

Note: Hospital—based on a semi-private room; Doctor—based on a general practitioner's routine exam of an established patient; Dentist—based on adult teeth cleaning and periodic oral exam.
Source: ACCRA, Cost of Living Index, 1st Quarter 1999

Distribution of Office-Based Physicians

Area	Family/Gen. Practitioners	Specialists		
		Medical	Surgical	Other
MSA[1]	381	1,044	780	843

Note: Data as of 12/31/97; (1) Metropolitan Statistical Area - see Appendix A for areas included
Source: American Medical Assn., Physician Characteristics & Distribution in the U.S., 1999

Hospitals

Cincinnati has 9 general medical and surgical hospitals, 1 psychiatric, 1 rehabilitation, 1 children's general, 1 children's other specialty. *AHA Guide to the Healthcare Field, 1998-99*

According to *U.S. News and World Report,* Cincinnati has 2 of the best hospitals in the U.S.: **Children's Hospital Medical Center**, noted for pediatrics; **Good Samaritan Hospital**, noted for cardiology, urology. U.S. News Online, "America's Best Hospitals," 10th Edition, www.usnews.com

EDUCATION

Public School District Statistics

District Name	Num. Sch.	Enroll.	Classroom Teachers	Pupils per Teacher	Minority Pupils (%)	Current Exp.[1] ($/pupil)
Cincinnati City SD	82	50,332	3,132	16.1	71.0	6,127
Deer Park Community City SD	4	1,580	85	18.6	n/a	n/a
Finneytown Local SD	6	1,959	119	16.5	n/a	n/a
Forest Hills Local SD	8	8,032	394	20.4	n/a	n/a
Great Oaks Inst of Technology	7	n/a	254	0.0	n/a	n/a
Hamilton Bd of Educ-Data Proc	n/a	n/a	n/a	n/a	n/a	n/a
Indian Hill Ex Vill SD	4	2,051	145	14.1	n/a	n/a
Lockland City SD	2	827	51	16.2	n/a	n/a
Madeira City SD	3	1,498	88	17.0	n/a	n/a
Mariemont City SD	5	1,715	104	16.5	n/a	n/a
Mount Healthy City SD	10	4,100	224	18.3	n/a	n/a
North College Hill City SD	5	1,626	81	20.1	n/a	n/a
Northwest Local SD	14	10,723	555	19.3	n/a	n/a
Oak Hills Local SD	8	8,300	391	21.2	n/a	n/a
Princeton City SD	11	6,989	513	13.6	n/a	n/a
Southwestern Ohio	n/a	n/a	n/a	n/a	n/a	n/a
St Bernard-Elmwood Place City	3	1,305	82	15.9	n/a	n/a
Sycamore Community City SD	8	6,405	385	16.6	n/a	n/a
West Clermont Local SD	13	9,271	504	18.4	n/a	n/a
Winton Woods City SD	8	4,487	287	15.6	n/a	n/a

Note: Data covers the 1997-1998 school year unless otherwise noted; (1) Data covers fiscal year 1996; SD = School District; ISD = Independent School District; n/a not available
Source: National Center for Education Statistics, Common Core of Data Public Education Agency Universe 1997-98; National Center for Education Statistics, Characteristics of the 100 Largest Public Elementary and Secondary School Districts in the United States: 1997-98, July 1999

Educational Quality

School District	Education Quotient[1]	Graduate Outcome[2]	Community Index[3]	Resource Index[4]
Cincinnati City	90.0	74.0	87.0	123.0

Note: Nearly 1,000 secondary school districts were rated in terms of educational quality. The scores range from a low of 50 to a high of 150; (1) Average of the Graduate Outcome, Community and Resource indexes; (2) Based on graduation rates and college board scores (SAT/ACT); (3) Based on the surrounding community's average level of education and the area's average income level; (4) Based on teacher salaries, per-pupil expenditures and student-teacher ratios.
Source: Expansion Management, Ratings Issue, 1998

Educational Attainment by Race

Area	High School Graduate (%)					Bachelor's Degree (%)				
	Total	White	Black	Other	Hisp.[2]	Total	White	Black	Other	Hisp.[2]
City	69.6	74.7	59.4	83.5	76.4	22.2	28.9	7.9	56.6	42.0
MSA[1]	74.9	76.5	62.7	82.7	79.2	20.5	21.6	9.8	46.8	34.9
U.S.	75.2	77.9	63.1	60.4	49.8	20.3	21.5	11.4	19.4	9.2

*Note: Figures shown cover persons 25 years old and over; (1) Metropolitan Statistical Area -
see Appendix A for areas included; (2) people of Hispanic origin can be of any race
Source: 1990 Census of Population and Housing, Summary Tape File 3C*

School Enrollment by Type

Area	Preprimary				Elementary/High School			
	Public		Private		Public		Private	
	Enrollment	%	Enrollment	%	Enrollment	%	Enrollment	%
City	3,651	56.7	2,789	43.3	45,797	81.3	10,524	18.7
MSA[1]	15,601	53.0	13,831	47.0	206,692	81.4	47,137	18.6
U.S.	2,679,029	59.5	1,824,256	40.5	38,379,689	90.2	4,187,099	9.8

*Note: Figures shown cover persons 3 years old and over;
(1) Metropolitan Statistical Area - see Appendix A for areas included
Source: 1990 Census of Population and Housing, Summary Tape File 3C*

School Enrollment by Race

Area	Preprimary (%)				Elementary/High School (%)			
	White	Black	Other	Hisp.[1]	White	Black	Other	Hisp.[1]
City	58.4	39.9	1.7	0.9	45.6	53.0	1.4	0.6
MSA[2]	86.4	12.5	1.0	0.7	82.4	16.3	1.3	0.7
U.S.	80.4	12.5	7.1	7.8	74.1	15.6	10.3	12.5

*Note: Figures shown cover persons 3 years old and over; (1) people of Hispanic origin can be of any
race; (2) Metropolitan Statistical Area - see Appendix A for areas included
Source: 1990 Census of Population and Housing, Summary Tape File 3C*

Classroom Teacher Salaries in Public Schools

District	B.A. Degree		M.A. Degree		Maximum	
	Min. ($)	Rank[1]	Max. ($)	Rank[1]	Max. ($)	Rank[1]
Cincinnati	28,114	31	50,605	18	55,383	21
Average	26,980	-	46,065	-	51,435	-

*Note: Salaries are for 1997-1998; (1) Rank ranges from 1 to 100
Source: American Federation of Teachers, Survey & Analysis of Salary Trends, 1998*

Higher Education

Two-Year Colleges		Four-Year Colleges		Medical Schools	Law Schools	Voc/ Tech
Public	Private	Public	Private			
2	4	1	7	1	1	28

*Source: College Blue Book, Occupational Education, 1997; Medical School Admission Requirements,
1999-2000; Peterson's Guide to Two-Year Colleges, 1999; Peterson's Guide to Four-Year Colleges,
2000; Barron's Guide to Law Schools, 1999*

MAJOR EMPLOYERS

Major Employers

Belcan Corp. (engineering)	Milacron (machinery)
Children's Hospital Medical Center	Cinergy Corp.
Cincinnati Gas & Electric	Fifth Third Bankcorp
Gibson Greetings	Jewish Hospital of Cincinnati
Procter & Gamble	Elizabeth Gamble Deaconess Home Assn.

*Note: Companies listed are located in the city
Source: Dun's Business Rankings, 1999; Ward's Business Directory, 1998*

PUBLIC SAFETY

Crime Rate

Area	All Crimes	Violent Crimes				Property Crimes		
		Murder	Forcible Rape	Robbery	Aggrav. Assault	Burglary	Larceny -Theft	Motor Vehicle Theft
City	7,616.7	8.9	87.4	492.2	499.4	1,577.7	4,445.7	505.5
Suburbs[1]	n/a	n/a	n/a	n/a	n/a	n/a	n/a	n/a
MSA[2]	n/a	n/a	n/a	n/a	n/a	n/a	n/a	n/a
U.S.	5,086.6	7.4	36.3	201.9	390.9	944.8	2,979.7	525.6

Note: Crime rate is the number of crimes per 100,000 pop.; (1) defined as all areas within the MSA but located outside the central city; (2) Metropolitan Statistical Area - see Appendix A for areas incl.
Source: FBI Uniform Crime Reports, 1996

RECREATION

Culture and Recreation

Museums	Symphony Orchestras	Opera Companies	Dance Companies	Professional Theatres	Zoos	Pro Sports Teams
6	2	1	2	3	1	2

Source: International Directory of the Performing Arts, 1997; Official Museum Directory, 1999; Stern's Performing Arts Directory, 1997; USA Today Four Sport Stadium Guide, 1997; Chamber of Commerce/Economic Development, 1999

Library System

The Public Library of Cincinnati & Hamilton County has 41 branches, holdings of 4,585,127 volumes, and a budget of $48,690,170 (1996). *American Library Directory, 1998-1999*

MEDIA

Newspapers

Name	Type	Freq.	Distribution	Circulation
Catholic Telegraph	Religious	1x/wk	Local	23,000
Cincinnati Carscope	General	1x/wk	Local	24,000
Cincinnati Court Index	n/a	5x/wk	Area	1,500
The Cincinnati Enquirer	General	7x/wk	Regional	201,711
Cincinnati Herald	Black	1x/wk	Area	10,000
The Cincinnati Post	n/a	6x/wk	Area	67,000

Note: Includes newspapers with circulations of 1,000 or more located in the city; n/a not available
Source: Burrelle's Media Directory, 1999 Edition

Television Stations

Name	Ch.	Affiliation	Type	Owner
WLWT	n/a	NBCT	Commercial	Hearst-Argyle Broadcasting
WCPO	n/a	ABCT	Commercial	Scripps Howard Broadcasting
WKRC	12	CBST	Commercial	Jacor Communications Inc.
WXIX	19	FBC	Commercial	Raycom Media Inc.
WCET	48	PBS	Public	Greater Cincinnati TV Education Foundation
WSTR	64	UPN	Commercial	Sinclair Communications Inc.

Note: Stations included broadcast in the Cincinnati metro area; n/a not available
Source: Burrelle's Media Directory, 1999 Edition

AM Radio Stations

Call Letters	Freq. (kHz)	Target Audience	Station Format	Music Format
WKRC	550	General	N/S/T	n/a
WLW	700	General	N/S/T	n/a
WNOP	740	General	M	Jazz
WBOB	1160	General	N/S/T	n/a
WUBE	1230	General	M	Adult Standards
WCKY	1360	General	S/T	n/a
WMOH	1450	General	N/S/T	n/a
WCIN	1480	General	M	Oldies
WSAI	1530	General	M/T	Adult Standards

Note: Stations included broadcast in the Cincinnati metro area; n/a not available
Target Audience: A=Asian; B=Black; C=Christian; E=Ethnic; F=French; G=General; H=Hispanic; M=Men; N=Native American; R=Religious; S=Senior Citizen; W=Women; Y=Young Adult; Z=Children
Station Format: E=Educational; M=Music; N=News; S=Sports; T=Talk
Source: Burrelle's Media Directory, 1999 Edition

FM Radio Stations

Call Letters	Freq. (mHz)	Target Audience	Station Format	Music Format
WAIF	88.3	General	M/N/S	Classic Rock/Gospel/Jazz
WJVS	88.3	General	M/N/S	Adult Contemporary
WOBO	88.7	General	E/M	Big Band/Country
WVXR	89.3	General	E/M/N/T	Alternative/Big Band/Jazz/World Music
WVXC	89.3	General	E/M/N/T	Alternative/Big Band/Jazz/World Music
WVXW	89.5	General	E/M/N/T	Alternative/Big Band/Jazz/World Music
WGUC	90.9	General	M/N	Classical
WVXU	91.7	General	E/M/N/T	Alternative/Big Band/Jazz/World Music
WOFX	92.5	General	Men	Native American
WAKW	93.3	General	E/M/S	Adult Contemporary/Christian
WVMX	94.1	General	M	Adult Contemporary
WVAE	94.9	General	M	Jazz
WVXG	95.1	General	E/M/N/T	Alternative/Big Band/Jazz/World Music
WYGY	96.5	General	M/N/S	Country
WRRM	98.5	General	M/N	Adult Contemporary
WIZF	100.9	Black	M/N/T	Urban Contemporary
WKRQ	101.9	General	M/N/T	Adult Contemporary
WEBN	102.7	General	M/N	AOR
WGRR	103.5	General	M/N/T	Oldies
WUBE	105.1	General	M/N/S	Country
WVXI	106.3	General	E/M/N/T	Alternative/Big Band/Jazz/World Music
WKFS	107.1	General	M/N/T	Adult Contemporary

Note: Stations included broadcast in the Cincinnati metro area
Station Format: E=Educational; M=Music; N=News; S=Sports; T=Talk
Target Audience: A=Asian; B=Black; C=Christian; E=Ethnic; F=French; G=General; H=Hispanic; M=Men; N=Native American; R=Religious; S=Senior Citizen; W=Women; Y=Young Adult; Z=Children
Music Format: AOR=Album Oriented Rock; MOR=Middle-of-the-Road
Source: Burrelle's Media Directory, 1999 Edition

CLIMATE

Average and Extreme Temperatures

Temperature	Jan	Feb	Mar	Apr	May	Jun	Jul	Aug	Sep	Oct	Nov	Dec	Yr.
Extreme High (°F)	74	72	84	89	93	102	103	102	102	89	81	75	103
Average High (°F)	38	42	52	64	74	82	86	85	78	67	53	42	64
Average Temp. (°F)	30	33	43	54	63	72	76	74	68	56	44	34	54
Average Low (°F)	21	24	33	43	52	61	65	63	56	45	35	26	44
Extreme Low (°F)	-25	-15	-11	17	27	39	47	43	33	16	0	-20	-25

Note: Figures cover the years 1948-1990
Source: National Climatic Data Center, International Station Meteorological Climate Summary, 3/95

Average Precipitation/Snowfall/Humidity

Precip./Humidity	Jan	Feb	Mar	Apr	May	Jun	Jul	Aug	Sep	Oct	Nov	Dec	Yr.
Avg. Precip. (in.)	3.2	2.9	3.9	3.5	4.0	3.9	4.2	3.1	2.8	2.8	3.4	3.1	40.9
Avg. Snowfall (in.)	7	5	4	1	Tr	0	0	0	0	Tr	2	4	23
Avg. Rel. Hum. 7am (%)	79	78	77	76	79	82	85	87	87	83	79	79	81
Avg. Rel. Hum. 4pm (%)	65	60	55	50	51	53	54	52	52	51	58	65	55

Note: Figures cover the years 1948-1990; Tr = Trace amounts (<0.05 in. of rain; <0.5 in. of snow)
Source: National Climatic Data Center, International Station Meteorological Climate Summary, 3/95

Weather Conditions

Temperature			Daytime Sky			Precipitation		
10°F & below	32°F & below	90°F & above	Clear	Partly cloudy	Cloudy	0.01 inch or more precip.	0.1 inch or more snow/ice	Thunder-storms
14	107	23	80	126	159	127	25	39

Note: Figures are average number of days per year and covers the years 1948-1990
Source: National Climatic Data Center, International Station Meteorological Climate Summary, 3/95

AIR & WATER QUALITY

Maximum Pollutant Concentrations

	Particulate Matter (ug/m^3)	Carbon Monoxide (ppm)	Sulfur Dioxide (ppm)	Nitrogen Dioxide (ppm)	Ozone (ppm)	Lead (ug/m^3)
MSA[1] Level	94	3	0.045	0.028	0.12	0.03
NAAQS[2]	150	9	0.140	0.053	0.12	1.50
Met NAAQS?	Yes	Yes	Yes	Yes	Yes	Yes

Note: (1) Metropolitan Statistical Area - see Appendix A for areas included; (2) National Ambient Air Quality Standards; ppm = parts per million; ug/m^3 = micrograms per cubic meter; n/a not available
Source: EPA, National Air Quality and Emissions Trends Report, 1997

Pollutant Standards Index

In the Cincinnati MSA (see Appendix A for areas included), the Pollutant Standards Index (PSI) exceeded 100 on 14 days in 1997. A PSI value greater than 100 indicates that air quality would be in the unhealthful range on that day. *EPA, National Air Quality and Emissions Trends Report, 1997*

Drinking Water

Water System Name	Pop. Served	Primary Water Source Type	Number of Violations in 1998	Type of Violation/ Contaminants
City of Cincinnati-Miller	686,400	Surface	None	None

Note: Data as of July 10, 1999
Source: EPA, Office of Ground Water and Drinking Water, Safe Drinking Water Information System

Cincinnati tap water is alkaline, hard and fluoridated.
Editor & Publisher Market Guide, 1999

Cleveland, Ohio

Background

Founded in 1796 by General Moses Cleveland, on what was known as the Western Reserve of Connecticut, Cleveland began with very modest resources. Of all the people that General Cleveland led on his expedition, only three remained in the area. However, the completion of the Erie and Ohio Canals brought people and industry, both of which were sorely needed to keep the area alive. By the 1840s, the population had grown by 500 percent from the decade before. While neighborhoods fell along racial and ethnic lines, the children of these immigrants intermarried, and surpassed their parents on socio-economic levels. Cleveland was a place where the American dream could be realized.

During World War I, a new wave of job seekers flooded Cleveland. These were largely blacks from Southern rural areas, and poor whites from the states of Kentucky, Tennessee, and West Virginia filling in for a shortage of workers in war goods production.

The next group of job seekers after the war did not have the same opportunities as their predecessors. There were fewer jobs to be had and the men were unskilled, thus making job competition difficult. These collapsing economic conditions set the stage for the urban unrest in the 1960s in the Hough neighborhood.

Cleveland has been undergoing an economic renaissance over the past five years with few projects representing more than $9 billion in capital investment. A public-private partnership has been responsible for the downtown sports complex, the Rock & Roll Hall of Fame, and a vibrant new entertainment district. In addition, construction is underway on a new football stadium for the Cleveland Browns and "40 percent of home buyers in the city of Cleveland are coming back from the suburbs," a reversal of national trends. The Port of Cleveland is the largest for overseas general cargo on Lake Erie, serving over 50 nations. Cleveland is also becoming a major biotechnology center with its renowned Cleveland Clinic supporting 500 ongoing research projects, and being one of only four facilities in the U.S. receiving government funding for research and development of an artificial heart. *Site Selection, Aug/Sept 1997*

The construction of the 360 million Gateway Project in downtown Cleveland, a combination open-air stadium and indoor arena, home to the Cleveland Indians and the Cavaliers basketball team was completed a few years ago.

Cleveland is on the south shore of Lake Erie in northeast Ohio. The metro area has a frontage of 31 miles. The Cuyahoga River runs through the city, bisecting it.

Summers are moderately warm and humid with occasional days when temperatures rise above 90 degrees. Winters are relatively cold and cloudy with weather changes occurring every few days due to passing cold fronts.

Precipitation varies widely from year to year, but is generally abundant throughout the year. Snowfalls fluctuate widely. Tornadoes occasionally occur in Cuyahoga County.

General Rankings and Evaluative Comments

■ Cleveland was ranked #2 out of 11 large, midwestern metropolitan areas in *Money's* 1998 survey of "The Best Places to Live in America." The survey was conducted by first contacting 512 representative households nationwide and asking them to rank 37 quality-of-life factors on a scale of 1 to 10. Next, a demographic profile was compiled on the 300 largest metropolitan statistical areas in the U.S. The numbers were crunched together to arrive at an overall ranking (things Americans consider most important, like clean air and water, low crime and good schools, received extra weight). Unlike previous years, the 1998 rankings were broken down by region (northeast, midwest, south, west) and population size (100,000 to 249,999; 250,000 to 999,999; 1 million plus). The city had a nationwide ranking of #163 out of 300 in 1997 and #146 out of 300 in 1996. *Money, July 1998; Money, July 1997; Money, September 1996*

■ *Ladies Home Journal* ranked America's 200 largest cities based on the qualities women care about most. Cleveland ranked #173 out of 200. Criteria: low crime rate, well-paying jobs, quality health and child care, good public schools, the presence of women in government, size of the gender wage gap, number of sexual-harassment and discrimination complaints filed, unemployment and divorce rates, commute times, population density, number of houses of worship, parks and cultural offerings, number of women's health specialists, how well a community's women cared for themselves, complexion kindness index based on UV radiation levels, odds of finding affordable fashions, rental rates for romance movies, champagne sales and other matters of the heart. *Ladies Home Journal, November 1998*

■ Zero Population Growth ranked 229 cities in terms of children's health, safety, and economic well-being. Cleveland was ranked #19 out of 25 major cities (main city in a metro area with population of greater than 2 million) and was given a grade of D. Criteria: total population, percent of population under 18 years of age, household language, percent population change, percent of births to teens, infant mortality rate, percent of low birth weights, dropout rate, enrollment in preprimary school, violent and property crime rates, unemployment rate, percent of children in poverty, percent of owner occupied units, number of bad air days, percent of public transportation commuters, and average travel time to work. *Zero Population Growth, Children's Environmental Index, Fall 1999*

■ Cleveland was ranked #40 out of 59 metro areas in *The Regional Economist's* "Rational Livability Ranking of 59 Large Metro Areas." The rankings were based on the metro area's total population change over the period 1990-97 divided by the number of people moving in from elsewhere in the United States (net domestic in-migration). *St. Louis Federal Reserve Bank of St. Louis, The Regional Economist, April 1999*

■ Cleveland was selected by *Yahoo! Internet Life* as one of "America's Most Wired Cities & Towns." The city ranked #30 out of 50. Criteria: home and work net use, domain density, hosts per capita, directory density and content quality. *Yahoo! Internet Life, March 1999*

■ Cognetics studied 273 metro areas in the United States, ranking them by entrepreneurial activity. Cleveland was ranked #34 out of the 50 largest metro areas. Criteria: Significant Starts (firms started in the last 10 years that still employ at least 5 people) and Young Growers (percent of firms 10 years old or less that grew significantly during the last 4 years). *Cognetics, "Entrepreneurial Hot Spots: The Best Places in America to Start and Grow a Company," 1998*

■ Cleveland was selected as one of the "Best American Cities to Start a Business" by *Point of View* magazine. Criteria: coolness, quality-of-life, and business concerns. The city was ranked #72 out of 75. *Point of View, November 1998*

■ Reliastar Financial Corp. ranked the 125 largest metropolitan areas according to the general financial security of residents. Cleveland was ranked #81 (tie) out of 125 with a score of -1.7. The score indicates the percentage a metropolitan area is above or below the metropolitan norm. A metro area with a score of 10.6 is 10.6% above the metro average. Criteria: Earnings and Wealth Potential (household income, education, net assets, cost of living); Safety Net (health insurance, retirement savings, life insurance, income support programs); Personal Threats (unemployment rate, low-income households, crime rate); Community Economic Vitality (cost of community services, job quality, job creation, housing costs). *Reliastar Financial Corp., "The Best Cities to Earn and Save Money," 1999 Edition*

Business Environment

STATE ECONOMY

State Economic Profile

"Ohio's expansion has started to decelerate. OH is expected to lag the nation in growth for some time. The slowdown in employment growth is concentrated in the manufacturing sector and outside of OH's larger metro areas. OH's weak demographic trends will constrain job growth and the housing market.

OH manufacturing shed about 7,000 jobs in 1998. A large share of these losses were in the Cleveland and Columbus areas, while Cincinnati managed to add a small number of manufacturing jobs. Job growth in the services sectors, particularly business, financial and health services, has helped to offset a slowdown in manufacturing in these urban areas. Bank merger and acquisition activity has resulted in jobs being shifted from rural and smaller areas to the larger metropolitan areas.

While OH's rural areas have suffered from a declining employment base, economic activity has also been shifting from the northern part of the state toward the middle and south. Last year's employment growth for Cincinnati was 2.5%, compared to only 1.6% for Columbus and 1.6% for Cleveland. Population growth has followed a similar pattern, although the state as a whole is among one of the weakest in the nation, losing a considerable number of younger households.

Ohio's housing market had a strong 1998, with sales up 8.6% and single family permits up 3.2%. Price appreciation was just below the nation and will likely remain modest given the increase in construction. Both construction and sales should contract in 1999 and 2000. Prices are likely to rise the most in Cincinnati, where construction has been modest and job growth strongest." *National Association of Realtors, Economic Profiles: The Fifty States and the District of Columbia, http://nar.realtor.com/databank/profiles.htm*

IMPORTS/EXPORTS

Total Export Sales

Area	1994 ($000)	1995 ($000)	1996 ($000)	1997 ($000)	% Chg. 1994-97	% Chg. 1996-97
MSA[1]	4,093,323	4,706,991	5,075,165	5,510,954	34.6	8.6
U.S.	512,415,609	583,030,524	622,827,063	687,597,999	34.2	10.4

Note: (1) Metropolitan Statistical Area - see Appendix A for areas included
Source: U.S. Department of Commerce, International Trade Association, Metropolitan Area Exports: An Export Performance Report on Over 250 U.S. Cities, November 10, 1998

CITY FINANCES

City Government Finances

Component	FY94 ($000)	FY94 (per capita $)
Revenue	796,925	1,584.56
Expenditure	950,156	1,889.24
Debt Outstanding	1,100,492	2,188.16
Cash & Securities	589,505	1,172.14

Source: U.S. Bureau of the Census, City Government Finances: 1993-94

City Government Revenue by Source

Source	FY94 ($000)	FY94 (per capita $)	FY94 (%)
From Federal Government	72,685	144.52	9.1
From State Governments	73,792	146.72	9.3
From Local Governments	1,307	2.60	0.2
Property Taxes	50,977	101.36	6.4
General Sales Taxes	0	0.00	0.0
Selective Sales Taxes	5,491	10.92	0.7
Income Taxes	218,574	434.60	27.4
Current Charges	99,232	197.31	12.5
Utility/Liquor Store	204,358	406.33	25.6
Employee Retirement[1]	0	0.00	0.0
Other	70,509	140.20	8.8

Note: (1) Excludes "city contributions," classified as "nonrevenue," intragovernmental transfers.
Source: U.S. Bureau of the Census, City Government Finances: 1993-94

City Government Expenditures by Function

Function	FY94 ($000)	FY94 (per capita $)	FY94 (%)
Educational Services	0	0.00	0.0
Employee Retirement[1]	0	0.00	0.0
Environment/Housing	157,034	312.24	16.5
Government Administration	45,516	90.50	4.8
Interest on General Debt	22,809	45.35	2.4
Public Safety	213,869	425.25	22.5
Social Services	23,251	46.23	2.4
Transportation	142,497	283.33	15.0
Utility/Liquor Store	307,088	610.60	32.3
Other	38,092	75.74	4.0

Note: (1) Payments to beneficiaries including withdrawal of contributions.
Source: U.S. Bureau of the Census, City Government Finances: 1993-94

Municipal Bond Ratings

Area	Moody's	S & P
Cleveland	n/a	n/a

Note: n/a not available; n/r not rated
Source: Moody's Bond Record, 6/99

POPULATION

Population Growth

Area	1980	1990	% Chg. 1980-90	July 1998 Estimate	% Chg. 1990-98
City	573,822	505,616	-11.9	495,817	-1.9
MSA[1]	1,898,825	1,831,122	-3.6	2,243,694	22.5
U.S.	226,545,805	248,765,170	9.8	270,299,000	8.7

Note: (1) Metropolitan Statistical Area - see Appendix A for areas included;
July 1998 MSA population estimate was calculated by the editors
Source: 1980/1990 Census of Housing and Population, Summary Tape File 3C;
Census Bureau Population Estimates 1998

Population Characteristics

Race	City 1980 Population	%	City 1990 Population	%	% Chg. 1980-90	MSA[1] 1990 Population	%
White	309,299	53.9	250,727	49.6	-18.9	1,435,694	78.4
Black	251,084	43.8	235,053	46.5	-6.4	355,237	19.4
Amer Indian/Esk/Aleut	1,282	0.2	1,531	0.3	19.4	3,396	0.2
Asian/Pacific Islander	3,372	0.6	4,885	1.0	44.9	20,376	1.1
Other	8,785	1.5	13,420	2.7	52.8	16,419	0.9
Hispanic Origin[2]	17,772	3.1	22,330	4.4	25.6	32,765	1.8

Note: (1) Metropolitan Statistical Area - see Appendix A for areas included;
(2) people of Hispanic origin can be of any race
Source: 1980/1990 Census of Housing and Population, Summary Tape File 3C

Ancestry

Area	German	Irish	English	Italian	U.S.	French	Polish	Dutch
City	14.2	11.1	4.1	5.3	2.9	1.2	6.4	1.0
MSA[1]	25.2	15.1	9.9	9.8	2.7	2.0	9.3	1.5
U.S.	23.3	15.6	13.1	5.9	5.3	4.2	3.8	2.5

Note: Figures are percentages and include persons that reported multiple ancestry (eg. if a person reported being Irish and Italian, they were included in both columns); (1) Metropolitan Statistical Area - see Appendix A for areas included
Source: 1990 Census of Population and Housing, Summary Tape File 3C

Age

Area	Median Age (Years)	Age Distribution (%) Under 5	Under 18	18-24	25-44	45-64	65+	80+
City	31.8	8.7	27.0	10.4	30.7	18.0	13.9	3.0
MSA[1]	34.7	7.1	24.6	9.0	31.7	20.1	14.6	3.0
U.S.	32.9	7.3	25.6	10.5	32.6	18.7	12.5	2.8

Note: (1) Metropolitan Statistical Area - see Appendix A for areas included
Source: 1990 Census of Population and Housing, Summary Tape File 3C

Male/Female Ratio

Area	Number of males per 100 females (all ages)	Number of males per 100 females (18 years old+)
City	88.2	83.4
MSA[1]	90.1	85.9
U.S.	95.0	91.9

Note: (1) Metropolitan Statistical Area - see Appendix A for areas included
Source: 1990 Census of Population, General Population Characteristics

INCOME

Per Capita/Median/Average Income

Area	Per Capita ($)	Median Household ($)	Average Household ($)
City	9,258	17,822	22,921
MSA[1]	15,092	30,560	38,413
U.S.	14,420	30,056	38,453

Note: All figures are for 1989; (1) Metropolitan Statistical Area - see Appendix A for areas included
Source: 1990 Census of Population and Housing, Summary Tape File 3C

Household Income Distribution by Race

Income ($)	City (%)					U.S. (%)				
	Total	White	Black	Other	Hisp.[1]	Total	White	Black	Other	Hisp.[1]
Less than 5,000	16.7	10.1	24.8	19.3	22.3	6.2	4.8	15.2	8.6	8.8
5,000 - 9,999	15.5	14.1	17.4	15.1	14.7	9.3	8.6	14.2	9.9	11.1
10,000 - 14,999	11.5	12.0	10.8	11.0	11.6	8.8	8.5	11.0	9.8	11.0
15,000 - 24,999	19.5	20.9	17.6	20.5	18.6	17.5	17.3	18.9	18.5	20.5
25,000 - 34,999	14.8	17.2	11.9	15.6	15.1	15.8	16.1	14.2	15.4	16.4
35,000 - 49,999	13.0	15.5	9.9	11.3	11.5	17.9	18.6	13.3	16.1	16.0
50,000 - 74,999	7.0	8.0	5.9	5.9	5.5	15.0	15.8	9.3	13.4	11.1
75,000 - 99,999	1.3	1.4	1.2	1.1	0.5	5.1	5.5	2.6	4.7	3.1
100,000+	0.7	0.9	0.4	0.1	0.3	4.4	4.8	1.3	3.7	1.9

Note: All figures are for 1989; (1) people of Hispanic origin can be of any race
Source: 1990 Census of Population and Housing, Summary Tape File 3C

Effective Buying Income

Area	Per Capita ($)	Median Household ($)	Average Household ($)
City	11,056	21,459	27,524
MSA[1]	17,431	35,328	44,743
U.S.	16,803	34,536	45,243

Note: Data as of 1/1/99; (1) Metropolitan Statistical Area - see Appendix A for areas included
Source: Standard Rate & Data Service, Newspaper Advertising Source, 9/99

Effective Household Buying Income Distribution

Area	% of Households Earning						
	$10,000 -$19,999	$20,000 -$34,999	$35,000 -$49,999	$50,000 -$74,999	$75,000 -$99,000	$100,000 -$124,999	$125,000 and up
City	21.2	23.1	15.2	10.8	2.6	0.5	0.4
MSA[1]	15.2	22.0	18.9	19.6	7.3	2.2	2.4
U.S.	16.0	22.6	18.2	18.9	7.2	2.4	2.7

Note: Data as of 1/1/99; (1) Metropolitan Statistical Area - see Appendix A for areas included
Source: Standard Rate & Data Service, Newspaper Advertising Source, 9/99

Poverty Rates by Race and Age

Area	Total (%)	By Race (%)				By Age (%)		
		White	Black	Other	Hisp.[2]	Under 5 years old	Under 18 years old	65 years and over
City	28.7	18.2	39.1	37.4	40.0	46.2	43.0	19.2
MSA[1]	11.8	6.8	31.0	22.0	30.6	20.5	18.1	9.5
U.S.	13.1	9.8	29.5	23.1	25.3	20.1	18.3	12.8

Note: Figures show the percent of people living below the poverty line in 1989. The average poverty threshold was $12,674 for a family of four in 1989; (1) Metropolitan Statistical Area - see Appendix A for areas included; (2) people of Hispanic origin can be of any race
Source: 1990 Census of Population and Housing, Summary Tape File 3C

EMPLOYMENT

Labor Force and Employment

Area	Civilian Labor Force			Workers Employed		
	Jun. 1998	Jun. 1999	% Chg.	Jun. 1998	Jun. 1999	% Chg.
City	205,997	212,986	3.4	188,055	193,306	2.8
MSA[1]	1,114,150	1,149,118	3.1	1,066,109	1,095,878	2.8
U.S.	138,798,000	140,666,000	1.3	132,265,000	134,395,000	1.6

Note: Data is not seasonally adjusted and covers workers 16 years of age and older; (1) Metropolitan Statistical Area - see Appendix A for areas included
Source: Bureau of Labor Statistics, http://stats.bls.gov

Unemployment Rate

Area	1998						1999					
	Jul.	Aug.	Sep.	Oct.	Nov.	Dec.	Jan.	Feb.	Mar.	Apr.	May.	Jun.
City	7.9	8.1	9.0	8.5	8.4	8.0	9.1	9.4	8.6	8.7	7.9	9.2
MSA[1]	4.4	4.2	4.3	4.1	4.1	4.0	5.0	5.0	4.5	4.3	3.9	4.6
U.S.	4.7	4.5	4.4	4.2	4.1	4.0	4.8	4.7	4.4	4.1	4.0	4.5

Note: Data is not seasonally adjusted and covers workers 16 years of age and older; all figures are percentages; (1) Metropolitan Statistical Area - see Appendix A for areas included
Source: Bureau of Labor Statistics, http://stats.bls.gov

Employment by Industry

Sector	MSA[1]		U.S.
	Number of Employees	Percent of Total	Percent of Total
Services	352,400	30.1	30.4
Retail Trade	200,800	17.1	17.7
Government	148,300	12.7	15.6
Manufacturing	220,500	18.8	14.3
Finance/Insurance/Real Estate	77,700	6.6	5.9
Wholesale Trade	76,500	6.5	5.4
Transportation/Public Utilities	46,800	4.0	5.3
Construction	47,800	4.1	5.0
Mining	900	0.1	0.4

Note: Figures cover non-farm employment as of 6/99 and are not seasonally adjusted; (1) Metropolitan Statistical Area - see Appendix A for areas included
Source: Bureau of Labor Statistics, http://stats.bls.gov

Employment by Occupation

Occupation Category	City (%)	MSA[1] (%)	U.S. (%)
White Collar	47.7	61.5	58.1
Executive/Admin./Management	7.6	13.0	12.3
Professional	8.8	14.6	14.1
Technical & Related Support	3.9	4.0	3.7
Sales	8.4	12.1	11.8
Administrative Support/Clerical	19.1	17.8	16.3
Blue Collar	33.3	25.3	26.2
Precision Production/Craft/Repair	10.7	10.7	11.3
Machine Operators/Assem./Insp.	11.8	7.4	6.8
Transportation/Material Movers	5.2	3.6	4.1
Cleaners/Helpers/Laborers	5.6	3.6	3.9
Services	18.3	12.3	13.2
Farming/Forestry/Fishing	0.7	0.8	2.5

Note: Figures cover employed persons 16 years old and over; (1) Metropolitan Statistical Area - see Appendix A for areas included
Source: 1990 Census of Population and Housing, Summary Tape File 3C

Occupational Employment Projections: 1996 - 2006

Occupations Expected to Have the Largest Job Growth (ranked by numerical growth)	Fast-Growing Occupations[1] (ranked by percent growth)
1. Cashiers	1. Systems analysts
2. Salespersons, retail	2. Occupational therapy assistants
3. Systems analysts	3. Desktop publishers
4. General managers & top executives	4. Paralegals
5. Truck drivers, light	5. Physical therapy assistants and aides
6. Registered nurses	6. Medical assistants
7. Food preparation workers	7. Personal and home care aides
8. Nursing aides/orderlies/attendants	8. Home health aides
9. Home health aides	9. Physical therapists
10. Marketing & sales, supervisors	10. Occupational therapists

Note: Projections cover Ohio; (1) Excludes occupations with total job growth less than 300
Source: U.S. Department of Labor, Employment and Training Administration, America's Labor Market Information System (ALMIS)

TAXES

Major State and Local Tax Rates

State Corp. Income (%)	State Personal Income (%)	Residential Property (effective rate per $100)	Sales & Use		State Gasoline (cents/ gallon)	State Cigarette (cents/ pack)
			State (%)	Local (%)		
5.1 - 8.5[a]	0.673 - 6.799	n/a	5.0	2.0	22.0	24.0

Note: Personal/corporate income, sales, gasoline and cigarette tax rates as of January 1999. Property tax rates as of 1997; (a) Or 4.0 mils times the value of the taxpayer's issued and outstanding share of stock ($150K max). An additional litter tax is imposed equal to 0.11% on the first $50,000 of taxable income, 0.22% on income over $50,000; or 0.14 mills on net worth
Source: Federation of Tax Administrators, www.taxadmin.org; Washington D.C. Department of Finance and Revenue, Tax Rates and Tax Burdens in the District of Columbia: A Nationwide Comparison, July 1998; Chamber of Commerce, 1999

Total Taxes Per Capita and as a Percent of Income

Area	Per Capita Income ($)	Per Capita Taxes ($)			Percent of Income (%)		
		Total	Federal	State/ Local	Total	Federal	State/ Local
Ohio	26,684	9,354	6,322	3,033	35.1	23.7	11.4
U.S.	27,876	9,881	6,690	3,191	35.4	24.0	11.4

Note: Figures are for 1998
Source: Tax Foundation, www.taxfoundation.org

Estimated Tax Burden

Area	State Income	Local Income	Property	Sales	Total
Cleveland	2,762	1,500	4,250	683	9,195

Note: The numbers are estimates of taxes paid by a married couple with two children and annual earnings of $75,000. Sales tax estimates assume they spend average amounts on food, clothing, household goods and gasoline. Property tax estimates assume they live in a $250,000 home.
Source: Kiplinger's Personal Finance Magazine, October 1998

COMMERCIAL REAL ESTATE

Office Market

Class/Location	Total Space (sq. ft.)	Vacant Space (sq. ft.)	Vac. Rate (%)	Under Constr. (sq. ft.)	Net Absorp. (sq. ft.)	Rental Rates ($/sq.ft./yr.)
Class A						
CBD	10,746,116	967,150	9.0	0	429,845	17.00-30.00
Outside CBD	3,495,962	276,181	7.9	400,000	455,015	16.00-24.00
Class B						
CBD	11,307,749	1,775,317	15.7	0	712,388	14.00-18.00
Outside CBD	10,594,014	1,377,222	13.0	250,000	-105,940	14.00-17.00

Note: Data as of 10/98 and covers Cleveland; CBD = Central Business District; n/a not available;
Source: Society of Industrial and Office Realtors, 1999 Comparative Statistics of Industrial and Office Real Estate Markets

"Major employers like Progressive Insurance and MBNA are expanding, and growth in major medical facilities, including the Cleveland Clinic and University Hospital is expected to support further market improvement in 1999. The banking merger and a consolidation by Amoco and BP threaten Cleveland headquarters jobs, which could reduce demand while throwing a quantity of sub-lease space on the market. Rental rates, having achieved peaks of $30 per sq. ft. downtown and $24 per sq. ft. for suburban space, should pause in their upward movement. The Duke REIT is aggressive on the development side, as office demand spills over into the flex space market. Several other office park developers are active as well. Our SIOR reporters see anchor commitments being required for new building to go forward in 1999." *Society of Industrial and Office Realtors, 1999 Comparative Statistics of Industrial and Office Real Estate Markets*

Industrial Market

Location	Total Space (sq. ft.)	Vacant Space (sq. ft.)	Vac. Rate (%)	Under Constr. (sq. ft.)	Net Absorp. (sq. ft.)	Gross Lease ($/sq.ft./yr.)
Central City	92,570,000	10,641,000	11.5	278,000	-968,000	2.00-4.75
Suburban	216,736,000	10,391,000	4.8	2,155,000	326,000	2.35-6.90

Note: Data as of 10/98 and covers Cleveland; n/a not available
Source: Society of Industrial and Office Realtors, 1999 Comparative Statistics of Industrial and Office Real Estate Markets

"Although 1999 begins with some tightness in supply, a number of industrial brokers report a slowdown in showings and new prospect inquiries. Expectations for the year are muted, especially for properties more than 100,000 sq. ft. Developers have been taking fairly aggressive positions on the few well-located and improved sites in the seven-county Greater Cleveland market. There are many projects on the drawing boards, but in the more restrictive financing environment of recent months, it is expected that a number of these deals will be either scaled back or put on hold. With Wall Street's capital well suddenly dry, commercial banks are stepping up their activity. Consolidation is reshaping the real estate services market as well, as industrial brokerages find themselves either part of large national and international firms or operating as boutiques." *Society of Industrial and Office Realtors, 1999 Comparative Statistics of Industrial and Office Real Estate Markets*

Retail Market

Shopping Center Inventory (sq. ft.)	Shopping Center Construction (sq. ft.)	Construction as a Percent of Inventory (%)	Torto Wheaton Rent Index[1] ($/sq. ft.)
36,832,000	0	0.0	9.72

Note: Data as of 1997 and covers the Metropolitan Statistical Area - see Appendix A for areas included; (1) Index is based on a model that predicts what the average rent should be for leases with certain characteristics, in certain locations during certain years.
Source: National Association of Realtors, 1997-1998 Market Conditions Report

"Beginning in 1994, a boom in business investment and strong consumer spending sparked activity in Cleveland's retail market. Large scale projects, such as Jacob's Field and Tower City Mall, added to the area's growing tourism industry.During the period, the retail rent index rose 17%. The boom, however, has cooled off, and many industry experts are watching closely to see if Cleveland can support new retail activity over the long haul. Indeed, the area's lackluster population growth, expected to be only 0.1% annually over the next five years, will be a major deterrent to economic growth." *National Association of Realtors, 1997-1998 Market Conditions Report*

COMMERCIAL UTILITIES

Typical Monthly Electric Bills

Area	Commercial Service ($/month)		Industrial Service ($/month)	
	12 kW demand 1,500 kWh	100 kW demand 30,000 kWh	1,000 kW demand 400,000 kWh	20,000 kW demand 10,000,000 kWh
City	194	3,423	35,353	572,471
U.S.	150	2,174	23,995	508,569

Note: Based on rates in effect January 1, 1999
Source: Edison Electric Institute, Typical Residential, Commercial and Industrial Bills, Winter 1999

TRANSPORTATION

Transportation Statistics

Average minutes to work	22.5
Interstate highways	I-71; I-77; I-80; I-90
Bus lines	
In-city	Greater Cleveland Regional TA, 762 vehicles
Inter-city	6
Passenger air service	
Airport	Cleveland-Hopkins International
Airlines	9
Aircraft departures	115,472 (1996)
Enplaned passengers	5,286,691 (1996)
Rail service	Amtrak; Light Rail
Motor freight carriers	99
Major waterways/ports	Lake Erie; Port of Cleveland

Source: Editor & Publisher Market Guide, 1999; FAA Airport Activity Statistics, 1997; Amtrak National Time Table, Northeast Timetable, Spring/Summer 1999; 1990 Census of Population and Housing, STF 3C; Chamber of Commerce/Economic Development 1999; Jane's Urban Transport Systems 1999-2000

Means of Transportation to Work

Area	Car/Truck/Van		Public Transportation			Bicycle	Walked	Other Means	Worked at Home
	Drove Alone	Car-pooled	Bus	Subway	Railroad				
City	64.8	14.0	13.0	0.6	0.1	0.1	5.0	1.2	1.2
MSA[1]	77.7	10.5	5.5	0.4	0.1	0.1	2.9	0.8	2.0
U.S.	73.2	13.4	3.0	1.5	0.5	0.4	3.9	1.2	3.0

Note: Figures shown are percentages and only include workers 16 years old and over;
(1) Metropolitan Statistical Area - see Appendix A for areas included
Source: 1990 Census of Population and Housing, Summary Tape File 3C

BUSINESSES

Major Business Headquarters

Company Name	1999 Rankings	
	Fortune 500	Forbes 500
Eaton	250	-
IMG	-	170
Jones Day Reavis & Pogue	-	478
Keycorp	238	-
LTV	362	-
MTD Products	-	338
National City Corp.	201	-
Parker Hannifin	336	-
Sherwin-Williams	322	-
TRW	142	-

Note: Companies listed are located in the city; dashes indicate no ranking
Fortune 500: Companies that produce a 10-K are ranked 1 to 500 based on 1998 revenue
Forbes 500: Private companies are ranked 1 to 500 based on 1997 revenue
Source: Forbes, November 30, 1998; Fortune, April 26, 1999

Best Companies to Work For

TRW Inc., headquartered in Cleveland, is among the "100 Best Companies for Working Mothers." Criteria: fair wages, opportunities for women to advance, support for child care, flexible work schedules, family-friendly benefits, and work/life supports. *Working Mother, October 1998*

The Lincoln Electric Co. (electronics/electrical) and Americal Greetings Corp. (retail), headquartered in Cleveland, are among the "100 Best Places to Work in IS." Criteria: compensation, turnover and training. *Computerworld, May 25, 1998*

Fast-Growing Businesses

According to *Fortune*, Cleveland is home to one of America's 100 fastest-growing companies: Century Business Services. Companies were ranked based on earnings-per-share growth, revenue growth and total return over the previous three years. Criteria for inclusion: public companies with sales of least $50 million. Companies that lost money in the most recent quarter, or ended in the red for the past four quarters as a whole, were not eligible. Limited partnerships and REITs were also not considered. *Fortune, "America's Fastest-Growing Companies," 1999*

Women-Owned Firms: Number, Employment and Sales

Area	Number of Firms	Employ-ment	Sales ($000)	Rank[2]
MSA[1]	68,800	320,500	31,437,200	23

Note: (1) Metropolitan Statistical Area - see Appendix A for areas included;
(2) Calculated on an averaging of the number of businesses, employment and sales
Source: The National Foundation for Women Business Owners, 1999 Facts on Women-Owned Businesses: Trends in the Top 50 Metropolitan Areas

Women-Owned Firms: Growth

Area	% change from 1992 to 1999			Rank[2]
	Number of Firms	Employ-ment	Sales	
MSA[1]	44.0	149.8	154.9	15

Note: (1) Metropolitan Statistical Area - see Appendix A for areas included; (2) Calculated on an averaging of the percent growth of number of businesses, employment and sales
Source: The National Foundation for Women Business Owners, 1999 Facts on Women-Owned Businesses: Trends in the Top 50 Metropolitan Areas

Minority Business Opportunity

Cleveland is home to one company which is on the Black Enterprise Industrial/Service 100 list (largest based on gross sales): Ozanne Construction Co. Inc. (general construction and construction mgmt.) . Criteria: operational in previous calendar year, at least 51% black-owned and manufactures/owns the product it sells or provides industrial or consumer services. Brokerages, real estate firms and firms that provide professional services are not eligible. *Black Enterprise, www.blackenterprise.com*

HOTELS & MOTELS

Hotels/Motels

Area	Hotels/ Motels	Rooms	Luxury-Level Hotels/Motels		Average Minimum Rates ($)		
			◆◆◆◆	◆◆◆◆◆	◆◆	◆◆◆	◆◆◆◆
City	13	3,462	2	0	n/a	124	187
Airport	21	2,812	0	0	n/a	n/a	n/a
Suburbs	56	6,291	0	0	n/a	n/a	n/a
Total	90	12,565	2	0	n/a	n/a	n/a

Note: n/a not available; classifications range from one diamond (budget properties with basic amenities) to five diamond (luxury properties with the finest service, rooms and facilities).
Source: OAG, Business Travel Planner, Winter 1998-99

CONVENTION CENTERS

Major Convention Centers

Center Name	Meeting Rooms	Exhibit Space (sq. ft.)
Cleveland Convention Center	37	375,000
Cleveland State University Convocation Center	n/a	300,000
International Expo Center	20	1,500,000
Sheraton Cleveland City Centre Hotel	1	n/a
The Forum Conference & Education Center	12	22,000

Note: n/a not available
Source: Trade Shows Worldwide, 1998; Meetings & Conventions, 4/15/99;
Sucessful Meetings, 3/31/98

Living Environment

COST OF LIVING

Cost of Living Index

Composite Index	Groceries	Housing	Utilities	Trans-portation	Health Care	Misc. Goods/ Services
112.6	108.8	117.7	135.0	115.0	122.4	102.6

Note: U.S. = 100
Source: ACCRA, Cost of Living Index, 1st Quarter 1999

HOUSING

Median Home Prices and Housing Affordability

Area	Median Price[2] 1st Qtr. 1999 ($)	HOI[3] 1st Qtr. 1999	Afford-ability Rank[4]
MSA[1]	107,000	78.1	70
U.S.	134,000	69.6	–

Note: (1) Metropolitan Statistical Area - see Appendix A for areas included; (2) U.S. figures calculated from the sales of 524,324 new and existing homes in 181 markets; (3) Housing Opportunity Index - percent of homes sold that were within the reach of the median income household at the prevailing mortgage interest rate; (4) Rank is from 1-181 with 1 being most affordable
Source: National Association of Home Builders, Housing Opportunity Index, 1st Quarter 1999

Median Home Price Projection

It is projected that the median price of existing single-family homes in the metro area will increase by 2.4% in 1999. Nationwide, home prices are projected to increase 3.8%.
Kiplinger's Personal Finance Magazine, January 1999

Average New Home Price

Area	Price ($)
City	164,650
U.S.	142,735

Note: Figures are based on a new home with 1,800 sq. ft. of living area on an 8,000 sq. ft. lot.
Source: ACCRA, Cost of Living Index, 1st Quarter 1999

Average Apartment Rent

Area	Rent ($/mth)
City	826
U.S.	601

Note: Figures are based on an unfurnished two bedroom, 1-1/2 or 2 bath apartment, approximately 950 sq. ft. in size, excluding all utilities except water
Source: ACCRA, Cost of Living Index, 1st Quarter 1999

RESIDENTIAL UTILITIES

Average Residential Utility Costs

Area	All Electric ($/mth)	Part Electric ($/mth)	Other Energy ($/mth)	Phone ($/mth)
City	–	82.27	55.21	22.25
U.S.	100.02	55.73	43.33	19.71

Source: ACCRA, Cost of Living Index, 1st Quarter 1999

HEALTH CARE

Average Health Care Costs

Area	Hospital ($/day)	Doctor ($/visit)	Dentist ($/visit)
City	662.00	62.00	77.80
U.S.	430.43	52.45	66.35

Note: Hospital—based on a semi-private room; Doctor—based on a general practitioner's routine exam of an established patient; Dentist—based on adult teeth cleaning and periodic oral exam.
Source: ACCRA, Cost of Living Index, 1st Quarter 1999

Distribution of Office-Based Physicians

Area	Family/Gen. Practitioners	Specialists		
		Medical	Surgical	Other
MSA[1]	359	1,811	1,244	1,372

Note: Data as of 12/31/97; (1) Metropolitan Statistical Area - see Appendix A for areas included
Source: American Medical Assn., Physician Characteristics & Distribution in the U.S., 1999

Hospitals

Cleveland has 1 general medical and surgical hospital, 1 alcoholism and other chemical dependency, 1 children's rehabilitation. *AHA Guide to the Healthcare Field, 1998-99*

According to *U.S. News and World Report,* Cleveland has 2 of the best hospitals in the U.S.: **Cleveland Clinic**, noted for cancer, cardiology, endocrinology, gastroenterology, geriatrics, gynecology, neurology, orthopedics, otolaryngology, pediatrics, pulmonology, rheumatology, urology; **University Hospitals of Cleveland**, noted for cancer, endocrinology, gastroenterology, geriatrics, gynecology, neurology, orthopedics, otolaryngology, pediatrics, pulmonology, rheumatology. *U.S. News Online, "America's Best Hospitals," 10th Edition, www.usnews.com*

EDUCATION

Public School District Statistics

District Name	Num. Sch.	Enroll.	Classroom Teachers	Pupils per Teacher	Minority Pupils (%)	Current Exp.[1] ($/pupil)
Cleveland City SD	125	76,504	4,611	16.6	79.7	6,616
Cuyahoga Heights Local SD	3	826	54	15.3	n/a	n/a
Garfield Heights City SD	5	3,368	184	18.3	n/a	n/a
Orange City SD	5	2,292	177	12.9	n/a	n/a
Polaris JVSD	1	n/a	48	0.0	n/a	n/a
Richmond Heights Local SD	3	971	48	20.2	n/a	n/a
Warrensville Heights City SD	7	3,107	177	17.6	n/a	n/a

Note: Data covers the 1997-1998 school year unless otherwise noted; (1) Data covers fiscal year 1996; SD = School District; ISD = Independent School District; n/a not available
Source: National Center for Education Statistics, Common Core of Data Public Education Agency Universe 1997-98; National Center for Education Statistics, Characteristics of the 100 Largest Public Elementary and Secondary School Districts in the United States: 1997-98, July 1999

Educational Quality

School District	Education Quotient[1]	Graduate Outcome[2]	Community Index[3]	Resource Index[4]
Cleveland City	78.0	50.0	81.0	134.0

Note: Nearly 1,000 secondary school districts were rated in terms of educational quality. The scores range from a low of 50 to a high of 150; (1) Average of the Graduate Outcome, Community and Resource indexes; (2) Based on graduation rates and college board scores (SAT/ACT); (3) Based on the surrounding community's average level of education and the area's average income level; (4) Based on teacher salaries, per-pupil expenditures and student-teacher ratios.
Source: Expansion Management, Ratings Issue, 1998

Educational Attainment by Race

Area	High School Graduate (%)					Bachelor's Degree (%)				
	Total	White	Black	Other	Hisp.[2]	Total	White	Black	Other	Hisp.[2]
City	58.8	61.9	55.6	49.3	44.7	8.1	10.2	5.0	13.9	6.2
MSA[1]	75.7	78.7	62.4	69.6	56.6	19.9	22.0	8.5	35.4	13.8
U.S.	75.2	77.9	63.1	60.4	49.8	20.3	21.5	11.4	19.4	9.2

Note: Figures shown cover persons 25 years old and over; (1) Metropolitan Statistical Area - see Appendix A for areas included; (2) people of Hispanic origin can be of any race
Source: 1990 Census of Population and Housing, Summary Tape File 3C

School Enrollment by Type

Area	Preprimary				Elementary/High School			
	Public		Private		Public		Private	
	Enrollment	%	Enrollment	%	Enrollment	%	Enrollment	%
City	4,923	62.6	2,939	37.4	69,894	78.7	18,875	21.3
MSA[1]	19,818	55.4	15,951	44.6	241,493	80.6	58,046	19.4
U.S.	2,679,029	59.5	1,824,256	40.5	38,379,689	90.2	4,187,099	9.8

Note: Figures shown cover persons 3 years old and over;
(1) Metropolitan Statistical Area - see Appendix A for areas included
Source: 1990 Census of Population and Housing, Summary Tape File 3C

School Enrollment by Race

Area	Preprimary (%)				Elementary/High School (%)			
	White	Black	Other	Hisp.[1]	White	Black	Other	Hisp.[1]
City	43.5	53.1	3.4	5.4	37.6	57.0	5.4	6.5
MSA[2]	80.4	17.1	2.4	2.0	71.5	25.4	3.1	2.7
U.S.	80.4	12.5	7.1	7.8	74.1	15.6	10.3	12.5

Note: Figures shown cover persons 3 years old and over; (1) people of Hispanic origin can be of any race; (2) Metropolitan Statistical Area - see Appendix A for areas included
Source: 1990 Census of Population and Housing, Summary Tape File 3C

Classroom Teacher Salaries in Public Schools

District	B.A. Degree		M.A. Degree		Maximum	
	Min. ($)	Rank[1]	Max. ($)	Rank[1]	Max. ($)	Rank[1]
Cleveland	26,628	46	51,242	16	52,186	39
Average	26,980	-	46,065	-	51,435	-

Note: Salaries are for 1997-1998; (1) Rank ranges from 1 to 100
Source: American Federation of Teachers, Survey & Analysis of Salary Trends, 1998

Higher Education

Two-Year Colleges		Four-Year Colleges		Medical Schools	Law Schools	Voc/ Tech
Public	Private	Public	Private			
1	3	1	5	1	2	16

Source: College Blue Book, Occupational Education, 1997; Medical School Admission Requirements, 1999-2000; Peterson's Guide to Two-Year Colleges, 1999; Peterson's Guide to Four-Year Colleges, 2000; Barron's Guide to Law Schools, 1999

MAJOR EMPLOYERS

Major Employers

American Greetings Corp.	Cleveland Clinic Foundation
Fairview Hospital	KeyCorp
Lincoln Electric Co.	Metrohealth System
Mt. Sinai Medical Center	Progressive Casualty Insurance
University Hospitals of Cleveland	Officemax

Note: Companies listed are located in the city
Source: Dun's Business Rankings, 1999; Ward's Business Directory, 1998

PUBLIC SAFETY

Crime Rate

Area	All Crimes	Violent Crimes				Property Crimes		
		Murder	Forcible Rape	Robbery	Aggrav. Assault	Burglary	Larceny -Theft	Motor Vehicle Theft
City	7,455.5	15.5	128.5	772.6	542.1	1,640.3	2,880.4	1,476.2
Suburbs[1]	n/a	n/a	n/a	n/a	n/a	n/a	n/a	n/a
MSA[2]	n/a	n/a	n/a	n/a	n/a	n/a	n/a	n/a
U.S.	4,922.7	6.8	35.9	186.1	382.0	919.6	2,886.5	505.8

Note: Crime rate is the number of crimes per 100,000 pop.; (1) defined as all areas within the MSA but located outside the central city; (2) Metropolitan Statistical Area - see Appendix A for areas incl.
Source: FBI Uniform Crime Reports, 1997

RECREATION

Culture and Recreation

Museums	Symphony Orchestras	Opera Companies	Dance Companies	Professional Theatres	Zoos	Pro Sports Teams
15	2	2	2	5	1	3

Source: International Directory of the Performing Arts, 1997; Official Museum Directory, 1999; Stern's Performing Arts Directory, 1997; USA Today Four Sport Stadium Guide, 1997; Chamber of Commerce/Economic Development, 1999

Library System

The Cleveland Public Library has 28 branches, holdings of 2,638,584 volumes, and a budget of $42,834,724 (1997). *American Library Directory, 1998-1999*

MEDIA

Newspapers

Name	Type	Freq.	Distribution	Circulation
Amerikanski Slovenec-Glasilo KSKJ	Religious	20x/yr	U.S.	10,700
Cincinnati Call and Post	General	1x/wk	Local	12,000
Cleveland Call and Post	Black	1x/wk	Local	20,000
Cleveland Free Times	General	1x/wk	Area	50,000
Cleveland Jewish News	Religious	1x/wk	Area	15,500
Euclid Sun Journal	General	1x/wk	Local	12,310
Garfield-Maple Sun	General	1x/wk	Local	11,079
Lakewood Sun Post	General	1x/wk	Local	10,978
The News Sun	n/a	1x/wk	Local	16,538
The Plain Dealer	n/a	7x/wk	Area	400,593
Solon Herald Sun	General	1x/wk	Local	18,127
State Edition Call and Post	General	1x/wk	State	10,000
The Sun Herald	General	1x/wk	Local	16,323
Sun Messenger	General	1x/wk	Local	15,033
Sun Press	General	1x/wk	Local	21,188
The Sun Star	General	1x/wk	Local	12,088
The West Geauga Sun	n/a	1x/wk	Local	12,126

Note: Includes newspapers with circulations of 10,000 or more located in the city; n/a not available
Source: Burrelle's Media Directory, 1999 Edition

Television Stations

Name	Ch.	Affiliation	Type	Owner
WKYC	n/a	NBCT	Commercial	Gannett Broadcasting
WEWS	n/a	ABCT	Commercial	Scripps Howard Broadcasting
WJW	n/a	FBC	Commercial	Fox Television Stations Inc.
WOIO	19	CBST	Commercial	Raycom Media Inc.
WVPX	23	n/a	Commercial	Paxson Communications Corporation
WVIZ	25	PBS	Public	Educational TV Association of Metro Cleveland
WUAB	43	n/a	Commercial	Raycom Media Inc.
WBNX	55	FKN/WB	Commercial	Winston Broadcasting Network Inc.
WQHS	61	n/a	Commercial	HSN Inc.
WOAC	67	n/a	Commercial	Shop at Home Inc.

Note: Stations included broadcast in the Cleveland metro area; n/a not available
Source: Burrelle's Media Directory, 1999 Edition

AM Radio Stations

Call Letters	Freq. (kHz)	Target Audience	Station Format	Music Format
WHLO	640	Religious	M/S/T	Christian
WRMR	850	General	M	Adult Standards/Big Band
WFUN	970	General	M/N/S/T	Oldies
WCCD	1000	General	M/T	Christian
WTAM	1100	General	N/S/T	n/a
WKNR	1220	General	S	n/a
WERE	1300	General	T	n/a
WHK	1420	General	N/T	n/a
WJMO	1490	General	M	Oldies/R&B
WABQ	1540	B/R	M/N/S/T	Christian

Note: Stations included broadcast in the Cleveland metro area; n/a not available
Target Audience: A=Asian; B=Black; C=Christian; E=Ethnic; F=French; G=General; H=Hispanic; M=Men; N=Native American; R=Religious; S=Senior Citizen; W=Women; Y=Young Adult; Z=Children
Station Format: E=Educational; M=Music; N=News; S=Sports; T=Talk
Source: Burrelle's Media Directory, 1999 Edition

FM Radio Stations

Call Letters	Freq. (mHz)	Target Audience	Station Format	Music Format
WBWC	88.3	General	M/N/S	n/a
WJCU	88.7	General	M/N/S	Alternative/AOR/Classic Rock/Country/Jazz/Oldies/Urban Contemporary
WCSB	89.3	General	E/M/T	n/a
WCPN	90.3	General	M/N/T	Blues/Jazz
WRUW	91.1	General	M	n/a
WKHR	91.5	General	E/M	Adult Standards/Big Band
WZJM	92.3	General	M/N/S	Oldies
WZAK	93.1	Black	M/N/S	n/a
WCLV	95.5	General	M/N/S	Classical
WREO	97.1	General	M	Adult Contemporary
WHK	98.1	Religious	T	n/a
WNCX	98.5	General	M	Classic Rock
WGAR	99.5	General	M	Country
WMMS	100.7	General	M/N/S	AOR
WDOK	102.1	General	M/N	Adult Contemporary
WCRF	103.3	General	E/M/T	Christian
WQAL	104.1	General	M/N/S	Adult Contemporary
WMJI	105.7	General	M/N/S	Oldies
WMVX	106.5	General	M/N/S/T	Adult Top 40/Classic Rock
WENZ	107.9	Young Adult	M/N/T	Alternative

Note: Stations included broadcast in the Cleveland metro area; n/a not available
Station Format: E=Educational; M=Music; N=News; S=Sports; T=Talk
Target Audience: A=Asian; B=Black; C=Christian; E=Ethnic; F=French; G=General; H=Hispanic; M=Men; N=Native American; R=Religious; S=Senior Citizen; W=Women; Y=Young Adult; Z=Children
Music Format: AOR=Album Oriented Rock; MOR=Middle-of-the-Road
Source: Burrelle's Media Directory, 1999 Edition

CLIMATE

Average and Extreme Temperatures

Temperature	Jan	Feb	Mar	Apr	May	Jun	Jul	Aug	Sep	Oct	Nov	Dec	Yr.
Extreme High (°F)	73	69	82	88	92	104	100	102	101	89	82	77	104
Average High (°F)	33	36	46	58	69	79	83	81	74	63	50	38	59
Average Temp. (°F)	26	28	37	49	59	68	73	71	64	54	43	31	50
Average Low (°F)	19	20	28	38	48	58	62	61	54	44	35	24	41
Extreme Low (°F)	-19	-15	-5	10	25	31	41	38	34	19	3	-15	-19

Note: Figures cover the years 1948-1990
Source: National Climatic Data Center, International Station Meteorological Climate Summary, 3/95

Average Precipitation/Snowfall/Humidity

Precip./Humidity	Jan	Feb	Mar	Apr	May	Jun	Jul	Aug	Sep	Oct	Nov	Dec	Yr.
Avg. Precip. (in.)	2.4	2.3	3.1	3.4	3.5	3.5	3.5	3.4	3.2	2.6	3.2	2.9	37.1
Avg. Snowfall (in.)	13	12	10	2	Tr	0	0	0	0	1	5	12	55
Avg. Rel. Hum. 7am (%)	79	79	78	76	77	78	81	85	84	81	78	78	79
Avg. Rel. Hum. 4pm (%)	70	67	62	56	54	55	55	58	58	58	65	70	61

Note: Figures cover the years 1948-1990; Tr = Trace amounts (<0.05 in. of rain; <0.5 in. of snow)
Source: National Climatic Data Center, International Station Meteorological Climate Summary, 3/95

Weather Conditions

Temperature			Daytime Sky			Precipitation		
5°F & below	32°F & below	90°F & above	Clear	Partly cloudy	Cloudy	0.01 inch or more precip.	0.1 inch or more snow/ice	Thunder-storms
11	123	12	63	127	175	157	48	34

Note: Figures are average number of days per year and covers the years 1948-1990
Source: National Climatic Data Center, International Station Meteorological Climate Summary, 3/95

AIR & WATER QUALITY

Maximum Pollutant Concentrations

	Particulate Matter (ug/m^3)	Carbon Monoxide (ppm)	Sulfur Dioxide (ppm)	Nitrogen Dioxide (ppm)	Ozone (ppm)	Lead (ug/m^3)
MSA[1] Level	133	6	0.057	0.028	0.12	0.05
NAAQS[2]	150	9	0.140	0.053	0.12	1.50
Met NAAQS?	Yes	Yes	Yes	Yes	Yes	Yes

Note: (1) Metropolitan Statistical Area - see Appendix A for areas included; (2) National Ambient Air Quality Standards; ppm = parts per million; ug/m^3 = micrograms per cubic meter; n/a not available
Source: EPA, National Air Quality and Emissions Trends Report, 1997

Pollutant Standards Index

In the Cleveland MSA (see Appendix A for areas included), the Pollutant Standards Index (PSI) exceeded 100 on 16 days in 1997. A PSI value greater than 100 indicates that air quality would be in the unhealthful range on that day. *EPA, National Air Quality and Emissions Trends Report, 1997*

Drinking Water

Water System Name	Pop. Served	Primary Water Source Type	Number of Violations in 1998	Type of Violation/ Contaminants
City of Cleveland-Baldwin Point	424,027	Surface	1	Arsenic
City of Cleveland-Crown Plant	198,665	Surface	1	Arsenic
City of Cleveland-Morgan Plant	352,888	Surface	1	Arsenic
City of Cleveland-Nottingham Pl.	326,846	Surface	1	Arsenic

Note: Data as of July 10, 1999
Source: EPA, Office of Ground Water and Drinking Water, Safe Drinking Water Information System

Cleveland tap water is alkaline, hard and fluoridated.
Editor & Publisher Market Guide, 1999

Greensboro, North Carolina

Background

Greensboro is a quiet community in northern North Carolina. The city, together with Winston-Salem and High Point, forms an urban triangle, and is the trio's largest member.

The city was the site of the Battle of Guilford Courthouse during the American Revolution on March 15, 1781, as well as the birthplace of such notable Americans as Dolly Madison, wife of the fourth President of the United States, James Madison, and William Sydney Porter, otherwise known as the author, O. Henry.

During the mid to late 19th century, the economy of the city was largely based upon textile production. While that still remains a vital role in Greensboro, petroleum, pharmaceutical products, furniture, tobacco, and electronic equipment have come into prominence as well. These industries give Greensboro about 500 manufacturing plants in its surrounding area.

Greensboro is one of the anchors of the newly emerging center for business opportunities in North Carolina, the Piedmont Triad. Along with Winston-Salem and High Point, it has become a major metro area for attracting new plants and facilities. The city is located in Guilford County, and saw over 2,000 new jobs created in 1996 by new and expanding companies. *Site Selection, June/July 1997*

Greensboro is the largest city in the Piedmont Triad region. Both winter temperatures and rainfall are modified by the Blue Ridge Mountain barrier on the northwest. The summer temperatures vary with cloudiness and shower activity, but are generally mild. Northwesterly winds rarely bring heavy or prolonged winter rain or snow.

Damaging storms are infrequent as are tornadoes. Hurricanes do produce heavy rainfall, but usually not winds of destructive force.

General Rankings and Evaluative Comments

- Greensboro was ranked #11 out of 19 large, southern metropolitan areas in *Money's* 1998 survey of "The Best Places to Live in America." The survey was conducted by first contacting 512 representative households nationwide and asking them to rank 37 quality-of-life factors on a scale of 1 to 10. Next, a demographic profile was compiled on the 300 largest metropolitan statistical areas in the U.S. The numbers were crunched together to arrive at an overall ranking (things Americans consider most important, like clean air and water, low crime and good schools, received extra weight). Unlike previous years, the 1998 rankings were broken down by region (northeast, midwest, south, west) and population size (100,000 to 249,999; 250,000 to 999,999; 1 million plus). The city had a nationwide ranking of #79 out of 300 in 1997 and #161 out of 300 in 1996. *Money, July 1998; Money, July 1997; Money, September 1996*

- *Ladies Home Journal* ranked America's 200 largest cities based on the qualities women care about most. Greensboro ranked #74 out of 200. Criteria: low crime rate, well-paying jobs, quality health and child care, good public schools, the presence of women in government, size of the gender wage gap, number of sexual-harassment and discrimination complaints filed, unemployment and divorce rates, commute times, population density, number of houses of worship, parks and cultural offerings, number of women's health specialists, how well a community's women cared for themselves, complexion kindness index based on UV radiation levels, odds of finding affordable fashions, rental rates for romance movies, champagne sales and other matters of the heart. *Ladies Home Journal, November 1998*

- Zero Population Growth ranked 229 cities in terms of children's health, safety, and economic well-being. Greensboro was ranked #37 out of 112 independent cities (cities with populations greater than 100,000 which were neither Major Cities nor Suburbs/Outer Cities) and was given a grade of C+. Criteria: total population, percent of population under 18 years of age, household language, percent population change, percent of births to teens, infant mortality rate, percent of low birth weights, dropout rate, enrollment in preprimary school, violent and property crime rates, unemployment rate, percent of children in poverty, percent of owner occupied units, number of bad air days, percent of public transportation commuters, and average travel time to work. *Zero Population Growth, Children's Environmental Index, Fall 1999*

- Greensboro was ranked #17 out of 59 metro areas in *The Regional Economist's* "Rational Livability Ranking of 59 Large Metro Areas." The rankings were based on the metro area's total population change over the period 1990-97 divided by the number of people moving in from elsewhere in the United States (net domestic in-migration). *St. Louis Federal Reserve Bank of St. Louis, The Regional Economist, April 1999*

- Greensboro was selected by *Yahoo! Internet Life* as one of "America's Most Wired Cities & Towns." The city ranked #48 out of 50. Criteria: home and work net use, domain density, hosts per capita, directory density and content quality. *Yahoo! Internet Life, March 1999*

- Cognetics studied 273 metro areas in the United States, ranking them by entrepreneurial activity. Greensboro was ranked #28 out of the 50 largest metro areas. Criteria: Significant Starts (firms started in the last 10 years that still employ at least 5 people) and Young Growers (percent of firms 10 years old or less that grew significantly during the last 4 years). *Cognetics, "Entrepreneurial Hot Spots: The Best Places in America to Start and Grow a Company," 1998*

- Reliastar Financial Corp. ranked the 125 largest metropolitan areas according to the general financial security of residents. Greensboro was ranked #13 out of 125 with a score of 10.1. The score indicates the percentage a metropolitan area is above or below the metropolitan norm. A metro area with a score of 10.6 is 10.6% above the metro average. Criteria: Earnings and Wealth Potential (household income, education, net assets, cost of living); Safety Net (health insurance, retirement savings, life insurance, income support programs); Personal Threats (unemployment rate, low-income households, crime rate); Community Economic Vitality (cost of community services, job quality, job creation, housing costs). *Reliastar Financial Corp., "The Best Cities to Earn and Save Money," 1999 Edition*

Business Environment

STATE ECONOMY

State Economic Profile

"In spite of declines in textiles and apparels, North Carolina has seen impressive job growth in the last few years. As NC continues to diversify its economy away from its traditional manufacturing base and toward its newer high-tech and financial services sectors, job growth will outpace the nation for a number of years to come, albeit at a slightly slower rate than those seen in 1997 and 1998.

Raleigh-Durham has been and will continue to be one of NC's growth engines. High-tech firms in the Research Triangle Park have expanded employment considerably. Cisco Systems, for one, is planning to expand its operations, adding as many as 4,000 jobs over the next three years. Raleigh's housing market has more than doubled in size during the 1990s. Price appreciation has been strong, although homes still remain affordable. 1999 should be another hot year for sales and new construction in Raleigh-Durham.

NC's other hot spot has been Charlotte. While many parts of the country have been hurt by consolidation in the financial services industry, many of these jobs have made their way to Charlotte. As this wave of consolidation has slowed, so has job growth in Charlotte, reflected in its 0.6% job growth rate in 1998, far below that of previous years. Continued restructuring in NC's textiles, apparel and furniture industries will slow job growth in the Charlotte area.

The outlook for NC, while a slowdown from its recent pace, is still one of impressive job growth, far outpacing the nation. With its business friendly atmosphere and the decision of Federal Express to locate its Mid-Atlantic hub here, NC will likely attract more corporate relocations. Its affordable housing markets and overall high quality of life will also attract residents, helping fuel job growth." *National Association of Realtors, Economic Profiles: The Fifty States and the District of Columbia, http://nar.realtor.com/databank/profiles.htm*

IMPORTS/EXPORTS

Total Export Sales

Area	1994 ($000)	1995 ($000)	1996 ($000)	1997 ($000)	% Chg. 1994-97	% Chg. 1996-97
MSA[1]	2,773,310	3,356,262	3,495,639	4,050,787	46.1	15.9
U.S.	512,415,609	583,030,524	622,827,063	687,597,999	34.2	10.4

Note: (1) Metropolitan Statistical Area - see Appendix A for areas included
Source: U.S. Department of Commerce, International Trade Association, Metropolitan Area Exports: An Export Performance Report on Over 250 U.S. Cities, November 10, 1998

CITY FINANCES

City Government Finances

Component	FY92 ($000)	FY92 (per capita $)
Revenue	176,995	938.64
Expenditure	187,686	995.34
Debt Outstanding	178,095	944.48
Cash & Securities	148,371	786.84

Source: U.S. Bureau of the Census, City Government Finances: 1991-92

City Government Revenue by Source

Source	FY92 ($000)	FY92 (per capita $)	FY92 (%)
From Federal Government	4,058	21.52	2.3
From State Governments	21,387	113.42	12.1
From Local Governments	17,967	95.28	10.2
Property Taxes	59,998	318.18	33.9
General Sales Taxes	0	0.00	0.0
Selective Sales Taxes	1,624	8.61	0.9
Income Taxes	0	0.00	0.0
Current Charges	26,089	138.36	14.7
Utility/Liquor Store	25,651	136.03	14.5
Employee Retirement[1]	0	0.00	0.0
Other	20,221	107.24	11.4

Note: (1) Excludes "city contributions," classified as "nonrevenue," intragovernmental transfers.
Source: U.S. Bureau of the Census, City Government Finances: 1991-92

City Government Expenditures by Function

Function	FY92 ($000)	FY92 (per capita $)	FY92 (%)
Educational Services	4,568	24.23	2.4
Employee Retirement[1]	0	0.00	0.0
Environment/Housing	57,606	305.50	30.7
Government Administration	12,096	64.15	6.4
Interest on General Debt	5,333	28.28	2.8
Public Safety	42,240	224.01	22.5
Social Services	357	1.89	0.2
Transportation	27,323	144.90	14.6
Utility/Liquor Store	28,392	150.57	15.1
Other	9,771	51.82	5.2

Note: (1) Payments to beneficiaries including withdrawal of contributions.
Source: U.S. Bureau of the Census, City Government Finances: 1991-92

Municipal Bond Ratings

Area	Moody's	S & P
Greensboro	Aa1	n/a

Note: n/a not available; n/r not rated
Source: Moody's Bond Record, 6/99

POPULATION

Population Growth

Area	1980	1990	% Chg. 1980-90	July 1998 Estimate	% Chg. 1990-98
City	155,684	183,521	17.9	197,910	7.8
MSA[1]	851,444	942,091	10.6	1,171,550	24.4
U.S.	226,545,805	248,765,170	9.8	270,299,000	8.7

Note: (1) Metropolitan Statistical Area - see Appendix A for areas included;
July 1998 MSA population estimate was calculated by the editors
Source: 1980/1990 Census of Housing and Population, Summary Tape File 3C;
Census Bureau Population Estimates 1998

Population Characteristics

Race	City 1980 Population	%	City 1990 Population	%	% Chg. 1980-90	MSA[1] 1990 Population	%
White	102,771	66.0	117,349	63.9	14.2	748,794	79.5
Black	51,207	32.9	62,356	34.0	21.8	181,869	19.3
Amer Indian/Esk/Aleut	659	0.4	779	0.4	18.2	3,186	0.3
Asian/Pacific Islander	748	0.5	2,573	1.4	244.0	6,373	0.7
Other	299	0.2	464	0.3	55.2	1,869	0.2
Hispanic Origin[2]	1,201	0.8	1,389	0.8	15.7	6,122	0.6

Note: (1) Metropolitan Statistical Area - see Appendix A for areas included;
(2) people of Hispanic origin can be of any race
Source: 1980/1990 Census of Housing and Population, Summary Tape File 3C

Ancestry

Area	German	Irish	English	Italian	U.S.	French	Polish	Dutch
City	15.7	11.7	15.4	2.1	7.2	2.1	1.2	2.0
MSA[1]	20.5	12.6	15.4	1.6	12.5	2.0	0.8	2.9
U.S.	23.3	15.6	13.1	5.9	5.3	4.2	3.8	2.5

Note: Figures are percentages and include persons that reported multiple ancestry (eg. if a person reported being Irish and Italian, they were included in both columns); (1) Metropolitan Statistical Area - see Appendix A for areas included
Source: 1990 Census of Population and Housing, Summary Tape File 3C

Age

Area	Median Age (Years)	Under 5	Under 18	18-24	25-44	45-64	65+	80+
City	32.2	6.4	21.6	14.8	33.8	18.0	11.8	2.5
MSA[1]	34.0	6.6	23.1	11.1	33.3	20.4	12.1	2.6
U.S.	32.9	7.3	25.6	10.5	32.6	18.7	12.5	2.8

Note: (1) Metropolitan Statistical Area - see Appendix A for areas included
Source: 1990 Census of Population and Housing, Summary Tape File 3C

Male/Female Ratio

Area	Number of males per 100 females (all ages)	Number of males per 100 females (18 years old+)
City	86.9	82.6
MSA[1]	91.7	87.9
U.S.	95.0	91.9

Note: (1) Metropolitan Statistical Area - see Appendix A for areas included
Source: 1990 Census of Population, General Population Characteristics

INCOME

Per Capita/Median/Average Income

Area	Per Capita ($)	Median Household ($)	Average Household ($)
City	15,644	29,184	37,886
MSA[1]	14,588	29,254	36,588
U.S.	14,420	30,056	38,453

Note: All figures are for 1989; (1) Metropolitan Statistical Area - see Appendix A for areas included
Source: 1990 Census of Population and Housing, Summary Tape File 3C

Household Income Distribution by Race

Income ($)	City (%)					U.S. (%)				
	Total	White	Black	Other	Hisp.[1]	Total	White	Black	Other	Hisp.[1]
Less than 5,000	5.9	3.8	10.5	9.5	4.9	6.2	4.8	15.2	8.6	8.8
5,000 - 9,999	8.4	7.2	11.1	6.9	10.0	9.3	8.6	14.2	9.9	11.1
10,000 - 14,999	9.2	7.7	12.8	6.3	13.5	8.8	8.5	11.0	9.8	11.0
15,000 - 24,999	19.2	17.5	22.9	23.9	28.1	17.5	17.3	18.9	18.5	20.5
25,000 - 34,999	16.9	16.8	17.1	18.4	11.2	15.8	16.1	14.2	15.4	16.4
35,000 - 49,999	18.1	19.3	15.3	14.2	12.6	17.9	18.6	13.3	16.1	16.0
50,000 - 74,999	13.8	16.4	7.9	15.0	12.3	15.0	15.8	9.3	13.4	11.1
75,000 - 99,999	4.2	5.1	2.0	4.4	4.2	5.1	5.5	2.6	4.7	3.1
100,000+	4.4	6.2	0.4	1.4	3.3	4.4	4.8	1.3	3.7	1.9

Note: All figures are for 1989; (1) people of Hispanic origin can be of any race
Source: 1990 Census of Population and Housing, Summary Tape File 3C

Effective Buying Income

Area	Per Capita ($)	Median Household ($)	Average Household ($)
City	17,604	33,765	42,964
MSA[1]	16,742	32,857	41,794
U.S.	16,803	34,536	45,243

Note: Data as of 1/1/99; (1) Metropolitan Statistical Area - see Appendix A for areas included
Source: Standard Rate & Data Service, Newspaper Advertising Source, 9/99

Effective Household Buying Income Distribution

Area	% of Households Earning						
	$10,000 -$19,999	$20,000 -$34,999	$35,000 -$49,999	$50,000 -$74,999	$75,000 -$99,000	$100,000 -$124,999	$125,000 and up
City	16.1	24.6	18.7	18.1	6.3	2.2	2.9
MSA[1]	16.8	25.0	19.4	18.1	5.4	1.7	2.0
U.S.	16.0	22.6	18.2	18.9	7.2	2.4	2.7

Note: Data as of 1/1/99; (1) Metropolitan Statistical Area - see Appendix A for areas included
Source: Standard Rate & Data Service, Newspaper Advertising Source, 9/99

Poverty Rates by Race and Age

Area	Total (%)	By Race (%)				By Age (%)		
		White	Black	Other	Hisp.[2]	Under 5 years old	Under 18 years old	65 years and over
City	11.6	6.8	20.7	17.0	15.0	18.6	15.6	12.1
MSA[1]	10.0	7.1	21.8	19.5	19.9	15.3	13.3	16.0
U.S.	13.1	9.8	29.5	23.1	25.3	20.1	18.3	12.8

Note: Figures show the percent of people living below the poverty line in 1989. The average poverty threshold was $12,674 for a family of four in 1989; (1) Metropolitan Statistical Area - see Appendix A for areas included; (2) people of Hispanic origin can be of any race
Source: 1990 Census of Population and Housing, Summary Tape File 3C

EMPLOYMENT

Labor Force and Employment

Area	Civilian Labor Force			Workers Employed		
	Jun. 1998	Jun. 1999	% Chg.	Jun. 1998	Jun. 1999	% Chg.
City	114,193	115,916	1.5	110,596	113,065	2.2
MSA[1]	634,700	645,205	1.7	616,819	630,586	2.2
U.S.	138,798,000	140,666,000	1.3	132,265,000	134,395,000	1.6

Note: Data is not seasonally adjusted and covers workers 16 years of age and older;
(1) Metropolitan Statistical Area - see Appendix A for areas included
Source: Bureau of Labor Statistics, http://stats.bls.gov

Unemployment Rate

Area	1998						1999					
	Jul.	Aug.	Sep.	Oct.	Nov.	Dec.	Jan.	Feb.	Mar.	Apr.	May.	Jun.
City	3.0	2.8	2.6	2.5	2.3	1.9	2.5	2.6	2.3	2.0	2.3	2.5
MSA[1]	2.8	3.1	2.3	2.3	2.2	1.8	2.4	2.5	2.2	1.8	2.1	2.3
U.S.	4.7	4.5	4.4	4.2	4.1	4.0	4.8	4.7	4.4	4.1	4.0	4.5

Note: Data is not seasonally adjusted and covers workers 16 years of age and older; all figures are percentages; (1) Metropolitan Statistical Area - see Appendix A for areas included
Source: Bureau of Labor Statistics, http://stats.bls.gov

Employment by Industry

Sector	MSA[1]		U.S.
	Number of Employees	Percent of Total	Percent of Total
Services	178,300	27.1	30.4
Retail Trade	111,400	16.9	17.7
Government	66,800	10.1	15.6
Manufacturing	160,900	24.4	14.3
Finance/Insurance/Real Estate	34,200	5.2	5.9
Wholesale Trade	36,800	5.6	5.4
Transportation/Public Utilities	36,400	5.5	5.3
Construction	n/a	n/a	5.0
Mining	n/a	n/a	0.4

Note: Figures cover non-farm employment as of 6/99 and are not seasonally adjusted; (1) Metropolitan Statistical Area - see Appendix A for areas included; n/a not available
Source: Bureau of Labor Statistics, http://stats.bls.gov

Employment by Occupation

Occupation Category	City (%)	MSA[1] (%)	U.S. (%)
White Collar	63.9	53.4	58.1
Executive/Admin./Management	13.5	11.1	12.3
Professional	14.7	12.0	14.1
Technical & Related Support	3.5	3.3	3.7
Sales	14.4	11.3	11.8
Administrative Support/Clerical	17.8	15.6	16.3
Blue Collar	22.7	34.3	26.2
Precision Production/Craft/Repair	8.2	12.9	11.3
Machine Operators/Assem./Insp.	7.4	12.8	6.8
Transportation/Material Movers	3.3	4.3	4.1
Cleaners/Helpers/Laborers	3.7	4.3	3.9
Services	12.5	10.8	13.2
Farming/Forestry/Fishing	0.8	1.5	2.5

Note: Figures cover employed persons 16 years old and over; (1) Metropolitan Statistical Area - see Appendix A for areas included
Source: 1990 Census of Population and Housing, Summary Tape File 3C

Occupational Employment Projections: 1996 - 2006

Occupations Expected to Have the Largest Job Growth (ranked by numerical growth)	Fast-Growing Occupations[1] (ranked by percent growth)
1. Cashiers	1. Occupational therapy assistants
2. Registered nurses	2. Computer engineers
3. General managers & top executives	3. Database administrators
4. Nursing aides/orderlies/attendants	4. Systems analysts
5. Salespersons, retail	5. Physical therapy assistants and aides
6. Child care workers, private household	6. Physical therapists
7. Food service workers	7. Occupational therapists
8. Marketing & sales, supervisors	8. Home health aides
9. Janitors/cleaners/maids, ex. priv. hshld.	9. Desktop publishers
10. Truck drivers, light	10. Respiratory therapists

Note: Projections cover North Carolina; (1) Excludes occupations with total job growth less than 300
Source: U.S. Department of Labor, Employment and Training Administration, America's Labor Market Information System (ALMIS)

TAXES

Major State and Local Tax Rates

State Corp. Income (%)	State Personal Income (%)	Residential Property (effective rate per $100)	Sales & Use		State Gasoline (cents/ gallon)	State Cigarette (cents/ pack)
			State (%)	Local (%)		
7.0	6.0 - 7.75	n/a	4.0	2.0	21.6	5.0

Note: Personal/corporate income, sales, gasoline and cigarette tax rates as of January 1999.
Property tax rates as of 1997.
Source: Federation of Tax Administrators, www.taxadmin.org; Washington D.C. Department of Finance and Revenue, Tax Rates and Tax Burdens in the District of Columbia: A Nationwide Comparison, July 1998; Chamber of Commerce, 1999

Total Taxes Per Capita and as a Percent of Income

Area	Per Capita Income ($)	Per Capita Taxes ($)			Percent of Income (%)		
		Total	Federal	State/ Local	Total	Federal	State/ Local
North Carolina	25,480	8,669	5,924	2,745	34.0	23.3	10.8
U.S.	27,876	9,881	6,690	3,191	35.4	24.0	11.4

Note: Figures are for 1998
Source: Tax Foundation, www.taxfoundation.org

COMMERCIAL REAL ESTATE

Office Market

Class/ Location	Total Space (sq. ft.)	Vacant Space (sq. ft.)	Vac. Rate (%)	Under Constr. (sq. ft.)	Net Absorp. (sq. ft.)	Rental Rates ($/sq.ft./yr.)
Class A						
CBD	2,415,346	53,062	2.2	19,100	-303	18.00-20.00
Outside CBD	3,759,569	511,407	13.6	383,000	284,157	16.00-21.00
Class B						
CBD	2,078,586	319,130	15.4	0	61,999	13.50-16.00
Outside CBD	5,927,247	975,432	16.5	21,300	23,083	14.50-17.00

Note: Data as of 10/98 and covers Piedmont Triad Area (Greensboro, High Point and Winston-Salem); CBD = Central Business District; n/a not available;
Source: Society of Industrial and Office Realtors, 1999 Comparative Statistics of Industrial and Office Real Estate Markets

"The new Federal Express hub and runway at the Piedmont Triad International Airport will have a profound effect on the local economy. In addition to the direct economic impact and creation of new jobs, approximately 315,000 sq. ft. of potential development could appear in the Airport sub-market. Furthermore, the facility will help attract other businesses, including high-technology firms and business service companies. Three office projects under construction include a 35,000 sq. ft. office addition in Greensboro, a 20,000 sq. ft. office building in High Point, and a 18,000 sq. ft. office building in Winston-Salem. All this activity should help lower the vacancy rate and increase rental rates in the suburbs. Net absorption of Class A space in the CBD should be positive during 1999." *Society of Industrial and Office Realtors, 1999 Comparative Statistics of Industrial and Office Real Estate Markets*

Industrial Market

Location	Total Space (sq. ft.)	Vacant Space (sq. ft.)	Vac. Rate (%)	Under Constr. (sq. ft.)	Net Absorp. (sq. ft.)	Net Lease ($/sq.ft./yr.)
Central City	n/a	n/a	n/a	n/a	n/a	n/a
Suburban	31,400,000	3,422,600	10.9	650,000	1,397,600	3.50-6.20

Note: Data as of 10/98 and covers Greensboro/High Point/Winston-Salem; n/a not available
Source: Society of Industrial and Office Realtors, 1999 Comparative Statistics of Industrial and Office Real Estate Markets

"Federal Express plans to open its East Coast hub at Piedmont Triad International Airport by 2003. This will have a substantial impact on the local economy. The facility will add more than $160 million into the local economy, including a new roadway for PTI, and 1,500 new jobs. A number of ancillary companies as well as large users of Federal Express, such as mail order companies, will follow FedEx into the area. In addition, there is approximately 600,000 sq. ft. proposed or underway that should be on line in early 1999. Samet Corporation is an active developer with a 120,000 sq. ft. project at Piedmont Center and an 87,000 sq. ft. project at Union Cross Business Park under construction. Highwoods Properties is currently constructing two buildings, 136,000 sq. ft. and 189,000 sq. ft. in size, at Air Park South." *Society of Industrial and Office Realtors, 1999 Comparative Statistics of Industrial and Office Real Estate Markets*

COMMERCIAL UTILITIES

Typical Monthly Electric Bills

Area	Commercial Service ($/month)		Industrial Service ($/month)	
	12 kW demand 1,500 kWh	100 kW demand 30,000 kWh	1,000 kW demand 400,000 kWh	20,000 kW demand 10,000,000 kWh
City	150	1,814	20,801	295,548
U.S.	150	2,174	23,995	508,569

Note: Based on rates in effect January 1, 1999
Source: Edison Electric Institute, Typical Residential, Commercial and Industrial Bills, Winter 1999

TRANSPORTATION

Transportation Statistics

Average minutes to work	16.7
Interstate highways	I-40; I-85
Bus lines	
In-city	Greensboro TA
Inter-city	2
Passenger air service	
Airport	Piedmont Triad International
Airlines	9
Aircraft departures	27,191 (1996)
Enplaned passengers	1,200,587 (1996)
Rail service	Amtrak
Motor freight carriers	n/a
Major waterways/ports	None

Source: Editor & Publisher Market Guide, 1999; FAA Airport Activity Statistics, 1997; Amtrak National Time Table, Northeast Timetable, Spring/Summer 1999; 1990 Census of Population and Housing, STF 3C; Chamber of Commerce/Economic Development 1999; Jane's Urban Transport Systems 1999-2000

Means of Transportation to Work

Area	Car/Truck/Van		Public Transportation			Bicycle	Walked	Other Means	Worked at Home
	Drove Alone	Car-pooled	Bus	Subway	Railroad				
City	79.1	12.5	1.5	0.0	0.0	0.3	3.6	1.2	1.8
MSA[1]	79.1	14.5	1.0	0.0	0.0	0.1	2.3	0.8	2.1
U.S.	73.2	13.4	3.0	1.5	0.5	0.4	3.9	1.2	3.0

Note: Figures shown are percentages and only include workers 16 years old and over;
(1) Metropolitan Statistical Area - see Appendix A for areas included
Source: 1990 Census of Population and Housing, Summary Tape File 3C

BUSINESSES

Major Business Headquarters

Company Name	1999 Rankings	
	Fortune 500	Forbes 500
VF	301	-

Note: Companies listed are located in the city; dashes indicate no ranking
Fortune 500: Companies that produce a 10-K are ranked 1 to 500 based on 1998 revenue
Forbes 500: Private companies are ranked 1 to 500 based on 1997 revenue
Source: Forbes, November 30, 1998; Fortune, April 26, 1999

Fast-Growing Businesses

According to *Inc.*, Greensboro is home to one of America's 100 fastest-growing private companies: RF Micro Devices. Criteria for inclusion: must be an independent, privately-held, U.S. corporation, proprietorship or partnership; sales of at least $200,000 in 1995; five-year operating/sales history; increase in 1999 sales over 1998 sales; holding companies, regulated banks, and utilities were excluded. Inc. 500, 1999

According to Deloitte & Touche LLP, Greensboro is home to one of America's 100 fastest-growing high-technology companies: RF Micro Devices. Companies are ranked by percentage growth in revenue over a five-year period. Criteria for inclusion: must be a U.S. company developing and/or providing technology products or services; company must have been in business for five years with 1993 revenues of at least $50,000. *Deloitte & Touche LLP, November 17, 1998*

Women-Owned Firms: Number, Employment and Sales

Area	Number of Firms	Employment	Sales ($000)	Rank[2]
MSA[1]	39,400	122,900	15,055,600	46

Note: (1) Metropolitan Statistical Area - see Appendix A for areas included;
(2) Calculated on an averaging of the number of businesses, employment and sales
Source: The National Foundation for Women Business Owners, 1999 Facts on Women-Owned Businesses: Trends in the Top 50 Metropolitan Areas

Women-Owned Firms: Growth

Area	% change from 1992 to 1999			Rank[2]
	Number of Firms	Employment	Sales	
MSA[1]	45.8	100.3	120.2	30

Note: (1) Metropolitan Statistical Area - see Appendix A for areas included; (2) Calculated on an averaging of the percent growth of number of businesses, employment and sales
Source: The National Foundation for Women Business Owners, 1999 Facts on Women-Owned Businesses: Trends in the Top 50 Metropolitan Areas

Minority Business Opportunity

Greensboro is home to one company which is on the Black Enterprise Industrial/Service 100 list (largest based on gross sales): Southeast Fuels Inc. (energy sales) . Criteria: operational in previous calendar year, at least 51% black-owned and manufactures/owns the product it sells or provides industrial or consumer services. Brokerages, real estate firms and firms that provide professional services are not eligible. *Black Enterprise, www.blackenterprise.com*

HOTELS & MOTELS

Hotels/Motels

Area	Hotels/Motels	Rooms	Luxury-Level Hotels/Motels		Average Minimum Rates ($)		
			♦♦♦♦	♦♦♦♦♦	♦♦	♦♦♦	♦♦♦♦
City	29	4,691	0	0	55	98	n/a
Airport	5	976	0	0	n/a	n/a	n/a
Suburbs	9	746	0	0	n/a	n/a	n/a
Total	43	6,413	0	0	n/a	n/a	n/a

Note: n/a not available; classifications range from one diamond (budget properties with basic amenities) to five diamond (luxury properties with the finest service, rooms and facilities).
Source: OAG, Business Travel Planner, Winter 1998-99

CONVENTION CENTERS

Major Convention Centers

Center Name	Meeting Rooms	Exhibit Space (sq. ft.)
Greensboro Coliseum Complex	2	140,000
Joseph S. Koury Convention Center	78	100,000

Source: Trade Shows Worldwide, 1998; Meetings & Conventions, 4/15/99; Sucessful Meetings, 3/31/98

Living Environment

COST OF LIVING

Cost of Living Index

Composite Index	Groceries	Housing	Utilities	Trans-portation	Health Care	Misc. Goods/Services
98.1	97.7	99.0	109.4	92.4	79.5	99.4

Note: U.S. = 100
Source: ACCRA, Cost of Living Index, 3rd Quarter 1998

HOUSING

Median Home Prices and Housing Affordability

Area	Median Price[2] 1st Qtr. 1999 ($)	HOI[3] 1st Qtr. 1999	Afford-ability Rank[4]
MSA[1]	102,000	81.5	40
U.S.	134,000	69.6	–

Note: (1) Metropolitan Statistical Area - see Appendix A for areas included; (2) U.S. figures calculated from the sales of 524,324 new and existing homes in 181 markets; (3) Housing Opportunity Index - percent of homes sold that were within the reach of the median income household at the prevailing mortgage interest rate; (4) Rank is from 1-181 with 1 being most affordable
Source: National Association of Home Builders, Housing Opportunity Index, 1st Quarter 1999

Median Home Price Projection

It is projected that the median price of existing single-family homes in the metro area will decrease by -1.0% in 1999. Nationwide, home prices are projected to increase 3.8%.
Kiplinger's Personal Finance Magazine, January 1999

Average New Home Price

Area	Price ($)
City	144,150
U.S.	138,988

Note: Figures are based on a new home with 1,800 sq. ft. of living area on an 8,000 sq. ft. lot.
Source: ACCRA, Cost of Living Index, 3rd Quarter 1998

Average Apartment Rent

Area	Rent ($/mth)
City	542
U.S.	586

Note: Figures are based on an unfurnished two bedroom, 1-1/2 or 2 bath apartment, approximately 950 sq. ft. in size, excluding all utilities except water
Source: ACCRA, Cost of Living Index, 3rd Quarter 1998

RESIDENTIAL UTILITIES

Average Residential Utility Costs

Area	All Electric ($/mth)	Part Electric ($/mth)	Other Energy ($/mth)	Phone ($/mth)
City	111.97	–	–	19.55
U.S.	103.76	55.93	43.48	19.86

Source: ACCRA, Cost of Living Index, 3rd Quarter 1998

HEALTH CARE

Average Health Care Costs

Area	Hospital ($/day)	Doctor ($/visit)	Dentist ($/visit)
City	187.00	47.60	49.40
U.S.	405.11	50.96	63.88

Note: Hospital—based on a semi-private room; Doctor—based on a general practitioner's routine exam of an established patient; Dentist—based on adult teeth cleaning and periodic oral exam.
Source: ACCRA, Cost of Living Index, 3rd Quarter 1998

Distribution of Office-Based Physicians

Area	Family/Gen. Practitioners	Specialists		
		Medical	Surgical	Other
MSA[1]	249	672	558	502

Note: Data as of 12/31/97; (1) Metropolitan Statistical Area - see Appendix A for areas included
Source: American Medical Assn., Physician Characteristics & Distribution in the U.S., 1999

Hospitals

Greensboro has 1 general medical and surgical hospital, 1 psychiatric, 1 other specialty. *AHA Guide to the Healthcare Field, 1998-99*

EDUCATION

Public School District Statistics

District Name	Num. Sch.	Enroll.	Classroom Teachers	Pupils per Teacher	Minority Pupils (%)	Current Exp.[1] ($/pupil)
Guilford County Schools	95	59,903	4,095	14.6	45.8	5,226

Note: Data covers the 1997-1998 school year unless otherwise noted; (1) Data covers fiscal year 1996; SD = School District; ISD = Independent School District; n/a not available
Source: National Center for Education Statistics, Common Core of Data Public Education Agency Universe 1997-98; National Center for Education Statistics, Characteristics of the 100 Largest Public Elementary and Secondary School Districts in the United States: 1997-98, July 1999

Educational Quality

School District	Education Quotient[1]	Graduate Outcome[2]	Community Index[3]	Resource Index[4]
Guilford County	78.0	85.0	94.0	61.0

Note: Nearly 1,000 secondary school districts were rated in terms of educational quality. The scores range from a low of 50 to a high of 150; (1) Average of the Graduate Outcome, Community and Resource indexes; (2) Based on graduation rates and college board scores (SAT/ACT); (3) Based on the surrounding community's average level of education and the area's average income level; (4) Based on teacher salaries, per-pupil expenditures and student-teacher ratios.
Source: Expansion Management, Ratings Issue, 1998

Educational Attainment by Race

Area	High School Graduate (%)					Bachelor's Degree (%)				
	Total	White	Black	Other	Hisp.[2]	Total	White	Black	Other	Hisp.[2]
City	79.2	83.3	70.6	63.6	75.0	29.9	35.0	17.7	35.1	29.3
MSA[1]	72.0	73.3	66.1	63.1	70.0	19.2	20.2	14.0	27.5	21.4
U.S.	75.2	77.9	63.1	60.4	49.8	20.3	21.5	11.4	19.4	9.2

Note: Figures shown cover persons 25 years old and over; (1) Metropolitan Statistical Area - see Appendix A for areas included; (2) people of Hispanic origin can be of any race
Source: 1990 Census of Population and Housing, Summary Tape File 3C

School Enrollment by Type

Area	Preprimary				Elementary/High School			
	Public		Private		Public		Private	
	Enrollment	%	Enrollment	%	Enrollment	%	Enrollment	%
City	1,840	54.1	1,564	45.9	23,934	92.5	1,927	7.5
MSA[1]	8,849	58.2	6,354	41.8	136,757	93.7	9,199	6.3
U.S.	2,679,029	59.5	1,824,256	40.5	38,379,689	90.2	4,187,099	9.8

Note: Figures shown cover persons 3 years old and over;
(1) Metropolitan Statistical Area - see Appendix A for areas included
Source: 1990 Census of Population and Housing, Summary Tape File 3C

School Enrollment by Race

Area	Preprimary (%)				Elementary/High School (%)			
	White	Black	Other	Hisp.[1]	White	Black	Other	Hisp.[1]
City	66.1	30.7	3.2	0.2	54.1	43.1	2.9	1.0
MSA[2]	78.2	20.4	1.4	1.0	74.1	24.2	1.7	0.8
U.S.	80.4	12.5	7.1	7.8	74.1	15.6	10.3	12.5

Note: Figures shown cover persons 3 years old and over; (1) people of Hispanic origin can be of any race; (2) Metropolitan Statistical Area - see Appendix A for areas included
Source: 1990 Census of Population and Housing, Summary Tape File 3C

Classroom Teacher Salaries in Public Schools

District	B.A. Degree		M.A. Degree		Maximum	
	Min. ($)	Rank[1]	Max. ($)	Rank[1]	Max. ($)	Rank[1]
Greensboro	24,310	80	46,960	37	49,840	55
Average	26,980	-	46,065	-	51,435	-

Note: Salaries are for 1997-1998; (1) Rank ranges from 1 to 100
Source: American Federation of Teachers, Survey & Analysis of Salary Trends, 1998

Higher Education

Two-Year Colleges		Four-Year Colleges		Medical Schools	Law Schools	Voc/Tech
Public	Private	Public	Private			
0	0	2	3	0	0	5

Source: College Blue Book, Occupational Education, 1997; Medical School Admission Requirements, 1999-2000; Peterson's Guide to Two-Year Colleges, 1999; Peterson's Guide to Four-Year Colleges, 2000; Barron's Guide to Law Schools, 1999

MAJOR EMPLOYERS

Major Employers

VF Jeanswear
Greensboro News & Record
Jefferson-Pilot Corp. (life insurance)
Triad International Maintenance Corp.
Standard Industrial Maintenence
Burlington Industries
Guilford Mills
Moses H. Cone Memorial Hospital
Sunstates Maintenance Corp.
Wesley Long Community Hospital

Note: Companies listed are located in the city
Source: Dun's Business Rankings, 1999; Ward's Business Directory, 1998

PUBLIC SAFETY

Crime Rate

Area	All Crimes	Violent Crimes				Property Crimes		
		Murder	Forcible Rape	Robbery	Aggrav. Assault	Burglary	Larceny -Theft	Motor Vehicle Theft
City	8,017.3	17.0	41.7	378.1	521.3	1,493.1	5,013.7	552.4
Suburbs[1]	5,494.8	5.5	35.5	147.2	348.5	1,320.7	3,321.0	316.2
MSA[2]	5,941.6	7.6	36.6	188.1	379.1	1,351.3	3,620.8	358.1
U.S.	4,922.7	6.8	35.9	186.1	382.0	919.6	2,886.5	505.8

Note: Crime rate is the number of crimes per 100,000 pop.; (1) defined as all areas within the MSA but located outside the central city; (2) Metropolitan Statistical Area - see Appendix A for areas incl.
Source: FBI Uniform Crime Reports, 1997

RECREATION

Culture and Recreation

Museums	Symphony Orchestras	Opera Companies	Dance Companies	Professional Theatres	Zoos	Pro Sports Teams
3	2	1	1	0	1	1

Source: International Directory of the Performing Arts, 1997; Official Museum Directory, 1999; Stern's Performing Arts Directory, 1997; USA Today Four Sport Stadium Guide, 1997; Chamber of Commerce/Economic Development, 1999

Library System

The Greensboro Public Library has eight branches, holdings of 759,831 volumes, and a budget of $5,728,877 (1995-1996). *American Library Directory, 1998-1999*

MEDIA

Newspapers

Name	Type	Freq.	Distribution	Circulation
Greensboro News & Record	General	7x/wk	Area	95,348

Note: Includes newspapers with circulations of 1,000 or more located in the city;
Source: Burrelle's Media Directory, 1999 Edition

Television Stations

Name	Ch.	Affiliation	Type	Owner
WFMY	n/a	CBST	Commercial	Gannett Broadcasting
WGHP	n/a	FBC	Commercial	Fox Television Stations Inc.
WXIV	14	n/a	Commercial	Carolina Blue Communications
WGPX	16	PAXTV	Commercial	Paxson Communications Corporation
WBFX	20	FKN/WB	Commercial	Pappas Telecasting Companies
WLXI	61	n/a	Non-comm.	Tri-State Christian Network

Note: Stations included broadcast in the Greensboro metro area; n/a not available
Source: Burrelle's Media Directory, 1999 Edition

AM Radio Stations

Call Letters	Freq. (kHz)	Target Audience	Station Format	Music Format
WPET	950	General	M	Gospel
WMFR	1230	General	N/T	n/a
WTCK	1320	General	S/T	n/a
WKEW	1400	General	N/S/T	n/a
WEAL	1510	Religious	M	Gospel

Note: Stations included broadcast in the Greensboro metro area; n/a not available
Target Audience: A=Asian; B=Black; C=Christian; E=Ethnic; F=French; G=General; H=Hispanic;
M=Men; N=Native American; R=Religious; S=Senior Citizen; W=Women; Y=Young Adult; Z=Children
Station Format: E=Educational; M=Music; N=News; S=Sports; T=Talk
Source: Burrelle's Media Directory, 1999 Edition

FM Radio Stations

Call Letters	Freq. (mHz)	Target Audience	Station Format	Music Format
WNAA	90.1	Black	M/T	Jazz/Oldies/Urban Contemporary
WWIH	90.3	General	M	n/a
WKRR	92.3	General	M	Classic Rock
WMQX	93.1	General	M/N	Oldies
WHPE	95.5	Religious	M	Christian
WQMG	97.1	Black	M	R&B
WIST	98.3	General	M/N/S/T	Adult Standards/Big Band/Country/Easy Listening/Jazz/Oldies
WKSI	98.7	General	M/N	Adult Contemporary
WMAG	99.5	General	M	Adult Contemporary
WHSL	100.3	General	M	Country/Oldies
WJMH	102.1	Young Adult	M/N/S/T	Urban Contemporary
WKZL	107.5	General	M	Alternative

Note: Stations included broadcast in the Greensboro metro area; n/a not available
Station Format: E=Educational; M=Music; N=News; S=Sports; T=Talk
Target Audience: A=Asian; B=Black; C=Christian; E=Ethnic; F=French; G=General; H=Hispanic;
M=Men; N=Native American; R=Religious; S=Senior Citizen; W=Women; Y=Young Adult; Z=Children
Source: Burrelle's Media Directory, 1999 Edition

CLIMATE

Average and Extreme Temperatures

Temperature	Jan	Feb	Mar	Apr	May	Jun	Jul	Aug	Sep	Oct	Nov	Dec	Yr.
Extreme High (°F)	78	81	89	91	96	102	102	103	100	95	85	78	103
Average High (°F)	48	51	60	70	78	84	87	86	80	70	60	50	69
Average Temp. (°F)	38	41	49	58	67	74	78	76	70	59	49	40	58
Average Low (°F)	28	30	37	46	55	63	67	66	59	47	37	30	47
Extreme Low (°F)	-8	-1	5	23	32	42	49	45	37	20	10	0	-8

Note: Figures cover the years 1948-1990
Source: National Climatic Data Center, International Station Meteorological Climate Summary, 3/95

Average Precipitation/Snowfall/Humidity

Precip./Humidity	Jan	Feb	Mar	Apr	May	Jun	Jul	Aug	Sep	Oct	Nov	Dec	Yr.
Avg. Precip. (in.)	3.2	3.4	3.7	3.1	3.7	3.8	4.5	4.2	3.4	3.4	2.9	3.3	42.5
Avg. Snowfall (in.)	4	3	2	Tr	0	0	0	0	0	0	Tr	1	10
Avg. Rel. Hum. 7am (%)	80	78	78	77	82	84	87	90	90	88	83	80	83
Avg. Rel. Hum. 4pm (%)	53	50	47	44	51	54	57	58	56	51	51	54	52

Note: Figures cover the years 1948-1990; Tr = Trace amounts (<0.05 in. of rain; <0.5 in. of snow)
Source: National Climatic Data Center, International Station Meteorological Climate Summary, 3/95

Weather Conditions

Temperature			Daytime Sky			Precipitation		
10°F & below	32°F & below	90°F & above	Clear	Partly cloudy	Cloudy	0.01 inch or more precip.	0.1 inch or more snow/ice	Thunder-storms
3	85	32	94	143	128	113	5	43

Note: Figures are average number of days per year and covers the years 1948-1990
Source: National Climatic Data Center, International Station Meteorological Climate Summary, 3/95

AIR & WATER QUALITY

Maximum Pollutant Concentrations

	Particulate Matter (ug/m^3)	Carbon Monoxide (ppm)	Sulfur Dioxide (ppm)	Nitrogen Dioxide (ppm)	Ozone (ppm)	Lead (ug/m^3)
MSA[1] Level	61	5	0.023	0.017	0.12	0.00
NAAQS[2]	150	9	0.140	0.053	0.12	1.50
Met NAAQS?	Yes	Yes	Yes	Yes	Yes	Yes

Note: (1) Metropolitan Statistical Area - see Appendix A for areas included; (2) National Ambient Air Quality Standards; ppm = parts per million; ug/m^3 = micrograms per cubic meter; n/a not available
Source: EPA, National Air Quality and Emissions Trends Report, 1997

Pollutant Standards Index

In the Greensboro MSA (see Appendix A for areas included), the Pollutant Standards Index (PSI) exceeded 100 on 17 days in 1997. A PSI value greater than 100 indicates that air quality would be in the unhealthful range on that day. *EPA, National Air Quality and Emissions Trends Report, 1997*

Drinking Water

Water System Name	Pop. Served	Primary Water Source Type	Number of Violations in 1998	Type of Violation/ Contaminants
City of Greensboro	218,463	Surface	None	None

Note: Data as of July 10, 1999
Source: EPA, Office of Ground Water and Drinking Water, Safe Drinking Water Information System

Greensboro tap water is alkaline, soft.
Editor & Publisher Market Guide, 1999

Lexington, Kentucky

Background

Lexington has managed to combine the frenzied pace of a major city with the slow tempo of a small town without losing the traditions and gentility of its southern heritage.

Since its settlement in 1775, Lexington has grown to become Kentucky's second largest city and the commercial center of the Bluegrass region. The town was founded in 1779 and incorporated in 1832.

It is noted for its training of thoroughbred horses and marketing of burley tobacco. Hemp was Lexington's major antebellum crop until the rope from which it was made was no longer used for ship rigging. After the Civil War the farmers in the area switched to tobacco as their primary crop.

The city is also the chief producer of bluegrass seed and white barley in the United States. Other products manufactured in Lexington include paper products, air-conditioning and heating equipment, electric typewriters, metal products, and bourbon whiskey.

Surrounded by horse farms and rolling Bluegrass meadows, Lexington was once known as the "Athens of the West" when a large number of early American artists, poets, musicians, and architects settled here. They all left their imprint on the city.

Lexington has a definite continental climate with a rather large daily temperature range. The climate is temperate and well suited to a varied plant and animal life. The area is subject to rather sudden and sweeping changes in temperature with the spells generally of short duration. Temperatures above 100 degrees and below zero degrees are relatively rare.

General Rankings and Evaluative Comments

- Lexington was ranked #9 out of 44 mid-sized, southern metropolitan areas in *Money's* 1998 survey of "The Best Places to Live in America." The survey was conducted by first contacting 512 representative households nationwide and asking them to rank 37 quality-of-life factors on a scale of 1 to 10. Next, a demographic profile was compiled on the 300 largest metropolitan statistical areas in the U.S. The numbers were crunched together to arrive at an overall ranking (things Americans consider most important, like clean air and water, low crime and good schools, received extra weight). Unlike previous years, the 1998 rankings were broken down by region (northeast, midwest, south, west) and population size (100,000 to 249,999; 250,000 to 999,999; 1 million plus). The city had a nationwide ranking of #165 out of 300 in 1997 and #143 out of 300 in 1996. *Money, July 1998; Money, July 1997; Money, September 1996*

- *Ladies Home Journal* ranked America's 200 largest cities based on the qualities women care about most. Lexington ranked #8 out of 200. Criteria: low crime rate, well-paying jobs, quality health and child care, good public schools, the presence of women in government, size of the gender wage gap, number of sexual-harassment and discrimination complaints filed, unemployment and divorce rates, commute times, population density, number of houses of worship, parks and cultural offerings, number of women's health specialists, how well a community's women cared for themselves, complexion kindness index based on UV radiation levels, odds of finding affordable fashions, rental rates for romance movies, champagne sales and other matters of the heart.

  "The cost of living is lower than the nation's average and job growth was in the top 15 percent last year." *Ladies Home Journal, November 1998*

- Zero Population Growth ranked 229 cities in terms of children's health, safety, and economic well-being. Lexington was ranked #28 out of 112 independent cities (cities with populations greater than 100,000 which were neither Major Cities nor Suburbs/Outer Cities) and was given a grade of B. Criteria: total population, percent of population under 18 years of age, household language, percent population change, percent of births to teens, infant mortality rate, percent of low birth weights, dropout rate, enrollment in preprimary school, violent and property crime rates, unemployment rate, percent of children in poverty, percent of owner occupied units, number of bad air days, percent of public transportation commuters, and average travel time to work. *Zero Population Growth, Children's Environmental Index, Fall 1999*

- Cognetics studied 273 metro areas in the United States, ranking them by entrepreneurial activity. Lexington was ranked #12 out of 134 smaller metro areas. Criteria: Significant Starts (firms started in the last 10 years that still employ at least 5 people) and Young Growers (percent of firms 10 years old or less that grew significantly during the last 4 years). *Cognetics, "Entrepreneurial Hot Spots: The Best Places in America to Start and Grow a Company," 1998*

- Reliastar Financial Corp. ranked the 125 largest metropolitan areas according to the general financial security of residents. Lexington was ranked #50 out of 125 with a score of 3.5. The score indicates the percentage a metropolitan area is above or below the metropolitan norm. A metro area with a score of 10.6 is 10.6% above the metro average. Criteria: Earnings and Wealth Potential (household income, education, net assets, cost of living); Safety Net (health insurance, retirement savings, life insurance, income support programs); Personal Threats (unemployment rate, low-income households, crime rate); Community Economic Vitality (cost of community services, job quality, job creation, housing costs). *Reliastar Financial Corp., "The Best Cities to Earn and Save Money," 1999 Edition*

Business Environment

STATE ECONOMY

State Economic Profile

"Kentucky has trailed the nation by a narrow margin in recent years. A continued slowdown in its manufacturing sector and weak population growth will widen that difference as Kentucky falls further below the nation in 1999 and 2000. Recent growth in home sales and price appreciation has attracted a tremendous amount of new construction, which will moderate future price appreciation.

The engine behind KY's economy has been Louisville. Almost 60% of state employment gains took place in Louisville, which added jobs at a rate almost twice that of the state. Within Louisville, the job engine has been UPS and associated companies. As the UPS hub, Louisville has managed to attract a wide range of wholesale and distribution companies, helping to offset its weak manufacturing sector.

Lexington has been the other source of growth. Employment gains were 2.4% in 1998, held back by only the extremely tight labor market (unemployment of 1.7%). Manufacturing employment growth in Kentucky will occur mostly in Lexington.

Both Lexington and Louisville witnessed a boom in multifamily housing activity in 1998. Multifamily permits rose over 100% in Louisville and 46% in Lexington. Considering KY's continued loss of younger households, it is likely that KY's rental markets will soften considerably in 1999.

Increased job growth has added relatively little to consumer spending. Job growth has been concentrated among lower-paying occupations, and declines in the unionized sector (especially steel) squeezed household income." *National Association of Realtors, Economic Profiles: The Fifty States and the District of Columbia, http://nar.realtor.com/databank/profiles.htm*

IMPORTS/EXPORTS

Total Export Sales

Area	1994 ($000)	1995 ($000)	1996 ($000)	1997 ($000)	% Chg. 1994-97	% Chg. 1996-97
MSA[1]	1,078,566	1,235,009	1,499,919	1,886,843	74.9	25.8
U.S.	512,415,609	583,030,524	622,827,063	687,597,999	34.2	10.4

Note: (1) Metropolitan Statistical Area - see Appendix A for areas included
Source: U.S. Department of Commerce, International Trade Association, Metropolitan Area Exports: An Export Performance Report on Over 250 U.S. Cities, November 10, 1998

CITY FINANCES

City Government Finances

Component	FY92 ($000)	FY92 (per capita $)
Revenue	221,415	953.66
Expenditure	203,486	876.44
Debt Outstanding	413,906	1,782.75
Cash & Securities	430,175	1,852.82

Source: U.S. Bureau of the Census, City Government Finances: 1991-92

City Government Revenue by Source

Source	FY92 ($000)	FY92 (per capita $)	FY92 (%)
From Federal Government	10,538	45.39	4.8
From State Governments	5,661	24.38	2.6
From Local Governments	141	0.61	0.1
Property Taxes	24,060	103.63	10.9
General Sales Taxes	0	0.00	0.0
Selective Sales Taxes	6,072	26.15	2.7
Income Taxes	59,819	257.65	27.0
Current Charges	59,224	255.09	26.7
Utility/Liquor Store	1,344	5.79	0.6
Employee Retirement[1]	23,369	100.65	10.6
Other	31,187	134.33	14.1

Note: (1) Excludes "city contributions," classified as "nonrevenue," intragovernmental transfers.
Source: U.S. Bureau of the Census, City Government Finances: 1991-92

City Government Expenditures by Function

Function	FY92 ($000)	FY92 (per capita $)	FY92 (%)
Educational Services	7,683	33.09	3.8
Employee Retirement[1]	8,728	37.59	4.3
Environment/Housing	48,352	208.26	23.8
Government Administration	14,131	60.86	6.9
Interest on General Debt	27,660	119.14	13.6
Public Safety	46,715	201.21	23.0
Social Services	17,762	76.50	8.7
Transportation	13,681	58.93	6.7
Utility/Liquor Store	4,890	21.06	2.4
Other	13,884	59.80	6.8

Note: (1) Payments to beneficiaries including withdrawal of contributions.
Source: U.S. Bureau of the Census, City Government Finances: 1991-92

Municipal Bond Ratings

Area	Moody's	S & P
Lexington	Aa2	n/a

Note: n/a not available; n/r not rated
Source: Moody's Bond Record, 6/99

POPULATION

Population Growth

Area	1980	1990	% Chg. 1980-90	July 1998 Estimate	% Chg. 1990-98
City	204,165	225,366	10.4	241,749	7.3
MSA[1]	317,629	348,428	9.7	452,785	30.0
U.S.	226,545,805	248,765,170	9.8	270,299,000	8.7

Note: (1) Metropolitan Statistical Area - see Appendix A for areas included;
July 1998 MSA population estimate was calculated by the editors
Source: 1980/1990 Census of Housing and Population, Summary Tape File 3C;
Census Bureau Population Estimates 1998

Population Characteristics

Race	City 1980 Population	%	City 1990 Population	%	% Chg. 1980-90	MSA[1] 1990 Population	%
White	174,934	85.7	190,795	84.7	9.1	305,969	87.8
Black	26,979	13.2	30,172	13.4	11.8	37,234	10.7
Amer Indian/Esk/Aleut	271	0.1	432	0.2	59.4	689	0.2
Asian/Pacific Islander	1,580	0.8	3,345	1.5	111.7	3,744	1.1
Other	401	0.2	622	0.3	55.1	792	0.2
Hispanic Origin[2]	1,279	0.6	2,358	1.0	84.4	2,994	0.9

Note: (1) Metropolitan Statistical Area - see Appendix A for areas included;
(2) people of Hispanic origin can be of any race
Source: 1980/1990 Census of Housing and Population, Summary Tape File 3C

Ancestry

Area	German	Irish	English	Italian	U.S.	French	Polish	Dutch
City	22.1	18.1	19.5	2.3	8.5	3.2	1.1	2.3
MSA[1]	21.2	17.9	18.8	1.9	10.9	3.0	1.0	2.3
U.S.	23.3	15.6	13.1	5.9	5.3	4.2	3.8	2.5

Note: Figures are percentages and include persons that reported multiple ancestry (eg. if a person reported being Irish and Italian, they were included in both columns); (1) Metropolitan Statistical Area - see Appendix A for areas included
Source: 1990 Census of Population and Housing, Summary Tape File 3C

Age

Area	Median Age (Years)	Age Distribution (%) Under 5	Under 18	18-24	25-44	45-64	65+	80+
City	31.2	6.7	22.4	14.5	36.4	16.8	9.9	2.0
MSA[1]	31.7	6.8	23.9	13.1	35.1	17.6	10.3	2.2
U.S.	32.9	7.3	25.6	10.5	32.6	18.7	12.5	2.8

Note: (1) Metropolitan Statistical Area - see Appendix A for areas included
Source: 1990 Census of Population and Housing, Summary Tape File 3C

Male/Female Ratio

Area	Number of males per 100 females (all ages)	Number of males per 100 females (18 years old+)
City	91.7	88.2
MSA[1]	92.3	88.7
U.S.	95.0	91.9

Note: (1) Metropolitan Statistical Area - see Appendix A for areas included
Source: 1990 Census of Population, General Population Characteristics

INCOME

Per Capita/Median/Average Income

Area	Per Capita ($)	Median Household ($)	Average Household ($)
City	14,962	28,056	36,979
MSA[1]	13,945	27,558	35,698
U.S.	14,420	30,056	38,453

Note: All figures are for 1989; (1) Metropolitan Statistical Area - see Appendix A for areas included
Source: 1990 Census of Population and Housing, Summary Tape File 3C

Household Income Distribution by Race

Income ($)	City (%)					U.S. (%)				
	Total	White	Black	Other	Hisp.[1]	Total	White	Black	Other	Hisp.[1]
Less than 5,000	7.7	5.8	20.5	9.1	8.3	6.2	4.8	15.2	8.6	8.8
5,000 - 9,999	9.1	8.1	15.8	14.1	11.5	9.3	8.6	14.2	9.9	11.1
10,000 - 14,999	9.4	8.8	13.3	13.3	8.7	8.8	8.5	11.0	9.8	11.0
15,000 - 24,999	18.1	18.0	18.8	18.6	21.6	17.5	17.3	18.9	18.5	20.5
25,000 - 34,999	16.1	16.8	11.8	9.7	7.0	15.8	16.1	14.2	15.4	16.4
35,000 - 49,999	17.1	18.0	10.8	12.8	16.1	17.9	18.6	13.3	16.1	16.0
50,000 - 74,999	13.9	14.9	7.1	10.1	19.3	15.0	15.8	9.3	13.4	11.1
75,000 - 99,999	4.5	4.9	1.4	5.1	4.3	5.1	5.5	2.6	4.7	3.1
100,000+	4.2	4.7	0.7	7.2	3.2	4.4	4.8	1.3	3.7	1.9

Note: All figures are for 1989; (1) people of Hispanic origin can be of any race
Source: 1990 Census of Population and Housing, Summary Tape File 3C

Effective Buying Income

Area	Per Capita ($)	Median Household ($)	Average Household ($)
City	18,027	34,366	44,662
MSA[1]	16,875	32,749	43,706
U.S.	16,803	34,536	45,243

Note: Data as of 1/1/99; (1) Metropolitan Statistical Area - see Appendix A for areas included
Source: Standard Rate & Data Service, Newspaper Advertising Source, 9/99

Effective Household Buying Income Distribution

Area	% of Households Earning						
	$10,000 -$19,999	$20,000 -$34,999	$35,000 -$49,999	$50,000 -$74,999	$75,000 -$99,000	$100,000 -$124,999	$125,000 and up
City	15.6	22.6	17.4	18.6	7.4	2.7	3.1
MSA[1]	16.7	22.7	17.5	18.1	6.8	2.1	2.4
U.S.	16.0	22.6	18.2	18.9	7.2	2.4	2.7

Note: Data as of 1/1/99; (1) Metropolitan Statistical Area - see Appendix A for areas included
Source: Standard Rate & Data Service, Newspaper Advertising Source, 9/99

Poverty Rates by Race and Age

Area	Total (%)	By Race (%)				By Age (%)		
		White	Black	Other	Hisp.[2]	Under 5 years old	Under 18 years old	65 years and over
City	14.1	10.9	34.0	22.1	26.4	19.9	18.8	13.2
MSA[1]	14.2	11.9	32.7	20.9	24.3	21.1	18.9	16.3
U.S.	13.1	9.8	29.5	23.1	25.3	20.1	18.3	12.8

Note: Figures show the percent of people living below the poverty line in 1989. The average poverty threshold was $12,674 for a family of four in 1989; (1) Metropolitan Statistical Area - see Appendix A for areas included; (2) people of Hispanic origin can be of any race
Source: 1990 Census of Population and Housing, Summary Tape File 3C

EMPLOYMENT

Labor Force and Employment

Area	Civilian Labor Force			Workers Employed		
	Jun. 1998	Jun. 1999	% Chg.	Jun. 1998	Jun. 1999	% Chg.
City	143,156	147,159	2.8	139,883	144,127	3.0
MSA[1]	255,746	262,781	2.8	249,642	257,216	3.0
U.S.	138,798,000	140,666,000	1.3	132,265,000	134,395,000	1.6

Note: Data is not seasonally adjusted and covers workers 16 years of age and older;
(1) Metropolitan Statistical Area - see Appendix A for areas included
Source: Bureau of Labor Statistics, http://stats.bls.gov

Unemployment Rate

Area	1998						1999					
	Jul.	Aug.	Sep.	Oct.	Nov.	Dec.	Jan.	Feb.	Mar.	Apr.	May.	Jun.
City	2.0	2.1	2.1	2.1	1.9	1.6	1.9	2.0	2.0	1.8	1.9	2.1
MSA[1]	2.1	2.1	2.1	2.0	1.9	1.7	2.2	2.3	2.2	2.0	2.0	2.1
U.S.	4.7	4.5	4.4	4.2	4.1	4.0	4.8	4.7	4.4	4.1	4.0	4.5

Note: Data is not seasonally adjusted and covers workers 16 years of age and older; all figures are percentages; (1) Metropolitan Statistical Area - see Appendix A for areas included
Source: Bureau of Labor Statistics, http://stats.bls.gov

Employment by Industry

Sector	MSA[1]		U.S.
	Number of Employees	Percent of Total	Percent of Total
Services	78,900	27.9	30.4
Retail Trade	50,900	18.0	17.7
Government	55,000	19.4	15.6
Manufacturing	49,500	17.5	14.3
Finance/Insurance/Real Estate	10,700	3.8	5.9
Wholesale Trade	12,300	4.3	5.4
Transportation/Public Utilities	11,200	4.0	5.3
Construction	14,500	5.1	5.0
Mining	300	0.1	0.4

Note: Figures cover non-farm employment as of 6/99 and are not seasonally adjusted;
(1) Metropolitan Statistical Area - see Appendix A for areas included
Source: Bureau of Labor Statistics, http://stats.bls.gov

Employment by Occupation

Occupation Category	City (%)	MSA[1] (%)	U.S. (%)
White Collar	66.3	61.0	58.1
Executive/Admin./Management	13.6	12.3	12.3
Professional	18.8	16.3	14.1
Technical & Related Support	4.8	4.3	3.7
Sales	13.4	12.3	11.8
Administrative Support/Clerical	15.7	15.8	16.3
Blue Collar	17.3	21.4	26.2
Precision Production/Craft/Repair	7.8	9.3	11.3
Machine Operators/Assem./Insp.	4.0	5.6	6.8
Transportation/Material Movers	3.0	3.4	4.1
Cleaners/Helpers/Laborers	2.6	3.1	3.9
Services	13.9	13.4	13.2
Farming/Forestry/Fishing	2.5	4.2	2.5

Note: Figures cover employed persons 16 years old and over;
(1) Metropolitan Statistical Area - see Appendix A for areas included
Source: 1990 Census of Population and Housing, Summary Tape File 3C

Occupational Employment Projections: 1996 - 2006

Occupations Expected to Have the Largest Job Growth (ranked by numerical growth)	Fast-Growing Occupations[1] (ranked by percent growth)
1. Cashiers	1. Personal and home care aides
2. Truck drivers, light	2. Systems analysts
3. General managers & top executives	3. Physical therapists
4. Salespersons, retail	4. Occupational therapists
5. Registered nurses	5. Medical assistants
6. Nursing aides/orderlies/attendants	6. Paralegals
7. Food service workers	7. Home health aides
8. Child care workers, private household	8. Surgical technologists
9. General office clerks	9. Numerical control machine tool oper.
10. Janitors/cleaners/maids, ex. priv. hshld.	10. Dental hygienists

Note: Projections cover Kentucky; (1) Excludes occupations with total job growth less than 300
Source: U.S. Department of Labor, Employment and Training Administration, America's Labor Market Information System (ALMIS)

TAXES

Major State and Local Tax Rates

State Corp. Income (%)	State Personal Income (%)	Residential Property (effective rate per $100)	Sales & Use		State Gasoline (cents/ gallon)	State Cigarette (cents/ pack)
			State (%)	Local (%)		
4.0 - 8.25	2.0 - 6.0	n/a	6.0	None	16.4[a]	3.0[b]

Note: Personal/corporate income, sales, gasoline and cigarette tax rates as of January 1999. Property tax rates as of 1997; (a) Rate is comprised of 15 cents excise and 1.4 cents motor carrier tax. Carriers pay an additional surcharge of 2%; (b) Dealers pay an additional enforcement and administrative fee of 0.1 cent per pack
Source: Federation of Tax Administrators, www.taxadmin.org; Washington D.C. Department of Finance and Revenue, Tax Rates and Tax Burdens in the District of Columbia: A Nationwide Comparison, July 1998; Chamber of Commerce, 1999

Total Taxes Per Capita and as a Percent of Income

Area	Per Capita Income ($)	Per Capita Taxes ($)			Percent of Income (%)		
		Total	Federal	State/ Local	Total	Federal	State/ Local
Kentucky	22,643	7,832	5,129	2,703	34.6	22.7	11.9
U.S.	27,876	9,881	6,690	3,191	35.4	24.0	11.4

Note: Figures are for 1998
Source: Tax Foundation, www.taxfoundation.org

Estimated Tax Burden

Area	State Income	Local Income	Property	Sales	Total
Lexington	3,500	1,500	2,500	585	8,085

Note: The numbers are estimates of taxes paid by a married couple with two children and annual earnings of $75,000. Sales tax estimates assume they spend average amounts on food, clothing, household goods and gasoline. Property tax estimates assume they live in a $250,000 home.
Source: Kiplinger's Personal Finance Magazine, October 1998

COMMERCIAL REAL ESTATE

Data not available at time of publication.

COMMERCIAL UTILITIES

Typical Monthly Electric Bills

Area	Commercial Service ($/month)		Industrial Service ($/month)	
	12 kW demand 1,500 kWh	100 kW demand 30,000 kWh	1,000 kW demand 400,000 kWh	20,000 kW demand 10,000,000 kWh
City	89	1,231	14,152	222,452
U.S.	150	2,174	23,995	508,569

Note: Based on rates in effect January 1, 1999
Source: Edison Electric Institute, Typical Residential, Commercial and Industrial Bills, Winter 1999

TRANSPORTATION

Transportation Statistics

Average minutes to work	17.5
Interstate highways	I-64; I-75
Bus lines	
In-city	Lexington TA
Inter-city	1
Passenger air service	
Airport	Bluegrass Airport
Airlines	9
Aircraft departures	9,943 (1996)
Enplaned passengers	368,768 (1996)
Rail service	No Amtrak service
Motor freight carriers	56
Major waterways/ports	None

Source: Editor & Publisher Market Guide, 1999; FAA Airport Activity Statistics, 1997; Amtrak National Time Table, Northeast Timetable, Spring/Summer 1999; 1990 Census of Population and Housing, STF 3C; Chamber of Commerce/Economic Development 1999; Jane's Urban Transport Systems 1999-2000

Means of Transportation to Work

Area	Car/Truck/Van		Public Transportation			Bicycle	Walked	Other Means	Worked at Home
	Drove Alone	Car-pooled	Bus	Subway	Railroad				
City	78.4	11.6	1.5	0.0	0.0	0.3	5.1	0.6	2.4
MSA[1]	77.9	12.7	1.0	0.0	0.0	0.2	4.7	0.6	2.8
U.S.	73.2	13.4	3.0	1.5	0.5	0.4	3.9	1.2	3.0

Note: Figures shown are percentages and only include workers 16 years old and over; (1) Metropolitan Statistical Area - see Appendix A for areas included
Source: 1990 Census of Population and Housing, Summary Tape File 3C

BUSINESSES

Major Business Headquarters

Company Name	1999 Rankings	
	Fortune 500	Forbes 500
Clark Material Handling	-	480
Lexmark International	486	-

Note: Companies listed are located in the city; dashes indicate no ranking
Fortune 500: Companies that produce a 10-K are ranked 1 to 500 based on 1998 revenue
Forbes 500: Private companies are ranked 1 to 500 based on 1997 revenue
Source: Forbes, November 30, 1998; Fortune, April 26, 1999

HOTELS & MOTELS

Hotels/Motels

Area	Hotels/Motels	Rooms	Luxury-Level Hotels/Motels		Average Minimum Rates ($)		
			♦♦♦♦	♦♦♦♦♦	♦♦	♦♦♦	♦♦♦♦
City	38	5,291	0	0	57	109	n/a
Airport	1	142	0	0	n/a	n/a	n/a
Total	39	5,433	0	0	n/a	n/a	n/a

Note: n/a not available; classifications range from one diamond (budget properties with basic amenities) to five diamond (luxury properties with the finest service, rooms and facilities).
Source: OAG, Business Travel Planner, Winter 1998-99

CONVENTION CENTERS

Major Convention Centers

Center Name	Meeting Rooms	Exhibit Space (sq. ft.)
Lexington Convention Center	10	66,000

Source: Trade Shows Worldwide, 1998; Meetings & Conventions, 4/15/99; Sucessful Meetings, 3/31/98

Living Environment

COST OF LIVING

Cost of Living Index

Composite Index	Groceries	Housing	Utilities	Trans- portation	Health Care	Misc. Goods/ Services
96.2	99.5	92.0	88.5	92.1	98.7	100.8

Note: U.S. = 100; Figures are for the Metropolitan Statistical Area - see Appendix A for areas included
Source: ACCRA, Cost of Living Index, 1st Quarter 1999

HOUSING

Median Home Prices and Housing Affordability

Area	Median Price[2] 1st Qtr. 1999 ($)	HOI[3] 1st Qtr. 1999	Afford- ability Rank[4]
MSA[1]	109,000	80.5	50
U.S.	134,000	69.6	–

Note: (1) Metropolitan Statistical Area - see Appendix A for areas included; (2) U.S. figures calculated from the sales of 524,324 new and existing homes in 181 markets; (3) Housing Opportunity Index - percent of homes sold that were within the reach of the median income household at the prevailing mortgage interest rate; (4) Rank is from 1-181 with 1 being most affordable
Source: National Association of Home Builders, Housing Opportunity Index, 1st Quarter 1999

Median Home Price Projection

It is projected that the median price of existing single-family homes in the metro area will decrease by -1.0% in 1999. Nationwide, home prices are projected to increase 3.8%.
Kiplinger's Personal Finance Magazine, January 1999

Average New Home Price

Area	Price ($)
MSA[1]	125,289
U.S.	142,735

Note: Figures are based on a new home with 1,800 sq. ft. of living area on an 8,000 sq. ft. lot; (1) Metropolitan Statistical Area - see Appendix A for areas included
Source: ACCRA, Cost of Living Index, 1st Quarter 1999

Average Apartment Rent

Area	Rent ($/mth)
MSA[1]	673
U.S.	601

Note: Figures are based on an unfurnished two bedroom, 1-1/2 or 2 bath apartment, approximately 950 sq. ft. in size, excluding all utilities except water; (1) Metropolitan Statistical Area - see Appendix A for areas included
Source: ACCRA, Cost of Living Index, 1st Quarter 1999

RESIDENTIAL UTILITIES

Average Residential Utility Costs

Area	All Electric ($/mth)	Part Electric ($/mth)	Other Energy ($/mth)	Phone ($/mth)
MSA[1]	–	32.96	49.13	24.89
U.S.	100.02	55.73	43.33	19.71

Note: (1) (1) Metropolitan Statistical Area - see Appendix A for areas included
Source: ACCRA, Cost of Living Index, 1st Quarter 1999

HEALTH CARE

Average Health Care Costs

Area	Hospital ($/day)	Doctor ($/visit)	Dentist ($/visit)
MSA[1]	387.13	51.25	67.40
U.S.	430.43	52.45	66.35

Note: Hospital—based on a semi-private room; Doctor—based on a general practitioner's routine exam of an established patient; Dentist—based on adult teeth cleaning and periodic oral exam; (1) Metropolitan Statistical Area - see Appendix A for areas included
Source: ACCRA, Cost of Living Index, 1st Quarter 1999

Distribution of Office-Based Physicians

Area	Family/Gen. Practitioners	Specialists Medical	Surgical	Other
MSA[1]	135	382	296	380

Note: Data as of 12/31/97; (1) Metropolitan Statistical Area - see Appendix A for areas included
Source: American Medical Assn., Physician Characteristics & Distribution in the U.S., 1999

Hospitals

Lexington has 6 general medical and surgical hospitals, 3 psychiatric, 1 rehabilitation, 1 children's orthopedic. *AHA Guide to the Healthcare Field, 1998-99*

According to *U.S. News and World Report,* Lexington has 1 of the best hospitals in the U.S.: **University of Kentucky Hospital,** noted for cancer, gynecology, urology. *U.S. News Online, "America's Best Hospitals," 10th Edition, www.usnews.com*

EDUCATION

Public School District Statistics

District Name	Num. Sch.	Enroll.	Classroom Teachers	Pupils per Teacher	Minority Pupils (%)	Current Exp.[1] ($/pupil)
Central Ky St Voc Tech Sch	n/a	n/a	n/a	n/a	n/a	n/a
Fayette Co	63	34,337	2,147	16.0	n/a	n/a

Note: Data covers the 1997-1998 school year unless otherwise noted; (1) Data covers fiscal year 1996; SD = School District; ISD = Independent School District; n/a not available
Source: National Center for Education Statistics, Common Core of Data Public Education Agency Universe 1997-98; National Center for Education Statistics, Characteristics of the 100 Largest Public Elementary and Secondary School Districts in the United States: 1997-98, July 1999

Educational Quality

School District	Education Quotient[1]	Graduate Outcome[2]	Community Index[3]	Resource Index[4]
Fayette County	114.0	118.0	111.0	108.0

Note: Nearly 1,000 secondary school districts were rated in terms of educational quality. The scores range from a low of 50 to a high of 150; (1) Average of the Graduate Outcome, Community and Resource indexes; (2) Based on graduation rates and college board scores (SAT/ACT); (3) Based on the surrounding community's average level of education and the area's average income level; (4) Based on teacher salaries, per-pupil expenditures and student-teacher ratios.
Source: Expansion Management, Ratings Issue, 1998

Educational Attainment by Race

Area	High School Graduate (%) Total	White	Black	Other	Hisp.[2]	Bachelor's Degree (%) Total	White	Black	Other	Hisp.[2]
City	80.2	82.5	63.1	86.6	72.4	30.6	32.8	10.3	59.5	24.4
MSA[1]	75.9	77.3	61.8	84.6	72.5	25.3	26.7	9.2	55.8	22.9
U.S.	75.2	77.9	63.1	60.4	49.8	20.3	21.5	11.4	19.4	9.2

Note: Figures shown cover persons 25 years old and over; (1) Metropolitan Statistical Area - see Appendix A for areas included; (2) people of Hispanic origin can be of any race
Source: 1990 Census of Population and Housing, Summary Tape File 3C

School Enrollment by Type

Area	Preprimary				Elementary/High School			
	Public		Private		Public		Private	
	Enrollment	%	Enrollment	%	Enrollment	%	Enrollment	%
City	1,718	45.0	2,100	55.0	29,574	90.0	3,284	10.0
MSA[1]	2,832	50.7	2,759	49.3	50,759	91.9	4,490	8.1
U.S.	2,679,029	59.5	1,824,256	40.5	38,379,689	90.2	4,187,099	9.8

Note: Figures shown cover persons 3 years old and over;
(1) Metropolitan Statistical Area - see Appendix A for areas included
Source: 1990 Census of Population and Housing, Summary Tape File 3C

School Enrollment by Race

Area	Preprimary (%)				Elementary/High School (%)			
	White	Black	Other	Hisp.[1]	White	Black	Other	Hisp.[1]
City	83.6	13.3	3.1	0.7	77.4	20.3	2.3	1.1
MSA[2]	86.2	11.1	2.7	0.7	83.7	14.7	1.7	0.9
U.S.	80.4	12.5	7.1	7.8	74.1	15.6	10.3	12.5

Note: Figures shown cover persons 3 years old and over; (1) people of Hispanic origin can be of any race; (2) Metropolitan Statistical Area - see Appendix A for areas included
Source: 1990 Census of Population and Housing, Summary Tape File 3C

Classroom Teacher Salaries in Public Schools

District	B.A. Degree		M.A. Degree		Maximum	
	Min. ($)	Rank[1]	Max. ($)	Rank[1]	Max. ($)	Rank[1]
Lexington	23,984	82	41,415	81	48,054	65
Average	26,980	-	46,065	-	51,435	-

Note: Salaries are for 1997-1998; (1) Rank ranges from 1 to 100
Source: American Federation of Teachers, Survey & Analysis of Salary Trends, 1998

Higher Education

Two-Year Colleges		Four-Year Colleges		Medical Schools	Law Schools	Voc/Tech
Public	Private	Public	Private			
1	3	1	2	1	1	6

Source: College Blue Book, Occupational Education, 1997; Medical School Admission Requirements, 1999-2000; Peterson's Guide to Two-Year Colleges, 1999; Peterson's Guide to Four-Year Colleges, 2000; Barron's Guide to Law Schools, 1999

MAJOR EMPLOYERS

Major Employers

Gall's Inc. (catalog & mail order)
Health Associates of Kentucky
Lexington Herald-Leader Co.
Link-Belt Construction Equip.
Lexmark International (computer equipment)
Interim Personnel of Central Kentucky
SuperAmerica Corp. (gasoline service stations)
Jimmy John's (eating places)
University of Kentucky Hospital
Phycor of Kentucky (medical clinics)

Note: Companies listed are located in the city
Source: Dun's Business Rankings, 1999; Ward's Business Directory, 1998

PUBLIC SAFETY

Crime Rate

Area	All Crimes	Violent Crimes				Property Crimes		
		Murder	Forcible Rape	Robbery	Aggrav. Assault	Burglary	Larceny -Theft	Motor Vehicle Theft
City	6,250.0	9.9	53.2	239.0	492.5	1,075.7	4,006.3	373.4
Suburbs[1]	n/a	n/a	n/a	n/a	n/a	n/a	n/a	n/a
MSA[2]	n/a	n/a	n/a	n/a	n/a	n/a	n/a	n/a
U.S.	4,922.7	6.8	35.9	186.1	382.0	919.6	2,886.5	505.8

Note: Crime rate is the number of crimes per 100,000 pop.; (1) defined as all areas within the MSA but located outside the central city; (2) Metropolitan Statistical Area - see Appendix A for areas incl.
Source: FBI Uniform Crime Reports, 1997

RECREATION

Culture and Recreation

Museums	Symphony Orchestras	Opera Companies	Dance Companies	Professional Theatres	Zoos	Pro Sports Teams
8	1	0	1	1	0	0

Source: International Directory of the Performing Arts, 1997; Official Museum Directory, 1999; Stern's Performing Arts Directory, 1997; USA Today Four Sport Stadium Guide, 1997; Chamber of Commerce/Economic Development, 1999

Library System

The Lexington Public Library has four branches, holdings of 605,543 volumes, and a budget of $7,455,469 (1996-1997). *American Library Directory, 1998-1999*

MEDIA

Newspapers

Name	Type	Freq.	Distribution	Circulation
The Kentucky Kernel	General	5x/wk	Camp/Comm	17,000
Lexington Herald-Leader	n/a	7x/wk	Area	130,000

Note: Includes newspapers with circulations of 1,000 or more located in the city; n/a not available
Source: Burrelle's Media Directory, 1999 Edition

Television Stations

Name	Ch.	Affiliation	Type	Owner
WLEX	18	NBCT	Commercial	Evening Post Publishing
WKMU	21	PBS	Public	Kentucky Authority for Educational TV
WKPI	22	PBS	Public	Kentucky Authority for Educational TV
WKZT	23	PBS	Public	Kentucky Authority for Educational TV
WKAS	25	PBS	Public	Kentucky Authority for Educational TV
WKYT	27	CBST	Commercial	Gray Kentucky Television
WKPD	29	PBS	Public	Kentucky Authority for Educational TV
WKSO	29	PBS	Public	Kentucky Authority for Educational TV
WKON	31	PBS	Public	Kentucky Authority for Educational TV
WKHA	35	PBS	Public	Kentucky Authority for Educational TV
WKMA	35	PBS	Public	Kentucky Authority for Educational TV
WTVQ	36	ABCT	Commercial	Media General Inc.
WKMR	38	PBS	Public	Kentucky Authority for Educational TV
WKLE	46	PBS	Public	Kentucky Authority for Educational TV
WKOH	52	PBS	Public	Kentucky Authority for Educational TV
WKGB	53	PBS	Public	Kentucky Authority for Educational TV
WCVN	54	PBS	Public	Kentucky Authority for Educational TV
WDKY	56	FBC	Commercial	Superior Communications Group Inc.
WKMJ	68	PBS	Public	Kentucky Authority for Educational TV

Note: Stations included broadcast in the Lexington metro area; n/a not available
Source: Burrelle's Media Directory, 1999 Edition

AM Radio Stations

Call Letters	Freq. (kHz)	Target Audience	Station Format	Music Format
WVLK	590	General	M	Adult Contemporary
WLAP	630	General	N/S/T	n/a
WCGW	770	General	M/N/S/T	Christian
WLXG	1300	General	N/S/T	n/a
WMJR	1380	Religious	M/T	Christian

Note: Stations included broadcast in the Lexington metro area; n/a not available
Target Audience: A=Asian; B=Black; C=Christian; E=Ethnic; F=French; G=General; H=Hispanic; M=Men; N=Native American; R=Religious; S=Senior Citizen; W=Women; Y=Young Adult; Z=Children
Station Format: E=Educational; M=Music; N=News; S=Sports; T=Talk
Source: Burrelle's Media Directory, 1999 Edition

FM Radio Stations

Call Letters	Freq. (mHz)	Target Audience	Station Format	Music Format
WRFL	88.1	General	M/N	Alternative
WUKY	91.3	General	M/N/S	Big Band/Jazz
WVLK	92.9	General	M/N/S	Country
WMXL	94.5	Women	M	Adult Contemporary
WKYI	96.1	n/a	n/a	n/a
WGKS	96.9	General	M	Adult Contemporary
WKQQ	98.1	General	M/N/S	AOR/Classic Rock/Jazz/Oldies
WMDJ	100.1	General	M/N/S	Classic Rock/Classical/Country
WLRO	101.5	General	M/N/S	Classic Rock/Oldies
WLTO	102.5	General	M	Oldies/R&B
WCDA	106.3	General	n/a	n/a

Note: Stations included broadcast in the Lexington metro area; n/a not available
Station Format: E=Educational; M=Music; N=News; S=Sports; T=Talk
Target Audience: A=Asian; B=Black; C=Christian; E=Ethnic; F=French; G=General; H=Hispanic;
M=Men; N=Native American; R=Religious; S=Senior Citizen; W=Women; Y=Young Adult; Z=Children
Music Format: AOR=Album Oriented Rock; MOR=Middle-of-the-Road
Source: Burrelle's Media Directory, 1999 Edition

CLIMATE

Average and Extreme Temperatures

Temperature	Jan	Feb	Mar	Apr	May	Jun	Jul	Aug	Sep	Oct	Nov	Dec	Yr.
Extreme High (°F)	76	75	82	88	92	101	103	103	103	91	83	75	103
Average High (°F)	40	44	54	66	75	83	86	85	79	68	55	44	65
Average Temp. (°F)	32	36	45	55	64	73	76	75	69	57	46	36	55
Average Low (°F)	24	26	34	44	54	62	66	65	58	46	36	28	45
Extreme Low (°F)	-21	-15	-2	18	26	39	47	42	35	20	-3	-19	-21

Note: Figures cover the years 1948-1990
Source: National Climatic Data Center, International Station Meteorological Climate Summary, 3/95

Average Precipitation/Snowfall/Humidity

Precip./Humidity	Jan	Feb	Mar	Apr	May	Jun	Jul	Aug	Sep	Oct	Nov	Dec	Yr.
Avg. Precip. (in.)	3.6	3.4	4.4	3.9	4.3	4.0	4.8	3.7	3.0	2.4	3.5	3.9	45.1
Avg. Snowfall (in.)	6	5	3	Tr	Tr	0	0	0	0	Tr	1	3	17
Avg. Rel. Hum. 7am (%)	81	80	77	75	78	80	83	85	85	83	81	81	81
Avg. Rel. Hum. 4pm (%)	67	61	55	51	54	54	56	55	54	53	60	66	57

Note: Figures cover the years 1948-1990; Tr = Trace amounts (<0.05 in. of rain; <0.5 in. of snow)
Source: National Climatic Data Center, International Station Meteorological Climate Summary, 3/95

Weather Conditions

Temperature			Daytime Sky			Precipitation		
10°F & below	32°F & below	90°F & above	Clear	Partly cloudy	Cloudy	0.01 inch or more precip.	0.1 inch or more snow/ice	Thunder-storms
11	96	22	86	136	143	129	17	44

Note: Figures are average number of days per year and covers the years 1948-1990
Source: National Climatic Data Center, International Station Meteorological Climate Summary, 3/95

AIR & WATER QUALITY

Maximum Pollutant Concentrations

	Particulate Matter (ug/m³)	Carbon Monoxide (ppm)	Sulfur Dioxide (ppm)	Nitrogen Dioxide (ppm)	Ozone (ppm)	Lead (ug/m³)
MSA[1] Level	62	5	0.016	0.014	0.10	0.02
NAAQS[2]	150	9	0.140	0.053	0.12	1.50
Met NAAQS?	Yes	Yes	Yes	Yes	Yes	Yes

Note: (1) Metropolitan Statistical Area - see Appendix A for areas included; (2) National Ambient Air Quality Standards; ppm = parts per million; ug/m³ = micrograms per cubic meter; n/a not available
Source: EPA, National Air Quality and Emissions Trends Report, 1997

Drinking Water

Water System Name	Pop. Served	Primary Water Source Type	Number of Violations in 1998	Type of Violation/ Contaminants
Kentucky-American Water Co.	281,094	Surface	None	None

Note: Data as of July 10, 1999
Source: EPA, Office of Ground Water and Drinking Water, Safe Drinking Water Information System

Lexington tap water is alkaline, medium and fluoridated.
Editor & Publisher Market Guide, 1999

Louisville, Kentucky

Background

Louisville began in 1778, when George Rogers Clark, on his way to capture British Fort Vincennes, established a base on an island above the Falls of the Ohio River. Shortly thereafter a settlement grew on the south side of the river. Two years later the Virginia state legislature named the town Louisville to pay homage to King Louis XIV of France, who had allied his country with America during the American Revolution.

The Falls forced people traveling down the Ohio to use the portage of Louisville, which helped the town grow in the early nineteenth century. Kentucky incorporated the town as a city in 1828. Two years later, the Portland Canal opened, allowing boats to go around the rapids. River traffic increased, assisting the city's growth. In the next several years the coming of the railroad would link the town to the much of the rest of the South. The cultivation of tobacco became important to the state in the 1830s and Louisville became an important processing site.

The Civil War was an interesting period in the city's history, as adherents to both the North and the South walked the city's streets. Yet the North had the upper hand, and Louisville quickly became a supply center for Union armies marching south.

The postwar period saw boom times for Louisville, and by the end of the nineteenth century the city's population topped 200,000. The city received a setback in 1937, when the Ohio River invaded the city's environs. Subsequently, a floodwall was built to prevent such a catastrophe from reoccurring. World War II saw the city rebound, as it became an important center for the production of munitions. After the war, the city desegregated its schools in a calm fashion, without the trouble seen in so many other areas.

The annual Run for the Roses horserace, The Kentucky Derby, has been hosted by Louisville since 1875, earning the city the nickname, Derby Town.

Although the city suffered the loss of some industries in the economic crunch of the 1980s, it still is a major center for manufacturing. The tobacco processing and production industry is still a vital part of the local economy, as is the distillation of gin and whiskey. Two Ford Motors factories, producing trucks and utility vehicles, are in Louisville. Other area concerns produce baseball bats, chemicals, paint, and electrical appliances.

The city serves as an important corporate command post. The headquarters of four Fortune 500 Companies are located in Louisville: Tricon Global Restaurants, Humana, Vencor, and LG&E Energy Corporation. Many other businesses also direct their operations from the city.

Louisville has maintained its importance as a vital center of transportation. The metropolitan area has two ports on the Ohio River; three interstate highways intersect the city; and it also has an international airport. The airport serves as the center for United Parcel Service's international flights. The Louisville metro area has many incentives to offer new businesses. These include a Foreign Trade Zone and an Enterprise Zone.

The city's climate is a typical continental one. Temperatures range in the winter from the twenties to the fifties, and in the summer from the fifties to the eighties. The yearly average rainfall is forty-four inches, a significant proportion of which comes in March. Snowfall tends to be around sixteen inches, much of it coming during the months of November through March.

General Rankings and Evaluative Comments

■ Louisville was ranked #5 out of 44 mid-sized, southern metropolitan areas in *Money's* 1998 survey of "The Best Places to Live in America." The survey was conducted by first contacting 512 representative households nationwide and asking them to rank 37 quality-of-life factors on a scale of 1 to 10. Next, a demographic profile was compiled on the 300 largest metropolitan statistical areas in the U.S. The numbers were crunched together to arrive at an overall ranking (things Americans consider most important, like clean air and water, low crime and good schools, received extra weight). Unlike previous years, the 1998 rankings were broken down by region (northeast, midwest, south, west) and population size (100,000 to 249,999; 250,000 to 999,999; 1 million plus). The city had a nationwide ranking of #280 out of 300 in 1997 and #234 out of 300 in 1996. *Money, July 1998; Money, July 1997; Money, September 1996*

■ *Ladies Home Journal* ranked America's 200 largest cities based on the qualities women care about most. Louisville ranked #125 out of 200. Criteria: low crime rate, well-paying jobs, quality health and child care, good public schools, the presence of women in government, size of the gender wage gap, number of sexual-harassment and discrimination complaints filed, unemployment and divorce rates, commute times, population density, number of houses of worship, parks and cultural offerings, number of women's health specialists, how well a community's women cared for themselves, complexion kindness index based on UV radiation levels, odds of finding affordable fashions, rental rates for romance movies, champagne sales and other matters of the heart. *Ladies Home Journal, November 1998*

■ Zero Population Growth ranked 229 cities in terms of children's health, safety, and economic well-being. Louisville was ranked #73 out of 112 independent cities (cities with populations greater than 100,000 which were neither Major Cities nor Suburbs/Outer Cities) and was given a grade of C-. Criteria: total population, percent of population under 18 years of age, household language, percent population change, percent of births to teens, infant mortality rate, percent of low birth weights, dropout rate, enrollment in preprimary school, violent and property crime rates, unemployment rate, percent of children in poverty, percent of owner occupied units, number of bad air days, percent of public transportation commuters, and average travel time to work. *Zero Population Growth, Children's Environmental Index, Fall 1999*

■ Louisville was ranked #31 out of 59 metro areas in *The Regional Economist's* "Rational Livability Ranking of 59 Large Metro Areas." The rankings were based on the metro area's total population change over the period 1990-97 divided by the number of people moving in from elsewhere in the United States (net domestic in-migration). *St. Louis Federal Reserve Bank of St. Louis, The Regional Economist, April 1999*

■ Louisville was selected by *Yahoo! Internet Life* as one of "America's Most Wired Cities & Towns." The city ranked #49 out of 50. Criteria: home and work net use, domain density, hosts per capita, directory density and content quality. *Yahoo! Internet Life, March 1999*

■ Cognetics studied 273 metro areas in the United States, ranking them by entrepreneurial activity. Louisville was ranked #16 out of the 50 largest metro areas. Criteria: Significant Starts (firms started in the last 10 years that still employ at least 5 people) and Young Growers (percent of firms 10 years old or less that grew significantly during the last 4 years). *Cognetics, "Entrepreneurial Hot Spots: The Best Places in America to Start and Grow a Company," 1998*

■ Louisville was included among *Entrepreneur* magazine's listing of the "20 Best Cities for Small Business." It was ranked #3 among mid-sized metro areas. Criteria: entrepreneurial activity, small-business growth, economic growth, and risk of failure. *Entrepreneur, October 1999*

■ Louisville was selected as one of the "Best American Cities to Start a Business" by *Point of View* magazine. Criteria: coolness, quality-of-life, and business concerns. The city was ranked #45 out of 75. *Point of View, November 1998*

■ Reliastar Financial Corp. ranked the 125 largest metropolitan areas according to the general financial security of residents. Louisville was ranked #64 out of 125 with a score of 1.6. The score indicates the percentage a metropolitan area is above or below the metropolitan norm. A metro area with a score of 10.6 is 10.6% above the metro average. Criteria: Earnings and Wealth Potential (household income, education, net assets, cost of living); Safety Net (health insurance, retirement savings, life insurance, income support programs); Personal Threats (unemployment rate, low-income households, crime rate); Community Economic Vitality (cost of community services, job quality, job creation, housing costs).
Reliastar Financial Corp., "The Best Cities to Earn and Save Money," 1999 Edition

Business Environment

STATE ECONOMY

State Economic Profile

"Kentucky has trailed the nation by a narrow margin in recent years. A continued slowdown in its manufacturing sector and weak population growth will widen that difference as Kentucky falls further below the nation in 1999 and 2000. Recent growth in home sales and price appreciation has attracted a tremendous amount of new construction, which will moderate future price appreciation.

The engine behind KY's economy has been Louisville. Almost 60% of state employment gains took place in Louisville, which added jobs at a rate almost twice that of the state. Within Louisville, the job engine has been UPS and associated companies. As the UPS hub, Louisville has managed to attract a wide range of wholesale and distribution companies, helping to offset its weak manufacturing sector.

Lexington has been the other source of growth. Employment gains were 2.4% in 1998, held back by only the extremely tight labor market (unemployment of 1.7%). Manufacturing employment growth in Kentucky will occur mostly in Lexington.

Both Lexington and Louisville witnessed a boom in multifamily housing activity in 1998. Multifamily permits rose over 100% in Louisville and 46% in Lexington. Considering KY's continued loss of younger households, it is likely that KY's rental markets will soften considerably in 1999.

Increased job growth has added relatively little to consumer spending. Job growth has been concentrated among lower-paying occupations, and declines in the unionized sector (especially steel) squeezed household income." *National Association of Realtors, Economic Profiles: The Fifty States and the District of Columbia, http://nar.realtor.com/databank/profiles.htm*

IMPORTS/EXPORTS

Total Export Sales

Area	1994 ($000)	1995 ($000)	1996 ($000)	1997 ($000)	% Chg. 1994-97	% Chg. 1996-97
MSA[1]	1,798,847	2,199,762	2,327,058	2,449,114	36.1	5.2
U.S.	512,415,609	583,030,524	622,827,063	687,597,999	34.2	10.4

Note: (1) Metropolitan Statistical Area - see Appendix A for areas included
Source: U.S. Department of Commerce, International Trade Association, Metropolitan Area Exports: An Export Performance Report on Over 250 U.S. Cities, November 10, 1998

CITY FINANCES

City Government Finances

Component	FY92 ($000)	FY92 (per capita $)
Revenue	316,963	1,183.35
Expenditure	291,317	1,087.60
Debt Outstanding	441,848	1,649.59
Cash & Securities	358,679	1,339.09

Source: U.S. Bureau of the Census, City Government Finances: 1991-92

City Government Revenue by Source

Source	FY92 ($000)	FY92 (per capita $)	FY92 (%)
From Federal Government	20,553	76.73	6.5
From State Governments	23,974	89.50	7.6
From Local Governments	12,235	45.68	3.9
Property Taxes	38,302	143.00	12.1
General Sales Taxes	0	0.00	0.0
Selective Sales Taxes	988	3.69	0.3
Income Taxes	88,543	330.57	27.9
Current Charges	21,336	79.66	6.7
Utility/Liquor Store	62,314	232.64	19.7
Employee Retirement[1]	0	0.00	0.0
Other	48,718	181.88	15.4

Note: (1) Excludes "city contributions," classified as "nonrevenue," intragovernmental transfers.
Source: U.S. Bureau of the Census, City Government Finances: 1991-92

City Government Expenditures by Function

Function	FY92 ($000)	FY92 (per capita $)	FY92 (%)
Educational Services	8,053	30.06	2.8
Employee Retirement[1]	0	0.00	0.0
Environment/Housing	52,665	196.62	18.1
Government Administration	14,106	52.66	4.8
Interest on General Debt	37,838	141.26	13.0
Public Safety	59,473	222.04	20.4
Social Services	18,059	67.42	6.2
Transportation	20,487	76.49	7.0
Utility/Liquor Store	36,603	136.65	12.6
Other	44,033	164.39	15.1

Note: (1) Payments to beneficiaries including withdrawal of contributions.
Source: U.S. Bureau of the Census, City Government Finances: 1991-92

Municipal Bond Ratings

Area	Moody's	S & P
Louisville	Aa3	n/a

Note: n/a not available; n/r not rated
Source: Moody's Bond Record, 6/99

POPULATION

Population Growth

Area	1980	1990	% Chg. 1980-90	July 1998 Estimate	% Chg. 1990-98
City	298,455	269,157	-9.8	255,045	-5.2
MSA[1]	956,756	952,662	-0.4	1,006,017	5.6
U.S.	226,545,805	248,765,170	9.8	270,299,000	8.7

Note: (1) Metropolitan Statistical Area - see Appendix A for areas included;
July 1998 MSA population estimate was calculated by the editors
Source: 1980/1990 Census of Housing and Population, Summary Tape File 3C;
Census Bureau Population Estimates 1998

Population Characteristics

Race	City 1980 Population	%	City 1990 Population	%	% Chg. 1980-90	MSA[1] 1990 Population	%
White	212,052	71.0	186,141	69.2	-12.2	818,577	85.9
Black	84,254	28.2	79,892	29.7	-5.2	124,711	13.1
Amer Indian/Esk/Aleut	408	0.1	694	0.3	70.1	1,767	0.2
Asian/Pacific Islander	1,327	0.4	2,006	0.7	51.2	6,045	0.6
Other	414	0.1	424	0.2	2.4	1,562	0.2
Hispanic Origin[2]	2,005	0.7	1,490	0.6	-25.7	4,979	0.5

Note: (1) Metropolitan Statistical Area - see Appendix A for areas included;
(2) people of Hispanic origin can be of any race
Source: 1980/1990 Census of Housing and Population, Summary Tape File 3C

Ancestry

Area	German	Irish	English	Italian	U.S.	French	Polish	Dutch
City	24.9	17.4	11.7	1.8	9.1	2.8	0.8	1.8
MSA[1]	31.8	20.8	14.7	2.1	10.4	3.7	1.0	2.4
U.S.	23.3	15.6	13.1	5.9	5.3	4.2	3.8	2.5

Note: Figures are percentages and include persons that reported multiple ancestry (eg. if a person reported being Irish and Italian, they were included in both columns); (1) Metropolitan Statistical Area - see Appendix A for areas included
Source: 1990 Census of Population and Housing, Summary Tape File 3C

Age

Area	Median Age (Years)	Age Distribution (%) Under 5	Under 18	18-24	25-44	45-64	65+	80+
City	34.3	6.8	23.5	9.9	31.9	18.2	16.6	4.3
MSA[1]	33.8	6.8	25.3	9.4	33.1	19.6	12.6	2.8
U.S.	32.9	7.3	25.6	10.5	32.6	18.7	12.5	2.8

Note: (1) Metropolitan Statistical Area - see Appendix A for areas included
Source: 1990 Census of Population and Housing, Summary Tape File 3C

Male/Female Ratio

Area	Number of males per 100 females (all ages)	Number of males per 100 females (18 years old+)
City	86.1	81.1
MSA[1]	91.1	86.8
U.S.	95.0	91.9

Note: (1) Metropolitan Statistical Area - see Appendix A for areas included
Source: 1990 Census of Population, General Population Characteristics

INCOME

Per Capita/Median/Average Income

Area	Per Capita ($)	Median Household ($)	Average Household ($)
City	11,527	20,141	26,993
MSA[1]	13,600	27,599	34,899
U.S.	14,420	30,056	38,453

Note: All figures are for 1989; (1) Metropolitan Statistical Area - see Appendix A for areas included
Source: 1990 Census of Population and Housing, Summary Tape File 3C

Household Income Distribution by Race

Income ($)	City (%)					U.S. (%)				
	Total	White	Black	Other	Hisp.[1]	Total	White	Black	Other	Hisp.[1]
Less than 5,000	13.0	8.5	24.9	25.1	17.7	6.2	4.8	15.2	8.6	8.8
5,000 - 9,999	14.2	12.8	18.3	11.8	9.6	9.3	8.6	14.2	9.9	11.1
10,000 - 14,999	11.8	11.3	12.9	18.8	11.3	8.8	8.5	11.0	9.8	11.0
15,000 - 24,999	20.2	21.2	17.8	14.7	19.4	17.5	17.3	18.9	18.5	20.5
25,000 - 34,999	14.9	16.5	10.6	11.2	15.3	15.8	16.1	14.2	15.4	16.4
35,000 - 49,999	13.3	14.7	9.7	11.0	17.0	17.9	18.6	13.3	16.1	16.0
50,000 - 74,999	8.5	10.1	4.5	5.4	1.1	15.0	15.8	9.3	13.4	11.1
75,000 - 99,999	2.1	2.6	0.9	1.0	3.8	5.1	5.5	2.6	4.7	3.1
100,000+	1.9	2.4	0.5	1.1	4.9	4.4	4.8	1.3	3.7	1.9

Note: All figures are for 1989; (1) people of Hispanic origin can be of any race
Source: 1990 Census of Population and Housing, Summary Tape File 3C

Effective Buying Income

Area	Per Capita ($)	Median Household ($)	Average Household ($)
City	14,544	25,558	34,024
MSA[1]	17,462	34,318	44,430
U.S.	16,803	34,536	45,243

Note: Data as of 1/1/99; (1) Metropolitan Statistical Area - see Appendix A for areas included
Source: Standard Rate & Data Service, Newspaper Advertising Source, 9/99

Effective Household Buying Income Distribution

Area	% of Households Earning						
	$10,000 -$19,999	$20,000 -$34,999	$35,000 -$49,999	$50,000 -$74,999	$75,000 -$99,000	$100,000 -$124,999	$125,000 and up
City	20.3	24.0	15.4	13.1	4.3	1.3	1.5
MSA[1]	15.8	23.0	18.5	19.1	7.1	2.2	2.2
U.S.	16.0	22.6	18.2	18.9	7.2	2.4	2.7

Note: Data as of 1/1/99; (1) Metropolitan Statistical Area - see Appendix A for areas included
Source: Standard Rate & Data Service, Newspaper Advertising Source, 9/99

Poverty Rates by Race and Age

Area	Total (%)	By Race (%)				By Age (%)		
		White	Black	Other	Hisp.[2]	Under 5 years old	Under 18 years old	65 years and over
City	22.6	15.0	39.5	40.6	28.8	40.5	35.4	17.0
MSA[1]	12.7	9.4	33.5	20.9	19.7	21.5	18.3	12.6
U.S.	13.1	9.8	29.5	23.1	25.3	20.1	18.3	12.8

Note: Figures show the percent of people living below the poverty line in 1989. The average poverty
threshold was $12,674 for a family of four in 1989; (1) Metropolitan Statistical Area - see Appendix A
for areas included; (2) people of Hispanic origin can be of any race
Source: 1990 Census of Population and Housing, Summary Tape File 3C

EMPLOYMENT

Labor Force and Employment

Area	Civilian Labor Force			Workers Employed		
	Jun. 1998	Jun. 1999	% Chg.	Jun. 1998	Jun. 1999	% Chg.
City	134,103	137,730	2.7	127,500	131,924	3.5
MSA[1]	557,959	577,788	3.6	538,073	554,920	3.1
U.S.	138,798,000	140,666,000	1.3	132,265,000	134,395,000	1.6

Note: Data is not seasonally adjusted and covers workers 16 years of age and older;
(1) Metropolitan Statistical Area - see Appendix A for areas included
Source: Bureau of Labor Statistics, http://stats.bls.gov

Unemployment Rate

Area	1998						1999					
	Jul.	Aug.	Sep.	Oct.	Nov.	Dec.	Jan.	Feb.	Mar.	Apr.	May.	Jun.
City	4.2	4.3	4.3	4.1	3.7	3.2	3.8	4.0	3.9	3.9	4.3	4.2
MSA[1]	3.1	3.1	3.1	3.1	2.8	2.5	3.1	3.0	2.9	2.8	3.2	4.0
U.S.	4.7	4.5	4.4	4.2	4.1	4.0	4.8	4.7	4.4	4.1	4.0	4.5

Note: Data is not seasonally adjusted and covers workers 16 years of age and older; all figures are percentages; (1) Metropolitan Statistical Area - see Appendix A for areas included
Source: Bureau of Labor Statistics, http://stats.bls.gov

Employment by Industry

Sector	MSA[1]		U.S.
	Number of Employees	Percent of Total	Percent of Total
Services	177,400	30.3	30.4
Retail Trade	111,800	19.1	17.7
Government	71,600	12.2	15.6
Manufacturing	88,000	15.0	14.3
Finance/Insurance/Real Estate	30,300	5.2	5.9
Wholesale Trade	32,200	5.5	5.4
Transportation/Public Utilities	43,300	7.4	5.3
Construction	30,700	5.2	5.0
Mining	700	0.1	0.4

Note: Figures cover non-farm employment as of 6/99 and are not seasonally adjusted; (1) Metropolitan Statistical Area - see Appendix A for areas included
Source: Bureau of Labor Statistics, http://stats.bls.gov

Employment by Occupation

Occupation Category	City (%)	MSA[1] (%)	U.S. (%)
White Collar	55.6	57.1	58.1
Executive/Admin./Management	9.7	11.4	12.3
Professional	14.5	12.7	14.1
Technical & Related Support	3.9	3.6	3.7
Sales	10.8	12.5	11.8
Administrative Support/Clerical	16.7	16.9	16.3
Blue Collar	26.2	28.4	26.2
Precision Production/Craft/Repair	9.7	11.5	11.3
Machine Operators/Assem./Insp.	7.6	8.0	6.8
Transportation/Material Movers	4.0	4.4	4.1
Cleaners/Helpers/Laborers	5.0	4.5	3.9
Services	17.4	13.1	13.2
Farming/Forestry/Fishing	0.8	1.4	2.5

Note: Figures cover employed persons 16 years old and over; (1) Metropolitan Statistical Area - see Appendix A for areas included
Source: 1990 Census of Population and Housing, Summary Tape File 3C

Occupational Employment Projections: 1996 - 2006

Occupations Expected to Have the Largest Job Growth (ranked by numerical growth)	Fast-Growing Occupations[1] (ranked by percent growth)
1. Cashiers	1. Personal and home care aides
2. Truck drivers, light	2. Systems analysts
3. General managers & top executives	3. Physical therapists
4. Salespersons, retail	4. Occupational therapists
5. Registered nurses	5. Medical assistants
6. Nursing aides/orderlies/attendants	6. Paralegals
7. Food service workers	7. Home health aides
8. Child care workers, private household	8. Surgical technologists
9. General office clerks	9. Numerical control machine tool oper.
10. Janitors/cleaners/maids, ex. priv. hshld.	10. Dental hygienists

Note: Projections cover Kentucky; (1) Excludes occupations with total job growth less than 300
Source: U.S. Department of Labor, Employment and Training Administration, America's Labor Market Information System (ALMIS)

TAXES

Major State and Local Tax Rates

State Corp. Income (%)	State Personal Income (%)	Residential Property (effective rate per $100)	Sales & Use State (%)	Sales & Use Local (%)	State Gasoline (cents/ gallon)	State Cigarette (cents/ pack)
4.0 - 8.25	2.0 - 6.0	1.12	6.0	None	16.4[a]	3.0[b]

Note: Personal/corporate income, sales, gasoline and cigarette tax rates as of January 1999. Property tax rates as of 1997; (a) Rate is comprised of 15 cents excise and 1.4 cents motor carrier tax. Carriers pay an additional surcharge of 2%; (b) Dealers pay an additional enforcement and administrative fee of 0.1 cent per pack
Source: Federation of Tax Administrators, www.taxadmin.org; Washington D.C. Department of Finance and Revenue, Tax Rates and Tax Burdens in the District of Columbia: A Nationwide Comparison, July 1998; Chamber of Commerce, 1999

Total Taxes Per Capita and as a Percent of Income

Area	Per Capita Income ($)	Per Capita Taxes ($) Total	Federal	State/ Local	Percent of Income (%) Total	Federal	State/ Local
Kentucky	22,643	7,832	5,129	2,703	34.6	22.7	11.9
U.S.	27,876	9,881	6,690	3,191	35.4	24.0	11.4

Note: Figures are for 1998
Source: Tax Foundation, www.taxfoundation.org

Estimated Tax Burden

Area	State Income	Local Income	Property	Sales	Total
Louisville	3,500	1,500	3,000	585	8,585

Note: The numbers are estimates of taxes paid by a married couple with two children and annual earnings of $75,000. Sales tax estimates assume they spend average amounts on food, clothing, household goods and gasoline. Property tax estimates assume they live in a $250,000 home.
Source: Kiplinger's Personal Finance Magazine, October 1998

COMMERCIAL REAL ESTATE

Office Market

Class/ Location	Total Space (sq. ft.)	Vacant Space (sq. ft.)	Vac. Rate (%)	Under Constr. (sq. ft.)	Net Absorp. (sq. ft.)	Rental Rates ($/sq.ft./yr.)
Class A						
CBD	3,536,000	106,000	3.0	n/a	64,000	17.00-21.00
Outside CBD	2,010,000	240,000	11.9	350,000	85,000	16.00-20.00
Class B						
CBD	4,500,000	1,125,000	25.0	n/a	175,000	10.00-15.00
Outside CBD	4,150,000	370,000	8.9	100,000	100,000	11.00-15.00

Note: Data as of 10/98 and covers Louisville; CBD = Central Business District; n/a not available;
Source: Society of Industrial and Office Realtors, 1999 Comparative Statistics of Industrial and Office Real Estate Markets

"The failed merger of Humana will keep several jobs in the Louisville area. Our SIOR reporter anticipates mild increases in absorption. New construction in 1998 will be one of the factors that might cause slight increases in vacancy rates in 1999. Rental rates are expected to increase slightly. Sales prices for all but suburban Class B buildings are expected to remain stable. Class B property sales prices could increase up to five percent. Another year of speculative development is expected in Louisville's east-end. This will be the fastest growing area in the county." *Society of Industrial and Office Realtors, 1999 Comparative Statistics of Industrial and Office Real Estate Markets*

Industrial Market

Location	Total Space (sq. ft.)	Vacant Space (sq. ft.)	Vac. Rate (%)	Under Constr. (sq. ft.)	Net Absorp. (sq. ft.)	Gross Lease ($/sq.ft./yr.)
Central City	7,400,000	300,000	4.1	60,000	170,000	3.20-4.00
Suburban	21,900,000	1,176,500	5.4	844,000	913,500	3.60-5.00

Note: Data as of 10/98 and covers Louisville; n/a not available
Source: Society of Industrial and Office Realtors, 1999 Comparative Statistics of Industrial and Office Real Estate Markets

"Demand for industrial space is expected to remain steady. Large amounts of 1998 construction will be absorbed before 1999 speculative development begins. The regional economy will grow at a reasonable pace. According to our local SIOR reporter, sales prices for warehouse/distribution space will increase up to 10 percent. Lease prices for warehouse/distribution space as well as manufacturing space will increase slightly. Absorption should remain level. The total dollar volume of sales will increase slightly. Low unemployment, a high quality of life, and a pro-growth environment will lead to population increases and industrial expansion. Local tax credits facilitate business expansion. Most of the industrial real estate markets will remain balanced in 1999." *Society of Industrial and Office Realtors, 1999 Comparative Statistics of Industrial and Office Real Estate Markets*

COMMERCIAL UTILITIES

Typical Monthly Electric Bills

Area	Commercial Service ($/month)		Industrial Service ($/month)	
	12 kW demand 1,500 kWh	100 kW demand 30,000 kWh	1,000 kW demand 400,000 kWh	20,000 kW demand 10,000,000 kWh
City[1]	96	1,707[a]	15,291	325,807
U.S.[2]	150	2,174	23,995	508,569

Note: (1) Based on rates in effect January 1, 1998; (2) Based on rates in effect January 1, 1999;
(a) Based on 120 kW demand and 30,000 kWh usage.
Source: Memphis Light, Gas and Water, 1998 Utility Bill Comparisons for Selected U.S. Cities;
Edison Electric Institute, Typical Residential, Commercial and Industrial Bills, Winter 1999

TRANSPORTATION

Transportation Statistics

Average minutes to work	19.5
Interstate highways	I-65; I-64; I-71
Bus lines	
In-city	Transit Authority of River City, 250 vehicles
Inter-city	1
Passenger air service	
Airport	Standiford Field
Airlines	11
Aircraft departures	54,941 (1996)
Enplaned passengers	1,713,487 (1996)
Rail service	Amtrak Thruway Motorcoach Connections
Motor freight carriers	n/a
Major waterways/ports	Ohio River

Source: Editor & Publisher Market Guide, 1999; FAA Airport Activity Statistics, 1997; Amtrak National Time Table, Northeast Timetable, Spring/Summer 1999; 1990 Census of Population and Housing, STF 3C; Chamber of Commerce/Economic Development 1999; Jane's Urban Transport Systems 1999-2000

Means of Transportation to Work

Area	Car/Truck/Van		Public Transportation			Bicycle	Walked	Other Means	Worked at Home
	Drove Alone	Car-pooled	Bus	Subway	Railroad				
City	72.0	13.3	8.3	0.0	0.0	0.2	3.8	0.8	1.5
MSA[1]	79.4	12.8	3.1	0.0	0.0	0.1	2.1	0.7	1.9
U.S.	73.2	13.4	3.0	1.5	0.5	0.4	3.9	1.2	3.0

Note: Figures shown are percentages and only include workers 16 years old and over; (1) Metropolitan Statistical Area - see Appendix A for areas included
Source: 1990 Census of Population and Housing, Summary Tape File 3C

BUSINESSES

Major Business Headquarters

Company Name	1999 Rankings	
	Fortune 500	Forbes 500
Humana	165	-
LG&E Energy	295	-
Tricon Global Restaurants	190	-
Vencor	464	-

Note: Companies listed are located in the city; dashes indicate no ranking
Fortune 500: Companies that produce a 10-K are ranked 1 to 500 based on 1998 revenue
Forbes 500: Private companies are ranked 1 to 500 based on 1997 revenue
Source: Forbes, November 30, 1998; Fortune, April 26, 1999

Fast-Growing Businesses

According to *Inc.*, Louisville is home to three of America's 100 fastest-growing private companies: UniDial Communications, Compression and Accent Marketing Services. Criteria for inclusion: must be an independent, privately-held, U.S. corporation, proprietorship or partnership; sales of at least $200,000 in 1995; five-year operating/sales history; increase in 1999 sales over 1998 sales; holding companies, regulated banks, and utilities were excluded. Inc. 500, 1999

Minority Business Opportunity

Louisville is home to four companies which are on the Black Enterprise Industrial/Service 100 list (largest based on gross sales): Active Transportation (transportation services); Dallas & Mavis Specialized Carrier Co. (transporation, warehousing, logistics); Bridgeman Foods (Wendy's franchisee); Automotive Carrier Services (transportation and logistics) . Criteria: operational in previous calendar year, at least 51% black-owned and manufactures/owns the product it sells or provides industrial or consumer services. Brokerages, real estate firms and firms that provide professional services are not eligible. *Black Enterprise, www.blackenterprise.com*

Louisville is home to one company which is on the Black Enterprise Auto Dealer 100 list (largest based on gross sales): Winston Pittman Enterprises (Toyota, Dodge) . Criteria: 1) operational in previous calendar year; 2) at least 51% black-owned. *Black Enterprise, www.blackenterprise.com*

Small Business Opportunity

According to *Forbes*, Louisville is home to one of America's 200 best small companies: Churchill Downs. Criteria: companies included must be publicly traded since November 1997 with a stock price of at least $5 per share and an average daily float of 1,000 shares. The company's latest 12-month sales must be between $5 and $350 million, return on equity (ROE) must be a minimum of 12% for both the past 5 years and the most recent four quarters, and five-year sales and EPS growth must average at least 10%. Companies with declining sales or earnings during the past year were dropped as well as businesses with debt/equity ratios over 1.25. Companies with negative operating cash flow in each of the past two years were also excluded. *Forbes, November 2, 1998*

HOTELS & MOTELS

Hotels/Motels

Area	Hotels/ Motels	Rooms	Luxury-Level Hotels/Motels		Average Minimum Rates ($)		
			◆◆◆◆	◆◆◆◆◆	◆◆	◆◆◆	◆◆◆◆
City	37	6,803	1	0	72	86	164
Airport	14	2,762	0	0	n/a	n/a	n/a
Suburbs	12	1,584	0	0	n/a	n/a	n/a
Total	63	11,149	1	0	n/a	n/a	n/a

Note: n/a not available; classifications range from one diamond (budget properties with basic amenities) to five diamond (luxury properties with the finest service, rooms and facilities).
Source: OAG, Business Travel Planner, Winter 1998-99

CONVENTION CENTERS

Major Convention Centers

Center Name	Meeting Rooms	Exhibit Space (sq. ft.)
Commonwealth Convention Center	37	100,000
Galt House Hotel	n/a	170,000
Kentucky Fair & Exposition Center	23	830,000
Louisville Gardens	4	22,500
Seelbach Hilton	19	n/a

Note: n/a not available
Source: Trade Shows Worldwide, 1998; Meetings & Conventions, 4/15/99;
Sucessful Meetings, 3/31/98

Living Environment

COST OF LIVING

Cost of Living Index

Composite Index	Groceries	Housing	Utilities	Trans- portation	Health Care	Misc. Goods/ Services
96.5	97.0	90.8	96.1	111.5	89.9	97.7

Note: U.S. = 100
Source: ACCRA, Cost of Living Index, 1st Quarter 1999

HOUSING

Median Home Prices and Housing Affordability

Area	Median Price[2] 1st Qtr. 1999 ($)	HOI[3] 1st Qtr. 1999	Afford- ability Rank[4]
MSA[1]	110,000	76.0	87
U.S.	134,000	69.6	–

Note: (1) Metropolitan Statistical Area - see Appendix A for areas included; (2) U.S. figures calculated from the sales of 524,324 new and existing homes in 181 markets; (3) Housing Opportunity Index - percent of homes sold that were within the reach of the median income household at the prevailing mortgage interest rate; (4) Rank is from 1-181 with 1 being most affordable
Source: National Association of Home Builders, Housing Opportunity Index, 1st Quarter 1999

Median Home Price Projection

It is projected that the median price of existing single-family homes in the metro area will increase by 2.1% in 1999. Nationwide, home prices are projected to increase 3.8%.
Kiplinger's Personal Finance Magazine, January 1999

Average New Home Price

Area	Price ($)
City	126,300
U.S.	142,735

Note: Figures are based on a new home with 1,800 sq. ft. of living area on an 8,000 sq. ft. lot.
Source: ACCRA, Cost of Living Index, 1st Quarter 1999

Average Apartment Rent

Area	Rent ($/mth)
City	609
U.S.	601

Note: Figures are based on an unfurnished two bedroom, 1-1/2 or 2 bath apartment, approximately 950 sq. ft. in size, excluding all utilities except water
Source: ACCRA, Cost of Living Index, 1st Quarter 1999

RESIDENTIAL UTILITIES

Average Residential Utility Costs

Area	All Electric ($/mth)	Part Electric ($/mth)	Other Energy ($/mth)	Phone ($/mth)
City	–	41.92	48.58	25.31
U.S.	100.02	55.73	43.33	19.71

Source: ACCRA, Cost of Living Index, 1st Quarter 1999

HEALTH CARE

Average Health Care Costs

Area	Hospital ($/day)	Doctor ($/visit)	Dentist ($/visit)
City	345.47	53.15	54.30
U.S.	430.43	52.45	66.35

Note: Hospital—based on a semi-private room; Doctor—based on a general practitioner's routine exam of an established patient; Dentist—based on adult teeth cleaning and periodic oral exam.
Source: ACCRA, Cost of Living Index, 1st Quarter 1999

Distribution of Office-Based Physicians

Area	Family/Gen. Practitioners	Specialists		
		Medical	Surgical	Other
MSA[1]	266	714	575	596

Note: Data as of 12/31/97; (1) Metropolitan Statistical Area - see Appendix A for areas included
Source: American Medical Assn., Physician Characteristics & Distribution in the U.S., 1999

Hospitals

Louisville has 1 general medical and surgical hospital, 4 psychiatric, 1 rehabilitation. *AHA Guide to the Healthcare Field, 1998-99*

According to *U.S. News and World Report,* Louisville has 2 of the best hospitals in the U.S.: **Jewish Hospital**, noted for neurology, pulmonology; **University of Louisville Hospital**, noted for rheumatology. *U.S. News Online, "America's Best Hospitals," 10th Edition, www.usnews.com*

EDUCATION

Public School District Statistics

District Name	Num. Sch.	Enroll.	Classroom Teachers	Pupils per Teacher	Minority Pupils (%)	Current Exp.[1] ($/pupil)
Jefferson Co	165	104,338	5,415	19.3	36.4	5,565
Jefferson St Voc Tech Sch	n/a	n/a	n/a	n/a	n/a	n/a
Ky School For The Blind	n/a	n/a	n/a	n/a	n/a	n/a

Note: Data covers the 1997-1998 school year unless otherwise noted; (1) Data covers fiscal year 1996; SD = School District; ISD = Independent School District; n/a not available
Source: National Center for Education Statistics, Common Core of Data Public Education Agency Universe 1997-98; National Center for Education Statistics, Characteristics of the 100 Largest Public Elementary and Secondary School Districts in the United States: 1997-98, July 1999

Educational Quality

School District	Education Quotient[1]	Graduate Outcome[2]	Community Index[3]	Resource Index[4]
Jefferson County	90.0	75.0	89.0	120.0

Note: Nearly 1,000 secondary school districts were rated in terms of educational quality. The scores range from a low of 50 to a high of 150; (1) Average of the Graduate Outcome, Community and Resource indexes; (2) Based on graduation rates and college board scores (SAT/ACT); (3) Based on the surrounding community's average level of education and the area's average income level; (4) Based on teacher salaries, per-pupil expenditures and student-teacher ratios.
Source: Expansion Management, Ratings Issue, 1998

Educational Attainment by Race

Area	High School Graduate (%)					Bachelor's Degree (%)				
	Total	White	Black	Other	Hisp.[2]	Total	White	Black	Other	Hisp.[2]
City	67.2	70.3	58.4	68.4	75.8	17.2	20.7	6.7	33.2	26.6
MSA[1]	73.5	74.8	64.0	74.2	79.5	17.3	18.3	9.1	33.3	25.4
U.S.	75.2	77.9	63.1	60.4	49.8	20.3	21.5	11.4	19.4	9.2

Note: Figures shown cover persons 25 years old and over; (1) Metropolitan Statistical Area - see Appendix A for areas included; (2) people of Hispanic origin can be of any race
Source: 1990 Census of Population and Housing, Summary Tape File 3C

School Enrollment by Type

Area	Preprimary				Elementary/High School			
	Public		Private		Public		Private	
	Enrollment	%	Enrollment	%	Enrollment	%	Enrollment	%
City	1,856	52.7	1,668	47.3	35,092	82.7	7,366	17.3
MSA[1]	7,734	53.4	6,738	46.6	138,085	83.6	27,168	16.4
U.S.	2,679,029	59.5	1,824,256	40.5	38,379,689	90.2	4,187,099	9.8

Note: Figures shown cover persons 3 years old and over;
(1) Metropolitan Statistical Area - see Appendix A for areas included
Source: 1990 Census of Population and Housing, Summary Tape File 3C

School Enrollment by Race

Area	Preprimary (%)				Elementary/High School (%)			
	White	Black	Other	Hisp.[1]	White	Black	Other	Hisp.[1]
City	69.6	29.0	1.4	0.2	56.1	42.4	1.5	0.9
MSA[2]	86.2	12.4	1.4	0.6	81.0	17.7	1.3	0.7
U.S.	80.4	12.5	7.1	7.8	74.1	15.6	10.3	12.5

Note: Figures shown cover persons 3 years old and over; (1) people of Hispanic origin can be of any race; (2) Metropolitan Statistical Area - see Appendix A for areas included
Source: 1990 Census of Population and Housing, Summary Tape File 3C

Classroom Teacher Salaries in Public Schools

District	B.A. Degree		M.A. Degree		Maximum	
	Min. ($)	Rank[1]	Max. ($)	Rank[1]	Max. ($)	Rank[1]
Louisville	22,843	90	42,260	76	47,172	76
Average	26,980	-	46,065	-	51,435	-

Note: Salaries are for 1997-1998; (1) Rank ranges from 1 to 100
Source: American Federation of Teachers, Survey & Analysis of Salary Trends, 1998

Higher Education

Two-Year Colleges		Four-Year Colleges		Medical Schools	Law Schools	Voc/Tech
Public	Private	Public	Private			
1	3	1	3	1	2	15

Source: College Blue Book, Occupational Education, 1997; Medical School Admission Requirements, 1999-2000; Peterson's Guide to Two-Year Colleges, 1999; Peterson's Guide to Four-Year Colleges, 2000; Barron's Guide to Law Schools, 1999

MAJOR EMPLOYERS

Major Employers

Papa John USA
Alliant Hospitals
Saint-Gobain Advanced Materials Corp.
Management Cleaning Controls
Bank One Kentucky

Humco (insurance)
Jewish Hospital Healthcare Services
Baptist Healthcare System
University Medical Center
UPS Aviation Services

Note: Companies listed are located in the city
Source: Dun's Business Rankings, 1999; Ward's Business Directory, 1998

PUBLIC SAFETY

Crime Rate

Area	All Crimes	Violent Crimes				Property Crimes		
		Murder	Forcible Rape	Robbery	Aggrav. Assault	Burglary	Larceny-Theft	Motor Vehicle Theft
City	6,906.7	22.4	46.3	559.0	484.5	1,620.9	3,150.0	1,023.6
Suburbs[1]	n/a	n/a	n/a	n/a	n/a	n/a	n/a	n/a
MSA[2]	n/a	n/a	n/a	n/a	n/a	n/a	n/a	n/a
U.S.	4,922.7	6.8	35.9	186.1	382.0	919.6	2,886.5	505.8

Note: Crime rate is the number of crimes per 100,000 pop.; (1) defined as all areas within the MSA but located outside the central city; (2) Metropolitan Statistical Area - see Appendix A for areas incl.
Source: FBI Uniform Crime Reports, 1997

RECREATION

Culture and Recreation

Museums	Symphony Orchestras	Opera Companies	Dance Companies	Professional Theatres	Zoos	Pro Sports Teams
8	1	1	2	2	1	0

Source: International Directory of the Performing Arts, 1997; Official Museum Directory, 1999; Stern's Performing Arts Directory, 1997; USA Today Four Sport Stadium Guide, 1997; Chamber of Commerce/Economic Development, 1999

Library System

The Louisville Public Library has 16 branches, holdings of 1,473,288 volumes, and a budget of $12,913,666 (1996-1997). *American Library Directory, 1998-1999*

MEDIA

Newspapers

Name	Type	Freq.	Distribution	Circulation
The American Baptist	Religious	1x/wk	Local	4,000
The Courier-Journal	General	7x/wk	Local	232,000
Louisville Defender	Black	1x/wk	Area	2,883
The Record	Religious	1x/wk	Area	66,906
The Voice-Tribune	General	1x/wk	Local	13,462
Western Recorder	Religious	1x/wk	State	50,000

Note: Includes newspapers with circulations of 1,000 or more located in the city;
Source: Burrelle's Media Directory, 1999 Edition

Television Stations

Name	Ch.	Affiliation	Type	Owner
WAVE	n/a	NBCT	Commercial	Cosmos Broadcasting Corporation
WHAS	11	ABCT	Commercial	A.H. Belo Corporation
WBNA	21	WB	Commercial	Word Broadcasters
WLKY	32	CBST	Commercial	Pulitzer Broadcasting Company
WDRB	41	FBC	Commercial	Blade Communications Inc.
WKMJ	68	PBS	Public	Kentucky Authority for Educational TV

Note: Stations included broadcast in the Louisville metro area; n/a not available
Source: Burrelle's Media Directory, 1999 Edition

AM Radio Stations

Call Letters	Freq. (kHz)	Target Audience	Station Format	Music Format
WTMT	620	General	S/T	n/a
WNAI	680	General	T	n/a
WWKY	790	General	N/S/T	n/a
WHAS	840	General	M/N/S/T	Adult Contemporary
WFIA	900	General	M/T	Christian
WLOU	1350	General	M	Christian

Note: Stations included broadcast in the Louisville metro area; n/a not available
Target Audience: A=Asian; B=Black; C=Christian; E=Ethnic; F=French; G=General; H=Hispanic; M=Men; N=Native American; R=Religious; S=Senior Citizen; W=Women; Y=Young Adult; Z=Children
Station Format: E=Educational; M=Music; N=News; S=Sports; T=Talk
Source: Burrelle's Media Directory, 1999 Edition

FM Radio Stations

Call Letters	Freq. (mHz)	Target Audience	Station Format	Music Format
WJIE	88.5	General	M/N/S	Adult Contemporary/Christian
WFPL	89.3	General	N	n/a
WUOL	90.5	General	M/N	Classical
WFPK	91.9	General	M	Alternative/Jazz
WQSH	93.1	General	M/N/T	Adult Contemporary
WLSY	94.7	General	M	Adult Contemporary
WQMF	95.7	General	M/N/S	Classic Rock
WGZB	96.5	General	n/a	n/a
WAMZ	97.5	General	M/N/S	Country
WHKW	98.9	General	M	Country
WDJX	99.7	General	M	Top 40
WTFX	100.5	n/a	n/a	n/a
WMJM	101.3	General	n/a	n/a
WLRS	102.3	General	M/N/T	Alternative
WRKA	103.1	General	M	Oldies
WMHX	103.9	General	n/a	n/a
WSJW	103.9	n/a	n/a	n/a
WVEZ	106.9	General	M/N	Adult Contemporary
WSFR	107.7	General	n/a	n/a

Note: Stations included broadcast in the Louisville metro area; n/a not available
Station Format: E=Educational; M=Music; N=News; S=Sports; T=Talk
Target Audience: A=Asian; B=Black; C=Christian; E=Ethnic; F=French; G=General; H=Hispanic; M=Men; N=Native American; R=Religious; S=Senior Citizen; W=Women; Y=Young Adult; Z=Children
Source: Burrelle's Media Directory, 1999 Edition

CLIMATE

Average and Extreme Temperatures

Temperature	Jan	Feb	Mar	Apr	May	Jun	Jul	Aug	Sep	Oct	Nov	Dec	Yr.
Extreme High (°F)	77	77	86	91	95	102	105	101	104	92	84	76	105
Average High (°F)	41	46	56	68	77	85	88	87	80	69	56	45	67
Average Temp. (°F)	33	37	46	57	66	74	78	77	70	58	47	37	57
Average Low (°F)	25	27	36	46	55	64	68	66	59	47	37	29	46
Extreme Low (°F)	-20	-9	-1	22	31	42	50	46	33	23	-1	-15	-20

Note: Figures cover the years 1948-1990
Source: National Climatic Data Center, International Station Meteorological Climate Summary, 3/95

Average Precipitation/Snowfall/Humidity

Precip./Humidity	Jan	Feb	Mar	Apr	May	Jun	Jul	Aug	Sep	Oct	Nov	Dec	Yr.
Avg. Precip. (in.)	3.4	3.5	4.5	4.0	4.5	3.7	4.2	3.2	3.0	2.6	3.7	3.6	43.9
Avg. Snowfall (in.)	5	4	3	Tr	Tr	0	0	0	0	Tr	1	2	17
Avg. Rel. Hum. 7am (%)	78	78	75	75	79	80	82	85	86	84	79	78	80
Avg. Rel. Hum. 4pm (%)	62	58	52	49	52	53	55	53	53	51	57	62	55

Note: Figures cover the years 1948-1990; Tr = Trace amounts (<0.05 in. of rain; <0.5 in. of snow)
Source: National Climatic Data Center, International Station Meteorological Climate Summary, 3/95

Weather Conditions

Temperature			Daytime Sky			Precipitation		
10°F & below	32°F & below	90°F & above	Clear	Partly cloudy	Cloudy	0.01 inch or more precip.	0.1 inch or more snow/ice	Thunder-storms
8	90	35	82	143	140	125	15	45

Note: Figures are average number of days per year and covers the years 1948-1990
Source: National Climatic Data Center, International Station Meteorological Climate Summary, 3/95

AIR & WATER QUALITY

Maximum Pollutant Concentrations

	Particulate Matter (ug/m³)	Carbon Monoxide (ppm)	Sulfur Dioxide (ppm)	Nitrogen Dioxide (ppm)	Ozone (ppm)	Lead (ug/m³)
MSA[1] Level	98	6	0.038	0.020	0.13	0.02
NAAQS[2]	150	9	0.140	0.053	0.12	1.50
Met NAAQS?	Yes	Yes	Yes	Yes	No	Yes

Note: (1) Metropolitan Statistical Area - see Appendix A for areas included; (2) National Ambient Air Quality Standards; ppm = parts per million; ug/m³ = micrograms per cubic meter; n/a not available
Source: EPA, National Air Quality and Emissions Trends Report, 1997

Pollutant Standards Index

In the Louisville MSA (see Appendix A for areas included), the Pollutant Standards Index (PSI) exceeded 100 on 18 days in 1997. A PSI value greater than 100 indicates that air quality would be in the unhealthful range on that day. *EPA, National Air Quality and Emissions Trends Report, 1997*

Drinking Water

Water System Name	Pop. Served	Primary Water Source Type	Number of Violations in 1998	Type of Violation/ Contaminants
Louisville Water Co.	769,899	Surface	None	None

Note: Data as of July 10, 1999
Source: EPA, Office of Ground Water and Drinking Water, Safe Drinking Water Information System

Louisville tap water is fluoridated.
Editor & Publisher Market Guide, 1999

Manchester, New Hampshire

Background

Pennacook Indians lived in the area that eventually became the city of Manchester. Originally Europeans, especially Scotch-Irish, began settling in the area in the early eighteenth century and established the village of Harrytown in 1722. Manchester's second incarnation was that of town of Derryfield, formed in 1751.

Businessman Samuel Blodget built a canal to bypass the Amoskeag Falls of the Merrimack River, giving the town access to Boston. Blodget's hope was to transform Derryfield into an industrial center, similar to Manchester, England. Thus, in 1811, it was renamed after the English city.

Manchester did indeed soon become a busy factory town. The Amoskeag Manufacturing Company began operations in 1838, building some of the largest cotton and woolen mills in the world, thirty in all. By the early 1900s, the company was the world's largest textile firm. After World War I, however, these textile mills began a downhill slide, and during the midst of the Great Depression, Amoskeag closed its doors.

After so many years of dependence mostly upon the mills, the city began to diversify its economy. Cigar, shoe, paper, and machine manufacturers, knitting mills, food processors, and other businesses began to revive local commerce. During the 1980s the region experienced phenomenal economic growth. Business slumped during the recession of the early 1990s, but the city had fully recovered by the middle of the decade.

In the late 1990s Manchester has a strong economy. It has been assisted by recent growth in local businesses, such as Jac Pac Foods and Velcro USA. The German Brita Corporation, famous for its water filters, placed its North American headquarters in Londonderry, part of the Manchester metropolitan area. Other manufacturers make shoes, boots, and cotton and woolen products.

Financial firms are significant in Manchester. Fidelity Investments moved into the area, due in part to the Manchester's sophisticated communications network. Other significant employers in the field are Citizens Bank and the Bank of New Hampshire.

In the post-industrial world, services are of growing importance to major cities, and Manchester is no exception. In this economic niche, Manchester health service firms employ the most people. High tech service businesses, such as software application companies, are also having a positive impact on the area's commerce.

Incentives to business are many. The state of New Hampshire has no sales, income, or capital gains tax, and has many programs to assist business, while Manchester has programs of its own. The city is a leader within the Regional Economic Development Initiative, a private sector project, which helps the region's local governments to maintain and grow their economies. Manchester also has the Intown Management Corporation, whose aim is to rejuvenate the city's core.

The climate is a mixture. Winters can be bitterly cold, as one would expect in northern New England, with temperatures ranging from the single digits to the middle forties. Snowfall is heavy, with annual accumulations usually around sixty inches, making for good skiing conditions. Summers tend be mild and Manchester enjoys low humidity during the season.

General Rankings and Evaluative Comments

■ Manchester was ranked #1 out of 21 small, northestern metropolitan areas in *Money's* 1998 survey of "The Best Places to Live in America." The survey was conducted by first contacting 512 representative households nationwide and asking them to rank 37 quality-of-life factors on a scale of 1 to 10. Next, a demographic profile was compiled on the 300 largest metropolitan statistical areas in the U.S. The numbers were crunched together to arrive at an overall ranking (things Americans consider most important, like clean air and water, low crime and good schools, received extra weight). Unlike previous years, the 1998 rankings were broken down by region (northeast, midwest, south, west) and population size (100,000 to 249,999; 250,000 to 999,999; 1 million plus). The city had a nationwide ranking of #6 out of 300 in 1997 and #50 out of 300 in 1996. *Money, July 1998; Money, July 1997; Money, September 1996*

■ *Ladies Home Journal* ranked America's 200 largest cities based on the qualities women care about most. Manchester ranked #50 out of 200. Criteria: low crime rate, well-paying jobs, quality health and child care, good public schools, the presence of women in government, size of the gender wage gap, number of sexual-harassment and discrimination complaints filed, unemployment and divorce rates, commute times, population density, number of houses of worship, parks and cultural offerings, number of women's health specialists, how well a community's women cared for themselves, complexion kindness index based on UV radiation levels, odds of finding affordable fashions, rental rates for romance movies, champagne sales and other matters of the heart. *Ladies Home Journal, November 1998*

■ Zero Population Growth ranked 229 cities in terms of children's health, safety, and economic well-being. Manchester was ranked #14 out of 112 independent cities (cities with populations greater than 100,000 which were neither Major Cities nor Suburbs/Outer Cities) and was given a grade of B+. Criteria: total population, percent of population under 18 years of age, household language, percent population change, percent of births to teens, infant mortality rate, percent of low birth weights, dropout rate, enrollment in preprimary school, violent and property crime rates, unemployment rate, percent of children in poverty, percent of owner occupied units, number of bad air days, percent of public transportation commuters, and average travel time to work. *Zero Population Growth, Children's Environmental Index, Fall 1999*

■ Cognetics studied 273 metro areas in the United States, ranking them by entrepreneurial activity. Manchester was ranked #22 out of 134 smaller metro areas. Criteria: Significant Starts (firms started in the last 10 years that still employ at least 5 people) and Young Growers (percent of firms 10 years old or less that grew significantly during the last 4 years). *Cognetics, "Entrepreneurial Hot Spots: The Best Places in America to Start and Grow a Company," 1998*

Business Environment

STATE ECONOMY

State Economic Profile

"After several years of fairly strong growth, the New Hampshire economy is beginning to cool. Job growth has slowed and in-migration has weakened. However, its low cost of living and doing business relative to the rest of New England will enable NH to continue to attract residents and businesses from its neighbors.

1998 was a good year for NH's housing market. Sales were strong and prices remained affordable. Southern NH, particularly Nashua and Manchester, benefited from the strong Boston economy. It is estimated that about 80,000 individuals working in Boston own a home in southern NH. This increase in demand has attracted some new construction, as construction employment increased almost 5% in 1998. This increase, however, is not enough to moderate the home price increases expected in 1999 and 2000.

New Hampshire's manufacturing industry continues to contract. Manufacturing employment decreased at a rate of almost 3% in 1998, shedding over 3,000 jobs. Substantial layoffs at Compaq and Cabletron characterized the state of New Hampshire's manufacturing. Manufacturing will continue to be weak in 1999 and 2000.

NH's tight labor markets allowed it to absorb declines in its manufacturing sector. The thin labor market, however, has restrained growth in the services sector. With one of the lowest unemployment rates in the region and strong labor demand on the part of its neighbors, particularly Boston, NH cannot create many new jobs.

NH's strong fundamentals, a low-tax burden and high quality of life indicate continued solid growth, albeit at a rate below recent years." *National Association of Realtors, Economic Profiles: The Fifty States and the District of Columbia, http://nar.realtor.com/databank/profiles.htm*

IMPORTS/EXPORTS

Total Export Sales

Area	1994 ($000)	1995 ($000)	1996 ($000)	1997 ($000)	% Chg. 1994-97	% Chg. 1996-97
MSA[1]	115,303	146,299	198,254	237,847	106.3	20.0
U.S.	512,415,609	583,030,524	622,827,063	687,597,999	34.2	10.4

Note: (1) Metropolitan Statistical Area - see Appendix A for areas included
Source: U.S. Department of Commerce, International Trade Association, Metropolitan Area Exports: An Export Performance Report on Over 250 U.S. Cities, November 10, 1998

CITY FINANCES

City Government Finances

Component	FY92 ($000)	FY92 (per capita $)
Revenue	160,145	1,608.33
Expenditure	176,700	1,774.60
Debt Outstanding	87,520	878.96
Cash & Securities	18,095	181.73

Source: U.S. Bureau of the Census, City Government Finances: 1991-92

City Government Revenue by Source

Source	FY92 ($000)	FY92 (per capita $)	FY92 (%)
From Federal Government	6,093	61.19	3.8
From State Governments	12,678	127.32	7.9
From Local Governments	43	0.43	0.0
Property Taxes	105,236	1,056.88	65.7
General Sales Taxes	0	0.00	0.0
Selective Sales Taxes	0	0.00	0.0
Income Taxes	0	0.00	0.0
Current Charges	19,635	197.19	12.3
Utility/Liquor Store	9,970	100.13	6.2
Employee Retirement[1]	0	0.00	0.0
Other	6,490	65.18	4.1

Note: (1) Excludes "city contributions," classified as "nonrevenue," intragovernmental transfers.
Source: U.S. Bureau of the Census, City Government Finances: 1991-92

City Government Expenditures by Function

Function	FY92 ($000)	FY92 (per capita $)	FY92 (%)
Educational Services	71,232	715.38	40.3
Employee Retirement[1]	0	0.00	0.0
Environment/Housing	10,956	110.03	6.2
Government Administration	8,578	86.15	4.9
Interest on General Debt	6,066	60.92	3.4
Public Safety	23,055	231.54	13.0
Social Services	5,057	50.79	2.9
Transportation	19,497	195.81	11.0
Utility/Liquor Store	9,821	98.63	5.6
Other	22,438	225.34	12.7

Note: (1) Payments to beneficiaries including withdrawal of contributions.
Source: U.S. Bureau of the Census, City Government Finances: 1991-92

Municipal Bond Ratings

Area	Moody's	S & P
Manchester	Aa2	n/a

Note: n/a not available; n/r not rated
Source: Moody's Bond Record, 6/99

POPULATION

Population Growth

Area	1980	1990	% Chg. 1980-90	July 1998 Estimate	% Chg. 1990-98
City	90,936	99,567	9.5	102,524	3.0
MSA[1]	142,527	147,867	3.7	184,969	25.1
U.S.	226,545,805	248,765,170	9.8	270,299,000	8.7

Note: (1) Metropolitan Statistical Area - see Appendix A for areas included;
July 1998 MSA population estimate was calculated by the editors
Source: 1980/1990 Census of Housing and Population, Summary Tape File 3C;
Census Bureau Population Estimates 1998

Population Characteristics

Race	City 1980 Population	%	City 1990 Population	%	% Chg. 1980-90	MSA[1] 1990 Population	%
White	89,906	98.9	96,314	96.7	7.1	143,946	97.3
Black	322	0.4	924	0.9	187.0	1,073	0.7
Amer Indian/Esk/Aleut	134	0.1	240	0.2	79.1	389	0.3
Asian/Pacific Islander	321	0.4	1,193	1.2	271.7	1,501	1.0
Other	253	0.3	896	0.9	254.2	958	0.6
Hispanic Origin[2]	1,109	1.2	2,142	2.2	93.1	2,418	1.6

Note: (1) Metropolitan Statistical Area - see Appendix A for areas included;
(2) people of Hispanic origin can be of any race
Source: 1980/1990 Census of Housing and Population, Summary Tape File 3C

Ancestry

Area	German	Irish	English	Italian	U.S.	French	Polish	Dutch
City	8.1	21.1	13.9	5.2	3.8	21.0	6.1	0.9
MSA[1]	8.5	21.2	15.6	5.5	3.8	20.5	6.0	1.0
U.S.	23.3	15.6	13.1	5.9	5.3	4.2	3.8	2.5

Note: Figures are percentages and include persons that reported multiple ancestry (eg. if a person reported being Irish and Italian, they were included in both columns); (1) Metropolitan Statistical Area - see Appendix A for areas included
Source: 1990 Census of Population and Housing, Summary Tape File 3C

Age

Area	Median Age (Years)	Under 5	Under 18	18-24	25-44	45-64	65+	80+
City	31.8	7.8	23.0	11.9	34.9	16.5	13.7	3.1
MSA[1]	32.2	7.7	24.1	11.4	35.0	17.1	12.3	2.9
U.S.	32.9	7.3	25.6	10.5	32.6	18.7	12.5	2.8

Note: (1) Metropolitan Statistical Area - see Appendix A for areas included
Source: 1990 Census of Population and Housing, Summary Tape File 3C

Male/Female Ratio

Area	Number of males per 100 females (all ages)	Number of males per 100 females (18 years old+)
City	92.0	88.9
MSA[1]	93.8	90.4
U.S.	95.0	91.9

Note: (1) Metropolitan Statistical Area - see Appendix A for areas included
Source: 1990 Census of Population, General Population Characteristics

INCOME

Per Capita/Median/Average Income

Area	Per Capita ($)	Median Household ($)	Average Household ($)
City	15,111	31,911	36,814
MSA[1]	16,278	35,866	42,004
U.S.	14,420	30,056	38,453

Note: All figures are for 1989; (1) Metropolitan Statistical Area - see Appendix A for areas included
Source: 1990 Census of Population and Housing, Summary Tape File 3C

Household Income Distribution by Race

Income ($)	City (%)					U.S. (%)				
	Total	White	Black	Other	Hisp.[1]	Total	White	Black	Other	Hisp.[1]
Less than 5,000	4.7	4.4	15.4	13.8	6.3	6.2	4.8	15.2	8.6	8.8
5,000 - 9,999	9.4	9.3	14.9	8.6	7.7	9.3	8.6	14.2	9.9	11.1
10,000 - 14,999	7.5	7.5	8.5	5.5	12.8	8.8	8.5	11.0	9.8	11.0
15,000 - 24,999	16.1	16.1	17.6	19.8	20.1	17.5	17.3	18.9	18.5	20.5
25,000 - 34,999	16.9	17.0	9.6	17.1	19.6	15.8	16.1	14.2	15.4	16.4
35,000 - 49,999	21.9	22.0	23.1	16.2	19.4	17.9	18.6	13.3	16.1	16.0
50,000 - 74,999	16.1	16.2	9.1	14.7	12.5	15.0	15.8	9.3	13.4	11.1
75,000 - 99,999	4.8	4.9	1.7	2.9	1.7	5.1	5.5	2.6	4.7	3.1
100,000+	2.5	2.6	0.0	1.4	0.0	4.4	4.8	1.3	3.7	1.9

Note: All figures are for 1989; (1) people of Hispanic origin can be of any race
Source: 1990 Census of Population and Housing, Summary Tape File 3C

Effective Buying Income

Area	Per Capita ($)	Median Household ($)	Average Household ($)
City	16,688	35,717	40,892
MSA[1]	19,286	44,613	51,228
U.S.	16,803	34,536	45,243

Note: Data as of 1/1/99; (1) Metropolitan Statistical Area - see Appendix A for areas included
Source: Standard Rate & Data Service, Newspaper Advertising Source, 9/99

Effective Household Buying Income Distribution

Area	% of Households Earning						
	$10,000 -$19,999	$20,000 -$34,999	$35,000 -$49,999	$50,000 -$74,999	$75,000 -$99,000	$100,000 -$124,999	$125,000 and up
City	14.4	22.8	21.1	20.5	6.4	1.7	1.4
MSA[1]	10.3	18.7	20.7	25.8	10.3	3.4	3.0
U.S.	16.0	22.6	18.2	18.9	7.2	2.4	2.7

Note: Data as of 1/1/99; (1) Metropolitan Statistical Area - see Appendix A for areas included
Source: Standard Rate & Data Service, Newspaper Advertising Source, 9/99

Poverty Rates by Race and Age

Area	Total (%)	By Race (%)				By Age (%)		
		White	Black	Other	Hisp.[2]	Under 5 years old	Under 18 years old	65 years and over
City	9.0	8.5	28.5	24.0	19.5	16.0	12.6	12.2
MSA[1]	7.1	6.7	24.4	20.3	17.5	11.6	9.0	11.5
U.S.	13.1	9.8	29.5	23.1	25.3	20.1	18.3	12.8

Note: Figures show the percent of people living below the poverty line in 1989. The average poverty threshold was $12,674 for a family of four in 1989; (1) Metropolitan Statistical Area - see Appendix A for areas included; (2) people of Hispanic origin can be of any race
Source: 1990 Census of Population and Housing, Summary Tape File 3C

EMPLOYMENT

Labor Force and Employment

Area	Civilian Labor Force			Workers Employed		
	Jun. 1998	Jun. 1999	% Chg.	Jun. 1998	Jun. 1999	% Chg.
City	56,445	58,556	3.7	54,868	57,166	4.2
MSA[1]	102,827	106,879	3.9	100,135	104,329	4.2
U.S.	138,798,000	140,666,000	1.3	132,265,000	134,395,000	1.6

Note: Data is not seasonally adjusted and covers workers 16 years of age and older;
(1) Metropolitan Statistical Area - see Appendix A for areas included
Source: Bureau of Labor Statistics, http://stats.bls.gov

Unemployment Rate

Area	1998						1999					
	Jul.	Aug.	Sep.	Oct.	Nov.	Dec.	Jan.	Feb.	Mar.	Apr.	May.	Jun.
City	2.3	2.6	2.7	2.3	2.7	2.3	3.0	3.2	3.1	2.2	2.0	2.4
MSA[1]	2.2	2.4	2.6	2.3	2.6	2.2	2.8	3.1	3.0	2.3	2.0	2.4
U.S.	4.7	4.5	4.4	4.2	4.1	4.0	4.8	4.7	4.4	4.1	4.0	4.5

Note: Data is not seasonally adjusted and covers workers 16 years of age and older; all figures are percentages; (1) Metropolitan Statistical Area - see Appendix A for areas included
Source: Bureau of Labor Statistics, http://stats.bls.gov

Employment by Industry

Sector	MSA[1]		U.S.
	Number of Employees	Percent of Total	Percent of Total
Services	32,500	31.8	30.4
Retail Trade	18,300	17.9	17.7
Government	11,300	11.1	15.6
Manufacturing	15,100	14.8	14.3
Finance/Insurance/Real Estate	7,000	6.8	5.9
Wholesale Trade	7,100	6.9	5.4
Transportation/Public Utilities	6,100	6.0	5.3
Construction	n/a	n/a	5.0
Mining	n/a	n/a	0.4

Note: Figures cover non-farm employment as of 6/99 and are not seasonally adjusted; (1) Metropolitan Statistical Area - see Appendix A for areas included; n/a not available
Source: Bureau of Labor Statistics, http://stats.bls.gov

Employment by Occupation

Occupation Category	City (%)	MSA[1] (%)	U.S. (%)
White Collar	60.5	63.0	58.1
Executive/Admin./Management	11.9	13.1	12.3
Professional	12.6	13.6	14.1
Technical & Related Support	3.5	3.6	3.7
Sales	12.9	13.5	11.8
Administrative Support/Clerical	19.5	19.1	16.3
Blue Collar	25.8	24.5	26.2
Precision Production/Craft/Repair	11.2	11.1	11.3
Machine Operators/Assem./Insp.	7.3	6.5	6.8
Transportation/Material Movers	3.7	3.5	4.1
Cleaners/Helpers/Laborers	3.6	3.3	3.9
Services	13.3	11.9	13.2
Farming/Forestry/Fishing	0.5	0.6	2.5

Note: Figures cover employed persons 16 years old and over; (1) Metropolitan Statistical Area - see Appendix A for areas included
Source: 1990 Census of Population and Housing, Summary Tape File 3C

Occupational Employment Projections: 1996 - 2006

Occupations Expected to Have the Largest Job Growth (ranked by numerical growth)	Fast-Growing Occupations[1] (ranked by percent growth)
1. Salespersons, retail	1. Systems analysts
2. Cashiers	2. Database administrators
3. General managers & top executives	3. Computer engineers
4. Teachers aides, clerical & paraprofess.	4. Personal and home care aides
5. Truck drivers, light	5. Paralegals
6. Registered nurses	6. Home health aides
7. Marketing & sales, supervisors	7. Teachers, special education
8. Systems analysts	8. Medical assistants
9. Teachers, secondary school	9. Occupational therapists
10. Computer engineers	10. Data processing equipment repairers

Note: Projections cover New Hampshire; (1) Excludes occupations with total job growth less than 300
Source: U.S. Department of Labor, Employment and Training Administration, America's Labor Market Information System (ALMIS)

TAXES

Major State and Local Tax Rates

| State Corp. Income (%) | State Personal Income (%) | Residential Property (effective rate per $100) | Sales & Use | | State Gasoline (cents/ gallon) | State Cigarette (cents/ pack) |
			State (%)	Local (%)		
7.0[a]	5.0[b]	3.40	None	None	18.7[c]	37.0

Note: Personal/corporate income, sales, gasoline and cigarette tax rates as of January 1999.
Property tax rates as of 1997; (b) Applies to interest and dividend income only; (a) Plus a 0.25% tax on the enterprise base (total compensation, interest and dividends paid). Business profits tax imposed on both corporations and unincorporated associations; (c) Rate is comprised of 18 cents excise and 0.7 cents motor carrier tax
Source: Federation of Tax Administrators, www.taxadmin.org; Washington D.C. Department of Finance and Revenue, Tax Rates and Tax Burdens in the District of Columbia: A Nationwide Comparison, July 1998; Chamber of Commerce, 1999

Total Taxes Per Capita and as a Percent of Income

| Area | Per Capita Income ($) | Per Capita Taxes ($) | | | Percent of Income (%) | | |
		Total	Federal	State/ Local	Total	Federal	State/ Local
New Hampshire	30,034	9,421	7,462	1,959	31.4	24.8	6.5
U.S.	27,876	9,881	6,690	3,191	35.4	24.0	11.4

Note: Figures are for 1998
Source: Tax Foundation, www.taxfoundation.org

Estimated Tax Burden

Area	State Income	Local Income	Property	Sales	Total
Manchester	0	0	6,500	0	6,500

Note: The numbers are estimates of taxes paid by a married couple with two children and annual earnings of $75,000. Sales tax estimates assume they spend average amounts on food, clothing, household goods and gasoline. Property tax estimates assume they live in a $250,000 home.
Source: Kiplinger's Personal Finance Magazine, October 1998

COMMERCIAL REAL ESTATE

Data not available at time of publication.

COMMERCIAL UTILITIES

Typical Monthly Electric Bills

Area	Commercial Service ($/month)		Industrial Service ($/month)	
	12 kW demand 1,500 kWh	100 kW demand 30,000 kWh	1,000 kW demand 400,000 kWh	20,000 kW demand 10,000,000 kWh
City	253	3,620	41,553	679,731
U.S.	150	2,174	23,995	508,569

Note: Based on rates in effect January 1, 1999
Source: Edison Electric Institute, Typical Residential, Commercial and Industrial Bills, Winter 1999

TRANSPORTATION

Transportation Statistics

Average minutes to work	18.8
Interstate highways	I-93
Bus lines	
In-city	Manchester TA, 25 city buses
Inter-city	2
Passenger air service	
Airport	Manchester Municipal
Airlines	9
Aircraft departures	10,217 (1996)
Enplaned passengers	381,292 (1996)
Rail service	No Amtrak service
Motor freight carriers	39
Major waterways/ports	Merrimack River

Source: Editor & Publisher Market Guide, 1999; FAA Airport Activity Statistics, 1997; Amtrak National Time Table, Northeast Timetable, Spring/Summer 1999; 1990 Census of Population and Housing, STF 3C; Chamber of Commerce/Economic Development 1999; Jane's Urban Transport Systems 1999-2000

Means of Transportation to Work

Area	Car/Truck/Van		Public Transportation			Bicycle	Walked	Other Means	Worked at Home
	Drove Alone	Car-pooled	Bus	Subway	Railroad				
City	76.9	14.2	1.3	0.0	0.0	0.3	4.5	0.7	2.0
MSA[1]	78.7	13.0	1.0	0.0	0.0	0.2	3.9	0.6	2.6
U.S.	73.2	13.4	3.0	1.5	0.5	0.4	3.9	1.2	3.0

Note: Figures shown are percentages and only include workers 16 years old and over;
(1) Metropolitan Statistical Area - see Appendix A for areas included
Source: 1990 Census of Population and Housing, Summary Tape File 3C

BUSINESSES

Major Business Headquarters

Company Name	1999 Rankings	
	Fortune 500	Forbes 500

No companies listed.
Note: Companies listed are located in the city; dashes indicate no ranking
Fortune 500: Companies that produce a 10-K are ranked 1 to 500 based on 1998 revenue
Forbes 500: Private companies are ranked 1 to 500 based on 1997 revenue
Source: Forbes, November 30, 1998; Fortune, April 26, 1999

Fast-Growing Businesses

According to Deloitte & Touche LLP, Manchester is home to one of America's 100 fast-growing high-technology companies: New Technology Partners. Companies are ranked by percentage growth in revenue over a five-year period. Criteria for inclusion: must be a U.S. company developing and/or providing technology products or services; company must have been in business for five years with 1993 revenues of at least $50,000. *Deloitte & Touche LLP, November 17, 1998*

HOTELS & MOTELS

Hotels/Motels

Area	Hotels/ Motels	Rooms	Luxury-Level Hotels/Motels		Average Minimum Rates ($)		
			♦♦♦♦	♦♦♦♦♦	♦♦	♦♦♦	♦♦♦♦
City	11	891	0	0	n/a	n/a	n/a
Airport	2	185	0	0	n/a	n/a	n/a
Total	13	1,076	0	0	n/a	n/a	n/a

Note: n/a not available; classifications range from one diamond (budget properties with basic amenities) to five diamond (luxury properties with the finest service, rooms and facilities).
Source: OAG, Business Travel Planner, Winter 1998-99

CONVENTION CENTERS

Major Convention Centers

Center Name	Meeting Rooms	Exhibit Space (sq. ft.)
Armory Exhibit Center at the Center of N.H.	10	12,000
Expo Center of New Hampshire	n/a	n/a
Holiday Inn	16	50,000

Note: n/a not available
Source: Trade Shows Worldwide, 1998; Meetings & Conventions, 4/15/99;
Sucessful Meetings, 3/31/98

Living Environment

COST OF LIVING

Cost of Living Index

Composite Index	Groceries	Housing	Utilities	Trans-portation	Health Care	Misc. Goods/ Services
110.3	98.7	114.7	146.8	94.0	114.6	107.7

Note: U.S. = 100
Source: ACCRA, Cost of Living Index, 1st Quarter 1999

HOUSING

Median Home Prices and Housing Affordability

Area	Median Price[2] 1st Qtr. 1999 ($)	HOI[3] 1st Qtr. 1999	Afford-ability Rank[4]
MSA[1]	n/a	n/a	n/a
U.S.	134,000	69.6	–

Note: (1) Metropolitan Statistical Area - see Appendix A for areas included; (2) U.S. figures calculated from the sales of 524,324 new and existing homes in 181 markets; (3) Housing Opportunity Index - percent of homes sold that were within the reach of the median income household at the prevailing mortgage interest rate; (4) Rank is from 1-181 with 1 being most affordable; n/a not available
Source: National Association of Home Builders, Housing Opportunity Index, 1st Quarter 1999

Median Home Price Projection

It is projected that the median price of existing single-family homes in the metro area will increase by 2.2% in 1999. Nationwide, home prices are projected to increase 3.8%.
Kiplinger's Personal Finance Magazine, January 1999

Average New Home Price

Area	Price ($)
City	154,950
U.S.	142,735

Note: Figures are based on a new home with 1,800 sq. ft. of living area on an 8,000 sq. ft. lot.
Source: ACCRA, Cost of Living Index, 1st Quarter 1999

Average Apartment Rent

Area	Rent ($/mth)
City	878
U.S.	601

Note: Figures are based on an unfurnished two bedroom, 1-1/2 or 2 bath apartment, approximately 950 sq. ft. in size, excluding all utilities except water
Source: ACCRA, Cost of Living Index, 1st Quarter 1999

RESIDENTIAL UTILITIES

Average Residential Utility Costs

Area	All Electric ($/mth)	Part Electric ($/mth)	Other Energy ($/mth)	Phone ($/mth)
City	–	82.96	68.78	21.39
U.S.	100.02	55.73	43.33	19.71

Source: ACCRA, Cost of Living Index, 1st Quarter 1999

HEALTH CARE

Average Health Care Costs

Area	Hospital ($/day)	Doctor ($/visit)	Dentist ($/visit)
City	493.00	68.00	67.00
U.S.	430.43	52.45	66.35

Note: Hospital—based on a semi-private room; Doctor—based on a general practitioner's routine exam of an established patient; Dentist—based on adult teeth cleaning and periodic oral exam.
Source: ACCRA, Cost of Living Index, 1st Quarter 1999

Distribution of Office-Based Physicians

Area	Family/Gen. Practitioners	Specialists		
		Medical	Surgical	Other
MSA[1]	64	196	155	155

Note: Data as of 12/31/97; (1) Metropolitan Statistical Area - see Appendix A for areas included
Source: American Medical Assn., Physician Characteristics & Distribution in the U.S., 1999

Hospitals

Manchester has 3 general medical and surgical hospitals. *AHA Guide to the Healthcare Field, 1998-99*

EDUCATION

Public School District Statistics

District Name	Num. Sch.	Enroll.	Classroom Teachers	Pupils per Teacher	Minority Pupils (%)	Current Exp.[1] ($/pupil)
Manchester Sch Dist	21	16,563	894	18.5	n/a	n/a

Note: Data covers the 1997-1998 school year unless otherwise noted; (1) Data covers fiscal year 1996; SD = School District; ISD = Independent School District; n/a not available
Source: National Center for Education Statistics, Common Core of Data Public Education Agency Universe 1997-98; National Center for Education Statistics, Characteristics of the 100 Largest Public Elementary and Secondary School Districts in the United States: 1997-98, July 1999

Educational Quality

School District	Education Quotient[1]	Graduate Outcome[2]	Community Index[3]	Resource Index[4]
Manchester SD	85.0	86.0	77.0	84.0

Note: Nearly 1,000 secondary school districts were rated in terms of educational quality. The scores range from a low of 50 to a high of 150; (1) Average of the Graduate Outcome, Community and Resource indexes; (2) Based on graduation rates and college board scores (SAT/ACT); (3) Based on the surrounding community's average level of education and the area's average income level; (4) Based on teacher salaries, per-pupil expenditures and student-teacher ratios.
Source: Expansion Management, Ratings Issue, 1998

Educational Attainment by Race

Area	High School Graduate (%)					Bachelor's Degree (%)				
	Total	White	Black	Other	Hisp.[2]	Total	White	Black	Other	Hisp.[2]
City	74.9	74.9	82.5	74.3	76.2	19.6	19.3	17.5	33.8	23.3
MSA[1]	77.5	77.6	79.3	73.6	78.8	21.5	21.3	14.7	36.3	26.3
U.S.	75.2	77.9	63.1	60.4	49.8	20.3	21.5	11.4	19.4	9.2

Note: Figures shown cover persons 25 years old and over; (1) Metropolitan Statistical Area - see Appendix A for areas included; (2) people of Hispanic origin can be of any race
Source: 1990 Census of Population and Housing, Summary Tape File 3C

School Enrollment by Type

Area	Preprimary				Elementary/High School			
	Public		Private		Public		Private	
	Enrollment	%	Enrollment	%	Enrollment	%	Enrollment	%
City	878	49.0	913	51.0	11,881	87.4	1,716	12.6
MSA[1]	1,274	42.6	1,718	57.4	19,200	87.6	2,720	12.4
U.S.	2,679,029	59.5	1,824,256	40.5	38,379,689	90.2	4,187,099	9.8

Note: Figures shown cover persons 3 years old and over;
(1) Metropolitan Statistical Area - see Appendix A for areas included
Source: 1990 Census of Population and Housing, Summary Tape File 3C

School Enrollment by Race

Area	Preprimary (%)				Elementary/High School (%)			
	White	Black	Other	Hisp.[1]	White	Black	Other	Hisp.[1]
City	97.9	0.3	1.7	1.3	95.1	1.4	3.5	3.9
MSA[2]	97.7	0.2	2.1	1.5	96.5	1.0	2.5	2.6
U.S.	80.4	12.5	7.1	7.8	74.1	15.6	10.3	12.5

Note: Figures shown cover persons 3 years old and over; (1) people of Hispanic origin can be of any race; (2) Metropolitan Statistical Area - see Appendix A for areas included
Source: 1990 Census of Population and Housing, Summary Tape File 3C

Classroom Teacher Salaries in Public Schools

District	B.A. Degree		M.A. Degree		Maximum	
	Min. ($)	Rank[1]	Max. ($)	Rank[1]	Max. ($)	Rank[1]
	n/a	n/a	n/a	n/a	n/a	n/a
Average	26,980	-	46,065	-	51,435	-

Note: Salaries are for 1997-1998; (1) Rank ranges from 1 to 100; n/a not available
Source: American Federation of Teachers, Survey & Analysis of Salary Trends, 1998

Higher Education

Two-Year Colleges		Four-Year Colleges		Medical Schools	Law Schools	Voc/ Tech
Public	Private	Public	Private			
1	1	1	3	0	0	6

Source: College Blue Book, Occupational Education, 1997; Medical School Admission Requirements, 1999-2000; Peterson's Guide to Two-Year Colleges, 1999; Peterson's Guide to Four-Year Colleges, 2000; Barron's Guide to Law Schools, 1999

MAJOR EMPLOYERS

Major Employers

Sunburst Hospitality Corp.	Optima Health-CMC
Elliot Hospital	Citizens Bank of New Hampshire
American Fast Ferries	New Hampshire Vermont Health Service
Public Service Co. of New Hampshire	NHIG Holding (insurance)
Union Leader Corp.	Velcro Inc.

Note: Companies listed are located in the city
Source: Dun's Business Rankings, 1999; Ward's Business Directory, 1998

PUBLIC SAFETY

Crime Rate

Area	All Crimes	Violent Crimes				Property Crimes		
		Murder	Forcible Rape	Robbery	Aggrav. Assault	Burglary	Larceny -Theft	Motor Vehicle Theft
City	5,178.9	1.0	55.5	138.3	45.4	845.1	3,664.3	429.1
Suburbs[1]	2,418.9	1.4	15.5	15.5	47.9	398.7	1,808.9	131.0
MSA[2]	4,026.6	1.2	38.8	87.0	46.5	658.7	2,889.7	304.7
U.S.	5,086.6	7.4	36.3	201.9	390.9	944.8	2,979.7	525.6

Note: Crime rate is the number of crimes per 100,000 pop.; (1) defined as all areas within the MSA but located outside the central city; (2) Metropolitan Statistical Area - see Appendix A for areas incl.
Source: FBI Uniform Crime Reports, 1996

RECREATION

Culture and Recreation

Museums	Symphony Orchestras	Opera Companies	Dance Companies	Professional Theatres	Zoos	Pro Sports Teams
3	2	0	0	0	0	0

Source: International Directory of the Performing Arts, 1997; Official Museum Directory, 1999; Stern's Performing Arts Directory, 1997; USA Today Four Sport Stadium Guide, 1997; Chamber of Commerce/Economic Development, 1999

Library System

The Manchester City Library has one branch, holdings of 312,790 volumes, and a budget of $1,412,984 (1996-1997). *American Library Directory, 1998-1999*

MEDIA

Newspapers

Name	Type	Freq.	Distribution	Circulation
The Union Leader	n/a	7x/wk	Area	89,000

Note: Includes newspapers with circulations of 500 or more located in the city; n/a not available
Source: Burrelle's Media Directory, 1999 Edition

Television Stations

Name	Ch.	Affiliation	Type	Owner
WMUR	n/a	ABCT	Commercial	Imes Communications Group
WPXB	60	n/a	Commercial	Paxson Communications Corporation

Note: Stations included broadcast in the Manchester metro area; n/a not available
Source: Burrelle's Media Directory, 1999 Edition

AM Radio Stations

Call Letters	Freq. (kHz)	Target Audience	Station Format	Music Format
WGIR	610	General	N/T	n/a
WMVU	900	General	N/S/T	n/a
WFEA	1370	General	M/N/S	Adult Standards
WSMN	1590	General	M/N/S/T	Adult Contemporary/Big Band/Country

Note: Stations included broadcast in the Manchester metro area; n/a not available
Target Audience: A=Asian; B=Black; C=Christian; E=Ethnic; F=French; G=General; H=Hispanic;
M=Men; N=Native American; R=Religious; S=Senior Citizen; W=Women; Y=Young Adult; Z=Children
Station Format: E=Educational; M=Music; N=News; S=Sports; T=Talk
Source: Burrelle's Media Directory, 1999 Edition

FM Radio Stations

Call Letters	Freq. (mHz)	Target Audience	Station Format	Music Format
WZID	95.7	General	M/N/S	Adult Contemporary
WQLL	96.5	General	n/a	n/a
WGIR	101.1	General	M	AOR
WHOB	106.3	General	M	Adult Top 40

Note: Stations included broadcast in the Manchester metro area; n/a not available
Station Format: E=Educational; M=Music; N=News; S=Sports; T=Talk
Target Audience: A=Asian; B=Black; C=Christian; E=Ethnic; F=French; G=General; H=Hispanic;
M=Men; N=Native American; R=Religious; S=Senior Citizen; W=Women; Y=Young Adult; Z=Children
Music Format: AOR=Album Oriented Rock; MOR=Middle-of-the-Road
Source: Burrelle's Media Directory, 1999 Edition

CLIMATE

Average and Extreme Temperatures

Temperature	Jan	Feb	Mar	Apr	May	Jun	Jul	Aug	Sep	Oct	Nov	Dec	Yr.
Extreme High (°F)	68	66	85	95	97	98	102	101	98	90	80	68	102
Average High (°F)	31	34	43	57	69	77	83	80	72	61	48	35	57
Average Temp. (°F)	20	23	33	44	56	65	70	68	59	48	38	25	46
Average Low (°F)	9	11	22	32	42	51	57	55	46	35	28	15	34
Extreme Low (°F)	-33	-27	-16	8	21	30	35	29	22	10	-5	-22	-33

Note: Figures cover the years 1948-1990
Source: National Climatic Data Center, International Station Meteorological Climate Summary, 3/95

Average Precipitation/Snowfall/Humidity

Precip./Humidity	Jan	Feb	Mar	Apr	May	Jun	Jul	Aug	Sep	Oct	Nov	Dec	Yr.
Avg. Precip. (in.)	2.8	2.5	2.9	3.1	3.2	3.1	3.1	3.3	2.9	3.1	3.8	3.2	36.9
Avg. Snowfall (in.)	18	15	11	2	Tr	0	0	0	0	Tr	4	14	63
Avg. Rel. Hum. 7am (%)	76	76	76	75	75	80	82	87	89	86	83	79	80
Avg. Rel. Hum. 4pm (%)	59	55	52	46	47	52	51	53	55	53	61	63	54

Note: Figures cover the years 1948-1990; Tr = Trace amounts (<0.05 in. of rain; <0.5 in. of snow)
Source: National Climatic Data Center, International Station Meteorological Climate Summary, 3/95

Weather Conditions

Temperature			Daytime Sky			Precipitation		
5°F & below	32°F & below	90°F & above	Clear	Partly cloudy	Cloudy	0.01 inch or more precip.	0.1 inch or more snow/ice	Thunder-storms
32	171	12	87	131	147	125	32	19

Note: Figures are average number of days per year and covers the years 1948-1990
Source: National Climatic Data Center, International Station Meteorological Climate Summary, 3/95

AIR & WATER QUALITY

Maximum Pollutant Concentrations

	Particulate Matter (ug/m^3)	Carbon Monoxide (ppm)	Sulfur Dioxide (ppm)	Nitrogen Dioxide (ppm)	Ozone (ppm)	Lead (ug/m^3)
MSA[1] Level	n/a	n/a	n/a	n/a	n/a	n/a
NAAQS[2]	150	9	0.140	0.053	0.12	1.50
Met NAAQS?	n/a	n/a	n/a	n/a	n/a	n/a

Note: (1) Metropolitan Statistical Area - see Appendix A for areas included; (2) National Ambient Air Quality Standards; ppm = parts per million; ug/m^3 = micrograms per cubic meter; n/a not available
Source: EPA, National Air Quality and Emissions Trends Report, 1997

Drinking Water

Water System Name	Pop. Served	Primary Water Source Type	Number of Violations in 1998	Type of Violation/ Contaminants
Manchester Water Works	128,000	Surface	None	None

Note: Data as of July 10, 1999
Source: EPA, Office of Ground Water and Drinking Water, Safe Drinking Water Information System

Manchester tap water is slightly acid, very soft.
Editor & Publisher Market Guide, 1999

New York, New York

Background

Few cities in the world can compare with New York's frenetic excitement. The city is snappy, quick, loaded with attitude, and beautiful, known for its famous skyline and the world's best known bridge, the Brooklyn Bridge.

New York is the largest city in New York State, and located on its southernmost extension, at the mouth of the Hudson River. The area was first explored by Giovanni De Verrazano in 1524, and then by Henry Hudson in 1609. The first Dutch settlers came in 1624, and by 1625, the area had become the permanent settlement of New Amsterdam. A year later, as the famous story goes, the island of Manhattan was bought for a mere $24 by Peter Minuit from the local tribes.

After New York was no longer the temporary capitals of both New York State and the United States, the city continued to grow in importance and stature. It became the city, where, according to singer Frank Sinatra, "If you can make it there, you'll make it anywhere." The city offers the very best in the arts—the Metropolitan Museum of Art, The Museum of Modern Art, and the Guggenheim Museum; education—New York University and Columbia University; finance—the New York and the American Stock Exchanges; plus fashion, theatres, restaurants, political activism, and more. New York is competitive, sometimes stressful, and home to over 7 million people.

Many projects are underway. Construction crews recently broke ground for a 48-story office tower at 42nd Street and Broadway. The Disney Corporation is renovating the New Amsterdam Theater. Madame Tussaud's Wax Museum is planning a major new attraction. AMC is building the city's largest movie house, with 25 screens. The 42nd Street project will create 2,800 jobs and more than $330 million in economic activity.

Another major project is Harlem USA, a $56 million, retail-entertainment complex that will house a Disney store, multi-screen movie theater, indoor ice-skating rink, health center and a 53,000-square-foot supermarket, all scheduled for a late 1999 opening.

Though New York City ranks low in job growth compared with other large metropolitan areas, like Atlanta and Dallas, and its unemployment rate is above the national rate, the city still continues to dominate high-paying industries ranging from advertising to broadcasting. It is still the world's undisputed financial capital and home to over 1,000 small companies in the software business. Being a center of cultural life gives the city a long-lasting allure. The overall crime rate is down to its lowest level in 30 years and The National Civic League named New York City as one of the country's 10 all-American cities in 1997. According to a 1997 Harris Poll, New York was ranked the city that most people wanted to live in or near.

The New York metro area is close to the path of most storm and frontal systems which move across the continent. The city can experience very high temperatures in summer and very low temperatures in winter, despite being on the coast. The passage of many weather systems helps to reduce the duration of both cold and warm spells and serves to circulate the air, reducing stagnation.

General Rankings and Evaluative Comments

- New York was ranked #3 out of 15 large, northeastern metropolitan areas in *Money's* 1998 survey of "The Best Places to Live in America." The survey was conducted by first contacting 512 representative households nationwide and asking them to rank 37 quality-of-life factors on a scale of 1 to 10. Next, a demographic profile was compiled on the 300 largest metropolitan statistical areas in the U.S. The numbers were crunched together to arrive at an overall ranking (things Americans consider most important, like clean air and water, low crime and good schools, received extra weight). Unlike previous years, the 1998 rankings were broken down by region (northeast, midwest, south, west) and population size (100,000 to 249,999; 250,000 to 999,999; 1 million plus). The city had a nationwide ranking of #151 out of 300 in 1997 and #231 out of 300 in 1996. *Money, July 1998; Money, July 1997; Money, September 1996*

- *Ladies Home Journal* ranked America's 200 largest cities based on the qualities women care about most. New York ranked #184 out of 200. Criteria: low crime rate, well-paying jobs, quality health and child care, good public schools, the presence of women in government, size of the gender wage gap, number of sexual-harassment and discrimination complaints filed, unemployment and divorce rates, commute times, population density, number of houses of worship, parks and cultural offerings, number of women's health specialists, how well a community's women cared for themselves, complexion kindness index based on UV radiation levels, odds of finding affordable fashions, rental rates for romance movies, champagne sales and other matters of the heart. *Ladies Home Journal, November 1998*

- Zero Population Growth ranked 229 cities in terms of children's health, safety, and economic well-being. New York was ranked #10 out of 25 major cities (main city in a metro area with population of greater than 2 million) and was given a grade of C+. Criteria: total population, percent of population under 18 years of age, household language, percent population change, percent of births to teens, infant mortality rate, percent of low birth weights, dropout rate, enrollment in preprimary school, violent and property crime rates, unemployment rate, percent of children in poverty, percent of owner occupied units, number of bad air days, percent of public transportation commuters, and average travel time to work. *Zero Population Growth, Children's Environmental Index, Fall 1999*

- New York was ranked #58 out of 59 metro areas in *The Regional Economist's* "Rational Livability Ranking of 59 Large Metro Areas." The rankings were based on the metro area's total population change over the period 1990-97 divided by the number of people moving in from elsewhere in the United States (net domestic in-migration). *St. Louis Federal Reserve Bank of St. Louis, The Regional Economist, April 1999*

- New York appeared on *Travel & Leisure's* list of the world's 100 best cities. It was ranked #3 in the U.S. and #9 in the world. Criteria: activities/attractions, culture/arts, people, restaurants/food, and value. *Travel & Leisure, 1998 World's Best Awards*

- *Conde Nast Traveler* polled 37,293 readers for travel satisfaction. Cities were ranked based on the following criteria: people/friendliness, environment/ambiance, cultural enrichment, restaurants and fun/energy. New York appeared in the top 25, ranking number 8, with an overall rating of 70.7 out of 100. *Conde Nast Traveler, Readers' Choice Poll 1998*

- New York was selected by *Yahoo! Internet Life* as one of "America's Most Wired Cities & Towns." The city ranked #16 out of 50. Criteria: home and work net use, domain density, hosts per capita, directory density and content quality. *Yahoo! Internet Life, March 1999*

- Cognetics studied 273 metro areas in the United States, ranking them by entrepreneurial activity. New York was ranked #47 out of the 50 largest metro areas. Criteria: Significant Starts (firms started in the last 10 years that still employ at least 5 people) and Young Growers (percent of firms 10 years old or less that grew significantly during the last 4 years). Cognetics, "Entrepreneurial Hot Spots: The Best Places in America to Start and Grow a Company," 1998

- New York was included among *Entrepreneur* magazine's listing of the "20 Best Cities for Small Business." It was ranked #2 among northeastern metro areas. Criteria: entrepreneurial activity, small-business growth, economic growth, and risk of failure. *Entrepreneur, October 1999*

- New York was selected as one of the "Best American Cities to Start a Business" by *Point of View* magazine. Criteria: coolness, quality-of-life, and business concerns. The city was ranked #50 out of 75. *Point of View, November 1998*

- *Computerworld* selected the best markets for IT job seekers based on their annual salary, skills, and hiring surveys. New York ranked #5 out of 10. *Computerworld, January 11, 1999*

- Reliastar Financial Corp. ranked the 125 largest metropolitan areas according to the general financial security of residents. New York was ranked #124 out of 125 with a score of -27.6. The score indicates the percentage a metropolitan area is above or below the metropolitan norm. A metro area with a score of 10.6 is 10.6% above the metro average. Criteria: Earnings and Wealth Potential (household income, education, net assets, cost of living); Safety Net (health insurance, retirement savings, life insurance, income support programs); Personal Threats (unemployment rate, low-income households, crime rate); Community Economic Vitality (cost of community services, job quality, job creation, housing costs). *Reliastar Financial Corp., "The Best Cities to Earn and Save Money," 1999 Edition*

Business Environment

STATE ECONOMY

State Economic Profile

"New York is starting to decelerate from its strongest performance in over a decade. Manufacturing employment continues to contract, particularly in upstate. Since most of its growth downstate is driven by Wall Street, NY's job outlook remains vulnerable to swings in the stock market. Population declines will continue to be one of NY's primary problems.

Almost all of 1998's job gains were in the New York City-Long Island area. NY state added some 140,800 jobs in 1998, 134,300 of those in NYC/Long Island. The bulk of these were concentrated in the services sector, particularly business and financial services. The raging bull market has done wonders for NYC and the surrounding suburbs. Since we do not expect a downturn in the stock market in 1999, job growth in NY will continue, albeit at a slower rate.

While NYC has been on a roll, upstate is only seeing some modest easing in its stagnant economy. Buffalo witnessed an increase of 0.2% job growth in 1998. Similar weak growth (0.3%) occurred in Rochester. Job cuts by Kodak and Xerox only added to the troubled upstate economy. Increased state tax revenues, largely from Wall Street, have allowed some government employment gains in Albany.

New York's primary constraint is its continued loss of residents, particularly among younger households. Although home sales rose 6% in 1998, appreciation has only been modest in the NYC area and weak upstate. Rising construction payrolls were largely concentrated in the NYC commercial market, with only an 8% increase in residential permits. As a result of declining population, NY is likely to lose two congressional seats in the post-2000 redistricting, pushing the decline of its political capital and accompanying federal dollars." *National Association of Realtors, Economic Profiles: The Fifty States and the District of Columbia, http://nar.realtor.com/databank/profiles.htm*

IMPORTS/EXPORTS

Total Export Sales

Area	1994 ($000)	1995 ($000)	1996 ($000)	1997 ($000)	% Chg. 1994-97	% Chg. 1996-97
MSA[1]	23,543,749	27,131,084	27,970,507	29,082,571	23.5	4.0
U.S.	512,415,609	583,030,524	622,827,063	687,597,999	34.2	10.4

Note: (1) Metropolitan Statistical Area - see Appendix A for areas included
Source: U.S. Department of Commerce, International Trade Association, Metropolitan Area Exports: An Export Performance Report on Over 250 U.S. Cities, November 10, 1998

CITY FINANCES

City Government Finances

Component	FY94 ($000)	FY94 (per capita $)
Revenue	44,930,293	6,101.76
Expenditure	49,002,330	6,654.76
Debt Outstanding	40,295,356	5,472.31
Cash & Securities	61,986,313	8,418.05

Source: U.S. Bureau of the Census, City Government Finances: 1993-94

City Government Revenue by Source

Source	FY94 ($000)	FY94 (per capita $)	FY94 (%)
From Federal Government	1,476,961	200.58	3.3
From State Governments	14,193,538	1,927.55	31.6
From Local Governments	141,530	19.22	0.3
Property Taxes	7,870,393	1,068.84	17.5
General Sales Taxes	2,503,646	340.01	5.6
Selective Sales Taxes	1,143,078	155.24	2.5
Income Taxes	6,069,153	824.22	13.5
Current Charges	4,252,073	577.45	9.5
Utility/Liquor Store	2,165,917	294.14	4.8
Employee Retirement[1]	3,267,783	443.78	7.3
Other	1,846,221	250.73	4.1

Note: (1) Excludes "city contributions," classified as "nonrevenue," intragovernmental transfers.
Source: U.S. Bureau of the Census, City Government Finances: 1993-94

City Government Expenditures by Function

Function	FY94 ($000)	FY94 (per capita $)	FY94 (%)
Educational Services	9,308,163	1,264.09	19.0
Employee Retirement[1]	3,731,065	506.70	7.6
Environment/Housing	4,526,245	614.69	9.2
Government Administration	1,250,636	169.84	2.6
Interest on General Debt	1,786,406	242.60	3.6
Public Safety	4,071,222	552.89	8.3
Social Services	11,807,299	1,603.49	24.1
Transportation	1,066,127	144.79	2.2
Utility/Liquor Store	4,420,933	600.38	9.0
Other	7,034,234	955.28	14.4

Note: (1) Payments to beneficiaries including withdrawal of contributions.
Source: U.S. Bureau of the Census, City Government Finances: 1993-94

Municipal Bond Ratings

Area	Moody's	S & P
New York	Aaa	n/a

Note: n/a not available; n/r not rated
Source: Moody's Bond Record, 6/99

POPULATION

Population Growth

Area	1980	1990	% Chg. 1980-90	July 1998 Estimate	% Chg. 1990-98
City	7,071,639	7,322,564	3.5	7,420,166	1.3
MSA[1]	8,274,961	8,546,846	3.3	8,675,635	1.5
U.S.	226,545,805	248,765,170	9.8	270,299,000	8.7

Note: (1) Metropolitan Statistical Area - see Appendix A for areas included;
July 1998 MSA population estimate was calculated by the editors
Source: 1980/1990 Census of Housing and Population, Summary Tape File 3C;
Census Bureau Population Estimates 1998

Population Characteristics

Race	City				% Chg. 1980-90	MSA[1]	
	1980		1990			1990	
	Population	%	Population	%		Population	%
White	4,348,605	61.5	3,831,907	52.3	-11.9	4,832,376	56.5
Black	1,788,377	25.3	2,107,137	28.8	17.8	2,254,576	26.4
Amer Indian/Esk/Aleut	13,400	0.2	22,718	0.3	69.5	24,822	0.3
Asian/Pacific Islander	245,759	3.5	510,549	7.0	107.7	553,987	6.5
Other	675,498	9.6	850,253	11.6	25.9	881,085	10.3
Hispanic Origin[2]	1,406,024	19.9	1,737,927	23.7	23.6	1,842,127	21.6

Note: (1) Metropolitan Statistical Area - see Appendix A for areas included;
(2) people of Hispanic origin can be of any race
Source: 1980/1990 Census of Housing and Population, Summary Tape File 3C

Ancestry

Area	German	Irish	English	Italian	U.S.	French	Polish	Dutch
City	5.4	7.3	2.4	11.5	2.1	0.9	4.1	0.3
MSA[1]	6.4	8.9	3.0	13.2	2.3	1.0	4.3	0.4
U.S.	23.3	15.6	13.1	5.9	5.3	4.2	3.8	2.5

Note: Figures are percentages and include persons that reported multiple ancestry (eg. if a person reported being Irish and Italian, they were included in both columns); (1) Metropolitan Statistical Area - see Appendix A for areas included
Source: 1990 Census of Population and Housing, Summary Tape File 3C

Age

Area	Median Age (Years)	Age Distribution (%)						
		Under 5	Under 18	18-24	25-44	45-64	65+	80+
City	33.6	6.9	23.0	10.3	33.9	19.8	13.0	3.1
MSA[1]	33.9	6.8	23.0	10.2	33.7	20.1	13.0	3.1
U.S.	32.9	7.3	25.6	10.5	32.6	18.7	12.5	2.8

Note: (1) Metropolitan Statistical Area - see Appendix A for areas included
Source: 1990 Census of Population and Housing, Summary Tape File 3C

Male/Female Ratio

Area	Number of males per 100 females (all ages)	Number of males per 100 females (18 years old+)
City	88.1	84.5
MSA[1]	88.6	85.0
U.S.	95.0	91.9

Note: (1) Metropolitan Statistical Area - see Appendix A for areas included
Source: 1990 Census of Population, General Population Characteristics

INCOME

Per Capita/Median/Average Income

Area	Per Capita ($)	Median Household ($)	Average Household ($)
City	16,281	29,823	41,741
MSA[1]	17,397	31,659	45,159
U.S.	14,420	30,056	38,453

Note: All figures are for 1989; (1) Metropolitan Statistical Area - see Appendix A for areas included
Source: 1990 Census of Population and Housing, Summary Tape File 3C

Household Income Distribution by Race

Income ($)	City (%)					U.S. (%)				
	Total	White	Black	Other	Hisp.[1]	Total	White	Black	Other	Hisp.[1]
Less than 5,000	8.9	6.1	13.4	12.9	14.4	6.2	4.8	15.2	8.6	8.8
5,000 - 9,999	11.3	10.1	12.6	13.5	16.3	9.3	8.6	14.2	9.9	11.1
10,000 - 14,999	7.5	7.1	7.8	9.0	9.4	8.8	8.5	11.0	9.8	11.0
15,000 - 24,999	15.2	13.5	17.9	17.7	18.1	17.5	17.3	18.9	18.5	20.5
25,000 - 34,999	14.1	13.7	14.7	14.5	14.5	15.8	16.1	14.2	15.4	16.4
35,000 - 49,999	15.9	16.7	14.9	14.5	13.7	17.9	18.6	13.3	16.1	16.0
50,000 - 74,999	14.6	16.4	12.3	11.5	9.5	15.0	15.8	9.3	13.4	11.1
75,000 - 99,999	6.0	7.5	4.1	3.6	2.7	5.1	5.5	2.6	4.7	3.1
100,000+	6.4	9.0	2.2	2.7	1.4	4.4	4.8	1.3	3.7	1.9

Note: All figures are for 1989; (1) people of Hispanic origin can be of any race
Source: 1990 Census of Population and Housing, Summary Tape File 3C

Effective Buying Income

Area	Per Capita ($)	Median Household ($)	Average Household ($)
City	18,062	35,069	47,683
MSA[1]	19,236	35,740	51,190
U.S.	16,803	34,536	45,243

Note: Data as of 1/1/99; (1) Metropolitan Statistical Area - see Appendix A for areas included
Source: Standard Rate & Data Service, Newspaper Advertising Source, 9/99

Effective Household Buying Income Distribution

Area	% of Households Earning						
	$10,000 -$19,999	$20,000 -$34,999	$35,000 -$49,999	$50,000 -$74,999	$75,000 -$99,000	$100,000 -$124,999	$125,000 and up
City	14.7	19.9	15.8	18.0	8.5	3.6	4.2
MSA[1]	14.4	19.7	16.1	18.3	8.3	3.4	4.7
U.S.	16.0	22.6	18.2	18.9	7.2	2.4	2.7

Note: Data as of 1/1/99; (1) Metropolitan Statistical Area - see Appendix A for areas included
Source: Standard Rate & Data Service, Newspaper Advertising Source, 9/99

Poverty Rates by Race and Age

Area	Total (%)	By Race (%)				By Age (%)		
		White	Black	Other	Hisp.[2]	Under 5 years old	Under 18 years old	65 years and over
City	19.3	12.3	25.3	29.4	33.2	30.5	30.1	16.5
MSA[1]	17.5	10.8	24.8	28.4	32.3	27.5	27.1	15.3
U.S.	13.1	9.8	29.5	23.1	25.3	20.1	18.3	12.8

Note: Figures show the percent of people living below the poverty line in 1989. The average poverty threshold was $12,674 for a family of four in 1989; (1) Metropolitan Statistical Area - see Appendix A for areas included; (2) people of Hispanic origin can be of any race
Source: 1990 Census of Population and Housing, Summary Tape File 3C

EMPLOYMENT

Labor Force and Employment

Area	Civilian Labor Force			Workers Employed		
	Jun. 1998	Jun. 1999	% Chg.	Jun. 1998	Jun. 1999	% Chg.
City	8,939,560	8,961,027	0.2	8,469,185	8,512,422	0.5
MSA[1]	4,097,393	4,073,782	-0.6	3,816,774	3,826,056	0.2
U.S.	138,798,000	140,666,000	1.3	132,265,000	134,395,000	1.6

Note: Data is not seasonally adjusted and covers workers 16 years of age and older; (1) Metropolitan Statistical Area - see Appendix A for areas included
Source: Bureau of Labor Statistics, http://stats.bls.gov

Unemployment Rate

Area	1998						1999					
	Jul.	Aug.	Sep.	Oct.	Nov.	Dec.	Jan.	Feb.	Mar.	Apr.	May.	Jun.
City	5.6	5.2	5.3	5.2	5.2	5.1	5.9	6.0	5.5	4.9	4.9	5.0
MSA[1]	7.3	6.9	6.9	7.2	7.0	6.8	7.3	7.3	6.3	5.9	5.8	6.1
U.S.	4.7	4.5	4.4	4.2	4.1	4.0	4.8	4.7	4.4	4.1	4.0	4.5

Note: Data is not seasonally adjusted and covers workers 16 years of age and older; all figures are percentages; (1) Metropolitan Statistical Area - see Appendix A for areas included
Source: Bureau of Labor Statistics, http://stats.bls.gov

Employment by Industry

Sector	MSA[1]		U.S.
	Number of Employees	Percent of Total	Percent of Total
Services	1,580,100	38.0	30.4
Retail Trade	495,300	11.9	17.7
Government	643,400	15.5	15.6
Manufacturing	312,800	7.5	14.3
Finance/Insurance/Real Estate	523,700	12.6	5.9
Wholesale Trade	223,200	5.4	5.4
Transportation/Public Utilities	237,400	5.7	5.3
Construction	n/a	n/a	5.0
Mining	n/a	n/a	0.4

Note: Figures cover non-farm employment as of 6/99 and are not seasonally adjusted; (1) Metropolitan Statistical Area - see Appendix A for areas included; n/a not available
Source: Bureau of Labor Statistics, http://stats.bls.gov

Employment by Occupation

Occupation Category	City (%)	MSA[1] (%)	U.S. (%)
White Collar	64.6	65.5	58.1
Executive/Admin./Management	13.5	14.2	12.3
Professional	17.0	17.5	14.1
Technical & Related Support	3.1	3.1	3.7
Sales	10.3	10.6	11.8
Administrative Support/Clerical	20.6	20.0	16.3
Blue Collar	19.2	18.7	26.2
Precision Production/Craft/Repair	7.5	7.7	11.3
Machine Operators/Assem./Insp.	4.9	4.5	6.8
Transportation/Material Movers	3.7	3.6	4.1
Cleaners/Helpers/Laborers	3.1	2.9	3.9
Services	16.0	15.4	13.2
Farming/Forestry/Fishing	0.3	0.4	2.5

Note: Figures cover employed persons 16 years old and over; (1) Metropolitan Statistical Area - see Appendix A for areas included
Source: 1990 Census of Population and Housing, Summary Tape File 3C

Occupational Employment Projections: 1996 - 2006

Occupations Expected to Have the Largest Job Growth (ranked by numerical growth)	Fast-Growing Occupations[1] (ranked by percent growth)
1. Salespersons, retail	1. Computer scientists
2. Home health aides	2. Systems analysts
3. Cashiers	3. Computer engineers
4. Teachers, secondary school	4. Computer support specialists
5. Systems analysts	5. Data processing equipment repairers
6. Teachers, special education	6. Database administrators
7. Personal and home care aides	7. Electronic pagination systems workers
8. Maintenance repairers, general utility	8. Teachers, special education
9. Guards	9. Medical assistants
10. Stock clerks, stockroom or warehouse	10. Physical therapy assistants and aides

Note: Projections cover New York State; (1) Excludes occupations with total job growth less than 1,000
Source: New York State Department of Labor, Occupational Outlook, Employment & Openings by Occupation, 1996-2006

TAXES

Major State and Local Tax Rates

State Corp. Income (%)	State Personal Income (%)	Residential Property (effective rate per $100)	Sales & Use		State Gasoline (cents/ gallon)	State Cigarette (cents/ pack)
			State (%)	Local (%)		
9.0[a]	4.0 - 6.85	0.75	4.0	4.25	8.0[b]	56.0

Note: Personal/corporate income, sales, gasoline and cigarette tax rates as of January 1999.
Property tax rates as of 1997; (a) Or 1.78 (0.1 for banks) mills per dollar of capital (up to $350,000; or 3.25% (3% after 7/1/99) (3% for banks) of the minimum taxable income; or a minimum of $100 to $1,500 depending on payroll size ($250 plus 2.5% surtax for banks); if any of these is greater than the tax computed on net income. An addition tax of 0.9 mills per dollar of subsidiary capital is imposed on corporations. Small businesses with income under $200,000 pay tax of 8% of income.; (b) Carriers pay an additional surcharge of 22.21 cents
Source: Federation of Tax Administrators, www.taxadmin.org; Washington D.C. Department of Finance and Revenue, Tax Rates and Tax Burdens in the District of Columbia: A Nationwide Comparison, July 1998; Chamber of Commerce, 1999

Total Taxes Per Capita and as a Percent of Income

Area	Per Capita Income ($)	Per Capita Taxes ($)			Percent of Income (%)		
		Total	Federal	State/ Local	Total	Federal	State/ Local
New York	33,564	12,439	7,876	4,564	37.1	23.5	13.6
U.S.	27,876	9,881	6,690	3,191	35.4	24.0	11.4

Note: Figures are for 1998
Source: Tax Foundation, www.taxfoundation.org

Estimated Tax Burden

Area	State Income	Local Income	Property	Sales	Total
New York	3,384	2,436	3,750	804	10,374

Note: The numbers are estimates of taxes paid by a married couple with two children and annual earnings of $75,000. Sales tax estimates assume they spend average amounts on food, clothing, household goods and gasoline. Property tax estimates assume they live in a $250,000 home.
Source: Kiplinger's Personal Finance Magazine, October 1998

COMMERCIAL REAL ESTATE

Office Market

Class/ Location	Total Space (sq. ft.)	Vacant Space (sq. ft.)	Vac. Rate (%)	Under Constr. (sq. ft.)	Net Absorp. (sq. ft.)	Rental Rates ($/sq.ft./yr.)
Class A						
CBD	178,187,000	10,457,000	5.9	1,478,000	4,917,000	19.00-100.00
Outside CBD	55,625,000	3,250,000	5.8	n/a	2,268,000	18.00-52.00
Class B						
CBD	66,732,000	5,789,000	8.7	n/a	2,434,000	13.00-60.00
Outside CBD	35,462,000	4,794,000	13.5	n/a	2,105,000	15.00-38.00

Note: Data as of 10/98 and covers Manhattan; CBD = Central Business District; n/a not available; Source: Society of Industrial and Office Realtors, 1999 Comparative Statistics of Industrial and Office Real Estate Markets

"Market fundamentals for 1999 add up to a good year. Absorption is expected to rise six to 10 percent, and vacancy rates will likely fall. Although no new speculative office buildings are planned, a number of new projects with substantial levels of pre-leased space have already been announced, particularly in Times Square and Columbus Circle. In those cases, the anchor tenants will be Time-Warner and Reuters. The SIOR reporter indicates that motion picture services are the fastest growing employment sector in Manhattan. Several new television and movie production studios have been proposed for Manhattan. They include Hudson River Studios at Hudson and West Street. However, the importance of the securities industry in Manhattan means that a downturn in employment in that sector would have a significant negative impact on the office market." *Society of Industrial and Office Realtors, 1999 Comparative Statistics of Industrial and Office Real Estate Markets*

Industrial Market

Location	Total Space (sq. ft.)	Vacant Space (sq. ft.)	Vac. Rate (%)	Under Constr. (sq. ft.)	Net Absorp. (sq. ft.)	Gross Lease ($/sq.ft./yr.)
Central City	217,385,480	21,802,687	10.0	n/a	6,949,779	n/a
Suburban	n/a	n/a	n/a	n/a	n/a	n/a

Note: Data as of 10/98 and covers Brooklyn/Queens; n/a not available
Source: Society of Industrial and Office Realtors, 1999 Comparative Statistics of Industrial and Office Real Estate Markets

"There is an enormous base of industrial space in the area—217.4 million sq. ft.—which tends to lend stability to this market. A tendency for Manhattan tenants to move to Brooklyn and Queens has recently occurred because of rising lease prices in their current locations, a desire for more efficient space, and the need for larger facilities. On the whole, more than 75 percent of the transactions have taken place with local companies who either purchase for their own use or enter into long-term leases with their landlords. In spite of the anticipated slow-down in economic and real estate activity, the local SIOR reporter sees improvements in nearly all categories. He indicates that absorption of warehouse and manufacturing space will rise by six to 10 percent and that lease prices for all types of industrial space will increase by one to five percent. He forecasts gains in construction of one to five percent for warehouse, manufacturing, and High Tech/R&D space." *Society of Industrial and Office Realtors, 1999 Comparative Statistics of Industrial and Office Real Estate Markets*

Retail Market

Shopping Center Inventory (sq. ft.)	Shopping Center Construction (sq. ft.)	Construction as a Percent of Inventory (%)	Torto Wheaton Rent Index[1] ($/sq. ft.)
n/a	n/a	n/a	n/a

Note: Data as of 1997 and covers the Metropolitan Statistical Area - see Appendix A for areas included; (1) Index is based on a model that predicts what the average rent should be for leases with certain characteristics, in certain locations during certain years.
Source: National Association of Realtors, 1997-1998 Market Conditions Report

" After four years of declines in retail sales, retailers bounced back with sales increasing roughly 3.0% per year during the last three years. The employment picture for New York City is a little misleading. During the past year, the unemployment rate has risen over one percentage point. However, employment growth is currently the highest this decade. Which is giving the more accurate picture? Both. The unemployment rate has increased due to a large jump in the share of people looking for jobs. This is occurring because of New York City's relatively healthy job market. The uptrend in employment growth has fueled retail sales somewhat; however, sales remain soft in comparison with the U.S. The retail sector could get a boost soon because the city is projected to finish the fiscal year with a $350 million surplus. Thus, burdensom state and local taxes should subside over the next few years." *National Association of Realtors, 1997-1998 Market Conditions Report*

COMMERCIAL UTILITIES

Typical Monthly Electric Bills

Area	Commercial Service ($/month)		Industrial Service ($/month)	
	12 kW demand 1,500 kWh	100 kW demand 30,000 kWh	1,000 kW demand 400,000 kWh	20,000 kW demand 10,000,000 kWh
City	340	3,890	39,422	561,364
U.S.	150	2,174	23,995	508,569

Note: Based on rates in effect January 1, 1999
Source: Edison Electric Institute, Typical Residential, Commercial and Industrial Bills, Winter 1999

TRANSPORTATION

Transportation Statistics

Average minutes to work	36.5
Interstate highways	I-78; I-87; I-95
Bus lines	
In-city	New York City TA, 4,037 vehicles
Inter-city	34
Passenger air service	
Airport	JFK International; LaGuardia; Newark International (NJ)
Airlines	90+
Aircraft departures	400,944 (1996)
Enplaned passengers	32,212,982 (1996)
Rail service	Amtrak; Metro-North; LIRR; Staten Island Rapid Transit
Motor freight carriers	369
Major waterways/ports	Port of New York/New Jersey

Source: Editor & Publisher Market Guide, 1999; FAA Airport Activity Statistics, 1997; Amtrak National Time Table, Northeast Timetable, Spring/Summer 1999; 1990 Census of Population and Housing, STF 3C; Chamber of Commerce/Economic Development 1999; Jane's Urban Transport Systems 1999-2000

Means of Transportation to Work

Area	Car/Truck/Van		Public Transportation			Bicycle	Walked	Other Means	Worked at Home
	Drove Alone	Car-pooled	Bus	Subway	Railroad				
City	24.0	8.5	12.7	36.7	1.7	0.3	10.7	2.9	2.4
MSA[1]	30.7	8.9	11.4	30.9	3.0	0.3	9.7	2.6	2.5
U.S.	73.2	13.4	3.0	1.5	0.5	0.4	3.9	1.2	3.0

Note: Figures shown are percentages and only include workers 16 years old and over;
(1) Metropolitan Statistical Area - see Appendix A for areas included
Source: 1990 Census of Population and Housing, Summary Tape File 3C

BUSINESSES

Major Business Headquarters

Company Name	1999 Rankings	
	Fortune 500	Forbes 500
AT&T	10	-
Advance Publications	-	46
Amerada Hess	251	-

Company Name	1999 Rankings	
	Fortune 500	Forbes 500
American Express	72	-
American Intl. Group	22	-
Andersen Worldwide	-	8
Avon Products	308	-
Bank of New York	285	-
Bankers Trust Corp.	140	-
Barnes & Noble	489	-
Bear Stearns	204	-
Bell Atlantic	25	-
Bloomberg LP	-	148
Bridge Information Systems	-	125
Bristol-Myers Squibb	77	-
CBS	172	-
Cendant	282	-
Chase Manhattan Corp.	23	-
Citigroup	7	-
Colgate-Palmolive	177	-
Consolidated Edison	239	-
Continental Grain	-	5
Deloitte Touche Tohmatsu	-	14
Dover	324	-
Eastman Kodak	121	-
Empire Beef	-	384
Ernst & Young	-	12
Estee Lauder	417	-
Gilman Investment	-	391
Goldman Sachs & Co	-	4
GoodTimes Entertainment	-	494
Gould Paper	-	272
Guardian Life of America	205	-
Hartz Group	-	354
Hearst	-	60
Helmsley Enterprises	-	199
Horsehead Industries	-	304
ICC Industries	-	173
Interpublic Group	387	-
J Crew	-	262
J.P. Morgan	76	-
KPMG Peat Marwick	-	11
Lehman Brothers	66	-
Loew's	60	-
M Fabrikant & Sons	-	289
MacAndrews & Forbes Holdings	-	54
MacManus Group	-	260
Marsh & Mclennan	232	-
McGraw-Hill	406	-
McKinsey & Co	-	66
Merrill Lynch	19	-
Metropolitan Life Insurance	39	-
Morgan Stanley Dean Witter	29	-
Neuberger Berman	-	466
New York Life Insurance	68	-
New York Times	495	-
Omnicom Group	378	-
Paine Webber Group	230	-
Parsons Brinckerhoff	-	294
Peerless Importers	-	373
Perry H Koplik & Sons	-	411
Pfizer	106	-

Company Name	1999 Rankings	
	Fortune 500	Forbes 500
Philip Morris	8	-
Price Waterhouse Coopers	-	6
RAB Holdings	-	444
RJR Nabisco Holdings	89	-
Red Apple Group	-	70
Reliance Group Holdings	437	-
Renco Group	-	50
Republic New York	424	-
Skadden Arps Slate Meagher & Flom	-	269
TIAA-CREF	18	-
Time Warner	108	-
Tishman Realty & Construction	-	226
Towers Perrin	-	165
Transammonia	-	71
Turner Corp.	375	-
United Auto Group	482	-
Venator	287	-
Viacom	138	-
Warren Equities	-	365
Wegmans Food Markets	-	61
Westvaco	499	-

Note: Companies listed are located in the city; dashes indicate no ranking
Fortune 500: Companies that produce a 10-K are ranked 1 to 500 based on 1998 revenue
Forbes 500: Private companies are ranked 1 to 500 based on 1997 revenue
Source: Forbes, November 30, 1998; Fortune, April 26, 1999

Best Companies to Work For

Goldman Sachs (brokerage), Merrill Lynch (brokerage) and Ernst & Young (accounting), headquartered in New York, are among the "100 Best Companies to Work for in America." Criteria: trust in management, pride in work/company, camaraderie, company responses to the Hewitt People Practices Inventory, and employee responses to their Great Place to Work survey. The companies also had to be at least 10 years old and have a minimum of 500 employees. *Fortune, January 11, 1999*

American Express, AT&T, BankersTrust, Bristol-Myers Squibb, Chase Manhattan Bank, Citicorp/Citibank, Coopers & Lybrand, Donaldson Lufkin & Jenrette, Ernst & Young, Merrill Lynch, J.P. Morgan, Pfizer and PriceWaterhouse, headquartered in New York, are among the "100 Best Companies for Working Mothers." Criteria: fair wages, opportunities for women to advance, support for child care, flexible work schedules, family-friendly benefits, and work/life supports. *Working Mother, October 1998*

Price Waterhouse LLP (professional services/consulting), AT&T Corp., Deloitte & Touche LLP (professional services/consulting), Ernst & Young (professional services/consulting), The Chase Manhattan Corp. (financial services), Metropolitan Life Insurance Co. (insurance), Brooklyn Union Gas (utility), New York Life Insurance Co. (insurance), TransAtlantic Holdings, Inc. (insurance), headquartered in New York, are among the "100 Best Places to Work in IS." Criteria: compensation, turnover and training. *Computerworld, May 25, 1998*

Avon Products, Scholastic Corp. and American Express Corp., headquartered in New York, are among the top public firms for executive women. Criteria: number of female directors, women in senior management positions and the ratio of female managers to female employees. *Working Women, September 1998*

Fast-Growing Businesses

According to *Inc.*, New York is home to three of America's 100 fastest-growing private companies: Jade Systems, International Transport Solutions and PC Ware International. Criteria for inclusion: must be an independent, privately-held, U.S. corporation, proprietorship or partnership; sales of at least $200,000 in 1995; five-year operating/sales history; increase in 1999 sales over 1998 sales; holding companies, regulated banks, and utilities were excluded. *Inc. 500, 1999*

New York is home to four of *Business Week's* "hot growth" companies: ASI Solutions, Healthworld, Medialink Worldwide and Kenneth Cole Productions. Criteria: increase in sales and profits, return on capital and stock price. *Business Week, 5/31/99*

According to *Fortune*, New York is home to two of America's 100 fastest-growing companies: Actrade International and Impath. Companies were ranked based on earnings-per-share growth, revenue growth and total return over the previous three years. Criteria for inclusion: public companies with sales of least $50 million. Companies that lost money in the most recent quarter, or ended in the red for the past four quarters as a whole, were not eligible. Limited partnerships and REITs were also not considered. *Fortune, "America's Fastest-Growing Companies," 1999*

According to Deloitte & Touche LLP, New York is home to one of America's 100 fastest-growing high-technology companies: Cellular Vision USA. Companies are ranked by percentage growth in revenue over a five-year period. Criteria for inclusion: must be a U.S. company developing and/or providing technology products or services; company must have been in business for five years with 1993 revenues of at least $50,000. *Deloitte & Touche LLP, November 17, 1998*

Women-Owned Firms: Number, Employment and Sales

Area	Number of Firms	Employ-ment	Sales ($000)	Rank[2]
MSA[1]	282,200	1,077,900	193,572,200	1

Note: (1) Metropolitan Statistical Area - see Appendix A for areas included;
(2) Calculated on an averaging of the number of businesses, employment and sales
Source: The National Foundation for Women Business Owners, 1999 Facts on Women-Owned Businesses: Trends in the Top 50 Metropolitan Areas

Women-Owned Firms: Growth

Area	% change from 1992 to 1999			Rank[2]
	Number of Firms	Employ-ment	Sales	
MSA[1]	38.3	96.5	116.2	43

Note: (1) Metropolitan Statistical Area - see Appendix A for areas included; (2) Calculated on an averaging of the percent growth of number of businesses, employment and sales
Source: The National Foundation for Women Business Owners, 1999 Facts on Women-Owned Businesses: Trends in the Top 50 Metropolitan Areas

Minority Business Opportunity

New York is home to seven companies which are on the Black Enterprise Industrial/Service 100 list (largest based on gross sales): TLC Beatrice International Holdings Inc. (manufacturing and distribution of grocery products); Granite Broadcasting Corp. (selling of commercial air-time); Essence Communications Inc. (magazine publishing, catalog sales and entertainment); Rush Communications (music, film, television, advertising, fashion and management); Earl G. Graves Ltd. (magazine publishing, conducts business and upscale recreational conferences); Inner City Broadcasting Corp. (radio broadcasting); Restoration Supermarket Corp. (supermarket and drugstore retail sales) . Criteria: operational in previous calendar year, at least 51% black-owned and manufactures/owns the product it sells or provides industrial or consumer services. Brokerages, real estate firms and firms that provide professional services are not eligible. *Black Enterprise, www.blackenterprise.com*

Eight of the 500 largest Hispanic-owned companies in the U.S. are located in New York. *Hispanic Business, June 1999*

New York is home to two companies which are on the Hispanic Business Fastest-Growing 100 list (greatest sales growth from 1994 to 1998): Delgado Design Inc. (graphic design svcs.); Urban Telecommunications Inc. (telecommunications contractor). *Hispanic Business, July/August 1999*

Small Business Opportunity

According to *Forbes*, New York is home to five of America's 200 best small companies: Actrade International, ASI Solutions, Kenneth Cole Productions, Medialink Worldwide and Richton International. Criteria: companies included must be publicly traded since November 1997 with a stock price of at least $5 per share and an average daily float of 1,000 shares. The company's latest 12-month sales must be between $5 and $350 million, return on equity (ROE) must be a minimum of 12% for both the past 5 years and the most recent four quarters, and five-year sales and EPS growth must average at least 10%. Companies with declining sales or earnings during the past year were dropped as well as businesses with debt/equity ratios over 1.25. Companies with negative operating cash flow in each of the past two years were also excluded. *Forbes, November 2, 1998*

HOTELS & MOTELS

Hotels/Motels

Area	Hotels/ Motels	Rooms	Luxury-Level Hotels/Motels		Average Minimum Rates ($)		
			♦♦♦♦	♦♦♦♦♦	♦♦	♦♦♦	♦♦♦♦
City	173	50,761	17	3	181	237	332
Airport	15	3,395	0	0	n/a	n/a	n/a
Suburbs	22	3,283	0	0	n/a	n/a	n/a
Total	210	57,439	17	3	n/a	n/a	n/a

Note: n/a not available; classifications range from one diamond (budget properties with basic amenities) to five diamond (luxury properties with the finest service, rooms and facilities).
Source: OAG, Business Travel Planner, Winter 1998-99

New York is home to one of the top 100 hotels in the world according to *Travel & Leisure*: Four Seasons (#73) . Criteria: value, rooms/ambience, location, facilities/activities and service. *Travel & Leisure, 1998 World's Best Awards, Best Hotels and Resorts*

CONVENTION CENTERS

Major Convention Centers

Center Name	Meeting Rooms	Exhibit Space (sq. ft.)
Chase Development Center	55	n/a
Chase MetroTech Conference Center (Brooklyn)	14	n/a
Downtown Executive Conference Center	10	n/a
Expo Center at Madison Square Garden	4	54,000
Grand Hyatt New York	49	18,500
Hotel Macklowe and Macklowe Conference Center	33	17,000
International Design Center/New York	11	88,000
Jacob K. Javits Convention Center	100	900,000
Lombardi-Center-Fordham University	6	45,000
Manhattan Center	2	25,000
Marriott-Frenchmen's Reef Beach Resort	13	n/a
New York Design Center	n/a	n/a
New York Hilton and Towers at Rockefeller Center	47	81,500
New York Merchandise Mart	n/a	n/a
Smith Barney Conference Center	25	n/a
The Coleman Center	9	n/a
The Show Piers New York Passenger Ship Terminal	n/a	12,000
Viacom Conference & Training Center	8	3,200
World Trade Institute	11	8,682

Note: n/a not available
Source: Trade Shows Worldwide, 1998; Meetings & Conventions, 4/15/99; Sucessful Meetings, 3/31/98

Living Environment

COST OF LIVING

Cost of Living Index

Composite Index	Groceries	Housing	Utilities	Trans-portation	Health Care	Misc. Goods/Services
232.1	150.2	455.6	163.2	125.4	187.0	137.9

Note: U.S. = 100; Figures are for Manhattan
Source: ACCRA, Cost of Living Index, 1st Quarter 1999

HOUSING

Median Home Prices and Housing Affordability

Area	Median Price[2] 1st Qtr. 1999 ($)	HOI[3] 1st Qtr. 1999	Afford-ability Rank[4]
MSA[1]	165,000	56.8	158
U.S.	134,000	69.6	–

Note: (1) Metropolitan Statistical Area - see Appendix A for areas included; (2) U.S. figures calculated from the sales of 524,324 new and existing homes in 181 markets; (3) Housing Opportunity Index - percent of homes sold that were within the reach of the median income household at the prevailing mortgage interest rate; (4) Rank is from 1-181 with 1 being most affordable
Source: National Association of Home Builders, Housing Opportunity Index, 1st Quarter 1999

Median Home Price Projection

It is projected that the median price of existing single-family homes in the metro area will increase by 4.5% in 1999. Nationwide, home prices are projected to increase 3.8%.
Kiplinger's Personal Finance Magazine, January 1999

Average New Home Price

Area	Price ($)
City[1]	621,667
U.S.	142,735

Note: Figures are based on a new home with 1,800 sq. ft. of living area on an 8,000 sq. ft. lot; (1) Manhattan
Source: ACCRA, Cost of Living Index, 1st Quarter 1999

Average Apartment Rent

Area	Rent ($/mth)
City[1]	3,220
U.S.	601

Note: Figures are based on an unfurnished two bedroom, 1-1/2 or 2 bath apartment, approximately 950 sq. ft. in size, excluding all utilities except water; (1) Manhattan
Source: ACCRA, Cost of Living Index, 1st Quarter 1999

RESIDENTIAL UTILITIES

Average Residential Utility Costs

Area	All Electric ($/mth)	Part Electric ($/mth)	Other Energy ($/mth)	Phone ($/mth)
City[1]	–	77.21	91.19	24.06
U.S.	100.02	55.73	43.33	19.71

Note: (1) Manhattan
Source: ACCRA, Cost of Living Index, 1st Quarter 1999

HEALTH CARE

Average Health Care Costs

Area	Hospital ($/day)	Doctor ($/visit)	Dentist ($/visit)
City[1]	1,462.60	91.00	98.00
U.S.	430.43	52.45	66.35

Note: Hospital—based on a semi-private room; Doctor—based on a general practitioner's routine exam of an established patient; Dentist—based on adult teeth cleaning and periodic oral exam; (1) (1) Manhattan
Source: ACCRA, Cost of Living Index, 1st Quarter 1999

Distribution of Office-Based Physicians

Area	Family/Gen. Practitioners	Specialists		
		Medical	Surgical	Other
MSA[1]	913	9,570	4,885	6,118

Note: Data as of 12/31/97; (1) Metropolitan Statistical Area - see Appendix A for areas included
Source: American Medical Assn., Physician Characteristics & Distribution in the U.S., 1999

Hospitals

New York has 56 general medical and surgical hospitals, 8 psychiatric, 2 eye, ear, nose and throat, 2 orthopedic, 2 chronic disease, 1 alcoholism and other chemical dependency, 2 other specialty, 2 children's psychiatric. *AHA Guide to the Healthcare Field, 1998-99*

According to *U.S. News and World Report,* New York has 10 of the best hospitals in the U.S.: **New York University Medical Center**, noted for gynecology, neurology, rehabilitation, rheumatology; **Mount Sinai Medical Center**, noted for gastroenterology, geriatrics, gynecology, neurology, otolaryngology, psychiatry, rehabilitation, rheumatology; **New York Presbyterian Medical Center**, noted for cancer, cardiology, endocrinology, gastroenterology, geriatrics, gynecology, neurology, orthopedics, otolaryngology, pediatrics, psychiatry, pulmonology, rehabilitation, rheumatology, urology; **Beth Israel Medical Center**, noted for neurology; **Memorial Sloan-Kettering Cancer Center**, noted for cancer, gastroenterology, gynecology, otolaryngology, urology; **Hospital for Special Surgery**, noted for orthopedics, rheumatology; **Hospital for Joint Diseases-Orthopedic Institute**, noted for orthopedics; **New York Eye & Ear Infirmary**, noted for ophthalmology; **Harlem Hospital Center**, noted for geriatrics; **Montefiore Medical Center**, noted for gastroenterology, rheumatology. *U.S. News Online, "America's Best Hospitals," 10th Edition, www.usnews.com*

EDUCATION

Public School District Statistics

District Name	Num. Sch.	Enroll.	Classroom Teachers	Pupils per Teacher	Minority Pupils (%)	Current Exp.[1] ($/pupil)
NYC-Chancellor's Office	1,153	1,071,853	59,718	17.9	84.3	7,428

Note: Data covers the 1997-1998 school year unless otherwise noted; (1) Data covers fiscal year 1996; SD = School District; ISD = Independent School District; n/a not available
Source: National Center for Education Statistics, Common Core of Data Public Education Agency Universe 1997-98; National Center for Education Statistics, Characteristics of the 100 Largest Public Elementary and Secondary School Districts in the United States: 1997-98, July 1999

Educational Quality

School District	Education Quotient[1]	Graduate Outcome[2]	Community Index[3]	Resource Index[4]
New York City	76.0	51.0	56.0	131.0

Note: Nearly 1,000 secondary school districts were rated in terms of educational quality. The scores range from a low of 50 to a high of 150; (1) Average of the Graduate Outcome, Community and Resource indexes; (2) Based on graduation rates and college board scores (SAT/ACT); (3) Based on the surrounding community's average level of education and the area's average income level; (4) Based on teacher salaries, per-pupil expenditures and student-teacher ratios.
Source: Expansion Management, Ratings Issue, 1998

Educational Attainment by Race

Area	High School Graduate (%)					Bachelor's Degree (%)				
	Total	White	Black	Other	Hisp.[2]	Total	White	Black	Other	Hisp.[2]
City	68.3	74.2	64.1	54.6	47.9	23.0	29.2	12.4	17.7	8.2
MSA[1]	70.3	76.1	64.4	55.7	48.6	24.6	30.6	12.7	18.9	8.6
U.S.	75.2	77.9	63.1	60.4	49.8	20.3	21.5	11.4	19.4	9.2

Note: Figures shown cover persons 25 years old and over; (1) Metropolitan Statistical Area -
see Appendix A for areas included; (2) people of Hispanic origin can be of any race
Source: 1990 Census of Population and Housing, Summary Tape File 3C

School Enrollment by Type

Area	Preprimary				Elementary/High School			
	Public		Private		Public		Private	
	Enrollment	%	Enrollment	%	Enrollment	%	Enrollment	%
City	54,891	55.5	43,933	44.5	934,140	79.1	246,344	20.9
MSA[1]	66,531	53.1	58,729	46.9	1,086,038	79.3	283,106	20.7
U.S.	2,679,029	59.5	1,824,256	40.5	38,379,689	90.2	4,187,099	9.8

Note: Figures shown cover persons 3 years old and over;
(1) Metropolitan Statistical Area - see Appendix A for areas included
Source: 1990 Census of Population and Housing, Summary Tape File 3C

School Enrollment by Race

Area	Preprimary (%)				Elementary/High School (%)			
	White	Black	Other	Hisp.[1]	White	Black	Other	Hisp.[1]
City	47.4	35.6	17.1	21.2	38.6	36.8	24.6	32.6
MSA[2]	55.0	30.1	14.9	18.2	43.6	34.0	22.5	29.7
U.S.	80.4	12.5	7.1	7.8	74.1	15.6	10.3	12.5

Note: Figures shown cover persons 3 years old and over; (1) people of Hispanic origin can be of any
race; (2) Metropolitan Statistical Area - see Appendix A for areas included
Source: 1990 Census of Population and Housing, Summary Tape File 3C

Classroom Teacher Salaries in Public Schools

District	B.A. Degree		M.A. Degree		Maximum	
	Min. ($)	Rank[1]	Max. ($)	Rank[1]	Max. ($)	Rank[1]
New York	29,611	21	57,964	6	61,801	7
Average	26,980	-	46,065	-	51,435	-

Note: Salaries are for 1997-1998; (1) Rank ranges from 1 to 100
Source: American Federation of Teachers, Survey & Analysis of Salary Trends, 1998

Higher Education

Two-Year Colleges		Four-Year Colleges		Medical Schools	Law Schools	Voc/Tech
Public	Private	Public	Private			
8	11	12	33	6	8	75

Source: College Blue Book, Occupational Education, 1997; Medical School Admission Requirements,
1999-2000; Peterson's Guide to Two-Year Colleges, 1999; Peterson's Guide to Four-Year Colleges,
2000; Barron's Guide to Law Schools, 1999

MAJOR EMPLOYERS

Major Employers

American Express	American International Group
Consolidated Edison	JP Morgan & Co.
Merrill Lynch & Co.	Metro North Commuter Railroad
Montefiore Medical Center	Morgan Guaranty Trust
Mount Sinai Hospital	Saatchi & Saatchi Advertising Worldwide

Note: Companies listed are located in the city
Source: Dun's Business Rankings, 1999; Ward's Business Directory, 1998

PUBLIC SAFETY

Crime Rate

Area	All Crimes	Violent Crimes				Property Crimes		
		Murder	Forcible Rape	Robbery	Aggrav. Assault	Burglary	Larceny -Theft	Motor Vehicle Theft
City	4,861.6	10.5	29.5	610.7	617.8	739.0	2,145.2	708.9
Suburbs[1]	3,144.1	2.6	11.3	139.8	177.9	480.8	1,994.3	337.3
MSA[2]	4,606.7	9.3	26.8	540.8	552.6	700.7	2,122.8	653.7
U.S.	4,922.7	6.8	35.9	186.1	382.0	919.6	2,886.5	505.8

Note: Crime rate is the number of crimes per 100,000 pop.; (1) defined as all areas within the MSA but located outside the central city; (2) Metropolitan Statistical Area - see Appendix A for areas incl.
Source: FBI Uniform Crime Reports, 1997

RECREATION

Culture and Recreation

Museums	Symphony Orchestras	Opera Companies	Dance Companies	Professional Theatres	Zoos	Pro Sports Teams
99	18	17	15	30	4	9

Source: International Directory of the Performing Arts, 1997; Official Museum Directory, 1999; Stern's Performing Arts Directory, 1997; USA Today Four Sport Stadium Guide, 1997; Chamber of Commerce/Economic Development, 1999

Library System

The New York Public Library has 80 branches, holdings of 5,465,081 volumes and a budget of $n/a (1996-97). The Brooklyn Public Library has 59 branches, holdings of 2,981,238 volumes and a budget of $63,000,557 (1996-97). The Queensborough Public Library has 62 branches, holdings of 8,668,404 volumes and a budget of $71,497,000 (1996-97). *American Library Directory, 1998-1999*

MEDIA

Newspapers

Name	Type	Freq.	Distribution	Circulation
China Daily	Asian	6x/wk	U.S./Int'l.	280,000
Downtown Resident	General	1x/wk	Local	200,000
The Marketeer Islander	General	1x/wk	Local	479,000
The New York Daily News	General	7x/wk	Area	787,089
New York Post	n/a	7x/wk	Area	418,255
The New York Times	General	7x/wk	U.S./Int'l.	1,110,143
Our Town	General	1x/wk	Local	119,000
The Wall Street Journal	n/a	5x/wk	U.S./Int'l.	1,774,870

Note: Includes newspapers with circulations of 100,000 or more located in the city; n/a not available
Source: Burrelle's Media Directory, 1999 Edition

Television Stations

Name	Ch.	Affiliation	Type	Owner
WCBS	n/a	CBST	Commercial	Westinghouse Broadcasting Company
WNBC	n/a	NBCT	Commercial	General Electric Corporation
WNYW	n/a	FBC	Commercial	Fox Television Stations Inc.
WABC	n/a	ABCT	Commercial	ABC Inc.
WPIX	11	n/a	Commercial	Tribune Broadcasting Company
WNET	13	PBS	Public	Educational Broadcasting Corporation
KLKE	24	ABCT	n/a	n/a
WNYE	25	PBS	Public	New York City Board of Education
WPXN	31	PAXTV	Commercial	Paxson Communications Corporation

Note: Stations included broadcast in the New York metro area; n/a not available
Source: Burrelle's Media Directory, 1999 Edition

FM Radio Stations

Call Letters	Freq. (mHz)	Target Audience	Station Format	Music Format
WARY	88.1	General	M	AOR
WNYK	88.7	Religious	M	Adult Contemporary/Alternative/Christian
WSIA	88.9	General	M/N/S	Alternative/Big Band/Blues/Jazz/Modern Rock/Reggae/R&B/World Music
WNYU	89.1	General	E/M/N/S/T	Alternative/Jazz/Latin/Urban Contemporary
WKCR	89.9	Z/G	E/M/N/S/T	Big Band/Classical/Country/Jazz/Latin/R&B
WHCR	90.3	General	M/N/S/T	Urban Contemporary
WFUV	90.7	General	M/N/S/T	Adult Contemporary/Alternative/AOR
WKRB	90.9	General	E/M/N/S/T	Classic Rock/Jazz/Latin/Reggae/Top 40/Urban Contemporary
WNYE	91.5	General	E/M/S	n/a
WXRK	92.3	General	M	Alternative/AOR/Modern Rock
WPAT	93.1	Hispanic	Women	M/N
WRTN	93.5	General	M	Big Band/Jazz
WNYC	93.9	General	M/N/S	Classical
WPLJ	95.5	General	M	Adult Contemporary
WQXR	96.3	General	M/N/S	Classical
WQHT	97.1	General	M	n/a
WSKQ	97.9	Hispanic	M	Latin
WRKS	98.7	General	M/N/T	Urban Contemporary
WBAI	99.5	General	E/M/N/T	Alternative/Jazz
WCBS	101.1	General	M/N/S/T	Oldies
WQCD	101.9	General	M/N	Jazz
WNEW	102.7	General	M	Alternative/Classic Rock/Modern Rock
WFAS	103.9	General	M	Adult Contemporary
WAXQ	104.3	General	M/N/T	Classic Rock
WTJM	105.1	General	M/N	Oldies
WCAA	105.9	Hispanic	M/N/T	Latin
WNWK	105.9	General	M/N/T	Latin
WZZN	106.3	General	M	MOR
WLTW	106.7	General	M/N/S	Adult Contemporary
WYNY	107.1	General	M	Country
WBLS	107.5	B/G	M	Urban Contemporary

Note: Stations included broadcast in the New York metro area; n/a not available
Station Format: E=Educational; M=Music; N=News; S=Sports; T=Talk
Target Audience: A=Asian; B=Black; C=Christian; E=Ethnic; F=French; G=General; H=Hispanic; M=Men; N=Native American; R=Religious; S=Senior Citizen; W=Women; Y=Young Adult; Z=Children
Music Format: AOR=Album Oriented Rock; MOR=Middle-of-the-Road
Source: Burrelle's Media Directory, 1999 Edition

AM Radio Stations

Call Letters	Freq. (kHz)	Target Audience	Station Format	Music Format
WLGC	590	General	M	n/a
WCCR	640	General	M/N/S	n/a
WFAN	660	General	S	n/a
WOR	710	General	T	n/a
WABC	770	General	N/S/T	n/a
WNYC	820	General	N/T	n/a
WCBS	880	General	N	n/a
WRKL	910	Ethnic	M/N/T	n/a
WINS	1010	General	N	n/a
WEVD	1050	General	N/T	n/a
WBBR	1130	General	N	n/a
WLIB	1190	General	T	n/a
WFAS	1230	General	N/S/T	n/a
WLIR	1300	General	M/N/S/T	Adult Standards/Big Band/Oldies
WVIP	1310	General	M/N/S/T	Adult Contemporary/Adult Standards
WZQR	1350	General	M	Country
WKDM	1380	Hispanic	M/T	Latin
WVOX	1460	General	M/N/S	n/a
WZRC	1480	Asian	M/N/T	n/a
WPUT	1510	General	M/N/S	Country
WQEW	1560	Children	E/M	Classic Rock/Top 40
WWRL	1600	General	M/T	R&B

Note: Stations included broadcast in the New York metro area; n/a not available
Target Audience: A=Asian; B=Black; C=Christian; E=Ethnic; F=French; G=General; H=Hispanic; M=Men; N=Native American; R=Religious; S=Senior Citizen; W=Women; Y=Young Adult; Z=Children
Station Format: E=Educational; M=Music; N=News; S=Sports; T=Talk
Source: Burrelle's Media Directory, 1999 Edition

CLIMATE

Average and Extreme Temperatures

Temperature	Jan	Feb	Mar	Apr	May	Jun	Jul	Aug	Sep	Oct	Nov	Dec	Yr.
Extreme High (°F)	68	75	85	96	97	101	104	99	99	88	81	72	104
Average High (°F)	38	41	50	61	72	80	85	84	76	65	54	43	62
Average Temp. (°F)	32	34	43	53	63	72	77	76	68	58	48	37	55
Average Low (°F)	26	27	35	44	54	63	68	67	60	49	41	31	47
Extreme Low (°F)	-2	-2	8	21	36	46	53	50	40	29	17	-1	-2

Note: Figures cover the years 1962-1992
Source: National Climatic Data Center, International Station Meteorological Climate Summary, 3/95

Average Precipitation/Snowfall/Humidity

Precip./Humidity	Jan	Feb	Mar	Apr	May	Jun	Jul	Aug	Sep	Oct	Nov	Dec	Yr.
Avg. Precip. (in.)	3.5	3.1	4.0	3.9	4.5	3.8	4.5	4.1	4.1	3.3	4.5	3.8	47.0
Avg. Snowfall (in.)	7	8	4	Tr	Tr	0	0	0	0	Tr	Tr	3	23
Avg. Rel. Hum. 7am (%)	67	67	66	64	72	74	74	76	78	75	72	69	71
Avg. Rel. Hum. 4pm (%)	55	53	50	45	52	55	53	54	56	55	57	58	53

Note: Figures cover the years 1962-1992; Tr = Trace amounts (<0.05 in. of rain; <0.5 in. of snow)
Source: National Climatic Data Center, International Station Meteorological Climate Summary, 3/95

Weather Conditions

Temperature			Daytime Sky			Precipitation		
32°F & below	45°F & below	90°F & above	Clear	Partly cloudy	Cloudy	0.01 inch or more precip.	0.1 inch or more snow/ice	Thunder-storms
75	170	18	85	166	114	120	11	20

Note: Figures are average number of days per year and covers the years 1962-1992
Source: National Climatic Data Center, International Station Meteorological Climate Summary, 3/95

AIR & WATER QUALITY

Maximum Pollutant Concentrations

	Particulate Matter (ug/m³)	Carbon Monoxide (ppm)	Sulfur Dioxide (ppm)	Nitrogen Dioxide (ppm)	Ozone (ppm)	Lead (ug/m³)
MSA[1] Level	101	6	0.043	0.040	0.16	0.16
NAAQS[2]	150	9	0.140	0.053	0.12	1.50
Met NAAQS?	Yes	Yes	Yes	Yes	No	Yes

Note: (1) Metropolitan Statistical Area - see Appendix A for areas included; (2) National Ambient Air Quality Standards; ppm = parts per million; ug/m³ = micrograms per cubic meter; n/a not available
Source: EPA, National Air Quality and Emissions Trends Report, 1997

Pollutant Standards Index

In the New York MSA (see Appendix A for areas included), the Pollutant Standards Index (PSI) exceeded 100 on 24 days in 1997. A PSI value greater than 100 indicates that air quality would be in the unhealthful range on that day. *EPA, National Air Quality and Emissions Trends Report, 1997*

Drinking Water

Water System Name	Pop. Served	Primary Water Source Type	Number of Violations in 1998	Type of Violation/ Contaminants
NYC - Catskill/Delaware System	6,552,718	Surface	None	None
NYC - Croton System	1,000,000	Surface	None	None
NYC - Jamaica Service Area	518,000	Ground	None	None

Note: Data as of July 10, 1999
Source: EPA, Office of Ground Water and Drinking Water, Safe Drinking Water Information System

New York City tap water has three major sources: the Catskills & Delaware subsytems (neutral, soft, average pH 7.0) and Croton subsystem (alkaline, moderately hard, average pH 7.1). All three supplies are fluoridated and chlorinated.
Editor & Publisher Market Guide, 1999

Norfolk, Virginia

Background

Because Norfolk possesses one of the finest harbors in the world, it is only natural that the city should center its economy and culture around the Navy and maritime trade.

Located 205 miles southeast of Washington, D.C., Norfolk is home to the largest naval installation in the world. Outside of San Diego, Norfolk has more naval officers, retired or otherwise, than any other city. Its 45-foot deep channel can accommodate the largest of ships, from nuclear supercarriers, to merchant ships carrying cargo of tobacco, coal, or petroleum.

The city was founded in 1682, when English settlers bought the land for 10,000 pounds of tobacco. The 18th century saw Norfolk enjoy a prosperous trade with the West Indies. However, British troops bombarded the city on January 1, 1771. To prevent further razing by the British, the Virginia Militia themselves destroyed what was left of the city.

Norfolk was once again the scene of fighting during the Civil War. The most famous battle during this period occurred between the *CSS Virginia (Merrimac)* and the *USS Monitor* in Hampton Roads, the natural channel through which the James River and its tributaries flow into the Chesapeake Bay.

In addition to the Navy providing the most jobs in Norfolk, the city has a diversified economy in food and beverage processing and the production of candy, peanuts, insecticides, flags, paint, furniture, and women's clothing.

The geographic location of the city allows for generally mild winters, beautiful springs and autumns, and summers which are warm and long but tempered by cool periods.

General Rankings and Evaluative Comments

- Norfolk was ranked #1 out of 19 large, southern metropolitan areas in *Money's* 1998 survey of "The Best Places to Live in America." The survey was conducted by first contacting 512 representative households nationwide and asking them to rank 37 quality-of-life factors on a scale of 1 to 10. Next, a demographic profile was compiled on the 300 largest metropolitan statistical areas in the U.S. The numbers were crunched together to arrive at an overall ranking (things Americans consider most important, like clean air and water, low crime and good schools, received extra weight). Unlike previous years, the 1998 rankings were broken down by region (northeast, midwest, south, west) and population size (100,000 to 249,999; 250,000 to 999,999; 1 million plus). The city had a nationwide ranking of #115 out of 300 in 1997 and #117 out of 300 in 1996. *Money, July 1998; Money, July 1997; Money, September 1996*

- *Ladies Home Journal* ranked America's 200 largest cities based on the qualities women care about most. Norfolk ranked #60 out of 200. Criteria: low crime rate, well-paying jobs, quality health and child care, good public schools, the presence of women in government, size of the gender wage gap, number of sexual-harassment and discrimination complaints filed, unemployment and divorce rates, commute times, population density, number of houses of worship, parks and cultural offerings, number of women's health specialists, how well a community's women cared for themselves, complexion kindness index based on UV radiation levels, odds of finding affordable fashions, rental rates for romance movies, champagne sales and other matters of the heart. *Ladies Home Journal, November 1998*

- Zero Population Growth ranked 229 cities in terms of children's health, safety, and economic well-being. Norfolk was ranked #96 out of 112 independent cities (cities with populations greater than 100,000 which were neither Major Cities nor Suburbs/Outer Cities) and was given a grade of D. Criteria: total population, percent of population under 18 years of age, household language, percent population change, percent of births to teens, infant mortality rate, percent of low birth weights, dropout rate, enrollment in preprimary school, violent and property crime rates, unemployment rate, percent of children in poverty, percent of owner occupied units, number of bad air days, percent of public transportation commuters, and average travel time to work. *Zero Population Growth, Children's Environmental Index, Fall 1999*

- Norfolk was ranked #33 out of 59 metro areas in *The Regional Economist's* "Rational Livability Ranking of 59 Large Metro Areas." The rankings were based on the metro area's total population change over the period 1990-97 divided by the number of people moving in from elsewhere in the United States (net domestic in-migration). *St. Louis Federal Reserve Bank of St. Louis, The Regional Economist, April 1999*

- Norfolk was selected by *Yahoo! Internet Life* as one of "America's Most Wired Cities & Towns." The city ranked #41 out of 50. Criteria: home and work net use, domain density, hosts per capita, directory density and content quality. *Yahoo! Internet Life, March 1999*

- Cognetics studied 273 metro areas in the United States, ranking them by entrepreneurial activity. Norfolk was ranked #32 out of the 50 largest metro areas. Criteria: Significant Starts (firms started in the last 10 years that still employ at least 5 people) and Young Growers (percent of firms 10 years old or less that grew significantly during the last 4 years). *Cognetics, "Entrepreneurial Hot Spots: The Best Places in America to Start and Grow a Company," 1998*

- Norfolk was included among *Entrepreneur* magazine's listing of the "20 Best Cities for Small Business." It was ranked #8 among large metro areas and #5 among southern metro areas. Criteria: entrepreneurial activity, small-business growth, economic growth, and risk of failure. *Entrepreneur, October 1999*

- Norfolk was selected as one of the "Best American Cities to Start a Business" by *Point of View* magazine. Criteria: coolness, quality-of-life, and business concerns. The city was ranked #59 out of 75. *Point of View, November 1998*

■ Reliastar Financial Corp. ranked the 125 largest metropolitan areas according to the general financial security of residents. Norfolk was ranked #74 (tie) out of 125 with a score of -1.0. The score indicates the percentage a metropolitan area is above or below the metropolitan norm. A metro area with a score of 10.6 is 10.6% above the metro average. Criteria: Earnings and Wealth Potential (household income, education, net assets, cost of living); Safety Net (health insurance, retirement savings, life insurance, income support programs); Personal Threats (unemployment rate, low-income households, crime rate); Community Economic Vitality (cost of community services, job quality, job creation, housing costs).
Reliastar Financial Corp., "The Best Cities to Earn and Save Money," 1999 Edition

Business Environment

STATE ECONOMY

State Economic Profile

"Virginia has begun to slow from its recent expansion. VA's above-average growth is largely a result of the expansion of high-tech firms in Northern Virginia. Slower growth in the Hampton Roads and Richmond areas stems from a slowdown in the manufacturing and farm sectors. VA's demographic situation is solid, and its housing and construction markets remain vibrant. Although a slowing US economy will be a drag on VA, the long-term outlook for Virginia is strong, above-average growth.

Northern Virginia has become less dependent upon defense spending as its economy has diversified into commercial internet and software development. The Tidewater area is a different story. Both consolidation among shipbuilders and declining Naval purchasers are likely to result in job losses in VA's shipbuilding industry. Job reductions have also taken place at the Port of Hampton Roads as VA's exports have fallen. The opening of the Gateway Plant will diversify southeastern VA's economy away from its dependence on military spending.

VA's housing market was one of the hottest in 1998. Home sales were up over 25% in 1998 with activity occurring in all parts of the state. Price appreciation was strong in northern, central and southeastern VA. While permit activity was flat in Richmond, both northern VA and Hampton Roads saw permit activity increase by at least 10%. Sales and starts should moderate slightly in 1999.

VA has some of the nation's strongest economic fundamentals: business friendly environment, an educated workforce, strong demographics and a diversified economy. VA's most immediate constraint is its tight labor market." *National Association of Realtors, Economic Profiles: The Fifty States and the District of Columbia, http://nar.realtor.com/databank/profiles.htm*

IMPORTS/EXPORTS

Total Export Sales

Area	1994 ($000)	1995 ($000)	1996 ($000)	1997 ($000)	% Chg. 1994-97	% Chg. 1996-97
MSA[1]	807,674	1,005,516	1,256,850	1,396,907	73.0	11.1
U.S.	512,415,609	583,030,524	622,827,063	687,597,999	34.2	10.4

Note: (1) Metropolitan Statistical Area - see Appendix A for areas included
Source: U.S. Department of Commerce, International Trade Association, Metropolitan Area Exports: An Export Performance Report on Over 250 U.S. Cities, November 10, 1998

CITY FINANCES

City Government Finances

Component	FY92 ($000)	FY92 (per capita $)
Revenue	633,413	2,497.27
Expenditure	645,970	2,546.78
Debt Outstanding	1,022,535	4,031.41
Cash & Securities	1,151,712	4,540.70

Source: U.S. Bureau of the Census, City Government Finances: 1991-92

City Government Revenue by Source

Source	FY92 ($000)	FY92 (per capita $)	FY92 (%)
From Federal Government	47,795	188.43	7.5
From State Governments	151,719	598.16	24.0
From Local Governments	11,379	44.86	1.8
Property Taxes	126,735	499.66	20.0
General Sales Taxes	19,068	75.18	3.0
Selective Sales Taxes	49,800	196.34	7.9
Income Taxes	0	0.00	0.0
Current Charges	93,327	367.95	14.7
Utility/Liquor Store	33,117	130.57	5.2
Employee Retirement[1]	34,162	134.69	5.4
Other	66,311	261.44	10.5

Note: (1) Excludes "city contributions," classified as "nonrevenue," intragovernmental transfers.
Source: U.S. Bureau of the Census, City Government Finances: 1991-92

City Government Expenditures by Function

Function	FY92 ($000)	FY92 (per capita $)	FY92 (%)
Educational Services	201,132	792.98	31.1
Employee Retirement[1]	15,304	60.34	2.4
Environment/Housing	111,589	439.95	17.3
Government Administration	35,498	139.95	5.5
Interest on General Debt	51,880	204.54	8.0
Public Safety	69,126	272.53	10.7
Social Services	61,425	242.17	9.5
Transportation	47,852	188.66	7.4
Utility/Liquor Store	44,376	174.96	6.9
Other	7,788	30.70	1.2

Note: (1) Payments to beneficiaries including withdrawal of contributions.
Source: U.S. Bureau of the Census, City Government Finances: 1991-92

Municipal Bond Ratings

Area	Moody's	S & P
Norfolk	Aaa	n/a

Note: n/a not available; n/r not rated
Source: Moody's Bond Record, 6/99

POPULATION

Population Growth

Area	1980	1990	% Chg. 1980-90	July 1998 Estimate	% Chg. 1990-98
City	266,979	261,229	-2.2	215,215	-17.6
MSA[1]	1,160,311	1,396,107	20.3	1,572,100	12.6
U.S.	226,545,805	248,765,170	9.8	270,299,000	8.7

Note: (1) Metropolitan Statistical Area - see Appendix A for areas included;
July 1998 MSA population estimate was calculated by the editors
Source: 1980/1990 Census of Housing and Population, Summary Tape File 3C;
Census Bureau Population Estimates 1998

Population Characteristics

Race	City 1980 Population	%	City 1990 Population	%	% Chg. 1980-90	MSA[1] 1990 Population	%
White	163,052	61.1	148,132	56.7	-9.2	947,500	67.9
Black	93,977	35.2	102,135	39.1	8.7	398,011	28.5
Amer Indian/Esk/Aleut	822	0.3	1,397	0.5	70.0	5,315	0.4
Asian/Pacific Islander	7,075	2.7	6,680	2.6	-5.6	34,897	2.5
Other	2,053	0.8	2,885	1.1	40.5	10,384	0.7
Hispanic Origin[2]	5,792	2.2	7,240	2.8	25.0	31,310	2.2

Note: (1) Metropolitan Statistical Area - see Appendix A for areas included;
(2) people of Hispanic origin can be of any race
Source: 1980/1990 Census of Housing and Population, Summary Tape File 3C

Ancestry

Area	German	Irish	English	Italian	U.S.	French	Polish	Dutch
City	14.6	11.9	11.0	3.5	5.9	2.9	1.8	1.6
MSA[1]	17.4	13.4	15.5	3.9	7.7	3.3	2.1	1.7
U.S.	23.3	15.6	13.1	5.9	5.3	4.2	3.8	2.5

Note: Figures are percentages and include persons that reported multiple ancestry (eg. if a person reported being Irish and Italian, they were included in both columns); (1) Metropolitan Statistical Area - see Appendix A for areas included
Source: 1990 Census of Population and Housing, Summary Tape File 3C

Age

Area	Median Age (Years)	Age Distribution (%) Under 5	Under 18	18-24	25-44	45-64	65+	80+
City	27.2	8.3	23.0	21.6	31.8	13.1	10.5	2.1
MSA[1]	29.7	8.3	26.4	13.6	34.8	16.2	9.0	1.6
U.S.	32.9	7.3	25.6	10.5	32.6	18.7	12.5	2.8

Note: (1) Metropolitan Statistical Area - see Appendix A for areas included
Source: 1990 Census of Population and Housing, Summary Tape File 3C

Male/Female Ratio

Area	Number of males per 100 females (all ages)	Number of males per 100 females (18 years old+)
City	114.0	117.8
MSA[1]	100.4	99.4
U.S.	95.0	91.9

Note: (1) Metropolitan Statistical Area - see Appendix A for areas included
Source: 1990 Census of Population, General Population Characteristics

INCOME

Per Capita/Median/Average Income

Area	Per Capita ($)	Median Household ($)	Average Household ($)
City	11,643	23,563	29,947
MSA[1]	13,495	30,841	36,794
U.S.	14,420	30,056	38,453

Note: All figures are for 1989; (1) Metropolitan Statistical Area - see Appendix A for areas included
Source: 1990 Census of Population and Housing, Summary Tape File 3C

Household Income Distribution by Race

Income ($)	City (%)					U.S. (%)				
	Total	White	Black	Other	Hisp.[1]	Total	White	Black	Other	Hisp.[1]
Less than 5,000	9.3	4.3	17.8	7.5	4.7	6.2	4.8	15.2	8.6	8.8
5,000 - 9,999	9.7	7.1	14.4	6.4	5.8	9.3	8.6	14.2	9.9	11.1
10,000 - 14,999	10.7	9.2	12.9	13.8	16.7	8.8	8.5	11.0	9.8	11.0
15,000 - 24,999	23.2	23.0	23.4	24.3	27.0	17.5	17.3	18.9	18.5	20.5
25,000 - 34,999	17.5	19.1	14.8	18.4	20.3	15.8	16.1	14.2	15.4	16.4
35,000 - 49,999	15.4	18.5	10.0	17.7	12.9	17.9	18.6	13.3	16.1	16.0
50,000 - 74,999	9.3	11.9	5.2	8.7	8.5	15.0	15.8	9.3	13.4	11.1
75,000 - 99,999	2.7	3.7	0.9	2.1	1.9	5.1	5.5	2.6	4.7	3.1
100,000+	2.2	3.3	0.6	1.0	2.2	4.4	4.8	1.3	3.7	1.9

Note: All figures are for 1989; (1) people of Hispanic origin can be of any race
Source: 1990 Census of Population and Housing, Summary Tape File 3C

Effective Buying Income

Area	Per Capita ($)	Median Household ($)	Average Household ($)
City	13,031	26,105	37,268
MSA[1]	14,627	32,849	40,596
U.S.	16,803	34,536	45,243

Note: Data as of 1/1/99; (1) Metropolitan Statistical Area - see Appendix A for areas included
Source: Standard Rate & Data Service, Newspaper Advertising Source, 9/99

Effective Household Buying Income Distribution

Area	% of Households Earning						
	$10,000 -$19,999	$20,000 -$34,999	$35,000 -$49,999	$50,000 -$74,999	$75,000 -$99,000	$100,000 -$124,999	$125,000 and up
City	20.5	28.2	17.2	12.0	3.4	1.1	1.3
MSA[1]	15.8	26.7	20.6	18.2	5.0	1.3	1.3
U.S.	16.0	22.6	18.2	18.9	7.2	2.4	2.7

Note: Data as of 1/1/99; (1) Metropolitan Statistical Area - see Appendix A for areas included
Source: Standard Rate & Data Service, Newspaper Advertising Source, 9/99

Poverty Rates by Race and Age

Area	Total (%)	By Race (%)				By Age (%)		
		White	Black	Other	Hisp.[2]	Under 5 years old	Under 18 years old	65 years and over
City	19.3	10.1	32.7	15.1	15.0	29.2	28.6	15.3
MSA[1]	11.5	5.9	25.1	9.5	10.5	17.8	16.4	12.5
U.S.	13.1	9.8	29.5	23.1	25.3	20.1	18.3	12.8

Note: Figures show the percent of people living below the poverty line in 1989. The average poverty threshold was $12,674 for a family of four in 1989; (1) Metropolitan Statistical Area - see Appendix A for areas included; (2) people of Hispanic origin can be of any race
Source: 1990 Census of Population and Housing, Summary Tape File 3C

EMPLOYMENT

Labor Force and Employment

Area	Civilian Labor Force			Workers Employed		
	Jun. 1998	Jun. 1999	% Chg.	Jun. 1998	Jun. 1999	% Chg.
City	87,345	89,839	2.9	81,872	84,321	3.0
MSA[1]	746,394	766,973	2.8	715,820	737,321	3.0
U.S.	138,798,000	140,666,000	1.3	132,265,000	134,395,000	1.6

Note: Data is not seasonally adjusted and covers workers 16 years of age and older;
(1) Metropolitan Statistical Area - see Appendix A for areas included
Source: Bureau of Labor Statistics, http://stats.bls.gov

Unemployment Rate

Area	1998						1999					
	Jul.	Aug.	Sep.	Oct.	Nov.	Dec.	Jan.	Feb.	Mar.	Apr.	May.	Jun.
City	5.2	5.4	5.8	4.9	5.0	4.8	4.9	4.9	4.4	4.3	5.5	6.1
MSA[1]	3.4	3.5	3.7	3.3	3.3	3.1	3.4	3.3	2.9	2.8	3.4	3.9
U.S.	4.7	4.5	4.4	4.2	4.1	4.0	4.8	4.7	4.4	4.1	4.0	4.5

Note: Data is not seasonally adjusted and covers workers 16 years of age and older; all figures are percentages; (1) Metropolitan Statistical Area - see Appendix A for areas included
Source: Bureau of Labor Statistics, http://stats.bls.gov

Employment by Industry

Sector	MSA[1]		U.S.
	Number of Employees	Percent of Total	Percent of Total
Services	213,600	30.9	30.4
Retail Trade	137,700	19.9	17.7
Government	143,800	20.8	15.6
Manufacturing	63,900	9.2	14.3
Finance/Insurance/Real Estate	34,300	5.0	5.9
Wholesale Trade	26,700	3.9	5.4
Transportation/Public Utilities	31,300	4.5	5.3
Construction	n/a	n/a	5.0
Mining	n/a	n/a	0.4

Note: Figures cover non-farm employment as of 6/99 and are not seasonally adjusted; (1) Metropolitan Statistical Area - see Appendix A for areas included; n/a not available
Source: Bureau of Labor Statistics, http://stats.bls.gov

Employment by Occupation

Occupation Category	City (%)	MSA[1] (%)	U.S. (%)
White Collar	54.8	59.3	58.1
Executive/Admin./Management	10.1	12.4	12.3
Professional	13.1	14.7	14.1
Technical & Related Support	3.9	4.3	3.7
Sales	11.5	12.3	11.8
Administrative Support/Clerical	16.2	15.6	16.3
Blue Collar	26.5	25.3	26.2
Precision Production/Craft/Repair	12.4	13.5	11.3
Machine Operators/Assem./Insp.	4.4	4.2	6.8
Transportation/Material Movers	5.2	3.9	4.1
Cleaners/Helpers/Laborers	4.4	3.7	3.9
Services	17.5	14.2	13.2
Farming/Forestry/Fishing	1.2	1.2	2.5

Note: Figures cover employed persons 16 years old and over; (1) Metropolitan Statistical Area - see Appendix A for areas included
Source: 1990 Census of Population and Housing, Summary Tape File 3C

Occupational Employment Projections: 1996 - 2006

Occupations Expected to Have the Largest Job Growth (ranked by numerical growth)	Fast-Growing Occupations[1] (ranked by percent growth)
1. Systems analysts	1. Desktop publishers
2. Cashiers	2. Personal and home care aides
3. Computer engineers	3. Physical therapy assistants and aides
4. General managers & top executives	4. Medical assistants
5. Salespersons, retail	5. Physical therapists
6. Janitors/cleaners/maids, ex. priv. hshld.	6. Occupational therapists
7. Database administrators	7. Home health aides
8. Receptionists and information clerks	8. Manicurists
9. Engineering/science/computer sys. mgrs.	9. Paralegals
10. Truck drivers, light	10. Bill and account collectors

Note: Projections cover Virginia; (1) Excludes occupations with total job growth less than 300
Source: U.S. Department of Labor, Employment and Training Administration, America's Labor Market Information System (ALMIS)

TAXES

Major State and Local Tax Rates

State Corp. Income (%)	State Personal Income (%)	Residential Property (effective rate per $100)	Sales & Use State (%)	Local (%)	State Gasoline (cents/ gallon)	State Cigarette (cents/ pack)
6.0	2.0 - 5.75	n/a	3.5	1.0	17.5[a]	2.5[b]

Note: Personal/corporate income, sales, gasoline and cigarette tax rates as of January 1999.
Property tax rates as of 1997; (a) Does not include a 2% local option tax; (b) Counties and cities may impose an additional tax of 2 - 15 cents per pack
Source: Federation of Tax Administrators, www.taxadmin.org; Washington D.C. Department of Finance and Revenue, Tax Rates and Tax Burdens in the District of Columbia: A Nationwide Comparison, July 1998; Chamber of Commerce, 1999

Total Taxes Per Capita and as a Percent of Income

Area	Per Capita Income ($)	Per Capita Taxes ($) Total	Federal	State/ Local	Percent of Income (%) Total	Federal	State/ Local
Virginia	28,326	9,650	6,727	2,923	34.1	23.7	10.3
U.S.	27,876	9,881	6,690	3,191	35.4	24.0	11.4

Note: Figures are for 1998
Source: Tax Foundation, www.taxfoundation.org

Estimated Tax Burden

Area	State Income	Local Income	Property	Sales	Total
Norfolk	3,181	0	3,250	673	7,104

Note: The numbers are estimates of taxes paid by a married couple with two children and annual earnings of $75,000. Sales tax estimates assume they spend average amounts on food, clothing, household goods and gasoline. Property tax estimates assume they live in a $250,000 home.
Source: Kiplinger's Personal Finance Magazine, October 1998

COMMERCIAL REAL ESTATE

Office Market

Class/ Location	Total Space (sq. ft.)	Vacant Space (sq. ft.)	Vac. Rate (%)	Under Constr. (sq. ft.)	Net Absorp. (sq. ft.)	Rental Rates ($/sq.ft./yr.)
Class A						
CBD	1,679,924	56,400	3.4	0	93,518	16.50-18.00
Outside CBD	4,619,162	164,458	3.6	721,000	511,661	16.50-18.50
Class B						
CBD	1,767,335	172,947	9.8	0	-4,062	12.75-15.00
Outside CBD	9,941,793	614,047	6.2	0	890,741	10.50-15.00

Note: Data as of 10/98 and covers Norfolk; CBD = Central Business District; n/a not available;
Source: Society of Industrial and Office Realtors, 1999 Comparative Statistics of Industrial and Office Real Estate Markets

"Demand for sales and rents should remain strong for 1999. There is concern about one million sq. ft. of new office space ready to enter the market within the next six months. The influx of so much space will likely soften the market. This will result in vacancy increases of up to ten percent. Absorption in 1999 will not keep up with the 11 to 15 percent increases in construction. Nevertheless, weighted average rental rates should increase as new space rents for higher prices than existing facilities. However, tenant work letters for the new space will result in lower effective rents for the new construction. Reflecting the health of the market, sales and rental rates should increase up to ten percent. There will be little or no development downtown, as rental rates have not yet reached levels that justify new construction." *Society of Industrial and Office Realtors, 1999 Comparative Statistics of Industrial and Office Real Estate Markets*

Industrial Market

Location	Total Space (sq. ft.)	Vacant Space (sq. ft.)	Vac. Rate (%)	Under Constr. (sq. ft.)	Net Absorp. (sq. ft.)	Net Lease ($/sq.ft./yr.)
Central City	5,788,785	193,212	3.3	0	n/a	2.75-4.25
Suburban	70,370,562	5,250,504	7.5	314,000	n/a	2.75-6.00

Note: Data as of 10/98 and covers Norfolk (Hampton Roads); n/a not available
Source: Society of Industrial and Office Realtors, 1999 Comparative Statistics of Industrial and Office Real Estate Markets

"There will be some speculative industrial development during 1999. Five or six projects will be located throughout the region. The regional economy should remain healthy in 1999 with the influx of additional military operations and support services. The port of Hampton Roads maintains its competitive edge. Tonnage is growing as facilities modernize and add capacity each year. Shipbuilding and ship repair fluctuate and remain a strong component of the market. Hampton Roads is pushing to become a solid base for high technology firms. Manufacturing and assembly jobs could potentially see steady growth via the expansion of existing corporations and a moderate influx of new companies. The market should see mild improvement during 1999, pending developments with the national and international economies." *Society of Industrial and Office Realtors, 1999 Comparative Statistics of Industrial and Office Real Estate Markets*

COMMERCIAL UTILITIES

Typical Monthly Electric Bills

Area	Commercial Service ($/month)		Industrial Service ($/month)	
	12 kW demand 1,500 kWh	100 kW demand 30,000 kWh	1,000 kW demand 400,000 kWh	20,000 kW demand 10,000,000 kWh
City	119	1,978	20,383	346,201
U.S.	150	2,174	23,995	508,569

Note: Based on rates in effect January 1, 1999
Source: Edison Electric Institute, Typical Residential, Commercial and Industrial Bills, Winter 1999

TRANSPORTATION

Transportation Statistics

Average minutes to work	20.6
Interstate highways	I-64
Bus lines	
In-city	Tidewater Regional Transit, 163 vehicles
Inter-city	1
Passenger air service	
Airport	Norfolk International Airport
Airlines	16
Aircraft departures	23,099 (1996)
Enplaned passengers	1,263,078 (1996)
Rail service	No Amtrak Service
Motor freight carriers	135
Major waterways/ports	Chesapeake Bay; Hampton Roads

Source: Editor & Publisher Market Guide, 1999; FAA Airport Activity Statistics, 1997; Amtrak National Time Table, Northeast Timetable, Spring/Summer 1999; 1990 Census of Population and Housing, STF 3C; Chamber of Commerce/Economic Development 1999; Jane's Urban Transport Systems 1999-2000

Means of Transportation to Work

Area	Car/Truck/Van		Public Transportation			Bicycle	Walked	Other Means	Worked at Home
	Drove Alone	Car-pooled	Bus	Subway	Railroad				
City	56.0	13.9	4.4	0.0	0.0	0.8	4.8	1.9	18.2
MSA[1]	72.7	14.1	2.0	0.0	0.0	0.5	3.7	1.6	5.3
U.S.	73.2	13.4	3.0	1.5	0.5	0.4	3.9	1.2	3.0

Note: Figures shown are percentages and only include workers 16 years old and over;
(1) Metropolitan Statistical Area - see Appendix A for areas included
Source: 1990 Census of Population and Housing, Summary Tape File 3C

BUSINESSES

Major Business Headquarters

Company Name	1999 Rankings	
	Fortune 500	Forbes 500
Landmark Communciations	-	392
Norfolk Southern	351	-

Note: Companies listed are located in the city; dashes indicate no ranking
Fortune 500: Companies that produce a 10-K are ranked 1 to 500 based on 1998 revenue
Forbes 500: Private companies are ranked 1 to 500 based on 1997 revenue
Source: Forbes, November 30, 1998; Fortune, April 26, 1999

Women-Owned Firms: Number, Employment and Sales

Area	Number of Firms	Employ-ment	Sales ($000)	Rank[2]
MSA[1]	41,300	89,500	16,716,300	44

Note: (1) Metropolitan Statistical Area - see Appendix A for areas included;
(2) Calculated on an averaging of the number of businesses, employment and sales
Source: The National Foundation for Women Business Owners, 1999 Facts on Women-Owned Businesses: Trends in the Top 50 Metropolitan Areas

Women-Owned Firms: Growth

Area	% change from 1992 to 1999			Rank[2]
	Number of Firms	Employ-ment	Sales	
MSA[1]	43.8	61.4	139.3	35

Note: (1) Metropolitan Statistical Area - see Appendix A for areas included; (2) Calculated on an averaging of the percent growth of number of businesses, employment and sales
Source: The National Foundation for Women Business Owners, 1999 Facts on Women-Owned Businesses: Trends in the Top 50 Metropolitan Areas

HOTELS & MOTELS

Hotels/Motels

Area	Hotels/ Motels	Rooms	Luxury-Level Hotels/Motels		Average Minimum Rates ($)		
			♦♦♦♦	♦♦♦♦♦	♦♦	♦♦♦	♦♦♦♦
City	22	2,934	0	0	55	99	n/a
Airport	11	2,014	0	0	n/a	n/a	n/a
Suburbs	87	8,567	0	0	n/a	n/a	n/a
Total	120	13,515	0	0	n/a	n/a	n/a

Note: n/a not available; classifications range from one diamond (budget properties with basic amenities) to five diamond (luxury properties with the finest service, rooms and facilities).
Source: OAG, Business Travel Planner, Winter 1998-99

CONVENTION CENTERS

Major Convention Centers

Center Name	Meeting Rooms	Exhibit Space (sq. ft.)
Norfolk SCOPE	6	85,000
Norfolk Waterside Convention	19	14,400
Old Dominion University Exhibition Hall	n/a	80,000
Omni Norfolk	15	18,440
Quality Inn Lake Wright Resort/Convention Center	12	21,812

Note: n/a not available
Source: Trade Shows Worldwide, 1998; Meetings & Conventions, 4/15/99;
Sucessful Meetings, 3/31/98

Living Environment

COST OF LIVING

Cost of Living Index

Composite Index	Groceries	Housing	Utilities	Trans-portation	Health Care	Misc. Goods/ Services
97.3	97.6	90.0	119.2	104.7	95.8	95.9

Note: U.S. = 100
Source: ACCRA, Cost of Living Index, 4th Quarter 1998

HOUSING

Median Home Prices and Housing Affordability

Area	Median Price[2] 1st Qtr. 1999 ($)	HOI[3] 1st Qtr. 1999	Afford-ability Rank[4]
MSA[1]	111,000	78.1	70
U.S.	134,000	69.6	–

Note: (1) Metropolitan Statistical Area - see Appendix A for areas included; (2) U.S. figures calculated from the sales of 524,324 new and existing homes in 181 markets; (3) Housing Opportunity Index - percent of homes sold that were within the reach of the median income household at the prevailing mortgage interest rate; (4) Rank is from 1-181 with 1 being most affordable
Source: National Association of Home Builders, Housing Opportunity Index, 1st Quarter 1999

Median Home Price Projection

It is projected that the median price of existing single-family homes in the metro area will increase by 3.7% in 1999. Nationwide, home prices are projected to increase 3.8%.
Kiplinger's Personal Finance Magazine, January 1999

Average New Home Price

Area	Price ($)
City	125,877
U.S.	141,438

Note: Figures are based on a new home with 1,800 sq. ft. of living area on an 8,000 sq. ft. lot.
Source: ACCRA, Cost of Living Index, 4th Quarter 1998

Average Apartment Rent

Area	Rent ($/mth)
City	582
U.S.	593

Note: Figures are based on an unfurnished two bedroom, 1-1/2 or 2 bath apartment, approximately 950 sq. ft. in size, excluding all utilities except water
Source: ACCRA, Cost of Living Index, 4th Quarter 1998

RESIDENTIAL UTILITIES

Average Residential Utility Costs

Area	All Electric ($/mth)	Part Electric ($/mth)	Other Energy ($/mth)	Phone ($/mth)
City	–	66.16	53.50	22.78
U.S.	101.64	55.45	43.56	19.81

Source: ACCRA, Cost of Living Index, 4th Quarter 1998

HEALTH CARE

Average Health Care Costs

Area	Hospital ($/day)	Doctor ($/visit)	Dentist ($/visit)
City	324.60	56.20	60.40
U.S.	417.46	51.94	64.89

Note: Hospital—based on a semi-private room; Doctor—based on a general practitioner's routine exam of an established patient; Dentist—based on adult teeth cleaning and periodic oral exam.
Source: ACCRA, Cost of Living Index, 4th Quarter 1998

Distribution of Office-Based Physicians

Area	Family/Gen. Practitioners	Specialists		
		Medical	Surgical	Other
MSA[1]	403	741	685	616

Note: Data as of 12/31/97; (1) Metropolitan Statistical Area - see Appendix A for areas included
Source: American Medical Assn., Physician Characteristics & Distribution in the U.S., 1999

Hospitals

Norfolk has 4 general medical and surgical hospitals, 1 psychiatric, 1 chronic disease, 1 children's general. *AHA Guide to the Healthcare Field, 1998-99*

According to *U.S. News and World Report*, Norfolk has 1 of the best hospitals in the U.S.: **Sentara Norfolk General Hospital**, noted for cardiology, rheumatology. *U.S. News Online, "America's Best Hospitals," 10th Edition, www.usnews.com*

EDUCATION

Public School District Statistics

District Name	Num. Sch.	Enroll.	Classroom Teachers	Pupils per Teacher	Minority Pupils (%)	Current Exp.[1] ($/pupil)
Governor's School For The Arts	1	n/a	n/a	n/a	n/a	n/a
Norfolk City Public Schls	61	38,014	n/a	n/a	n/a	n/a
Southeast Coop. Ed. Prg.	1	n/a	n/a	n/a	n/a	n/a

Note: Data covers the 1997-1998 school year unless otherwise noted; (1) Data covers fiscal year 1996; SD = School District; ISD = Independent School District; n/a not available
Source: National Center for Education Statistics, Common Core of Data Public Education Agency Universe 1997-98; National Center for Education Statistics, Characteristics of the 100 Largest Public Elementary and Secondary School Districts in the United States: 1997-98, July 1999

Educational Quality

School District	Education Quotient[1]	Graduate Outcome[2]	Community Index[3]	Resource Index[4]
Norfolk City	112.0	105.0	63.0	142.0

Note: Nearly 1,000 secondary school districts were rated in terms of educational quality. The scores range from a low of 50 to a high of 150; (1) Average of the Graduate Outcome, Community and Resource indexes; (2) Based on graduation rates and college board scores (SAT/ACT); (3) Based on the surrounding community's average level of education and the area's average income level; (4) Based on teacher salaries, per-pupil expenditures and student-teacher ratios.
Source: Expansion Management, Ratings Issue, 1998

Educational Attainment by Race

Area	High School Graduate (%)					Bachelor's Degree (%)				
	Total	White	Black	Other	Hisp.[2]	Total	White	Black	Other	Hisp.[2]
City	72.7	80.7	58.8	77.8	84.2	16.8	21.8	7.9	23.5	16.0
MSA[1]	79.1	84.2	64.9	80.0	85.6	20.1	23.3	11.3	22.3	16.1
U.S.	75.2	77.9	63.1	60.4	49.8	20.3	21.5	11.4	19.4	9.2

Note: Figures shown cover persons 25 years old and over; (1) Metropolitan Statistical Area - see Appendix A for areas included; (2) people of Hispanic origin can be of any race
Source: 1990 Census of Population and Housing, Summary Tape File 3C

School Enrollment by Type

Area	Preprimary				Elementary/High School			
	Public		Private		Public		Private	
	Enrollment	%	Enrollment	%	Enrollment	%	Enrollment	%
City	2,322	59.2	1,600	40.8	33,000	91.0	3,245	9.0
MSA[1]	14,319	54.5	11,942	45.5	218,089	92.8	16,852	7.2
U.S.	2,679,029	59.5	1,824,256	40.5	38,379,689	90.2	4,187,099	9.8

Note: Figures shown cover persons 3 years old and over;
(1) Metropolitan Statistical Area - see Appendix A for areas included
Source: 1990 Census of Population and Housing, Summary Tape File 3C

School Enrollment by Race

Area	Preprimary (%)				Elementary/High School (%)			
	White	Black	Other	Hisp.[1]	White	Black	Other	Hisp.[1]
City	60.5	35.6	3.9	3.4	41.5	54.4	4.1	2.5
MSA[2]	71.3	25.7	2.9	2.7	60.2	35.5	4.3	2.3
U.S.	80.4	12.5	7.1	7.8	74.1	15.6	10.3	12.5

Note: Figures shown cover persons 3 years old and over; (1) people of Hispanic origin can be of any race; (2) Metropolitan Statistical Area - see Appendix A for areas included
Source: 1990 Census of Population and Housing, Summary Tape File 3C

Classroom Teacher Salaries in Public Schools

District	B.A. Degree		M.A. Degree		Maximum	
	Min. ($)	Rank[1]	Max. ($)	Rank[1]	Max. ($)	Rank[1]
Norfolk	26,800	43	45,040	51	47,740	69
Average	26,980	-	46,065	-	51,435	-

Note: Salaries are for 1997-1998; (1) Rank ranges from 1 to 100
Source: American Federation of Teachers, Survey & Analysis of Salary Trends, 1998

Higher Education

Two-Year Colleges		Four-Year Colleges		Medical Schools	Law Schools	Voc/Tech
Public	Private	Public	Private			
0	2	2	1	1	0	8

Source: College Blue Book, Occupational Education, 1997; Medical School Admission Requirements, 1999-2000; Peterson's Guide to Two-Year Colleges, 1999; Peterson's Guide to Four-Year Colleges, 2000; Barron's Guide to Law Schools, 1999

MAJOR EMPLOYERS

Major Employers

Children's Hospital of the Kings Daughters
Trader Publishing
Bon-Secours-DePaul Medical Center
United States Marine Repair
Tarmac Mid-Atlantic (ready-mixed concrete)
Dollar Tree Stores
Virginia International Terminals
Landmark Communications
Norfolk Shipbuilding & Drydock Corp.
Tidewater Construction Corp.

Note: Companies listed are located in the city
Source: Dun's Business Rankings, 1999; Ward's Business Directory, 1998

PUBLIC SAFETY

Crime Rate

Area	All Crimes	Violent Crimes				Property Crimes		
		Murder	Forcible Rape	Robbery	Aggrav. Assault	Burglary	Larceny-Theft	Motor Vehicle Theft
City	7,598.8	22.2	55.6	476.8	419.5	1,018.8	5,086.0	519.9
Suburbs[1]	4,789.0	6.8	32.7	180.6	204.8	775.2	3,268.8	320.1
MSA[2]	5,232.1	9.2	36.3	227.3	238.7	813.6	3,555.3	351.6
U.S.	4,922.7	6.8	35.9	186.1	382.0	919.6	2,886.5	505.8

Note: Crime rate is the number of crimes per 100,000 pop.; (1) defined as all areas within the MSA but located outside the central city; (2) Metropolitan Statistical Area - see Appendix A for areas incl.
Source: FBI Uniform Crime Reports, 1997

RECREATION

Culture and Recreation

Museums	Symphony Orchestras	Opera Companies	Dance Companies	Professional Theatres	Zoos	Pro Sports Teams
6	1	1	0	1	1	0

Source: International Directory of the Performing Arts, 1997; Official Museum Directory, 1999; Stern's Performing Arts Directory, 1997; USA Today Four Sport Stadium Guide, 1997; Chamber of Commerce/Economic Development, 1999

Library System

The Norfolk Public Library has 11 branches, holdings of 909,565 volumes, and a budget of $4,394,844 (1996-1997). *American Library Directory, 1998-1999*

MEDIA

Newspapers

Name	Type	Freq.	Distribution	Circulation
The Compass	General	1x/wk	Local	40,000
The Flag Ship	n/a	1x/wk	Area	40,000
Hampton Roads Metro Weekender	Black	1x/wk	Local	40,000
New Journal & Guide	Black	1x/wk	U.S.	30,000
The Virginian-Pilot	General	7x/wk	Area	201,236

Note: Includes newspapers with circulations of 1,000 or more located in the city; n/a not available
Source: Burrelle's Media Directory, 1999 Edition

Television Stations

Name	Ch.	Affiliation	Type	Owner
WTKR	n/a	CBST	Commercial	New York Times Company
WVEC	13	ABCT	Commercial	A.H. Belo Corporation
WHRO	15	PBS	Public	Hampton Roads Educational Telecom. Assn.
WTVZ	33	FBC/WB	Commercial	Sinclair Communications Inc.

Note: Stations included broadcast in the Norfolk metro area; n/a not available
Source: Burrelle's Media Directory, 1999 Edition

AM Radio Stations

Call Letters	Freq. (kHz)	Target Audience	Station Format	Music Format
WTAR	790	General	N/S/T	n/a
WNIS	850	General	N/T	n/a
WPCE	1400	General	M/N/S	Christian
WCPK	1600	General	M	n/a

Note: Stations included broadcast in the Norfolk metro area; n/a not available
Target Audience: A=Asian; B=Black; C=Christian; E=Ethnic; F=French; G=General; H=Hispanic; M=Men; N=Native American; R=Religious; S=Senior Citizen; W=Women; Y=Young Adult; Z=Children
Station Format: E=Educational; M=Music; N=News; S=Sports; T=Talk
Source: Burrelle's Media Directory, 1999 Edition

FM Radio Stations

Call Letters	Freq. (mHz)	Target Audience	Station Format	Music Format
WHRV	89.5	General	M/N	Alternative/Jazz
WHRO	90.3	General	M	Classical
WNSB	91.1	General	n/a	n/a
WSZY	92.1	General	M/N/S	n/a
WFOG	92.9	G/W	M/N/S	Adult Contemporary
WLTY	95.7	General	M/N/S	Country
WROX	96.1	General	M	Alternative
WOWI	102.9	General	M/N/T	Urban Contemporary
WJCD	105.3	General	M/N/S	Adult Contemporary/Jazz

Note: Stations included broadcast in the Norfolk metro area; n/a not available
Station Format: E=Educational; M=Music; N=News; S=Sports; T=Talk
Target Audience: A=Asian; B=Black; C=Christian; E=Ethnic; F=French; G=General; H=Hispanic; M=Men; N=Native American; R=Religious; S=Senior Citizen; W=Women; Y=Young Adult; Z=Children
Source: Burrelle's Media Directory, 1999 Edition

CLIMATE

Average and Extreme Temperatures

Temperature	Jan	Feb	Mar	Apr	May	Jun	Jul	Aug	Sep	Oct	Nov	Dec	Yr.
Extreme High (°F)	78	81	88	97	97	101	103	104	99	95	86	80	104
Average High (°F)	48	50	58	68	76	84	87	86	80	70	61	52	68
Average Temp. (°F)	40	42	49	58	67	75	79	78	72	62	53	44	60
Average Low (°F)	32	33	40	48	57	66	70	70	64	53	43	35	51
Extreme Low (°F)	-3	8	18	28	36	45	54	49	45	27	20	7	-3

Note: Figures cover the years 1948-1990
Source: National Climatic Data Center, International Station Meteorological Climate Summary, 3/95

Average Precipitation/Snowfall/Humidity

Precip./Humidity	Jan	Feb	Mar	Apr	May	Jun	Jul	Aug	Sep	Oct	Nov	Dec	Yr.
Avg. Precip. (in.)	3.6	3.4	3.7	3.1	3.8	3.6	5.1	5.4	4.0	3.3	3.0	3.2	45.0
Avg. Snowfall (in.)	3	3	1	Tr	0	0	0	0	0	0	Tr	1	8
Avg. Rel. Hum. 7am (%)	74	74	74	73	77	79	82	84	83	82	79	75	78
Avg. Rel. Hum. 4pm (%)	59	57	54	51	56	57	60	63	62	61	58	59	58

Note: Figures cover the years 1948-1990; Tr = Trace amounts (<0.05 in. of rain; <0.5 in. of snow)
Source: National Climatic Data Center, International Station Meteorological Climate Summary, 3/95

Weather Conditions

Temperature			Daytime Sky			Precipitation		
10°F & below	32°F & below	90°F & above	Clear	Partly cloudy	Cloudy	0.01 inch or more precip.	0.1 inch or more snow/ice	Thunderstorms
< 1	54	32	89	149	127	115	6	37

Note: Figures are average number of days per year and covers the years 1948-1990
Source: National Climatic Data Center, International Station Meteorological Climate Summary, 3/95

AIR & WATER QUALITY

Maximum Pollutant Concentrations

	Particulate Matter (ug/m³)	Carbon Monoxide (ppm)	Sulfur Dioxide (ppm)	Nitrogen Dioxide (ppm)	Ozone (ppm)	Lead (ug/m³)
MSA[1] Level	68	5	0.026	0.019	0.11	0.01
NAAQS[2]	150	9	0.140	0.053	0.12	1.50
Met NAAQS?	Yes	Yes	Yes	Yes	Yes	Yes

Note: (1) Metropolitan Statistical Area - see Appendix A for areas included; (2) National Ambient Air Quality Standards; ppm = parts per million; ug/m³ = micrograms per cubic meter; n/a not available
Source: EPA, National Air Quality and Emissions Trends Report, 1997

Pollutant Standards Index

In the Norfolk MSA (see Appendix A for areas included), the Pollutant Standards Index (PSI) exceeded 100 on 17 days in 1997. A PSI value greater than 100 indicates that air quality would be in the unhealthful range on that day. *EPA, National Air Quality and Emissions Trends Report, 1997*

Drinking Water

Water System Name	Pop. Served	Primary Water Source Type	Number of Violations in 1998	Type of Violation/ Contaminants
Norfolk City Moores Bridges	295,000	Surface	None	None

Note: Data as of July 10, 1999
Source: EPA, Office of Ground Water and Drinking Water, Safe Drinking Water Information System

Norfolk tap water is slightly soft, fluoridated and has low alkalinity.
Editor & Publisher Market Guide, 1999

Philadelphia, Pennsylvania

Background

Philadelphia, "The City of Brotherly Love," was not founded upon brotherly love at all. The largest city in Pennsylvania was settled by Swedes and Finns in 1638, in a settlement known as New Sweden. The settlement was seized in 1655 by Peter Stuyvesant, Director General of New Amsterdam for the Dutch Crown. In turn, King Charles II of England conferred land between the Connecticut and Delaware Rivers, upon his brother, the Duke of York inconsiderate of any previous claims by the Dutch. Naturally, the two countries went to war. However, thanks to a generous loan by Admiral Sir William Penn, the land fell permanently into English hands. To repay the loan, the King gave Sir William's son, also named William, sole proprietorship of the state of present day Pennsylvania. This also rid him of a subject heavily influenced by a dissenting religious sect known as the Society of Friends, or Quakers.

Pennsylvania's landlord had the vision and the financial means with which to carry out a simple but radical experiment for the times: a city built upon religious tolerance. Amazingly enough, the place of religious outcasts prospered. Thanks to forests abundant in natural resources, and ports busy with international trade, Philadelphia, in the state's southeast corner, was a bustling, ideal American city.

While the region's manufacturing activities have been declining for the last few years, the service sector has emerged as the predominant economic force driving current and future growth in the city. Greater Philadelphia has the second largest health care industry in the nation. It has become a major materials development and processing center. More than 100,000 individuals are involved in the manufacture of chemicals, advanced materials, glass, plastics, industrial gases, metals, composites, and textiles.

According to the Association of University Related Research Parks, Philadelphia's University City Science Center is ranked #3 out of the top 10 research parks in the U.S. with 140 companies. *World Trade, 4/97*

The city claimed firsts in many cultural, educational, and political arenas. The Pennsylvania Academy of Fine Arts is the oldest museum and fine arts school in the country; the University of Pennsylvania, which Benjamin Franklin helped found, is the oldest university in the country; and of course, on July 4, 1776, the United States had been born, when "longhaired radicals" such as Thomas Jefferson, George Washington, and John Hancock signed The Declaration of Independence in the city, breaking away from the mother country forever.

The Appalachian Mountains to the west and the Atlantic Ocean to the east have a moderating effect on the city's climate. Temperatures below zero or above 100 degrees are a rarity.

General Rankings and Evaluative Comments

■ Philadelphia was ranked #9 out of 15 large, northeastern metropolitan areas in *Money's* 1998 survey of "The Best Places to Live in America." The survey was conducted by first contacting 512 representative households nationwide and asking them to rank 37 quality-of-life factors on a scale of 1 to 10. Next, a demographic profile was compiled on the 300 largest metropolitan statistical areas in the U.S. The numbers were crunched together to arrive at an overall ranking (things Americans consider most important, like clean air and water, low crime and good schools, received extra weight). Unlike previous years, the 1998 rankings were broken down by region (northeast, midwest, south, west) and population size (100,000 to 249,999; 250,000 to 999,999; 1 million plus). The city had a nationwide ranking of #187 out of 300 in 1997 and #233 out of 300 in 1996. *Money, July 1998; Money, July 1997; Money, September 1996*

■ *Ladies Home Journal* ranked America's 200 largest cities based on the qualities women care about most. Philadelphia ranked #199 out of 200. Criteria: low crime rate, well-paying jobs, quality health and child care, good public schools, the presence of women in government, size of the gender wage gap, number of sexual-harassment and discrimination complaints filed, unemployment and divorce rates, commute times, population density, number of houses of worship, parks and cultural offerings, number of women's health specialists, how well a community's women cared for themselves, complexion kindness index based on UV radiation levels, odds of finding affordable fashions, rental rates for romance movies, champagne sales and other matters of the heart. *Ladies Home Journal, November 1998*

■ Zero Population Growth ranked 229 cities in terms of children's health, safety, and economic well-being. Philadelphia was ranked #16 out of 25 major cities (main city in a metro area with population of greater than 2 million) and was given a grade of C-. Criteria: total population, percent of population under 18 years of age, household language, percent population change, percent of births to teens, infant mortality rate, percent of low birth weights, dropout rate, enrollment in preprimary school, violent and property crime rates, unemployment rate, percent of children in poverty, percent of owner occupied units, number of bad air days, percent of public transportation commuters, and average travel time to work. *Zero Population Growth, Children's Environmental Index, Fall 1999*

■ Philadelphia was ranked #48 out of 59 metro areas in *The Regional Economist's* "Rational Livability Ranking of 59 Large Metro Areas." The rankings were based on the metro area's total population change over the period 1990-97 divided by the number of people moving in from elsewhere in the United States (net domestic in-migration). *St. Louis Federal Reserve Bank of St. Louis, The Regional Economist, April 1999*

■ Philadelphia appeared on *Travel & Leisure's* list of the world's 100 best cities. It was ranked #19 in the U.S. and #70 in the world. Criteria: activities/attractions, culture/arts, people, restaurants/food, and value. *Travel & Leisure, 1998 World's Best Awards*

■ Philadelphia was selected by *Yahoo! Internet Life* as one of "America's Most Wired Cities & Towns." The city ranked #21 out of 50. Criteria: home and work net use, domain density, hosts per capita, directory density and content quality. *Yahoo! Internet Life, March 1999*

■ Philadelphia was chosen as one of "America's 10 Best Bike Towns." Rank: #9 out of 10. Criteria: marked bike lanes, municipal bike racks, bicycle access to bridges and public transportation, employment of a local government bicycle coordinator, area cycling advocacy efforts, bike-safety programs, budget for cycling programs, and local cycling culture.

"The enormously popular annual U.S. Pro Cycling Championships, which winds through Philadelphia's once-struggling Manayunk district, was a catalyst for pumping new life into this old working-class neighborhood. 'The race gave pride and recognition to Manayunk,' says Sue McNamara of the Bicycle Coalition of the Delaware Valley. 'Now it's the most chichi shopping area in the region.'

The city has spent $850,000 over the past four years planning 300 miles of bike lanes, with another $2.4 million tagged for construction through '99. In '94, bicycles were granted access to the subway system after 7 p.m. 'We're now working to get the hour restriction lifted,' says McNamara. Likewise, bike racks are being mounted to the fronts of city buses." *Bicycling, March 1999*

■ Cognetics studied 273 metro areas in the United States, ranking them by entrepreneurial activity. Philadelphia was ranked #44 out of the 50 largest metro areas. Criteria: Significant Starts (firms started in the last 10 years that still employ at least 5 people) and Young Growers (percent of firms 10 years old or less that grew significantly during the last 4 years). *Cognetics, "Entrepreneurial Hot Spots: The Best Places in America to Start and Grow a Company," 1998*

■ Philadelphia was selected as one of the "Best American Cities to Start a Business" by *Point of View* magazine. Criteria: coolness, quality-of-life, and business concerns. The city was ranked #51 out of 75. *Point of View, November 1998*

■ Reliastar Financial Corp. ranked the 125 largest metropolitan areas according to the general financial security of residents. Philadelphia was ranked #81 (tie) out of 125 with a score of -1.7. The score indicates the percentage a metropolitan area is above or below the metropolitan norm. A metro area with a score of 10.6 is 10.6% above the metro average. Criteria: Earnings and Wealth Potential (household income, education, net assets, cost of living); Safety Net (health insurance, retirement savings, life insurance, income support programs); Personal Threats (unemployment rate, low-income households, crime rate); Community Economic Vitality (cost of community services, job quality, job creation, housing costs). *Reliastar Financial Corp., "The Best Cities to Earn and Save Money," 1999 Edition*

Business Environment

STATE ECONOMY

State Economic Profile

"Pennsylvania's economy has lagged the nation for several years, a trend that will only get worse. While Philadelphia has seen some resurgence, it has not been enough to offset declines in the rest of the state. PA's poor demographic outlook will confine it to slow growth at best in 1999 and 2000. Expansions by high-tech and biotech firms, such as Lucent, SAP and SmithKline Beecham, will help PA's weak job outlook, although these gains will be limited to the eastern part of the state.

PA employment grew at the low rate of 0.8% in 1998, driven largely by the 1.0% increase in Philadelphia. In contrast, Pittsburgh lost jobs at a rate of 0.1%. While many areas of the country are experiencing declining manufacturing employment, due to weak export demand and long-term restructuring, Pittsburgh is one of the few urban areas that is also losing service jobs, at a rate of 0.4% in 1998. Services employment for PA grew 1.3% and 1.9% for Philadelphia in 1998.

Some of western PA's problems stem from its declining steel sector. Weak steel prices, over-capacity and a flood of cheap imports have undermined PA's steel industry. Even with import restraints and renewed world demand, the outlook for PA's steel industry remains bleak. PA's steel producers' biggest problem is US mini-mills that are sweeping the industry. Further declines in PA's steel industry are likely in 1999 and 2000.

Few states lose more residents every year than PA. Its continued loss of younger households will constrain labor market growth and pose problems for its housing market. Home sales were flat in 1998, and residential permits were up only 3%. Both sales and starts should contract in 1999." *National Association of Realtors, Economic Profiles: The Fifty States and the District of Columbia, http://nar.realtor.com/databank/profiles.htm*

IMPORTS/EXPORTS

Total Export Sales

Area	1994 ($000)	1995 ($000)	1996 ($000)	1997 ($000)	% Chg. 1994-97	% Chg. 1996-97
MSA[1]	6,545,836	7,896,893	7,727,940	8,027,797	22.6	3.9
U.S.	512,415,609	583,030,524	622,827,063	687,597,999	34.2	10.4

Note: (1) Metropolitan Statistical Area - see Appendix A for areas included
Source: U.S. Department of Commerce, International Trade Association, Metropolitan Area Exports: An Export Performance Report on Over 250 U.S. Cities, November 10, 1998

CITY FINANCES

City Government Finances

Component	FY94 ($000)	FY94 (per capita $)
Revenue	3,979,708	2,614.14
Expenditure	3,998,386	2,626.40
Debt Outstanding	3,673,489	2,412.99
Cash & Securities	3,362,497	2,208.71

Source: U.S. Bureau of the Census, City Government Finances: 1993-94

City Government Revenue by Source

Source	FY94 ($000)	FY94 (per capita $)	FY94 (%)
From Federal Government	214,513	140.91	5.4
From State Governments	772,904	507.69	19.4
From Local Governments	84,002	55.18	2.1
Property Taxes	343,202	225.44	8.6
General Sales Taxes	83,690	54.97	2.1
Selective Sales Taxes	47,270	31.05	1.2
Income Taxes	821,701	539.75	20.6
Current Charges	420,978	276.53	10.6
Utility/Liquor Store	675,216	443.53	17.0
Employee Retirement[1]	158,189	103.91	4.0
Other	358,043	235.19	9.0

Note: (1) Excludes "city contributions," classified as "nonrevenue," intragovernmental transfers.
Source: U.S. Bureau of the Census, City Government Finances: 1993-94

City Government Expenditures by Function

Function	FY94 ($000)	FY94 (per capita $)	FY94 (%)
Educational Services	53,039	34.84	1.3
Employee Retirement[1]	330,636	217.18	8.3
Environment/Housing	424,265	278.69	10.6
Government Administration	398,688	261.88	10.0
Interest on General Debt	92,596	60.82	2.3
Public Safety	663,376	435.75	16.6
Social Services	628,790	413.03	15.7
Transportation	173,895	114.23	4.3
Utility/Liquor Store	711,727	467.51	17.8
Other	521,374	342.47	13.0

Note: (1) Payments to beneficiaries including withdrawal of contributions.
Source: U.S. Bureau of the Census, City Government Finances: 1993-94

Municipal Bond Ratings

Area	Moody's	S & P
Philadelphia	Aaa	n/a

Note: n/a not available; n/r not rated
Source: Moody's Bond Record, 6/99

POPULATION

Population Growth

Area	1980	1990	% Chg. 1980-90	July 1998 Estimate	% Chg. 1990-98
City	1,688,210	1,585,577	-6.1	1,436,287	-9.4
MSA[1]	4,716,818	4,856,881	3.0	4,963,153	2.2
U.S.	226,545,805	248,765,170	9.8	270,299,000	8.7

Note: (1) Metropolitan Statistical Area - see Appendix A for areas included;
July 1998 MSA population estimate was calculated by the editors
Source: 1980/1990 Census of Housing and Population, Summary Tape File 3C;
Census Bureau Population Estimates 1998

Population Characteristics

Race	City 1980 Population	%	City 1990 Population	%	% Chg. 1980-90	MSA[1] 1990 Population	%
White	988,337	58.5	848,894	53.5	-14.1	3,718,464	76.6
Black	638,788	37.8	632,430	39.9	-1.0	930,017	19.1
Amer Indian/Esk/Aleut	2,799	0.2	3,325	0.2	18.8	8,851	0.2
Asian/Pacific Islander	19,950	1.2	43,174	2.7	116.4	103,234	2.1
Other	38,336	2.3	57,754	3.6	50.7	96,315	2.0
Hispanic Origin[2]	63,570	3.8	84,186	5.3	32.4	164,601	3.4

Note: (1) Metropolitan Statistical Area - see Appendix A for areas included;
(2) people of Hispanic origin can be of any race
Source: 1980/1990 Census of Housing and Population, Summary Tape File 3C

Ancestry

Area	German	Irish	English	Italian	U.S.	French	Polish	Dutch
City	13.0	16.9	4.7	11.2	1.7	1.0	5.8	0.5
MSA[1]	23.6	22.8	11.3	14.4	2.1	2.1	6.5	1.5
U.S.	23.3	15.6	13.1	5.9	5.3	4.2	3.8	2.5

Note: Figures are percentages and include persons that reported multiple ancestry (eg. if a person reported being Irish and Italian, they were included in both columns); (1) Metropolitan Statistical Area - see Appendix A for areas included
Source: 1990 Census of Population and Housing, Summary Tape File 3C

Age

Area	Median Age (Years)	Age Distribution (%) Under 5	Under 18	18-24	25-44	45-64	65+	80+
City	33.1	7.3	23.9	11.4	30.8	18.6	15.2	3.4
MSA[1]	33.7	7.3	24.4	10.3	32.4	19.5	13.5	2.9
U.S.	32.9	7.3	25.6	10.5	32.6	18.7	12.5	2.8

Note: (1) Metropolitan Statistical Area - see Appendix A for areas included
Source: 1990 Census of Population and Housing, Summary Tape File 3C

Male/Female Ratio

Area	Number of males per 100 females (all ages)	Number of males per 100 females (18 years old+)
City	86.8	82.6
MSA[1]	91.8	88.0
U.S.	95.0	91.9

Note: (1) Metropolitan Statistical Area - see Appendix A for areas included
Source: 1990 Census of Population, General Population Characteristics

INCOME

Per Capita/Median/Average Income

Area	Per Capita ($)	Median Household ($)	Average Household ($)
City	12,091	24,603	31,208
MSA[1]	16,386	35,437	44,191
U.S.	14,420	30,056	38,453

Note: All figures are for 1989; (1) Metropolitan Statistical Area - see Appendix A for areas included
Source: 1990 Census of Population and Housing, Summary Tape File 3C

Household Income Distribution by Race

Income ($)	City (%)					U.S. (%)				
	Total	White	Black	Other	Hisp.[1]	Total	White	Black	Other	Hisp.[1]
Less than 5,000	10.0	6.4	14.6	18.6	19.1	6.2	4.8	15.2	8.6	8.8
5,000 - 9,999	12.7	11.2	14.9	15.3	18.0	9.3	8.6	14.2	9.9	11.1
10,000 - 14,999	9.9	9.3	10.4	12.5	12.4	8.8	8.5	11.0	9.8	11.0
15,000 - 24,999	18.0	17.3	19.0	19.6	19.4	17.5	17.3	18.9	18.5	20.5
25,000 - 34,999	15.2	15.8	14.5	13.5	12.9	15.8	16.1	14.2	15.4	16.4
35,000 - 49,999	16.4	18.0	14.5	11.2	10.4	17.9	18.6	13.3	16.1	16.0
50,000 - 74,999	12.2	14.6	9.2	6.5	6.1	15.0	15.8	9.3	13.4	11.1
75,000 - 99,999	3.3	4.3	2.0	1.5	1.1	5.1	5.5	2.6	4.7	3.1
100,000+	2.2	3.0	0.9	1.2	0.6	4.4	4.8	1.3	3.7	1.9

Note: All figures are for 1989; (1) people of Hispanic origin can be of any race
Source: 1990 Census of Population and Housing, Summary Tape File 3C

Effective Buying Income

Area	Per Capita ($)	Median Household ($)	Average Household ($)
City	14,405	29,561	37,708
MSA[1]	20,205	42,969	54,762
U.S.	16,803	34,536	45,243

Note: Data as of 1/1/99; (1) Metropolitan Statistical Area - see Appendix A for areas included
Source: Standard Rate & Data Service, Newspaper Advertising Source, 9/99

Effective Household Buying Income Distribution

Area	% of Households Earning						
	$10,000 -$19,999	$20,000 -$34,999	$35,000 -$49,999	$50,000 -$74,999	$75,000 -$99,000	$100,000 -$124,999	$125,000 and up
City	17.8	22.0	16.7	16.7	6.0	1.7	1.5
MSA[1]	12.2	18.7	17.7	22.7	10.6	4.0	4.4
U.S.	16.0	22.6	18.2	18.9	7.2	2.4	2.7

Note: Data as of 1/1/99; (1) Metropolitan Statistical Area - see Appendix A for areas included
Source: Standard Rate & Data Service, Newspaper Advertising Source, 9/99

Poverty Rates by Race and Age

Area	Total (%)	By Race (%)				By Age (%)		
		White	Black	Other	Hisp.[2]	Under 5 years old	Under 18 years old	65 years and over
City	20.3	11.1	29.0	41.6	45.3	31.9	30.3	16.3
MSA[1]	10.4	5.6	25.5	30.1	35.2	15.9	15.0	10.4
U.S.	13.1	9.8	29.5	23.1	25.3	20.1	18.3	12.8

Note: Figures show the percent of people living below the poverty line in 1989. The average poverty threshold was $12,674 for a family of four in 1989; (1) Metropolitan Statistical Area - see Appendix A for areas included; (2) people of Hispanic origin can be of any race
Source: 1990 Census of Population and Housing, Summary Tape File 3C

EMPLOYMENT

Labor Force and Employment

Area	Civilian Labor Force			Workers Employed		
	Jun. 1998	Jun. 1999	% Chg.	Jun. 1998	Jun. 1999	% Chg.
City	643,721	651,326	1.2	603,420	612,656	1.5
MSA[1]	2,504,231	2,538,751	1.4	2,393,935	2,430,685	1.5
U.S.	138,798,000	140,666,000	1.3	132,265,000	134,395,000	1.6

Note: Data is not seasonally adjusted and covers workers 16 years of age and older; (1) Metropolitan Statistical Area - see Appendix A for areas included
Source: Bureau of Labor Statistics, http://stats.bls.gov

Unemployment Rate

Area	1998						1999					
	Jul.	Aug.	Sep.	Oct.	Nov.	Dec.	Jan.	Feb.	Mar.	Apr.	May.	Jun.
City	6.5	6.2	6.6	6.1	6.0	4.9	5.6	5.7	5.7	5.4	5.4	5.9
MSA[1]	4.7	4.4	4.4	4.0	3.9	3.4	4.1	4.1	4.1	3.8	3.8	4.3
U.S.	4.7	4.5	4.4	4.2	4.1	4.0	4.8	4.7	4.4	4.1	4.0	4.5

Note: Data is not seasonally adjusted and covers workers 16 years of age and older; all figures are percentages; (1) Metropolitan Statistical Area - see Appendix A for areas included
Source: Bureau of Labor Statistics, http://stats.bls.gov

Employment by Industry

Sector	MSA[1]		U.S.
	Number of Employees	Percent of Total	Percent of Total
Services	863,600	36.8	30.4
Retail Trade	384,400	16.4	17.7
Government	290,000	12.4	15.6
Manufacturing	302,400	12.9	14.3
Finance/Insurance/Real Estate	165,800	7.1	5.9
Wholesale Trade	129,500	5.5	5.4
Transportation/Public Utilities	111,800	4.8	5.3
Construction	n/a	n/a	5.0
Mining	n/a	n/a	0.4

Note: Figures cover non-farm employment as of 6/99 and are not seasonally adjusted;
(1) Metropolitan Statistical Area - see Appendix A for areas included; n/a not available
Source: Bureau of Labor Statistics, http://stats.bls.gov

Employment by Occupation

Occupation Category	City (%)	MSA[1] (%)	U.S. (%)
White Collar	60.0	64.5	58.1
Executive/Admin./Management	10.3	13.6	12.3
Professional	14.5	15.9	14.1
Technical & Related Support	3.8	4.1	3.7
Sales	9.7	12.0	11.8
Administrative Support/Clerical	21.8	18.9	16.3
Blue Collar	23.2	22.6	26.2
Precision Production/Craft/Repair	9.0	10.3	11.3
Machine Operators/Assem./Insp.	6.2	5.2	6.8
Transportation/Material Movers	3.9	3.6	4.1
Cleaners/Helpers/Laborers	4.0	3.5	3.9
Services	16.3	11.9	13.2
Farming/Forestry/Fishing	0.5	1.0	2.5

Note: Figures cover employed persons 16 years old and over;
(1) Metropolitan Statistical Area - see Appendix A for areas included
Source: 1990 Census of Population and Housing, Summary Tape File 3C

Occupational Employment Projections: 1994 - 2005

High Demand Occupations (ranked by annual openings)	Fast-Growing Occupations[1] (ranked by percent growth)
1. Cashiers	1. Personal and home care aides
2. Salespersons, retail	2. Electronic pagination systems workers
3. Waiters & waitresses	3. Computer engineers
4. Registered nurses	4. Systems analysts
5. General managers & top executives	5. Home health aides
6. Janitors/cleaners/maids, ex. priv. hshld.	6. Human services workers
7. Secretaries, except legal & medical	7. Teachers, preschool and kindergarten
8. General office clerks	8. Computer support specialists
9. Teachers, secondary school	9. Physical therapists
10. Marketing & sales, supervisors	10. Residential counselors

Note: Projections cover Pennsylvania; (1) Excludes occupations with total job growth less than 300
Source: Pennsylvania Workforce 2005, Winter 1997-98

TAXES

Major State and Local Tax Rates

State Corp. Income (%)	State Personal Income (%)	Residential Property (effective rate per $100)	Sales & Use		State Gasoline (cents/gallon)	State Cigarette (cents/pack)
			State (%)	Local (%)		
9.99	2.8	2.64	6.0	1.0	30.77[a]	31.0

Note: Personal/corporate income, sales, gasoline and cigarette tax rates as of January 1999.
Property tax rates as of 1997; (a) Rate is comprised of 12 cents excise and 18.77 cents motor carrier tax. Carriers pay an additional surcharge of 6 cents
Source: Federation of Tax Administrators, www.taxadmin.org; Washington D.C. Department of Finance and Revenue, Tax Rates and Tax Burdens in the District of Columbia: A Nationwide Comparison, July 1998; Chamber of Commerce, 1999

Total Taxes Per Capita and as a Percent of Income

Area	Per Capita Income ($)	Per Capita Taxes ($)			Percent of Income (%)		
		Total	Federal	State/Local	Total	Federal	State/Local
Pennsylvania	26,194	9,782	6,750	3,013	35.2	23.7	11.5
U.S.	27,876	9,881	6,690	3,191	35.4	24.0	11.4

Note: Figures are for 1998
Source: Tax Foundation, www.taxfoundation.org

Estimated Tax Burden

Area	State Income	Local Income	Property	Sales	Total
Philadelphia	2,100	3,720	4,500	683	11,003

Note: The numbers are estimates of taxes paid by a married couple with two children and annual earnings of $75,000. Sales tax estimates assume they spend average amounts on food, clothing, household goods and gasoline. Property tax estimates assume they live in a $250,000 home.
Source: Kiplinger's Personal Finance Magazine, October 1998

COMMERCIAL REAL ESTATE

Office Market

Class/Location	Total Space (sq. ft.)	Vacant Space (sq. ft.)	Vac. Rate (%)	Under Constr. (sq. ft.)	Net Absorp. (sq. ft.)	Rental Rates ($/sq.ft./yr.)
Class A						
CBD	25,700,611	2,210,369	8.6	0	484,649	16.25-31.75
Outside CBD	23,072,408	1,666,207	7.2	1,111,909	768,817	15.00-34.25
Class B						
CBD	13,195,155	2,247,966	17.0	0	-1,409,292	9.75-23.00
Outside CBD	23,549,181	1,416,981	6.0	n/a	2,047,870	12.75-26.00

Note: Data as of 10/98 and covers Philadelphia; CBD = Central Business District; n/a not available;
Source: Society of Industrial and Office Realtors, 1999 Comparative Statistics of Industrial and Office Real Estate Markets

"Little new office development is expected in Philadelphia in 1999; there is at least a five-year supply of office space in Philadelphia at current absorption rates. Employment growth is relatively modest, and most of the growth in office-using employment will take place in the suburbs. The strongest markets in 1999 are likely to be in the suburbs. Especially tight at the end 1998 were Bala Cynwyd, Radnor, Conshohocken sections of the 202 corridor, and Plymouth Meeting. However, a significant amount of new construction may be completed in the suburbs during 1999. Slower economic growth in 1999 and more stringent underwriting standards by lenders are likely to have a negative impact on both new demand and new construction." *Society of Industrial and Office Realtors, 1999 Comparative Statistics of Industrial and Office Real Estate Markets*

Industrial Market

Location	Total Space (sq. ft.)	Vacant Space (sq. ft.)	Vac. Rate (%)	Under Constr. (sq. ft.)	Net Absorp. (sq. ft.)	Lease ($/sq.ft./yr.)
Central City	94,788,789	13,199,870	13.9	n/a	700,880	2.00-4.00
Suburban	148,356,933	14,669,121	9.9	613,217	1,207,339	3.25-6.25

Note: Data as of 10/98 and covers Philadelphia. Net absorption reflects reduction of inventory; n/a not available
Source: Society of Industrial and Office Realtors, 1999 Comparative Statistics of Industrial and Office Real Estate Markets

"Total employment gains in Philadelphia will average 16,000 new jobs in 1999, down from 21,000 jobs in 1998. Employment in manufacturing will decline by an estimated 4,000 jobs. Nevertheless, a significant portion of Philadelphia's inventory of industrial space—50 percent—will continue to be dedicated to manufacturing and High Tech/R&D purposes. Demand for modern, technologically efficient space will continue to be strong in 1999 because of the large number of high-tech firms in the area, particularly in the chemical and drug industries. The local SIOR reporters indicate that there will continue to be a moderate shortage of High Tech/R&D space, which accounts for 15 percent of the total inventory. Construction will increase by one to five percent, a sharp reduction from the rate of growth in 1998. Rental rates for High-Tech/R&D space will increase by one to five percent in 1999." *Society of Industrial and Office Realtors, 1999 Comparative Statistics of Industrial and Office Real Estate Markets*

Retail Market

Shopping Center Inventory (sq. ft.)	Shopping Center Construction (sq. ft.)	Construction as a Percent of Inventory (%)	Torto Wheaton Rent Index[1] ($/sq. ft.)
73,675,000	410,000	0.6	15.09

Note: Data as of 1997 and covers the Metropolitan Statistical Area - see Appendix A for areas included; (1) Index is based on a model that predicts what the average rent should be for leases with certain characteristics, in certain locations during certain years.
Source: National Association of Realtors, 1997-1998 Market Conditions Report

"Philadelphia's retail market is faring poorly. Philadelphia's rents have remained relatively flat over the past five years, but are still among the highest rents in the nation. Construction has fallen dramatically during the last two years, and is the lowest of the northeast metros as a percent of inventory. This has occured due to the double-edged sword of an outflow of residents and slow income growth. Combined with tepid employment growth due to cutbacks in the healt hcare and telecommunications industries and severe job losses at the Naval Shipyard the last few years, this should restrict retail activity in the near-term." *National Association of Realtors, 1997-1998 Market Conditions Report*

COMMERCIAL UTILITIES

Typical Monthly Electric Bills

Area	Commercial Service ($/month)		Industrial Service ($/month)	
	12 kW demand 1,500 kWh	100 kW demand 30,000 kWh	1,000 kW demand 400,000 kWh	20,000 kW demand 10,000,000 kWh
City	256	3,193	34,623	633,393
U.S.	150	2,174	23,995	508,569

Note: Based on rates in effect January 1, 1999
Source: Edison Electric Institute, Typical Residential, Commercial and Industrial Bills, Winter 1999

TRANSPORTATION

Transportation Statistics

Average minutes to work	27.4
Interstate highways	I-76; I-95
Bus lines	
In-city	Southeastern PTA, 1,272 vehicles
Inter-city	2
Passenger air service	
Airport	Philadelphia International
Airlines	17
Aircraft departures	134,133 (1996)
Enplaned passengers	8,571,564 (1996)
Rail service	Amtrak; Light Rail; Metro
Motor freight carriers	100
Major waterways/ports	Port of Philadelphia

Source: Editor & Publisher Market Guide, 1999; FAA Airport Activity Statistics, 1997; Amtrak National Time Table, Northeast Timetable, Spring/Summer 1999; 1990 Census of Population and Housing, STF 3C; Chamber of Commerce/Economic Development 1999; Jane's Urban Transport Systems 1999-2000

Means of Transportation to Work

Area	Car/Truck/Van		Public Transportation			Bicycle	Walked	Other Means	Worked at Home
	Drove Alone	Car-pooled	Bus	Subway	Railroad				
City	44.7	13.2	18.5	7.0	1.8	0.6	10.4	2.1	1.8
MSA[1]	67.8	11.9	6.3	2.7	2.1	0.3	5.4	1.2	2.3
U.S.	73.2	13.4	3.0	1.5	0.5	0.4	3.9	1.2	3.0

Note: Figures shown are percentages and only include workers 16 years old and over;
(1) Metropolitan Statistical Area - see Appendix A for areas included
Source: 1990 Census of Population and Housing, Summary Tape File 3C

BUSINESSES

Major Business Headquarters

Company Name	1999 Rankings	
	Fortune 500	Forbes 500
Aramark	262	18
Berwind Group	-	157
Cigna	57	-
Comcast	292	-
Crown Cork & Seal	198	-
Day & Zimmermann	-	175
Pacifico Group	-	396
Peco Energy	309	-
Rohm & Haas	408	-
Sunoco	240	-

Note: Companies listed are located in the city; dashes indicate no ranking
Fortune 500: Companies that produce a 10-K are ranked 1 to 500 based on 1998 revenue
Forbes 500: Private companies are ranked 1 to 500 based on 1997 revenue
Source: Forbes, November 30, 1998; Fortune, April 26, 1999

Best Companies to Work For

CIGNA, headquartered in Philadelphia, is among the "100 Best Companies for Working Mothers." Criteria: fair wages, opportunities for women to advance, support for child care, flexible work schedules, family-friendly benefits, and work/life supports. *Working Mother, October 1998*

Peco Energy Co. (utilities), headquartered in Philadelphia, is among the "100 Best Places to Work in IS." Criteria: compensation, turnover and training. *Computerworld, May 25, 1998*

Fast-Growing Businesses

According to *Inc.*, Philadelphia is home to one of America's 100 fastest-growing private companies: Western Sky Industries. Criteria for inclusion: must be an independent, privately-held, U.S. corporation, proprietorship or partnership; sales of at least $200,000 in 1995; five-year operating/sales history; increase in 1999 sales over 1998 sales; holding companies, regulated banks, and utilities were excluded. *Inc. 500, 1999*

According to *Fortune*, Philadelphia is home to one of America's 100 fastest-growing companies: Resource America. Companies were ranked based on earnings-per-share growth, revenue growth and total return over the previous three years. Criteria for inclusion: public companies with sales of least $50 million. Companies that lost money in the most recent quarter, or ended in the red for the past four quarters as a whole, were not eligible. Limited partnerships and REITs were also not considered. *Fortune, "America's Fastest-Growing Companies," 1999*

Women-Owned Firms: Number, Employment and Sales

Area	Number of Firms	Employ-ment	Sales ($000)	Rank[2]
MSA[1]	144,600	695,900	90,231,000	4

Note: (1) Metropolitan Statistical Area - see Appendix A for areas included;
(2) Calculated on an averaging of the number of businesses, employment and sales
Source: The National Foundation for Women Business Owners, 1999 Facts on Women-Owned Businesses: Trends in the Top 50 Metropolitan Areas

Women-Owned Firms: Growth

Area	% change from 1992 to 1999			Rank[2]
	Number of Firms	Employ-ment	Sales	
MSA[1]	39.3	122.6	133.4	32

Note: (1) Metropolitan Statistical Area - see Appendix A for areas included; (2) Calculated on an averaging of the percent growth of number of businesses, employment and sales
Source: The National Foundation for Women Business Owners, 1999 Facts on Women-Owned Businesses: Trends in the Top 50 Metropolitan Areas

Minority Business Opportunity

Philadelphia is home to two companies which are on the Black Enterprise Industrial/Service 100 list (largest based on gross sales): Philadelphia Coca-Cola Bottling Co. Inc. (soft drink bottling); PRWT Services Inc. (transaction services, payment and document processing) . Criteria: operational in previous calendar year, at least 51% black-owned and manufactures/owns the product it sells or provides industrial or consumer services. Brokerages, real estate firms and firms that provide professional services are not eligible. *Black Enterprise, www.blackenterprise.com*

Small Business Opportunity

According to *Forbes*, Philadelphia is home to two of America's 200 best small companies: CMAC Investment and Urban Outfitters. Criteria: companies included must be publicly traded since November 1997 with a stock price of at least $5 per share and an average daily float of 1,000 shares. The company's latest 12-month sales must be between $5 and $350 million, return on equity (ROE) must be a minimum of 12% for both the past 5 years and the most recent four quarters, and five-year sales and EPS growth must average at least 10%. Companies with declining sales or earnings during the past year were dropped as well as businesses with debt/equity ratios over 1.25. Companies with negative operating cash flow in each of the past two years were also excluded. *Forbes, November 2, 1998*

HOTELS & MOTELS

Hotels/Motels

Area	Hotels/ Motels	Rooms	Luxury-Level Hotels/Motels		Average Minimum Rates ($)		
			♦♦♦♦	♦♦♦♦♦	♦♦	♦♦♦	♦♦♦♦
City	34	8,801	4	0	84	136	257
Airport	15	3,558	0	0	n/a	n/a	n/a
Suburbs	61	8,749	0	0	n/a	n/a	n/a
Total	110	21,108	4	0	n/a	n/a	n/a

Note: n/a not available; classifications range from one diamond (budget properties with basic amenities) to five diamond (luxury properties with the finest service, rooms and facilities).
Source: OAG, Business Travel Planner, Winter 1998-99

Philadelphia is home to two of the top 100 hotels in the world according to *Travel & Leisure*: Four Seasons (#64) and Ritz-Carlton (#77) . Criteria: value, rooms/ambience, location, facilities/activities and service. *Travel & Leisure, 1998 World's Best Awards, Best Hotels and Resorts*

CONVENTION CENTERS

Major Convention Centers

Center Name	Meeting Rooms	Exhibit Space (sq. ft.)
Marketplace Design Center	4	20,000
Pennsylvania Convention Center	52	440,000
Philadelphia Civic Center	30	382,000
Sugarloaf-Albert M. Greenfield Conference Center	20	n/a
Wyndham Franklin Plaza	28	60,000

Note: n/a not available
Source: Trade Shows Worldwide, 1998; Meetings & Conventions, 4/15/99;
Sucessful Meetings, 3/31/98

Living Environment

COST OF LIVING

Cost of Living Index

Composite Index	Groceries	Housing	Utilities	Trans-portation	Health Care	Misc. Goods/ Services
120.5	109.2	139.3	144.2	120.4	99.2	107.6

Note: U.S. = 100
Source: ACCRA, Cost of Living Index, 1st Quarter 1999

HOUSING

Median Home Prices and Housing Affordability

Area	Median Price[2] 1st Qtr. 1999 ($)	HOI[3] 1st Qtr. 1999	Afford-ability Rank[4]
MSA[1]	105,000	77.4	78
U.S.	134,000	69.6	–

Note: (1) Metropolitan Statistical Area - see Appendix A for areas included; (2) U.S. figures calculated from the sales of 524,324 new and existing homes in 181 markets; (3) Housing Opportunity Index - percent of homes sold that were within the reach of the median income household at the prevailing mortgage interest rate; (4) Rank is from 1-181 with 1 being most affordable
Source: National Association of Home Builders, Housing Opportunity Index, 1st Quarter 1999

Median Home Price Projection

It is projected that the median price of existing single-family homes in the metro area will increase by 2.5% in 1999. Nationwide, home prices are projected to increase 3.8%.
Kiplinger's Personal Finance Magazine, January 1999

Average New Home Price

Area	Price ($)
City	197,999
U.S.	142,735

Note: Figures are based on a new home with 1,800 sq. ft. of living area on an 8,000 sq. ft. lot.
Source: ACCRA, Cost of Living Index, 1st Quarter 1999

Average Apartment Rent

Area	Rent ($/mth)
City	733
U.S.	601

Note: Figures are based on an unfurnished two bedroom, 1-1/2 or 2 bath apartment, approximately 950 sq. ft. in size, excluding all utilities except water
Source: ACCRA, Cost of Living Index, 1st Quarter 1999

RESIDENTIAL UTILITIES

Average Residential Utility Costs

Area	All Electric ($/mth)	Part Electric ($/mth)	Other Energy ($/mth)	Phone ($/mth)
City	–	94.02	58.49	16.51
U.S.	100.02	55.73	43.33	19.71

Source: ACCRA, Cost of Living Index, 1st Quarter 1999

HEALTH CARE

Average Health Care Costs

Area	Hospital ($/day)	Doctor ($/visit)	Dentist ($/visit)
City	452.00	50.50	63.75
U.S.	430.43	52.45	66.35

Note: Hospital—based on a semi-private room; Doctor—based on a general practitioner's routine exam of an established patient; Dentist—based on adult teeth cleaning and periodic oral exam.
Source: ACCRA, Cost of Living Index, 1st Quarter 1999

Distribution of Office-Based Physicians

Area	Family/Gen. Practitioners	Specialists		
		Medical	Surgical	Other
MSA[1]	917	4,113	2,607	3,299

Note: Data as of 12/31/97; (1) Metropolitan Statistical Area - see Appendix A for areas included
Source: American Medical Assn., Physician Characteristics & Distribution in the U.S., 1999

Hospitals

Philadelphia has 26 general medical and surgical hospitals, 3 psychiatric, 3 other specialty, 2 children's general, 1 children's orthopedic, 1 children's rehabilitation. *AHA Guide to the Healthcare Field, 1998-99*

According to *U.S. News and World Report,* Philadelphia has 8 of the best hospitals in the U.S.: **Hospital of the University of Pennsylvania**, noted for cancer, endocrinology, gastroenterology, geriatrics, gynecology, neurology, orthopedics, otolaryngology, pulmonology, rheumatology, urology; **Thomas Jefferson University Hospital**, noted for cancer, cardiology, gastroenterology, geriatrics, gynecology, neurology, orthopedics, otolaryngology, pulmonology, rehabilitation, rheumatology, urology; **Fox Chase Cancer Center**, noted for cancer; **Temple University Hospital**, noted for gastroenterology; **Wills Eye Hospital**, noted for ophthalmology; **Children's Hospital of Philadelphia**, noted for pediatrics; **Albert Einstein Medical Center (Moss Rehab Hospital)**, noted for rehabilitation; **Magee Rehabilitation Hospital**, noted for rehabilitation. *U.S. News Online, "America's Best Hospitals," 10th Edition, www.usnews.com*

EDUCATION

Public School District Statistics

District Name	Num. Sch.	Enroll.	Classroom Teachers	Pupils per Teacher	Minority Pupils (%)	Current Exp.[1] ($/pupil)
Phila Community Acad A Pa Cs	1	180	7	25.7	n/a	n/a
Phila Harambee Inst Sci/Tec Cs	1	220	12	18.3	n/a	n/a
Phila World Comm Hs Cs	1	270	9	30.0	n/a	n/a
Philadelphia City SD	259	212,865	10,913	19.5	81.0	5,575
Youth Build Phila Cs	1	149	6	24.8	n/a	n/a

Note: Data covers the 1997-1998 school year unless otherwise noted; (1) Data covers fiscal year 1996; SD = School District; ISD = Independent School District; n/a not available
Source: National Center for Education Statistics, Common Core of Data Public Education Agency Universe 1997-98; National Center for Education Statistics, Characteristics of the 100 Largest Public Elementary and Secondary School Districts in the United States: 1997-98, July 1999

Educational Quality

School District	Education Quotient[1]	Graduate Outcome[2]	Community Index[3]	Resource Index[4]
Philadelphia City	66.0	55.0	54.0	89.0

Note: Nearly 1,000 secondary school districts were rated in terms of educational quality. The scores range from a low of 50 to a high of 150; (1) Average of the Graduate Outcome, Community and Resource indexes; (2) Based on graduation rates and college board scores (SAT/ACT); (3) Based on the surrounding community's average level of education and the area's average income level; (4) Based on teacher salaries, per-pupil expenditures and student-teacher ratios.
Source: Expansion Management, Ratings Issue, 1998

Educational Attainment by Race

Area	High School Graduate (%)					Bachelor's Degree (%)				
	Total	White	Black	Other	Hisp.[2]	Total	White	Black	Other	Hisp.[2]
City	64.3	68.1	60.2	51.4	44.7	15.2	19.0	9.1	17.3	8.2
MSA[1]	75.9	79.2	63.8	62.6	51.8	22.8	25.2	10.9	26.5	11.7
U.S.	75.2	77.9	63.1	60.4	49.8	20.3	21.5	11.4	19.4	9.2

Note: Figures shown cover persons 25 years old and over; (1) Metropolitan Statistical Area - see Appendix A for areas included; (2) people of Hispanic origin can be of any race
Source: 1990 Census of Population and Housing, Summary Tape File 3C

School Enrollment by Type

Area	Preprimary				Elementary/High School			
	Public		Private		Public		Private	
	Enrollment	%	Enrollment	%	Enrollment	%	Enrollment	%
City	13,314	55.4	10,702	44.6	179,728	70.8	74,032	29.2
MSA[1]	48,214	48.5	51,171	51.5	595,382	76.8	179,754	23.2
U.S.	2,679,029	59.5	1,824,256	40.5	38,379,689	90.2	4,187,099	9.8

Note: Figures shown cover persons 3 years old and over;
(1) Metropolitan Statistical Area - see Appendix A for areas included
Source: 1990 Census of Population and Housing, Summary Tape File 3C

School Enrollment by Race

Area	Preprimary (%)				Elementary/High School (%)			
	White	Black	Other	Hisp.[1]	White	Black	Other	Hisp.[1]
City	49.3	44.6	6.0	4.7	41.6	48.6	9.8	8.4
MSA[2]	79.3	16.9	3.8	3.0	69.7	23.9	6.4	5.3
U.S.	80.4	12.5	7.1	7.8	74.1	15.6	10.3	12.5

Note: Figures shown cover persons 3 years old and over; (1) people of Hispanic origin can be of any
race; (2) Metropolitan Statistical Area - see Appendix A for areas included
Source: 1990 Census of Population and Housing, Summary Tape File 3C

Classroom Teacher Salaries in Public Schools

District	B.A. Degree		M.A. Degree		Maximum	
	Min. ($)	Rank[1]	Max. ($)	Rank[1]	Max. ($)	Rank[1]
Philadelphia	28,599	26	50,434	20	57,198	16
Average	26,980	-	46,065	-	51,435	-

Note: Salaries are for 1997-1998; (1) Rank ranges from 1 to 100
Source: American Federation of Teachers, Survey & Analysis of Salary Trends, 1998

Higher Education

Two-Year Colleges		Four-Year Colleges		Medical Schools	Law Schools	Voc/Tech
Public	Private	Public	Private			
1	6	1	14	4	3	48

Source: College Blue Book, Occupational Education, 1997; Medical School Admission Requirements,
1999-2000; Peterson's Guide to Two-Year Colleges, 1999; Peterson's Guide to Four-Year Colleges,
2000; Barron's Guide to Law Schools, 1999

MAJOR EMPLOYERS

Major Employers

Albert Einstein Medical Center
Corestates Bank
Independence Blue Cross
Crown Beverage Packaging
Questpoint (data processing)

Children's Hospital of Philadelphia
Connecticut General Fire & Casualty Insurance
Food Distribution Center
Reliance Insurance
Atlantic Petroleum Corp.

Note: Companies listed are located in the city
Source: Dun's Business Rankings, 1999; Ward's Business Directory, 1998

PUBLIC SAFETY

Crime Rate

Area	All Crimes	Violent Crimes				Property Crimes		
		Murder	Forcible Rape	Robbery	Aggrav. Assault	Burglary	Larceny -Theft	Motor Vehicle Theft
City	6,920.0	27.1	46.1	1,013.1	442.6	1,060.2	2,817.6	1,513.4
Suburbs[1]	3,613.2	2.7	21.1	130.0	225.8	586.1	2,223.5	423.9
MSA[2]	4,630.8	10.2	28.8	401.8	292.5	732.0	2,406.3	759.2
U.S.	5,086.6	7.4	36.3	201.9	390.9	944.8	2,979.7	525.6

Note: Crime rate is the number of crimes per 100,000 pop.; (1) defined as all areas within the MSA but
located outside the central city; (2) Metropolitan Statistical Area - see Appendix A for areas incl.
Source: FBI Uniform Crime Reports, 1996

RECREATION

Culture and Recreation

Museums	Symphony Orchestras	Opera Companies	Dance Companies	Professional Theatres	Zoos	Pro Sports Teams
25	4	3	5	8	1	4

Source: International Directory of the Performing Arts, 1997; Official Museum Directory, 1999; Stern's Performing Arts Directory, 1997; USA Today Four Sport Stadium Guide, 1997; Chamber of Commerce/Economic Development, 1999

Library System

The Free Library of Philadelphia has 49 branches, holdings of 7,983,088 volumes, and a budget of $63,767,334 (1996-1997). *American Library Directory, 1998-1999*

MEDIA

Newspapers

Name	Type	Freq.	Distribution	Circulation
Catholic Standard & Times	Religious	1x/wk	Area	71,962
The Leader	General	1x/wk	Local	29,000
Olney Times	General	1x/wk	Area	25,000
Philadelphia Daily News	General	6x/wk	Area	180,000
Philadelphia Inquirer	General	7x/wk	Area	433,489
Philadelphia New Observer Newspaper	Black	1x/wk	Local	80,000
Philadelphia Tribune	Black	3x/wk	Area	126,000
Scoop U.S.A.	Black	1x/wk	Local	30,000
South Philadelphia Review	General	1x/wk	Local	72,000

Note: Includes newspapers with circulations of 25,000 or more located in the city;
Source: Burrelle's Media Directory, 1999 Edition

Television Stations

Name	Ch.	Affiliation	Type	Owner
KYW	n/a	CBST	Commercial	Westinghouse Broadcasting Company
WPVI	n/a	ABCT	Commercial	ABC Inc.
WHYY	12	PBS	Public	WHYY Inc.
WPHL	17	WB	Commercial	Chicago Tribune Magazines
WTXF	29	FBC	Commercial	Fox Television Stations Inc.
WYBE	35	n/a	Public	Independence Public Media of Philadelphia Inc.
WGTW	48	n/a	Commercial	Brunson Communications
WPSG	57	UPN	Commercial	Paramount Communications Inc.
WPPX	61	n/a	Commercial	Paxson Communications Corporation

Note: Stations included broadcast in the Philadelphia metro area; n/a not available
Source: Burrelle's Media Directory, 1999 Edition

AM Radio Stations

Call Letters	Freq. (kHz)	Target Audience	Station Format	Music Format
WFIL	560	G/R	E/M/N/S/T	Adult Contemporary/Christian/Easy Listening
WIP	610	General	S/T	n/a
WPHE	690	Hispanic	M/N/T	Latin
WURD	900	Hispanic	M/N/T	Latin
KYW	1060	General	N	n/a
WHAT	1340	B/R	E/M/S/T	Christian

Note: Stations included broadcast in the Philadelphia metro area; n/a not available
Target Audience: A=Asian; B=Black; C=Christian; E=Ethnic; F=French; G=General; H=Hispanic; M=Men; N=Native American; R=Religious; S=Senior Citizen; W=Women; Y=Young Adult; Z=Children
Station Format: E=Educational; M=Music; N=News; S=Sports; T=Talk
Source: Burrelle's Media Directory, 1999 Edition

FM Radio Stations

Call Letters	Freq. (mHz)	Target Audience	Station Format	Music Format
WXPH	88.1	General	M/N/S	Adult Standards/Alternative
WSJR	88.1	n/a	M	Alternative
WPEB	88.1	Z/G	E/M/T	n/a
WXPN	88.5	General	M	Adult Contemporary
WRTI	90.1	General	E/M/N/S	Classical/Jazz
WHYY	90.9	General	N	n/a
WRTY	91.1	Black	E/M/N/S	Classical/Jazz
WRTQ	91.3	n/a	M	Classical/Jazz
WJAZ	91.7	General	E/M/N/S/T	Classical/Jazz
WKDU	91.7	General	M	n/a
WXTU	92.5	General	M/N/S	Country
WMMR	93.3	General	M/N/S	AOR/Classic Rock/Modern Rock
WYSP	94.1	Men	M/N/S	AOR
WXXM	95.7	General	M	Oldies
WUSL	98.9	Black	M/N/T	Gospel/Reggae/R&B/Urban Contemporary
WBEB	101.1	General	M	Adult Contemporary
WPHI	103.9	General	M	Urban Contemporary
WJJZ	106.1	General	M/N/S	Jazz

Note: Stations included broadcast in the Philadelphia metro area; n/a not available
Station Format: E=Educational; M=Music; N=News; S=Sports; T=Talk
Target Audience: A=Asian; B=Black; C=Christian; E=Ethnic; F=French; G=General; H=Hispanic;
M=Men; N=Native American; R=Religious; S=Senior Citizen; W=Women; Y=Young Adult; Z=Children
Music Format: AOR=Album Oriented Rock; MOR=Middle-of-the-Road
Source: Burrelle's Media Directory, 1999 Edition

CLIMATE

Average and Extreme Temperatures

Temperature	Jan	Feb	Mar	Apr	May	Jun	Jul	Aug	Sep	Oct	Nov	Dec	Yr.
Extreme High (°F)	74	74	85	94	96	100	104	101	100	89	84	72	104
Average High (°F)	39	42	51	63	73	82	86	85	78	67	55	43	64
Average Temp. (°F)	32	34	42	53	63	72	77	76	68	57	47	36	55
Average Low (°F)	24	26	33	43	53	62	67	66	59	47	38	28	45
Extreme Low (°F)	-7	-4	7	19	28	44	51	44	35	25	15	1	-7

Note: Figures cover the years 1948-1990
Source: National Climatic Data Center, International Station Meteorological Climate Summary, 3/95

Average Precipitation/Snowfall/Humidity

Precip./Humidity	Jan	Feb	Mar	Apr	May	Jun	Jul	Aug	Sep	Oct	Nov	Dec	Yr.
Avg. Precip. (in.)	3.2	2.8	3.7	3.5	3.7	3.6	4.1	4.0	3.3	2.7	3.4	3.3	41.4
Avg. Snowfall (in.)	7	7	4	Tr	Tr	0	0	0	0	Tr	1	4	22
Avg. Rel. Hum. 7am (%)	74	73	73	72	75	77	80	82	84	83	79	75	77
Avg. Rel. Hum. 4pm (%)	60	55	51	48	51	52	54	55	55	54	57	60	54

Note: Figures cover the years 1948-1990; Tr = Trace amounts (<0.05 in. of rain; <0.5 in. of snow)
Source: National Climatic Data Center, International Station Meteorological Climate Summary, 3/95

Weather Conditions

Temperature			Daytime Sky			Precipitation		
10°F & below	32°F & below	90°F & above	Clear	Partly cloudy	Cloudy	0.01 inch or more precip.	0.1 inch or more snow/ice	Thunder-storms
5	94	23	81	146	138	117	14	27

Note: Figures are average number of days per year and covers the years 1948-1990
Source: National Climatic Data Center, International Station Meteorological Climate Summary, 3/95

AIR & WATER QUALITY

Maximum Pollutant Concentrations

	Particulate Matter (ug/m³)	Carbon Monoxide (ppm)	Sulfur Dioxide (ppm)	Nitrogen Dioxide (ppm)	Ozone (ppm)	Lead (ug/m³)
MSA[1] Level	264	5	0.048	0.032	0.14	0.81
NAAQS[2]	150	9	0.140	0.053	0.12	1.50
Met NAAQS?	No	Yes	Yes	Yes	No	Yes

Note: (1) Metropolitan Statistical Area - see Appendix A for areas included; (2) National Ambient Air Quality Standards; ppm = parts per million; ug/m³ = micrograms per cubic meter; n/a not available
Source: EPA, National Air Quality and Emissions Trends Report, 1997

Pollutant Standards Index

In the Philadelphia MSA (see Appendix A for areas included), the Pollutant Standards Index (PSI) exceeded 100 on 39 days in 1997. A PSI value greater than 100 indicates that air quality would be in the unhealthful range on that day. *EPA, National Air Quality and Emissions Trends Report, 1997*

Drinking Water

Water System Name	Pop. Served	Primary Water Source Type	Number of Violations in 1998	Type of Violation/ Contaminants
Philadelphia Water Dept.	1,755,000	Surface	None	None

Note: Data as of July 10, 1999
Source: EPA, Office of Ground Water and Drinking Water, Safe Drinking Water Information System

Philadelphia tap water is slightly acid, moderately hard (Schuykill River), moderately soft (Delaware River); fluoridated.
Editor & Publisher Market Guide, 1999

Pittsburgh, Pennsylvania

Background

Pittsburgh was once the creaking, croaking, belching giant of heavy industry. Thanks to a plentiful supply of bituminous coal beds and limestone deposits nearby, the city had forged a prosperous economy based upon steel, glass, rubber, petroleum, and machinery. However, unregulated spews of soot into the air by these factories earned Pittsburgh the title of "Smoky City." Concerned citizens and politicians passed smoke-control laws. Today, Pittsburgh's renaissance is a result of these citizen's unflagging faith in their city.

In the 18th century, the area in and around the Ohio Valley and the Allegheny River, where present day Pittsburgh lies, was claimed by both British and French flags. After being lobbed back and forth between the two, the land finally fell into British hands. The city was named Pittsborough, for the British Prime Minister at the time, William Pitt.

Almost immediately, the city showed signs of what it was to become. In 1792, the first blast furnace was built by George Anschulz. In 1797, the first glass factory was opened, and in 1804, the first cotton factory was opened. Irish, Scottish, and a smattering of English immigrants provided the labor pool for these factories. During the Civil War, this labor pool was augmented by a wave of German immigrants. Finally, during the late 19th century, Poles, Czechs, Slovaks, Italians, Russians, and Hungarians completed the picture in the colorful quilt of Pittsburgh's workforce. The last wave particularly contributed their sweat and toil to the fortunes of captains of industry such as Andrew Carnegie, Henry Clay Frick, and Charles M. Schwab.

Fortunately for Pittsburgh, these industrialists gave back to the city in the form of their cultural and educational patronage. The Carnegie Institute is renowned for the Museum of Art and the Museum of Natural History. The Frick Art Museum is a noted private collection featuring such artists as Rubens, Tintoretto, Fragonard, and Boucher.

In 1997, Pittsburgh was at a crossroads of progress. Technology and health care services, their manufacturing counterparts, and financial institutions have become dominant forces behind a steadily diversifying economy. New Internet software and computer software companies have set up operations in or near Pittsburgh. In all, 3,600 high-tech companies have created 100,000 jobs in the past 10 years. Real estate costs and crime rates are among the lowest of any large city in the country. The city has plans to expand the Convention Center and construct two downtown stadiums, one for baseball (the Pirates) and one for football (the Steelers).

The city is a little over 100 miles southeast of Lake Erie. Its nearness to the Great Lakes and to the Atlantic Seaboard helps to modify its humid continental type of climate. Winter is influenced primarily by Canadian air masses which are infrequently tempered by air from the Gulf of Mexico. During the summer, Gulf air brings warm humid weather. Once every four years, the Monongahela and Ohio Rivers combine, causing the Ohio River to reach the 25 foot flood stage.

General Rankings and Evaluative Comments

■ Pittsburgh was ranked #7 out of 15 large, northeastern metropolitan areas in *Money's* 1998 survey of "The Best Places to Live in America." The survey was conducted by first contacting 512 representative households nationwide and asking them to rank 37 quality-of-life factors on a scale of 1 to 10. Next, a demographic profile was compiled on the 300 largest metropolitan statistical areas in the U.S. The numbers were crunched together to arrive at an overall ranking (things Americans consider most important, like clean air and water, low crime and good schools, received extra weight). Unlike previous years, the 1998 rankings were broken down by region (northeast, midwest, south, west) and population size (100,000 to 249,999; 250,000 to 999,999; 1 million plus). The city had a nationwide ranking of #164 out of 300 in 1997 and #149 out of 300 in 1996. *Money, July 1998; Money, July 1997; Money, September 1996*

■ *Ladies Home Journal* ranked America's 200 largest cities based on the qualities women care about most. Pittsburgh ranked #114 out of 200. Criteria: low crime rate, well-paying jobs, quality health and child care, good public schools, the presence of women in government, size of the gender wage gap, number of sexual-harassment and discrimination complaints filed, unemployment and divorce rates, commute times, population density, number of houses of worship, parks and cultural offerings, number of women's health specialists, how well a community's women cared for themselves, complexion kindness index based on UV radiation levels, odds of finding affordable fashions, rental rates for romance movies, champagne sales and other matters of the heart. *Ladies Home Journal, November 1998*

■ Zero Population Growth ranked 229 cities in terms of children's health, safety, and economic well-being. Pittsburgh was ranked #6 out of 25 major cities (main city in a metro area with population of greater than 2 million) and was given a grade of B. Criteria: total population, percent of population under 18 years of age, household language, percent population change, percent of births to teens, infant mortality rate, percent of low birth weights, dropout rate, enrollment in preprimary school, violent and property crime rates, unemployment rate, percent of children in poverty, percent of owner occupied units, number of bad air days, percent of public transportation commuters, and average travel time to work. *Zero Population Growth, Children's Environmental Index, Fall 1999*

■ Pittsburgh was ranked #38 out of 59 metro areas in *The Regional Economist's* "Rational Livability Ranking of 59 Large Metro Areas." The rankings were based on the metro area's total population change over the period 1990-97 divided by the number of people moving in from elsewhere in the United States (net domestic in-migration). *St. Louis Federal Reserve Bank of St. Louis, The Regional Economist, April 1999*

■ Pittsburgh was selected by *Yahoo! Internet Life* as one of "America's Most Wired Cities & Towns." The city ranked #40 out of 50. Criteria: home and work net use, domain density, hosts per capita, directory density and content quality. *Yahoo! Internet Life, March 1999*

■ Cognetics studied 273 metro areas in the United States, ranking them by entrepreneurial activity. Pittsburgh was ranked #46 out of the 50 largest metro areas. Criteria: Significant Starts (firms started in the last 10 years that still employ at least 5 people) and Young Growers (percent of firms 10 years old or less that grew significantly during the last 4 years). *Cognetics, "Entrepreneurial Hot Spots: The Best Places in America to Start and Grow a Company," 1998*

■ Pittsburgh was selected as one of the "Best American Cities to Start a Business" by *Point of View* magazine. Criteria: coolness, quality-of-life, and business concerns. The city was ranked #37 out of 75. *Point of View, November 1998*

■ Reliastar Financial Corp. ranked the 125 largest metropolitan areas according to the general financial security of residents. Pittsburgh was ranked #57 out of 125 with a score of 2.6. The score indicates the percentage a metropolitan area is above or below the metropolitan norm. A metro area with a score of 10.6 is 10.6% above the metro average. Criteria: Earnings and Wealth Potential (household income, education, net assets, cost of living); Safety Net (health insurance, retirement savings, life insurance, income support programs); Personal Threats (unemployment rate, low-income households, crime rate); Community Economic Vitality (cost of community services, job quality, job creation, housing costs). *Reliastar Financial Corp., "The Best Cities to Earn and Save Money," 1999 Edition*

Business Environment

STATE ECONOMY

State Economic Profile

"Pennsylvania's economy has lagged the nation for several years, a trend that will only get worse. While Philadelphia has seen some resurgence, it has not been enough to offset declines in the rest of the state. PA's poor demographic outlook will confine it to slow growth at best in 1999 and 2000. Expansions by high-tech and biotech firms, such as Lucent, SAP and SmithKline Beecham, will help PA's weak job outlook, although these gains will be limited to the eastern part of the state.

PA employment grew at the low rate of 0.8% in 1998, driven largely by the 1.0% increase in Philadelphia. In contrast, Pittsburgh lost jobs at a rate of 0.1%. While many areas of the country are experiencing declining manufacturing employment, due to weak export demand and long-term restructuring, Pittsburgh is one of the few urban areas that is also losing service jobs, at a rate of 0.4% in 1998. Services employment for PA grew 1.3% and 1.9% for Philadelphia in 1998.

Some of western PA's problems stem from its declining steel sector. Weak steel prices, over-capacity and a flood of cheap imports have undermined PA's steel industry. Even with import restraints and renewed world demand, the outlook for PA's steel industry remains bleak. PA's steel producers' biggest problem is US mini-mills that are sweeping the industry. Further declines in PA's steel industry are likely in 1999 and 2000.

Few states lose more residents every year than PA. Its continued loss of younger households will constrain labor market growth and pose problems for its housing market. Home sales were flat in 1998, and residential permits were up only 3%. Both sales and starts should contract in 1999." *National Association of Realtors, Economic Profiles: The Fifty States and the District of Columbia, http://nar.realtor.com/databank/profiles.htm*

IMPORTS/EXPORTS

Total Export Sales

Area	1994 ($000)	1995 ($000)	1996 ($000)	1997 ($000)	% Chg. 1994-97	% Chg. 1996-97
MSA[1]	3,150,610	3,982,169	3,933,687	4,352,159	38.1	10.6
U.S.	512,415,609	583,030,524	622,827,063	687,597,999	34.2	10.4

Note: (1) Metropolitan Statistical Area - see Appendix A for areas included
Source: U.S. Department of Commerce, International Trade Association, Metropolitan Area Exports: An Export Performance Report on Over 250 U.S. Cities, November 10, 1998

CITY FINANCES

City Government Finances

Component	FY92 ($000)	FY92 (per capita $)
Revenue	406,994	1,112.32
Expenditure	428,721	1,171.70
Debt Outstanding	660,819	1,806.03
Cash & Securities	399,269	1,091.21

Source: U.S. Bureau of the Census, City Government Finances: 1991-92

City Government Revenue by Source

Source	FY92 ($000)	FY92 (per capita $)	FY92 (%)
From Federal Government	20,818	56.90	5.1
From State Governments	21,444	58.61	5.3
From Local Governments	48,331	132.09	11.9
Property Taxes	121,850	333.02	29.9
General Sales Taxes	0	0.00	0.0
Selective Sales Taxes	29,155	79.68	7.2
Income Taxes	36,625	100.10	9.0
Current Charges	12,361	33.78	3.0
Utility/Liquor Store	0	0.00	0.0
Employee Retirement[1]	33,792	92.35	8.3
Other	82,618	225.80	20.3

Note: (1) Excludes "city contributions," classified as "nonrevenue," intragovernmental transfers.
Source: U.S. Bureau of the Census, City Government Finances: 1991-92

City Government Expenditures by Function

Function	FY92 ($000)	FY92 (per capita $)	FY92 (%)
Educational Services	5,708	15.60	1.3
Employee Retirement[1]	33,864	92.55	7.9
Environment/Housing	64,532	176.37	15.1
Government Administration	29,821	81.50	7.0
Interest on General Debt	44,618	121.94	10.4
Public Safety	102,810	280.98	24.0
Social Services	7,147	19.53	1.7
Transportation	21,694	59.29	5.1
Utility/Liquor Store	16,232	44.36	3.8
Other	102,295	279.57	23.9

Note: (1) Payments to beneficiaries including withdrawal of contributions.
Source: U.S. Bureau of the Census, City Government Finances: 1991-92

Municipal Bond Ratings

Area	Moody's	S & P
Pittsburgh	n/a	n/a

Note: n/a not available; n/r not rated
Source: Moody's Bond Record, 6/99

POPULATION

Population Growth

Area	1980	1990	% Chg. 1980-90	July 1998 Estimate	% Chg. 1990-98
City	423,938	369,879	-12.8	340,520	-7.9
MSA[1]	2,218,870	2,056,705	-7.3	2,374,277	15.4
U.S.	226,545,805	248,765,170	9.8	270,299,000	8.7

Note: (1) Metropolitan Statistical Area - see Appendix A for areas included;
July 1998 MSA population estimate was calculated by the editors
Source: 1980/1990 Census of Housing and Population, Summary Tape File 3C;
Census Bureau Population Estimates 1998

Population Characteristics

Race	City 1980 Population	%	City 1990 Population	%	% Chg. 1980-90	MSA[1] 1990 Population	%
White	318,287	75.1	266,636	72.1	-16.2	1,867,837	90.8
Black	101,549	24.0	95,635	25.9	-5.8	168,568	8.2
Amer Indian/Esk/Aleut	584	0.1	662	0.2	13.4	2,161	0.1
Asian/Pacific Islander	2,818	0.7	5,780	1.6	105.1	14,766	0.7
Other	700	0.2	1,166	0.3	66.6	3,373	0.2
Hispanic Origin[2]	3,196	0.8	3,415	0.9	6.9	10,451	0.5

Note: (1) Metropolitan Statistical Area - see Appendix A for areas included;
(2) people of Hispanic origin can be of any race
Source: 1980/1990 Census of Housing and Population, Summary Tape File 3C

Ancestry

Area	German	Irish	English	Italian	U.S.	French	Polish	Dutch
City	25.4	17.8	5.9	12.4	1.5	1.5	9.5	0.6
MSA[1]	33.6	20.0	11.1	15.4	1.8	2.2	10.0	1.8
U.S.	23.3	15.6	13.1	5.9	5.3	4.2	3.8	2.5

Note: Figures are percentages and include persons that reported multiple ancestry (eg. if a person reported being Irish and Italian, they were included in both columns); (1) Metropolitan Statistical Area - see Appendix A for areas included
Source: 1990 Census of Population and Housing, Summary Tape File 3C

Age

Area	Median Age (Years)	Under 5	Under 18	18-24	25-44	45-64	65+	80+
City	34.5	6.1	19.9	13.7	30.3	18.2	17.9	3.9
MSA[1]	36.9	6.2	21.7	9.2	30.6	21.0	17.4	3.5
U.S.	32.9	7.3	25.6	10.5	32.6	18.7	12.5	2.8

Note: (1) Metropolitan Statistical Area - see Appendix A for areas included
Source: 1990 Census of Population and Housing, Summary Tape File 3C

Male/Female Ratio

Area	Number of males per 100 females (all ages)	Number of males per 100 females (18 years old+)
City	86.8	82.9
MSA[1]	89.4	85.5
U.S.	95.0	91.9

Note: (1) Metropolitan Statistical Area - see Appendix A for areas included
Source: 1990 Census of Population, General Population Characteristics

INCOME

Per Capita/Median/Average Income

Area	Per Capita ($)	Median Household ($)	Average Household ($)
City	12,580	20,747	29,587
MSA[1]	14,052	26,700	34,902
U.S.	14,420	30,056	38,453

Note: All figures are for 1989; (1) Metropolitan Statistical Area - see Appendix A for areas included
Source: 1990 Census of Population and Housing, Summary Tape File 3C

Household Income Distribution by Race

Income ($)	City (%)					U.S. (%)				
	Total	White	Black	Other	Hisp.[1]	Total	White	Black	Other	Hisp.[1]
Less than 5,000	10.9	7.3	21.3	24.6	12.7	6.2	4.8	15.2	8.6	8.8
5,000 - 9,999	15.9	13.9	22.5	13.1	11.0	9.3	8.6	14.2	9.9	11.1
10,000 - 14,999	11.5	11.3	11.9	13.1	14.8	8.8	8.5	11.0	9.8	11.0
15,000 - 24,999	19.2	19.8	17.5	18.1	16.2	17.5	17.3	18.9	18.5	20.5
25,000 - 34,999	14.8	15.9	11.5	12.6	16.5	15.8	16.1	14.2	15.4	16.4
35,000 - 49,999	13.3	14.8	9.0	7.3	15.1	17.9	18.6	13.3	16.1	16.0
50,000 - 74,999	8.9	10.3	4.7	6.1	7.9	15.0	15.8	9.3	13.4	11.1
75,000 - 99,999	2.6	3.1	1.0	1.3	3.3	5.1	5.5	2.6	4.7	3.1
100,000+	2.9	3.6	0.7	3.7	2.5	4.4	4.8	1.3	3.7	1.9

Note: All figures are for 1989; (1) people of Hispanic origin can be of any race
Source: 1990 Census of Population and Housing, Summary Tape File 3C

Effective Buying Income

Area	Per Capita ($)	Median Household ($)	Average Household ($)
City	16,372	27,250	38,797
MSA[1]	18,576	34,238	46,122
U.S.	16,803	34,536	45,243

Note: Data as of 1/1/99; (1) Metropolitan Statistical Area - see Appendix A for areas included
Source: Standard Rate & Data Service, Newspaper Advertising Source, 9/99

Effective Household Buying Income Distribution

Area	% of Households Earning						
	$10,000 -$19,999	$20,000 -$34,999	$35,000 -$49,999	$50,000 -$74,999	$75,000 -$99,000	$100,000 -$124,999	$125,000 and up
City	20.3	22.3	15.4	13.8	5.4	1.9	2.7
MSA[1]	16.9	22.2	17.7	18.5	7.6	2.5	2.7
U.S.	16.0	22.6	18.2	18.9	7.2	2.4	2.7

Note: Data as of 1/1/99; (1) Metropolitan Statistical Area - see Appendix A for areas included
Source: Standard Rate & Data Service, Newspaper Advertising Source, 9/99

Poverty Rates by Race and Age

Area	Total (%)	By Race (%)				By Age (%)		
		White	Black	Other	Hisp.[2]	Under 5 years old	Under 18 years old	65 years and over
City	21.4	14.0	40.9	38.1	23.6	37.0	32.5	14.4
MSA[1]	12.2	10.0	35.9	23.2	19.4	20.4	17.9	10.5
U.S.	13.1	9.8	29.5	23.1	25.3	20.1	18.3	12.8

Note: Figures show the percent of people living below the poverty line in 1989. The average poverty threshold was $12,674 for a family of four in 1989; (1) Metropolitan Statistical Area - see Appendix A for areas included; (2) people of Hispanic origin can be of any race
Source: 1990 Census of Population and Housing, Summary Tape File 3C

EMPLOYMENT

Labor Force and Employment

Area	Civilian Labor Force			Workers Employed		
	Jun. 1998	Jun. 1999	% Chg.	Jun. 1998	Jun. 1999	% Chg.
City	163,920	166,286	1.4	156,347	159,004	1.7
MSA[1]	1,166,299	1,182,118	1.4	1,114,249	1,133,191	1.7
U.S.	138,798,000	140,666,000	1.3	132,265,000	134,395,000	1.6

Note: Data is not seasonally adjusted and covers workers 16 years of age and older;
(1) Metropolitan Statistical Area - see Appendix A for areas included
Source: Bureau of Labor Statistics, http://stats.bls.gov

Unemployment Rate

Area	1998						1999					
	Jul.	Aug.	Sep.	Oct.	Nov.	Dec.	Jan.	Feb.	Mar.	Apr.	May.	Jun.
City	4.9	4.7	4.6	4.2	4.1	3.6	4.5	4.5	4.5	4.0	4.0	4.4
MSA[1]	4.5	4.2	4.2	4.0	4.2	3.9	5.2	5.0	4.9	4.1	3.8	4.1
U.S.	4.7	4.5	4.4	4.2	4.1	4.0	4.8	4.7	4.4	4.1	4.0	4.5

Note: Data is not seasonally adjusted and covers workers 16 years of age and older; all figures are percentages; (1) Metropolitan Statistical Area - see Appendix A for areas included
Source: Bureau of Labor Statistics, http://stats.bls.gov

Employment by Industry

Sector	MSA[1]		U.S.
	Number of Employees	Percent of Total	Percent of Total
Services	395,800	35.4	30.4
Retail Trade	204,600	18.3	17.7
Government	123,800	11.1	15.6
Manufacturing	140,600	12.6	14.3
Finance/Insurance/Real Estate	66,500	6.0	5.9
Wholesale Trade	58,000	5.2	5.4
Transportation/Public Utilities	69,800	6.2	5.3
Construction	54,100	4.8	5.0
Mining	4,300	0.4	0.4

Note: Figures cover non-farm employment as of 6/99 and are not seasonally adjusted; (1) Metropolitan Statistical Area - see Appendix A for areas included
Source: Bureau of Labor Statistics, http://stats.bls.gov

Employment by Occupation

Occupation Category	City (%)	MSA[1] (%)	U.S. (%)
White Collar	63.3	61.9	58.1
Executive/Admin./Management	10.4	12.2	12.3
Professional	17.8	15.7	14.1
Technical & Related Support	4.9	4.3	3.7
Sales	10.6	12.6	11.8
Administrative Support/Clerical	19.7	17.1	16.3
Blue Collar	17.7	23.1	26.2
Precision Production/Craft/Repair	7.4	10.4	11.3
Machine Operators/Assem./Insp.	3.6	4.6	6.8
Transportation/Material Movers	3.3	4.0	4.1
Cleaners/Helpers/Laborers	3.5	4.0	3.9
Services	18.5	14.1	13.2
Farming/Forestry/Fishing	0.5	0.9	2.5

Note: Figures cover employed persons 16 years old and over; (1) Metropolitan Statistical Area - see Appendix A for areas included
Source: 1990 Census of Population and Housing, Summary Tape File 3C

Occupational Employment Projections: 1994 - 2005

High Demand Occupations (ranked by annual openings)	Fast-Growing Occupations[1] (ranked by percent growth)
1. Cashiers	1. Personal and home care aides
2. Salespersons, retail	2. Electronic pagination systems workers
3. Waiters & waitresses	3. Computer engineers
4. Registered nurses	4. Systems analysts
5. General managers & top executives	5. Home health aides
6. Janitors/cleaners/maids, ex. priv. hshld.	6. Human services workers
7. Secretaries, except legal & medical	7. Teachers, preschool and kindergarten
8. General office clerks	8. Computer support specialists
9. Teachers, secondary school	9. Physical therapists
10. Marketing & sales, supervisors	10. Residential counselors

Note: Projections cover Pennsylvania; (1) Excludes occupations with total job growth less than 300
Source: Pennsylvania Workforce 2005, Winter 1997-98

TAXES

Major State and Local Tax Rates

State Corp. Income (%)	State Personal Income (%)	Residential Property (effective rate per $100)	Sales & Use		State Gasoline (cents/ gallon)	State Cigarette (cents/ pack)
			State (%)	Local (%)		
9.99	2.8	n/a	6.0	1.0	30.77[a]	31.0

Note: Personal/corporate income, sales, gasoline and cigarette tax rates as of January 1999.
Property tax rates as of 1997; (a) Rate is comprised of 12 cents excise and 18.77 cents motor carrier tax. Carriers pay an additional surcharge of 6 cents
Source: Federation of Tax Administrators, www.taxadmin.org; Washington D.C. Department of Finance and Revenue, Tax Rates and Tax Burdens in the District of Columbia: A Nationwide Comparison, July 1998; Chamber of Commerce, 1999

Total Taxes Per Capita and as a Percent of Income

Area	Per Capita Income ($)	Per Capita Taxes ($)			Percent of Income (%)		
		Total	Federal	State/ Local	Total	Federal	State/ Local
Pennsylvania	26,194	9,782	6,750	3,013	35.2	23.7	11.5
U.S.	27,876	9,881	6,690	3,191	35.4	24.0	11.4

Note: Figures are for 1998
Source: Tax Foundation, www.taxfoundation.org

Estimated Tax Burden

Area	State Income	Local Income	Property	Sales	Total
Pittsburgh	2,100	2,156	2,500	683	7,439

Note: The numbers are estimates of taxes paid by a married couple with two children and annual earnings of $75,000. Sales tax estimates assume they spend average amounts on food, clothing, household goods and gasoline. Property tax estimates assume they live in a $250,000 home.
Source: Kiplinger's Personal Finance Magazine, October 1998

COMMERCIAL REAL ESTATE

Office Market

Class/ Location	Total Space (sq. ft.)	Vacant Space (sq. ft.)	Vac. Rate (%)	Under Constr. (sq. ft.)	Net Absorp. (sq. ft.)	Rental Rates ($/sq.ft./yr.)
Class A						
CBD	13,992,899	1,523,136	10.9	n/a	-529,573	15.00-30.00
Outside CBD	10,469,266	1,254,887	12.0	240,600	511,085	11.00-24.00
Class B						
CBD	2,600,974	510,638	19.6	n/a	-4,977	12.00-18.50
Outside CBD	6,538,420	818,355	12.5	n/a	-610,416	7.00-21.75

Note: Data as of 10/98 and covers Pittsburgh; CBD = Central Business District; n/a not available;
Source: Society of Industrial and Office Realtors, 1999 Comparative Statistics of Industrial and Office Real Estate Markets

"The Pittsburgh metropolitan area expects further gains in economic growth in 1999. Anticipated growth by many companies could support the construction of new office space. Among the factors expected to influence this regional growth is the hotly debated $800 million 'Plan B' development program. This is expected to pave the way for the construction of two stadiums for professional football and baseball as well as an expanded convention center. The level of leasing activity in the Pittsburgh CBD could increase in 1999. However, this increase will not be dramatic. Substantial interest in the Parkway West office sub-market will result in speculative development. The other hot suburban market is Washington County. More than 500,000 sq. ft. of office space is proposed at these two locations." *Society of Industrial and Office Realtors, 1999 Comparative Statistics of Industrial and Office Real Estate Markets*

Industrial Market

Location	Total Space (sq. ft.)	Vacant Space (sq. ft.)	Vac. Rate (%)	Under Constr. (sq. ft.)	Net Absorp. (sq. ft.)	Gross Lease ($/sq.ft./yr.)
Central City	n/a	n/a	n/a	n/a	n/a	3.75-5.00
Suburban	130,000,000	19,000,000	14.6	2,000,000	3,000,000	3.75-5.00

Note: Data as of 10/98 and covers Pittsburgh; n/a not available
Source: Society of Industrial and Office Realtors, 1999 Comparative Statistics of Industrial and Office Real Estate Markets

"Warehouse construction will reach some 610,000 sq. ft. in 1999 as developers work to modernize Pittsburgh's inventory of warehouse space. SIOR's reporter indicates that absorption of manufacturing, warehouse and distribution space will rise one to five percent while the demand for High Tech/R&D buildings will increase by six to 10 percent. However, shortages of warehouses will persist in 1999. The vacancy rate for warehouses is expected to fall below 12 percent. This will tend to cause lease prices for warehouse and distribution space to rise significantly—by as much as six percent to 10 percent. The shortage of space will be particularly acute in properties larger than 100,000 sq. ft. Demand for space will be strongest for properties with good access to employees, customers, and raw materials." *Society of Industrial and Office Realtors, 1999 Comparative Statistics of Industrial and Office Real Estate Markets*

COMMERCIAL UTILITIES — Typical Monthly Electric Bills

Area	Commercial Service ($/month) 12 kW demand 1,500 kWh	100 kW demand 30,000 kWh	Industrial Service ($/month) 1,000 kW demand 400,000 kWh	20,000 kW demand 10,000,000 kWh
City	314	2,906	29,037	447,295
U.S.	150	2,174	23,995	508,569

Note: Based on rates in effect January 1, 1999
Source: Edison Electric Institute, Typical Residential, Commercial and Industrial Bills, Winter 1999

TRANSPORTATION

Transportation Statistics

Average minutes to work	21.1
Interstate highways	I-70; I-76; I-79
Bus lines	
In-city	Port Authority of Allegheny County, 1,058 vehicles
Inter-city	11
Passenger air service	
Airport	Pittsburgh International Airport
Airlines	6
Aircraft departures	153,084 (1996)
Enplaned passengers	9,348,090 (1996)
Rail service	Amtrak; Tramway/Light Rail
Motor freight carriers	163
Major waterways/ports	Port of Pittsburgh

Source: Editor & Publisher Market Guide, 1999; FAA Airport Activity Statistics, 1997; Amtrak National Time Table, Northeast Timetable, Spring/Summer 1999; 1990 Census of Population and Housing, STF 3C; Chamber of Commerce/Economic Development 1999; Jane's Urban Transport Systems 1999-2000

Means of Transportation to Work

Area	Car/Truck/Van		Public Transportation			Bicycle	Walked	Other Means	Worked at Home
	Drove Alone	Car-pooled	Bus	Subway	Railroad				
City	48.9	13.5	21.1	0.3	0.0	0.4	12.6	1.3	1.8
MSA[1]	70.7	12.9	7.7	0.2	0.0	0.1	5.1	1.1	2.1
U.S.	73.2	13.4	3.0	1.5	0.5	0.4	3.9	1.2	3.0

Note: Figures shown are percentages and only include workers 16 years old and over; (1) Metropolitan Statistical Area - see Appendix A for areas included
Source: 1990 Census of Population and Housing, Summary Tape File 3C

BUSINESSES

Major Business Headquarters

Company Name	1999 Rankings	
	Fortune 500	Forbes 500
Alcoa	96	-
Allegheny Teledyne	391	-
CNG	420	-
Dick Corp	-	418
Giant Eagle	-	29
H.J. Heinz	170	-
Koppers Industries	-	382
Mellon Bank	283	-
PNC Bank Corp.	209	-
PPG Industries	221	-
USX	47	-
Wesco Distribution	485	48

Note: Companies listed are located in the city; dashes indicate no ranking
Fortune 500: Companies that produce a 10-K are ranked 1 to 500 based on 1998 revenue
Forbes 500: Private companies are ranked 1 to 500 based on 1997 revenue
Source: Forbes, November 30, 1998; Fortune, April 26, 1999

Best Companies to Work For

UPMC Health System (research/teaching center), headquartered in Pittsburgh, is among the "100 Best Companies for Working Mothers." Criteria: fair wages, opportunities for women to advance, support for child care, flexible work schedules, family-friendly benefits, and work/life supports. *Working Mother, October 1998*

Women-Owned Firms: Number, Employment and Sales

Area	Number of Firms	Employ-ment	Sales ($000)	Rank[2]
MSA[1]	62,300	201,000	27,673,000	27

Note: (1) Metropolitan Statistical Area - see Appendix A for areas included;
(2) Calculated on an averaging of the number of businesses, employment and sales
Source: The National Foundation for Women Business Owners, 1999 Facts on Women-Owned
Businesses: Trends in the Top 50 Metropolitan Areas

Women-Owned Firms: Growth

Area	% change from 1992 to 1999			Rank[2]
	Number of Firms	Employ-ment	Sales	
MSA[1]	38.6	93.7	126.6	41

Note: (1) Metropolitan Statistical Area - see Appendix A for areas included; (2) Calculated on an
averaging of the percent growth of number of businesses, employment and sales
Source: The National Foundation for Women Business Owners, 1999 Facts on Women-Owned
Businesses: Trends in the Top 50 Metropolitan Areas

HOTELS & MOTELS

Hotels/Motels

Area	Hotels/Motels	Rooms	Luxury-Level Hotels/Motels		Average Minimum Rates ($)		
			♦♦♦♦	♦♦♦♦♦	♦♦	♦♦♦	♦♦♦♦
City	32	6,743	1	0	81	120	n/a
Airport	9	1,327	0	0	n/a	n/a	n/a
Suburbs	21	2,091	0	0	n/a	n/a	n/a
Total	62	10,161	1	0	n/a	n/a	n/a

Note: n/a not available; classifications range from one diamond (budget properties with basic
amenities) to five diamond (luxury properties with the finest service, rooms and facilities).
Source: OAG, Business Travel Planner, Winter 1998-99

CONVENTION CENTERS

Major Convention Centers

Center Name	Meeting Rooms	Exhibit Space (sq. ft.)
David L. Lawrence Convention Center	25	131,000
Expomart Radisson	22	106,000
Pittsburgh Civic Arena	5	n/a
Pittsburgh Expo Mart	21	106,154

Note: n/a not available
Source: Trade Shows Worldwide, 1998; Meetings & Conventions, 4/15/99;
Sucessful Meetings, 3/31/98

Living Environment

COST OF LIVING

Cost of Living Index

Composite Index	Groceries	Housing	Utilities	Trans-portation	Health Care	Misc. Goods/ Services
108.4	102.6	111.0	132.5	112.6	98.8	103.8

Note: U.S. = 100
Source: ACCRA, Cost of Living Index, 1st Quarter 1997

HOUSING

Median Home Prices and Housing Affordability

Area	Median Price[2] 1st Qtr. 1999 ($)	HOI[3] 1st Qtr. 1999	Afford-ability Rank[4]
MSA[1]	87,000	71.7	106
U.S.	134,000	69.6	–

Note: (1) Metropolitan Statistical Area - see Appendix A for areas included; (2) U.S. figures calculated from the sales of 524,324 new and existing homes in 181 markets; (3) Housing Opportunity Index - percent of homes sold that were within the reach of the median income household at the prevailing mortgage interest rate; (4) Rank is from 1-181 with 1 being most affordable
Source: National Association of Home Builders, Housing Opportunity Index, 1st Quarter 1999

Median Home Price Projection

It is projected that the median price of existing single-family homes in the metro area will increase by 2.6% in 1999. Nationwide, home prices are projected to increase 3.8%.
Kiplinger's Personal Finance Magazine, January 1999

Average New Home Price

Area	Price ($)
City	151,450
U.S.	133,782

Note: Figures are based on a new home with 1,800 sq. ft. of living area on an 8,000 sq. ft. lot.
Source: ACCRA, Cost of Living Index, 1st Quarter 1997

Average Apartment Rent

Area	Rent ($/mth)
City	598
U.S.	563

Note: Figures are based on an unfurnished two bedroom, 1-1/2 or 2 bath apartment, approximately 950 sq. ft. in size, excluding all utilities except water
Source: ACCRA, Cost of Living Index, 1st Quarter 1997

RESIDENTIAL UTILITIES

Average Residential Utility Costs

Area	All Electric ($/mth)	Part Electric ($/mth)	Other Energy ($/mth)	Phone ($/mth)
City	–	80.62	62.61	20.13
U.S.	110.19	56.83	45.14	19.36

Source: ACCRA, Cost of Living Index, 1st Quarter 1997

HEALTH CARE

Average Health Care Costs

Area	Hospital ($/day)	Doctor ($/visit)	Dentist ($/visit)
City	518.33	36.60	60.60
U.S.	385.60	47.34	59.26

Note: Hospital—based on a semi-private room; Doctor—based on a general practitioner's routine exam of an established patient; Dentist—based on adult teeth cleaning and periodic oral exam.
Source: ACCRA, Cost of Living Index, 1st Quarter 1997

Distribution of Office-Based Physicians

| Area | Family/Gen. Practitioners | Specialists | | |
		Medical	Surgical	Other
MSA[1]	572	1,808	1,297	1,403

Note: Data as of 12/31/97; (1) Metropolitan Statistical Area - see Appendix A for areas included
Source: American Medical Assn., Physician Characteristics & Distribution in the U.S., 1999

Hospitals

Pittsburgh has 1 general medical and surgical hospital, 1 obstetrics and gynecology, 2 rehabilitation, 3 other specialty, 1 children's general, 1 children's psychiatric, 1 children's other specialty. *AHA Guide to the Healthcare Field, 1998-99*

According to *U.S. News and World Report,* Pittsburgh has 5 of the best hospitals in the U.S.: **University of Pittsburgh Medical Center**, noted for cancer, cardiology, endocrinology, gastroenterology, geriatrics, gynecology, neurology, orthopedics, otolaryngology, psychiatry, pulmonology, rheumatology; **Children's Hospital of Pittsburgh**, noted for pediatrics; **Allegheny University Hospitals**, noted for cancer, gastroenterology, geriatrics, neurology, orthopedics, otolaryngology, rheumatology, urology; **Magee-Womens Hospital**, noted for gynecology; **Western Pennsylvania Hospital**, noted for endocrinology. *U.S. News Online, "America's Best Hospitals," 10th Edition, www.usnews.com*

EDUCATION

Public School District Statistics

District Name	Num. Sch.	Enroll.	Classroom Teachers	Pupils per Teacher	Minority Pupils (%)	Current Exp.[1] ($/pupil)
Allegheny IU 3	n/a	n/a	n/a	n/a	n/a	n/a
Avonworth SD	2	1,303	68	19.2	n/a	n/a
Baldwin-Whitehall SD	5	4,801	267	18.0	n/a	n/a
Brentwood Borough SD	4	1,461	78	18.7	n/a	n/a
Chartiers Valley SD	4	3,074	197	15.6	n/a	n/a
Fox Chapel Area SD	6	4,470	317	14.1	n/a	n/a
Keystone Oaks SD	5	2,883	191	15.1	n/a	n/a
Mt Lebanon SD	9	5,665	348	16.3	n/a	n/a
North Allegheny SD	13	8,422	502	16.8	n/a	n/a
North Hills SD	9	5,085	301	16.9	n/a	n/a
Northgate SD	3	1,695	94	18.0	n/a	n/a
Penn Hills SD	8	6,027	364	16.6	n/a	n/a
Pittsburgh SD	91	40,181	2,506	16.0	n/a	n/a
Upper Saint Clair SD	6	3,925	235	16.7	n/a	n/a
West Jefferson Hills SD	5	2,995	151	19.8	n/a	n/a
Woodland Hills SD	9	6,153	337	18.3	n/a	n/a

Note: Data covers the 1997-1998 school year unless otherwise noted; (1) Data covers fiscal year 1996; SD = School District; ISD = Independent School District; n/a not available
Source: National Center for Education Statistics, Common Core of Data Public Education Agency Universe 1997-98; National Center for Education Statistics, Characteristics of the 100 Largest Public Elementary and Secondary School Districts in the United States: 1997-98, July 1999

Educational Quality

School District	Education Quotient[1]	Graduate Outcome[2]	Community Index[3]	Resource Index[4]
Pittsburgh SD	119.0	112.0	62.0	145.0

Note: Nearly 1,000 secondary school districts were rated in terms of educational quality. The scores range from a low of 50 to a high of 150; (1) Average of the Graduate Outcome, Community and Resource indexes; (2) Based on graduation rates and college board scores (SAT/ACT); (3) Based on the surrounding community's average level of education and the area's average income level; (4) Based on teacher salaries, per-pupil expenditures and student-teacher ratios.
Source: Expansion Management, Ratings Issue, 1998

Educational Attainment by Race

Area	High School Graduate (%)					Bachelor's Degree (%)				
	Total	White	Black	Other	Hisp.[2]	Total	White	Black	Other	Hisp.[2]
City	72.4	74.0	66.3	87.7	78.4	20.1	22.6	8.8	62.2	39.2
MSA[1]	77.4	78.0	68.6	86.1	80.6	19.5	19.9	10.1	56.1	30.0
U.S.	75.2	77.9	63.1	60.4	49.8	20.3	21.5	11.4	19.4	9.2

Note: Figures shown cover persons 25 years old and over; (1) Metropolitan Statistical Area - see Appendix A for areas included; (2) people of Hispanic origin can be of any race
Source: 1990 Census of Population and Housing, Summary Tape File 3C

School Enrollment by Type

Area	Preprimary				Elementary/High School			
	Public		Private		Public		Private	
	Enrollment	%	Enrollment	%	Enrollment	%	Enrollment	%
City	3,400	58.5	2,412	41.5	36,244	75.8	11,549	24.2
MSA[1]	20,226	54.8	16,696	45.2	254,093	86.0	41,306	14.0
U.S.	2,679,029	59.5	1,824,256	40.5	38,379,689	90.2	4,187,099	9.8

Note: Figures shown cover persons 3 years old and over;
(1) Metropolitan Statistical Area - see Appendix A for areas included
Source: 1990 Census of Population and Housing, Summary Tape File 3C

School Enrollment by Race

Area	Preprimary (%)				Elementary/High School (%)			
	White	Black	Other	Hisp.[1]	White	Black	Other	Hisp.[1]
City	66.4	31.4	2.2	1.4	59.1	38.9	2.1	1.1
MSA[2]	89.5	9.1	1.4	0.8	87.5	11.3	1.3	0.6
U.S.	80.4	12.5	7.1	7.8	74.1	15.6	10.3	12.5

Note: Figures shown cover persons 3 years old and over; (1) people of Hispanic origin can be of any race; (2) Metropolitan Statistical Area - see Appendix A for areas included
Source: 1990 Census of Population and Housing, Summary Tape File 3C

Classroom Teacher Salaries in Public Schools

District	B.A. Degree		M.A. Degree		Maximum	
	Min. ($)	Rank[1]	Max. ($)	Rank[1]	Max. ($)	Rank[1]
Pittsburgh	32,800	4	62,648	3	64,248	4
Average	26,980	-	46,065	-	51,435	-

Note: Salaries are for 1997-1998; (1) Rank ranges from 1 to 100
Source: American Federation of Teachers, Survey & Analysis of Salary Trends, 1998

Higher Education

Two-Year Colleges		Four-Year Colleges		Medical Schools	Law Schools	Voc/ Tech
Public	Private	Public	Private			
1	10	1	6	1	2	22

Source: College Blue Book, Occupational Education, 1997; Medical School Admission Requirements, 1999-2000; Peterson's Guide to Two-Year Colleges, 1999; Peterson's Guide to Four-Year Colleges, 2000; Barron's Guide to Law Schools, 1999

MAJOR EMPLOYERS

Major Employers

Allegheny General Hospital	Jefferson Health Services
Bayer Corp.	Consol
Mellon Bank Corp.	Mercy Hospital of Pittsburgh
St. Francis Medical Center	UPMC Presbyterian
Western Pennsylvania Hospital	Federated Investors

Note: Companies listed are located in the city
Source: Dun's Business Rankings, 1999; Ward's Business Directory, 1998

PUBLIC SAFETY

Crime Rate

Area	All Crimes	Violent Crimes				Property Crimes		
		Murder	Forcible Rape	Robbery	Aggrav. Assault	Burglary	Larceny -Theft	Motor Vehicle Theft
City	5,817.7	14.2	49.5	436.8	285.9	950.9	3,283.2	797.2
Suburbs[1]	2,260.3	2.2	18.3	46.3	161.1	362.2	1,460.9	209.3
MSA[2]	2,783.4	4.0	22.9	103.7	179.5	448.7	1,728.9	295.7
U.S.	4,922.7	6.8	35.9	186.1	382.0	919.6	2,886.5	505.8

Note: Crime rate is the number of crimes per 100,000 pop.; (1) defined as all areas within the MSA but located outside the central city; (2) Metropolitan Statistical Area - see Appendix A for areas incl.
Source: FBI Uniform Crime Reports, 1997

RECREATION

Culture and Recreation

Museums	Symphony Orchestras	Opera Companies	Dance Companies	Professional Theatres	Zoos	Pro Sports Teams
7	2	3	2	3	1	3

Source: International Directory of the Performing Arts, 1997; Official Museum Directory, 1999; Stern's Performing Arts Directory, 1997; USA Today Four Sport Stadium Guide, 1997; Chamber of Commerce/Economic Development, 1999

Library System

The Carnegie Library of Pittsburgh has 17 branches and holdings of 1,999,783 volumes.
American Library Directory, 1998-1999

MEDIA

Newspapers

Name	Type	Freq.	Distribution	Circulation
Green Sheet Advertiser	General	1x/wk	Local	300,000
New Pittsburgh Courier	Black	2x/wk	Local	31,923
The Pitt News	n/a	5x/wk	Camp/Comm	14,000
Pittsburgh City Paper	Alternative	1x/wk	Local	55,000
Pittsburgh Legal Journal	n/a	5x/wk	Local	1,700
Pittsburgh Post-Gazette	General	7x/wk	Area	241,798
Pittsburgh Union	General	24x/yr	U.S.	13,000
South Hills Record	General	1x/wk	Local	8,032

Note: Includes newspapers with circulations of 1,000 or more located in the city; n/a not available
Source: Burrelle's Media Directory, 1999 Edition

Television Stations

Name	Ch.	Affiliation	Type	Owner
KDKA	n/a	CBST	Commercial	n/a
WTAE	n/a	ABCT	Commercial	Hearst-Argyle Broadcasting
WPXI	11	NBCT	Commercial	Cox Enterprises Inc.
WQED	13	PBS	Public	WQED
WQEX	16	PBS	Public	WQED
WNPA	19	UPN	Commercial	Century Technologies
WCWB	22	WB	Commercial	Eddie Edwards Sr.
WBPA	29	UPN/WB	Commercial	Venture Technology Group Inc.
WPCB	40	n/a	Commercial	Cornerstone Television Inc.
WPGH	53	FBC	Commercial	Sinclair Communications Inc.
WNEU	63	n/a	Commercial	Bon-Tele Network Inc.

Note: Stations included broadcast in the Pittsburgh metro area; n/a not available
Source: Burrelle's Media Directory, 1999 Edition

AM Radio Stations

Call Letters	Freq. (kHz)	Target Audience	Station Format	Music Format
WPIT	730	General	M/T	Christian
WEDO	810	General	M/N/S/T	n/a
WYJZ	860	General	M/N/S	Oldies
WWSW	970	General	M	Oldies
KDKA	1020	General	N/S/T	n/a
WEAE	1250	General	S	n/a
WJAS	1320	General	M	Big Band/MOR
WPTT	1360	General	T	n/a
KQV	1410	General	N	n/a
WXVX	1510	General	M/N	Gospel
WCXJ	1550	General	M/T	Christian/Urban Contemporary
WZUM	1590	General	M	Adult Contemporary

Note: Stations included broadcast in the Pittsburgh metro area; n/a not available
Target Audience: A=Asian; B=Black; C=Christian; E=Ethnic; F=French; G=General; H=Hispanic; M=Men; N=Native American; R=Religious; S=Senior Citizen; W=Women; Y=Young Adult; Z=Children
Station Format: E=Educational; M=Music; N=News; S=Sports; T=Talk
Music Format: AOR=Album Oriented Rock; MOR=Middle-of-the-Road
Source: Burrelle's Media Directory, 1999 Edition

FM Radio Stations

Call Letters	Freq. (mHz)	Target Audience	Station Format	Music Format
WRCT	88.3	General	M/N/S	Alternative/Big Band/Christian/Classical/Jazz/Latin/R&B/Urban Contemporary
WQED	89.3	General	M	Classical
WDUQ	90.5	General	M/N	Jazz
WYEP	91.3	General	E/M	Alternative/Blues/Classic Rock/Modern Rock/Reggae/R&B/World Music
WPTS	92.1	General	M/N/S/T	Alternative/Jazz/Reggae/Urban Contemporary
WLTJ	92.9	G/W	M/N/S	Adult Contemporary
WBZZ	93.7	General	M	n/a
WWSW	94.5	General	M	Oldies
WDRV	96.1	General	M/S/T	Adult Contemporary/Alternative
WVTY	96.1	Women	M	Adult Contemporary/Alternative
WRRK	96.9	General	M	Classic Rock
WSHH	99.7	General	M	Adult Contemporary
WZPT	100.7	General	M/N/S	Oldies
WORD	101.5	General	M/T	Christian
WDVE	102.5	General	M/S	AOR
WJJJ	104.7	General	n/a	n/a
WXDX	105.9	General	M/T	Alternative
WAMO	106.7	Black	M/N/S	Urban Contemporary
WSSZ	107.1	General	M/N	Urban Contemporary
WDSY	107.9	General	M	Country

Note: Stations included broadcast in the Pittsburgh metro area; n/a not available
Station Format: E=Educational; M=Music; N=News; S=Sports; T=Talk
Target Audience: A=Asian; B=Black; C=Christian; E=Ethnic; F=French; G=General; H=Hispanic; M=Men; N=Native American; R=Religious; S=Senior Citizen; W=Women; Y=Young Adult; Z=Children
Music Format: AOR=Album Oriented Rock; MOR=Middle-of-the-Road
Source: Burrelle's Media Directory, 1999 Edition

CLIMATE

Average and Extreme Temperatures

Temperature	Jan	Feb	Mar	Apr	May	Jun	Jul	Aug	Sep	Oct	Nov	Dec	Yr.
Extreme High (°F)	75	69	83	89	91	98	103	100	97	89	82	74	103
Average High (°F)	35	38	48	61	71	79	83	81	75	63	50	39	60
Average Temp. (°F)	28	30	39	50	60	68	73	71	64	53	42	32	51
Average Low (°F)	20	22	29	39	49	57	62	61	54	43	34	25	41
Extreme Low (°F)	-18	-12	-1	14	26	34	42	39	31	16	-1	-12	-18

Note: Figures cover the years 1948-1990
Source: National Climatic Data Center, International Station Meteorological Climate Summary, 3/95

Average Precipitation/Snowfall/Humidity

Precip./Humidity	Jan	Feb	Mar	Apr	May	Jun	Jul	Aug	Sep	Oct	Nov	Dec	Yr.
Avg. Precip. (in.)	2.8	2.4	3.4	3.3	3.6	3.9	3.8	3.2	2.8	2.4	2.7	2.8	37.1
Avg. Snowfall (in.)	11	9	8	2	Tr	0	0	0	0	Tr	4	8	43
Avg. Rel. Hum. 7am (%)	76	75	75	73	76	79	82	86	85	81	78	77	79
Avg. Rel. Hum. 4pm (%)	64	60	54	49	50	51	53	54	55	53	60	66	56

Note: Figures cover the years 1948-1990; Tr = Trace amounts (<0.05 in. of rain; <0.5 in. of snow)
Source: National Climatic Data Center, International Station Meteorological Climate Summary, 3/95

Weather Conditions

Temperature			Daytime Sky			Precipitation		
5°F & below	32°F & below	90°F & above	Clear	Partly cloudy	Cloudy	0.01 inch or more precip.	0.1 inch or more snow/ice	Thunder-storms
9	121	8	62	137	166	154	42	35

Note: Figures are average number of days per year and covers the years 1948-1990
Source: National Climatic Data Center, International Station Meteorological Climate Summary, 3/95

AIR & WATER QUALITY

Maximum Pollutant Concentrations

	Particulate Matter (ug/m^3)	Carbon Monoxide (ppm)	Sulfur Dioxide (ppm)	Nitrogen Dioxide (ppm)	Ozone (ppm)	Lead (ug/m^3)
MSA[1] Level	133	4	0.078	0.029	0.13	0.08
NAAQS[2]	150	9	0.140	0.053	0.12	1.50
Met NAAQS?	Yes	Yes	Yes	Yes	No	Yes

Note: (1) Metropolitan Statistical Area - see Appendix A for areas included; (2) National Ambient Air Quality Standards; ppm = parts per million; ug/m^3 = micrograms per cubic meter; n/a not available
Source: EPA, National Air Quality and Emissions Trends Report, 1997

Pollutant Standards Index

In the Pittsburgh MSA (see Appendix A for areas included), the Pollutant Standards Index (PSI) exceeded 100 on 21 days in 1997. A PSI value greater than 100 indicates that air quality would be in the unhealthful range on that day. *EPA, National Air Quality and Emissions Trends Report, 1997*

Drinking Water

Water System Name	Pop. Served	Primary Water Source Type	Number of Violations in 1998	Type of Violation/ Contaminants
PA American Water Co.-Pittsburgh	569,328	Surface	None	None
Pittsburgh Water & Sewer Auth.	370,000	Surface	None	None
West View Boro Muni Authority	200,000	Surface	None	None

Note: Data as of July 10, 1999
Source: EPA, Office of Ground Water and Drinking Water, Safe Drinking Water Information System

Pittsburgh tap water is alkaline, soft 9 months, hard 3 months (June, July, August); fluoridated. *Editor & Publisher Market Guide, 1999*

Providence, Rhode Island

Background

Providence has enjoyed a resurgence in recent years, making it a great place to live and do business.

Before whites began to arrive in the seventeenth century, Narragansetts lived in the area . After his banishment from Massachusetts Bay Colony because of his radical beliefs, Roger Williams established the settlement in 1636, naming it Providence because of his belief that God had led him to that spot on Narrangansett Bay. Williams made Providence a refuge for the religiously unorthodox. He guaranteed tolerance and forbade the state establishment of any church. Providence residents were involved in the protests against the British government prior to the American Revolution. They burned the British customs ship *Gaspee,* which had run aground off the coast of Rhode Island. After the war, Providence businesses successfully opened up a trade with the Chinese in silks and spices.

Providence was an early leader in manufacturing. In 1787 the first manual cotton-spinning machine in the nation was constructed there. Samuel Slater established in 1790 the country's first water-powered cotton spinner in Pawtucket, just down the road from Providence, which soon became a leader in the textile industry.

In 1794, local entrepreneur Nehemiah Dodge discovered how to make a new type of jewelry by coating inexpensive metals with more expensive ones. Soon thereafter, jewelry production would become a vital part of the Providence economy. As the town became an important textile and jewelry producer, the population grew, and in 1832, Rhode Island officially made Providence a city. For many years, Rhode Island had maintained a few cities as its capital, but in 1900, Providence was selected as the one place where the state government's leaders would be located.

During the two world wars, Providence was an important manufacturer of military supplies. In the interwar and postwar eras, many of the city's textile factories began to move to the South, where it found the cost of doing business much less expensive. The city's population began to shrink.

Presently, Providence is still one of the country's largest jewelry producers. Other concerns make electronic equipment, marine devices, scientific instruments, machinery, silverware, and some textiles. The city has excellent port facilities, to which tankers bring large amounts of fuel, for use throughout the southern half of New England.

Services are important to the city's vitality. There are three major banks in the city: Citizens, Fleet, and Bank Boston. Six hospitals, including Rhode Island Hospital, also employ many people. And since Providence is the capital of Rhode Island and the seat of Providence County, government at all levels is a large employer.

Since the early 1990s, the city has done much to breath new life into its downtown. It created Water Place Park, in which an old railroad yard was transformed into a beautiful waterfront, lined with shops and traversing gondolas. Business incentives include the best investment and research and development tax credits in the United States.

The climate in Providence is moderate, with relatively mild winters and summers. Winter temperatures range from the teens to the forties and from the fifties to eighties in the summer. This is because of the city's location on Narrangansett Bay and proximity to the Atlantic Ocean. There is an even distribution of the yearly average rainfall of forty-five inches, while most of the thirty-five annual inches of snowfall occurs in January and February.

General Rankings and Evaluative Comments

- Providence was ranked #15 out of 15 large, northeastern metropolitan areas in *Money's* 1998 survey of "The Best Places to Live in America." The survey was conducted by first contacting 512 representative households nationwide and asking them to rank 37 quality-of-life factors on a scale of 1 to 10. Next, a demographic profile was compiled on the 300 largest metropolitan statistical areas in the U.S. The numbers were crunched together to arrive at an overall ranking (things Americans consider most important, like clean air and water, low crime and good schools, received extra weight). Unlike previous years, the 1998 rankings were broken down by region (northeast, midwest, south, west) and population size (100,000 to 249,999; 250,000 to 999,999; 1 million plus). The city had a nationwide ranking of #240 out of 300 in 1997 and #198 out of 300 in 1996. *Money, July 1998; Money, July 1997; Money, September 1996*

- *Ladies Home Journal* ranked America's 200 largest cities based on the qualities women care about most. Providence ranked #177 out of 200. Criteria: low crime rate, well-paying jobs, quality health and child care, good public schools, the presence of women in government, size of the gender wage gap, number of sexual-harassment and discrimination complaints filed, unemployment and divorce rates, commute times, population density, number of houses of worship, parks and cultural offerings, number of women's health specialists, how well a community's women cared for themselves, complexion kindness index based on UV radiation levels, odds of finding affordable fashions, rental rates for romance movies, champagne sales and other matters of the heart. *Ladies Home Journal, November 1998*

- Zero Population Growth ranked 229 cities in terms of children's health, safety, and economic well-being. Providence was ranked #90 out of 112 independent cities (cities with populations greater than 100,000 which were neither Major Cities nor Suburbs/Outer Cities) and was given a grade of D. Criteria: total population, percent of population under 18 years of age, household language, percent population change, percent of births to teens, infant mortality rate, percent of low birth weights, dropout rate, enrollment in preprimary school, violent and property crime rates, unemployment rate, percent of children in poverty, percent of owner occupied units, number of bad air days, percent of public transportation commuters, and average travel time to work. *Zero Population Growth, Children's Environmental Index, Fall 1999*

- Providence was selected by *Yahoo! Internet Life* as one of "America's Most Wired Cities & Towns." The city ranked #46 out of 50. Criteria: home and work net use, domain density, hosts per capita, directory density and content quality. *Yahoo! Internet Life, March 1999*

- Cognetics studied 273 metro areas in the United States, ranking them by entrepreneurial activity. Providence was ranked #104 out of 134 smaller metro areas. Criteria: Significant Starts (firms started in the last 10 years that still employ at least 5 people) and Young Growers (percent of firms 10 years old or less that grew significantly during the last 4 years). *Cognetics, "Entrepreneurial Hot Spots: The Best Places in America to Start and Grow a Company," 1998*

- Providence was selected as one of the "Best American Cities to Start a Business" by *Point of View* magazine. Criteria: coolness, quality-of-life, and business concerns. The city was ranked #63 out of 75. *Point of View, November 1998*

- Reliastar Financial Corp. ranked the 125 largest metropolitan areas according to the general financial security of residents. Providence was ranked #91 (tie) out of 125 with a score of -3.1. The score indicates the percentage a metropolitan area is above or below the metropolitan norm. A metro area with a score of 10.6 is 10.6% above the metro average. Criteria: Earnings and Wealth Potential (household income, education, net assets, cost of living); Safety Net (health insurance, retirement savings, life insurance, income support programs); Personal Threats (unemployment rate, low-income households, crime rate); Community Economic Vitality (cost of community services, job quality, job creation, housing costs). *Reliastar Financial Corp., "The Best Cities to Earn and Save Money," 1999 Edition*

Business Environment

STATE ECONOMY

State Economic Profile

"The outlook for Rhode Island is not bright. Economic growth has been slow and will likely get slower. Current job growth, driven by construction and financial services, is not sustainable. Manufacturing continues its long-term decline. Adding to its economic woes is RI's weak demographic situation.

The RI economy added 3,200 jobs in 1998, a growth rate of 0.7%. Of those, 2,700 were in the construction industry. The manufacturing sector actually shed some 2,300 jobs. With RI's current negative population growth and weak employment growth, the present wave of construction activity is not sustainable. Construction employment should contract in 1999 and 2000, taking a good deal of the economy's strength with it. Potential growth in the transportation sector (via development of the Quonset seaport) could add to job growth.

One of RI's more vibrant sectors has been tourism. RI offers a much lower-cost and more easily accessible alternative to other New England attractions. RI's tourism industry, as a result of rapid growth, has become the state's second largest industry. Given the projected slowdown in the US and northeast economies in 1999 and 2000, RI's tourism industry will be hit particularly hard. This engine of job growth should stall over the next few years.

RI's housing market has experienced some recent growth in spite of demographic constraints. Sales were up over 15%, and single-family residential starts grew by 9% in 1998. Strong demand for beachfront properties and second homes was driving much of this activity. Sales and permits will likely decline as the RI and US economies cool in 1999-2000." *National Association of Realtors, Economic Profiles: The Fifty States and the District of Columbia, http://nar.realtor.com/databank/profiles.htm*

IMPORTS/EXPORTS

Total Export Sales

Area	1994 ($000)	1995 ($000)	1996 ($000)	1997 ($000)	% Chg. 1994-97	% Chg. 1996-97
MSA[1]	1,246,010	1,241,014	1,296,244	1,601,815	28.6	23.6
U.S.	512,415,609	583,030,524	622,827,063	687,597,999	34.2	10.4

Note: (1) Metropolitan Statistical Area - see Appendix A for areas included
Source: U.S. Department of Commerce, International Trade Association, Metropolitan Area Exports: An Export Performance Report on Over 250 U.S. Cities, November 10, 1998

CITY FINANCES

City Government Finances

Component	FY92 ($000)	FY92 (per capita $)
Revenue	332,588	2,104.14
Expenditure	324,579	2,053.47
Debt Outstanding	108,127	684.07
Cash & Securities	130,551	825.94

Source: U.S. Bureau of the Census, City Government Finances: 1991-92

City Government Revenue by Source

Source	FY92 ($000)	FY92 (per capita $)	FY92 (%)
From Federal Government	10,012	63.34	3.0
From State Governments	88,027	556.91	26.5
From Local Governments	1,423	9.00	0.4
Property Taxes	165,821	1,049.08	49.9
General Sales Taxes	0	0.00	0.0
Selective Sales Taxes	0	0.00	0.0
Income Taxes	0	0.00	0.0
Current Charges	18,714	118.40	5.6
Utility/Liquor Store	19,653	124.34	5.9
Employee Retirement[1]	17,718	112.09	5.3
Other	11,220	70.98	3.4

Note: (1) Excludes "city contributions," classified as "nonrevenue," intragovernmental transfers.
Source: U.S. Bureau of the Census, City Government Finances: 1991-92

City Government Expenditures by Function

Function	FY92 ($000)	FY92 (per capita $)	FY92 (%)
Educational Services	135,432	856.82	41.7
Employee Retirement[1]	18,567	117.47	5.7
Environment/Housing	28,178	178.27	8.7
Government Administration	15,095	95.50	4.7
Interest on General Debt	2,891	18.29	0.9
Public Safety	50,319	318.35	15.5
Social Services	15,289	96.73	4.7
Transportation	4,056	25.66	1.2
Utility/Liquor Store	13,658	86.41	4.2
Other	41,094	259.98	12.7

Note: (1) Payments to beneficiaries including withdrawal of contributions.
Source: U.S. Bureau of the Census, City Government Finances: 1991-92

Municipal Bond Ratings

Area	Moody's	S & P
Providence	Aaa	n/a

Note: n/a not available; n/r not rated
Source: Moody's Bond Record, 6/99

POPULATION

Population Growth

Area	1980	1990	% Chg. 1980-90	July 1998 Estimate	% Chg. 1990-98
City	156,804	160,728	2.5	150,890	-6.1
MSA[1]	618,514	654,869	5.9	1,120,608	71.1
U.S.	226,545,805	248,765,170	9.8	270,299,000	8.7

Note: (1) Metropolitan Statistical Area - see Appendix A for areas included;
July 1998 MSA population estimate was calculated by the editors
Source: 1980/1990 Census of Housing and Population, Summary Tape File 3C;
Census Bureau Population Estimates 1998

Population Characteristics

Race	City 1980 Population	%	City 1990 Population	%	% Chg. 1980-90	MSA[1] 1990 Population	%
White	128,798	82.1	112,893	70.2	-12.3	591,626	90.3
Black	18,679	11.9	23,387	14.6	25.2	29,824	4.6
Amer Indian/Esk/Aleut	1,208	0.8	1,598	1.0	32.3	3,379	0.5
Asian/Pacific Islander	3,012	1.9	9,599	6.0	218.7	14,385	2.2
Other	5,107	3.3	13,251	8.2	159.5	15,655	2.4
Hispanic Origin[2]	8,648	5.5	23,744	14.8	174.6	29,929	4.6

Note: (1) Metropolitan Statistical Area - see Appendix A for areas included;
(2) people of Hispanic origin can be of any race
Source: 1980/1990 Census of Housing and Population, Summary Tape File 3C

Ancestry

Area	German	Irish	English	Italian	U.S.	French	Polish	Dutch
City	5.6	15.3	8.1	19.3	1.8	6.0	3.0	0.5
MSA[1]	7.3	21.5	16.1	24.0	2.0	11.3	4.1	0.6
U.S.	23.3	15.6	13.1	5.9	5.3	4.2	3.8	2.5

Note: Figures are percentages and include persons that reported multiple ancestry (eg. if a person reported being Irish and Italian, they were included in both columns); (1) Metropolitan Statistical Area - see Appendix A for areas included
Source: 1990 Census of Population and Housing, Summary Tape File 3C

Age

Area	Median Age (Years)	Under 5	Under 18	18-24	25-44	45-64	65+	80+
City	29.2	7.8	24.0	17.6	30.1	14.7	13.6	3.6
MSA[1]	34.0	6.5	22.1	12.3	31.9	18.5	15.1	3.5
U.S.	32.9	7.3	25.6	10.5	32.6	18.7	12.5	2.8

Note: (1) Metropolitan Statistical Area - see Appendix A for areas included
Source: 1990 Census of Population and Housing, Summary Tape File 3C

Male/Female Ratio

Area	Number of males per 100 females (all ages)	Number of males per 100 females (18 years old+)
City	89.0	86.6
MSA[1]	91.5	88.1
U.S.	95.0	91.9

Note: (1) Metropolitan Statistical Area - see Appendix A for areas included
Source: 1990 Census of Population, General Population Characteristics

INCOME

Per Capita/Median/Average Income

Area	Per Capita ($)	Median Household ($)	Average Household ($)
City	11,838	22,147	31,465
MSA[1]	15,135	32,340	39,842
U.S.	14,420	30,056	38,453

Note: All figures are for 1989; (1) Metropolitan Statistical Area - see Appendix A for areas included
Source: 1990 Census of Population and Housing, Summary Tape File 3C

Household Income Distribution by Race

Income ($)	City (%)					U.S. (%)				
	Total	White	Black	Other	Hisp.[1]	Total	White	Black	Other	Hisp.[1]
Less than 5,000	8.1	7.1	10.8	12.0	11.6	6.2	4.8	15.2	8.6	8.8
5,000 - 9,999	17.1	16.2	18.5	21.9	22.9	9.3	8.6	14.2	9.9	11.1
10,000 - 14,999	10.3	9.5	13.6	12.0	12.3	8.8	8.5	11.0	9.8	11.0
15,000 - 24,999	19.2	18.8	20.3	20.1	20.8	17.5	17.3	18.9	18.5	20.5
25,000 - 34,999	14.0	13.8	15.2	13.8	13.1	15.8	16.1	14.2	15.4	16.4
35,000 - 49,999	14.9	16.1	10.6	11.9	10.4	17.9	18.6	13.3	16.1	16.0
50,000 - 74,999	9.7	10.6	8.2	5.8	6.6	15.0	15.8	9.3	13.4	11.1
75,000 - 99,999	3.2	3.6	2.0	1.9	1.1	5.1	5.5	2.6	4.7	3.1
100,000+	3.5	4.3	0.9	0.7	1.2	4.4	4.8	1.3	3.7	1.9

Note: All figures are for 1989; (1) people of Hispanic origin can be of any race
Source: 1990 Census of Population and Housing, Summary Tape File 3C

Effective Buying Income

Area	Per Capita ($)	Median Household ($)	Average Household ($)
City	13,394	26,161	36,975
MSA[1]	16,896	36,075	44,792
U.S.	16,803	34,536	45,243

Note: Data as of 1/1/99; (1) Metropolitan Statistical Area - see Appendix A for areas included
Source: Standard Rate & Data Service, Newspaper Advertising Source, 9/99

Effective Household Buying Income Distribution

Area	% of Households Earning						
	$10,000 -$19,999	$20,000 -$34,999	$35,000 -$49,999	$50,000 -$74,999	$75,000 -$99,000	$100,000 -$124,999	$125,000 and up
City	20.6	22.3	16.0	13.5	4.5	1.7	2.5
MSA[1]	15.7	21.3	19.2	20.4	7.3	2.2	2.3
U.S.	16.0	22.6	18.2	18.9	7.2	2.4	2.7

Note: Data as of 1/1/99; (1) Metropolitan Statistical Area - see Appendix A for areas included
Source: Standard Rate & Data Service, Newspaper Advertising Source, 9/99

Poverty Rates by Race and Age

Area	Total (%)	By Race (%)				By Age (%)		
		White	Black	Other	Hisp.[2]	Under 5 years old	Under 18 years old	65 years and over
City	23.0	17.7	31.1	38.4	36.5	36.1	35.0	19.2
MSA[1]	10.1	8.0	27.1	32.0	31.7	16.4	14.5	11.3
U.S.	13.1	9.8	29.5	23.1	25.3	20.1	18.3	12.8

Note: Figures show the percent of people living below the poverty line in 1989. The average poverty threshold was $12,674 for a family of four in 1989; (1) Metropolitan Statistical Area - see Appendix A for areas included; (2) people of Hispanic origin can be of any race
Source: 1990 Census of Population and Housing, Summary Tape File 3C

EMPLOYMENT

Labor Force and Employment

Area	Civilian Labor Force			Workers Employed		
	Jun. 1998	Jun. 1999	% Chg.	Jun. 1998	Jun. 1999	% Chg.
City	68,159	69,186	1.5	64,208	65,904	2.6
MSA[1]	569,431	576,695	1.3	543,836	555,716	2.2
U.S.	138,798,000	140,666,000	1.3	132,265,000	134,395,000	1.6

Note: Data is not seasonally adjusted and covers workers 16 years of age and older;
(1) Metropolitan Statistical Area - see Appendix A for areas included
Source: Bureau of Labor Statistics, http://stats.bls.gov

Unemployment Rate

Area	1998						1999					
	Jul.	Aug.	Sep.	Oct.	Nov.	Dec.	Jan.	Feb.	Mar.	Apr.	May.	Jun.
City	5.9	5.7	6.5	6.4	5.0	4.9	6.2	6.0	4.4	3.6	4.5	4.7
MSA[1]	4.5	4.4	4.8	4.6	3.9	3.7	5.5	5.2	4.0	3.1	3.5	3.6
U.S.	4.7	4.5	4.4	4.2	4.1	4.0	4.8	4.7	4.4	4.1	4.0	4.5

Note: Data is not seasonally adjusted and covers workers 16 years of age and older; all figures are percentages; (1) Metropolitan Statistical Area - see Appendix A for areas included
Source: Bureau of Labor Statistics, http://stats.bls.gov

Employment by Industry

Sector	MSA[1]		U.S.
	Number of Employees	Percent of Total	Percent of Total
Services	168,600	32.1	30.4
Retail Trade	97,500	18.6	17.7
Government	65,700	12.5	15.6
Manufacturing	101,400	19.3	14.3
Finance/Insurance/Real Estate	31,800	6.1	5.9
Wholesale Trade	22,200	4.2	5.4
Transportation/Public Utilities	18,900	3.6	5.3
Construction	19,100	3.6	5.0
Mining	300	0.1	0.4

Note: Figures cover non-farm employment as of 6/99 and are not seasonally adjusted;
(1) Metropolitan Statistical Area - see Appendix A for areas included
Source: Bureau of Labor Statistics, http://stats.bls.gov

Employment by Occupation

Occupation Category	City (%)	MSA[1] (%)	U.S. (%)
White Collar	53.5	59.1	58.1
Executive/Admin./Management	9.4	12.2	12.3
Professional	16.1	15.2	14.1
Technical & Related Support	3.4	3.6	3.7
Sales	8.5	11.5	11.8
Administrative Support/Clerical	16.1	16.8	16.3
Blue Collar	28.9	26.1	26.2
Precision Production/Craft/Repair	10.7	11.7	11.3
Machine Operators/Assem./Insp.	12.3	8.0	6.8
Transportation/Material Movers	2.5	3.3	4.1
Cleaners/Helpers/Laborers	3.4	3.1	3.9
Services	16.8	13.6	13.2
Farming/Forestry/Fishing	0.8	1.2	2.5

Note: Figures cover employed persons 16 years old and over;
(1) Metropolitan Statistical Area - see Appendix A for areas included
Source: 1990 Census of Population and Housing, Summary Tape File 3C

Occupational Employment Projections: 1996 - 2006

Occupations Expected to Have the Largest Job Growth (ranked by numerical growth)	Fast-Growing Occupations[1] (ranked by percent growth)
1. Cashiers	1. Securities, financial services sales
2. Registered nurses	2. Computer engineers
3. Nursing aides/orderlies/attendants	3. Systems analysts
4. Systems analysts	4. Database administrators
5. Home health aides	5. Credit analysts
6. Securities, financial services sales	6. Home health aides
7. Salespersons, retail	7. Medical assistants
8. General managers & top executives	8. Loan officers & counselors
9. Clerical supervisors	9. Human services workers
10. Marketing & sales, supervisors	10. Engineers

Note: Projections cover Rhode Island; (1) Excludes occupations with total job growth less than 300
Source: U.S. Department of Labor, Employment and Training Administration, America's Labor Market Information System (ALMIS)

TAXES

Major State and Local Tax Rates

State Corp. Income (%)	State Personal Income (%)	Residential Property (effective rate per $100)	Sales & Use		State Gasoline (cents/ gallon)	State Cigarette (cents/ pack)
			State (%)	Local (%)		
9.0[a]	(b)	3.20	7.0	None	29.0[c]	71.0

Note: Personal/corporate income, sales, gasoline and cigarette tax rates as of January 1999. Property tax rates as of 1997; (b) 26.5% Federal tax liability; (a) Minimum tax is $250; (c) Rate is comprised of 28 cents excise and 1 cent motor carrier tax
Source: Federation of Tax Administrators, www.taxadmin.org; Washington D.C. Department of Finance and Revenue, Tax Rates and Tax Burdens in the District of Columbia: A Nationwide Comparison, July 1998; Chamber of Commerce, 1999

Total Taxes Per Capita and as a Percent of Income

Area	Per Capita Income ($)	Per Capita Taxes ($)			Percent of Income (%)		
		Total	Federal	State/ Local	Total	Federal	State/ Local
Rhode Island	27,639	9,921	6,625	3,296	35.9	24.0	11.9
U.S.	27,876	9,881	6,690	3,191	35.4	24.0	11.4

Note: Figures are for 1998
Source: Tax Foundation, www.taxfoundation.org

Estimated Tax Burden

Area	State Income	Local Income	Property	Sales	Total
Providence	1,959	0	6,750	683	9,392

Note: The numbers are estimates of taxes paid by a married couple with two children and annual earnings of $75,000. Sales tax estimates assume they spend average amounts on food, clothing, household goods and gasoline. Property tax estimates assume they live in a $250,000 home.
Source: Kiplinger's Personal Finance Magazine, October 1998

COMMERCIAL REAL ESTATE

Office Market

Class/ Location	Total Space (sq. ft.)	Vacant Space (sq. ft.)	Vac. Rate (%)	Under Constr. (sq. ft.)	Net Absorp. (sq. ft.)	Rental Rates ($/sq.ft./yr.)
Class A						
CBD	1,948,302	200,675	10.3	0	206,750	20.00-30.00
Outside CBD	4,931,377	483,505	9.8	45,000	130,993	14.50-19.00
Class B						
CBD	2,260,620	262,232	11.6	0	317,757	15.00-19.00
Outside CBD	n/a	n/a	n/a	n/a	n/a	12.00-15.00

Note: Data as of 10/98 and covers Providence; CBD = Central Business District; n/a not available;
Source: Society of Industrial and Office Realtors, 1999 Comparative Statistics of Industrial and Office Real Estate Markets

"The market appeared to lose some velocity in late 1998, as the financial markets suffered well-publicized upheavals. Under the circumstances, 1999 might be a little rocky. The downtown market, which has improved significantly over the past few years, may see an uptick in Class A vacancy as demand softens. On a positive note, there is potential for some large-scale relocations from Boston. Not only would this provide a boost to absorption, but favorable attention to this smaller New England market. Speculative construction is not likely in the CBD, but some suburban projects are going forward. Improvements at T.F. Green airport are stimulating office development in its vicinity. Also, the Providence Place Mall will be opening in August 1999, providing yet another locational anchor." *Society of Industrial and Office Realtors, 1999 Comparative Statistics of Industrial and Office Real Estate Markets*

Industrial Market

Location	Total Space (sq. ft.)	Vacant Space (sq. ft.)	Vac. Rate (%)	Under Constr. (sq. ft.)	Net Absorp. (sq. ft.)	Net Lease ($/sq.ft./yr.)
Central City	5,685,217	210,233	3.7	0	84,629	1.00-3.50
Suburban	17,208,363	842,172	4.9	176,240	144,080	2.25-5.00

Note: Data as of 10/98 and covers Providence; n/a not available
Source: Society of Industrial and Office Realtors, 1999 Comparative Statistics of Industrial and Office Real Estate Markets

"With demand high and supply low, companies are looking at build-to-suit projects for the first time in years. Rhode Island has little history of speculative development and yet some modest activity on this front is occurring, as in the case of a 10,000 sq. ft. flex property in the Centre of New England Commerce Park. Rhode Island's public officials recognize Providence as a secondary market, and offer tax incentives for firms moving into the state. It is a major coup that Fidelity Investments recently opened a 500,000 sq. ft. facility in Smithfield. With a substantial shortage of space in all size categories, substantial increases in most transaction variables are seen for 1999. A rather robust increase in construction is also anticipated." *Society of Industrial and Office Realtors, 1999 Comparative Statistics of Industrial and Office Real Estate Markets*

COMMERCIAL UTILITIES

Typical Monthly Electric Bills

Area	Commercial Service ($/month)		Industrial Service ($/month)	
	12 kW demand 1,500 kWh	100 kW demand 30,000 kWh	1,000 kW demand 400,000 kWh	20,000 kW demand 10,000,000 kWh
City	153	2,326	26,937	374,051
U.S.	150	2,174	23,995	508,569

Note: Based on rates in effect January 1, 1999
Source: Edison Electric Institute, Typical Residential, Commercial and Industrial Bills, Winter 1999

TRANSPORTATION

Transportation Statistics

Average minutes to work	17.0
Interstate highways	I-95; I-195
Bus lines	
In-city	Rhode Island PTA, 242 vehicles
Inter-city	5
Passenger air service	
Airport	Theodore Francis Green State Airport
Airlines	14
Aircraft departures	18,525 (1996)
Enplaned passengers	1,128,679 (1996)
Rail service	Amtrak
Motor freight carriers	400
Major waterways/ports	Providence River

Source: Editor & Publisher Market Guide, 1999; FAA Airport Activity Statistics, 1997; Amtrak National Time Table, Northeast Timetable, Spring/Summer 1999; 1990 Census of Population and Housing, STF 3C; Chamber of Commerce/Economic Development 1999; Jane's Urban Transport Systems 1999-2000

Means of Transportation to Work

Area	Car/Truck/Van		Public Transportation			Bicycle	Walked	Other Means	Worked at Home
	Drove Alone	Car-pooled	Bus	Subway	Railroad				
City	62.2	16.1	6.6	0.1	0.6	0.4	10.8	1.1	2.0
MSA[1]	78.2	11.9	2.7	0.0	0.3	0.2	4.2	0.7	1.8
U.S.	73.2	13.4	3.0	1.5	0.5	0.4	3.9	1.2	3.0

Note: Figures shown are percentages and only include workers 16 years old and over; (1) Metropolitan Statistical Area - see Appendix A for areas included
Source: 1990 Census of Population and Housing, Summary Tape File 3C

BUSINESSES

Major Business Headquarters

Company Name	1999 Rankings	
	Fortune 500	Forbes 500
Gilbane Building	-	80
Textron	144	-

Note: Companies listed are located in the city; dashes indicate no ranking
Fortune 500: Companies that produce a 10-K are ranked 1 to 500 based on 1998 revenue
Forbes 500: Private companies are ranked 1 to 500 based on 1997 revenue
Source: Forbes, November 30, 1998; Fortune, April 26, 1999

Small Business Opportunity

According to *Forbes*, Providence is home to one of America's 200 best small companies: AFC Cable Systems. Criteria: companies included must be publicly traded since November 1997 with a stock price of at least $5 per share and an average daily float of 1,000 shares. The company's latest 12-month sales must be between $5 and $350 million, return on equity (ROE) must be a minimum of 12% for both the past 5 years and the most recent four quarters, and five-year sales and EPS growth must average at least 10%. Companies with declining sales or earnings during the past year were dropped as well as businesses with debt/equity ratios over 1.25. Companies with negative operating cash flow in each of the past two years were also excluded. *Forbes, November 2, 1998*

HOTELS & MOTELS

Hotels/Motels

| Area | Hotels/ Motels | Rooms | Luxury-Level Hotels/Motels | | Average Minimum Rates ($) | | |
			♦♦♦♦	♦♦♦♦♦	♦♦	♦♦♦	♦♦♦♦
City	6	1,236	0	0	n/a	n/a	n/a
Airport	9	1,121	0	0	n/a	n/a	n/a
Suburbs	24	2,117	0	0	n/a	n/a	n/a
Total	39	4,474	0	0	n/a	n/a	n/a

Note: n/a not available; classifications range from one diamond (budget properties with basic amenities) to five diamond (luxury properties with the finest service, rooms and facilities).
Source: OAG, Business Travel Planner, Winter 1998-99

CONVENTION CENTERS

Major Convention Centers

Center Name	Meeting Rooms	Exhibit Space (sq. ft.)
Providence Civic Center	5	88,700
Rhode Island Convention Center	24	100,000

Source: Trade Shows Worldwide, 1998; Meetings & Conventions, 4/15/99; Sucessful Meetings, 3/31/98

Living Environment

COST OF LIVING

Cost of Living Index

Composite Index	Groceries	Housing	Utilities	Trans-portation	Health Care	Misc. Goods/ Services
116.0	101.5	134.9	134.3	109.7	118.6	103.9

Note: U.S. = 100
Source: ACCRA, Cost of Living Index, 3rd Quarter 1996

HOUSING

Median Home Prices and Housing Affordability

Area	Median Price[2] 1st Qtr. 1999 ($)	HOI[3] 1st Qtr. 1999	Afford-ability Rank[4]
MSA[1]	n/a	n/a	n/a
U.S.	134,000	69.6	–

Note: (1) Metropolitan Statistical Area - see Appendix A for areas included; (2) U.S. figures calculated from the sales of 524,324 new and existing homes in 181 markets; (3) Housing Opportunity Index - percent of homes sold that were within the reach of the median income household at the prevailing mortgage interest rate; (4) Rank is from 1-181 with 1 being most affordable; n/a not available
Source: National Association of Home Builders, Housing Opportunity Index, 1st Quarter 1999

Median Home Price Projection

It is projected that the median price of existing single-family homes in the metro area will increase by 3.3% in 1999. Nationwide, home prices are projected to increase 3.8%.
Kiplinger's Personal Finance Magazine, January 1999

Average New Home Price

Area	Price ($)
City	165,593
U.S.	131,626

Note: Figures are based on a new home with 1,800 sq. ft. of living area on an 8,000 sq. ft. lot.
Source: ACCRA, Cost of Living Index, 3rd Quarter 1996

Average Apartment Rent

Area	Rent ($/mth)
City	925
U.S.	556

Note: Figures are based on an unfurnished two bedroom, 1-1/2 or 2 bath apartment, approximately 950 sq. ft. in size, excluding all utilities except water
Source: ACCRA, Cost of Living Index, 3rd Quarter 1996

RESIDENTIAL UTILITIES

Average Residential Utility Costs

Area	All Electric ($/mth)	Part Electric ($/mth)	Other Energy ($/mth)	Phone ($/mth)
City	–	74.16	65.65	23.46
U.S.	110.28	56.34	42.21	19.45

Source: ACCRA, Cost of Living Index, 3rd Quarter 1996

HEALTH CARE

Average Health Care Costs

Area	Hospital ($/day)	Doctor ($/visit)	Dentist ($/visit)
City	554.56	45.30	74.00
U.S.	381.46	46.47	58.18

Note: Hospital—based on a semi-private room; Doctor—based on a general practitioner's routine exam of an established patient; Dentist—based on adult teeth cleaning and periodic oral exam.
Source: ACCRA, Cost of Living Index, 3rd Quarter 1996

Distribution of Office-Based Physicians

Area	Family/Gen. Practitioners	Specialists		
		Medical	Surgical	Other
MSA[1]	126	779	505	471

Note: Data as of 12/31/97; (1) Metropolitan Statistical Area - see Appendix A for areas included
Source: American Medical Assn., Physician Characteristics & Distribution in the U.S., 1999

Hospitals

Providence has 5 general medical and surgical hospitals, 1 psychiatric, 1 obstetrics and gynecology. *AHA Guide to the Healthcare Field, 1998-99*

According to *U.S. News and World Report,* Providence has 1 of the best hospitals in the U.S.: **Rhode Island Hospital**, noted for pulmonology. *U.S. News Online, "America's Best Hospitals," 10th Edition, www.usnews.com*

EDUCATION

Public School District Statistics

District Name	Num. Sch.	Enroll.	Classroom Teachers	Pupils per Teacher	Minority Pupils (%)	Current Exp.[1] ($/pupil)
Board of Regents Schs	3	965	109	8.9	n/a	n/a
Providence Sch Dist	46	25,611	n/a	n/a	n/a	n/a

Note: Data covers the 1997-1998 school year unless otherwise noted; (1) Data covers fiscal year 1996; SD = School District; ISD = Independent School District; n/a not available
Source: National Center for Education Statistics, Common Core of Data Public Education Agency Universe 1997-98; National Center for Education Statistics, Characteristics of the 100 Largest Public Elementary and Secondary School Districts in the United States: 1997-98, July 1999

Educational Quality

School District	Education Quotient[1]	Graduate Outcome[2]	Community Index[3]	Resource Index[4]
Providence SD	74.0	57.0	54.0	113.0

Note: Nearly 1,000 secondary school districts were rated in terms of educational quality. The scores range from a low of 50 to a high of 150; (1) Average of the Graduate Outcome, Community and Resource indexes; (2) Based on graduation rates and college board scores (SAT/ACT); (3) Based on the surrounding community's average level of education and the area's average income level; (4) Based on teacher salaries, per-pupil expenditures and student-teacher ratios.
Source: Expansion Management, Ratings Issue, 1998

Educational Attainment by Race

Area	High School Graduate (%)					Bachelor's Degree (%)				
	Total	White	Black	Other	Hisp.[2]	Total	White	Black	Other	Hisp.[2]
City	62.8	66.1	61.6	41.9	42.0	21.6	25.4	10.1	9.5	6.6
MSA[1]	72.7	73.9	65.3	51.4	46.6	22.3	23.0	13.2	15.7	9.3
U.S.	75.2	77.9	63.1	60.4	49.8	20.3	21.5	11.4	19.4	9.2

Note: Figures shown cover persons 25 years old and over; (1) Metropolitan Statistical Area - see Appendix A for areas included; (2) people of Hispanic origin can be of any race
Source: 1990 Census of Population and Housing, Summary Tape File 3C

School Enrollment by Type

Area	Preprimary				Elementary/High School			
	Public		Private		Public		Private	
	Enrollment	%	Enrollment	%	Enrollment	%	Enrollment	%
City	1,469	56.4	1,137	43.6	20,203	82.8	4,199	17.2
MSA[1]	5,933	54.0	5,054	46.0	81,761	85.9	13,463	14.1
U.S.	2,679,029	59.5	1,824,256	40.5	38,379,689	90.2	4,187,099	9.8

Note: Figures shown cover persons 3 years old and over;
(1) Metropolitan Statistical Area - see Appendix A for areas included
Source: 1990 Census of Population and Housing, Summary Tape File 3C

School Enrollment by Race

Area	Preprimary (%)				Elementary/High School (%)			
	White	Black	Other	Hisp.[1]	White	Black	Other	Hisp.[1]
City	58.9	23.2	17.9	15.2	51.5	23.5	24.9	24.7
MSA[2]	87.8	6.8	5.4	4.3	84.8	7.2	8.1	7.6
U.S.	80.4	12.5	7.1	7.8	74.1	15.6	10.3	12.5

Note: Figures shown cover persons 3 years old and over; (1) people of Hispanic origin can be of any race; (2) Metropolitan Statistical Area - see Appendix A for areas included
Source: 1990 Census of Population and Housing, Summary Tape File 3C

Classroom Teacher Salaries in Public Schools

District	B.A. Degree		M.A. Degree		Maximum	
	Min. ($)	Rank[1]	Max. ($)	Rank[1]	Max. ($)	Rank[1]
	n/a	n/a	n/a	n/a	n/a	n/a
Average	26,980	-	46,065	-	51,435	-

Note: Salaries are for 1997-1998; (1) Rank ranges from 1 to 100; n/a not available
Source: American Federation of Teachers, Survey & Analysis of Salary Trends, 1998

Higher Education

Two-Year Colleges		Four-Year Colleges		Medical Schools	Law Schools	Voc/ Tech
Public	Private	Public	Private			
0	0	1	4	1	0	4

Source: College Blue Book, Occupational Education, 1997; Medical School Admission Requirements, 1999-2000; Peterson's Guide to Two-Year Colleges, 1999; Peterson's Guide to Four-Year Colleges, 2000; Barron's Guide to Law Schools, 1999

MAJOR EMPLOYERS

Major Employers

Rhode Island Hospital
Roger Williams Medical Center
St. Joseph Health Services of Rhode Island
Butler Hospital
Rhode Island Public Tranportation Authority

Women & Infants Hospital of Rhode Island
Miriam Hospital
K&M Associates (costume jewelry)
Hirsch Speidel (jewelry)
Narragansett Electric Co.

Note: Companies listed are located in the city
Source: Dun's Business Rankings, 1999; Ward's Business Directory, 1998

PUBLIC SAFETY

Crime Rate

Area	All Crimes	Violent Crimes				Property Crimes		
		Murder	Forcible Rape	Robbery	Aggrav. Assault	Burglary	Larceny -Theft	Motor Vehicle Theft
City	7,575.9	8.0	67.6	281.9	317.3	1,551.2	3,937.2	1,412.6
Suburbs[1]	2,959.5	1.1	28.8	33.5	216.2	553.8	1,850.7	275.4
MSA[2]	3,686.1	2.2	34.9	72.6	232.1	710.8	2,179.1	454.4
U.S.	4,922.7	6.8	35.9	186.1	382.0	919.6	2,886.5	505.8

Note: Crime rate is the number of crimes per 100,000 pop.; (1) defined as all areas within the MSA but located outside the central city; (2) Metropolitan Statistical Area - see Appendix A for areas incl.
Source: FBI Uniform Crime Reports, 1997

RECREATION

Culture and Recreation

Museums	Symphony Orchestras	Opera Companies	Dance Companies	Professional Theatres	Zoos	Pro Sports Teams
10	3	0	0	5	1	0

Source: International Directory of the Performing Arts, 1997; Official Museum Directory, 1999; Stern's Performing Arts Directory, 1997; USA Today Four Sport Stadium Guide, 1997; Chamber of Commerce/Economic Development, 1999

Library System

The Providence Public Library has nine branches, holdings of 1,215,202 volumes, and a budget of $6,110,062 (1997-1998). *American Library Directory, 1998-1999*

MEDIA

Newspapers

Name	Type	Freq.	Distribution	Circulation
Brown Daily Herald	General	5x/wk	Camp/Comm	5,000
The East Providence Post	n/a	1x/wk	Local	12,000
East Side Monthly	General	1x/mo	Local	14,000
Federal Hill Gazette	n/a	1x/mo	Regional	30,000
The Providence American	Black	2x/mo	Area	5,000
The Providence Journal-Bulletin	General	7x/wk	Area	164,400
The Providence Phoenix	n/a	1x/wk	Local	60,000
The Providence Visitor	Religious	1x/wk	State	40,000
The Seekonk Star	n/a	1x/wk	Local	4,000

Note: Includes newspapers with circulations of 1,000 or more located in the city; n/a not available
Source: Burrelle's Media Directory, 1999 Edition

Television Stations

Name	Ch.	Affiliation	Type	Owner
WLNE	n/a	ABCT/CBST	Commercial	Freedom Communications Inc.
WPRI	12	CBST	Commercial	Clear Channel Broadcasting Inc.
WRIW	23	UPN	Commercial	Viking Communications Inc.
WSBE	36	PBS	Public	Rhode Island Public Telecommunication Auth.
WNAC	64	FBC	Commercial	Sunrise Television Corp.
WPXQ	69	n/a	Commercial	Ocean State TV L.L.C.

Note: Stations included broadcast in the Providence metro area; n/a not available
Source: Burrelle's Media Directory, 1999 Edition

AM Radio Stations

Call Letters	Freq. (kHz)	Target Audience	Station Format	Music Format
WHJJ	920	General	N/S/T	n/a
WALE	990	E/G	E/M/N/S/T	n/a
WPMZ	1110	General	n/a	n/a
WRIB	1220	G/H	M	Christian/Latin
WDYZ	1450	Children	M/N/S	Oldies/Top 40

Note: Stations included broadcast in the Providence metro area; n/a not available
Target Audience: A=Asian; B=Black; C=Christian; E=Ethnic; F=French; G=General; H=Hispanic; M=Men; N=Native American; R=Religious; S=Senior Citizen; W=Women; Y=Young Adult; Z=Children
Station Format: E=Educational; M=Music; N=News; S=Sports; T=Talk
Source: Burrelle's Media Directory, 1999 Edition

FM Radio Stations

Call Letters	Freq. (mHz)	Target Audience	Station Format	Music Format
WELH	88.1	n/a	n/a	n/a
WDOM	91.3	General	M	n/a
WPRO	92.3	General	M	n/a
WSNE	93.3	General	M	Adult Contemporary
WHJY	94.1	General	M/N/S	AOR
WBRU	95.5	General	M/N	Alternative
WCTK	98.1	General	M/T	Country
WWBB	101.5	General	M	Oldies
WWRX	103.7	General	M	Classic Rock

Note: Stations included broadcast in the Providence metro area; n/a not available
Station Format: E=Educational; M=Music; N=News; S=Sports; T=Talk
Target Audience: A=Asian; B=Black; C=Christian; E=Ethnic; F=French; G=General; H=Hispanic; M=Men; N=Native American; R=Religious; S=Senior Citizen; W=Women; Y=Young Adult; Z=Children
Music Format: AOR=Album Oriented Rock; MOR=Middle-of-the-Road
Source: Burrelle's Media Directory, 1999 Edition

CLIMATE

Average and Extreme Temperatures

Temperature	Jan	Feb	Mar	Apr	May	Jun	Jul	Aug	Sep	Oct	Nov	Dec	Yr.
Extreme High (°F)	66	72	80	98	94	97	102	104	100	88	81	70	104
Average High (°F)	37	39	46	58	68	77	82	80	73	63	52	41	60
Average Temp. (°F)	29	30	38	48	58	67	73	71	64	54	44	33	51
Average Low (°F)	20	22	29	39	48	57	63	62	54	43	35	25	42
Extreme Low (°F)	-13	-7	1	14	29	41	48	40	32	20	6	-10	-13

Note: Figures cover the years 1948-1992
Source: National Climatic Data Center, International Station Meteorological Climate Summary, 3/95

Average Precipitation/Snowfall/Humidity

Precip./Humidity	Jan	Feb	Mar	Apr	May	Jun	Jul	Aug	Sep	Oct	Nov	Dec	Yr.
Avg. Precip. (in.)	3.9	3.6	4.2	4.1	3.7	2.9	3.2	4.0	3.5	3.6	4.5	4.3	45.3
Avg. Snowfall (in.)	10	10	7	1	Tr	0	0	0	0	Tr	1	7	35
Avg. Rel. Hum. 7am (%)	71	71	71	70	73	75	78	81	83	81	78	74	75
Avg. Rel. Hum. 4pm (%)	58	56	54	51	55	58	58	60	60	58	60	60	57

Note: Figures cover the years 1948-1992; Tr = Trace amounts (<0.05 in. of rain; <0.5 in. of snow)
Source: National Climatic Data Center, International Station Meteorological Climate Summary, 3/95

Weather Conditions

Temperature			Daytime Sky			Precipitation		
5°F & below	32°F & below	90°F & above	Clear	Partly cloudy	Cloudy	0.01 inch or more precip.	0.1 inch or more snow/ice	Thunder-storms
6	117	9	85	134	146	123	21	21

Note: Figures are average number of days per year and covers the years 1948-1992
Source: National Climatic Data Center, International Station Meteorological Climate Summary, 3/95

AIR & WATER QUALITY

Maximum Pollutant Concentrations

	Particulate Matter (ug/m³)	Carbon Monoxide (ppm)	Sulfur Dioxide (ppm)	Nitrogen Dioxide (ppm)	Ozone (ppm)	Lead (ug/m³)
MSA[1] Level	62	6	0.037	0.025	0.12	n/a
NAAQS[2]	150	9	0.140	0.053	0.12	1.50
Met NAAQS?	Yes	Yes	Yes	Yes	Yes	n/a

Note: (1) Metropolitan Statistical Area - see Appendix A for areas included; (2) National Ambient Air Quality Standards; ppm = parts per million; ug/m³ = micrograms per cubic meter; n/a not available
Source: EPA, National Air Quality and Emissions Trends Report, 1997

Pollutant Standards Index

In the Providence MSA (see Appendix A for areas included), the Pollutant Standards Index (PSI) exceeded 100 on 11 days in 1997. A PSI value greater than 100 indicates that air quality would be in the unhealthful range on that day. *EPA, National Air Quality and Emissions Trends Report, 1997*

Drinking Water

Water System Name	Pop. Served	Primary Water Source Type	Number of Violations in 1998	Type of Violation/ Contaminants
City of Pawtucket	110,000	Surface	None	None

Note: Data as of July 10, 1999
Source: EPA, Office of Ground Water and Drinking Water, Safe Drinking Water Information System

Providence tap water is alkaline, very soft.
Editor & Publisher Market Guide, 1999

Raleigh, North Carolina

Background

Raleigh is named for Queen Elizabeth I's swashbuckling favorite, Sir Walter Raleigh. In her name, he plundered Spanish ships for gold in the New World, and founded the first English settlement along the North Carolina coast. His excessive piracy led to his execution in 1618.

Raleigh is the capital of North Carolina, and its cultural and educational center. Located 120 miles west of the Atlantic Ocean, Raleigh is the retail and wholesale locus of eastern North Carolina. Its number of federal, state, and local government offices provide jobs for the economy of the surrounding area. The construction of the Research Triangle Park—a complex of research laboratories between the cities of Raleigh, Durham, and Chapel Hill—has pumped money into the local economy as well.

Since 1992, the city has been home to high-tech businesses and first rate universities like North Carolina State, Duke, and the University of North Carolina. The region has a high business start up rate, a low unemployment rate and average wages above the state level. The Research Triangle Park is the largest university-affiliated research park in the world, with 99 companies employing over 36,000 workers. It is home to such companies as IBM, DuPont, Motorola, and Harris Microelectronics. *Site Selection, June/July 1997*

Called the "City of Oaks," for its tree-lined streets, the city offers the modern architecture of Edward Durrell Stone's North Carolina Museum of Art, (he also designed the John F. Kennedy Center in Washington, D.C.), and antebellum structures, such as the Greek Revival Capitol Building, reconstructed in 1840 after the first capitol building burned down in 1831. The city's grid design streets makes exploration of this fine city simple.

Because it is centrally located between the mountains on the west and the coast on the south and east, the Raleigh area enjoys a pleasant climate. The mountains form a partial barrier to cold air masses moving from the west. As a result, there are few winter days when the temperature falls below 20 degrees. In the summer, tropical air is present over the eastern and central sections of North Carolina bringing warm temperatures and rather high humidity to the area. Raleigh is situated far enough from the coast so that the bad weather effects of coastal storms are reduced. While snow and sleet usually occur each year, excessive accumulations of snow are rare.

General Rankings and Evaluative Comments

■ Raleigh was ranked #2 out of 19 large, southern metropolitan areas in *Money's* 1998 survey of "The Best Places to Live in America." The survey was conducted by first contacting 512 representative households nationwide and asking them to rank 37 quality-of-life factors on a scale of 1 to 10. Next, a demographic profile was compiled on the 300 largest metropolitan statistical areas in the U.S. The numbers were crunched together to arrive at an overall ranking (things Americans consider most important, like clean air and water, low crime and good schools, received extra weight). Unlike previous years, the 1998 rankings were broken down by region (northeast, midwest, south, west) and population size (100,000 to 249,999; 250,000 to 999,999; 1 million plus). The city had a nationwide ranking of #16 out of 300 in 1997 and #24 out of 300 in 1996. *Money, July 1998; Money, July 1997; Money, September 1996*

■ Raleigh appeared on *Fortune's* list of "The Best Cities for Business." Rank: #6 out of 10. One hundred and sixty cities worldwide were analyzed by Arthur Andersen's Business Location Service. The North American research focused on cities creating new wealth and opportunities. *Fortune* made the final selection of the top 10 cities in the U.S. *Fortune, November 1998*

■ *Ladies Home Journal* ranked America's 200 largest cities based on the qualities women care about most. Raleigh ranked #37 out of 200. Criteria: low crime rate, well-paying jobs, quality health and child care, good public schools, the presence of women in government, size of the gender wage gap, number of sexual-harassment and discrimination complaints filed, unemployment and divorce rates, commute times, population density, number of houses of worship, parks and cultural offerings, number of women's health specialists, how well a community's women cared for themselves, complexion kindness index based on UV radiation levels, odds of finding affordable fashions, rental rates for romance movies, champagne sales and other matters of the heart. *Ladies Home Journal, November 1998*

■ Raleigh was selected as one of the 10 healthiest cities for women by *American Health*. It was ranked #8 out of America's 120 most populous metro areas. Criteria: number and quality of doctors and hospitals, quality of women's health centers, number of recreational opportunities, rate of violent crimes, cleanliness of air and water, percentage of women-owned businesses, and the number of family-friendly employers. *American Health, 1998*

■ Zero Population Growth ranked 229 cities in terms of children's health, safety, and economic well-being. Raleigh was ranked #19 out of 112 independent cities (cities with populations greater than 100,000 which were neither Major Cities nor Suburbs/Outer Cities) and was given a grade of B. Criteria: total population, percent of population under 18 years of age, household language, percent population change, percent of births to teens, infant mortality rate, percent of low birth weights, dropout rate, enrollment in preprimary school, violent and property crime rates, unemployment rate, percent of children in poverty, percent of owner occupied units, number of bad air days, percent of public transportation commuters, and average travel time to work. *Zero Population Growth, Children's Environmental Index, Fall 1999*

■ Raleigh appeared on *New Mobility's* list of "10 Disability Friendly Cities." Rank: #5 out of 10. Criteria: affordable and accessible housing, transportation, quality medical care, personal assistance services and strong advocacy.

"Raleigh's Capitol Area Transit's mainline transportation is fully accessible, while Accessible Raleigh Transportation System operates a two-tiered paratransit service." *New Mobility, December 1997*

■ Raleigh was ranked #5 out of 59 metro areas in *The Regional Economist's* "Rational Livability Ranking of 59 Large Metro Areas." The rankings were based on the metro area's total population change over the period 1990-97 divided by the number of people moving in from elsewhere in the United States (net domestic in-migration). *St. Louis Federal Reserve Bank of St. Louis, The Regional Economist, April 1999*

■ Raleigh was selected by *Yahoo! Internet Life* as one of "America's Most Wired Cities & Towns." The city ranked #18 out of 50. Criteria: home and work net use, domain density, hosts per capita, directory density and content quality. *Yahoo! Internet Life, March 1999*

■ Cognetics studied 273 metro areas in the United States, ranking them by entrepreneurial activity. Raleigh was ranked #3 out of the 50 largest metro areas. Criteria: Significant Starts (firms started in the last 10 years that still employ at least 5 people) and Young Growers (percent of firms 10 years old or less that grew significantly during the last 4 years). *Cognetics, "Entrepreneurial Hot Spots: The Best Places in America to Start and Grow a Company," 1998*

■ Raleigh was included among *Entrepreneur* magazine's listing of the "20 Best Cities for Small Business." It was ranked #3 among large metro areas and #2 among southern metro areas. Criteria: entrepreneurial activity, small-business growth, economic growth, and risk of failure. *Entrepreneur, October 1999*

■ Raleigh was selected as one of the "Best American Cities to Start a Business" by *Point of View* magazine. Criteria: coolness, quality-of-life, and business concerns. The city was ranked #7 out of 75. *Point of View, November 1998*

■ Raleigh appeared on *Sales & Marketing Management's* list of the "20 Hottest Cities for Selling." Rank: #16 out of 20. *S&MM* editors looked at Metropolitan Statistical Areas with populations of more than 150,000. The areas were ranked based on population increases, retail sales increases, effective buying income, increase in both residential and commercial building permits issued, unemployment rates, job growth, mix of industries, tax rates, number of corporate relocations, and the number of new corporations. *Sales & Marketing Management, April 1999*

■ Reliastar Financial Corp. ranked the 125 largest metropolitan areas according to the general financial security of residents. Raleigh was ranked #17 out of 125 with a score of 9.0. The score indicates the percentage a metropolitan area is above or below the metropolitan norm. A metro area with a score of 10.6 is 10.6% above the metro average. Criteria: Earnings and Wealth Potential (household income, education, net assets, cost of living); Safety Net (health insurance, retirement savings, life insurance, income support programs); Personal Threats (unemployment rate, low-income households, crime rate); Community Economic Vitality (cost of community services, job quality, job creation, housing costs). *Reliastar Financial Corp., "The Best Cities to Earn and Save Money," 1999 Edition*

Business Environment

STATE ECONOMY

State Economic Profile

"In spite of declines in textiles and apparels, North Carolina has seen impressive job growth in the last few years. As NC continues to diversify its economy away from its traditional manufacturing base and toward its newer high-tech and financial services sectors, job growth will outpace the nation for a number of years to come, albeit at a slightly slower rate than those seen in 1997 and 1998.

Raleigh-Durham has been and will continue to be one of NC's growth engines. High-tech firms in the Research Triangle Park have expanded employment considerably. Cisco Systems, for one, is planning to expand its operations, adding as many as 4,000 jobs over the next three years. Raleigh's housing market has more than doubled in size during the 1990s. Price appreciation has been strong, although homes still remain affordable. 1999 should be another hot year for sales and new construction in Raleigh-Durham.

NC's other hot spot has been Charlotte. While many parts of the country have been hurt by consolidation in the financial services industry, many of these jobs have made their way to Charlotte. As this wave of consolidation has slowed, so has job growth in Charlotte, reflected in its 0.6% job growth rate in 1998, far below that of previous years. Continued restructuring in NC's textiles, apparel and furniture industries will slow job growth in the Charlotte area.

The outlook for NC, while a slowdown from its recent pace, is still one of impressive job growth, far outpacing the nation. With its business friendly atmosphere and the decision of Federal Express to locate its Mid-Atlantic hub here, NC will likely attract more corporate relocations. Its affordable housing markets and overall high quality of life will also attract residents, helping fuel job growth." *National Association of Realtors, Economic Profiles: The Fifty States and the District of Columbia, http://nar.realtor.com/databank/profiles.htm*

IMPORTS/EXPORTS

Total Export Sales

Area	1994 ($000)	1995 ($000)	1996 ($000)	1997 ($000)	% Chg. 1994-97	% Chg. 1996-97
MSA[1]	1,758,673	2,093,206	2,609,828	2,713,071	54.3	4.0
U.S.	512,415,609	583,030,524	622,827,063	687,597,999	34.2	10.4

Note: (1) Metropolitan Statistical Area - see Appendix A for areas included
Source: U.S. Department of Commerce, International Trade Association, Metropolitan Area Exports: An Export Performance Report on Over 250 U.S. Cities, November 10, 1998

CITY FINANCES

City Government Finances

Component	FY92 ($000)	FY92 (per capita $)
Revenue	187,923	840.65
Expenditure	196,961	881.08
Debt Outstanding	154,545	691.33
Cash & Securities	165,666	741.08

Source: U.S. Bureau of the Census, City Government Finances: 1991-92

City Government Revenue by Source

Source	FY92 ($000)	FY92 (per capita $)	FY92 (%)
From Federal Government	3,011	13.47	1.6
From State Governments	22,117	98.94	11.8
From Local Governments	21,945	98.17	11.7
Property Taxes	68,750	307.54	36.6
General Sales Taxes	0	0.00	0.0
Selective Sales Taxes	1,949	8.72	1.0
Income Taxes	0	0.00	0.0
Current Charges	27,908	124.84	14.9
Utility/Liquor Store	17,984	80.45	9.6
Employee Retirement[1]	0	0.00	0.0
Other	24,259	108.52	12.9

Note: (1) Excludes "city contributions," classified as "nonrevenue," intragovernmental transfers.
Source: U.S. Bureau of the Census, City Government Finances: 1991-92

City Government Expenditures by Function

Function	FY92 ($000)	FY92 (per capita $)	FY92 (%)
Educational Services	0	0.00	0.0
Employee Retirement[1]	0	0.00	0.0
Environment/Housing	57,812	258.61	29.4
Government Administration	9,473	42.38	4.8
Interest on General Debt	6,204	27.75	3.1
Public Safety	37,283	166.78	18.9
Social Services	993	4.44	0.5
Transportation	24,808	110.97	12.6
Utility/Liquor Store	33,200	148.52	16.9
Other	27,188	121.62	13.8

Note: (1) Payments to beneficiaries including withdrawal of contributions.
Source: U.S. Bureau of the Census, City Government Finances: 1991-92

Municipal Bond Ratings

Area	Moody's	S & P
Raleigh	Aaa	n/a

Note: n/a not available; n/r not rated
Source: Moody's Bond Record, 6/99

POPULATION

Population Growth

Area	1980	1990	% Chg. 1980-90	July 1998 Estimate	% Chg. 1990-98
City	150,255	207,951	38.4	259,423	24.8
MSA[1]	561,222	735,480	31.0	1,080,843	47.0
U.S.	226,545,805	248,765,170	9.8	270,299,000	8.7

Note: (1) Metropolitan Statistical Area - see Appendix A for areas included;
July 1998 MSA population estimate was calculated by the editors
Source: 1980/1990 Census of Housing and Population, Summary Tape File 3C;
Census Bureau Population Estimates 1998

Population Characteristics

Race	City				% Chg. 1980-90	MSA[1]	
	1980		1990			1990	
	Population	%	Population	%		Population	%
White	106,574	70.9	144,193	69.3	35.3	533,421	72.5
Black	41,241	27.4	57,236	27.5	38.8	183,225	24.9
Amer Indian/Esk/Aleut	209	0.1	604	0.3	189.0	2,017	0.3
Asian/Pacific Islander	1,556	1.0	5,131	2.5	229.8	13,940	1.9
Other	675	0.4	787	0.4	16.6	2,877	0.4
Hispanic Origin[2]	1,382	0.9	2,454	1.2	77.6	8,386	1.1

Note: (1) Metropolitan Statistical Area - see Appendix A for areas included;
(2) people of Hispanic origin can be of any race
Source: 1980/1990 Census of Housing and Population, Summary Tape File 3C

Ancestry

Area	German	Irish	English	Italian	U.S.	French	Polish	Dutch
City	16.5	11.4	19.5	2.6	5.3	2.7	1.6	1.3
MSA[1]	16.3	12.4	19.0	2.6	7.5	2.8	1.7	1.5
U.S.	23.3	15.6	13.1	5.9	5.3	4.2	3.8	2.5

Note: Figures are percentages and include persons that reported multiple ancestry (eg. if a person reported being Irish and Italian, they were included in both columns); (1) Metropolitan Statistical Area - see Appendix A for areas included
Source: 1990 Census of Population and Housing, Summary Tape File 3C

Age

Area	Median Age (Years)	Age Distribution (%)						
		Under 5	Under 18	18-24	25-44	45-64	65+	80+
City	30.2	6.2	19.5	17.5	38.6	15.6	8.8	1.9
MSA[1]	31.2	6.8	22.5	14.0	37.6	16.9	8.9	2.0
U.S.	32.9	7.3	25.6	10.5	32.6	18.7	12.5	2.8

Note: (1) Metropolitan Statistical Area - see Appendix A for areas included
Source: 1990 Census of Population and Housing, Summary Tape File 3C

Male/Female Ratio

Area	Number of males per 100 females (all ages)	Number of males per 100 females (18 years old+)
City	93.6	92.8
MSA[1]	92.9	90.5
U.S.	95.0	91.9

Note: (1) Metropolitan Statistical Area - see Appendix A for areas included
Source: 1990 Census of Population, General Population Characteristics

INCOME

Per Capita/Median/Average Income

Area	Per Capita ($)	Median Household ($)	Average Household ($)
City	16,896	32,451	40,243
MSA[1]	16,170	33,290	40,686
U.S.	14,420	30,056	38,453

Note: All figures are for 1989; (1) Metropolitan Statistical Area - see Appendix A for areas included
Source: 1990 Census of Population and Housing, Summary Tape File 3C

Household Income Distribution by Race

Income ($)	City (%)					U.S. (%)				
	Total	White	Black	Other	Hisp.[1]	Total	White	Black	Other	Hisp.[1]
Less than 5,000	5.6	3.5	11.2	13.9	5.8	6.2	4.8	15.2	8.6	8.8
5,000 - 9,999	6.7	5.2	11.4	5.6	7.0	9.3	8.6	14.2	9.9	11.1
10,000 - 14,999	7.7	6.3	11.8	11.5	7.2	8.8	8.5	11.0	9.8	11.0
15,000 - 24,999	17.7	16.4	21.5	16.5	17.0	17.5	17.3	18.9	18.5	20.5
25,000 - 34,999	16.1	15.5	18.0	15.0	13.9	15.8	16.1	14.2	15.4	16.4
35,000 - 49,999	18.9	19.8	16.0	18.7	18.4	17.9	18.6	13.3	16.1	16.0
50,000 - 74,999	17.0	20.1	7.8	12.7	22.7	15.0	15.8	9.3	13.4	11.1
75,000 - 99,999	5.6	7.1	1.5	2.1	2.2	5.1	5.5	2.6	4.7	3.1
100,000+	4.7	6.1	0.8	4.0	5.8	4.4	4.8	1.3	3.7	1.9

Note: All figures are for 1989; (1) people of Hispanic origin can be of any race
Source: 1990 Census of Population and Housing, Summary Tape File 3C

Effective Buying Income

Area	Per Capita ($)	Median Household ($)	Average Household ($)
City	19,531	38,129	46,674
MSA[1]	18,992	38,166	47,652
U.S.	16,803	34,536	45,243

Note: Data as of 1/1/99; (1) Metropolitan Statistical Area - see Appendix A for areas included
Source: Standard Rate & Data Service, Newspaper Advertising Source, 9/99

Effective Household Buying Income Distribution

Area	% of Households Earning						
	$10,000 -$19,999	$20,000 -$34,999	$35,000 -$49,999	$50,000 -$74,999	$75,000 -$99,000	$100,000 -$124,999	$125,000 and up
City	13.5	22.7	18.4	21.3	8.6	2.9	2.9
MSA[1]	13.8	21.9	18.7	21.7	8.4	2.8	2.6
U.S.	16.0	22.6	18.2	18.9	7.2	2.4	2.7

Note: Data as of 1/1/99; (1) Metropolitan Statistical Area - see Appendix A for areas included
Source: Standard Rate & Data Service, Newspaper Advertising Source, 9/99

Poverty Rates by Race and Age

Area	Total (%)	By Race (%)				By Age (%)		
		White	Black	Other	Hisp.[2]	Under 5 years old	Under 18 years old	65 years and over
City	11.8	7.4	21.7	24.4	17.4	17.4	14.7	13.0
MSA[1]	10.2	6.5	20.5	18.2	15.9	13.3	11.5	15.3
U.S.	13.1	9.8	29.5	23.1	25.3	20.1	18.3	12.8

Note: Figures show the percent of people living below the poverty line in 1989. The average poverty threshold was $12,674 for a family of four in 1989; (1) Metropolitan Statistical Area - see Appendix A for areas included; (2) people of Hispanic origin can be of any race
Source: 1990 Census of Population and Housing, Summary Tape File 3C

EMPLOYMENT

Labor Force and Employment

Area	Civilian Labor Force			Workers Employed		
	Jun. 1998	Jun. 1999	% Chg.	Jun. 1998	Jun. 1999	% Chg.
City	164,765	171,135	3.9	161,548	168,571	4.3
MSA[1]	619,408	643,338	3.9	607,454	633,863	4.3
U.S.	138,798,000	140,666,000	1.3	132,265,000	134,395,000	1.6

Note: Data is not seasonally adjusted and covers workers 16 years of age and older; (1) Metropolitan Statistical Area - see Appendix A for areas included
Source: Bureau of Labor Statistics, http://stats.bls.gov

Unemployment Rate

Area	1998						1999					
	Jul.	Aug.	Sep.	Oct.	Nov.	Dec.	Jan.	Feb.	Mar.	Apr.	May.	Jun.
City	1.9	1.9	1.7	1.8	1.7	1.3	1.7	1.7	1.5	1.3	1.5	1.5
MSA[1]	1.9	1.8	1.6	1.6	1.5	1.3	1.6	1.6	1.5	1.3	1.5	1.5
U.S.	4.7	4.5	4.4	4.2	4.1	4.0	4.8	4.7	4.4	4.1	4.0	4.5

Note: Data is not seasonally adjusted and covers workers 16 years of age and older; all figures are percentages; (1) Metropolitan Statistical Area - see Appendix A for areas included
Source: Bureau of Labor Statistics, http://stats.bls.gov

Employment by Industry

Sector	MSA[1]		U.S.
	Number of Employees	Percent of Total	Percent of Total
Services	214,800	32.0	30.4
Retail Trade	108,800	16.2	17.7
Government	130,900	19.5	15.6
Manufacturing	84,100	12.5	14.3
Finance/Insurance/Real Estate	30,700	4.6	5.9
Wholesale Trade	32,000	4.8	5.4
Transportation/Public Utilities	29,300	4.4	5.3
Construction	n/a	n/a	5.0
Mining	n/a	n/a	0.4

Note: Figures cover non-farm employment as of 6/99 and are not seasonally adjusted;
(1) Metropolitan Statistical Area - see Appendix A for areas included; n/a not available
Source: Bureau of Labor Statistics, http://stats.bls.gov

Employment by Occupation

Occupation Category	City (%)	MSA[1] (%)	U.S. (%)
White Collar	73.4	68.9	58.1
Executive/Admin./Management	16.0	14.3	12.3
Professional	19.5	19.3	14.1
Technical & Related Support	6.6	6.5	3.7
Sales	14.2	11.8	11.8
Administrative Support/Clerical	17.2	16.9	16.3
Blue Collar	14.1	18.5	26.2
Precision Production/Craft/Repair	6.7	9.1	11.3
Machine Operators/Assem./Insp.	2.8	4.3	6.8
Transportation/Material Movers	2.3	2.5	4.1
Cleaners/Helpers/Laborers	2.5	2.6	3.9
Services	11.7	11.1	13.2
Farming/Forestry/Fishing	0.8	1.4	2.5

Note: Figures cover employed persons 16 years old and over;
(1) Metropolitan Statistical Area - see Appendix A for areas included
Source: 1990 Census of Population and Housing, Summary Tape File 3C

Occupational Employment Projections: 1996 - 2006

Occupations Expected to Have the Largest Job Growth (ranked by numerical growth)	Fast-Growing Occupations[1] (ranked by percent growth)
1. Cashiers	1. Occupational therapy assistants
2. Registered nurses	2. Computer engineers
3. General managers & top executives	3. Database administrators
4. Nursing aides/orderlies/attendants	4. Systems analysts
5. Salespersons, retail	5. Physical therapy assistants and aides
6. Child care workers, private household	6. Physical therapists
7. Food service workers	7. Occupational therapists
8. Marketing & sales, supervisors	8. Home health aides
9. Janitors/cleaners/maids, ex. priv. hshld.	9. Desktop publishers
10. Truck drivers, light	10. Respiratory therapists

Note: Projections cover North Carolina; (1) Excludes occupations with total job growth less than 300
Source: U.S. Department of Labor, Employment and Training Administration, America's Labor Market Information System (ALMIS)

TAXES

Major State and Local Tax Rates

State Corp. Income (%)	State Personal Income (%)	Residential Property (effective rate per $100)	Sales & Use State (%)	Local (%)	State Gasoline (cents/gallon)	State Cigarette (cents/pack)
7.0	6.0 - 7.75	n/a	4.0	2.0	21.6	5.0

Note: Personal/corporate income, sales, gasoline and cigarette tax rates as of January 1999. Property tax rates as of 1997.
Source: Federation of Tax Administrators, www.taxadmin.org; Washington D.C. Department of Finance and Revenue, Tax Rates and Tax Burdens in the District of Columbia: A Nationwide Comparison, July 1998; Chamber of Commerce, 1999

Total Taxes Per Capita and as a Percent of Income

Area	Per Capita Income ($)	Per Capita Taxes ($) Total	Federal	State/Local	Percent of Income (%) Total	Federal	State/Local
North Carolina	25,480	8,669	5,924	2,745	34.0	23.3	10.8
U.S.	27,876	9,881	6,690	3,191	35.4	24.0	11.4

Note: Figures are for 1998
Source: Tax Foundation, www.taxfoundation.org

Estimated Tax Burden

Area	State Income	Local Income	Property	Sales	Total
Raleigh	3,498	0	2,750	897	7,145

Note: The numbers are estimates of taxes paid by a married couple with two children and annual earnings of $75,000. Sales tax estimates assume they spend average amounts on food, clothing, household goods and gasoline. Property tax estimates assume they live in a $250,000 home.
Source: Kiplinger's Personal Finance Magazine, October 1998

**COMMERCIAL
REAL ESTATE**

Office Market

Class/ Location	Total Space (sq. ft.)	Vacant Space (sq. ft.)	Vac. Rate (%)	Under Constr. (sq. ft.)	Net Absorp. (sq. ft.)	Rental Rates ($/sq.ft./yr.)
Class A						
CBD	2,316,946	215,106	9.3	28,000	-1,973	15.50-20.00
Outside CBD	13,001,589	603,606	4.6	2,282,940	2,015,343	17.50-23.00
Class B						
CBD	1,057,874	87,562	8.3	0	-154,802	12.00-15.00
Outside CBD	6,265,748	328,534	5.2	0	253,230	14.50-17.00

Note: Data as of 10/98 and covers Raleigh, Cary, Chapel Hill, Durham and the Research Triangle; CBD = Central Business District; n/a not available;
Source: Society of Industrial and Office Realtors, 1999 Comparative Statistics of Industrial and Office Real Estate Markets

"More than 2.3 million sq. ft. of space is under Construction in the area. An additional 2.5 million sq. ft. is proposed, although not all will be built. While caution is the word around the town, Weeks/Lichton Corp. has plans for Paramount Center, a 160-acre office park in the 1-40 corridor near the Raleigh-Durham International Airport. The first phase of the project will be a 152,000 sq. ft. building for Tekelec, a telecommunications network equipment maker. Other major plans for the area include the construction of the $700 million, six-lane, 71-mile outer loop highway through North Raleigh that will open up new opportunities in that sub-market. While the local economy has been good, by mid-1999 the after effects of the international economy will become more evident." *Society of Industrial and Office Realtors, 1999 Comparative Statistics of Industrial and Office Real Estate Markets*

Industrial Market

Location	Total Space (sq. ft.)	Vacant Space (sq. ft.)	Vac. Rate (%)	Under Constr. (sq. ft.)	Net Absorp. (sq. ft.)	Net Lease ($/sq.ft./yr.)
Central City	n/a	n/a	n/a	n/a	n/a	n/a
Suburban	21,450,000	1,329,900	6.2	1,104,500	480,100	2.85-4.75

Note: Data as of 10/98 and covers Raleigh; n/a not available
Source: Society of Industrial and Office Realtors, 1999 Comparative Statistics of Industrial and Office Real Estate Markets

"Overall, growth in 1999 should be moderate compared to the runaway pace of the past few years. The market continues to prosper, but there are a few potential issues facing the area. One local official acknowledges that two of the area's largest developers, Highwoods Properties and Weeks/Lichtin, have begun to be more cautious about future developments by stepping away from purely speculative construction and demanding at least one or two definite tenants before beginning construction. The challenge of finding labor is a threat to the growth of the industrial sector. But some local officials have turned to the impact of electric deregulation as one possible solution to growth issues. Defenders of electric deregulation claim industrial development and industrial rates are directly linked, believing lower rates mean more industry and lower unemployment. Others feel that deregulation will eventually drive prices up." *Society of Industrial and Office Realtors, 1999 Comparative Statistics of Industrial and Office Real Estate Markets*

COMMERCIAL UTILITIES

Typical Monthly Electric Bills

Area	Commercial Service ($/month)		Industrial Service ($/month)	
	12 kW demand 1,500 kWh	100 kW demand 30,000 kWh	1,000 kW demand 400,000 kWh	20,000 kW demand 10,000,000 kWh
City	128	1,667	24,794	421,160
U.S.	150	2,174	23,995	508,569

Note: Based on rates in effect January 1, 1999
Source: Edison Electric Institute, Typical Residential, Commercial and Industrial Bills, Winter 1999

TRANSPORTATION

Transportation Statistics

Average minutes to work	18.1
Interstate highways	I-40; I-85
Bus lines	
In-city	Capital Area Transit
Inter-city	2
Passenger air service	
Airport	Raleigh-Durham International
Airlines	19
Aircraft departures	45,843 (1996)
Enplaned passengers	2,879,935 (1996)
Rail service	Amtrak
Motor freight carriers	34
Major waterways/ports	None

Source: Editor & Publisher Market Guide, 1999; FAA Airport Activity Statistics, 1997; Amtrak National Time Table, Northeast Timetable, Spring/Summer 1999; 1990 Census of Population and Housing, STF 3C; Chamber of Commerce/Economic Development 1999; Jane's Urban Transport Systems 1999-2000

Means of Transportation to Work

Area	Car/Truck/Van		Public Transportation			Bicycle	Walked	Other Means	Worked at Home
	Drove Alone	Car-pooled	Bus	Subway	Railroad				
City	79.0	11.3	2.7	0.0	0.0	0.4	3.5	1.1	2.0
MSA[1]	78.0	13.3	1.8	0.0	0.0	0.4	3.1	1.0	2.3
U.S.	73.2	13.4	3.0	1.5	0.5	0.4	3.9	1.2	3.0

Note: Figures shown are percentages and only include workers 16 years old and over;
(1) Metropolitan Statistical Area - see Appendix A for areas included
Source: 1990 Census of Population and Housing, Summary Tape File 3C

BUSINESSES

Major Business Headquarters

Company Name	1999 Rankings	
	Fortune 500	Forbes 500
Carolina Power & Light	465	-
General Parts	-	178

Note: Companies listed are located in the city; dashes indicate no ranking
Fortune 500: Companies that produce a 10-K are ranked 1 to 500 based on 1998 revenue
Forbes 500: Private companies are ranked 1 to 500 based on 1997 revenue
Source: Forbes, November 30, 1998; Fortune, April 26, 1999

Best Companies to Work For

Rex Healthcare, headquartered in Raleigh, is among the "100 Best Companies for Working Mothers." Criteria: fair wages, opportunities for women to advance, support for child care, flexible work schedules, family-friendly benefits, and work/life supports. *Working Mother, October 1998*

Fast-Growing Businesses

According to Deloitte & Touche LLP, Raleigh is home to one of America's 100 fastest-growing high-technology companies: Alliance of Professionals & Consultants. Companies are ranked by percentage growth in revenue over a five-year period. Criteria for inclusion: must be a U.S. company developing and/or providing technology products or services; company must have been in business for five years with 1993 revenues of at least $50,000. *Deloitte & Touche LLP, November 17, 1998*

HOTELS & MOTELS

Hotels/Motels

Area	Hotels/ Motels	Rooms	Luxury-Level Hotels/Motels		Average Minimum Rates ($)		
			♦♦♦♦	♦♦♦♦♦	♦♦	♦♦♦	♦♦♦♦
City	41	5,576	0	0	65	94	n/a
Airport	20	2,516	0	0	n/a	n/a	n/a
Suburbs	4	338	0	0	n/a	n/a	n/a
Total	65	8,430	0	0	n/a	n/a	n/a

Note: n/a not available; classifications range from one diamond (budget properties with basic amenities) to five diamond (luxury properties with the finest service, rooms and facilities).
Source: OAG, Business Travel Planner, Winter 1998-99

CONVENTION CENTERS

Major Convention Centers

Center Name	Meeting Rooms	Exhibit Space (sq. ft.)
Gov. W. Kerr Scott Bldg.	2	19,000
J.S. Dorton Arena	n/a	25,000
McKimmon Conference Center/NC State University	14	11,800
North Carolina State Fairgrounds	n/a	136,500
Raleigh Convention & Conference Center	23	106,500

Note: n/a not available
Source: Trade Shows Worldwide, 1998; Meetings & Conventions, 4/15/99; Sucessful Meetings, 3/31/98

Living Environment

COST OF LIVING

Cost of Living Index

Composite Index	Groceries	Housing	Utilities	Trans-portation	Health Care	Misc. Goods/ Services
100.8	99.4	106.0	102.6	93.0	104.4	98.5

Note: U.S. = 100; Figures are for Raleigh-Durham
Source: ACCRA, Cost of Living Index, 1st Quarter 1999

HOUSING

Median Home Prices and Housing Affordability

Area	Median Price[2] 1st Qtr. 1999 ($)	HOI[3] 1st Qtr. 1999	Afford-ability Rank[4]
MSA[1]	153,000	69.4	120
U.S.	134,000	69.6	–

Note: (1) Metropolitan Statistical Area - see Appendix A for areas included; (2) U.S. figures calculated from the sales of 524,324 new and existing homes in 181 markets; (3) Housing Opportunity Index - percent of homes sold that were within the reach of the median income household at the prevailing mortgage interest rate; (4) Rank is from 1-181 with 1 being most affordable
Source: National Association of Home Builders, Housing Opportunity Index, 1st Quarter 1999

Median Home Price Projection

It is projected that the median price of existing single-family homes in the metro area will increase by 4.5% in 1999. Nationwide, home prices are projected to increase 3.8%.
Kiplinger's Personal Finance Magazine, January 1999

Average New Home Price

Area	Price ($)
City[1]	148,691
U.S.	142,735

Note: Figures are based on a new home with 1,800 sq. ft. of living area on an 8,000 sq. ft. lot; (1) Raleigh-Durham
Source: ACCRA, Cost of Living Index, 1st Quarter 1999

Average Apartment Rent

Area	Rent ($/mth)
City[1]	756
U.S.	601

Note: Figures are based on an unfurnished two bedroom, 1-1/2 or 2 bath apartment, approximately 950 sq. ft. in size, excluding all utilities except water; (1) Raleigh-Durham
Source: ACCRA, Cost of Living Index, 1st Quarter 1999

RESIDENTIAL UTILITIES

Average Residential Utility Costs

Area	All Electric ($/mth)	Part Electric ($/mth)	Other Energy ($/mth)	Phone ($/mth)
City[1]	104.07	–	–	17.44
U.S.	100.02	55.73	43.33	19.71

Note: (1) Raleigh-Durham
Source: ACCRA, Cost of Living Index, 1st Quarter 1999

HEALTH CARE

Average Health Care Costs

Area	Hospital ($/day)	Doctor ($/visit)	Dentist ($/visit)
City[1]	345.49	59.25	73.50
U.S.	430.43	52.45	66.35

Note: Hospital—based on a semi-private room; Doctor—based on a general practitioner's routine exam of an established patient; Dentist—based on adult teeth cleaning and periodic oral exam; (1) (1) Raleigh-Durham
Source: ACCRA, Cost of Living Index, 1st Quarter 1999

Distribution of Office-Based Physicians

Area	Family/Gen. Practitioners	Specialists		
		Medical	Surgical	Other
MSA[1]	276	922	641	887

Note: Data as of 12/31/97; (1) Metropolitan Statistical Area - see Appendix A for areas included
Source: American Medical Assn., Physician Characteristics & Distribution in the U.S., 1999

Hospitals

Raleigh has 3 general medical and surgical hospitals, 2 psychiatric, 1 alcoholism and other chemical dependency, 1 prison hospital. *AHA Guide to the Healthcare Field, 1998-99*

EDUCATION

Public School District Statistics

District Name	Num. Sch.	Enroll.	Classroom Teachers	Pupils per Teacher	Minority Pupils (%)	Current Exp.[1] ($/pupil)
Bonner Academy	1	75	n/a	n/a	n/a	n/a
Exploris	1	53	n/a	n/a	n/a	n/a
John H Baker Jr High	1	25	n/a	n/a	n/a	n/a
Magellan Charter	1	292	n/a	n/a	n/a	n/a
NC Schools For The Deaf/Blind	4	870	224	3.9	n/a	n/a
Wake County Schools	105	89,772	6,024	14.9	33.2	4,661

Note: Data covers the 1997-1998 school year unless otherwise noted; (1) Data covers fiscal year 1996; SD = School District; ISD = Independent School District; n/a not available
Source: National Center for Education Statistics, Common Core of Data Public Education Agency Universe 1997-98; National Center for Education Statistics, Characteristics of the 100 Largest Public Elementary and Secondary School Districts in the United States: 1997-98, July 1999

Educational Quality

School District	Education Quotient[1]	Graduate Outcome[2]	Community Index[3]	Resource Index[4]
Wake County	114.0	110.0	141.0	115.0

Note: Nearly 1,000 secondary school districts were rated in terms of educational quality. The scores range from a low of 50 to a high of 150; (1) Average of the Graduate Outcome, Community and Resource indexes; (2) Based on graduation rates and college board scores (SAT/ACT); (3) Based on the surrounding community's average level of education and the area's average income level; (4) Based on teacher salaries, per-pupil expenditures and student-teacher ratios.
Source: Expansion Management, Ratings Issue, 1998

Educational Attainment by Race

Area	High School Graduate (%)					Bachelor's Degree (%)				
	Total	White	Black	Other	Hisp.[2]	Total	White	Black	Other	Hisp.[2]
City	86.6	92.1	70.3	85.6	81.8	40.6	47.0	19.9	55.4	45.0
MSA[1]	82.4	87.2	66.0	86.3	77.2	34.8	39.2	17.8	55.6	36.6
U.S.	75.2	77.9	63.1	60.4	49.8	20.3	21.5	11.4	19.4	9.2

Note: Figures shown cover persons 25 years old and over; (1) Metropolitan Statistical Area - see Appendix A for areas included; (2) people of Hispanic origin can be of any race
Source: 1990 Census of Population and Housing, Summary Tape File 3C

School Enrollment by Type

Area	Preprimary				Elementary/High School			
	Public		Private		Public		Private	
	Enrollment	%	Enrollment	%	Enrollment	%	Enrollment	%
City	1,680	44.8	2,074	55.2	24,478	93.2	1,782	6.8
MSA[1]	6,751	46.9	7,652	53.1	99,864	92.8	7,735	7.2
U.S.	2,679,029	59.5	1,824,256	40.5	38,379,689	90.2	4,187,099	9.8

Note: Figures shown cover persons 3 years old and over;
(1) Metropolitan Statistical Area - see Appendix A for areas included
Source: 1990 Census of Population and Housing, Summary Tape File 3C

School Enrollment by Race

Area	Preprimary (%)				Elementary/High School (%)			
	White	Black	Other	Hisp.[1]	White	Black	Other	Hisp.[1]
City	75.4	21.2	3.4	1.9	59.1	37.3	3.6	1.2
MSA[2]	78.1	19.4	2.6	1.2	65.4	31.9	2.7	1.2
U.S.	80.4	12.5	7.1	7.8	74.1	15.6	10.3	12.5

Note: Figures shown cover persons 3 years old and over; (1) people of Hispanic origin can be of any
race; (2) Metropolitan Statistical Area - see Appendix A for areas included
Source: 1990 Census of Population and Housing, Summary Tape File 3C

Classroom Teacher Salaries in Public Schools

District	B.A. Degree		M.A. Degree		Maximum	
	Min. ($)	Rank[1]	Max. ($)	Rank[1]	Max. ($)	Rank[1]
Raleigh	24,365	79	48,613	30	51,504	42
Average	26,980	-	46,065	-	51,435	-

Note: Salaries are for 1997-1998; (1) Rank ranges from 1 to 100
Source: American Federation of Teachers, Survey & Analysis of Salary Trends, 1998

Higher Education

Two-Year Colleges		Four-Year Colleges		Medical Schools	Law Schools	Voc/ Tech
Public	Private	Public	Private			
1	0	1	4	0	0	6

Source: College Blue Book, Occupational Education, 1997; Medical School Admission Requirements,
1999-2000; Peterson's Guide to Two-Year Colleges, 1999; Peterson's Guide to Four-Year Colleges,
2000; Barron's Guide to Law Schools, 1999

MAJOR EMPLOYERS

Major Employers

Exide Electronics Group
HCA Raleigh Community Hospital
News & Observer Publishing
Amerimark Building Products
Wakemed (hospitals)

GE Capital Mortgage Corp.
Long Group (help supply services)
Penncorp Financial
Rex Hospital
RDS Corp. (building maintenance services)

Note: Companies listed are located in the city
Source: Dun's Business Rankings, 1999; Ward's Business Directory, 1998

PUBLIC SAFETY

Crime Rate

Area	All Crimes	Violent Crimes				Property Crimes		
		Murder	Forcible Rape	Robbery	Aggrav. Assault	Burglary	Larceny -Theft	Motor Vehicle Theft
City	7,747.3	9.3	41.0	292.4	564.8	1,468.3	4,805.9	565.6
Suburbs[1]	5,822.7	8.1	28.7	232.1	280.8	1,304.0	3,518.4	450.6
MSA[2]	6,295.1	8.4	31.7	246.9	350.5	1,344.4	3,834.4	478.8
U.S.	4,922.7	6.8	35.9	186.1	382.0	919.6	2,886.5	505.8

Note: Crime rate is the number of crimes per 100,000 pop.; (1) defined as all areas within the MSA but
located outside the central city; (2) Metropolitan Statistical Area - see Appendix A for areas incl.
Source: FBI Uniform Crime Reports, 1997

RECREATION

Culture and Recreation

Museums	Symphony Orchestras	Opera Companies	Dance Companies	Professional Theatres	Zoos	Pro Sports Teams
5	1	1	0	2	0	0

Source: International Directory of the Performing Arts, 1997; Official Museum Directory, 1999; Stern's Performing Arts Directory, 1997; USA Today Four Sport Stadium Guide, 1997; Chamber of Commerce/Economic Development, 1999

Library System

The Wake County Public Library System has 17 branches, holdings of 1,072,645 volumes, and a budget of $9,132,210 (1995-1996). *American Library Directory, 1998-1999*

MEDIA

Newspapers

Name	Type	Freq.	Distribution	Circulation
Baptist Informer	Black	1x/mo	Local	9,000
The Carolinian	Black	2x/wk	Area	17,700
Middle American News	General	1x/mo	U.S.	100,000
The News & Observer	General	7x/wk	Local	159,844

Note: Includes newspapers with circulations of 1,000 or more located in the city;
Source: Burrelle's Media Directory, 1999 Edition

Television Stations

Name	Ch.	Affiliation	Type	Owner
WRAL	n/a	CBST	Commercial	Capitol Broadcasting Company Inc.
WNCN	17	NBCT	Commercial	General Electric Corporation
WLFL	22	FBC/UPN	Commercial	Sinclair Communications Inc.
WRDC	28	FBC/UPN	Commercial	Glencairn Communications
WRPX	47	PAXTV	Commercial	DP Media Inc.
WRAZ	50	FBC	Commercial	Carolina Broadcasting Services Inc.

Note: Stations included broadcast in the Raleigh metro area; n/a not available
Source: Burrelle's Media Directory, 1999 Edition

AM Radio Stations

Call Letters	Freq. (kHz)	Target Audience	Station Format	Music Format
WETC	540	G/M	M/N	Christian/Country/Latin
WRDT	570	General	M/N/S/T	R&B
WPTF	680	General	T	n/a
WRBZ	850	General	N/S/T	n/a
WPJL	1240	G/R	M/N/S	Christian
WCRY	1460	General	M	Christian
WDUR	1490	General	M	Gospel
WCLY	1550	Religious	M	Christian

Note: Stations included broadcast in the Raleigh metro area; n/a not available
Target Audience: A=Asian; B=Black; C=Christian; E=Ethnic; F=French; G=General; H=Hispanic; M=Men; N=Native American; R=Religious; S=Senior Citizen; W=Women; Y=Young Adult; Z=Children
Station Format: E=Educational; M=Music; N=News; S=Sports; T=Talk
Source: Burrelle's Media Directory, 1999 Edition

FM Radio Stations

Call Letters	Freq. (mHz)	Target Audience	Station Format	Music Format
WKNC	88.1	General	E/M/N/S	Alternative/AOR/Christian/Classic Rock/Jazz/MOR/R&B/Urban Contemporary
WSHA	88.9	General	M	Christian/Jazz/R&B
WCPE	89.7	General	E/M	Classical
WRSN	93.9	General	M/N	Adult Contemporary
WQDR	94.7	General	M	Country
WBBB	96.1	n/a	M	Classic Rock
WKIX	96.9	General	M	Country
WQOK	97.5	B/G	M/N/S	Urban Contemporary
WTRG	100.7	General	M/N/S	Oldies
WRAL	101.5	General	M	Adult Contemporary
WNNL	103.9	B/G/R	M	Gospel
WFXK	104.3	B/G	M	Urban Contemporary
WDCG	105.1	General	M	Top 40
WRDU	106.1	General	M/N/S	AOR
WFXC	107.1	B/G	M	Urban Contemporary

Note: Stations included broadcast in the Raleigh metro area; n/a not available
Station Format: E=Educational; M=Music; N=News; S=Sports; T=Talk
Target Audience: A=Asian; B=Black; C=Christian; E=Ethnic; F=French; G=General; H=Hispanic; M=Men; N=Native American; R=Religious; S=Senior Citizen; W=Women; Y=Young Adult; Z=Children
Music Format: AOR=Album Oriented Rock; MOR=Middle-of-the-Road
Source: Burrelle's Media Directory, 1999 Edition

CLIMATE

Average and Extreme Temperatures

Temperature	Jan	Feb	Mar	Apr	May	Jun	Jul	Aug	Sep	Oct	Nov	Dec	Yr.
Extreme High (°F)	79	84	90	95	97	104	105	105	104	98	88	79	105
Average High (°F)	50	53	61	72	79	86	89	87	81	72	62	53	71
Average Temp. (°F)	40	43	50	59	67	75	78	77	71	60	51	42	60
Average Low (°F)	29	31	38	46	55	63	68	67	60	48	39	32	48
Extreme Low (°F)	-9	5	11	23	29	38	48	46	37	19	11	4	-9

Note: Figures cover the years 1948-1990
Source: National Climatic Data Center, International Station Meteorological Climate Summary, 3/95

Average Precipitation/Snowfall/Humidity

Precip./Humidity	Jan	Feb	Mar	Apr	May	Jun	Jul	Aug	Sep	Oct	Nov	Dec	Yr.
Avg. Precip. (in.)	3.4	3.6	3.6	2.9	3.9	3.6	4.4	4.4	3.2	2.9	3.0	3.1	42.0
Avg. Snowfall (in.)	2	3	1	Tr	0	0	0	0	0	0	Tr	1	8
Avg. Rel. Hum. 7am (%)	79	79	79	80	84	86	88	91	91	90	84	81	84
Avg. Rel. Hum. 4pm (%)	53	49	46	43	51	54	57	59	57	53	51	53	52

Note: Figures cover the years 1948-1990; Tr = Trace amounts (<0.05 in. of rain; <0.5 in. of snow)
Source: National Climatic Data Center, International Station Meteorological Climate Summary, 3/95

Weather Conditions

Temperature			Daytime Sky			Precipitation		
32°F & below	45°F & below	90°F & above	Clear	Partly cloudy	Cloudy	0.01 inch or more precip.	0.1 inch or more snow/ice	Thunder-storms
77	160	39	98	143	124	110	3	42

Note: Figures are average number of days per year and covers the years 1948-1990
Source: National Climatic Data Center, International Station Meteorological Climate Summary, 3/95

AIR & WATER QUALITY

Maximum Pollutant Concentrations

	Particulate Matter (ug/m³)	Carbon Monoxide (ppm)	Sulfur Dioxide (ppm)	Nitrogen Dioxide (ppm)	Ozone (ppm)	Lead (ug/m³)
MSA[1] Level	59	7	n/a	n/a	0.12	0.00
NAAQS[2]	150	9	0.140	0.053	0.12	1.50
Met NAAQS?	Yes	Yes	n/a	n/a	Yes	Yes

Note: (1) Metropolitan Statistical Area - see Appendix A for areas included; (2) National Ambient Air Quality Standards; ppm = parts per million; ug/m³ = micrograms per cubic meter; n/a not available
Source: EPA, National Air Quality and Emissions Trends Report, 1997

Pollutant Standards Index

In the Raleigh MSA (see Appendix A for areas included), the Pollutant Standards Index (PSI) exceeded 100 on 24 days in 1997. A PSI value greater than 100 indicates that air quality would be in the unhealthful range on that day. *EPA, National Air Quality and Emissions Trends Report, 1997*

Drinking Water

Water System Name	Pop. Served	Primary Water Source Type	Number of Violations in 1998	Type of Violation/ Contaminants
City of Raleigh	273,011	Surface	None	None

Note: Data as of July 10, 1999
Source: EPA, Office of Ground Water and Drinking Water, Safe Drinking Water Information System

Raleigh tap water is neutral, soft and fluoridated.
Editor & Publisher Market Guide, 1999

Richmond, Virginia

Background

Richmond is the genteel and aristocratic capital of Virginia. Home to blueblooded old families such as the Byrds, Lees, and Davises, Richmond has played a vital role in both U.S. and Confederate histories.

Richmond was first claimed in 1607 as English territory by John Smith—of Pocahantas fame—and Christopher Newport. In 1679, the area was granted to William Byrd I, with the understanding that he establish a settlement. His son, William Byrd II continued his father's work, and along with William Mayo, surveyed lots for what was to be named Richmond.

During the Revolutionary War, Richmond played host to two Virginia Conventions. These Conventions, which held founding fathers, such as George Washington, Thomas Jefferson, Benjamin Harrison, and Patrick Henry in the same room, ratified the Constitution as the law of the land for the emerging nation.

No sooner, however, had the United States congealed as a nation when dissension split the nation in two, causing fragmentation once again. During this time, Richmond was called upon to serve as the Confederate States' Capital, although the city was one of the most reluctant to secede. From the Roman Temple inspired Capitol, designed by Thomas Jefferson, Jefferson Davis ruled as President of the Confederacy.

Not surprisingly, today Richmond ranks high in its position as an authority on both Southern and Virginia history. The Virginia State Library, the Confederate Museum, The Virginia Historical Society, and its state capitol attest to this.

After its moments in the spotlight, Richmond wisely stepped down to a position of economic stability. Richmond witnessed low unemployment rates during both the depression and the late 1970s. With restoration of historic districts such as Jackson Ward—a neighborhood that saw its first Black-owned banks and insurance companies, Shockoe Slip—an old milling and tobacco center, and The Fan District—a neighborhood of 19th century townhouses and the Virginia Commonwealth University, whose streets fan out to the west, a new vitality has come to downtown Richmond.

Virginia has experienced recent economic growth because of its attraction to companies involved in high-technology. There was over $4 billion in economic development activity in 1995 with the northern part of the state being home to 300 high-tech companies. Richmond is the site of a $3 billion Motorola microprocessor facility, and the company, along with Siemens, will invest over another billion in the White Oak Semiconductor Plant, also in Richmond. One of the new research and development parks, the Virginia Biotechnology Research Park, is also located in Richmond. *World Trade, 4/97*

Richmond's climate is classified as modified continental with its warm summer and humid, mild winters. Snow only remains on the ground for a day or so. Ice storms are not uncommon but are not usually severe enough to cause considerable damage.

Hurricanes and tropical storms, when they occur, are responsible for the flooding during the summer and early fall months. Tornadoes are infrequent but some notable occurrences have been observed in the Richmond area.

General Rankings and Evaluative Comments

- Richmond was ranked #1 out of 44 mid-sized, southern metropolitan areas in *Money's* 1998 survey of "The Best Places to Live in America." The survey was conducted by first contacting 512 representative households nationwide and asking them to rank 37 quality-of-life factors on a scale of 1 to 10. Next, a demographic profile was compiled on the 300 largest metropolitan statistical areas in the U.S. The numbers were crunched together to arrive at an overall ranking (things Americans consider most important, like clean air and water, low crime and good schools, received extra weight). Unlike previous years, the 1998 rankings were broken down by region (northeast, midwest, south, west) and population size (100,000 to 249,999; 250,000 to 999,999; 1 million plus). The city had a nationwide ranking of #160 out of 300 in 1997 and #135 out of 300 in 1996. *Money, July 1998; Money, July 1997; Money, September 1996*

- *Ladies Home Journal* ranked America's 200 largest cities based on the qualities women care about most. Richmond ranked #46 out of 200. Criteria: low crime rate, well-paying jobs, quality health and child care, good public schools, the presence of women in government, size of the gender wage gap, number of sexual-harassment and discrimination complaints filed, unemployment and divorce rates, commute times, population density, number of houses of worship, parks and cultural offerings, number of women's health specialists, how well a community's women cared for themselves, complexion kindness index based on UV radiation levels, odds of finding affordable fashions, rental rates for romance movies, champagne sales and other matters of the heart. *Ladies Home Journal, November 1998*

- Zero Population Growth ranked 229 cities in terms of children's health, safety, and economic well-being. Richmond was ranked #101 out of 112 independent cities (cities with populations greater than 100,000 which were neither Major Cities nor Suburbs/Outer Cities) and was given a grade of D. Criteria: total population, percent of population under 18 years of age, household language, percent population change, percent of births to teens, infant mortality rate, percent of low birth weights, dropout rate, enrollment in preprimary school, violent and property crime rates, unemployment rate, percent of children in poverty, percent of owner occupied units, number of bad air days, percent of public transportation commuters, and average travel time to work. *Zero Population Growth, Children's Environmental Index, Fall 1999*

- Cognetics studied 273 metro areas in the United States, ranking them by entrepreneurial activity. Richmond was ranked #30 out of the 50 largest metro areas. Criteria: Significant Starts (firms started in the last 10 years that still employ at least 5 people) and Young Growers (percent of firms 10 years old or less that grew significantly during the last 4 years). *Cognetics, "Entrepreneurial Hot Spots: The Best Places in America to Start and Grow a Company," 1998*

- Reliastar Financial Corp. ranked the 125 largest metropolitan areas according to the general financial security of residents. Richmond was ranked #44 out of 125 with a score of 4.8. The score indicates the percentage a metropolitan area is above or below the metropolitan norm. A metro area with a score of 10.6 is 10.6% above the metro average. Criteria: Earnings and Wealth Potential (household income, education, net assets, cost of living); Safety Net (health insurance, retirement savings, life insurance, income support programs); Personal Threats (unemployment rate, low-income households, crime rate); Community Economic Vitality (cost of community services, job quality, job creation, housing costs). *Reliastar Financial Corp., "The Best Cities to Earn and Save Money," 1999 Edition*

Business Environment

STATE ECONOMY

State Economic Profile

" Virginia has begun to slow from its recent expansion. VA's above-average growth is largely a result of the expansion of high-tech firms in Northern Virginia. Slower growth in the Hampton Roads and Richmond areas stems from a slowdown in the manufacturing and farm sectors. VA's demographic situation is solid, and its housing and construction markets remain vibrant. Although a slowing US economy will be a drag on VA, the long-term outlook for Virginia is strong, above-average growth.

Northern Virginia has become less dependent upon defense spending as its economy has diversified into commercial internet and software development. The Tidewater area is a different story. Both consolidation among shipbuilders and declining Naval purchasers are likely to result in job losses in VA's shipbuilding industry. Job reductions have also taken place at the Port of Hampton Roads as VA's exports have fallen. The opening of the Gateway Plant will diversify southeastern VA's economy away from its dependence on military spending.

VA's housing market was one of the hottest in 1998. Home sales were up over 25% in 1998 with activity occurring in all parts of the state. Price appreciation was strong in northern, central and southeastern VA. While permit activity was flat in Richmond, both northern VA and Hampton Roads saw permit activity increase by at least 10%. Sales and starts should moderate slightly in 1999.

VA has some of the nation's strongest economic fundamentals: business friendly environment, an educated workforce, strong demographics and a diversified economy. VA's most immediate constraint is its tight labor market." *National Association of Realtors, Economic Profiles: The Fifty States and the District of Columbia, http://nar.realtor.com/databank/profiles.htm*

IMPORTS/EXPORTS

Total Export Sales

Area	1994 ($000)	1995 ($000)	1996 ($000)	1997 ($000)	% Chg. 1994-97	% Chg. 1996-97
MSA[1]	5,260,571	5,389,333	5,609,352	5,571,698	5.9	-0.7
U.S.	512,415,609	583,030,524	622,827,063	687,597,999	34.2	10.4

Note: (1) Metropolitan Statistical Area - see Appendix A for areas included
Source: U.S. Department of Commerce, International Trade Association, Metropolitan Area Exports: An Export Performance Report on Over 250 U.S. Cities, November 10, 1998

CITY FINANCES

City Government Finances

Component	FY92 ($000)	FY92 (per capita $)
Revenue	715,137	3,571.27
Expenditure	739,700	3,693.94
Debt Outstanding	1,004,338	5,015.50
Cash & Securities	685,531	3,423.43

Source: U.S. Bureau of the Census, City Government Finances: 1991-92

City Government Revenue by Source

Source	FY92 ($000)	FY92 (per capita $)	FY92 (%)
From Federal Government	36,987	184.71	5.2
From State Governments	159,005	794.04	22.2
From Local Governments	1,948	9.73	0.3
Property Taxes	165,944	828.70	23.2
General Sales Taxes	20,321	101.48	2.8
Selective Sales Taxes	40,968	204.59	5.7
Income Taxes	0	0.00	0.0
Current Charges	89,623	447.56	12.5
Utility/Liquor Store	123,694	617.71	17.3
Employee Retirement[1]	19,169	95.73	2.7
Other	57,478	287.04	8.0

Note: (1) Excludes "city contributions," classified as "nonrevenue," intragovernmental transfers.
Source: U.S. Bureau of the Census, City Government Finances: 1991-92

City Government Expenditures by Function

Function	FY92 ($000)	FY92 (per capita $)	FY92 (%)
Educational Services	184,048	919.10	24.9
Employee Retirement[1]	22,315	111.44	3.0
Environment/Housing	135,238	675.36	18.3
Government Administration	31,063	155.12	4.2
Interest on General Debt	33,199	165.79	4.5
Public Safety	95,459	476.71	12.9
Social Services	56,666	282.98	7.7
Transportation	18,848	94.12	2.5
Utility/Liquor Store	142,172	709.98	19.2
Other	20,692	103.33	2.8

Note: (1) Payments to beneficiaries including withdrawal of contributions.
Source: U.S. Bureau of the Census, City Government Finances: 1991-92

Municipal Bond Ratings

Area	Moody's	S & P
Richmond	A1	n/a

Note: n/a not available; n/r not rated
Source: Moody's Bond Record, 6/99

POPULATION

Population Growth

Area	1980	1990	% Chg. 1980-90	July 1998 Estimate	% Chg. 1990-98
City	219,214	203,056	-7.4	194,173	-4.4
MSA[1]	761,311	865,640	13.7	958,352	10.7
U.S.	226,545,805	248,765,170	9.8	270,299,000	8.7

Note: (1) Metropolitan Statistical Area - see Appendix A for areas included;
July 1998 MSA population estimate was calculated by the editors
Source: 1980/1990 Census of Housing and Population, Summary Tape File 3C;
Census Bureau Population Estimates 1998

Population Characteristics

Race	City 1980 Population	%	City 1990 Population	%	% Chg. 1980-90	MSA[1] 1990 Population	%
White	104,984	47.9	87,928	43.3	-16.2	595,909	68.8
Black	112,426	51.3	112,406	55.4	-0.0	252,376	29.2
Amer Indian/Esk/Aleut	330	0.2	441	0.2	33.6	2,610	0.3
Asian/Pacific Islander	1,110	0.5	1,664	0.8	49.9	11,768	1.4
Other	364	0.2	617	0.3	69.5	2,977	0.3
Hispanic Origin[2]	2,210	1.0	1,744	0.9	-21.1	8,788	1.0

Note: (1) Metropolitan Statistical Area - see Appendix A for areas included;
(2) people of Hispanic origin can be of any race
Source: 1980/1990 Census of Housing and Population, Summary Tape File 3C

Ancestry

Area	German	Irish	English	Italian	U.S.	French	Polish	Dutch
City	9.3	7.4	13.2	1.8	4.2	1.8	1.0	0.9
MSA[1]	15.8	12.4	18.9	2.8	8.0	2.8	1.5	1.5
U.S.	23.3	15.6	13.1	5.9	5.3	4.2	3.8	2.5

Note: Figures are percentages and include persons that reported multiple ancestry (eg. if a person reported being Irish and Italian, they were included in both columns); (1) Metropolitan Statistical Area - see Appendix A for areas included
Source: 1990 Census of Population and Housing, Summary Tape File 3C

Age

Area	Median Age (Years)	Age Distribution (%) Under 5	Under 18	18-24	25-44	45-64	65+	80+
City	33.1	6.9	20.8	12.9	33.9	17.1	15.3	3.7
MSA[1]	33.2	7.2	24.3	10.3	35.4	18.7	11.3	2.3
U.S.	32.9	7.3	25.6	10.5	32.6	18.7	12.5	2.8

Note: (1) Metropolitan Statistical Area - see Appendix A for areas included
Source: 1990 Census of Population and Housing, Summary Tape File 3C

Male/Female Ratio

Area	Number of males per 100 females (all ages)	Number of males per 100 females (18 years old+)
City	83.9	80.0
MSA[1]	90.7	87.1
U.S.	95.0	91.9

Note: (1) Metropolitan Statistical Area - see Appendix A for areas included
Source: 1990 Census of Population, General Population Characteristics

INCOME

Per Capita/Median/Average Income

Area	Per Capita ($)	Median Household ($)	Average Household ($)
City	13,993	23,551	32,497
MSA[1]	15,848	33,489	40,785
U.S.	14,420	30,056	38,453

Note: All figures are for 1989; (1) Metropolitan Statistical Area - see Appendix A for areas included
Source: 1990 Census of Population and Housing, Summary Tape File 3C

Household Income Distribution by Race

Income ($)	City (%)					U.S. (%)				
	Total	White	Black	Other	Hisp.[1]	Total	White	Black	Other	Hisp.[1]
Less than 5,000	10.6	5.0	16.4	12.1	3.6	6.2	4.8	15.2	8.6	8.8
5,000 - 9,999	11.1	9.5	13.1	4.7	8.5	9.3	8.6	14.2	9.9	11.1
10,000 - 14,999	10.9	8.9	12.9	10.3	12.5	8.8	8.5	11.0	9.8	11.0
15,000 - 24,999	19.8	18.8	20.6	27.9	30.4	17.5	17.3	18.9	18.5	20.5
25,000 - 34,999	15.5	16.1	14.9	16.9	19.6	15.8	16.1	14.2	15.4	16.4
35,000 - 49,999	15.1	17.3	12.9	15.1	8.2	17.9	18.6	13.3	16.1	16.0
50,000 - 74,999	10.1	12.9	7.3	8.3	10.2	15.0	15.8	9.3	13.4	11.1
75,000 - 99,999	3.4	5.3	1.5	2.5	3.0	5.1	5.5	2.6	4.7	3.1
100,000+	3.4	6.2	0.5	2.3	4.0	4.4	4.8	1.3	3.7	1.9

Note: All figures are for 1989; (1) people of Hispanic origin can be of any race
Source: 1990 Census of Population and Housing, Summary Tape File 3C

Effective Buying Income

Area	Per Capita ($)	Median Household ($)	Average Household ($)
City	14,718	25,049	34,283
MSA[1]	17,593	36,893	45,150
U.S.	16,803	34,536	45,243

Note: Data as of 1/1/99; (1) Metropolitan Statistical Area - see Appendix A for areas included
Source: Standard Rate & Data Service, Newspaper Advertising Source, 9/99

Effective Household Buying Income Distribution

Area	% of Households Earning						
	$10,000 -$19,999	$20,000 -$34,999	$35,000 -$49,999	$50,000 -$74,999	$75,000 -$99,000	$100,000 -$124,999	$125,000 and up
City	20.7	25.2	15.8	11.8	3.7	1.4	1.8
MSA[1]	14.3	23.0	19.9	21.5	7.1	2.1	2.1
U.S.	16.0	22.6	18.2	18.9	7.2	2.4	2.7

Note: Data as of 1/1/99; (1) Metropolitan Statistical Area - see Appendix A for areas included
Source: Standard Rate & Data Service, Newspaper Advertising Source, 9/99

Poverty Rates by Race and Age

Area	Total (%)	By Race (%)				By Age (%)		
		White	Black	Other	Hisp.[2]	Under 5 years old	Under 18 years old	65 years and over
City	20.9	10.3	28.9	19.0	17.1	37.6	35.8	16.5
MSA[1]	9.8	5.0	21.1	10.9	11.1	16.1	14.0	11.3
U.S.	13.1	9.8	29.5	23.1	25.3	20.1	18.3	12.8

Note: Figures show the percent of people living below the poverty line in 1989. The average poverty threshold was $12,674 for a family of four in 1989; (1) Metropolitan Statistical Area - see Appendix A for areas included; (2) people of Hispanic origin can be of any race
Source: 1990 Census of Population and Housing, Summary Tape File 3C

EMPLOYMENT

Labor Force and Employment

Area	Civilian Labor Force			Workers Employed		
	Jun. 1998	Jun. 1999	% Chg.	Jun. 1998	Jun. 1999	% Chg.
City	97,181	100,150	3.1	92,839	96,159	3.6
MSA[1]	510,747	527,636	3.3	494,988	512,688	3.6
U.S.	138,798,000	140,666,000	1.3	132,265,000	134,395,000	1.6

Note: Data is not seasonally adjusted and covers workers 16 years of age and older; (1) Metropolitan Statistical Area - see Appendix A for areas included
Source: Bureau of Labor Statistics, http://stats.bls.gov

Unemployment Rate

Area	1998						1999					
	Jul.	Aug.	Sep.	Oct.	Nov.	Dec.	Jan.	Feb.	Mar.	Apr.	May.	Jun.
City	3.8	4.0	4.3	4.1	3.7	3.3	3.4	3.2	3.1	2.9	3.5	4.0
MSA[1]	2.6	2.7	2.9	2.7	2.5	2.3	2.4	2.3	2.1	2.0	2.5	2.8
U.S.	4.7	4.5	4.4	4.2	4.1	4.0	4.8	4.7	4.4	4.1	4.0	4.5

Note: Data is not seasonally adjusted and covers workers 16 years of age and older; all figures are percentages; (1) Metropolitan Statistical Area - see Appendix A for areas included
Source: Bureau of Labor Statistics, http://stats.bls.gov

Employment by Industry

Sector	MSA[1]		U.S.
	Number of Employees	Percent of Total	Percent of Total
Services	145,300	26.4	30.4
Retail Trade	96,700	17.6	17.7
Government	103,200	18.8	15.6
Manufacturing	60,700	11.0	14.3
Finance/Insurance/Real Estate	47,000	8.6	5.9
Wholesale Trade	32,000	5.8	5.4
Transportation/Public Utilities	29,700	5.4	5.3
Construction	34,000	6.2	5.0
Mining	800	0.1	0.4

Note: Figures cover non-farm employment as of 6/99 and are not seasonally adjusted;
(1) Metropolitan Statistical Area - see Appendix A for areas included
Source: Bureau of Labor Statistics, http://stats.bls.gov

Employment by Occupation

Occupation Category	City (%)	MSA[1] (%)	U.S. (%)
White Collar	59.9	63.1	58.1
Executive/Admin./Management	11.5	13.9	12.3
Professional	15.9	14.3	14.1
Technical & Related Support	3.7	4.1	3.7
Sales	11.0	12.3	11.8
Administrative Support/Clerical	17.9	18.5	16.3
Blue Collar	21.4	23.5	26.2
Precision Production/Craft/Repair	7.3	10.9	11.3
Machine Operators/Assem./Insp.	6.0	5.2	6.8
Transportation/Material Movers	4.0	3.8	4.1
Cleaners/Helpers/Laborers	4.0	3.6	3.9
Services	17.9	12.4	13.2
Farming/Forestry/Fishing	0.9	1.1	2.5

Note: Figures cover employed persons 16 years old and over;
(1) Metropolitan Statistical Area - see Appendix A for areas included
Source: 1990 Census of Population and Housing, Summary Tape File 3C

Occupational Employment Projections: 1996 - 2006

Occupations Expected to Have the Largest Job Growth (ranked by numerical growth)	Fast-Growing Occupations[1] (ranked by percent growth)
1. Systems analysts	1. Desktop publishers
2. Cashiers	2. Personal and home care aides
3. Computer engineers	3. Physical therapy assistants and aides
4. General managers & top executives	4. Medical assistants
5. Salespersons, retail	5. Physical therapists
6. Janitors/cleaners/maids, ex. priv. hshld.	6. Occupational therapists
7. Database administrators	7. Home health aides
8. Receptionists and information clerks	8. Manicurists
9. Engineering/science/computer sys. mgrs.	9. Paralegals
10. Truck drivers, light	10. Bill and account collectors

Note: Projections cover Virginia; (1) Excludes occupations with total job growth less than 300
Source: U.S. Department of Labor, Employment and Training Administration, America's Labor Market Information System (ALMIS)

TAXES

Major State and Local Tax Rates

State Corp. Income (%)	State Personal Income (%)	Residential Property (effective rate per $100)	Sales & Use State (%)	Sales & Use Local (%)	State Gasoline (cents/ gallon)	State Cigarette (cents/ pack)
6.0	2.0 - 5.75	n/a	3.5	1.0	17.5[a]	2.5[b]

Note: Personal/corporate income, sales, gasoline and cigarette tax rates as of January 1999. Property tax rates as of 1997; (a) Does not include a 2% local option tax; (b) Counties and cities may impose an additional tax of 2 - 15 cents per pack
Source: Federation of Tax Administrators, www.taxadmin.org; Washington D.C. Department of Finance and Revenue, Tax Rates and Tax Burdens in the District of Columbia: A Nationwide Comparison, July 1998; Chamber of Commerce, 1999

Total Taxes Per Capita and as a Percent of Income

Area	Per Capita Income ($)	Per Capita Taxes ($) Total	Federal	State/ Local	Percent of Income (%) Total	Federal	State/ Local
Virginia	28,326	9,650	6,727	2,923	34.1	23.7	10.3
U.S.	27,876	9,881	6,690	3,191	35.4	24.0	11.4

Note: Figures are for 1998
Source: Tax Foundation, www.taxfoundation.org

COMMERCIAL REAL ESTATE

Office Market

Class/ Location	Total Space (sq. ft.)	Vacant Space (sq. ft.)	Vac. Rate (%)	Under Constr. (sq. ft.)	Net Absorp. (sq. ft.)	Rental Rates ($/sq.ft./yr.)
Class A						
CBD	4,736,302	171,136	3.6	0	-1,166	16.00-22.00
Outside CBD	7,721,439	363,706	4.7	187,000	581,735	15.25-17.00
Class B						
CBD	2,608,327	664,346	25.5	0	-297,187	11.50-16.50
Outside CBD	4,283,115	445,867	10.4	55,000	114,396	13.00-15.75

Note: Data as of 10/98 and covers Richmond; CBD = Central Business District; n/a not available; Source: Society of Industrial and Office Realtors, 1999 Comparative Statistics of Industrial and Office Real Estate Markets

"Because most Class A space in Richmond's CBD has already been purchased by REITs, fewer deals will be made in 1999. Approximately 279,000 sq. ft. of office space in three new buildings are slated to reach the market in 1999. These buildings should lease up rapidly as the demand for Class A space tightens, indicating possible demand for additional speculative development. Construction of such space is likely to originate from privately held development groups. Outstanding growth companies, including LandAmerica Financial,

Capital One, and GE Capital, will be major absorbers of space. Motorola's delay in completing its semiconductor plant in West Creek will slow growth some, particularly for semiconductor related companies. Total absorption is expected to increase up to 15 percent, leading to slight decreases in vacancies." *Society of Industrial and Office Realtors, 1999 Comparative Statistics of Industrial and Office Real Estate Markets*

Industrial Market

Location	Total Space (sq. ft.)	Vacant Space (sq. ft.)	Vac. Rate (%)	Under Constr. (sq. ft.)	Net Absorp. (sq. ft.)	Gross Lease ($/sq.ft./yr.)
Central City	5,866,612	413,558	7.0	n/a	1,466,900	2.25-5.50
Suburban	18,440,988	2,102,918	11.4	522,250	1,522,764	3.00-6.00

Note: Data as of 10/98 and covers Richmond; n/a not available
Source: Society of Industrial and Office Realtors, 1999 Comparative Statistics of Industrial and Office Real Estate Markets

"Both Liberty Property Trust and Highwoods Properties have either new product coming on line or already under construction. The existing REITs have recently reduced their appetite for new land purchases. Instead they are seeking to develop what land holdings they already possess, particularly when they can build at no additional cost per sq. ft. Hewlett-Packard recently announced a new $35 million printer assembly and distribution center located on 93 acres in the White Oak Technology Park. This site is adjacent to the new White Oak Semiconductor Complex, east of Richmond International Airport. The project consists of three buildings totaling 832,000 sq. ft., scheduled to be completed in 1999. Several distribution and manufacturing companies have recently offered warehouse space for sublease—a signal that some companies are experiencing or anticipating a slowdown in business." *Society of Industrial and Office Realtors, 1999 Comparative Statistics of Industrial and Office Real Estate Markets*

COMMERCIAL UTILITIES

Typical Monthly Electric Bills

Area	Commercial Service ($/month)		Industrial Service ($/month)	
	12 kW demand 1,500 kWh	100 kW demand 30,000 kWh	1,000 kW demand 400,000 kWh	20,000 kW demand 10,000,000 kWh
City	119	1,978	20,383	346,201
U.S.	150	2,174	23,995	508,569

Note: Based on rates in effect January 1, 1999
Source: Edison Electric Institute, Typical Residential, Commercial and Industrial Bills, Winter 1999

TRANSPORTATION

Transportation Statistics

Average minutes to work	20.1
Interstate highways	I-64; I-85; I-95
Bus lines	
In-city	Greater Richmond Transit Co.
Inter-city	4
Passenger air service	
Airport	Richmond International
Airlines	13
Aircraft departures	21,232 (1996)
Enplaned passengers	992,861 (1996)
Rail service	Amtrak
Motor freight carriers	80
Major waterways/ports	Port of Richmond

Source: Editor & Publisher Market Guide, 1999; FAA Airport Activity Statistics, 1997; Amtrak National Time Table, Northeast Timetable, Spring/Summer 1999; 1990 Census of Population and Housing, STF 3C; Chamber of Commerce/Economic Development 1999; Jane's Urban Transport Systems 1999-2000

Means of Transportation to Work

| Area | Car/Truck/Van | | Public Transportation | | | Bicycle | Walked | Other Means | Worked at Home |
	Drove Alone	Car-pooled	Bus	Subway	Railroad				
City	64.5	13.8	12.5	0.0	0.0	1.0	5.4	1.1	1.7
MSA[1]	77.2	13.4	3.5	0.0	0.0	0.3	2.5	0.9	2.1
U.S.	73.2	13.4	3.0	1.5	0.5	0.4	3.9	1.2	3.0

Note: Figures shown are percentages and only include workers 16 years old and over;
(1) Metropolitan Statistical Area - see Appendix A for areas included
Source: 1990 Census of Population and Housing, Summary Tape File 3C

BUSINESSES

Major Business Headquarters

| Company Name | 1999 Rankings | |
	Fortune 500	Forbes 500
CSX	162	-
Carpenter	-	245
Circuit City Group	182	-
Dominion Resources	271	-
Pittston	403	-
Reynolds Metals	281	-
Ukrop's Super Markets	-	460
Universal	361	-

Note: Companies listed are located in the city; dashes indicate no ranking
Fortune 500: Companies that produce a 10-K are ranked 1 to 500 based on 1998 revenue
Forbes 500: Private companies are ranked 1 to 500 based on 1997 revenue
Source: Forbes, November 30, 1998; Fortune, April 26, 1999

Best Companies to Work For

CSX Corp. (transportation) and Circuit City Stores (retail/electronics), headquartered in Richmond, are among the "100 Best Places to Work in IS." Criteria: compensation, turnover and training. *Computerworld, May 25, 1998*

Minority Business Opportunity

Richmond is home to one company which is on the Black Enterprise Industrial/Service 100 list (largest based on gross sales): Community Pride Food Stores (supermarket) . Criteria: operational in previous calendar year, at least 51% black-owned and manufactures/owns the product it sells or provides industrial or consumer services. Brokerages, real estate firms and firms that provide professional services are not eligible. *Black Enterprise, www.blackenterprise.com*

HOTELS & MOTELS

Hotels/Motels

| Area | Hotels/ Motels | Rooms | Luxury-Level Hotels/Motels | | Average Minimum Rates ($) | | |
			♦♦♦♦	♦♦♦♦♦	♦♦	♦♦♦	♦♦♦♦
City	42	5,782	1	0	65	105	150
Airport	8	1,011	0	0	n/a	n/a	n/a
Suburbs	26	3,142	0	0	n/a	n/a	n/a
Total	76	9,935	1	0	n/a	n/a	n/a

Note: n/a not available; classifications range from one diamond (budget properties with basic amenities) to five diamond (luxury properties with the finest service, rooms and facilities).
Source: OAG, Business Travel Planner, Winter 1998-99

CONVENTION CENTERS   **Major Convention Centers**

Center Name	Meeting Rooms	Exhibit Space (sq. ft.)
Hyatt Richmond	19	15,837
Richmond Centre for Conventions and Exhibitions	9	62,216
Richmond Coliseum	12	36,000
Richmond Marriott	26	22,773
Richmond Mosque	4	18,000
Virginia State Fairgrounds at Strawberry Hill	n/a	200,000

Note: n/a not available
Source: Trade Shows Worldwide, 1998; Meetings & Conventions, 4/15/99;
Sucessful Meetings, 3/31/98

Living Environment

COST OF LIVING

Cost of Living Index

Composite Index	Groceries	Housing	Utilities	Trans-portation	Health Care	Misc. Goods/ Services
105.6	98.4	107.5	126.3	106.1	100.9	103.0

Note: U.S. = 100
Source: ACCRA, Cost of Living Index, 1st Quarter 1999

HOUSING

Median Home Prices and Housing Affordability

Area	Median Price[2] 1st Qtr. 1999 ($)	HOI[3] 1st Qtr. 1999	Afford-ability Rank[4]
MSA[1]	126,000	79.8	59
U.S.	134,000	69.6	–

Note: (1) Metropolitan Statistical Area - see Appendix A for areas included; (2) U.S. figures calculated from the sales of 524,324 new and existing homes in 181 markets; (3) Housing Opportunity Index - percent of homes sold that were within the reach of the median income household at the prevailing mortgage interest rate; (4) Rank is from 1-181 with 1 being most affordable
Source: National Association of Home Builders, Housing Opportunity Index, 1st Quarter 1999

Median Home Price Projection

It is projected that the median price of existing single-family homes in the metro area will increase by 3.9% in 1999. Nationwide, home prices are projected to increase 3.8%.
Kiplinger's Personal Finance Magazine, January 1999

Average New Home Price

Area	Price ($)
City	155,250
U.S.	142,735

Note: Figures are based on a new home with 1,800 sq. ft. of living area on an 8,000 sq. ft. lot.
Source: ACCRA, Cost of Living Index, 1st Quarter 1999

Average Apartment Rent

Area	Rent ($/mth)
City	737
U.S.	601

Note: Figures are based on an unfurnished two bedroom, 1-1/2 or 2 bath apartment, approximately 950 sq. ft. in size, excluding all utilities except water
Source: ACCRA, Cost of Living Index, 1st Quarter 1999

RESIDENTIAL UTILITIES

Average Residential Utility Costs

Area	All Electric ($/mth)	Part Electric ($/mth)	Other Energy ($/mth)	Phone ($/mth)
City	129.12	–	–	20.25
U.S.	100.02	55.73	43.33	19.71

Source: ACCRA, Cost of Living Index, 1st Quarter 1999

HEALTH CARE

Average Health Care Costs

Area	Hospital ($/day)	Doctor ($/visit)	Dentist ($/visit)
City	440.00	51.86	67.14
U.S.	430.43	52.45	66.35

Note: Hospital—based on a semi-private room; Doctor—based on a general practitioner's routine exam of an established patient; Dentist—based on adult teeth cleaning and periodic oral exam.
Source: ACCRA, Cost of Living Index, 1st Quarter 1999

Distribution of Office-Based Physicians

Area	Family/Gen. Practitioners	Specialists		
		Medical	Surgical	Other
MSA[1]	267	673	482	488

Note: Data as of 12/31/97; (1) Metropolitan Statistical Area - see Appendix A for areas included
Source: American Medical Assn., Physician Characteristics & Distribution in the U.S., 1999

Hospitals

Richmond has 1 general medical and surgical hospital, 2 psychiatric, 1 eye, ear, nose and throat, 2 rehabilitation, 1 children's general. *AHA Guide to the Healthcare Field, 1998-99*

According to *U.S. News and World Report,* Richmond has 1 of the best hospitals in the U.S.: **Medical College of Virginia Hospitals**, noted for gastroenterology, neurology, orthopedics, pulmonology. *U.S. News Online, "America's Best Hospitals," 10th Edition, www.usnews.com*

EDUCATION

Public School District Statistics

District Name	Num. Sch.	Enroll.	Classroom Teachers	Pupils per Teacher	Minority Pupils (%)	Current Exp.[1] ($/pupil)
Henrico Cnty Public Schls	60	39,073	n/a	n/a	n/a	n/a
Richmond City Public Schls	60	27,787	n/a	n/a	n/a	n/a

Note: Data covers the 1997-1998 school year unless otherwise noted; (1) Data covers fiscal year 1996; SD = School District; ISD = Independent School District; n/a not available
Source: National Center for Education Statistics, Common Core of Data Public Education Agency Universe 1997-98; National Center for Education Statistics, Characteristics of the 100 Largest Public Elementary and Secondary School Districts in the United States: 1997-98, July 1999

Educational Quality

School District	Education Quotient[1]	Graduate Outcome[2]	Community Index[3]	Resource Index[4]
Richmond City	97.0	75.0	59.0	148.0

Note: Nearly 1,000 secondary school districts were rated in terms of educational quality. The scores range from a low of 50 to a high of 150; (1) Average of the Graduate Outcome, Community and Resource indexes; (2) Based on graduation rates and college board scores (SAT/ACT); (3) Based on the surrounding community's average level of education and the area's average income level; (4) Based on teacher salaries, per-pupil expenditures and student-teacher ratios.
Source: Expansion Management, Ratings Issue, 1998

Educational Attainment by Race

Area	High School Graduate (%)					Bachelor's Degree (%)				
	Total	White	Black	Other	Hisp.[2]	Total	White	Black	Other	Hisp.[2]
City	68.1	80.1	56.3	76.2	75.1	24.2	39.4	9.5	33.2	26.9
MSA[1]	75.8	81.1	61.5	75.3	79.5	23.8	28.1	11.9	32.4	27.9
U.S.	75.2	77.9	63.1	60.4	49.8	20.3	21.5	11.4	19.4	9.2

Note: Figures shown cover persons 25 years old and over; (1) Metropolitan Statistical Area - see Appendix A for areas included; (2) people of Hispanic origin can be of any race
Source: 1990 Census of Population and Housing, Summary Tape File 3C

School Enrollment by Type

Area	Preprimary				Elementary/High School			
	Public		Private		Public		Private	
	Enrollment	%	Enrollment	%	Enrollment	%	Enrollment	%
City	1,849	62.6	1,105	37.4	24,399	89.2	2,946	10.8
MSA[1]	9,730	59.5	6,628	40.5	130,034	93.0	9,840	7.0
U.S.	2,679,029	59.5	1,824,256	40.5	38,379,689	90.2	4,187,099	9.8

Note: Figures shown cover persons 3 years old and over;
(1) Metropolitan Statistical Area - see Appendix A for areas included
Source: 1990 Census of Population and Housing, Summary Tape File 3C

School Enrollment by Race

Area	Preprimary (%)				Elementary/High School (%)			
	White	Black	Other	Hisp.[1]	White	Black	Other	Hisp.[1]
City	34.4	63.4	2.2	0.7	20.0	79.0	1.0	1.0
MSA[2]	72.2	26.1	1.7	1.2	61.8	35.5	2.7	1.2
U.S.	80.4	12.5	7.1	7.8	74.1	15.6	10.3	12.5

Note: Figures shown cover persons 3 years old and over; (1) people of Hispanic origin can be of any race; (2) Metropolitan Statistical Area - see Appendix A for areas included
Source: 1990 Census of Population and Housing, Summary Tape File 3C

Classroom Teacher Salaries in Public Schools

District	B.A. Degree		M.A. Degree		Maximum	
	Min. ($)	Rank[1]	Max. ($)	Rank[1]	Max. ($)	Rank[1]
Richmond	25,572	59	43,464	64	46,534	79
Average	26,980	-	46,065	-	51,435	-

Note: Salaries are for 1997-1998; (1) Rank ranges from 1 to 100
Source: American Federation of Teachers, Survey & Analysis of Salary Trends, 1998

Higher Education

Two-Year Colleges		Four-Year Colleges		Medical Schools	Law Schools	Voc/ Tech
Public	Private	Public	Private			
1	2	1	2	1	1	15

Source: College Blue Book, Occupational Education, 1997; Medical School Admission Requirements, 1999-2000; Peterson's Guide to Two-Year Colleges, 1999; Peterson's Guide to Four-Year Colleges, 2000; Barron's Guide to Law Schools, 1999

MAJOR EMPLOYERS

Major Employers

Bon Secours Memorial Regional Medical Ctr.
HCA Health Services of VA
Trigon Insurance
Reynolds Metals
St. Mary's Hospital of Richmond
Federal Reserve Bank of Richmond
Health Corp of VA
Overnite Transportation Co.
Viasystems Technologies Corp.
Virginia Electric Power

Note: Companies listed are located in the city
Source: Dun's Business Rankings, 1999; Ward's Business Directory, 1998

PUBLIC SAFETY

Crime Rate

Area	All Crimes	Violent Crimes				Property Crimes		
		Murder	Forcible Rape	Robbery	Aggrav. Assault	Burglary	Larceny -Theft	Motor Vehicle Theft
City	9,395.1	67.2	54.2	741.7	812.3	1,720.0	4,706.0	1,293.7
Suburbs[1]	4,358.3	6.8	26.9	104.0	168.6	675.4	3,127.6	249.0
MSA[2]	5,463.4	20.1	32.9	243.9	309.8	904.6	3,473.9	478.2
U.S.	4,922.7	6.8	35.9	186.1	382.0	919.6	2,886.5	505.8

Note: Crime rate is the number of crimes per 100,000 pop.; (1) defined as all areas within the MSA but located outside the central city; (2) Metropolitan Statistical Area - see Appendix A for areas incl.
Source: FBI Uniform Crime Reports, 1997

RECREATION

Culture and Recreation

Museums	Symphony Orchestras	Opera Companies	Dance Companies	Professional Theatres	Zoos	Pro Sports Teams
9	1	0	3	2	0	0

Source: International Directory of the Performing Arts, 1997; Official Museum Directory, 1999; Stern's Performing Arts Directory, 1997; USA Today Four Sport Stadium Guide, 1997; Chamber of Commerce/Economic Development, 1999

Library System

The Richmond Public Library has eight branches, holdings of 758,906 volumes, and a budget of $3,681,650 (1996-1997). *American Library Directory, 1998-1999*

MEDIA

Newspapers

Name	Type	Freq.	Distribution	Circulation
Catholic Virginian	Religious	26x/yr	State	60,000
Richmond Times-Dispatch	General	7x/wk	Area	211,598

Note: Includes newspapers with circulations of 1,000 or more located in the city;
Source: Burrelle's Media Directory, 1999 Edition

Television Stations

Name	Ch.	Affiliation	Type	Owner
WTVR	n/a	CBST	Commercial	Raycom Media Inc.
WRIC	n/a	ABCT	Commercial	Young Broadcasting Inc.
WWBT	12	NBCT	Commercial	Jefferson-Pilot Communications Company
WCVE	23	PBS	Non-comm.	Central Virginia Educational Telecom. Corp.
WRLH	35	FBC	Commercial	Sinclair Communications Inc.
WCVW	57	PBS	Non-comm.	Central Virginia Educational Telecom. Corp.
WUPV	65	UPN	Commercial	Lockwood Broadcasting Inc.

Note: Stations included broadcast in the Richmond metro area; n/a not available
Source: Burrelle's Media Directory, 1999 Edition

AM Radio Stations

Call Letters	Freq. (kHz)	Target Audience	Station Format	Music Format
WGGM	820	R/W	M/N/S	Christian
WRNL	910	General	N/S	n/a
WXGI	950	General	M/S	Country
WRVA	1140	General	N/T	n/a
WLEE	1320	n/a	n/a	n/a
WTVR	1380	G/W	M/N/S	Adult Standards/Big Band/MOR
WREJ	1540	General	M	Christian/Gospel
WFTH	1590	General	M	Christian

Note: Stations included broadcast in the Richmond metro area; n/a not available
Target Audience: A=Asian; B=Black; C=Christian; E=Ethnic; F=French; G=General; H=Hispanic; M=Men; N=Native American; R=Religious; S=Senior Citizen; W=Women; Y=Young Adult; Z=Children
Station Format: E=Educational; M=Music; N=News; S=Sports; T=Talk
Music Format: AOR=Album Oriented Rock; MOR=Middle-of-the-Road
Source: Burrelle's Media Directory, 1999 Edition

FM Radio Stations

Call Letters	Freq. (mHz)	Target Audience	Station Format	Music Format
WCVE	88.9	G/M/W	E/M/N	Classical/Jazz
WDCE	90.1	General	E/M/N/S/T	Alternative/Classical/Jazz/Latin/ Urban Contemporary/World Music
WCDX	92.1	General	M/N	Urban Contemporary
WRVQ	94.5	General	M/N/S	n/a
WKHK	95.3	General	M	Country
WKLR	96.5	General	M	Classic Rock
WTVR	98.1	General	M/N	Adult Contemporary
WPLZ	99.3	General	M/N/T	Oldies/R&B/Urban Contemporary
WSOJ	100.3	Black	M/N/S	Urban Contemporary
WRXL	102.1	General	M/N/S	Alternative/AOR/Classic Rock
WMXB	103.7	General	M/N/S	Adult Contemporary
WKJS	104.7	General	M/N/S	Urban Contemporary
WJRV	105.7	General	n/a	n/a
WRCL	106.5	General	M	Alternative

Note: Stations included broadcast in the Richmond metro area; n/a not available
Station Format: E=Educational; M=Music; N=News; S=Sports; T=Talk
Target Audience: A=Asian; B=Black; C=Christian; E=Ethnic; F=French; G=General; H=Hispanic; M=Men; N=Native American; R=Religious; S=Senior Citizen; W=Women; Y=Young Adult; Z=Children
Music Format: AOR=Album Oriented Rock; MOR=Middle-of-the-Road
Source: Burrelle's Media Directory, 1999 Edition

CLIMATE

Average and Extreme Temperatures

Temperature	Jan	Feb	Mar	Apr	May	Jun	Jul	Aug	Sep	Oct	Nov	Dec	Yr.
Extreme High (°F)	80	82	91	96	98	104	105	103	103	99	86	80	105
Average High (°F)	47	50	59	69	78	85	88	86	81	71	60	50	69
Average Temp. (°F)	38	40	48	58	66	75	78	77	71	60	50	41	58
Average Low (°F)	28	30	37	45	55	63	68	67	60	48	38	31	48
Extreme Low (°F)	-6	-8	11	19	31	40	51	47	35	21	14	1	-8

Note: Figures cover the years 1921-1990
Source: National Climatic Data Center, International Station Meteorological Climate Summary, 3/95

Average Precipitation/Snowfall/Humidity

Precip./Humidity	Jan	Feb	Mar	Apr	May	Jun	Jul	Aug	Sep	Oct	Nov	Dec	Yr.
Avg. Precip. (in.)	3.3	3.0	3.5	3.1	3.7	3.7	5.2	4.9	3.3	3.1	2.9	3.1	43.0
Avg. Snowfall (in.)	5	4	2	Tr	0	0	0	0	0	Tr	1	2	13
Avg. Rel. Hum. 7am (%)	79	79	78	76	81	82	85	89	90	89	84	80	83
Avg. Rel. Hum. 4pm (%)	54	51	46	43	51	53	56	58	57	53	51	55	52

Note: Figures cover the years 1921-1990; Tr = Trace amounts (<0.05 in. of rain; <0.5 in. of snow)
Source: National Climatic Data Center, International Station Meteorological Climate Summary, 3/95

Weather Conditions

Temperature			Daytime Sky			Precipitation		
10°F & below	32°F & below	90°F & above	Clear	Partly cloudy	Cloudy	0.01 inch or more precip.	0.1 inch or more snow/ice	Thunder-storms
3	79	41	90	147	128	115	7	43

Note: Figures are average number of days per year and covers the years 1921-1990
Source: National Climatic Data Center, International Station Meteorological Climate Summary, 3/95

AIR & WATER QUALITY

Maximum Pollutant Concentrations

	Particulate Matter (ug/m³)	Carbon Monoxide (ppm)	Sulfur Dioxide (ppm)	Nitrogen Dioxide (ppm)	Ozone (ppm)	Lead (ug/m³)
MSA[1] Level	59	4	0.024	0.021	0.13	0.01
NAAQS[2]	150	9	0.140	0.053	0.12	1.50
Met NAAQS?	Yes	Yes	Yes	Yes	No	Yes

Note: (1) Metropolitan Statistical Area - see Appendix A for areas included; (2) National Ambient Air Quality Standards; ppm = parts per million; ug/m³ = micrograms per cubic meter; n/a not available
Source: EPA, National Air Quality and Emissions Trends Report, 1997

Pollutant Standards Index

In the Richmond MSA (see Appendix A for areas included), the Pollutant Standards Index (PSI) exceeded 100 on 21 days in 1997. A PSI value greater than 100 indicates that air quality would be in the unhealthful range on that day. *EPA, National Air Quality and Emissions Trends Report, 1997*

Drinking Water

Water System Name	Pop. Served	Primary Water Source Type	Number of Violations in 1998	Type of Violation/ Contaminants
City of Richmond WTP	209,000	Surface	41	None

Note: Data as of July 10, 1999; (1) System failed to conduct initial or repeat sampling, or to accurately report an analytical result for 41 specific contaminants.
Source: EPA, Office of Ground Water and Drinking Water, Safe Drinking Water Information System

Richmond tap water is alkaline, soft and fluoridated.
Editor & Publisher Market Guide, 1999

Rochester, New York

Background

The city of Rochester is on the Genesee River and lies close to Lake Ontario. The first to live in the area were the Algonquins, soon to be followed by the Seneca, one of the Five Nations of the Iroquois. The first white man to live in the area, Ebenezer Allen, came in 1789 and built a flour mill for the local natives. In 1812, a Maryland entrepreneur, Nathaniel Rochester, founded a village in 1812 on land that he had bought earlier along the Genesee. In 1817, the settlement was given a town charter with the name Rochesterville, which was changed to Rochester five years later. After the Erie Canal reached the city in 1823, the city's population quickly grew. Numerous flour mills were built on the banks of the Genesee River, and soon Rochester earned the sobriquet Flour City.

New York incorporated Rochester as a city in 1834. The economy diversified in the years before the Civil War. Henry Lomb and John Jacob Bausch established an eyeglass store. Shortly thereafter an optical equipment industry was set up in the city. Rochester became an important place in the antebellum abolitionist movement, when Frederick Douglass began publishing there his newspaper, The North Star. Another reformer, women's rights activist Susan B. Anthony, also lived in the city.

After the war, George Eastman in 1880 built a photographic plate-making firm. Eight years later he began to manufacture and sell the famous Kodak camera.

In the early twentieth century, a major dredging of the city's harbor took place and the port facilities were upgraded. The opening of the St. Lawrence Seaway in 1959 allowed ocean-going vessels to reach Rochester.

City leaders undertook a substantial effort in the 1960s and 1970s to rejuvenate the city's downtown. This included the construction of an enclosed shopping mall in the city's core, Midtown Plaza, the first such facility in the country.

Eastman Kodak maintains a significant presence in the city, with five manufacturing (cameras, film, and related products), research, training, and sales facilities. The company's headquarters are also in Rochester. Xerox Corporation also has a major presence, with several facilities in the immediate region. Xerox makes a variety of business machines and copiers in the Rochester area. Other manufactures include clothing, processed foods, chemicals, rubber, metal, machinery, and stone, clay, and glass products. Manufacturing firms make up seven percent of the businesses in the area and employ about twenty-eight percent of the work force. Rochester's largest industry sector is service, with thirty-six percent of businesses and thirty-four percent of the work force.

Rochester has available incentives to encourage business. The city has an Economic Development Zone to assist new businesses set up and old ones grow. Other incentives include a Targeted Business Assistance Program for small businesses, and a Targeted Industrial Renovation Program for manufacturers.

The city's proximity to Lake Ontario affects its climate with longer than usual summers and winters. Summertime temperatures range from the fifties to the eighties; those in the winter go from the teens to the forties. Rainfall averages thirty-one inches a year. Lake effect snows have a great effect on Rochester, and the city usually sees nearly ninety inches of it each year.

General Rankings and Evaluative Comments

- Rochester was ranked #10 out of 15 large, northeastern metropolitan areas in *Money's* 1998 survey of "The Best Places to Live in America." The survey was conducted by first contacting 512 representative households nationwide and asking them to rank 37 quality-of-life factors on a scale of 1 to 10. Next, a demographic profile was compiled on the 300 largest metropolitan statistical areas in the U.S. The numbers were crunched together to arrive at an overall ranking (things Americans consider most important, like clean air and water, low crime and good schools, received extra weight). Unlike previous years, the 1998 rankings were broken down by region (northeast, midwest, south, west) and population size (100,000 to 249,999; 250,000 to 999,999; 1 million plus). The city had a nationwide ranking of #248 out of 300 in 1997 and #253 out of 300 in 1996. *Money, July 1998; Money, July 1997; Money, September 1996*

- *Ladies Home Journal* ranked America's 200 largest cities based on the qualities women care about most. Rochester ranked #57 out of 200. Criteria: low crime rate, well-paying jobs, quality health and child care, good public schools, the presence of women in government, size of the gender wage gap, number of sexual-harassment and discrimination complaints filed, unemployment and divorce rates, commute times, population density, number of houses of worship, parks and cultural offerings, number of women's health specialists, how well a community's women cared for themselves, complexion kindness index based on UV radiation levels, odds of finding affordable fashions, rental rates for romance movies, champagne sales and other matters of the heart. *Ladies Home Journal, November 1998*

- Zero Population Growth ranked 229 cities in terms of children's health, safety, and economic well-being. Rochester was ranked #91 out of 112 independent cities (cities with populations greater than 100,000 which were neither Major Cities nor Suburbs/Outer Cities) and was given a grade of D. Criteria: total population, percent of population under 18 years of age, household language, percent population change, percent of births to teens, infant mortality rate, percent of low birth weights, dropout rate, enrollment in preprimary school, violent and property crime rates, unemployment rate, percent of children in poverty, percent of owner occupied units, number of bad air days, percent of public transportation commuters, and average travel time to work. *Zero Population Growth, Children's Environmental Index, Fall 1999*

- Rochester was ranked #43 out of 59 metro areas in *The Regional Economist's* "Rational Livability Ranking of 59 Large Metro Areas." The rankings were based on the metro area's total population change over the period 1990-97 divided by the number of people moving in from elsewhere in the United States (net domestic in-migration). *St. Louis Federal Reserve Bank of St. Louis, The Regional Economist, April 1999*

- Rochester was selected by *Yahoo! Internet Life* as one of "America's Most Wired Cities & Towns." The city ranked #34 out of 50. Criteria: home and work net use, domain density, hosts per capita, directory density and content quality. *Yahoo! Internet Life, March 1999*

- Cognetics studied 273 metro areas in the United States, ranking them by entrepreneurial activity. Rochester was ranked #50 out of the 50 largest metro areas. Criteria: Significant Starts (firms started in the last 10 years that still employ at least 5 people) and Young Growers (percent of firms 10 years old or less that grew significantly during the last 4 years). *Cognetics, "Entrepreneurial Hot Spots: The Best Places in America to Start and Grow a Company," 1998*

- Rochester appeared on *Sales & Marketing Management's* list of the "20 Hottest Cities for Selling." Rank: #18 out of 20. *S&MM* editors looked at Metropolitan Statistical Areas with populations of more than 150,000. The areas were ranked based on population increases, retail sales increases, effective buying income, increase in both residential and commercial building permits issued, unemployment rates, job growth, mix of industries, tax rates, number of corporate relocations, and the number of new corporations.
Sales & Marketing Management, April 1999

■ Reliastar Financial Corp. ranked the 125 largest metropolitan areas according to the general financial security of residents. Rochester was ranked #39 out of 125 with a score of 5.4. The score indicates the percentage a metropolitan area is above or below the metropolitan norm. A metro area with a score of 10.6 is 10.6% above the metro average. Criteria: Earnings and Wealth Potential (household income, education, net assets, cost of living); Safety Net (health insurance, retirement savings, life insurance, income support programs); Personal Threats (unemployment rate, low-income households, crime rate); Community Economic Vitality (cost of community services, job quality, job creation, housing costs).
Reliastar Financial Corp., "The Best Cities to Earn and Save Money," 1999 Edition

Business Environment

STATE ECONOMY

State Economic Profile

"New York is starting to decelerate from its strongest performance in over a decade. Manufacturing employment continues to contract, particularly in upstate. Since most of its growth downstate is driven by Wall Street, NY's job outlook remains vulnerable to swings in the stock market. Population declines will continue to be one of NY's primary problems.

Almost all of 1998's job gains were in the New York City-Long Island area. NY state added some 140,800 jobs in 1998, 134,300 of those in NYC/Long Island. The bulk of these were concentrated in the services sector, particularly business and financial services. The raging bull market has done wonders for NYC and the surrounding suburbs. Since we do not expect a downturn in the stock market in 1999, job growth in NY will continue, albeit at a slower rate.

While NYC has been on a roll, upstate is only seeing some modest easing in its stagnant economy. Buffalo witnessed an increase of 0.2% job growth in 1998. Similar weak growth (0.3%) occurred in Rochester. Job cuts by Kodak and Xerox only added to the troubled upstate economy. Increased state tax revenues, largely from Wall Street, have allowed some government employment gains in Albany.

New York's primary constraint is its continued loss of residents, particularly among younger households. Although home sales rose 6% in 1998, appreciation has only been modest in the NYC area and weak upstate. Rising construction payrolls were largely concentrated in the NYC commercial market, with only an 8% increase in residential permits. As a result of declining population, NY is likely to lose two congressional seats in the post-2000 redistricting, pushing the decline of its political capital and accompanying federal dollars." *National Association of Realtors, Economic Profiles: The Fifty States and the District of Columbia, http://nar.realtor.com/databank/profiles.htm*

IMPORTS/EXPORTS

Total Export Sales

Area	1994 ($000)	1995 ($000)	1996 ($000)	1997 ($000)	% Chg. 1994-97	% Chg. 1996-97
MSA[1]	3,143,662	3,860,521	4,307,694	4,694,459	49.3	9.0
U.S.	512,415,609	583,030,524	622,827,063	687,597,999	34.2	10.4

Note: (1) Metropolitan Statistical Area - see Appendix A for areas included
Source: U.S. Department of Commerce, International Trade Association, Metropolitan Area Exports: An Export Performance Report on Over 250 U.S. Cities, November 10, 1998

CITY FINANCES

City Government Finances

Component	FY92 ($000)	FY92 (per capita $)
Revenue	641,243	2,791.53
Expenditure	645,441	2,809.81
Debt Outstanding	284,426	1,238.20
Cash & Securities	191,302	832.80

Source: U.S. Bureau of the Census, City Government Finances: 1991-92

City Government Revenue by Source

Source	FY92 ($000)	FY92 (per capita $)	FY92 (%)
From Federal Government	53,965	234.93	8.4
From State Governments	219,365	954.96	34.2
From Local Governments	88,724	386.24	13.8
Property Taxes	125,539	546.51	19.6
General Sales Taxes	0	0.00	0.0
Selective Sales Taxes	11,204	48.77	1.7
Income Taxes	0	0.00	0.0
Current Charges	65,537	285.30	10.2
Utility/Liquor Store	25,989	113.14	4.1
Employee Retirement[1]	0	0.00	0.0
Other	50,920	221.67	7.9

Note: (1) Excludes "city contributions," classified as "nonrevenue," intragovernmental transfers.
Source: U.S. Bureau of the Census, City Government Finances: 1991-92

City Government Expenditures by Function

Function	FY92 ($000)	FY92 (per capita $)	FY92 (%)
Educational Services	329,818	1,435.80	51.1
Employee Retirement[1]	0	0.00	0.0
Environment/Housing	95,051	413.79	14.7
Government Administration	17,750	77.27	2.8
Interest on General Debt	16,687	72.64	2.6
Public Safety	67,153	292.34	10.4
Social Services	0	0.00	0.0
Transportation	19,649	85.54	3.0
Utility/Liquor Store	17,219	74.96	2.7
Other	82,114	357.47	12.7

Note: (1) Payments to beneficiaries including withdrawal of contributions.
Source: U.S. Bureau of the Census, City Government Finances: 1991-92

Municipal Bond Ratings

Area	Moody's	S & P
Rochester	A1	n/a

Note: n/a not available; n/r not rated
Source: Moody's Bond Record, 6/99

POPULATION

Population Growth

Area	1980	1990	% Chg. 1980-90	July 1998 Estimate	% Chg. 1990-98
City	241,741	231,636	-4.2	216,887	-6.4
MSA[1]	971,230	1,002,410	3.2	1,096,559	9.4
U.S.	226,545,805	248,765,170	9.8	270,299,000	8.7

Note: (1) Metropolitan Statistical Area - see Appendix A for areas included;
July 1998 MSA population estimate was calculated by the editors
Source: 1980/1990 Census of Housing and Population, Summary Tape File 3C;
Census Bureau Population Estimates 1998

Population Characteristics

| Race | City | | | | | MSA[1] | |
| | 1980 | | 1990 | | % Chg. 1980-90 | 1990 | |
	Population	%	Population	%		Population	%
White	169,510	70.1	141,952	61.3	-16.3	878,195	87.6
Black	62,256	25.8	73,102	31.6	17.4	93,088	9.3
Amer Indian/Esk/Aleut	1,145	0.5	1,033	0.4	-9.8	2,605	0.3
Asian/Pacific Islander	1,698	0.7	3,752	1.6	121.0	13,225	1.3
Other	7,132	3.0	11,797	5.1	65.4	15,297	1.5
Hispanic Origin[2]	13,153	5.4	18,936	8.2	44.0	29,330	2.9

Note: (1) Metropolitan Statistical Area - see Appendix A for areas included;
(2) people of Hispanic origin can be of any race
Source: 1980/1990 Census of Housing and Population, Summary Tape File 3C

Ancestry

Area	German	Irish	English	Italian	U.S.	French	Polish	Dutch
City	19.1	13.7	9.3	12.9	2.0	3.5	4.0	2.5
MSA[1]	30.0	19.4	18.6	17.0	2.5	4.8	5.4	5.7
U.S.	23.3	15.6	13.1	5.9	5.3	4.2	3.8	2.5

Note: Figures are percentages and include persons that reported multiple ancestry (eg. if a person
reported being Irish and Italian, they were included in both columns); (1) Metropolitan Statistical Area -
see Appendix A for areas included
Source: 1990 Census of Population and Housing, Summary Tape File 3C

Age

| Area | Median Age (Years) | Age Distribution (%) | | | | | | |
		Under 5	Under 18	18-24	25-44	45-64	65+	80+
City	29.7	9.5	26.0	13.0	35.1	14.0	11.9	3.3
MSA[1]	32.9	7.6	25.0	11.2	33.1	18.4	12.3	2.8
U.S.	32.9	7.3	25.6	10.5	32.6	18.7	12.5	2.8

Note: (1) Metropolitan Statistical Area - see Appendix A for areas included
Source: 1990 Census of Population and Housing, Summary Tape File 3C

Male/Female Ratio

Area	Number of males per 100 females (all ages)	Number of males per 100 females (18 years old+)
City	89.1	84.7
MSA[1]	93.5	89.9
U.S.	95.0	91.9

Note: (1) Metropolitan Statistical Area - see Appendix A for areas included
Source: 1990 Census of Population, General Population Characteristics

INCOME

Per Capita/Median/Average Income

Area	Per Capita ($)	Median Household ($)	Average Household ($)
City	11,704	22,785	28,286
MSA[1]	15,355	34,234	40,554
U.S.	14,420	30,056	38,453

Note: All figures are for 1989; (1) Metropolitan Statistical Area - see Appendix A for areas included
Source: 1990 Census of Population and Housing, Summary Tape File 3C

Household Income Distribution by Race

Income ($)	City (%)					U.S. (%)				
	Total	White	Black	Other	Hisp.[1]	Total	White	Black	Other	Hisp.[1]
Less than 5,000	9.4	5.9	16.2	21.3	21.4	6.2	4.8	15.2	8.6	8.8
5,000 - 9,999	15.0	13.9	17.2	18.2	21.4	9.3	8.6	14.2	9.9	11.1
10,000 - 14,999	10.5	10.1	11.7	10.9	10.9	8.8	8.5	11.0	9.8	11.0
15,000 - 24,999	18.2	18.8	17.1	16.6	16.3	17.5	17.3	18.9	18.5	20.5
25,000 - 34,999	15.9	17.0	13.5	13.3	13.3	15.8	16.1	14.2	15.4	16.4
35,000 - 49,999	16.0	17.5	13.1	11.5	9.3	17.9	18.6	13.3	16.1	16.0
50,000 - 74,999	10.8	12.0	8.7	6.9	6.2	15.0	15.8	9.3	13.4	11.1
75,000 - 99,999	2.7	3.1	1.9	0.7	0.7	5.1	5.5	2.6	4.7	3.1
100,000+	1.4	1.7	0.6	0.6	0.6	4.4	4.8	1.3	3.7	1.9

Note: All figures are for 1989; (1) people of Hispanic origin can be of any race
Source: 1990 Census of Population and Housing, Summary Tape File 3C

Effective Buying Income

Area	Per Capita ($)	Median Household ($)	Average Household ($)
City	12,386	24,368	30,463
MSA[1]	15,933	35,791	42,374
U.S.	16,803	34,536	45,243

Note: Data as of 1/1/99; (1) Metropolitan Statistical Area - see Appendix A for areas included
Source: Standard Rate & Data Service, Newspaper Advertising Source, 9/99

Effective Household Buying Income Distribution

Area	% of Households Earning						
	$10,000 -$19,999	$20,000 -$34,999	$35,000 -$49,999	$50,000 -$74,999	$75,000 -$99,000	$100,000 -$124,999	$125,000 and up
City	21.0	24.4	16.8	12.8	2.9	0.6	0.5
MSA[1]	15.4	22.9	20.2	21.0	6.6	1.9	1.5
U.S.	16.0	22.6	18.2	18.9	7.2	2.4	2.7

Note: Data as of 1/1/99; (1) Metropolitan Statistical Area - see Appendix A for areas included
Source: Standard Rate & Data Service, Newspaper Advertising Source, 9/99

Poverty Rates by Race and Age

Area	Total (%)	By Race (%)				By Age (%)		
		White	Black	Other	Hisp.[2]	Under 5 years old	Under 18 years old	65 years and over
City	23.5	14.8	35.9	41.6	45.2	41.2	38.4	13.3
MSA[1]	9.8	6.8	32.2	27.9	36.1	17.0	14.4	7.5
U.S.	13.1	9.8	29.5	23.1	25.3	20.1	18.3	12.8

Note: Figures show the percent of people living below the poverty line in 1989. The average poverty threshold was $12,674 for a family of four in 1989; (1) Metropolitan Statistical Area - see Appendix A for areas included; (2) people of Hispanic origin can be of any race
Source: 1990 Census of Population and Housing, Summary Tape File 3C

EMPLOYMENT

Labor Force and Employment

Area	Civilian Labor Force			Workers Employed		
	Jun. 1998	Jun. 1999	% Chg.	Jun. 1998	Jun. 1999	% Chg.
City	115,351	115,982	0.5	108,353	107,959	-0.4
MSA[1]	583,719	583,940	0.0	562,227	560,184	-0.4
U.S.	138,798,000	140,666,000	1.3	132,265,000	134,395,000	1.6

Note: Data is not seasonally adjusted and covers workers 16 years of age and older;
(1) Metropolitan Statistical Area - see Appendix A for areas included
Source: Bureau of Labor Statistics, http://stats.bls.gov

Unemployment Rate

Area	1998						1999					
	Jul.	Aug.	Sep.	Oct.	Nov.	Dec.	Jan.	Feb.	Mar.	Apr.	May.	Jun.
City	7.9	6.3	6.7	5.8	5.6	5.4	6.4	7.1	7.0	6.4	7.0	6.9
MSA[1]	4.3	3.5	3.8	3.3	3.5	3.6	4.4	4.8	4.7	4.0	4.2	4.1
U.S.	4.7	4.5	4.4	4.2	4.1	4.0	4.8	4.7	4.4	4.1	4.0	4.5

Note: Data is not seasonally adjusted and covers workers 16 years of age and older; all figures are percentages; (1) Metropolitan Statistical Area - see Appendix A for areas included
Source: Bureau of Labor Statistics, http://stats.bls.gov

Employment by Industry

Sector	MSA[1]		U.S.
	Number of Employees	Percent of Total	Percent of Total
Services	170,100	31.0	30.4
Retail Trade	94,000	17.1	17.7
Government	82,300	15.0	15.6
Manufacturing	119,600	21.8	14.3
Finance/Insurance/Real Estate	21,400	3.9	5.9
Wholesale Trade	23,300	4.2	5.4
Transportation/Public Utilities	17,700	3.2	5.3
Construction	20,100	3.7	5.0
Mining	400	0.1	0.4

Note: Figures cover non-farm employment as of 6/99 and are not seasonally adjusted; (1) Metropolitan Statistical Area - see Appendix A for areas included
Source: Bureau of Labor Statistics, http://stats.bls.gov

Employment by Occupation

Occupation Category	City (%)	MSA[1] (%)	U.S. (%)
White Collar	54.9	60.3	58.1
Executive/Admin./Management	9.7	12.3	12.3
Professional	15.2	16.7	14.1
Technical & Related Support	4.6	4.4	3.7
Sales	9.0	10.7	11.8
Administrative Support/Clerical	16.5	16.2	16.3
Blue Collar	27.0	25.5	26.2
Precision Production/Craft/Repair	10.4	11.2	11.3
Machine Operators/Assem./Insp.	9.6	7.9	6.8
Transportation/Material Movers	3.5	3.3	4.1
Cleaners/Helpers/Laborers	3.5	3.1	3.9
Services	17.7	12.7	13.2
Farming/Forestry/Fishing	0.4	1.4	2.5

Note: Figures cover employed persons 16 years old and over; (1) Metropolitan Statistical Area - see Appendix A for areas included
Source: 1990 Census of Population and Housing, Summary Tape File 3C

Occupational Employment Projections: 1996 - 2006

Occupations Expected to Have the Largest Job Growth (ranked by numerical growth)	Fast-Growing Occupations[1] (ranked by percent growth)
1. Salespersons, retail	1. Computer scientists
2. Home health aides	2. Systems analysts
3. Cashiers	3. Computer engineers
4. Teachers, secondary school	4. Computer support specialists
5. Systems analysts	5. Data processing equipment repairers
6. Teachers, special education	6. Database administrators
7. Personal and home care aides	7. Electronic pagination systems workers
8. Maintenance repairers, general utility	8. Teachers, special education
9. Guards	9. Medical assistants
10. Stock clerks, stockroom or warehouse	10. Physical therapy assistants and aides

Note: Projections cover New York State; (1) Excludes occupations with total job growth less than 1,000
Source: New York State Department of Labor, Occupational Outlook, Employment & Openings by Occupation, 1996-2006

TAXES

Major State and Local Tax Rates

State Corp. Income (%)	State Personal Income (%)	Residential Property (effective rate per $100)	Sales & Use		State Gasoline (cents/ gallon)	State Cigarette (cents/ pack)
			State (%)	Local (%)		
9.0[a]	4.0 - 6.85	n/a	4.0	4.0	8.0[b]	56.0

Note: Personal/corporate income, sales, gasoline and cigarette tax rates as of January 1999. Property tax rates as of 1997; (a) Or 1.78 (0.1 for banks) mills per dollar of capital (up to $350,000; or 3.25% (3% after 7/1/99) (3% for banks) of the minimum taxable income; or a minimum of $100 to $1,500 depending on payroll size ($250 plus 2.5% surtax for banks); if any of these is greater than the tax computed on net income. An addition tax of 0.9 mills per dollar of subsidiary capital is imposed on corporations. Small businesses with income under $200,000 pay tax of 8% of income.; (b) Carriers pay an additional surcharge of 22.21 cents
Source: Federation of Tax Administrators, www.taxadmin.org; Washington D.C. Department of Finance and Revenue, Tax Rates and Tax Burdens in the District of Columbia: A Nationwide Comparison, July 1998; Chamber of Commerce, 1999

Total Taxes Per Capita and as a Percent of Income

Area	Per Capita Income ($)	Per Capita Taxes ($)			Percent of Income (%)		
		Total	Federal	State/ Local	Total	Federal	State/ Local
New York	33,564	12,439	7,876	4,564	37.1	23.5	13.6
U.S.	27,876	9,881	6,690	3,191	35.4	24.0	11.4

Note: Figures are for 1998
Source: Tax Foundation, www.taxfoundation.org

COMMERCIAL REAL ESTATE

Office Market

Class/ Location	Total Space (sq. ft.)	Vacant Space (sq. ft.)	Vac. Rate (%)	Under Constr. (sq. ft.)	Net Absorp. (sq. ft.)	Rental Rates ($/sq.ft./yr.)
Class A						
CBD	2,333,300	244,600	10.5	300,000	-62,230	18.00-28.50
Outside CBD	2,515,600	62,600	2.5	140,000	236,700	17.50-21.50
Class B						
CBD	6,015,300	953,400	15.8	0	127,400	10.00-18.00
Outside CBD	2,579,200	228,900	8.9	37,000	-600	12.50-17.00

Note: Data as of 10/98 and covers Rochester; CBD = Central Business District; n/a not available;
Source: Society of Industrial and Office Realtors, 1999 Comparative Statistics of Industrial and Office Real Estate Markets

"The SIOR local reporter expects significant levels of new construction in 1999. Construction in the metropolitan area as a whole could go up by five percent. In the suburban office market, new construction will consist largely of Class A space where the vacancy rate fell from 5.9

percent in 1997 to 2.5 percent in 1998. Net absorption of office space in the metropolitan area is expected to increase by as much as five percent. Vacancy rates are forecasted to remain at significantly lower levels in the suburbs than in the CBD. Average rental rate increases will be in the low single-digit levels in downtown for less desirable Class A buildings." *Society of Industrial and Office Realtors, 1999 Comparative Statistics of Industrial and Office Real Estate Markets*

Industrial Market

Location	Total Space (sq. ft.)	Vacant Space (sq. ft.)	Vac. Rate (%)	Under Constr. (sq. ft.)	Net Absorp. (sq. ft.)	Net Lease ($/sq.ft./yr.)
Central City	5,000,000	200,000	4.0	200,000	0	2.75-4.00
Suburban	5,000,000	200,000	4.0	200,000	0	3.25-6.00

Note: Data as of 10/98 and covers Rochester; n/a not available
Source: Society of Industrial and Office Realtors, 1999 Comparative Statistics of Industrial and Office Real Estate Markets

"Both population and employment are expected to decline in the Rochester metropolitan area in 1999. The slowdown in economic activity in the nation as a whole will have only a moderate impact on the Rochester metropolitan area. Many of the people employed in the industries in the area are not subject to strong cyclical forces since the hulk of highly cost-sensitive jobs have moved to less expensive locations. Nevertheless, our SIOR reporter indicates that some industrial migration out of the area will continue. Some of the growth in the high-tech industry will be displaced outside local Rochester. Absorption, lease prices, and new construction for the various types of industrial land uses will remain at about the same level as in 1998." *Society of Industrial and Office Realtors, 1999 Comparative Statistics of Industrial and Office Real Estate Markets*

COMMERCIAL UTILITIES

Typical Monthly Electric Bills

Area	Commercial Service ($/month)		Industrial Service ($/month)	
	12 kW demand 1,500 kWh	100 kW demand 30,000 kWh	1,000 kW demand 400,000 kWh	20,000 kW demand 10,000,000 kWh
City	224	3,077	35,238	513,813
U.S.	150	2,174	23,995	508,569

Note: Based on rates in effect January 1, 1999
Source: Edison Electric Institute, Typical Residential, Commercial and Industrial Bills, Winter 1999

TRANSPORTATION

Transportation Statistics

Average minutes to work	18.0
Interstate highways	I-390; I-490 to I-90
Bus lines	
In-city	Regional Transit Service, 337 vehicles
Inter-city	4
Passenger air service	
Airport	Rochester-Monroe County
Airlines	6
Aircraft departures	22,606 (1996)
Enplaned passengers	1,041,628 (1996)
Rail service	Amtrak
Motor freight carriers	91
Major waterways/ports	Lake Ontario

Source: Editor & Publisher Market Guide, 1999; FAA Airport Activity Statistics, 1997; Amtrak National Time Table, Northeast Timetable, Spring/Summer 1999; 1990 Census of Population and Housing, STF 3C; Chamber of Commerce/Economic Development 1999; Jane's Urban Transport Systems 1999-2000

Means of Transportation to Work

| Area | Car/Truck/Van | | Public Transportation | | | Bicycle | Walked | Other Means | Worked at Home |
	Drove Alone	Car-pooled	Bus	Subway	Railroad				
City	65.4	13.3	10.5	0.0	0.0	0.5	7.6	0.9	1.8
MSA[1]	77.7	11.6	3.1	0.0	0.0	0.2	4.3	0.5	2.4
U.S.	73.2	13.4	3.0	1.5	0.5	0.4	3.9	1.2	3.0

Note: Figures shown are percentages and only include workers 16 years old and over;
(1) Metropolitan Statistical Area - see Appendix A for areas included
Source: 1990 Census of Population and Housing, Summary Tape File 3C

BUSINESSES

Major Business Headquarters

| Company Name | 1999 Rankings | |
	Fortune 500	Forbes 500
Eastman Kodak	121	-
Empire Beef	-	384
Wegmans Food Markets	-	61

Note: Companies listed are located in the city; dashes indicate no ranking
Fortune 500: Companies that produce a 10-K are ranked 1 to 500 based on 1998 revenue
Forbes 500: Private companies are ranked 1 to 500 based on 1997 revenue
Source: Forbes, November 30, 1998; Fortune, April 26, 1999

Best Companies to Work For

Wegmans (supermarket), headquartered in Rochester, is among the "100 Best Companies to Work for in America." Criteria: trust in management, pride in work/company, camaraderie, company responses to the Hewitt People Practices Inventory, and employee responses to their Great Place to Work survey. The companies also had to be at least 10 years old and have a minimum of 500 employees. *Fortune, January 11, 1999*

Bausch & Lomb and Eastman Kodak, headquartered in Rochester, are among the "100 Best Companies for Working Mothers." Criteria: fair wages, opportunities for women to advance, support for child care, flexible work schedules, family-friendly benefits, and work/life supports. *Working Mother, October 1998*

Frontier Corp. (telecommunications), headquartered in Rochester, is among the "100 Best Places to Work in IS." Criteria: compensation, turnover and training. *Computerworld, May 25, 1998*

Fast-Growing Businesses

Rochester is home to one of *Business Week's* "hot growth" companies: Performance Technologies. Criteria: increase in sales and profits, return on capital and stock price. *Business Week, 5/31/99*

Minority Business Opportunity

Rochester is home to one company which is on the Black Enterprise Auto Dealer 100 list (largest based on gross sales): Bob Johnson Chevrolet (Ford, Chevrolet) . Criteria: 1) operational in previous calendar year; 2) at least 51% black-owned. *Black Enterprise, www.blackenterprise.com*

HOTELS & MOTELS

Hotels/Motels

Area	Hotels/ Motels	Rooms	Luxury-Level Hotels/Motels		Average Minimum Rates ($)		
			♦♦♦♦	♦♦♦♦♦	♦♦	♦♦♦	♦♦♦♦
City	16	2,430	0	0	83	127	n/a
Airport	4	513	0	0	n/a	n/a	n/a
Suburbs	30	2,861	0	0	n/a	n/a	n/a
Total	50	5,804	0	0	n/a	n/a	n/a

Note: n/a not available; classifications range from one diamond (budget properties with basic amenities) to five diamond (luxury properties with the finest service, rooms and facilities).
Source: OAG, Business Travel Planner, Winter 1998-99

CONVENTION CENTERS

Major Convention Centers

Center Name	Meeting Rooms	Exhibit Space (sq. ft.)
Rochester Community War Memorial	12	80,000
Rochester Riverside Convention Center	22	100,000

Source: Trade Shows Worldwide, 1998; Meetings & Conventions, 4/15/99; Sucessful Meetings, 3/31/98

Living Environment

COST OF LIVING

Cost of Living Index

Composite Index	Groceries	Housing	Utilities	Trans-portation	Health Care	Misc. Goods/ Services
102.2	117.0	86.9	127.9	118.9	89.2	99.5

Note: U.S. = 100; Figures are for the Metropolitan Statistical Area - see Appendix A for areas included
Source: ACCRA, Cost of Living Index, 3rd Quarter 1996

HOUSING

Median Home Prices and Housing Affordability

Area	Median Price[2] 1st Qtr. 1999 ($)	HOI[3] 1st Qtr. 1999	Afford- ability Rank[4]
MSA[1]	85,000	83.3	31
U.S.	134,000	69.6	–

Note: (1) Metropolitan Statistical Area - see Appendix A for areas included; (2) U.S. figures calculated from the sales of 524,324 new and existing homes in 181 markets; (3) Housing Opportunity Index - percent of homes sold that were within the reach of the median income household at the prevailing mortgage interest rate; (4) Rank is from 1-181 with 1 being most affordable
Source: National Association of Home Builders, Housing Opportunity Index, 1st Quarter 1999

Median Home Price Projection

It is projected that the median price of existing single-family homes in the metro area will increase by 2.6% in 1999. Nationwide, home prices are projected to increase 3.8%.
Kiplinger's Personal Finance Magazine, January 1999

Average New Home Price

Area	Price ($)
MSA[1]	112,110
U.S.	131,626

Note: Figures are based on a new home with 1,800 sq. ft. of living area on an 8,000 sq. ft. lot; (1) Metropolitan Statistical Area - see Appendix A for areas included
Source: ACCRA, Cost of Living Index, 3rd Quarter 1996

Average Apartment Rent

Area	Rent ($/mth)
MSA[1]	484
U.S.	556

Note: Figures are based on an unfurnished two bedroom, 1-1/2 or 2 bath apartment, approximately 950 sq. ft. in size, excluding all utilities except water; (1) Metropolitan Statistical Area - see Appendix A for areas included
Source: ACCRA, Cost of Living Index, 3rd Quarter 1996

RESIDENTIAL UTILITIES

Average Residential Utility Costs

Area	All Electric ($/mth)	Part Electric ($/mth)	Other Energy ($/mth)	Phone ($/mth)
MSA[1]	–	67.43	67.14	20.68
U.S.	110.28	56.34	42.21	19.45

Note: (1) (1) Metropolitan Statistical Area - see Appendix A for areas included
Source: ACCRA, Cost of Living Index, 3rd Quarter 1996

HEALTH CARE

Average Health Care Costs

Area	Hospital ($/day)	Doctor ($/visit)	Dentist ($/visit)
MSA[1]	494.00	35.00	44.43
U.S.	381.46	46.47	58.18

Note: Hospital—based on a semi-private room; Doctor—based on a general practitioner's routine exam of an established patient; Dentist—based on adult teeth cleaning and periodic oral exam; (1) Metropolitan Statistical Area - see Appendix A for areas included
Source: ACCRA, Cost of Living Index, 3rd Quarter 1996

Distribution of Office-Based Physicians

Area	Family/Gen. Practitioners	Specialists		
		Medical	Surgical	Other
MSA[1]	147	922	520	541

Note: Data as of 12/31/97; (1) Metropolitan Statistical Area - see Appendix A for areas included
Source: American Medical Assn., Physician Characteristics & Distribution in the U.S., 1999

Hospitals

Rochester has 6 general medical and surgical hospitals, 1 psychiatric, 1 other specialty. *AHA Guide to the Healthcare Field, 1998-99*

According to *U.S. News and World Report*, Rochester has 1 of the best hospitals in the U.S.: **Strong Memorial Hospital-Rochester University**, noted for gynecology, neurology. *U.S. News Online, "America's Best Hospitals," 10th Edition, www.usnews.com*

EDUCATION

Public School District Statistics

District Name	Num. Sch.	Enroll.	Classroom Teachers	Pupils per Teacher	Minority Pupils (%)	Current Exp.[1] ($/pupil)
Brighton CSD	4	3,344	217	15.4	n/a	n/a
East Irondequoit CSD	6	3,301	212	15.6	n/a	n/a
Gates-Chili CSD	7	5,411	332	16.3	n/a	n/a
Rochester City SD	58	38,345	2,642	14.5	n/a	n/a
West Irondequoit CSD	10	4,019	217	18.5	n/a	n/a

Note: Data covers the 1997-1998 school year unless otherwise noted; (1) Data covers fiscal year 1996; SD = School District; ISD = Independent School District; n/a not available
Source: National Center for Education Statistics, Common Core of Data Public Education Agency Universe 1997-98; National Center for Education Statistics, Characteristics of the 100 Largest Public Elementary and Secondary School Districts in the United States: 1997-98, July 1999

Educational Quality

School District	Education Quotient[1]	Graduate Outcome[2]	Community Index[3]	Resource Index[4]
Rochester City	88.0	54.0	116.0	149.0

Note: Nearly 1,000 secondary school districts were rated in terms of educational quality. The scores range from a low of 50 to a high of 150; (1) Average of the Graduate Outcome, Community and Resource indexes; (2) Based on graduation rates and college board scores (SAT/ACT); (3) Based on the surrounding community's average level of education and the area's average income level; (4) Based on teacher salaries, per-pupil expenditures and student-teacher ratios.
Source: Expansion Management, Ratings Issue, 1998

Educational Attainment by Race

Area	High School Graduate (%)					Bachelor's Degree (%)				
	Total	White	Black	Other	Hisp.[2]	Total	White	Black	Other	Hisp.[2]
City	68.8	74.4	57.7	49.1	44.4	19.0	23.6	7.5	13.9	5.7
MSA[1]	79.1	81.1	60.3	61.6	53.6	23.4	24.4	10.3	27.5	11.7
U.S.	75.2	77.9	63.1	60.4	49.8	20.3	21.5	11.4	19.4	9.2

Note: Figures shown cover persons 25 years old and over; (1) Metropolitan Statistical Area - see Appendix A for areas included; (2) people of Hispanic origin can be of any race
Source: 1990 Census of Population and Housing, Summary Tape File 3C

School Enrollment by Type

Area	Preprimary				Elementary/High School			
	Public		Private		Public		Private	
	Enrollment	%	Enrollment	%	Enrollment	%	Enrollment	%
City	2,983	63.5	1,711	36.5	31,066	85.5	5,277	14.5
MSA[1]	12,739	59.0	8,851	41.0	146,730	89.9	16,489	10.1
U.S.	2,679,029	59.5	1,824,256	40.5	38,379,689	90.2	4,187,099	9.8

Note: Figures shown cover persons 3 years old and over;
(1) Metropolitan Statistical Area - see Appendix A for areas included
Source: 1990 Census of Population and Housing, Summary Tape File 3C

School Enrollment by Race

Area	Preprimary (%)				Elementary/High School (%)			
	White	Black	Other	Hisp.[1]	White	Black	Other	Hisp.[1]
City	55.9	35.8	8.3	10.0	38.9	49.3	11.8	14.2
MSA[2]	86.9	9.6	3.4	3.3	81.3	13.9	4.9	4.8
U.S.	80.4	12.5	7.1	7.8	74.1	15.6	10.3	12.5

Note: Figures shown cover persons 3 years old and over; (1) people of Hispanic origin can be of any race; (2) Metropolitan Statistical Area - see Appendix A for areas included
Source: 1990 Census of Population and Housing, Summary Tape File 3C

Classroom Teacher Salaries in Public Schools

District	B.A. Degree		M.A. Degree		Maximum	
	Min. ($)	Rank[1]	Max. ($)	Rank[1]	Max. ($)	Rank[1]
Rochester	31,250	11	60,258	4	71,281	3
Average	26,980	-	46,065	-	51,435	-

Note: Salaries are for 1997-1998; (1) Rank ranges from 1 to 100
Source: American Federation of Teachers, Survey & Analysis of Salary Trends, 1998

Higher Education

Two-Year Colleges		Four-Year Colleges		Medical Schools	Law Schools	Voc/ Tech
Public	Private	Public	Private			
0	3	0	7	1	0	7

Source: College Blue Book, Occupational Education, 1997; Medical School Admission Requirements, 1999-2000; Peterson's Guide to Two-Year Colleges, 1999; Peterson's Guide to Four-Year Colleges, 2000; Barron's Guide to Law Schools, 1999

MAJOR EMPLOYERS

Major Employers

Eastman Kodak
Park Ridge Health System
Highland Hospital of Rochester
Doyle Group (detective & armored car svcs.)
Paychex
Genesee Hospital
V&J National Enterprises (eating places)
St. Mary's Hospital of the Sisters of Charity
Gleason Corp. (machine tools)
Rochester Gas & Electric

Note: Companies listed are located in the city
Source: Dun's Business Rankings, 1999; Ward's Business Directory, 1998

PUBLIC SAFETY

Crime Rate

Area	All Crimes	Violent Crimes				Property Crimes		
		Murder	Forcible Rape	Robbery	Aggrav. Assault	Burglary	Larceny -Theft	Motor Vehicle Theft
City	8,617.1	23.0	55.9	674.7	288.6	1,631.1	4,746.5	1,197.3
Suburbs[1]	2,993.6	1.2	15.7	38.8	68.7	421.9	2,306.1	141.2
MSA[2]	4,187.6	5.8	24.2	173.8	115.4	678.7	2,824.3	365.5
U.S.	4,922.7	6.8	35.9	186.1	382.0	919.6	2,886.5	505.8

Note: Crime rate is the number of crimes per 100,000 pop.; (1) defined as all areas within the MSA but located outside the central city; (2) Metropolitan Statistical Area - see Appendix A for areas incl.
Source: FBI Uniform Crime Reports, 1997

RECREATION

Culture and Recreation

Museums	Symphony Orchestras	Opera Companies	Dance Companies	Professional Theatres	Zoos	Pro Sports Teams
6	2	0	1	2	1	0

Source: International Directory of the Performing Arts, 1997; Official Museum Directory, 1999; Stern's Performing Arts Directory, 1997; USA Today Four Sport Stadium Guide, 1997; Chamber of Commerce/Economic Development, 1999

Library System

The Rochester Public Library has 10 branches, holdings of 1,073,867 volumes, and a budget of $11,123,338 (1996). *American Library Directory, 1998-1999*

MEDIA

Newspapers

Name	Type	Freq.	Distribution	Circulation
Ad Net Community News - Gates/Chili Ed.	General	1x/wk	Local	16,000
Ad Net Community News - Greece Edition	General	1x/wk	Local	30,000
Daily Record	n/a	5x/wk	Area	2,860
Democrat and Chronicle	General	7x/wk	Area	143,689
Gates/Chili News	General	1x/wk	Local	9,800
Irondequoit Shopper	n/a	1x/wk	Local	20,000
Jewish Ledger	Religious	1x/wk	Area	8,000

Note: Includes newspapers with circulations of 1,000 or more located in the city; n/a not available
Source: Burrelle's Media Directory, 1999 Edition

Television Stations

Name	Ch.	Affiliation	Type	Owner
WROC	n/a	CBST	Commercial	SunRise Broadcasting Corporation
WHEC	10	NBCT	Commercial	Hubbard Broadcasting Inc.
WOKR	13	ABCT	Commercial	Gannett Broadcasting
WXXI	21	PBS	Public	Public Broadcasting Council of Central New York
WUHF	31	FBC	Commercial	Sullivan Broadcasting Company

Note: Stations included broadcast in the Rochester metro area; n/a not available
Source: Burrelle's Media Directory, 1999 Edition

AM Radio Stations

Call Letters	Freq. (kHz)	Target Audience	Station Format	Music Format
WEZO	950	General	M/N/S	Adult Standards
WDCZ	990	General	M/T	Christian
WHAM	1180	General	N/T	n/a
WHTK	1280	Men	S/T	n/a
WXXI	1370	General	M/N/T	Jazz
WWWG	1460	Religious	M/N/T	Gospel

Note: Stations included broadcast in the Rochester metro area; n/a not available
Target Audience: A=Asian; B=Black; C=Christian; E=Ethnic; F=French; G=General; H=Hispanic;
M=Men; N=Native American; R=Religious; S=Senior Citizen; W=Women; Y=Young Adult; Z=Children
Station Format: E=Educational; M=Music; N=News; S=Sports; T=Talk
Source: Burrelle's Media Directory, 1999 Edition

FM Radio Stations

Call Letters	Freq. (mHz)	Target Audience	Station Format	Music Format
WRUR	88.5	General	M/N/S	Alternative/Big Band/Christian/Classical/Jazz/ Latin/R&B/Urban Contemporary
WITR	89.7	General	E/M	Alternative/Jazz
WGMC	90.1	General	M	Big Band/Jazz/Latin
WXXI	91.5	General	E/M	Classical
WBEE	92.5	General	M/N	Country
WQRV	93.3	General	M	Classic Rock
WZNE	94.1	General	M	Adult Contemporary/Alternative
WNVE	95.1	General	M/T	Alternative
WCMF	96.5	General	M/N/S/T	Alternative/AOR/Classic Rock
WPXY	97.9	General	M	Top 40
WBBF	98.9	General	M	Oldies
WVOR	100.5	General	M	Adult Contemporary/Adult Top 40
WRMM	101.3	General	M	Adult Contemp./AOR/Classic Rock/Easy Listening
WDCZ	102.7	General	M/T	Christian
WDKX	103.9	Black	M/N/S	Blues/Jazz/R&B/Urban Contemporary
WIRQ	104.7	General	M/N/S	Alternative
WMAX	106.7	General	M/N/S	Oldies

Note: Stations included broadcast in the Rochester metro area
Station Format: E=Educational; M=Music; N=News; S=Sports; T=Talk
Target Audience: A=Asian; B=Black; C=Christian; E=Ethnic; F=French; G=General; H=Hispanic;
M=Men; N=Native American; R=Religious; S=Senior Citizen; W=Women; Y=Young Adult; Z=Children
Music Format: AOR=Album Oriented Rock; MOR=Middle-of-the-Road
Source: Burrelle's Media Directory, 1999 Edition

CLIMATE

Average and Extreme Temperatures

Temperature	Jan	Feb	Mar	Apr	May	Jun	Jul	Aug	Sep	Oct	Nov	Dec	Yr.
Extreme High (°F)	74	67	83	93	94	100	98	99	99	91	81	72	100
Average High (°F)	31	33	42	56	68	78	82	80	72	61	48	36	57
Average Temp. (°F)	24	25	34	46	57	67	72	70	62	52	41	29	48
Average Low (°F)	17	17	25	36	46	56	60	59	52	42	33	23	39
Extreme Low (°F)	-16	-19	-6	13	26	35	42	36	30	20	5	-12	-19

Note: Figures cover the years 1945-1990
Source: National Climatic Data Center, International Station Meteorological Climate Summary, 3/95

Average Precipitation/Snowfall/Humidity

Precip./Humidity	Jan	Feb	Mar	Apr	May	Jun	Jul	Aug	Sep	Oct	Nov	Dec	Yr.
Avg. Precip. (in.)	2.2	2.3	2.5	2.6	2.7	2.8	2.6	3.3	2.8	2.5	2.8	2.6	31.8
Avg. Snowfall (in.)	24	23	14	4	Tr	0	0	0	Tr	Tr	7	20	92
Avg. Rel. Hum. 7am (%)	79	80	80	78	77	79	82	87	88	85	82	81	81
Avg. Rel. Hum. 4pm (%)	71	69	63	56	53	53	52	55	59	61	69	74	61

Note: Figures cover the years 1945-1990; Tr = Trace amounts (<0.05 in. of rain; <0.5 in. of snow)
Source: National Climatic Data Center, International Station Meteorological Climate Summary, 3/95

Weather Conditions

Temperature			Daytime Sky			Precipitation		
5°F & below	32°F & below	90°F & above	Clear	Partly cloudy	Cloudy	0.01 inch or more precip.	0.1 inch or more snow/ice	Thunder-storms
13	135	11	58	137	170	157	65	27

Note: Figures are average number of days per year and covers the years 1945-1990
Source: National Climatic Data Center, International Station Meteorological Climate Summary, 3/95

AIR & WATER QUALITY

Maximum Pollutant Concentrations

	Particulate Matter (ug/m3)	Carbon Monoxide (ppm)	Sulfur Dioxide (ppm)	Nitrogen Dioxide (ppm)	Ozone (ppm)	Lead (ug/m3)
MSA[1] Level	47	2	0.050	n/a	0.10	n/a
NAAQS[2]	150	9	0.140	0.053	0.12	1.50
Met NAAQS?	Yes	Yes	Yes	n/a	Yes	n/a

Note: (1) Metropolitan Statistical Area - see Appendix A for areas included; (2) National Ambient Air Quality Standards; ppm = parts per million; ug/m3 = micrograms per cubic meter; n/a not available
Source: EPA, National Air Quality and Emissions Trends Report, 1997

Pollutant Standards Index

In the Rochester MSA (see Appendix A for areas included), the Pollutant Standards Index (PSI) exceeded 100 on 6 days in 1997. A PSI value greater than 100 indicates that air quality would be in the unhealthful range on that day. *EPA, National Air Quality and Emissions Trends Report, 1997*

Drinking Water

Water System Name	Pop. Served	Primary Water Source Type	Number of Violations in 1998	Type of Violation/ Contaminants
Rochester City	220,000	Surface	None	None

Note: Data as of July 10, 1999
Source: EPA, Office of Ground Water and Drinking Water, Safe Drinking Water Information System

Rochester tap water is neutral, soft.
Editor & Publisher Market Guide, 1999

Washington, DC

Background

The city and federal district of Washington, D.C. with it foreign Embassies and Consulates, is definitely cosmopolitan. However, underlying this international worldliness, is a decidedly patrician and Yankee air.

The small sliver of land designated as our country's capital grew out of a section of land carved from the state of Maryland, after many years of arguing. The Father of our country, George Washington, silenced bickering voices, and chose the present site we know today as Washington, D.C. In 1793, the first cornerstone of the White House was laid. In 1800, the north wing had been completed, and a drifting Congress found its home. President John Adams was the first President to reside at the White House. The building was burned down by the British during the War of 1812, and its final reconstruction was not completed until 1891!

The young Capital, which grows more confident and worldly every year, is a breathtaking collection of architectural styles—Greek Revival, Federal-Style, Victorian, and Baroque. All this blends in with the monuments and other sites that we know so well—Washington Monument, Lincoln Memorial, White House, and Jefferson Memorial.

As the political machine of the country, the main industry is, of course, government. This economic sector employs roughly 2.8 million people. With 20 million visitors a year, tourism has become Washington's second largest income producer. Economic activity not withstanding, Washington is also the home of four major universities—American, Georgetown, George Washington and Howard.

The District of Columbia is operating under a Congressional legislation that created a financial control board in 1995 to oversea the District's budget. The new 1998 budget bill has expanded the powers of the board in exchange for nearly $1 billion in federal aid over the next five years.

The authority of the Mayor and City Council to run major city agencies is now in the hands of the Board and this shift in power has already accelerated some new economic development: an increase of jobs in the private sector of nearly 9,000; new retail development; an increase in revenue due to aggressive tax collection; a positive "credit watch" status from Standard & Poor; an opera house, plans for a new convention center downtown; and construction of a new $100 million downtown sports arena—The MCI Center—which opened in December of 1997. *New York Times, 8/8/97, 12/3/97; USA Today, 11/18/97*

Summertime in Washington is warm and humid and winter is cold, but not severe.

General Rankings and Evaluative Comments

■ Washington was ranked #1 out of 15 large, northeastern metropolitan areas in *Money's* 1998 survey of "The Best Places to Live in America." The survey was conducted by first contacting 512 representative households nationwide and asking them to rank 37 quality-of-life factors on a scale of 1 to 10. Next, a demographic profile was compiled on the 300 largest metropolitan statistical areas in the U.S. The numbers were crunched together to arrive at an overall ranking (things Americans consider most important, like clean air and water, low crime and good schools, received extra weight). Unlike previous years, the 1998 rankings were broken down by region (northeast, midwest, south, west) and population size (100,000 to 249,999; 250,000 to 999,999; 1 million plus). The city had a nationwide ranking of #162 out of 300 in 1997 and #128 out of 300 in 1996. *Money, July 1998; Money, July 1997; Money, September 1996*

■ *Ladies Home Journal* ranked America's 200 largest cities based on the qualities women care about most. Washington ranked #23 out of 200. Criteria: low crime rate, well-paying jobs, quality health and child care, good public schools, the presence of women in government, size of the gender wage gap, number of sexual-harassment and discrimination complaints filed, unemployment and divorce rates, commute times, population density, number of houses of worship, parks and cultural offerings, number of women's health specialists, how well a community's women cared for themselves, complexion kindness index based on UV radiation levels, odds of finding affordable fashions, rental rates for romance movies, champagne sales and other matters of the heart. *Ladies Home Journal, November 1998*

■ Washington was selected as one of the 10 healthiest cities for women by *American Health*. It was ranked #4 out of America's 120 most populous metro areas. Criteria: number and quality of doctors and hospitals, quality of women's health centers, number of recreational opportunities, rate of violent crimes, cleanliness of air and water, percentage of women-owned businesses, and the number of family-friendly employers.

"Washington has upped its safety measures for its citizens. Thanks to crime prevention programs, the rate of violent crime has drastically declined in recent years, and currently stands at 7% above the national average." *American Health, 1998*

■ Zero Population Growth ranked 229 cities in terms of children's health, safety, and economic well-being. Washington was ranked #22 out of 25 major cities (main city in a metro area with population of greater than 2 million) and was given a grade of D. Criteria: total population, percent of population under 18 years of age, household language, percent population change, percent of births to teens, infant mortality rate, percent of low birth weights, dropout rate, enrollment in preprimary school, violent and property crime rates, unemployment rate, percent of children in poverty, percent of owner occupied units, number of bad air days, percent of public transportation commuters, and average travel time to work. Zero Population Growth, Children's Environmental Index, Fall 1999

■ Washington was ranked #39 out of 59 metro areas in *The Regional Economist's* "Rational Livability Ranking of 59 Large Metro Areas." The rankings were based on the metro area's total population change over the period 1990-97 divided by the number of people moving in from elsewhere in the United States (net domestic in-migration). *St. Louis Federal Reserve Bank of St. Louis, The Regional Economist, April 1999*

■ Washington appeared on *Travel & Leisure's* list of the world's 100 best cities. It was ranked #7 in the U.S. and #17 in the world. Criteria: activities/attractions, culture/arts, people, restaurants/food, and value. *Travel & Leisure, 1998 World's Best Awards*

■ *Conde Nast Traveler* polled 37,293 readers for travel satisfaction. Cities were ranked based on the following criteria: people/friendliness, environment/ambiance, cultural enrichment, restaurants and fun/energy. Washington appeared in the top 25, ranking number 14, with an overall rating of 66.1 out of 100. *Conde Nast Traveler, Readers' Choice Poll 1998*

■ Washington was selected by *Yahoo! Internet Life* as one of "America's Most Wired Cities & Towns." The city ranked #4 out of 50. Criteria: home and work net use, domain density, hosts per capita, directory density and content quality. *Yahoo! Internet Life, March 1999*

- Cognetics studied 273 metro areas in the United States, ranking them by entrepreneurial activity. Washington was ranked #10 out of the 50 largest metro areas. Criteria: Significant Starts (firms started in the last 10 years that still employ at least 5 people) and Young Growers (percent of firms 10 years old or less that grew significantly during the last 4 years). *Cognetics, "Entrepreneurial Hot Spots: The Best Places in America to Start and Grow a Company," 1998*

- Washington was included among *Entrepreneur* magazine's listing of the "20 Best Cities for Small Business." It was ranked #10 among large metro areas. Criteria: entrepreneurial activity, small-business growth, economic growth, and risk of failure. *Entrepreneur, October 1999*

- Washington was selected as one of the "Best American Cities to Start a Business" by *Point of View* magazine. Criteria: coolness, quality-of-life, and business concerns. The city was ranked #33 out of 75. *Point of View, November 1998*

- *Computerworld* selected the best markets for IT job seekers based on their annual salary, skills, and hiring surveys. Washington ranked #4 out of 10. *Computerworld, January 11, 1999*

- Reliastar Financial Corp. ranked the 125 largest metropolitan areas according to the general financial security of residents. Washington was ranked #47 out of 125 with a score of 4.0. The score indicates the percentage a metropolitan area is above or below the metropolitan norm. A metro area with a score of 10.6 is 10.6% above the metro average. Criteria: Earnings and Wealth Potential (household income, education, net assets, cost of living); Safety Net (health insurance, retirement savings, life insurance, income support programs); Personal Threats (unemployment rate, low-income households, crime rate); Community Economic Vitality (cost of community services, job quality, job creation, housing costs). *Reliastar Financial Corp., "The Best Cities to Earn and Save Money," 1999 Edition*

Business Environment

STATE ECONOMY

State Economic Profile

"The District of Columbia's economy is looking its brightest in some years. Job cutbacks by the federal government have slowed and private employment growth has increased. In addition, in 1998 DC saw its hottest housing and office market in years. New development will provide additional jobs in 1999.

DC's new mayor, Anthony Williams, has instilled the city with a new sense of optimism. The city government is actively focusing on private sector growth via tax cuts and streamlining the city government operations and employment. Some city job cuts are expected, but should be offset by increases in private employment. Much of DC's economic prospects rides on Williams' ability to reform the DC government.

DC's commercial and residential properties are finally coming to life after years of stagnation. Last year saw the best housing market in decades, with record sales and strong appreciation. The $5,000 federal tax credit for first-time homebuyers has helped to attract some new households into the city. The next 2 years should see strong sales and appreciation, with modest residential construction. One constraint upon the market will be the large inventory of vacant properties and continued loss of residents to the suburbs.

After years of decline, DC has begun to stabilize. The downtown area around the MCI center is seeing development interest. The city's flood of residents moving into the suburbs has slowed. DC's rebound, however, depends upon continued reform of the city government. DC's outlook is for stable, steady growth in 1999 and 2000." *National Association of Realtors, Economic Profiles: The Fifty States and the District of Columbia, http://nar.realtor.com/databank/profiles.htm*

IMPORTS/EXPORTS

Total Export Sales

Area	1994 ($000)	1995 ($000)	1996 ($000)	1997 ($000)	% Chg. 1994-97	% Chg. 1996-97
MSA[1]	7,969,303	8,350,435	8,083,517	7,980,732	0.1	-1.3
U.S.	512,415,609	583,030,524	622,827,063	687,597,999	34.2	10.4

Note: (1) Metropolitan Statistical Area - see Appendix A for areas included
Source: U.S. Department of Commerce, International Trade Association, Metropolitan Area Exports: An Export Performance Report on Over 250 U.S. Cities, November 10, 1998

CITY FINANCES

City Government Finances

Component	FY94 ($000)	FY94 (per capita $)
Revenue	4,991,420	8,787.37
Expenditure	5,285,531	9,305.15
Debt Outstanding	4,110,029	7,235.69
Cash & Securities	3,323,561	5,851.11

Source: U.S. Bureau of the Census, City Government Finances: 1993-94

City Government Revenue by Source

Source	FY94 ($000)	FY94 (per capita $)	FY94 (%)
From Federal Government	1,623,802	2,858.70	32.5
From State Governments	0	0.00	0.0
From Local Governments	72,642	127.89	1.5
Property Taxes	811,009	1,427.78	16.2
General Sales Taxes	472,540	831.90	9.5
Selective Sales Taxes	307,461	541.28	6.2
Income Taxes	798,725	1,406.15	16.0
Current Charges	271,473	477.93	5.4
Utility/Liquor Store	53,086	93.46	1.1
Employee Retirement[1]	231,923	408.30	4.6
Other	348,759	613.99	7.0

Note: (1) Excludes "city contributions," classified as "nonrevenue," intragovernmental transfers.
Source: U.S. Bureau of the Census, City Government Finances: 1993-94

City Government Expenditures by Function

Function	FY94 ($000)	FY94 (per capita $)	FY94 (%)
Educational Services	763,471	1,344.09	14.4
Employee Retirement[1]	279,576	492.19	5.3
Environment/Housing	458,065	806.42	8.7
Government Administration	294,420	518.32	5.6
Interest on General Debt	302,791	533.06	5.7
Public Safety	727,983	1,281.61	13.8
Social Services	1,606,811	2,828.78	30.4
Transportation	160,749	283.00	3.0
Utility/Liquor Store	101,997	179.57	1.9
Other	589,668	1,038.11	11.2

Note: (1) Payments to beneficiaries including withdrawal of contributions.
Source: U.S. Bureau of the Census, City Government Finances: 1993-94

Municipal Bond Ratings

Area	Moody's	S & P
Washington	Ba1	n/a

Note: n/a not available; n/r not rated
Source: Moody's Bond Record, 6/99

POPULATION

Population Growth

Area	1980	1990	% Chg. 1980-90	July 1998 Estimate	% Chg. 1990-98
City	638,333	606,900	-4.9	523,124	-13.8
MSA[1]	3,250,822	3,923,574	20.7	4,676,555	19.2
U.S.	226,545,805	248,765,170	9.8	270,299,000	8.7

Note: (1) Metropolitan Statistical Area - see Appendix A for areas included;
July 1998 MSA population estimate was calculated by the editors
Source: 1980/1990 Census of Housing and Population, Summary Tape File 3C;
Census Bureau Population Estimates 1998

Population Characteristics

Race	City				% Chg. 1980-90	MSA[1]	
	1980		1990			1990	
	Population	%	Population	%		Population	%
White	174,705	27.4	179,690	29.6	2.9	2,580,207	65.8
Black	448,370	70.2	399,751	65.9	-10.8	1,042,210	26.6
Amer Indian/Esk/Aleut	1,014	0.2	1,559	0.3	53.7	12,115	0.3
Asian/Pacific Islander	6,883	1.1	11,233	1.9	63.2	201,502	5.1
Other	7,361	1.2	14,667	2.4	99.3	87,540	2.2
Hispanic Origin[2]	17,679	2.8	31,358	5.2	77.4	218,256	5.6

Note: (1) Metropolitan Statistical Area - see Appendix A for areas included;
(2) people of Hispanic origin can be of any race
Source: 1980/1990 Census of Housing and Population, Summary Tape File 3C

Ancestry

Area	German	Irish	English	Italian	U.S.	French	Polish	Dutch
City	6.5	5.7	5.6	1.9	1.9	1.4	1.6	0.6
MSA[1]	19.0	14.2	14.2	4.7	3.0	2.9	3.0	1.5
U.S.	23.3	15.6	13.1	5.9	5.3	4.2	3.8	2.5

Note: Figures are percentages and include persons that reported multiple ancestry (eg. if a person
reported being Irish and Italian, they were included in both columns); (1) Metropolitan Statistical Area -
see Appendix A for areas included
Source: 1990 Census of Population and Housing, Summary Tape File 3C

Age

Area	Median Age (Years)	Age Distribution (%)						
		Under 5	Under 18	18-24	25-44	45-64	65+	80+
City	33.4	6.0	19.2	13.4	35.9	18.7	12.8	2.8
MSA[1]	32.4	7.2	23.5	10.9	38.2	19.0	8.5	1.7
U.S.	32.9	7.3	25.6	10.5	32.6	18.7	12.5	2.8

Note: (1) Metropolitan Statistical Area - see Appendix A for areas included
Source: 1990 Census of Population and Housing, Summary Tape File 3C

Male/Female Ratio

Area	Number of males per 100 females (all ages)	Number of males per 100 females (18 years old+)
City	87.2	84.0
MSA[1]	94.8	92.2
U.S.	95.0	91.9

Note: (1) Metropolitan Statistical Area - see Appendix A for areas included
Source: 1990 Census of Population, General Population Characteristics

INCOME

Per Capita/Median/Average Income

Area	Per Capita ($)	Median Household ($)	Average Household ($)
City	18,881	30,727	44,413
MSA[1]	21,416	46,884	56,799
U.S.	14,420	30,056	38,453

Note: All figures are for 1989; (1) Metropolitan Statistical Area - see Appendix A for areas included
Source: 1990 Census of Population and Housing, Summary Tape File 3C

Household Income Distribution by Race

Income ($)	City (%)					U.S. (%)				
	Total	White	Black	Other	Hisp.[1]	Total	White	Black	Other	Hisp.[1]
Less than 5,000	8.7	3.5	11.7	10.2	8.1	6.2	4.8	15.2	8.6	8.8
5,000 - 9,999	7.8	3.6	10.2	8.8	8.0	9.3	8.6	14.2	9.9	11.1
10,000 - 14,999	7.2	4.4	8.7	8.5	11.2	8.8	8.5	11.0	9.8	11.0
15,000 - 24,999	17.3	12.3	20.2	19.2	19.5	17.5	17.3	18.9	18.5	20.5
25,000 - 34,999	14.7	13.4	15.3	18.0	19.6	15.8	16.1	14.2	15.4	16.4
35,000 - 49,999	15.6	16.5	15.0	16.5	15.3	17.9	18.6	13.3	16.1	16.0
50,000 - 74,999	14.4	18.6	12.2	10.5	10.3	15.0	15.8	9.3	13.4	11.1
75,000 - 99,999	6.4	10.4	4.3	3.5	4.0	5.1	5.5	2.6	4.7	3.1
100,000+	7.8	17.3	2.4	4.8	4.0	4.4	4.8	1.3	3.7	1.9

Note: All figures are for 1989; (1) people of Hispanic origin can be of any race
Source: 1990 Census of Population and Housing, Summary Tape File 3C

Effective Buying Income

Area	Per Capita ($)	Median Household ($)	Average Household ($)
City	22,594	37,950	53,623
MSA[1]	22,621	49,996	60,948
U.S.	16,803	34,536	45,243

Note: Data as of 1/1/99; (1) Metropolitan Statistical Area - see Appendix A for areas included
Source: Standard Rate & Data Service, Newspaper Advertising Source, 9/99

Effective Household Buying Income Distribution

Area	% of Households Earning						
	$10,000 -$19,999	$20,000 -$34,999	$35,000 -$49,999	$50,000 -$74,999	$75,000 -$99,000	$100,000 -$124,999	$125,000 and up
City	12.4	21.6	15.9	17.7	9.4	4.4	5.9
MSA[1]	8.0	17.6	18.8	26.1	13.5	5.4	5.0
U.S.	16.0	22.6	18.2	18.9	7.2	2.4	2.7

Note: Data as of 1/1/99; (1) Metropolitan Statistical Area - see Appendix A for areas included
Source: Standard Rate & Data Service, Newspaper Advertising Source, 9/99

Poverty Rates by Race and Age

Area	Total (%)	By Race (%)				By Age (%)		
		White	Black	Other	Hisp.[2]	Under 5 years old	Under 18 years old	65 years and over
City	16.9	8.2	20.2	21.9	20.4	27.0	25.5	17.2
MSA[1]	6.4	3.6	12.6	9.9	12.0	8.3	7.9	8.6
U.S.	13.1	9.8	29.5	23.1	25.3	20.1	18.3	12.8

Note: Figures show the percent of people living below the poverty line in 1989. The average poverty threshold was $12,674 for a family of four in 1989; (1) Metropolitan Statistical Area - see Appendix A for areas included; (2) people of Hispanic origin can be of any race
Source: 1990 Census of Population and Housing, Summary Tape File 3C

EMPLOYMENT

Labor Force and Employment

Area	Civilian Labor Force			Workers Employed		
	Jun. 1998	Jun. 1999	% Chg.	Jun. 1998	Jun. 1999	% Chg.
City	275,247	278,781	1.3	248,084	259,418	4.6
MSA[1]	2,583,291	2,679,400	3.7	2,491,215	2,600,374	4.4
U.S.	138,798,000	140,666,000	1.3	132,265,000	134,395,000	1.6

Note: Data is not seasonally adjusted and covers workers 16 years of age and older; (1) Metropolitan Statistical Area - see Appendix A for areas included
Source: Bureau of Labor Statistics, http://stats.bls.gov

Unemployment Rate

Area	1998						1999					
	Jul.	Aug.	Sep.	Oct.	Nov.	Dec.	Jan.	Feb.	Mar.	Apr.	May.	Jun.
City	9.6	8.9	8.5	8.3	8.0	7.2	7.7	7.8	7.1	6.3	6.3	6.9
MSA[1]	3.2	3.1	3.2	3.0	2.8	2.5	2.8	2.9	2.6	2.5	2.7	2.9
U.S.	4.7	4.5	4.4	4.2	4.1	4.0	4.8	4.7	4.4	4.1	4.0	4.5

Note: Data is not seasonally adjusted and covers workers 16 years of age and older; all figures are percentages; (1) Metropolitan Statistical Area - see Appendix A for areas included
Source: Bureau of Labor Statistics, http://stats.bls.gov

Employment by Industry

Sector	MSA[1]		U.S.
	Number of Employees	Percent of Total	Percent of Total
Services	1,048,900	39.8	30.4
Retail Trade	400,400	15.2	17.7
Government	591,500	22.5	15.6
Manufacturing	104,800	4.0	14.3
Finance/Insurance/Real Estate	143,000	5.4	5.9
Wholesale Trade	81,200	3.1	5.4
Transportation/Public Utilities	124,100	4.7	5.3
Construction	139,600	5.3	5.0
Mining	1,200	<0.1	0.4

Note: Figures cover non-farm employment as of 6/99 and are not seasonally adjusted; (1) Metropolitan Statistical Area - see Appendix A for areas included
Source: Bureau of Labor Statistics, http://stats.bls.gov

Employment by Occupation

Occupation Category	City (%)	MSA[1] (%)	U.S. (%)
White Collar	71.1	73.2	58.1
Executive/Admin./Management	17.2	20.1	12.3
Professional	21.9	20.1	14.1
Technical & Related Support	4.9	5.1	3.7
Sales	6.7	9.7	11.8
Administrative Support/Clerical	20.4	18.1	16.3
Blue Collar	11.9	14.5	26.2
Precision Production/Craft/Repair	4.5	7.7	11.3
Machine Operators/Assem./Insp.	1.7	1.8	6.8
Transportation/Material Movers	3.3	2.7	4.1
Cleaners/Helpers/Laborers	2.4	2.3	3.9
Services	16.6	11.5	13.2
Farming/Forestry/Fishing	0.4	0.9	2.5

Note: Figures cover employed persons 16 years old and over; (1) Metropolitan Statistical Area - see Appendix A for areas included
Source: 1990 Census of Population and Housing, Summary Tape File 3C

Occupational Employment Projections: 1994 - 2005

High Demand Occupations (ranked by annual openings)	Fast-Growing Occupations[1] (ranked by percent growth)
1. Janitors/cleaners/maids, ex. priv. hshld.	1. Child care workers, private household
2. Secretaries, except legal & medical	2. Residential counselors
3. General managers & top executives	3. Home health aides
4. Waiters & waitresses	4. Teachers, preschool and kindergarten
5. General office clerks	5. Human services workers
6. Lawyers	6. Personal and home care aides
7. Guards	7. Instructors, adult (nonvocational) educ.
8. Receptionists and information clerks	8. Janitors/cleaners/maids, ex. priv. hshld.
9. Clerical supervisors	9. Social workers, exc. med. & psych.
10. Food preparation, fast food	10. Artists and commercial artists

Note: Projections cover DC; (1) Based on employment growth of 100 or more jobs
Source: Department of Employment Services, Occupational Employment Projections - Year 2005, District of Columbia

TAXES

Major State and Local Tax Rates

State Corp. Income (%)	State Personal Income (%)	Residential Property (effective rate per $100)	Sales & Use State (%)	Sales & Use Local (%)	State Gasoline (cents/ gallon)	State Cigarette (cents/ pack)
9.975 [a]	6.0 - 9.5	0.96	5.75	None	20.0	65.0

Note: Personal/corporate income, sales, gasoline and cigarette tax rates as of January 1999. Property tax rates as of 1997; (a) A 5.0% surtax is also imposed. Minimum tax is $100
Source: Federation of Tax Administrators, www.taxadmin.org; Washington D.C. Department of Finance and Revenue, Tax Rates and Tax Burdens in the District of Columbia: A Nationwide Comparison, July 1998; Chamber of Commerce, 1999

Total Taxes Per Capita and as a Percent of Income

Area	Per Capita Income ($)	Per Capita Taxes ($) Total	Per Capita Taxes ($) Federal	Per Capita Taxes ($) State/ Local	Percent of Income (%) Total	Percent of Income (%) Federal	Percent of Income (%) State/ Local
DC	37,876	15,543	8,689	6,854	41.0	22.9	18.1
U.S.	27,876	9,881	6,690	3,191	35.4	24.0	11.4

Note: Figures are for 1998
Source: Tax Foundation, www.taxfoundation.org

Estimated Tax Burden

Area	State Income	Local Income	Property	Sales	Total
Washington	4,964	0	3,000	561	8,525

Note: The numbers are estimates of taxes paid by a married couple with two children and annual earnings of $75,000. Sales tax estimates assume they spend average amounts on food, clothing, household goods and gasoline. Property tax estimates assume they live in a $250,000 home.
Source: Kiplinger's Personal Finance Magazine, October 1998

COMMERCIAL REAL ESTATE

Office Market

Class/ Location	Total Space (sq. ft.)	Vacant Space (sq. ft.)	Vac. Rate (%)	Under Constr. (sq. ft.)	Net Absorp. (sq. ft.)	Rental Rates ($/sq.ft./yr.)
Class A						
CBD	45,636,466	1,888,503	4.1	1,852,146	1,055,690	34.00-55.00
Outside CBD	97,229,037	3,270,752	3.4	9,961,837	1,167,854	25.00-32.00
Class B						
CBD	41,579,727	2,556,285	6.1	n/a	756,025	25.00-36.00
Outside CBD	56,578,309	4,146,051	7.3	79,000	219,403	18.00-25.00

Note: Data as of 10/98 and covers District of Columbia; CBD = Central Business District; n/a not available;
Source: Society of Industrial and Office Realtors, 1999 Comparative Statistics of Industrial and Office Real Estate Markets

"The demand for Class A space will remain strong in 1999. Given the current uncertainty about the national economy, a few projects scheduled as speculative have reverted back to build-to-suit. There is approximately 750,000 sq. ft. of proposed space in the District. Several large speculative projects should be able to satisfy the continued demand for new office space. The majority of the new development is occurring in the East End, CBD, and Capital Hill sub-markets. Solid growth in business and professional services will hopefully sustain absorption over the new year, especially if the area can attract more high-technology employees. As capital markets adjust to the overseas turmoil, domestic pension funds will once again become a major player in the real estate market." *Society of Industrial and Office Realtors, 1999 Comparative Statistics of Industrial and Office Real Estate Markets*

Industrial Market

Location	Total Space (sq. ft.)	Vacant Space (sq. ft.)	Vac. Rate (%)	Under Constr. (sq. ft.)	Net Absorp. (sq. ft.)	Lease ($/sq.ft./yr.)
Central City	n/a	n/a	n/a	n/a	n/a	n/a
Suburban	69,761,840	6,989,879	10.0	1,253,492	1,552,821	3.75-6.00

Note: Data as of 10/98 and covers Suburban Maryland (Prince Georges, Montgomery and Frederick Counties); n/a not available
Source: Society of Industrial and Office Realtors, 1999 Comparative Statistics of Industrial and Office Real Estate Markets

"Steady growth should be the trend in suburban Maryland, resulting in stable to slow lease price increases in 1999. Industrial growth in Frederick County is expected to escalate. About 1.7 million sq. ft. of new space is in the pipeline, and this could drive vacancy up to 10.5 percent by year-end 1999. Manekin is developing two flex/warehouses in Beltsville—a healthy Prince Georges County niche. Two R&D properties are also planned in Montgomery County—the heart of the local bio-tech community. Sales prices for prime buildings have been exceptionally strong, in the $60 to $70 per square foot range, with high-tech space commanding nearly $100 per sq. ft. Further price increases are envisioned. As vacancy rises, look for warehouse construction to pull back sharply. It is hard to predict a more active year for investment sales, but leasing volume should grow modestly in 1999." *Society of Industrial and Office Realtors, 1999 Comparative Statistics of Industrial and Office Real Estate Markets*

Retail Market

Shopping Center Inventory (sq. ft.)	Shopping Center Construction (sq. ft.)	Construction as a Percent of Inventory (%)	Torto Wheaton Rent Index[1] ($/sq. ft.)
84,389,000	1,162,000	1.4	16.67

Note: Data as of 1997 and covers the Metropolitan Statistical Area - see Appendix A for areas included; (1) Index is based on a model that predicts what the average rent should be for leases with certain characteristics, in certain locations during certain years.
Source: National Association of Realtors, 1997-1998 Market Conditions Report

"An easing of federal government cutbacks, coupled with a strong tourism industry, helped make 1997 a good year for the Washington D.C. area retail market. The area's retail rent index climbed 5.8% while shopping center completions remained robust. The addition of the new $200 million MCI Arena Downtown will be a boon to retailers in the area. Furthermore, Washington ranks near the top of the most eligible list in all of the most relevant demographic categories analyzed by restaurants. National retailers have recently stormed into the area, led by Minneapolis-based Target stores, which opened 15 stores between Baltimore and Washington. However, many brokers expect activity to level off in the near future." *National Association of Realtors, 1997-1998 Market Conditions Report*

COMMERCIAL UTILITIES

Typical Monthly Electric Bills

Area	Commercial Service ($/month)		Industrial Service ($/month)	
	12 kW demand 1,500 kWh	100 kW demand 30,000 kWh	1,000 kW demand 400,000 kWh	20,000 kW demand 10,000,000 kWh
City	142	2,080	21,953	378,227
U.S.	150	2,174	23,995	508,569

Note: Based on rates in effect January 1, 1999
Source: Edison Electric Institute, Typical Residential, Commercial and Industrial Bills, Winter 1999

TRANSPORTATION

Transportation Statistics

Average minutes to work	27.1
Interstate highways	I-66; I-95
Bus lines	
In-city	Washington Metropolitan Area TA, 1,557 vehicles
Inter-city	9
Passenger air service	
Airport	Dulles International; Ronald Reagan Washington National Airport
Airlines	25
Aircraft departures	150,226 (1996)
Enplaned passengers	11,522,295 (1996)
Rail service	Amtrak; Metro (subway)
Motor freight carriers	n/a
Major waterways/ports	Potomac River

Source: Editor & Publisher Market Guide, 1999; FAA Airport Activity Statistics, 1997; Amtrak National Time Table, Northeast Timetable, Spring/Summer 1999; 1990 Census of Population and Housing, STF 3C; Chamber of Commerce/Economic Development 1999; Jane's Urban Transport Systems 1999-2000

Means of Transportation to Work

Area	Car/Truck/Van		Public Transportation			Bicycle	Walked	Other Means	Worked at Home
	Drove Alone	Car-pooled	Bus	Subway	Railroad				
City	35.0	12.0	22.3	12.9	0.2	0.8	11.8	2.0	3.0
MSA[1]	62.9	15.8	6.6	6.5	0.2	0.3	3.9	1.0	2.8
U.S.	73.2	13.4	3.0	1.5	0.5	0.4	3.9	1.2	3.0

Note: Figures shown are percentages and only include workers 16 years old and over;
(1) Metropolitan Statistical Area - see Appendix A for areas included
Source: 1990 Census of Population and Housing, Summary Tape File 3C

BUSINESSES

Major Business Headquarters

Company Name	1999 Rankings	
	Fortune 500	Forbes 500
Danaher	498	-
Fannie Mae	26	-
U.S. Office Products	419	-

Note: Companies listed are located in the city; dashes indicate no ranking
Fortune 500: Companies that produce a 10-K are ranked 1 to 500 based on 1998 revenue
Forbes 500: Private companies are ranked 1 to 500 based on 1997 revenue
Source: Forbes, November 30, 1998; Fortune, April 26, 1999

Best Companies to Work For

Marriott International (hotels) and Bureau of National Affairs (specialty publishing), headquartered in Washington, are among the "100 Best Companies to Work for in America." Criteria: trust in management, pride in work/company, camaraderie, company responses to the Hewitt People Practices Inventory, and employee responses to their Great Place to Work survey. The companies also had to be at least 10 years old and have a minimum of 500 employees. *Fortune, January 11, 1999*

The Bureau of National Affairs, Fannie Mae and Marriott International, headquartered in Washington, are among the "100 Best Companies for Working Mothers." Criteria: fair wages, opportunities for women to advance, support for child care, flexible work schedules, family-friendly benefits, and work/life supports. *Working Mother, October 1998*

Student Loan Marketing Assn. (financial services) and Fannie Mae (financial services), headquartered in Washington, are among the "100 Best Places to Work in IS." Criteria: compensation, turnover and training. *Computerworld, May 25, 1998*

Fannie Mae Corp., headquartered in Washington, is among the top public firms for executive women. Criteria: number of female directors, women in senior management positions and the ratio of female managers to female employees. *Working Women, September 1998*

Fast-Growing Businesses

Washington is home to one of *Business Week's* "hot growth" companies: Strayer Education. Criteria: increase in sales and profits, return on capital and stock price. *Business Week, 5/31/99*

According to *Fortune*, Washington is home to one of America's 100 fastest-growing companies: Federal Agricultural Mortgage. Companies were ranked based on earnings-per-share growth, revenue growth and total return over the previous three years. Criteria for inclusion: public companies with sales of least $50 million. Companies that lost money in the most recent quarter, or ended in the red for the past four quarters as a whole, were not eligible. Limited partnerships and REITs were also not considered. *Fortune, "America's Fastest-Growing Companies," 1999*

Women-Owned Firms: Number, Employment and Sales

Area	Number of Firms	Employ-ment	Sales ($000)	Rank[2]
MSA[1]	193,600	440,000	56,644,000	6

Note: (1) Metropolitan Statistical Area - see Appendix A for areas included;
(2) Calculated on an averaging of the number of businesses, employment and sales
Source: The National Foundation for Women Business Owners, 1999 Facts on Women-Owned Businesses: Trends in the Top 50 Metropolitan Areas

Women-Owned Firms: Growth

Area	% change from 1992 to 1999			Rank[2]
	Number of Firms	Employment	Sales	
MSA[1]	45.8	105.1	115.5	28

Note: (1) Metropolitan Statistical Area - see Appendix A for areas included; (2) Calculated on an averaging of the percent growth of number of businesses, employment and sales
Source: The National Foundation for Women Business Owners, 1999 Facts on Women-Owned Businesses: Trends in the Top 50 Metropolitan Areas

Minority Business Opportunity

Washington is home to one company which is on the Black Enterprise Industrial/Service 100 list (largest based on gross sales): BET Holdings II Inc. (cable television programming, magazine publishing) . Criteria: operational in previous calendar year, at least 51% black-owned and manufactures/owns the product it sells or provides industrial or consumer services. Brokerages, real estate firms and firms that provide professional services are not eligible. *Black Enterprise, www.blackenterprise.com*

Seven of the 500 largest Hispanic-owned companies in the U.S. are located in Washington. *Hispanic Business, June 1999*

Small Business Opportunity

According to *Forbes*, Washington is home to one of America's 200 best small companies: Strayer Education. Criteria: companies included must be publicly traded since November 1997 with a stock price of at least $5 per share and an average daily float of 1,000 shares. The company's latest 12-month sales must be between $5 and $350 million, return on equity (ROE) must be a minimum of 12% for both the past 5 years and the most recent four quarters, and five-year sales and EPS growth must average at least 10%. Companies with declining sales or earnings during the past year were dropped as well as businesses with debt/equity ratios over 1.25. Companies with negative operating cash flow in each of the past two years were also excluded. *Forbes, November 2, 1998*

HOTELS & MOTELS

Hotels/Motels

Area	Hotels/ Motels	Rooms	Luxury-Level Hotels/Motels		Average Minimum Rates ($)		
			♦♦♦♦	♦♦♦♦♦	♦♦	♦♦♦	♦♦♦♦
City	87	21,380	11	1	99	151	229
Airport	45	11,792	2	0	n/a	n/a	n/a
Suburbs	137	23,009	2	0	n/a	n/a	n/a
Total	269	56,181	15	1	n/a	n/a	n/a

Note: n/a not available; classifications range from one diamond (budget properties with basic amenities) to five diamond (luxury properties with the finest service, rooms and facilities).
Source: OAG, Business Travel Planner, Winter 1998-99

CONVENTION CENTERS

Major Convention Centers

Center Name	Meeting Rooms	Exhibit Space (sq. ft.)
District of Columbia Armory	n/a	124,771
Washington Convention Center	40	381,000

Note: n/a not available
Source: Trade Shows Worldwide, 1998; Meetings & Conventions, 4/15/99; Sucessful Meetings, 3/31/98

Living Environment

COST OF LIVING

Cost of Living Index

Composite Index	Groceries	Housing	Utilities	Trans-portation	Health Care	Misc. Goods/ Services
123.7	112.2	146.4	95.5	129.9	123.6	115.5

Note: U.S. = 100; Figures are for the Metropolitan Statistical Area - see Appendix A for areas included
Source: ACCRA, Cost of Living Index, 1st Quarter 1999

HOUSING

Median Home Prices and Housing Affordability

Area	Median Price[2] 1st Qtr. 1999 ($)	HOI[3] 1st Qtr. 1999	Afford-ability Rank[4]
MSA[1]	158,000	84.0	26
U.S.	134,000	69.6	–

Note: (1) Metropolitan Statistical Area - see Appendix A for areas included; (2) U.S. figures calculated from the sales of 524,324 new and existing homes in 181 markets; (3) Housing Opportunity Index - percent of homes sold that were within the reach of the median income household at the prevailing mortgage interest rate; (4) Rank is from 1-181 with 1 being most affordable
Source: National Association of Home Builders, Housing Opportunity Index, 1st Quarter 1999

Median Home Price Projection

It is projected that the median price of existing single-family homes in the metro area will increase by 3.8% in 1999. Nationwide, home prices are projected to increase 3.8%.
Kiplinger's Personal Finance Magazine, January 1999

Average New Home Price

Area	Price ($)
MSA[1]	203,023
U.S.	142,735

Note: Figures are based on a new home with 1,800 sq. ft. of living area on an 8,000 sq. ft. lot; (1) Metropolitan Statistical Area - see Appendix A for areas included
Source: ACCRA, Cost of Living Index, 1st Quarter 1999

Average Apartment Rent

Area	Rent ($/mth)
MSA[1]	1,098
U.S.	601

Note: Figures are based on an unfurnished two bedroom, 1-1/2 or 2 bath apartment, approximately 950 sq. ft. in size, excluding all utilities except water; (1) Metropolitan Statistical Area - see Appendix A for areas included
Source: ACCRA, Cost of Living Index, 1st Quarter 1999

RESIDENTIAL UTILITIES

Average Residential Utility Costs

Area	All Electric ($/mth)	Part Electric ($/mth)	Other Energy ($/mth)	Phone ($/mth)
MSA[1]	–	57.63	35.70	20.86
U.S.	100.02	55.73	43.33	19.71

Note: (1) (1) Metropolitan Statistical Area - see Appendix A for areas included
Source: ACCRA, Cost of Living Index, 1st Quarter 1999

HEALTH CARE

Average Health Care Costs

Area	Hospital ($/day)	Doctor ($/visit)	Dentist ($/visit)
MSA[1]	520.60	67.70	80.90
U.S.	430.43	52.45	66.35

Note: Hospital—based on a semi-private room; Doctor—based on a general practitioner's routine exam of an established patient; Dentist—based on adult teeth cleaning and periodic oral exam; (1) Metropolitan Statistical Area - see Appendix A for areas included
Source: ACCRA, Cost of Living Index, 1st Quarter 1999

Distribution of Office-Based Physicians

Area	Family/Gen. Practitioners	Specialists		
		Medical	Surgical	Other
MSA[1]	888	4,007	2,489	2,864

Note: Data as of 12/31/97; (1) Metropolitan Statistical Area - see Appendix A for areas included
Source: American Medical Assn., Physician Characteristics & Distribution in the U.S., 1999

Hospitals

Washington has 1 general medical and surgical hospital, 2 psychiatric, 1 obstetrics and gynecology, 1 rehabilitation, 1 children's general, 1 children's rehabilitation. *AHA Guide to the Healthcare Field, 1998-99*

According to *U.S. News and World Report*, Washington has 5 of the best hospitals in the U.S.: **Georgetown University Hospital**, noted for cardiology, gynecology, neurology, orthopedics, otolaryngology; **Children's National Medical Center**, noted for pediatrics; **National Rehabilitation Hospital**, noted for rehabilitation; **Howard University Hospital**, noted for endocrinology, rheumatology; **Washington Hospital Center**, noted for endocrinology. *U.S. News Online, "America's Best Hospitals," 10th Edition, www.usnews.com*

EDUCATION

Public School District Statistics

District Name	Num. Sch.	Enroll.	Classroom Teachers	Pupils per Teacher	Minority Pupils (%)	Current Exp.[1] ($/pupil)
District of Columbia Pub Schls	171	77,111	n/a	n/a	96.0	8,510

Note: Data covers the 1997-1998 school year unless otherwise noted; (1) Data covers fiscal year 1996; SD = School District; ISD = Independent School District; n/a not available
Source: National Center for Education Statistics, Common Core of Data Public Education Agency Universe 1997-98; National Center for Education Statistics, Characteristics of the 100 Largest Public Elementary and Secondary School Districts in the United States: 1997-98, July 1999

Educational Quality

School District	Education Quotient[1]	Graduate Outcome[2]	Community Index[3]	Resource Index[4]
District of Columbia	98.0	93.0	75.0	112.0

Note: Nearly 1,000 secondary school districts were rated in terms of educational quality. The scores range from a low of 50 to a high of 150; (1) Average of the Graduate Outcome, Community and Resource indexes; (2) Based on graduation rates and college board scores (SAT/ACT); (3) Based on the surrounding community's average level of education and the area's average income level; (4) Based on teacher salaries, per-pupil expenditures and student-teacher ratios.
Source: Expansion Management, Ratings Issue, 1998

Educational Attainment by Race

Area	High School Graduate (%)					Bachelor's Degree (%)				
	Total	White	Black	Other	Hisp.[2]	Total	White	Black	Other	Hisp.[2]
City	73.1	93.1	63.8	61.0	52.6	33.3	69.0	15.3	31.8	24.0
MSA[1]	85.2	90.1	74.5	75.7	64.5	38.5	45.3	19.9	38.4	23.8
U.S.	75.2	77.9	63.1	60.4	49.8	20.3	21.5	11.4	19.4	9.2

Note: Figures shown cover persons 25 years old and over; (1) Metropolitan Statistical Area - see Appendix A for areas included; (2) people of Hispanic origin can be of any race
Source: 1990 Census of Population and Housing, Summary Tape File 3C

School Enrollment by Type

Area	Preprimary				Elementary/High School			
	Public		Private		Public		Private	
	Enrollment	%	Enrollment	%	Enrollment	%	Enrollment	%
City	5,532	61.8	3,425	38.2	67,278	83.9	12,882	16.1
MSA[1]	39,352	48.2	42,299	51.8	522,711	87.4	75,692	12.6
U.S.	2,679,029	59.5	1,824,256	40.5	38,379,689	90.2	4,187,099	9.8

Note: Figures shown cover persons 3 years old and over;
(1) Metropolitan Statistical Area - see Appendix A for areas included
Source: 1990 Census of Population and Housing, Summary Tape File 3C

School Enrollment by Race

Area	Preprimary (%)				Elementary/High School (%)			
	White	Black	Other	Hisp.[1]	White	Black	Other	Hisp.[1]
City	25.0	71.2	3.8	3.4	12.6	82.2	5.2	6.5
MSA[2]	70.9	23.1	6.0	4.4	58.9	31.6	9.5	6.7
U.S.	80.4	12.5	7.1	7.8	74.1	15.6	10.3	12.5

Note: Figures shown cover persons 3 years old and over; (1) people of Hispanic origin can be of any race; (2) Metropolitan Statistical Area - see Appendix A for areas included
Source: 1990 Census of Population and Housing, Summary Tape File 3C

Classroom Teacher Salaries in Public Schools

District	B.A. Degree		M.A. Degree		Maximum	
	Min. ($)	Rank[1]	Max. ($)	Rank[1]	Max. ($)	Rank[1]
Washington	27,104	37	48,469	31	51,342	43
Average	26,980	-	46,065	-	51,435	-

Note: Salaries are for 1997-1998; (1) Rank ranges from 1 to 100
Source: American Federation of Teachers, Survey & Analysis of Salary Trends, 1998

Higher Education

Two-Year Colleges		Four-Year Colleges		Medical Schools	Law Schools	Voc/ Tech
Public	Private	Public	Private			
0	0	2	12	3	6	10

Source: College Blue Book, Occupational Education, 1997; Medical School Admission Requirements, 1999-2000; Peterson's Guide to Two-Year Colleges, 1999; Peterson's Guide to Four-Year Colleges, 2000; Barron's Guide to Law Schools, 1999

MAJOR EMPLOYERS

Major Employers

Children's National Medical Center
Federal National Mortgage Association
International Bank for Reconstruction & Development
Marriott International Hotels
Meristar Hotels & Resorts

Federal Deposit Insurance Corp.
GEICO Corp.
International Monetary Fund

CTF Holdings (hotels & motels)
Washington Metropolitan Area Transit Authority

Note: Companies listed are located in the city
Source: Dun's Business Rankings, 1999; Ward's Business Directory, 1998

PUBLIC SAFETY

Crime Rate

Area	All Crimes	Violent Crimes				Property Crimes		
		Murder	Forcible Rape	Robbery	Aggrav. Assault	Burglary	Larceny -Theft	Motor Vehicle Theft
City	9,827.2	56.9	41.2	850.5	1,075.2	1,316.3	5,056.3	1,430.8
Suburbs[1]	4,222.4	4.1	25.0	149.6	205.7	574.4	2,787.1	476.5
MSA[2]	4,879.2	10.3	26.9	231.7	307.6	661.4	3,053.0	588.4
U.S.	4,922.7	6.8	35.9	186.1	382.0	919.6	2,886.5	505.8

Note: Crime rate is the number of crimes per 100,000 pop.; (1) defined as all areas within the MSA but located outside the central city; (2) Metropolitan Statistical Area - see Appendix A for areas incl.
Source: FBI Uniform Crime Reports, 1997

RECREATION

Culture and Recreation

Museums	Symphony Orchestras	Opera Companies	Dance Companies	Professional Theatres	Zoos	Pro Sports Teams
31	3	3	8	11	1	3

Source: International Directory of the Performing Arts, 1997; Official Museum Directory, 1999; Stern's Performing Arts Directory, 1997; USA Today Four Sport Stadium Guide, 1997; Chamber of Commerce/Economic Development, 1999

Library System

The District of Columbia Public Library has 25 branches and holdings of 2,165,154 volumes. *American Library Directory, 1998-1999*

MEDIA

Newspapers

Name	Type	Freq.	Distribution	Circulation
Aerospace Daily	n/a	5x/wk	U.S./Int'l.	22,000
Capital Spotlight Newspaper	Blk/Gen/Rel	1x/wk	Local	50,000
La Nacion	Hispanic	1x/wk	Area	22,000
The Rock Creek Current	General	1x/wk	Local	32,500
Washington Informer	Black	1x/wk	Regional	27,000
The Washington New Observer	Black	1x/wk	Area	20,000
Washington Post	General	7x/wk	Area	834,641
The Washington Post National Weekly	General	1x/wk	U.S.	118,000
The Washington Times	General	7x/wk	Local	101,243
Washington Times (National Weekly Edition)	General	1x/wk	U.S.	100,196

Note: Includes newspapers with circulations of 10,000 or more located in the city; n/a not available
Source: Burrelle's Media Directory, 1999 Edition

Television Stations

Name	Ch.	Affiliation	Type	Owner
WRC	n/a	NBCT	Commercial	General Electric Corporation
WTTG	n/a	FBC	Commercial	Fox Television Stations Inc.
WJLA	n/a	ABCT	Commercial	Allbritton Communications Company
WUSA	n/a	CBST	Commercial	Gannett Broadcasting
WHMM	32	PBS	Public	Howard University
WBDC	50	n/a	Commercial	Jasas Corporation

Note: Stations included broadcast in the Washington metro area; n/a not available
Source: Burrelle's Media Directory, 1999 Edition

AM Radio Stations

Call Letters	Freq. (kHz)	Target Audience	Station Format	Music Format
WMAL	630	G/S	N/T	n/a
WTOP	1500	General	N/S	n/a

Note: Stations included broadcast in the Washington metro area; n/a not available
Target Audience: A=Asian; B=Black; C=Christian; E=Ethnic; F=French; G=General; H=Hispanic;
M=Men; N=Native American; R=Religious; S=Senior Citizen; W=Women; Y=Young Adult; Z=Children
Station Format: E=Educational; M=Music; N=News; S=Sports; T=Talk
Source: Burrelle's Media Directory, 1999 Edition

FM Radio Stations

Call Letters	Freq. (mHz)	Target Audience	Station Format	Music Format
WAMU	88.5	General	M/N/T	Country
WPFW	89.3	General	E/M/N/T	Jazz/Oldies/R&B
WDCU	90.1	General	M	Christian/Jazz/R&B
WHUR	96.3	n/a	M	Adult Contemporary
WGMS	103.5	General	M	Classical
WJZW	105.9	B/G/H	M/N/S	Jazz
WRQX	107.3	General	M/N/T	Adult Contemporary/Adult Top 40
WTOP	107.7	General	N/S/T	n/a

Note: Stations included broadcast in the Washington metro area; n/a not available
Station Format: E=Educational; M=Music; N=News; S=Sports; T=Talk
Target Audience: A=Asian; B=Black; C=Christian; E=Ethnic; F=French; G=General; H=Hispanic;
M=Men; N=Native American; R=Religious; S=Senior Citizen; W=Women; Y=Young Adult; Z=Children
Source: Burrelle's Media Directory, 1999 Edition

CLIMATE

Average and Extreme Temperatures

Temperature	Jan	Feb	Mar	Apr	May	Jun	Jul	Aug	Sep	Oct	Nov	Dec	Yr.
Extreme High (°F)	79	82	89	95	97	101	104	103	101	94	86	75	104
Average High (°F)	43	46	55	67	76	84	88	86	80	69	58	47	67
Average Temp. (°F)	36	38	46	57	66	75	79	78	71	60	49	39	58
Average Low (°F)	28	30	37	46	56	65	70	69	62	50	40	31	49
Extreme Low (°F)	-5	4	14	24	34	47	54	49	39	29	16	3	-5

Note: Figures cover the years 1945-1990
Source: National Climatic Data Center, International Station Meteorological Climate Summary, 3/95

Average Precipitation/Snowfall/Humidity

Precip./Humidity	Jan	Feb	Mar	Apr	May	Jun	Jul	Aug	Sep	Oct	Nov	Dec	Yr.
Avg. Precip. (in.)	2.8	2.6	3.3	2.9	4.0	3.4	4.1	4.2	3.3	2.9	3.0	3.1	39.5
Avg. Snowfall (in.)	6	6	2	Tr	0	0	0	0	0	Tr	1	3	18
Avg. Rel. Hum. 7am (%)	71	70	70	70	74	75	77	80	82	80	76	72	75
Avg. Rel. Hum. 4pm (%)	54	50	46	45	51	52	53	54	54	53	53	55	52

Note: Figures cover the years 1945-1990; Tr = Trace amounts (<0.05 in. of rain; <0.5 in. of snow)
Source: National Climatic Data Center, International Station Meteorological Climate Summary, 3/95

Weather Conditions

Temperature			Daytime Sky			Precipitation		
10°F & below	32°F & below	90°F & above	Clear	Partly cloudy	Cloudy	0.01 inch or more precip.	0.1 inch or more snow/ice	Thunder- storms
2	71	34	84	144	137	112	9	30

Note: Figures are average number of days per year and covers the years 1945-1990
Source: National Climatic Data Center, International Station Meteorological Climate Summary, 3/95

AIR & WATER QUALITY

Maximum Pollutant Concentrations

	Particulate Matter (ug/m³)	Carbon Monoxide (ppm)	Sulfur Dioxide (ppm)	Nitrogen Dioxide (ppm)	Ozone (ppm)	Lead (ug/m³)
MSA[1] Level	54	7	0.024	0.026	0.14	0.02
NAAQS[2]	150	9	0.140	0.053	0.12	1.50
Met NAAQS?	Yes	Yes	Yes	Yes	No	Yes

Note: (1) Metropolitan Statistical Area - see Appendix A for areas included; (2) National Ambient Air Quality Standards; ppm = parts per million; ug/m³ = micrograms per cubic meter; n/a not available
Source: EPA, National Air Quality and Emissions Trends Report, 1997

Pollutant Standards Index

In the Washington MSA (see Appendix A for areas included), the Pollutant Standards Index (PSI) exceeded 100 on 31 days in 1997. A PSI value greater than 100 indicates that air quality would be in the unhealthful range on that day. *EPA, National Air Quality and Emissions Trends Report, 1997*

Drinking Water

Water System Name	Pop. Served	Primary Water Source Type	Number of Violations in 1998	Type of Violation/ Contaminants
Water and Sewer Utility Admin	595,000	Purchased surface	None	None

Note: Data as of July 10, 1999
Source: EPA, Office of Ground Water and Drinking Water, Safe Drinking Water Information System

Washington tap water is slightly alkaline and medium soft.
Editor & Publisher Market Guide, 1999

Comparative Statistics

Population Growth: City

City	Population			% Change	
	1980	1990	1998[1]	1980-90	1990-98
Akron	237,177	223,019	215,712	-6.0	-3.3
Baltimore	786,775	736,014	645,593	-6.5	-12.3
Boston	562,994	574,283	555,447	2.0	-3.3
Charlotte	314,447	396,003	504,637	25.9	27.4
Cincinnati	385,457	364,040	336,400	-5.6	-7.6
Cleveland	573,822	505,616	495,817	-11.9	-1.9
Greensboro	155,684	183,521	197,910	17.9	7.8
Lexington	204,165	225,366	241,749	10.4	7.3
Louisville	298,455	269,157	255,045	-9.8	-5.2
Manchester	90,936	99,567	102,524	9.5	3.0
New York	7,071,639	7,322,564	7,420,166	3.5	1.3
Norfolk	266,979	261,229	215,215	-2.2	-17.6
Philadelphia	1,688,210	1,585,577	1,436,287	-6.1	-9.4
Pittsburgh	423,938	369,879	340,520	-12.8	-7.9
Providence	156,804	160,728	150,890	2.5	-6.1
Raleigh	150,255	207,951	259,423	38.4	24.8
Richmond	219,214	203,056	194,173	-7.4	-4.4
Rochester	241,741	231,636	216,887	-4.2	-6.4
Washington	638,333	606,900	523,124	-4.9	-13.8
U.S.	**226,545,805**	**248,765,170**	**270,299,000**	**9.8**	**8.7**

Note: (1) Census Bureau estimate as of 7/98
Source: 1980 Census; 1990 Census of Population and Housing, Summary Tape File 3C

Population Growth: Metro Area

MSA[1]	Population			% Change	
	1980	1990	1998[2]	1980-90	1990-98
Akron	660,328	657,575	687,664	-0.4	4.6
Baltimore	2,199,531	2,382,172	2,504,766	8.3	5.1
Boston	2,805,911	2,870,650	3,274,844	2.3	14.1
Charlotte	971,391	1,162,093	1,374,044	19.6	18.2
Cincinnati	1,401,491	1,452,645	1,621,106	3.6	11.6
Cleveland	1,898,825	1,831,122	2,243,694	-3.6	22.5
Greensboro	851,444	942,091	1,171,550	10.6	24.4
Lexington	317,629	348,428	452,785	9.7	30.0
Louisville	956,756	952,662	1,006,017	-0.4	5.6
Manchester	142,527	147,867	184,969	3.7	25.1
New York	8,274,961	8,546,846	8,675,635	3.3	1.5
Norfolk	1,160,311	1,396,107	1,572,100	20.3	12.6
Philadelphia	4,716,818	4,856,881	4,963,153	3.0	2.2
Pittsburgh	2,218,870	2,056,705	2,374,277	-7.3	15.4
Providence	618,514	654,869	1,120,608	5.9	71.1
Raleigh	561,222	735,480	1,080,843	31.0	47.0
Richmond	761,311	865,640	958,352	13.7	10.7
Rochester	971,230	1,002,410	1,096,559	3.2	9.4
Washington	3,250,822	3,923,574	4,676,555	20.7	19.2
U.S.	**226,545,805**	**248,765,170**	**270,299,000**	**9.8**	**8.7**

Note: (1) Metropolitan Statistical Area - see Appendix A for areas included; (2) Pop. estimates calculated by the editors
Source: 1980 Census; 1990 Census of Population and Housing, Summary Tape File 3C

Population Characteristics: City

City	1990 Percent of Total (%)					
	White	Black	American Indian/ Esk./Aleut.	Asian/ Pacific Islander	Other	Hispanic Origin[1]
Akron	73.9	24.4	0.3	1.1	0.3	0.7
Baltimore	39.1	59.2	0.3	1.1	0.3	1.0
Boston	63.0	25.5	0.3	5.3	5.9	10.4
Charlotte	65.6	31.9	0.4	1.7	0.5	1.3
Cincinnati	60.5	37.9	0.2	1.1	0.3	0.6
Cleveland	49.6	46.5	0.3	1.0	2.7	4.4
Greensboro	63.9	34.0	0.4	1.4	0.3	0.8
Lexington	84.7	13.4	0.2	1.5	0.3	1.0
Louisville	69.2	29.7	0.3	0.7	0.2	0.6
Manchester	96.7	0.9	0.2	1.2	0.9	2.2
New York	52.3	28.8	0.3	7.0	11.6	23.7
Norfolk	56.7	39.1	0.5	2.6	1.1	2.8
Philadelphia	53.5	39.9	0.2	2.7	3.6	5.3
Pittsburgh	72.1	25.9	0.2	1.6	0.3	0.9
Providence	70.2	14.6	1.0	6.0	8.2	14.8
Raleigh	69.3	27.5	0.3	2.5	0.4	1.2
Richmond	43.3	55.4	0.2	0.8	0.3	0.9
Rochester	61.3	31.6	0.4	1.6	5.1	8.2
Washington	29.6	65.9	0.3	1.9	2.4	5.2
U.S.	**80.3**	**12.0**	**0.8**	**2.9**	**3.9**	**8.8**

Note: (1) People of Hispanic origin can be of any race
Source: 1990 Census of Population and Housing, Summary Tape File 3C

Population Characteristics: Metro Area

MSA[1]	1990 Percent of Total (%)					
	White	Black	American Indian/ Esk./Aleut.	Asian/ Pacific Islander	Other	Hispanic Origin[2]
Akron	88.8	9.8	0.2	0.9	0.2	0.6
Baltimore	71.8	25.8	0.3	1.8	0.3	1.2
Boston	87.2	7.2	0.2	3.3	2.1	4.3
Charlotte	78.5	19.9	0.4	0.9	0.3	0.8
Cincinnati	85.8	13.1	0.2	0.8	0.2	0.5
Cleveland	78.4	19.4	0.2	1.1	0.9	1.8
Greensboro	79.5	19.3	0.3	0.7	0.2	0.6
Lexington	87.8	10.7	0.2	1.1	0.2	0.9
Louisville	85.9	13.1	0.2	0.6	0.2	0.5
Manchester	97.3	0.7	0.3	1.0	0.6	1.6
New York	56.5	26.4	0.3	6.5	10.3	21.6
Norfolk	67.9	28.5	0.4	2.5	0.7	2.2
Philadelphia	76.6	19.1	0.2	2.1	2.0	3.4
Pittsburgh	90.8	8.2	0.1	0.7	0.2	0.5
Providence	90.3	4.6	0.5	2.2	2.4	4.6
Raleigh	72.5	24.9	0.3	1.9	0.4	1.1
Richmond	68.8	29.2	0.3	1.4	0.3	1.0
Rochester	87.6	9.3	0.3	1.3	1.5	2.9
Washington	65.8	26.6	0.3	5.1	2.2	5.6
U.S.	**80.3**	**12.0**	**0.8**	**2.9**	**3.9**	**8.8**

Note: (1) Metropolitan Statistical Area - see Appendix A for areas included;
(2) People of Hispanic origin can be of any race
Source: 1990 Census of Population and Housing, Summary Tape File 3C

Age: City

City	Median Age (Years)	Age Distribution (%)						
		Under 5	Under 18	18-24	25-44	45-64	65+	80+
Akron	32.5	7.5	24.5	12.1	31.6	16.9	14.8	3.4
Baltimore	32.5	7.7	24.5	11.1	32.9	17.9	13.7	3.0
Boston	30.2	6.2	19.1	17.3	36.8	15.3	11.5	2.9
Charlotte	32.0	7.5	24.3	10.6	37.3	18.0	9.8	2.0
Cincinnati	30.8	8.4	25.0	12.8	32.6	15.7	13.9	3.7
Cleveland	31.8	8.7	27.0	10.4	30.7	18.0	13.9	3.0
Greensboro	32.2	6.4	21.6	14.8	33.8	18.0	11.8	2.5
Lexington	31.2	6.7	22.4	14.5	36.4	16.8	9.9	2.0
Louisville	34.3	6.8	23.5	9.9	31.9	18.2	16.6	4.3
Manchester	31.8	7.8	23.0	11.9	34.9	16.5	13.7	3.1
New York	33.6	6.9	23.0	10.3	33.9	19.8	13.0	3.1
Norfolk	27.2	8.3	23.0	21.6	31.8	13.1	10.5	2.1
Philadelphia	33.1	7.3	23.9	11.4	30.8	18.6	15.2	3.4
Pittsburgh	34.5	6.1	19.9	13.7	30.3	18.2	17.9	3.9
Providence	29.2	7.8	24.0	17.6	30.1	14.7	13.6	3.6
Raleigh	30.2	6.2	19.5	17.5	38.6	15.6	8.8	1.9
Richmond	33.1	6.9	20.8	12.9	33.9	17.1	15.3	3.7
Rochester	29.7	9.5	26.0	13.0	35.1	14.0	11.9	3.3
Washington	33.4	6.0	19.2	13.4	35.9	18.7	12.8	2.8
U.S.	**32.9**	**7.3**	**25.6**	**10.5**	**32.6**	**18.7**	**12.5**	**2.8**

Source: 1990 Census of Population and Housing, Summary Tape File 3C

Age: Metro Area

MSA[1]	Median Age (Years)	Age Distribution (%)						
		Under 5	Under 18	18-24	25-44	45-64	65+	80+
Akron	33.4	6.9	24.5	11.6	31.9	19.2	12.8	2.7
Baltimore	33.3	7.4	24.2	10.2	34.6	19.4	11.7	2.4
Boston	33.3	6.4	20.8	12.4	35.1	18.9	12.9	3.1
Charlotte	32.7	7.2	24.8	10.9	34.2	19.3	10.9	2.2
Cincinnati	32.4	7.9	26.8	10.1	32.6	18.4	12.0	2.8
Cleveland	34.7	7.1	24.6	9.0	31.7	20.1	14.6	3.0
Greensboro	34.0	6.6	23.1	11.1	33.3	20.4	12.1	2.6
Lexington	31.7	6.8	23.9	13.1	35.1	17.6	10.3	2.2
Louisville	33.8	6.8	25.3	9.4	33.1	19.6	12.6	2.8
Manchester	32.2	7.7	24.1	11.4	35.0	17.1	12.3	2.9
New York	33.9	6.8	23.0	10.2	33.7	20.1	13.0	3.1
Norfolk	29.7	8.3	26.4	13.6	34.8	16.2	9.0	1.6
Philadelphia	33.7	7.3	24.4	10.3	32.4	19.5	13.5	2.9
Pittsburgh	36.9	6.2	21.7	9.2	30.6	21.0	17.4	3.5
Providence	34.0	6.5	22.1	12.3	31.9	18.5	15.1	3.5
Raleigh	31.2	6.8	22.5	14.0	37.6	16.9	8.9	2.0
Richmond	33.2	7.2	24.3	10.3	35.4	18.7	11.3	2.3
Rochester	32.9	7.6	25.0	11.2	33.1	18.4	12.3	2.8
Washington	32.4	7.2	23.5	10.9	38.2	19.0	8.5	1.7
U.S.	**32.9**	**7.3**	**25.6**	**10.5**	**32.6**	**18.7**	**12.5**	**2.8**

Note: (1) Metropolitan Statistical Area - see Appendix A for areas included
Source: 1990 Census of Population and Housing, Summary Tape File 3C

Male/Female Ratio: City

City	Number of males per 100 females (all ages)	Number of males per 100 females (18 years old+)
Akron	88.7	84.7
Baltimore	87.7	83.1
Boston	91.4	90.3
Charlotte	90.2	86.7
Cincinnati	87.2	81.7
Cleveland	88.2	83.4
Greensboro	86.9	82.6
Lexington	91.7	88.2
Louisville	86.1	81.1
Manchester	92.0	88.9
New York	88.1	84.5
Norfolk	114.0	117.8
Philadelphia	86.8	82.6
Pittsburgh	86.8	82.9
Providence	89.0	86.6
Raleigh	93.6	92.8
Richmond	83.9	80.0
Rochester	89.1	84.7
Washington	87.2	84.0
U.S.	**95.0**	**91.9**

Source: 1990 Census of Population, General Population Characteristics

Male/Female Ratio: Metro Area

MSA[1]	Number of males per 100 females (all ages)	Number of males per 100 females (18 years old+)
Akron	92.4	88.8
Baltimore	93.5	90.2
Boston	92.0	89.2
Charlotte	93.0	89.8
Cincinnati	92.1	87.8
Cleveland	90.1	85.9
Greensboro	91.7	87.9
Lexington	92.3	88.7
Louisville	91.1	86.8
Manchester	93.8	90.4
New York	88.6	85.0
Norfolk	100.4	99.4
Philadelphia	91.8	88.0
Pittsburgh	89.4	85.5
Providence	91.5	88.1
Raleigh	92.9	90.5
Richmond	90.7	87.1
Rochester	93.5	89.9
Washington	94.8	92.2
U.S.	**95.0**	**91.9**

Note: (1) Metropolitan Statistical Area - see Appendix A for areas included
Source: 1990 Census of Population, General Population Characteristics

Educational Attainment by Race: City

City	High School Graduate (%)					Bachelor's Degree (%)				
	Total	White	Black	Other	Hisp.[1]	Total	White	Black	Other	Hisp.[1]
Akron	72.9	74.9	65.3	71.5	77.5	14.9	16.6	7.0	36.1	18.8
Baltimore	60.7	64.4	57.3	72.5	66.7	15.5	23.5	8.6	32.7	25.3
Boston	75.7	81.5	66.7	55.8	52.8	30.0	36.7	14.0	20.3	13.9
Charlotte	81.0	86.9	66.5	71.9	73.2	28.4	34.5	12.5	27.7	21.9
Cincinnati	69.6	74.7	59.4	83.5	76.4	22.2	28.9	7.9	56.6	42.0
Cleveland	58.8	61.9	55.6	49.3	44.7	8.1	10.2	5.0	13.9	6.2
Greensboro	79.2	83.3	70.6	63.6	75.0	29.9	35.0	17.7	35.1	29.3
Lexington	80.2	82.5	63.1	86.6	72.4	30.6	32.8	10.3	59.5	24.4
Louisville	67.2	70.3	58.4	68.4	75.8	17.2	20.7	6.7	33.2	26.6
Manchester	74.9	74.9	82.5	74.3	76.2	19.6	19.3	17.5	33.8	23.3
New York	68.3	74.2	64.1	54.6	47.9	23.0	29.2	12.4	17.7	8.2
Norfolk	72.7	80.7	58.8	77.8	84.2	16.8	21.8	7.9	23.5	16.0
Philadelphia	64.3	68.1	60.2	51.4	44.7	15.2	19.0	9.1	17.3	8.2
Pittsburgh	72.4	74.0	66.3	87.7	78.4	20.1	22.6	8.8	62.2	39.2
Providence	62.8	66.1	61.6	41.9	42.0	21.6	25.4	10.1	9.5	6.6
Raleigh	86.6	92.1	70.3	85.6	81.8	40.6	47.0	19.9	55.4	45.0
Richmond	68.1	80.1	56.3	76.2	75.1	24.2	39.4	9.5	33.2	26.9
Rochester	68.8	74.4	57.7	49.1	44.4	19.0	23.6	7.5	13.9	5.7
Washington	73.1	93.1	63.8	61.0	52.6	33.3	69.0	15.3	31.8	24.0
U.S.	**75.2**	**77.9**	**63.1**	**60.4**	**49.8**	**20.3**	**21.5**	**11.4**	**19.4**	**9.2**

Note: Figures shown cover persons 25 years old and over; (1) people of Hispanic origin can be of any race
Source: 1990 Census of Population and Housing, Summary Tape File 3C

Educational Attainment by Race: Metro Area

MSA[1]	High School Graduate (%)					Bachelor's Degree (%)				
	Total	White	Black	Other	Hisp.[2]	Total	White	Black	Other	Hisp.[2]
Akron	78.5	79.6	66.8	80.2	82.7	19.3	20.0	8.5	44.4	23.6
Baltimore	74.7	78.2	63.0	80.4	79.7	23.1	26.2	12.0	39.5	30.6
Boston	83.7	85.4	70.7	68.0	58.8	33.1	34.1	17.9	33.9	18.2
Charlotte	72.5	74.8	61.7	68.7	69.5	19.6	21.4	10.5	24.5	19.9
Cincinnati	74.9	76.5	62.7	82.7	79.2	20.5	21.6	9.8	46.8	34.9
Cleveland	75.7	78.7	62.4	69.6	56.6	19.9	22.0	8.5	35.4	13.8
Greensboro	72.0	73.3	66.1	63.1	70.0	19.2	20.2	14.0	27.5	21.4
Lexington	75.9	77.3	61.8	84.6	72.5	25.3	26.7	9.2	55.8	22.9
Louisville	73.5	74.8	64.0	74.2	79.5	17.3	18.3	9.1	33.3	25.4
Manchester	77.5	77.6	79.3	73.6	78.8	21.5	21.3	14.7	36.3	26.3
New York	70.3	76.1	64.4	55.7	48.6	24.6	30.6	12.7	18.9	8.6
Norfolk	79.1	84.2	64.9	80.0	85.6	20.1	23.3	11.3	22.3	16.1
Philadelphia	75.9	79.2	63.8	62.6	51.8	22.8	25.2	10.9	26.5	11.7
Pittsburgh	77.4	78.0	68.6	86.1	80.6	19.5	19.9	10.1	56.1	30.0
Providence	72.7	73.9	65.3	51.4	46.6	22.3	23.0	13.2	15.7	9.3
Raleigh	82.4	87.2	66.0	86.3	77.2	34.8	39.2	17.8	55.6	36.6
Richmond	75.8	81.1	61.5	75.3	79.5	23.8	28.1	11.9	32.4	27.9
Rochester	79.1	81.1	60.3	61.6	53.6	23.4	24.4	10.3	27.5	11.7
Washington	85.2	90.1	74.5	75.7	64.5	38.5	45.3	19.9	38.4	23.8
U.S.	**75.2**	**77.9**	**63.1**	**60.4**	**49.8**	**20.3**	**21.5**	**11.4**	**19.4**	**9.2**

Note: Figures shown cover persons 25 years old and over; (1) Metropolitan Statistical Area - see Appendix A for areas included; (2) people of Hispanic origin can be of any race
Source: 1990 Census of Population and Housing, Summary Tape File 3C

Per Capita/Median/Average Income: City

City	Per Capita ($)	Median Household ($)	Average Household ($)
Akron	12,015	22,279	29,376
Baltimore	11,994	24,045	31,415
Boston	15,581	29,180	37,907
Charlotte	16,793	31,873	41,578
Cincinnati	12,547	21,006	29,010
Cleveland	9,258	17,822	22,921
Greensboro	15,644	29,184	37,886
Lexington	14,962	28,056	36,979
Louisville	11,527	20,141	26,993
Manchester	15,111	31,911	36,814
New York	16,281	29,823	41,741
Norfolk	11,643	23,563	29,947
Philadelphia	12,091	24,603	31,208
Pittsburgh	12,580	20,747	29,587
Providence	11,838	22,147	31,465
Raleigh	16,896	32,451	40,243
Richmond	13,993	23,551	32,497
Rochester	11,704	22,785	28,286
Washington	18,881	30,727	44,413
U.S.	**14,420**	**30,056**	**38,453**

Note: Figures are for 1989
Source: 1990 Census of Population and Housing, Summary Tape File 3C

Per Capita/Median/Average Income: Metro Area

MSA[1]	Per Capita ($)	Median Household ($)	Average Household ($)
Akron	13,997	29,280	36,513
Baltimore	16,596	36,550	44,405
Boston	19,288	40,491	50,478
Charlotte	14,611	31,125	38,214
Cincinnati	14,610	30,691	38,344
Cleveland	15,092	30,560	38,413
Greensboro	14,588	29,254	36,588
Lexington	13,945	27,558	35,698
Louisville	13,600	27,599	34,899
Manchester	16,278	35,866	42,004
New York	17,397	31,659	45,159
Norfolk	13,495	30,841	36,794
Philadelphia	16,386	35,437	44,191
Pittsburgh	14,052	26,700	34,902
Providence	15,135	32,340	39,842
Raleigh	16,170	33,290	40,686
Richmond	15,848	33,489	40,785
Rochester	15,355	34,234	40,554
Washington	21,416	46,884	56,799
U.S.	**14,420**	**30,056**	**38,453**

Note: Figures are for 1989; (1) Metropolitan Statistical Area - see Appendix A for areas included
Source: 1990 Census of Population and Housing, Summary Tape File 3C

Household Income Distribution: City

City	\$ of Households Earning								
	Less than \$5,000	\$5,000 -\$9,999	\$10,000 -\$14,999	\$15,000 -\$24,999	\$25,000 -\$34,999	\$35,000 -\$49,999	\$50,000 -\$74,999	\$75,000 -\$99,999	\$100,000 and up
Akron	10.2	13.3	10.7	20.8	16.8	14.7	8.9	2.5	2.0
Baltimore	11.7	11.6	9.5	18.7	15.7	15.9	11.3	3.2	2.4
Boston	8.0	12.5	7.4	15.8	14.6	16.2	15.3	5.4	4.8
Charlotte	5.5	6.7	7.5	18.0	17.2	18.8	15.7	5.6	5.1
Cincinnati	13.5	13.6	10.7	19.3	14.7	14.1	8.8	2.7	2.6
Cleveland	16.7	15.5	11.5	19.5	14.8	13.0	7.0	1.3	0.7
Greensboro	5.9	8.4	9.2	19.2	16.9	18.1	13.8	4.2	4.4
Lexington	7.7	9.1	9.4	18.1	16.1	17.1	13.9	4.5	4.2
Louisville	13.0	14.2	11.8	20.2	14.9	13.3	8.5	2.1	1.9
Manchester	4.7	9.4	7.5	16.1	16.9	21.9	16.1	4.8	2.5
New York	8.9	11.3	7.5	15.2	14.1	15.9	14.6	6.0	6.4
Norfolk	9.3	9.7	10.7	23.2	17.5	15.4	9.3	2.7	2.2
Philadelphia	10.0	12.7	9.9	18.0	15.2	16.4	12.2	3.3	2.2
Pittsburgh	10.9	15.9	11.5	19.2	14.8	13.3	8.9	2.6	2.9
Providence	8.1	17.1	10.3	19.2	14.0	14.9	9.7	3.2	3.5
Raleigh	5.6	6.7	7.7	17.7	16.1	18.9	17.0	5.6	4.7
Richmond	10.6	11.1	10.9	19.8	15.5	15.1	10.1	3.4	3.4
Rochester	9.4	15.0	10.5	18.2	15.9	16.0	10.8	2.7	1.4
Washington	8.7	7.8	7.2	17.3	14.7	15.6	14.4	6.4	7.8
U.S.	**6.2**	**9.3**	**8.8**	**17.5**	**15.8**	**17.9**	**15.0**	**5.1**	**4.4**

Note: Figures are for 1989
Source: 1990 Census of Population and Housing, Summary Tape File 3C

Household Income Distribution: Metro Area

MSA[1]	\$ of Households Earning								
	Less than \$5,000	\$5,000 -\$9,999	\$10,000 -\$14,999	\$15,000 -\$24,999	\$25,000 -\$34,999	\$35,000 -\$49,999	\$50,000 -\$74,999	\$75,000 -\$99,999	\$100,000 and up
Akron	6.2	9.6	8.6	18.1	16.9	18.3	14.6	4.4	3.4
Baltimore	5.4	6.5	6.3	14.4	14.9	19.8	19.5	7.6	5.6
Boston	4.2	8.0	5.6	12.2	13.0	17.7	20.8	9.5	9.0
Charlotte	5.2	7.9	8.0	18.1	17.1	19.2	15.9	4.9	3.6
Cincinnati	6.7	8.6	8.1	17.2	16.0	19.1	15.5	4.8	4.0
Cleveland	6.9	8.9	8.3	16.9	15.9	18.6	15.5	4.9	4.1
Greensboro	5.9	8.3	9.1	19.0	17.3	18.8	14.1	3.9	3.6
Lexington	7.7	9.5	9.6	18.3	16.3	17.3	13.6	4.1	3.6
Louisville	7.2	9.5	9.5	18.8	16.7	18.0	13.4	3.9	2.9
Manchester	4.1	8.0	6.6	14.2	15.6	22.3	18.9	6.1	4.2
New York	8.2	10.5	7.2	14.5	13.6	15.9	15.5	6.8	7.8
Norfolk	6.0	6.5	7.6	19.0	17.9	20.1	15.7	4.4	2.9
Philadelphia	5.2	7.8	7.0	14.7	14.6	19.2	18.6	6.9	5.9
Pittsburgh	6.3	11.7	10.1	18.8	16.1	16.9	12.8	3.9	3.4
Providence	4.3	10.6	7.8	15.7	15.3	19.5	16.7	5.7	4.4
Raleigh	5.5	6.7	7.6	16.6	15.9	19.2	17.8	6.0	4.6
Richmond	5.3	6.7	7.5	16.5	16.1	20.0	18.1	5.7	4.2
Rochester	4.1	8.3	7.5	15.6	15.6	20.1	18.5	6.2	4.2
Washington	3.2	3.4	3.8	10.9	13.0	19.2	23.7	12.0	10.7
U.S.	**6.2**	**9.3**	**8.8**	**17.5**	**15.8**	**17.9**	**15.0**	**5.1**	**4.4**

Note: Figures are for 1989; (1) Metropolitan Statistical Area - see Appendix A for areas included
Source: 1990 Census of Population and Housing, Summary Tape File 3C

Effective Buying Income: City

City	Per Capita ($)	Median Household ($)	Average Household ($)
Akron	14,488	27,173	35,222
Baltimore	13,022	26,878	34,728
Boston	18,614	36,460	47,456
Charlotte	20,063	39,155	49,348
Cincinnati	15,477	26,169	35,902
Cleveland	11,056	21,459	27,524
Greensboro	17,604	33,765	42,964
Lexington	18,027	34,366	44,662
Louisville	14,544	25,558	34,024
Manchester	16,688	35,717	40,892
New York	18,062	35,069	47,683
Norfolk	13,031	26,105	37,268
Philadelphia	14,405	29,561	37,708
Pittsburgh	16,372	27,250	38,797
Providence	13,394	26,161	36,975
Raleigh	19,531	38,129	46,674
Richmond	14,718	25,049	34,283
Rochester	12,386	24,368	30,463
Washington	22,594	37,950	53,623
U.S.	**16,803**	**34,536**	**45,243**

Note: Data as of 1/1/99
Source: Standard Rate & Data Service, Newspaper Advertising Source, 9/99

Effective Buying Income: Metro Area

MSA[1]	Per Capita ($)	Median Household ($)	Average Household ($)
Akron	17,264	34,762	44,532
Baltimore	18,025	40,160	48,394
Boston	19,850	43,852	52,960
Charlotte	17,835	36,772	46,411
Cincinnati	17,989	36,959	47,155
Cleveland	17,431	35,328	44,743
Greensboro	16,742	32,857	41,794
Lexington	16,875	32,749	43,706
Louisville	17,462	34,318	44,430
Manchester	19,286	44,613	51,228
New York	19,236	35,740	51,190
Norfolk	14,627	32,849	40,596
Philadelphia	20,205	42,969	54,762
Pittsburgh	18,576	34,238	46,122
Providence	16,896	36,075	44,792
Raleigh	18,992	38,166	47,652
Richmond	17,593	36,893	45,150
Rochester	15,933	35,791	42,374
Washington	22,621	49,996	60,948
U.S.	**16,803**	**34,536**	**45,243**

Note: Data as of 1/1/99; (1) Metropolitan Statistical Area - see Appendix A for areas included; (2) Boston-Worcester-Lawrence-Lowell-Brockton; (3) New Haven-Bridgeport-Stamford-Danbury-Waterbury
Source: Standard Rate & Data Service, Newspaper Advertising Source, 9/99

Effective Household Buying Income Distribution: City

City	% of Households Earning						
	$10,000 -$19,999	$20,000 -$34,999	$35,000 -$49,999	$50,000 -$74,999	$75,000 -$99,000	$100,000 -$124,999	$125,000 and up
Akron	19.3	25.4	16.9	13.9	3.8	1.3	1.4
Baltimore	18.4	23.8	16.8	14.4	4.2	1.2	1.4
Boston	14.8	19.3	16.3	19.2	9.1	3.6	3.5
Charlotte	12.5	22.9	18.8	21.0	8.8	3.4	3.6
Cincinnati	20.0	22.9	15.3	13.7	4.7	1.6	2.1
Cleveland	21.2	23.1	15.2	10.8	2.6	0.5	0.4
Greensboro	16.1	24.6	18.7	18.1	6.3	2.2	2.9
Lexington	15.6	22.6	17.4	18.6	7.4	2.7	3.1
Louisville	20.3	24.0	15.4	13.1	4.3	1.3	1.5
Manchester	14.4	22.8	21.1	20.5	6.4	1.7	1.4
New York	14.7	19.9	15.8	18.0	8.5	3.6	4.2
Norfolk	20.5	28.2	17.2	12.0	3.4	1.1	1.3
Philadelphia	17.8	22.0	16.7	16.7	6.0	1.7	1.5
Pittsburgh	20.3	22.3	15.4	13.8	5.4	1.9	2.7
Providence	20.6	22.3	16.0	13.5	4.5	1.7	2.5
Raleigh	13.5	22.7	18.4	21.3	8.6	2.9	2.9
Richmond	20.7	25.2	15.8	11.8	3.7	1.4	1.8
Rochester	21.0	24.4	16.8	12.8	2.9	0.6	0.5
Washington	12.4	21.6	15.9	17.7	9.4	4.4	5.9
U.S.	**16.0**	**22.6**	**18.2**	**18.9**	**7.2**	**2.4**	**2.7**

Note: Data as of 1/1/99
Source: Standard Rate & Data Service, Newspaper Advertising Source, 9/99

Effective Household Buying Income Distribution: Metro Area

MSA[1]	% of Households Earning						
	$10,000 -$19,999	$20,000 -$34,999	$35,000 -$49,999	$50,000 -$74,999	$75,000 -$99,000	$100,000 -$124,999	$125,000 and up
Akron	15.5	22.9	18.6	19.4	7.0	2.3	2.3
Baltimore	12.4	21.0	20.0	23.0	8.9	2.7	2.6
Boston	11.9	17.9	17.8	23.8	11.0	4.0	3.8
Charlotte	14.4	23.1	19.4	20.7	7.7	2.4	2.3
Cincinnati	14.3	21.6	18.6	20.5	8.1	2.6	2.7
Cleveland	15.2	22.0	18.9	19.6	7.3	2.2	2.4
Greensboro	16.8	25.0	19.4	18.1	5.4	1.7	2.0
Lexington	16.7	22.7	17.5	18.1	6.8	2.1	2.4
Louisville	15.8	23.0	18.5	19.1	7.1	2.2	2.2
Manchester	10.3	18.7	20.7	25.8	10.3	3.4	3.0
New York	14.4	19.7	16.1	18.3	8.3	3.4	4.7
Norfolk	15.8	26.7	20.6	18.2	5.0	1.3	1.3
Philadelphia	12.2	18.7	17.7	22.7	10.6	4.0	4.4
Pittsburgh	16.9	22.2	17.7	18.5	7.6	2.5	2.7
Providence	15.7	21.3	19.2	20.4	7.3	2.2	2.3
Raleigh	13.8	21.9	18.7	21.7	8.4	2.8	2.6
Richmond	14.3	23.0	19.9	21.5	7.1	2.1	2.1
Rochester	15.4	22.9	20.2	21.0	6.6	1.9	1.5
Washington	8.0	17.6	18.8	26.1	13.5	5.4	5.0
U.S.	**16.0**	**22.6**	**18.2**	**18.9**	**7.2**	**2.4**	**2.7**

Note: Data as of 1/1/99; (1) Metropolitan Statistical Area - see Appendix A for areas included; (2) Boston-Worcester-Lawrence-Lowell-Brockton; (3) New Haven-Bridgeport-Stamford-Danbury-Waterbury
Source: Standard Rate & Data Service, Newspaper Advertising Source, 9/99

Poverty Rates by Race and Age: City

City	Total (%)	By Race (%)				By Age (%)		
		White	Black	Other	Hisp.[1]	Under 5 years old	Under 18 years old	65 years and over
Akron	20.5	15.0	36.0	35.3	25.7	35.6	31.2	11.4
Baltimore	21.9	12.6	27.9	25.2	21.5	34.3	32.5	19.3
Boston	18.7	13.9	24.2	32.0	33.9	27.9	28.3	15.3
Charlotte	10.8	5.1	22.5	12.2	9.9	18.4	16.0	13.8
Cincinnati	24.3	14.7	39.4	24.8	29.7	42.0	37.4	17.3
Cleveland	28.7	18.2	39.1	37.4	40.0	46.2	43.0	19.2
Greensboro	11.6	6.8	20.7	17.0	15.0	18.6	15.6	12.1
Lexington	14.1	10.9	34.0	22.1	26.4	19.9	18.8	13.2
Louisville	22.6	15.0	39.5	40.6	28.8	40.5	35.4	17.0
Manchester	9.0	8.5	28.5	24.0	19.5	16.0	12.6	12.2
New York	19.3	12.3	25.3	29.4	33.2	30.5	30.1	16.5
Norfolk	19.3	10.1	32.7	15.1	15.0	29.2	28.6	15.3
Philadelphia	20.3	11.1	29.0	41.6	45.3	31.9	30.3	16.3
Pittsburgh	21.4	14.0	40.9	38.1	23.6	37.0	32.5	14.4
Providence	23.0	17.7	31.1	38.4	36.5	36.1	35.0	19.2
Raleigh	11.8	7.4	21.7	24.4	17.4	17.4	14.7	13.0
Richmond	20.9	10.3	28.9	19.0	17.1	37.6	35.8	16.5
Rochester	23.5	14.8	35.9	41.6	45.2	41.2	38.4	13.3
Washington	16.9	8.2	20.2	21.9	20.4	27.0	25.5	17.2
U.S.	**13.1**	**9.8**	**29.5**	**23.1**	**25.3**	**20.1**	**18.3**	**12.8**

Note: Figures show the percent of people living below the poverty line in 1989. The average poverty threshold was $12,674 for a family of four in 1989; (1) People of Hispanic origin can be of any race
Source: 1990 Census of Population and Housing, Summary Tape File 3C

Poverty Rates by Race and Age: Metro Area

MSA[1]	Total (%)	By Race (%)				By Age (%)		
		White	Black	Other	Hisp.[2]	Under 5 years old	Under 18 years old	65 years and over
Akron	12.1	9.5	34.2	23.0	15.6	20.1	17.1	8.7
Baltimore	10.1	5.4	23.2	10.8	11.5	15.3	14.4	11.6
Boston	8.3	6.3	21.7	23.4	28.4	12.1	11.5	9.2
Charlotte	9.6	6.2	22.9	11.6	11.1	14.3	12.9	15.2
Cincinnati	11.4	8.0	34.0	14.1	18.3	19.4	16.4	11.0
Cleveland	11.8	6.8	31.0	22.0	30.6	20.5	18.1	9.5
Greensboro	10.0	7.1	21.8	19.5	19.9	15.3	13.3	16.0
Lexington	14.2	11.9	32.7	20.9	24.3	21.1	18.9	16.3
Louisville	12.7	9.4	33.5	20.9	19.7	21.5	18.3	12.6
Manchester	7.1	6.7	24.4	20.3	17.5	11.6	9.0	11.5
New York	17.5	10.8	24.8	28.4	32.3	27.5	27.1	15.3
Norfolk	11.5	5.9	25.1	9.5	10.5	17.8	16.4	12.5
Philadelphia	10.4	5.6	25.5	30.1	35.2	15.9	15.0	10.4
Pittsburgh	12.2	10.0	35.9	23.2	19.4	20.4	17.9	10.5
Providence	10.1	8.0	27.1	32.0	31.7	16.4	14.5	11.3
Raleigh	10.2	6.5	20.5	18.2	15.9	13.3	11.5	15.3
Richmond	9.8	5.0	21.1	10.9	11.1	16.1	14.0	11.3
Rochester	9.8	6.8	32.2	27.9	36.1	17.0	14.4	7.5
Washington	6.4	3.6	12.6	9.9	12.0	8.3	7.9	8.6
U.S.	**13.1**	**9.8**	**29.5**	**23.1**	**25.3**	**20.1**	**18.3**	**12.8**

Note: Figures show the percent of people living below the poverty line in 1989. The average poverty threshold was $12,674 for a family of four in 1989; (1) Metropolitan Statistical Area - see Appendix A for areas included;
(2) People of Hispanic origin can be of any race
Source: 1990 Census of Population and Housing, Summary Tape File 3C

Major State and Local Tax Rates

City	State Corp. Income (%)	State Personal Income (%)	Residential Property (effective rate per $100)	Sales & Use State (%)	Sales & Use Local (%)	State Gasoline (cents/ gallon)	State Cigarette (cents/ pack)
Akron	5.1 - 8.5[i]	0.673 - 6.799	n/a	5.0	0.75	22.0	24.0
Baltimore	7.0	2.0 - 4.85	2.42	5.0	None	23.5	36.0
Boston	9.5[c]	5.95	1.35	5.0	None	21.0	76.0
Charlotte	7.0	6.0 - 7.75	1.08	4.0	2.0	21.6	5.0
Cincinnati	5.1 - 8.5[i]	0.673 - 6.799	n/a	5.0	1.0	22.0	24.0
Cleveland	5.1 - 8.5[i]	0.673 - 6.799	n/a	5.0	2.0	22.0	24.0
Greensboro	7.0	6.0 - 7.75	n/a	4.0	2.0	21.6	5.0
Lexington	4.0 - 8.25	2.0 - 6.0	n/a	6.0	None	16.4[a]	3.0[b]
Louisville	4.0 - 8.25	2.0 - 6.0	1.12	6.0	None	16.4[a]	3.0[b]
Manchester	7.0[d]	5.0[e]	3.40	None	None	18.7[f]	37.0
New York	9.0[g]	4.0 - 6.85	0.75	4.0	4.25	8.0[h]	56.0
Norfolk	6.0	2.0 - 5.75	n/a	3.5	1.0	17.5[n]	2.5[o]
Philadelphia	9.99	2.8	2.64	6.0	1.0	30.77[j]	31.0
Pittsburgh	9.99	2.8	n/a	6.0	1.0	30.77[j]	31.0
Providence	9.0[k]	(l)	3.20	7.0	None	29.0[m]	71.0
Raleigh	7.0	6.0 - 7.75	n/a	4.0	2.0	21.6	5.0
Richmond	6.0	2.0 - 5.75	n/a	3.5	1.0	17.5[n]	2.5[o]
Rochester	9.0[g]	4.0 - 6.85	n/a	4.0	4.0	8.0[h]	56.0
Washington	9.975 [p]	6.0 - 9.5	0.96	5.75	None	20.0	65.0

Note: (a) Rate is comprised of 15 cents excise and 1.4 cents motor carrier tax. Carriers pay an additional surcharge of 2%; (b) Dealers pay an additional enforcement and administrative fee of 0.1 cent per pack; (c) Rate includes a 14% surtax, as does the following: an additional tax of $7.00 per $1,000 on taxable tangible property (or net worth allocable to state for intangible property corporations). Minimum tax is $456; (d) Plus a 0.25% tax on the enterprise base (total compensation, interest and dividends paid). Business profits tax imposed on both corporations and unincorporated associations; (e) Applies to interest and dividend income only; (f) Rate is comprised of 18 cents excise and 0.7 cents motor carrier tax; (g) Or 1.78 (0.1 for banks) mills per dollar of capital (up to $350,000); or 3.00% of the minimum taxable income; or a minimum of $100 to $1,500 depending on payroll size ($250 plus 2.5% surtax for banks); if any of these are greater than the tax computed on net income, an additional tax of 0.9 mills per dollar of subsidiary capital is imposed on corporations. Small businesses with income under $200,000 pay tax of 8% of income; (h) Carriers pay an additional surcharge of 22.21 cents; (i) Or 4.0 mils times the value of the taxpayer's issued and outstanding share of stock ($150K max). An additional litter tax is imposed equal to 0.11% on the first $50,000 of taxable income, 0.22% on income over $50,000; or 0.14 mills on net worth; (j) Rate is comprised of 12 cents excise and 18.77 cents motor carrier tax. Carriers pay an additional surcharge of 6 cents; (k) Minimum tax is $250; (l) 26.5% Federal tax liability; (m) Rate is comprised of 28 cents excise and 1 cent motor carrier tax; (n) Does not include a 2% local option tax; (o) Counties and cities may impose an additional tax of 2 - 15 cents per pack; (p) A 5.0% surtax is also imposed. Minimum tax is $100.
Source: Source: Federation of Tax Administrators, www.taxadmin.org; Washington D.C. Dept. of Finance and Revenue, Tax Rates and Tax Burdens in the District of Columbia: A Nationwide Comparison, July 1999; Chambers of Commerce, 1999

Employment by Industry

MSA[1]	Services	Retail	Gov't.	Manuf.	Finance/ Ins./R.E.	Whole-sale	Transp./ Utilities	Constr.	Mining
Akron	28.2	18.9	13.6	19.5	4.1	6.3	4.6	4.6	0.2
Baltimore	34.6	17.2	18.0	8.2	6.2	5.4	4.9	5.4	<0.1
Boston	39.4	15.8	12.0	10.9	8.4	5.7	4.4	3.4	<0.1
Charlotte	27.0	16.2	11.1	17.6	8.2	7.2	6.3	n/a	n/a
Cincinnati	30.4	18.8	11.6	16.1	6.4	6.7	5.3	4.6	0.1
Cleveland	30.1	17.1	12.7	18.8	6.6	6.5	4.0	4.1	0.1
Greensboro	27.1	16.9	10.1	24.4	5.2	5.6	5.5	n/a	n/a
Lexington	27.9	18.0	19.4	17.5	3.8	4.3	4.0	5.1	0.1
Louisville	30.3	19.1	12.2	15.0	5.2	5.5	7.4	5.2	0.1
Manchester	31.8	17.9	11.1	14.8	6.8	6.9	6.0	n/a	n/a
New York	38.0	11.9	15.5	7.5	12.6	5.4	5.7	n/a	n/a
Norfolk	30.9	19.9	20.8	9.2	5.0	3.9	4.5	n/a	n/a
Philadelphia	36.8	16.4	12.4	12.9	7.1	5.5	4.8	n/a	n/a
Pittsburgh	35.4	18.3	11.1	12.6	6.0	5.2	6.2	4.8	0.4
Providence	32.1	18.6	12.5	19.3	6.1	4.2	3.6	3.6	0.1
Raleigh	32.0	16.2	19.5	12.5	4.6	4.8	4.4	n/a	n/a
Richmond	26.4	17.6	18.8	11.0	8.6	5.8	5.4	6.2	0.1
Rochester	31.0	17.1	15.0	21.8	3.9	4.2	3.2	3.7	0.1
Washington	39.8	15.2	22.5	4.0	5.4	3.1	4.7	5.3	<0.1
U.S.	**30.4**	**17.7**	**15.6**	**14.3**	**5.9**	**5.4**	**5.3**	**5.0**	**0.4**

Note: All figures are percentages covering non-farm employment as of 6/99 and are not seasonally adjusted; (1) Metropolitan Statistical Area - see Appendix A for areas included; n/a not available
Source: Bureau of Labor Statistics, http://stats.bls.gov

Labor Force, Employment and Job Growth: City

Area	Civilian Labor Force			Workers Employed		
	Jun. 1998	Jun. 1999	% Chg.	Jun. 1998	Jun. 1999	% Chg.
Akron	110,736	115,170	4.0	104,318	108,318	3.8
Baltimore	307,395	312,138	1.5	276,940	286,254	3.4
Boston	302,404	302,266	-0.0	290,922	292,119	0.4
Charlotte	270,372	275,617	1.9	262,695	269,672	2.7
Cincinnati	175,852	184,751	5.1	166,085	174,713	5.2
Cleveland	205,997	212,986	3.4	188,055	193,306	2.8
Greensboro	114,193	115,916	1.5	110,596	113,065	2.2
Lexington	143,156	147,159	2.8	139,883	144,127	3.0
Louisville	134,103	137,730	2.7	127,500	131,924	3.5
Manchester	56,445	58,556	3.7	54,868	57,166	4.2
New York	8,939,560	8,961,027	0.2	8,469,185	8,512,422	0.5
Norfolk	87,345	89,839	2.9	81,872	84,321	3.0
Philadelphia	643,721	651,326	1.2	603,420	612,656	1.5
Pittsburgh	163,920	166,286	1.4	156,347	159,004	1.7
Providence	68,159	69,186	1.5	64,208	65,904	2.6
Raleigh	164,765	171,135	3.9	161,548	168,571	4.3
Richmond	97,181	100,150	3.1	92,839	96,159	3.6
Rochester	115,351	115,982	0.5	108,353	107,959	-0.4
Washington	275,247	278,781	1.3	248,084	259,418	4.6
U.S.	**138,798,000**	**140,666,000**	**1.3**	**132,265,000**	**134,395,000**	**1.6**

Note: Data is not seasonally adjusted and covers workers 16 years of age and older
Source: Bureau of Labor Statistics, http://stats.bls.gov

Labor Force, Employment and Job Growth: Metro Area

Area	Civilian Labor Force			Workers Employed		
	Jun. '98	Jun. '99	% Chg.	Jun. '98	Jun. '99	% Chg.
Akron	354,940	369,193	4.0	340,651	353,716	3.8
Baltimore	1,308,390	1,336,571	2.2	1,233,127	1,274,601	3.4
Boston	1,834,847	1,837,503	0.1	1,780,127	1,787,579	0.4
Charlotte	752,534	766,779	1.9	729,609	747,580	2.5
Cincinnati	846,760	885,339	4.6	814,672	852,921	4.7
Cleveland	1,114,150	1,149,118	3.1	1,066,109	1,095,878	2.8
Greensboro	634,700	645,205	1.7	616,819	630,586	2.2
Lexington	255,746	262,781	2.8	249,642	257,216	3.0
Louisville	557,959	577,788	3.6	538,073	554,920	3.1
Manchester	102,827	106,879	3.9	100,135	104,329	4.2
New York	4,097,393	4,073,782	-0.6	3,816,774	3,826,056	0.2
Norfolk	746,394	766,973	2.8	715,820	737,321	3.0
Philadelphia	2,504,231	2,538,751	1.4	2,393,935	2,430,685	1.5
Pittsburgh	1,166,299	1,182,118	1.4	1,114,249	1,133,191	1.7
Providence	569,431	576,695	1.3	543,836	555,716	2.2
Raleigh	619,408	643,338	3.9	607,454	633,863	4.3
Richmond	510,747	527,636	3.3	494,988	512,688	3.6
Rochester	583,719	583,940	0.0	562,227	560,184	-0.4
Washington	2,583,291	2,679,400	3.7	2,491,215	2,600,374	4.4
U.S.	**138,798,000**	**140,666,000**	**1.3**	**132,265,000**	**134,395,000**	**1.6**

Note: Data is not seasonally adjusted and covers workers 16 years of age and older;
(1) Metropolitan Statistical Area - see Appendix A for areas included
Source: Bureau of Labor Statistics, http://stats.bls.gov

Unemployment Rate: City

Area	1998						1999					
	Jul.	Aug.	Sep.	Oct.	Nov.	Dec.	Jan.	Feb.	Mar.	Apr.	May.	Jun.
Akron	5.1	4.8	5.4	5.1	5.4	5.2	6.7	6.6	6.1	5.6	5.0	5.9
Baltimore	10.3	9.7	8.6	8.3	7.9	6.8	7.2	7.6	6.8	6.9	7.6	8.3
Boston	3.6	3.4	3.8	3.0	2.7	2.6	3.4	2.9	3.0	2.7	3.0	3.4
Charlotte	2.7	2.6	2.4	2.3	2.2	1.8	2.3	2.2	2.0	1.7	2.0	2.2
Cincinnati	4.2	5.0	5.4	5.1	4.9	4.3	4.8	4.7	4.3	4.5	4.4	5.4
Cleveland	7.9	8.1	9.0	8.5	8.4	8.0	9.1	9.4	8.6	8.7	7.9	9.2
Greensboro	3.0	2.8	2.6	2.5	2.3	1.9	2.5	2.6	2.3	2.0	2.3	2.5
Lexington	2.0	2.1	2.1	2.1	1.9	1.6	1.9	2.0	2.0	1.8	1.9	2.1
Louisville	4.2	4.3	4.3	4.1	3.7	3.2	3.8	4.0	3.9	3.9	4.3	4.2
Manchester	2.3	2.6	2.7	2.3	2.7	2.3	3.0	3.2	3.1	2.2	2.0	2.4
New York	5.6	5.2	5.3	5.2	5.2	5.1	5.9	6.0	5.5	4.9	4.9	5.0
Norfolk	5.2	5.4	5.8	4.9	5.0	4.8	4.9	4.9	4.4	4.3	5.5	6.1
Philadelphia	6.5	6.2	6.6	6.1	6.0	4.9	5.6	5.7	5.7	5.4	5.4	5.9
Pittsburgh	4.9	4.7	4.6	4.2	4.1	3.6	4.5	4.5	4.5	4.0	4.0	4.4
Providence	5.9	5.7	6.5	6.4	5.0	4.9	6.2	6.0	4.4	3.6	4.5	4.7
Raleigh	1.9	1.9	1.7	1.8	1.7	1.3	1.7	1.7	1.5	1.3	1.5	1.5
Richmond	3.8	4.0	4.3	4.1	3.7	3.3	3.4	3.2	3.1	2.9	3.5	4.0
Rochester	7.9	6.3	6.7	5.8	5.6	5.4	6.4	7.1	7.0	6.4	7.0	6.9
Washington	9.6	8.9	8.5	8.3	8.0	7.2	7.7	7.8	7.1	6.3	6.3	6.9
U.S.	4.7	4.5	4.4	4.2	4.1	4.0	4.8	4.7	4.4	4.1	4.0	4.5

Note: All figures are percentages, are not seasonally adjusted and covers workers 16 years of age and older
Source: Bureau of Labor Statistics, http://stats.bls.gov

Unemployment Rate: Metro Area

Area	1998						1999					
	Jul.	Aug.	Sep.	Oct.	Nov.	Dec.	Jan.	Feb.	Mar.	Apr.	May.	Jun.
Akron	3.7	3.4	3.7	3.6	3.8	3.6	4.8	4.7	4.4	4.0	3.5	4.2
Baltimore	5.7	5.3	4.9	4.6	4.5	3.9	4.3	4.6	4.0	3.9	4.2	4.6
Boston	2.7	2.6	3.0	2.4	2.3	2.2	3.0	2.6	2.7	2.3	2.5	2.7
Charlotte	3.0	2.9	2.6	2.5	2.3	2.0	2.5	2.6	2.2	2.0	2.4	2.5
Cincinnati	3.1	3.3	3.5	3.4	3.2	2.9	3.7	3.5	3.1	3.0	2.9	3.7
Cleveland	4.4	4.2	4.3	4.1	4.1	4.0	5.0	5.0	4.5	4.3	3.9	4.6
Greensboro	2.8	3.1	2.3	2.3	2.2	1.8	2.4	2.5	2.2	1.8	2.1	2.3
Lexington	2.1	2.1	2.1	2.0	1.9	1.7	2.2	2.3	2.2	2.0	2.0	2.1
Louisville	3.1	3.1	3.1	3.1	2.8	2.5	3.1	3.0	2.9	2.8	3.2	4.0
Manchester	2.2	2.4	2.6	2.3	2.6	2.2	2.8	3.1	3.0	2.3	2.0	2.4
New York	7.3	6.9	6.9	7.2	7.0	6.8	7.3	7.3	6.3	5.9	5.8	6.1
Norfolk	3.4	3.5	3.7	3.3	3.3	3.1	3.4	3.3	2.9	2.8	3.4	3.9
Philadelphia	4.7	4.4	4.4	4.0	3.9	3.4	4.1	4.1	4.1	3.8	3.8	4.3
Pittsburgh	4.5	4.2	4.2	4.0	4.2	3.9	5.2	5.0	4.9	4.1	3.8	4.1
Providence	4.5	4.4	4.8	4.6	3.9	3.7	5.5	5.2	4.0	3.1	3.5	3.6
Raleigh	1.9	1.8	1.6	1.6	1.5	1.3	1.6	1.6	1.5	1.3	1.5	1.5
Richmond	2.6	2.7	2.9	2.7	2.5	2.3	2.4	2.3	2.1	2.0	2.5	2.8
Rochester	4.3	3.5	3.8	3.3	3.5	3.6	4.4	4.8	4.7	4.0	4.2	4.1
Washington	3.2	3.1	3.2	3.0	2.8	2.5	2.8	2.9	2.6	2.5	2.7	2.9
U.S.	4.7	4.5	4.4	4.2	4.1	4.0	4.8	4.7	4.4	4.1	4.0	4.5

Note: All figures are percentages, are not seasonally adjusted and covers workers 16 years of age and older
(1) Metropolitan Statistical Area - see Appendix A for areas included
Source: Bureau of Labor Statistics, http://stats.bls.gov

Average Hourly Wages: Occupations A - C

MSA[1]	Accountants/ Auditors	Assemblers/ Fabricators	Automotive Mechanics	Book- keepers	Carpenters	Cashiers	Clerks, Gen. Office
Akron	19.36	9.02	12.16	10.83	13.62	6.63	9.45
Baltimore	19.74	11.14	15.08	11.78	14.21	7.85	10.15
Boston	20.28	9.68	14.67	12.79	20.37	7.42	11.19
Charlotte	19.04	9.19	15.04	11.19	11.94	6.79	9.42
Cincinnati	17.73	10.03	14.05	10.82	14.06	6.81	9.35
Cleveland	20.76	14.08	13.42	11.25	15.49	6.92	9.62
Greensboro	20.25	9.58	14.19	11.33	11.29	6.70	9.57
Lexington	17.67	-	11.93	10.42	11.74	7.34	8.93
Louisville	19.41	15.87	13.11	10.50	13.59	6.96	8.96
Manchester	20.37	9.84	14.20	11.58	14.01	6.90	10.20
New York	23.13	9.41	14.23	14.57	21.97	7.18	11.19
Norfolk	16.90	8.47	12.28	10.76	12.43	6.23	9.24
Philadelphia	19.64	9.53	14.65	12.24	18.18	7.93	10.23
Pittsburgh	18.11	9.09	12.00	10.37	15.32	6.24	8.92
Providence	20.43	8.16	12.71	11.43	14.64	7.01	9.75
Raleigh	18.92	9.38	14.46	11.68	11.43	6.77	10.33
Richmond	17.64	8.87	13.90	11.28	12.46	6.49	9.58
Rochester	17.53	8.91	11.90	10.76	14.97	6.25	9.68
Washington	22.54	9.70	16.71	13.58	14.63	7.85	13.34

Notes: Wage data is for 1997 and covers the Metropolitan Statistical Area - see Appendix A for areas included; dashes indicate that data was not available
Source: Bureau of Labor Statistics, 1997 Metro Area Occupational Employment and Wage Estimates

Average Hourly Wages: Occupations C - F

MSA[1]	Clerks, Ship./Rec.	Computer Program.	Computer Support Specialists	Cooks, Restaurant	Electricians	Financial Managers	First-Line Supervisor/ Mgr., Sales
Akron	10.94	20.74	18.22	7.65	18.67	24.66	14.54
Baltimore	12.09	23.17	19.61	8.39	16.49	26.45	15.87
Boston	11.42	27.95	21.61	9.47	21.16	32.40	19.34
Charlotte	11.04	24.39	18.88	7.77	14.19	27.78	17.36
Cincinnati	11.57	21.92	19.99	7.93	15.81	26.06	15.54
Cleveland	11.50	23.71	16.80	8.18	17.13	26.17	16.92
Greensboro	10.60	21.03	18.92	8.25	12.56	26.69	16.22
Lexington	10.52	17.96	16.09	7.58	15.47	24.27	13.71
Louisville	11.01	17.77	13.79	7.60	13.02	25.51	15.43
Manchester	9.34	22.55	20.87	9.11	15.32	27.31	15.22
New York	12.86	29.21	23.19	10.15	24.14	-	23.67
Norfolk	10.55	20.82	13.95	7.13	13.91	24.48	13.98
Philadelphia	12.26	23.36	19.11	8.84	20.24	29.78	17.38
Pittsburgh	11.71	23.11	15.84	7.13	19.56	24.58	15.64
Providence	9.91	24.78	18.02	8.27	17.72	27.71	16.18
Raleigh	10.41	26.21	18.26	8.09	12.82	26.84	16.51
Richmond	11.69	21.19	17.89	7.77	15.76	26.15	15.95
Rochester	11.03	20.94	18.63	8.71	19.22	26.92	14.32
Washington	12.65	22.67	18.76	9.54	18.55	28.05	17.21

Notes: Wage data is for 1997 and covers the Metropolitan Statistical Area - see Appendix A for areas included; dashes indicate that data was not available
Source: Bureau of Labor Statistics, 1997 Metro Area Occupational Employment and Wage Estimates

Average Hourly Wages: Occupations F - L

MSA[1]	Food Preparation Worker	General Managers/ Top Exec.	Guards	Hand Packers	Janitors/ Cleaners	Laborers, Land- scaping	Lawyers
Akron	7.00	28.76	7.22	7.54	7.79	8.90	36.47
Baltimore	7.95	29.14	8.36	8.20	7.41	8.88	31.00
Boston	7.84	36.69	8.38	7.63	9.15	11.20	37.10
Charlotte	6.81	30.23	7.90	7.82	7.17	8.24	33.89
Cincinnati	7.11	29.46	8.19	7.80	7.73	8.70	34.72
Cleveland	6.79	29.74	8.51	7.56	8.49	9.84	32.50
Greensboro	6.81	28.00	8.04	7.61	6.95	8.54	30.70
Lexington	6.83	25.11	7.95	7.25	7.61	7.80	26.49
Louisville	7.39	27.99	8.44	7.78	7.61	8.79	30.08
Manchester	7.38	30.29	8.22	7.55	7.96	9.68	36.97
New York	8.09	-	9.36	8.23	11.57	13.96	-
Norfolk	6.30	24.21	7.03	6.28	7.20	7.73	34.35
Philadelphia	7.71	33.17	8.59	8.18	9.22	10.20	36.50
Pittsburgh	6.87	29.21	8.03	7.51	8.52	9.57	35.87
Providence	7.62	27.80	8.56	7.05	9.16	11.44	38.75
Raleigh	7.25	29.07	8.46	7.56	7.52	8.07	33.28
Richmond	7.22	27.76	10.12	7.03	6.85	8.44	39.94
Rochester	6.28	-	9.69	8.19	7.95	9.09	26.27
Washington	7.91	33.14	10.08	7.55	8.19	9.05	38.46

Notes: Wage data is for 1997 and covers the Metropolitan Statistical Area - see Appendix A for areas included; dashes indicate that data was not available
Source: Bureau of Labor Statistics, 1997 Metro Area Occupational Employment and Wage Estimates

Average Hourly Wages: Occupations M - P

MSA[1]	Maids/ House- keepers	Main- tenance Repairers	Marketing/ Advertising/ P.R. Mgrs.	Nurses, Licensed Practical	Nurses, Registered	Nursing Aides/ Orderlies/ Attendants	Physicians/ Surgeons
Akron	6.87	11.51	26.13	12.87	20.07	8.73	-
Baltimore	7.54	12.13	25.65	14.85	20.79	8.45	41.30
Boston	8.69	14.40	31.53	16.51	23.60	9.51	49.43
Charlotte	6.96	12.10	25.39	13.11	18.38	8.11	56.73
Cincinnati	7.06	12.36	27.35	13.22	17.09	7.73	-
Cleveland	6.81	11.86	28.13	14.11	19.23	8.11	-
Greensboro	7.01	11.77	26.42	13.22	18.97	7.38	55.28
Lexington	6.74	13.65	24.52	11.68	17.70	7.61	43.78
Louisville	7.12	11.64	25.97	12.73	19.12	7.71	46.75
Manchester	7.85	11.48	26.76	14.21	19.01	10.13	51.53
New York	10.78	14.08	-	15.41	25.93	10.66	-
Norfolk	6.24	10.70	23.80	11.11	18.74	7.37	50.37
Philadelphia	8.13	13.30	29.48	15.68	21.13	9.43	-
Pittsburgh	7.28	12.06	25.96	12.66	21.72	8.63	47.17
Providence	7.69	11.27	28.16	15.97	20.42	8.79	45.14
Raleigh	7.05	12.02	27.53	13.46	26.39	7.35	40.24
Richmond	6.87	11.80	27.61	12.40	19.77	7.85	45.93
Rochester	7.00	13.15	28.50	12.47	17.58	8.23	-
Washington	7.68	12.40	26.70	15.30	20.48	8.12	42.43

Notes: Wage data is for 1997 and covers the Metropolitan Statistical Area - see Appendix A for areas included; dashes indicate that data was not available
Source: Bureau of Labor Statistics, 1997 Metro Area Occupational Employment and Wage Estimates

Average Hourly Wages: Occupations R - S

MSA[1]	Receptionists/ Info. Clerks	Sales Reps., Except Scien./Retail	Sales Reps., Scientific/ Exc. Retail	Sales- persons, Retail	Secretaries, Except Leg./Med.	Stock Clerk, Sales Floor	Systems Analysts
Akron	8.11	18.14	23.57	8.60	10.33	7.65	22.68
Baltimore	8.80	19.41	23.05	8.77	11.79	8.90	25.27
Boston	10.21	21.56	25.09	8.99	14.23	8.42	26.07
Charlotte	9.51	19.35	24.02	8.92	11.25	7.56	23.64
Cincinnati	8.78	19.70	24.35	8.53	10.68	7.33	27.65
Cleveland	8.41	19.98	22.21	8.31	11.23	7.29	23.78
Greensboro	8.95	19.45	21.36	8.66	10.67	7.60	27.18
Lexington	7.99	18.12	20.14	8.25	9.97	7.28	21.51
Louisville	8.13	19.23	19.90	8.16	10.48	7.89	23.79
Manchester	9.02	18.92	27.94	8.75	12.29	8.43	27.00
New York	10.97	23.34	25.35	9.74	15.32	8.10	26.35
Norfolk	7.90	16.62	21.20	7.71	9.97	7.16	22.21
Philadelphia	9.64	20.90	25.29	8.80	12.64	8.54	24.24
Pittsburgh	8.19	18.16	21.27	7.87	10.51	6.48	21.16
Providence	9.58	18.38	22.01	8.25	11.57	7.75	24.43
Raleigh	8.93	19.47	21.40	8.74	11.87	7.73	23.44
Richmond	8.48	18.29	20.28	8.54	11.31	7.83	24.55
Rochester	8.68	19.57	21.67	8.17	11.32	6.94	24.96
Washington	9.69	19.72	21.83	8.87	13.55	9.33	27.82

Notes: Wage data is for 1997 and covers the Metropolitan Statistical Area - see Appendix A for areas included; dashes indicate that data was not available
Source: Bureau of Labor Statistics, 1997 Metro Area Occupational Employment and Wage Estimates

Average Hourly Wages: Occupations T - Z

MSA[1]	Teacher Aides	Teachers, Elementary School	Teachers, Secondary School	Telemar- keters	Truck Driv., Heavy/ Trac. Trail.	Truck Drivers, Light	Waiters/ Waitresses
Akron	8.26	18.26	19.20	8.35	16.86	10.97	5.61
Baltimore	7.96	16.29	20.64	9.64	14.82	11.25	6.42
Boston	8.85	19.04	16.06	11.17	14.98	10.89	6.36
Charlotte	7.95	15.84	15.14	10.39	14.20	11.38	5.68
Cincinnati	8.31	17.51	19.35	10.12	14.19	10.12	6.07
Cleveland	7.90	19.96	22.10	9.79	15.51	9.67	6.12
Greensboro	7.76	15.02	15.79	8.80	13.42	9.84	6.20
Lexington	7.21	16.00	16.67	8.83	13.74	9.44	5.41
Louisville	-	17.44	-	8.51	14.78	9.09	5.88
Manchester	8.64	23.55	24.45	10.16	15.51	9.72	5.36
New York	8.46	20.30	20.95	10.78	18.16	11.85	6.85
Norfolk	6.78	15.63	16.87	6.71	11.18	8.57	5.74
Philadelphia	9.67	23.70	23.75	8.82	15.27	12.00	5.92
Pittsburgh	7.92	24.01	23.31	7.26	13.08	11.14	5.56
Providence	7.65	20.15	19.71	8.22	15.11	10.46	5.89
Raleigh	9.44	15.02	14.57	9.12	12.01	10.22	5.86
Richmond	5.89	14.84	15.25	9.61	13.87	10.93	5.68
Rochester	7.95	20.07	20.75	13.00	13.31	12.29	6.24
Washington	8.17	16.25	20.28	8.50	14.12	11.38	6.74

Notes: Wage data is for 1997 and covers the Metropolitan Statistical Area - see Appendix A for areas included; hourly wages for elementary and secondary school teachers were calculated by the editors from annual wage data assuming a 40 hour work week; dashes indicate that data was not available
Source: Bureau of Labor Statistics, 1997 Metro Area Occupational Employment and Wage Estimates

Means of Transportation to Work: City

City	Car/Truck/Van Drove Alone	Car-pooled	Bus	Subway	Railroad	Bicycle	Walked	Other Means	Worked at Home
Akron	78.8	11.9	3.2	0.0	0.0	0.1	3.5	0.7	1.8
Baltimore	50.9	16.8	19.3	1.6	0.4	0.2	7.4	1.7	1.6
Boston	40.1	10.5	13.6	13.2	1.0	0.9	14.0	4.5	2.2
Charlotte	77.2	12.9	4.3	0.0	0.0	0.2	2.2	1.0	2.2
Cincinnati	67.4	12.6	10.9	0.0	0.0	0.2	5.9	0.9	2.0
Cleveland	64.8	14.0	13.0	0.6	0.1	0.1	5.0	1.2	1.2
Greensboro	79.1	12.5	1.5	0.0	0.0	0.3	3.6	1.2	1.8
Lexington	78.4	11.6	1.5	0.0	0.0	0.3	5.1	0.6	2.4
Louisville	72.0	13.3	8.3	0.0	0.0	0.2	3.8	0.8	1.5
Manchester	76.9	14.2	1.3	0.0	0.0	0.3	4.5	0.7	2.0
New York	24.0	8.5	12.7	36.7	1.7	0.3	10.7	2.9	2.4
Norfolk	56.0	13.9	4.4	0.0	0.0	0.8	4.8	1.9	18.2
Philadelphia	44.7	13.2	18.5	7.0	1.8	0.6	10.4	2.1	1.8
Pittsburgh	48.9	13.5	21.1	0.3	0.0	0.4	12.6	1.3	1.8
Providence	62.2	16.1	6.6	0.1	0.6	0.4	10.8	1.1	2.0
Raleigh	79.0	11.3	2.7	0.0	0.0	0.4	3.5	1.1	2.0
Richmond	64.5	13.8	12.5	0.0	0.0	1.0	5.4	1.1	1.7
Rochester	65.4	13.3	10.5	0.0	0.0	0.5	7.6	0.9	1.8
Washington	35.0	12.0	22.3	12.9	0.2	0.8	11.8	2.0	3.0
U.S.	**73.2**	**13.4**	**3.0**	**1.5**	**0.5**	**0.4**	**3.9**	**1.2**	**3.0**

Note: Figures shown are percentages and only include workers 16 years old and over
Source: 1990 Census of Population and Housing, Summary Tape File 3C

Means of Transportation to Work: Metro Area

MSA[1]	Car/Truck/Van Drove Alone	Car-pooled	Bus	Subway	Railroad	Bicycle	Walked	Other Means	Worked at Home
Akron	83.1	9.6	1.5	0.0	0.0	0.1	3.1	0.6	2.0
Baltimore	70.9	14.2	6.2	0.8	0.3	0.2	4.0	1.1	2.3
Boston	65.8	9.8	5.4	5.9	1.4	0.5	6.5	2.0	2.6
Charlotte	78.8	14.5	1.7	0.0	0.0	0.1	2.1	1.0	1.9
Cincinnati	78.6	11.6	4.1	0.0	0.0	0.1	2.8	0.7	2.1
Cleveland	77.7	10.5	5.5	0.4	0.1	0.1	2.9	0.8	2.0
Greensboro	79.1	14.5	1.0	0.0	0.0	0.1	2.3	0.8	2.1
Lexington	77.9	12.7	1.0	0.0	0.0	0.2	4.7	0.6	2.8
Louisville	79.4	12.8	3.1	0.0	0.0	0.1	2.1	0.7	1.9
Manchester	78.7	13.0	1.0	0.0	0.0	0.2	3.9	0.6	2.6
New York	30.7	8.9	11.4	30.9	3.0	0.3	9.7	2.6	2.5
Norfolk	72.7	14.1	2.0	0.0	0.0	0.5	3.7	1.6	5.3
Philadelphia	67.8	11.9	6.3	2.7	2.1	0.3	5.4	1.2	2.3
Pittsburgh	70.7	12.9	7.7	0.2	0.0	0.1	5.1	1.1	2.1
Providence	78.2	11.9	2.7	0.0	0.3	0.2	4.2	0.7	1.8
Raleigh	78.0	13.3	1.8	0.0	0.0	0.4	3.1	1.0	2.3
Richmond	77.2	13.4	3.5	0.0	0.0	0.3	2.5	0.9	2.1
Rochester	77.7	11.6	3.1	0.0	0.0	0.2	4.3	0.5	2.4
Washington	62.9	15.8	6.6	6.5	0.2	0.3	3.9	1.0	2.8
U.S.	**73.2**	**13.4**	**3.0**	**1.5**	**0.5**	**0.4**	**3.9**	**1.2**	**3.0**

Note: Figures shown are percentages and only include workers 16 years old and over;
(1) Metropolitan Statistical Area - see Appendix A for areas included
Source: 1990 Census of Population and Housing, Summary Tape File 3C

Cost of Living Index

Area	Composite	Groceries	Housing	Utilities	Transp.	Health	Misc.
Akron[6]	96.7	101.3	88.3	119.2	101.9	98.9	94.2
Baltimore	95.3	94.8	93.5	118.6	102.2	91.9	89.9
Boston[1]	136.6	112.9	182.3	141.6	116.5	134.0	114.7
Charlotte	101.1	102.2	101.0	97.3	100.2	92.7	103.0
Cincinnati	98.7	94.4	98.1	109.3	102.1	92.1	98.6
Cleveland	112.6	108.8	117.7	135.0	115.0	122.4	102.6
Greensboro[6]	98.1	97.7	99.0	109.4	92.4	79.5	99.4
Lexington[1]	96.2	99.5	92.0	88.5	92.1	98.7	100.8
Louisville	96.5	97.0	90.8	96.1	111.5	89.9	97.7
Manchester	110.3	98.7	114.7	146.8	94.0	114.6	107.7
New York[3]	232.1	150.2	455.6	163.2	125.4	187.0	137.9
Norfolk[4,5]	97.3	97.6	90.0	119.2	104.7	95.8	95.9
Philadelphia	120.5	109.2	139.3	144.2	120.4	99.2	107.6
Pittsburgh[7]	108.4	102.6	111.0	132.5	112.6	98.8	103.8
Providence[8]	116.0	101.5	134.9	134.3	109.7	118.6	103.9
Raleigh[2]	100.8	99.4	106.0	102.6	93.0	104.4	98.5
Richmond	105.6	98.4	107.5	126.3	106.1	100.9	103.0
Rochester[1,8]	102.2	117.0	86.9	127.9	118.9	89.2	99.5
Washington[1]	123.7	112.2	146.4	95.5	129.9	123.6	115.5
U.S.	**100.0**	**100.0**	**100.0**	**100.0**	**100.0**	**100.0**	**100.0**

Note: n/a not available; (1) Metropolitan Statistical Area (MSA) - see Appendix A for areas included;
(2) Raleigh-Durham; (3) Manhattan; (4) Hampton Roads/SE Virginia; (5) 4th Quarter 1998; (6) 3rd Quarter 1998; (7) 1st Quarter 1997; (8) 3rd Quarter 1996
Source: ACCRA, Cost of Living Index, 1st Quarter 1999 unless otherwise noted

Median Home Prices and Housing Affordability

MSA[1]	Median Price[2] 1st Qtr. 1999 ($)	HOI[3] 1st Qtr. 1999	Afford-ability Rank[4]
Akron	105,000	74.8	93
Baltimore	125,000	79.6	60
Boston	170,000	66.7	133
Charlotte	142,000	68.8	122
Cincinnati	112,000	80.4	53
Cleveland	107,000	78.1	70
Greensboro	102,000	81.5	40
Lexington	109,000	80.5	50
Louisville	110,000	76.0	87
Manchester	n/a	n/a	n/a
New York	165,000	56.8	158
Norfolk	111,000	78.1	70
Philadelphia	105,000	77.4	78
Pittsburgh	87,000	71.7	106
Providence	n/a	n/a	n/a
Raleigh	153,000	69.4	120
Richmond	126,000	79.8	59
Rochester	85,000	83.3	31
Washington	158,000	84.0	26
U.S.	**134,000**	**69.6**	**–**

Note: (1) Metropolitan Statistical Area - see Appendix A for areas included; (2) U.S. figures calculated from the sales of 524,324 new and existing homes in 181 markets; (3) Housing Opportunity Index - percent of homes sold that were within the reach of the median income household at the prevailing mortgage interest rate; (4) Rank is from 1-181 with 1 being most affordable; n/a not available
Source: National Association of Home Builders, Housing News Service, 1st Quarter 1999

Average Home Prices

Area	Price ($)
Akron[6]	120,000
Baltimore	134,896
Boston[1]	249,550
Charlotte	148,500
Cincinnati	139,847
Cleveland	164,650
Greensboro[6]	144,150
Lexington[1]	125,289
Louisville	126,300
Manchester	154,950
New York[3]	621,667
Norfolk[4,5]	125,877
Philadelphia	197,999
Pittsburgh[7]	151,450
Providence[8]	165,593
Raleigh[2]	148,691
Richmond	155,250
Rochester[1,8]	112,110
Washington[1]	203,023
U.S.	**142,735**

Note: Figures are based on a new home with 1,800 sq. ft. of living area on an 8,000 sq. ft. lot; n/a not available; (1) Metropolitan Statistical Area (MSA) - see Appendix A for areas included; (2) Raleigh-Durham; (3) Manhattan; (4) Hampton Roads/SE Virginia; (5) 4th Quarter 1998; (6) 3rd Quarter 1998; (7) 1st Quarter 1997; (8) 3rd Quarter 1996
Source: ACCRA, Cost of Living Index, 1st Quarter 1999 unless otherwise noted

Average Apartment Rent

Area	Rent ($/mth)
Akron[6]	563
Baltimore	534
Boston[1]	1,246
Charlotte	548
Cincinnati	647
Cleveland	826
Greensboro[6]	542
Lexington[1]	673
Louisville	609
Manchester	878
New York[3]	3,220
Norfolk[4,5]	582
Philadelphia	733
Pittsburgh[7]	598
Providence[8]	925
Raleigh[2]	756
Richmond	737
Rochester[1,8]	484
Washington[1]	1,098
U.S.	**601**

Note: Figures are based on an unfurnished two bedroom, 1-1/2 or 2 bath apartment, approximately 950 sq. ft. in size, excluding all utilities except water; n/a not available; (1) Metropolitan Statistical Area (MSA) - see Appendix A for areas included; (2) Raleigh-Durham; (3) Manhattan; (4) Hampton Roads/SE Virginia; (5) 4th Quarter 1998; (6) 3rd Quarter 1998; (7) 1st Quarter 1997; (8) 3rd Quarter 1996
Source: ACCRA, Cost of Living Index, 1st Quarter 1999 unless otherwise noted

Average Residential Utility Costs

Area	All Electric ($/mth)	Part Electric ($/mth)	Other Energy ($/mth)	Phone ($/mth)
Akron[6]	-	77.66	43.45	22.45
Baltimore	-	64.54	54.30	22.01
Boston[1]	-	79.14	65.30	23.03
Charlotte	97.99	-	-	17.51
Cincinnati	-	63.97	44.13	22.13
Cleveland	-	82.27	55.21	22.25
Greensboro[6]	111.97	-	-	19.55
Lexington[1]	-	32.96	49.13	24.89
Louisville	-	41.92	48.58	25.31
Manchester	-	82.96	68.78	21.39
New York[3]	-	77.21	91.19	24.06
Norfolk[4,5]	-	66.16	53.50	22.78
Philadelphia	-	94.02	58.49	16.51
Pittsburgh[7]	-	80.62	62.61	20.13
Providence[8]	-	74.16	65.65	23.46
Raleigh[2]	104.07	-	-	17.44
Richmond	129.12	-	-	20.25
Rochester[1,8]	-	67.43	67.14	20.68
Washington[1]	-	57.63	35.70	20.86
U.S.	**100.02**	**55.73**	**43.33**	**19.71**

Note: Dashes indicate data not applicable; n/a not available;
(1) Metropolitan Statistical Area (MSA) - see Appendix A for areas included; (2) Raleigh-Durham; (3) Manhattan; (4) Hampton Roads/SE Virginia; (5) 4th Quarter 1998; (6) 3rd Quarter 1998; (7) 1st Quarter 1997; (8) 3rd Quarter 1996
Source: ACCRA, Cost of Living Index, 1st Quarter 1999 unless otherwise noted

Average Health Care Costs

Area	Hospital ($/day)	Doctor ($/visit)	Dentist ($/visit)
Akron[6]	523.60	46.00	58.00
Baltimore	551.00	45.40	52.50
Boston[1]	694.00	74.50	79.20
Charlotte	396.67	53.00	56.80
Cincinnati	409.80	48.80	58.40
Cleveland	662.00	62.00	77.80
Greensboro[6]	187.00	47.60	49.40
Lexington[1]	387.13	51.25	67.40
Louisville	345.47	53.15	54.30
Manchester	493.00	68.00	67.00
New York[3]	1,462.60	91.00	98.00
Norfolk[4,5]	324.60	56.20	60.40
Philadelphia	452.00	50.50	63.75
Pittsburgh[7]	518.33	36.60	60.60
Providence[8]	554.56	45.30	74.00
Raleigh[2]	345.49	59.25	73.50
Richmond	440.00	51.86	67.14
Rochester[1,8]	494.00	35.00	44.43
Washington[1]	520.60	67.70	80.90
U.S.	**430.43**	**52.45**	**66.35**

Note: n/a not available; Hospital—based on a semi-private room; Doctor—based on a general practitioner's routine exam of an established patient; Dentist—based on adult teeth cleaning and periodic oral exam; (1) Metropolitan Statistical Area (MSA) - see Appendix A for areas included; (2) Raleigh-Durham; (3) Manhattan; (4) Hampton Roads/SE Virginia; (5) 4th Quarter 1998; (6) 3rd Quarter 1998; (7) 1st Quarter 1997; (8) 3rd Quarter 1996
Source: ACCRA, Cost of Living Index, 1st Quarter 1999 unless otherwise noted

Distribution of Office-Based Physicians

MSA[1]	General Practitioners	Specialists		
		Medical	Surgical	Other
Akron	128	318	269	268
Baltimore	402	2,286	1,567	1,633
Boston	487	4,439	2,350	3,395
Charlotte	282	711	657	516
Cincinnati	381	1,044	780	843
Cleveland	359	1,811	1,244	1,372
Greensboro	249	672	558	502
Lexington	135	382	296	380
Louisville	266	714	575	596
Manchester	64	196	155	155
New York	913	9,570	4,885	6,118
Norfolk	403	741	685	616
Philadelphia	917	4,113	2,607	3,299
Pittsburgh	572	1,808	1,297	1,403
Providence	126	779	505	471
Raleigh	276	922	641	887
Richmond	267	673	482	488
Rochester	147	922	520	541
Washington	888	4,007	2,489	2,864

Note: Data as of 12/31/97; (1) Metropolitan Statistical Area - see Appendix A for areas included
Source: Physician Characteristics & Distribution in the U.S., 1999

Educational Quality

City	School District	Education Quotient[1]	Graduate Outcome[2]	Community Index[3]	Resource Index[4]
Akron	Akron City	76.0	67.0	90.0	90.0
Baltimore	Baltimore City	n/a	n/a	n/a	n/a
Boston	Boston SD	79.0	54.0	69.0	131.0
Charlotte	Charlotte-Mecklenburg	82.0	85.0	129.0	68.0
Cincinnati	Cincinnati City	90.0	74.0	87.0	123.0
Cleveland	Cleveland City	78.0	50.0	81.0	134.0
Greensboro	Guilford County	78.0	85.0	94.0	61.0
Lexington	Fayette County	114.0	118.0	111.0	108.0
Louisville	Jefferson County	90.0	75.0	89.0	120.0
Manchester	Manchester SD	85.0	86.0	77.0	84.0
New York	New York City	76.0	51.0	56.0	131.0
Norfolk	Norfolk City	112.0	105.0	63.0	142.0
Philadelphia	Philadelphia City	66.0	55.0	54.0	89.0
Pittsburgh	Pittsburgh SD	119.0	112.0	62.0	145.0
Providence	Providence SD	74.0	57.0	54.0	113.0
Raleigh	Wake County	114.0	110.0	141.0	115.0
Richmond	Richmond City	97.0	75.0	59.0	148.0
Rochester	Rochester City	88.0	54.0	116.0	149.0
Washington	District of Columbia	98.0	93.0	75.0	112.0

Note: Nearly 1,000 secondary school districts were rated in terms of educational quality. The scores range from a low of 50 to a high of 150; (1) Average of the Graduate Outcome, Community and Resource indexes; (2) Based on graduation rates and college board scores (SAT/ACT); (3) Based on the surrounding community's average level of education and the area's average income level; (4) Based on teacher salaries, per-pupil expenditures and student-teacher ratios.
Source: Expansion Management, Ratings Issue 1998

School Enrollment by Type: City

City	Preprimary Public Enrollment	%	Preprimary Private Enrollment	%	Elementary/High School Public Enrollment	%	Elementary/High School Private Enrollment	%
Akron	2,292	61.2	1,452	38.8	31,965	88.9	3,982	11.1
Baltimore	7,935	67.4	3,830	32.6	102,104	85.5	17,364	14.5
Boston	3,504	56.5	2,698	43.5	58,244	77.2	17,231	22.8
Charlotte	4,071	53.5	3,540	46.5	55,638	89.3	6,640	10.7
Cincinnati	3,651	56.7	2,789	43.3	45,797	81.3	10,524	18.7
Cleveland	4,923	62.6	2,939	37.4	69,894	78.7	18,875	21.3
Greensboro	1,840	54.1	1,564	45.9	23,934	92.5	1,927	7.5
Lexington	1,718	45.0	2,100	55.0	29,574	90.0	3,284	10.0
Louisville	1,856	52.7	1,668	47.3	35,092	82.7	7,366	17.3
Manchester	878	49.0	913	51.0	11,881	87.4	1,716	12.6
New York	54,891	55.5	43,933	44.5	934,140	79.1	246,344	20.9
Norfolk	2,322	59.2	1,600	40.8	33,000	91.0	3,245	9.0
Philadelphia	13,314	55.4	10,702	44.6	179,728	70.8	74,032	29.2
Pittsburgh	3,400	58.5	2,412	41.5	36,244	75.8	11,549	24.2
Providence	1,469	56.4	1,137	43.6	20,203	82.8	4,199	17.2
Raleigh	1,680	44.8	2,074	55.2	24,478	93.2	1,782	6.8
Richmond	1,849	62.6	1,105	37.4	24,399	89.2	2,946	10.8
Rochester	2,983	63.5	1,711	36.5	31,066	85.5	5,277	14.5
Washington	5,532	61.8	3,425	38.2	67,278	83.9	12,882	16.1
U.S.	**2,679,029**	**59.5**	**1,824,256**	**40.5**	**38,379,689**	**90.2**	**4,187,099**	**9.8**

Note: Figures shown cover persons 3 years old and over
Source: 1990 Census of Population and Housing, Summary Tape File 3C

School Enrollment by Type: Metro Area

MSA[1]	Preprimary Public Enrollment	%	Preprimary Private Enrollment	%	Elementary/High School Public Enrollment	%	Elementary/High School Private Enrollment	%
Akron	7,419	57.9	5,400	42.1	97,708	89.9	11,025	10.1
Baltimore	25,147	55.8	19,929	44.2	320,507	86.2	51,108	13.8
Boston	27,026	49.3	27,803	50.7	331,757	85.6	55,619	14.4
Charlotte	10,978	56.1	8,605	43.9	176,791	92.7	13,957	7.3
Cincinnati	15,601	53.0	13,831	47.0	206,692	81.4	47,137	18.6
Cleveland	19,818	55.4	15,951	44.6	241,493	80.6	58,046	19.4
Greensboro	8,849	58.2	6,354	41.8	136,757	93.7	9,199	6.3
Lexington	2,832	50.7	2,759	49.3	50,759	91.9	4,490	8.1
Louisville	7,734	53.4	6,738	46.6	138,085	83.6	27,168	16.4
Manchester	1,274	42.6	1,718	57.4	19,200	87.6	2,720	12.4
New York	66,531	53.1	58,729	46.9	1,086,038	79.3	283,106	20.7
Norfolk	14,319	54.5	11,942	45.5	218,089	92.8	16,852	7.2
Philadelphia	48,214	48.5	51,171	51.5	595,382	76.8	179,754	23.2
Pittsburgh	20,226	54.8	16,696	45.2	254,093	86.0	41,306	14.0
Providence	5,933	54.0	5,054	46.0	81,761	85.9	13,463	14.1
Raleigh	6,751	46.9	7,652	53.1	99,864	92.8	7,735	7.2
Richmond	9,730	59.5	6,628	40.5	130,034	93.0	9,840	7.0
Rochester	12,739	59.0	8,851	41.0	146,730	89.9	16,489	10.1
Washington	39,352	48.2	42,299	51.8	522,711	87.4	75,692	12.6
U.S.	**2,679,029**	**59.5**	**1,824,256**	**40.5**	**38,379,689**	**90.2**	**4,187,099**	**9.8**

Note: Figures shown cover persons 3 years old and over;
(1) Metropolitan Statistical Area - see Appendix A for areas included
Source: 1990 Census of Population and Housing, Summary Tape File 3C

School Enrollment by Race: City

City	Preprimary (%)				Elementary/High School (%)			
	White	Black	Other	Hisp.[1]	White	Black	Other	Hisp.[1]
Akron	72.7	24.9	2.4	1.7	62.6	35.1	2.3	1.0
Baltimore	34.8	63.7	1.4	1.4	26.1	72.4	1.5	1.1
Boston	50.0	37.8	12.2	11.7	39.1	42.1	18.8	17.4
Charlotte	67.5	30.4	2.0	1.3	53.0	43.8	3.2	1.4
Cincinnati	58.4	39.9	1.7	0.9	45.6	53.0	1.4	0.6
Cleveland	43.5	53.1	3.4	5.4	37.6	57.0	5.4	6.5
Greensboro	66.1	30.7	3.2	0.2	54.1	43.1	2.9	1.0
Lexington	83.6	13.3	3.1	0.7	77.4	20.3	2.3	1.1
Louisville	69.6	29.0	1.4	0.2	56.1	42.4	1.5	0.9
Manchester	97.9	0.3	1.7	1.3	95.1	1.4	3.5	3.9
New York	47.4	35.6	17.1	21.2	38.6	36.8	24.6	32.6
Norfolk	60.5	35.6	3.9	3.4	41.5	54.4	4.1	2.5
Philadelphia	49.3	44.6	6.0	4.7	41.6	48.6	9.8	8.4
Pittsburgh	66.4	31.4	2.2	1.4	59.1	38.9	2.1	1.1
Providence	58.9	23.2	17.9	15.2	51.5	23.5	24.9	24.7
Raleigh	75.4	21.2	3.4	1.9	59.1	37.3	3.6	1.2
Richmond	34.4	63.4	2.2	0.7	20.0	79.0	1.0	1.0
Rochester	55.9	35.8	8.3	10.0	38.9	49.3	11.8	14.2
Washington	25.0	71.2	3.8	3.4	12.6	82.2	5.2	6.5
U.S.	**80.4**	**12.5**	**7.1**	**7.8**	**74.1**	**15.6**	**10.3**	**12.5**

Note: Figures shown cover persons 3 years old and over; (1) People of Hispanic origin can be of any race
Source: 1990 Census of Population and Housing, Summary Tape File 3C

School Enrollment by Race: Metro Area

MSA[1]	Preprimary (%)				Elementary/High School (%)			
	White	Black	Other	Hisp.[2]	White	Black	Other	Hisp.[2]
Akron	88.8	9.2	2.0	0.9	84.3	13.9	1.8	0.9
Baltimore	73.5	24.2	2.4	1.6	64.4	32.6	3.0	1.5
Boston	88.2	6.8	5.1	3.7	80.9	11.0	8.2	6.6
Charlotte	78.5	19.9	1.6	0.8	71.2	26.7	2.0	1.0
Cincinnati	86.4	12.5	1.0	0.7	82.4	16.3	1.3	0.7
Cleveland	80.4	17.1	2.4	2.0	71.5	25.4	3.1	2.7
Greensboro	78.2	20.4	1.4	1.0	74.1	24.2	1.7	0.8
Lexington	86.2	11.1	2.7	0.7	83.7	14.7	1.7	0.9
Louisville	86.2	12.4	1.4	0.6	81.0	17.7	1.3	0.7
Manchester	97.7	0.2	2.1	1.5	96.5	1.0	2.5	2.6
New York	55.0	30.1	14.9	18.2	43.6	34.0	22.5	29.7
Norfolk	71.3	25.7	2.9	2.7	60.2	35.5	4.3	2.3
Philadelphia	79.3	16.9	3.8	3.0	69.7	23.9	6.4	5.3
Pittsburgh	89.5	9.1	1.4	0.8	87.5	11.3	1.3	0.6
Providence	87.8	6.8	5.4	4.3	84.8	7.2	8.1	7.6
Raleigh	78.1	19.4	2.6	1.2	65.4	31.9	2.7	1.2
Richmond	72.2	26.1	1.7	1.2	61.8	35.5	2.7	1.2
Rochester	86.9	9.6	3.4	3.3	81.3	13.9	4.9	4.8
Washington	70.9	23.1	6.0	4.4	58.9	31.6	9.5	6.7
U.S.	**80.4**	**12.5**	**7.1**	**7.8**	**74.1**	**15.6**	**10.3**	**12.5**

Note: Figures shown cover persons 3 years old and over; (1) Metropolitan Statistical Area - see Appendix A for areas included; (2) People of Hispanic origin can be of any race
Source: 1990 Census of Population and Housing, Summary Tape File 3C

Crime Rate: City

City	All Crimes	Violent Crimes				Property Crimes		
		Murder	Forcible Rape	Robbery	Aggrav. Assault	Burglary	Larceny -Theft	Motor Vehicle Theft
Akron	7,168.3	6.3	86.9	363.2	593.8	1,283.5	3,924.3	910.4
Baltimore	10,783.3	43.4	66.7	1,199.2	1,111.1	1,772.5	5,363.2	1,227.2
Boston	6,817.4	7.7	63.1	491.5	858.5	774.9	3,228.7	1,392.9
Charlotte	9,409.9	10.5	61.4	483.3	1,075.6	1,852.8	5,146.2	780.1
Cincinnati	7,616.7	8.9	87.4	492.2	499.4	1,577.7	4,445.7	505.5
Cleveland	7,455.5	15.5	128.5	772.6	542.1	1,640.3	2,880.4	1,476.2
Greensboro	8,017.3	17.0	41.7	378.1	521.3	1,493.1	5,013.7	552.4
Lexington	6,250.0	9.9	53.2	239.0	492.5	1,075.7	4,006.3	373.4
Louisville	6,906.7	22.4	46.3	559.0	484.5	1,620.9	3,150.0	1,023.6
Manchester	5,178.9	1.0	55.5	138.3	45.4	845.1	3,664.3	429.1
New York	4,861.6	10.5	29.5	610.7	617.8	739.0	2,145.2	708.9
Norfolk	7,598.8	22.2	55.6	476.8	419.5	1,018.8	5,086.0	519.9
Philadelphia	6,920.0	27.1	46.1	1,013.1	442.6	1,060.2	2,817.6	1,513.4
Pittsburgh	5,817.7	14.2	49.5	436.8	285.9	950.9	3,283.2	797.2
Providence	7,575.9	8.0	67.6	281.9	317.3	1,551.2	3,937.2	1,412.6
Raleigh	7,747.3	9.3	41.0	292.4	564.8	1,468.3	4,805.9	565.6
Richmond	9,395.1	67.2	54.2	741.7	812.3	1,720.0	4,706.0	1,293.7
Rochester	8,617.1	23.0	55.9	674.7	288.6	1,631.1	4,746.5	1,197.3
Washington	9,827.2	56.9	41.2	850.5	1,075.2	1,316.3	5,056.3	1,430.8
U.S.	**4,922.7**	**6.8**	**35.9**	**186.1**	**382.0**	**919.6**	**2,886.5**	**505.8**

Note: Crime rate is the number of crimes per 100,000 population; n/a not available;
Source: FBI Uniform Crime Reports 1997

Crime Rate: Suburbs

Suburbs[1]	All Crimes	Violent Crimes				Property Crimes		
		Murder	Forcible Rape	Robbery	Aggrav. Assault	Burglary	Larceny -Theft	Motor Vehicle Theft
Akron	3,254.4	2.0	25.7	48.7	126.3	522.1	2,338.5	191.2
Baltimore	4,927.5	2.5	26.5	199.0	397.6	834.8	3,053.7	413.5
Boston	2,801.3	1.3	16.6	58.1	295.7	489.4	1,618.5	321.7
Charlotte	4,949.9	8.4	28.5	120.6	432.6	1,131.4	3,011.4	217.0
Cincinnati	n/a	n/a	n/a	n/a	n/a	n/a	n/a	n/a
Cleveland	n/a	n/a	n/a	n/a	n/a	n/a	n/a	n/a
Greensboro	5,494.8	5.5	35.5	147.2	348.5	1,320.7	3,321.0	316.2
Lexington	n/a	n/a	n/a	n/a	n/a	n/a	n/a	n/a
Louisville	n/a	n/a	n/a	n/a	n/a	n/a	n/a	n/a
Manchester	2,418.9	1.4	15.5	15.5	47.9	398.7	1,808.9	131.0
New York	3,144.1	2.6	11.3	139.8	177.9	480.8	1,994.3	337.3
Norfolk	4,789.0	6.8	32.7	180.6	204.8	775.2	3,268.8	320.1
Philadelphia	3,613.2	2.7	21.1	130.0	225.8	586.1	2,223.5	423.9
Pittsburgh	2,260.3	2.2	18.3	46.3	161.1	362.2	1,460.9	209.3
Providence	2,959.5	1.1	28.8	33.5	216.2	553.8	1,850.7	275.4
Raleigh	5,822.7	8.1	28.7	232.1	280.8	1,304.0	3,518.4	450.6
Richmond	4,358.3	6.8	26.9	104.0	168.6	675.4	3,127.6	249.0
Rochester	2,993.6	1.2	15.7	38.8	68.7	421.9	2,306.1	141.2
Washington	4,222.4	4.1	25.0	149.6	205.7	574.4	2,787.1	476.5
U.S.	**4,922.7**	**6.8**	**35.9**	**186.1**	**382.0**	**919.6**	**2,886.5**	**505.8**

Note: Crime rate is the number of crimes per 100,000 population; n/a not available; (1) Defined as all areas within the MSA but located outside the central city
Source: FBI Uniform Crime Reports 1997

Crime Rate: Metro Area

MSA[1]	All Crimes	Violent Crimes				Property Crimes		
		Murder	Forcible Rape	Robbery	Aggrav. Assault	Burglary	Larceny -Theft	Motor Vehicle Theft
Akron	4,548.6	3.4	45.9	152.7	280.9	773.9	2,862.9	429.0
Baltimore	6,609.0	14.2	38.1	486.2	602.5	1,104.1	3,716.9	647.1
Boston	3,445.9	2.3	24.1	127.6	386.1	535.2	1,876.9	493.6
Charlotte	6,847.8	9.3	42.5	274.9	706.2	1,438.4	3,919.8	456.6
Cincinnati	n/a	n/a	n/a	n/a	n/a	n/a	n/a	n/a
Cleveland	n/a	n/a	n/a	n/a	n/a	n/a	n/a	n/a
Greensboro	5,941.6	7.6	36.6	188.1	379.1	1,351.3	3,620.8	358.1
Lexington	n/a	n/a	n/a	n/a	n/a	n/a	n/a	n/a
Louisville	n/a	n/a	n/a	n/a	n/a	n/a	n/a	n/a
Manchester	4,026.6	1.2	38.8	87.0	46.5	658.7	2,889.7	304.7
New York	4,606.7	9.3	26.8	540.8	552.6	700.7	2,122.8	653.7
Norfolk	5,232.1	9.2	36.3	227.3	238.7	813.6	3,555.3	351.6
Philadelphia	4,630.8	10.2	28.8	401.8	292.5	732.0	2,406.3	759.2
Pittsburgh	2,783.4	4.0	22.9	103.7	179.5	448.7	1,728.9	295.7
Providence	3,686.1	2.2	34.9	72.6	232.1	710.8	2,179.1	454.4
Raleigh	6,295.1	8.4	31.7	246.9	350.5	1,344.4	3,834.4	478.8
Richmond	5,463.4	20.1	32.9	243.9	309.8	904.6	3,473.9	478.2
Rochester	4,187.6	5.8	24.2	173.8	115.4	678.7	2,824.3	365.5
Washington	4,879.2	10.3	26.9	231.7	307.6	661.4	3,053.0	588.4
U.S.	**4,922.7**	**6.8**	**35.9**	**186.1**	**382.0**	**919.6**	**2,886.5**	**505.8**

Note: Crime rate is the number of crimes per 100,000 population; n/a not available;
(1) Metropolitan Statistical Area - see Appendix A for areas included
Source: FBI Uniform Crime Reports 1997

Temperature & Precipitation: Yearly Averages and Extremes

City	Extreme Low (°F)	Average Low (°F)	Average Temp. (°F)	Average High (°F)	Extreme High (°F)	Average Precip. (in.)	Average Snow (in.)
Akron	-24	40	50	59	101	36.7	47
Baltimore	-7	45	56	65	105	41.2	21
Boston	-12	44	52	59	102	42.9	41
Charlotte	-5	50	61	71	104	42.8	6
Cincinnati	-25	44	54	64	103	40.9	23
Cleveland	-19	41	50	59	104	37.1	55
Greensboro	-8	47	58	69	103	42.5	10
Lexington	-21	45	55	65	103	45.1	17
Louisville	-20	46	57	67	105	43.9	17
Manchester	-33	34	46	57	102	36.9	63
New York	-2	47	55	62	104	47.0	23
Norfolk	-3	51	60	68	104	45.0	8
Philadelphia	-7	45	55	64	104	41.4	22
Pittsburgh	-18	41	51	60	103	37.1	43
Providence	-13	42	51	60	104	45.3	35
Raleigh	-9	48	60	71	105	42.0	8
Richmond	-8	48	58	69	105	43.0	13
Rochester	-19	39	48	57	100	31.8	92
Washington	-5	49	58	67	104	39.5	18

Note: Tr = Trace
Source: National Climatic Data Center, International Station Meteorological Climate Summary, 3/95

Weather Conditions

City	Temperature 10°F & below	32°F & below	90°F & above	Daytime Sky Clear	Partly cloudy	Cloudy	Precipitation .01 inch or more precip.	1.0 inch or more snow/ice	Thunder-storms
Akron	(a)	129	8	67	134	164	153	48	38
Baltimore	6	97	31	91	143	131	113	13	27
Boston	(a)	97	12	88	127	150	253	48	18
Charlotte	1	65	44	98	142	125	113	3	41
Cincinnati	14	107	23	80	126	159	127	25	39
Cleveland	(a)	123	12	63	127	175	157	48	34
Greensboro	3	85	32	94	143	128	113	5	43
Lexington	11	96	22	86	136	143	129	17	44
Louisville	8	90	35	82	143	140	125	15	45
Manchester	(a)	171	12	87	131	147	125	32	19
New York	(a)	(b)	18	85	166	114	120	11	20
Norfolk	< 1	54	32	89	149	127	115	6	37
Philadelphia	5	94	23	81	146	138	117	14	27
Pittsburgh	(a)	121	8	62	137	166	154	42	35
Providence	(a)	117	9	85	134	146	123	21	21
Raleigh	(a)	(b)	39	98	143	124	110	3	42
Richmond	3	79	41	90	147	128	115	7	43
Rochester	(a)	135	11	58	137	170	157	65	27
Washington	2	71	34	84	144	137	112	9	30

Note: Figures are average number of days per year; (a) Figures for 10 degrees and below are not available; (b) Figures for 32 degrees and below are not available
Source: National Climatic Data Center, International Station Meteorological Climate Summary, 3/95

Air Quality

MSA[1]	PSI>100[2] (days)	Ozone (ppm)	Carbon Monoxide (ppm)	Sulfur Dioxide (ppm)	Nitrogen Dioxide (ppm)	Particulate Matter (ug/m3)	Lead (ug/m3)
Akron	6	0.11	3	0.072	n/a	63	0.04
Baltimore	30	0.16	5	0.026	0.026	63	0.01
Boston	10	0.12	5	0.049	0.030	59	n/a
Charlotte	31	0.13	6	0.016	0.018	61	0.01
Cincinnati	14	0.12	3	0.045	0.028	94	0.03
Cleveland	16	0.12	6	0.057	0.028	133	0.05
Greensboro	17	0.12	5	0.023	0.017	61	0.00
Lexington	n/a	0.10	5	0.016	0.014	62	0.02
Louisville	18	0.13	6	0.038	0.020	98	0.02
Manchester	n/a	n/a	n/a	n/a	n/a	n/a	n/a
New York	24	0.16	6	0.043	0.040	101	0.16
Norfolk	17	0.11	5	0.026	0.019	68	0.01
Philadelphia	39	0.14	5	0.048	0.032	264	0.81
Pittsburgh	21	0.13	4	0.078	0.029	133	0.08
Providence	11	0.12	6	0.037	0.025	62	n/a
Raleigh	24	0.12	7	n/a	n/a	59	0.00
Richmond	21	0.13	4	0.024	0.021	59	0.01
Rochester	6	0.10	2	0.050	n/a	47	n/a
Washington	31	0.14	7	0.024	0.026	54	0.02
NAAQS[3]	-	0.12	9	0.140	0.053	150	1.50

Note: (1) Metropolitan Statistical Area - see Appendix A for areas included; (2) Number of days the Pollutant Standards Index (PSI) exceeded 100 in 1997. A PSI value greater than 100 indicates that air quality would be in the unhealthful range on that day; (3) National Ambient Air Quality Standard; ppm = parts per million; ug/m^3 = micrograms per cubic meter; n/a not available
Source: EPA, National Air Quality and Emissions Trends Report, 1997

Water Quality

City	Tap Water
Akron	Alkaline, soft
Baltimore	Alkaline, very soft and fluoridated
Boston	The Metropolitan Water District (combined sources, Quabbin Reservoir and Wachusett Reservoir) supplies municipal Boston and the ABC City Zone. Water is soft and slightly acid
Charlotte	Alkaline, very soft and fluoridated
Cincinnati	Alkaline, hard and fluoridated
Cleveland	Alkaline, hard and fluoridated
Greensboro	Alkaline, soft
Lexington	Alkaline, medium and fluoridated
Louisville	Fluoridated
Manchester	Slightly acid, very soft
New York	New York City tap water has three major sources: the Catskills & Delaware subsytems (neutral, soft, average pH 7.0) and Croton subsystem (alkaline, moderately hard, average pH 7.1). All three supplies are fluoridated and chlorinated
Norfolk	Slightly soft, fluoridated and has low alkalinity
Philadelphia	Slightly acid, moderately hard (Schuykill River), moderately soft (Delaware River); fluoridated
Pittsburgh	Alkaline, soft 9 months, hard 3 months (June, July, August); fluoridated
Providence	Alkaline, very soft
Raleigh	Neutral, soft and fluoridated
Richmond	Alkaline, soft and fluoridated
Rochester	Neutral, soft
Washington	Slightly alkaline and medium soft

Source: Editor & Publisher Market Guide 1999

Appendix B

Metropolitan Statistical Areas

Akron, OH

Includes Portage and Summit Counties

Baltimore, MD

Includes Baltimore City; Anne Arundel, Baltimore, Carroll, Harford, Howard and Queen Anne's Counties

Boston, MA-NH

Includes parts of Bristol, Essex, Middlesex, Norfolk, Plymouth and Worcester Counties, MA; and all of Suffolk County, MA; Part of Rockhingham County, NH (as of 6/30/93)

Includes parts of Bristol, Essex, Middlesex, Norfolk, Plymouth and Worcester Counties; and all of Suffolk County (prior to 6/30/93)

Charlotte-Gastonia-Rock Hill, NC-SC

Includes Cabarrus, Gaston, Lincoln, Mcklenburg, Rowan and Union Counties, NC; York County, SC

Cincinnati, OH-KY-IN

Includes Brown, Clermont, Hamilton and Warren Counties, OH; Boone, Campbell, Gallatin, Grant, Kenton and Pendleton Counties, KY; Dearborn and Ohio Counties, IN (as of 6/30/93)

Includes Clermont, Hamilton and Warren Counties, OH; Boone, Campbell and Kenton Counties, KY; Dearborn County, IN (prior to 6/30/93)

Cleveland, OH

Includes Ashtabula, Cuyahoga, Geauga, Lake, Lrain and Medina Counties (as of 6/30/93)

Includes Cuyahoga, Geauga, Lake and Medina Counties (prior to 6/30/93)

Greensboro-Winston-Salem-High Point, NC

Includes Alamance, Davidson, Davie, Forsyth, Guilford, Randolph, Stokes and Yadkin Counties (as of 6/30/93)

Includes Davison, David, Forsyth, Guilford, Randolph, Stokes and Yadkin Counties (prior to 6/30/93)

Lexington, KY

Includes Bourbon, Clark, Fayette, Jessamine, Madison, Scott and Woodford Counties (as of 6/30/93)

Includes Bourbon, Clark, Fayette, Jessamine, Scott and Woodford Counties (prior to 6/30/93)

Louisville, KY

Includes Clark, Floyd, Harrison and Scott Counties, IN; Bullitt, Jefferson and Oldham Counties, KY

Manchester, NH

Includes Hillsborough, Merrimak and Rockingham Counties

New York, NY

Includes Bronx, Kings, New York, Putnam, Queens, Richmond, Rockland and Westchester Counties

Norfolk-Virginia Beach-Newport News, VA-NC

Includes Chesapeake, Hampton, Newport News, Norfolk, Poquoson, Portsmouth, Suffolk, Virginia Beach and Williamsburg Cities, VA; Gloucester, Isle of Wright, James City, Mathews and York Counties, VA; Currituck County, NC (as of 6/30/93)

Includes Chespeake, Hampton, Newsport News, Norfolk, Poquoson, Portsmouth, Suffolk, Virginia Beach and Williamsburg Cities; Gloucester, James City and York Counties (prior to 6/30/93)

Philadelphia, PA-NJ

Includes Bucks, Chester, Delaware, Montgomery and Philadelphia Counties, PA; Burlington, Camden, Gloucester and Salem Counties, NJ (as of 6/30/93)

Includes Bucks, Chester, Delaware, Montgomery and Philadelphia Counties, PA; Burlington, Camden and Gloucester Counties, NJ (prior to 6/30/93)

Pittsburgh, PA

Includes Allegheny, Beaver, Butler, Fayette, Washington and Westmoreland Counties (as of 6/30/93)

Includes Allegheny, Fayette, Washington and Westmoreland Counties (prior to 6/30/93)

Providence, RI

Includes Providence County

Raleigh-Durham-Chapel Hill, NC

Includes Chatham, Durham, Franklin, Johnston, Orange and Wake Counties (as of 6/30/93)

Includes Durham, Franklin, Orange and Wake Counties (prior to 6/30/93)

Richmond-Petersburg, VA

Includes Colonial Heights, Hopewell, Petersburg and Richmond Cities; Charles City, Chesterfield, Dinwiddie, Goochland, Hanover, Henrico, New Kent, Powhatan and Prince George Counties

Rochester, NY

Includes Genesee, Livingston, Monroe, Ontario, Orleans and Wayne Counties

Washington, DC-MD-VA-WV

Includes District of Columbia; Clavert, Charles, Frederick, Montgomery and Prince George Counties, MD; Alexandria, Fairvax, Falls Church, Fredericksburg, Manassas and Manassas Park Cities, and Arlington, Clarke, Culpepper, Fairfax, Fauquier, King George, Loudon, Prince William, Spotsylvania, Stafford and Warren Counties, VA; Berkeley and Jefferson Counties; WV (as of 6/30/93)

Includes District of Columbia; Calvert, Charles, Frederick, Montgomery and Prince George Counties; MD; Alexandria, Fairfax, Falls Church, Manassas and Manassas Park Cities, and Arlington, Fairfax, Loudoun, Prince William and Stafford Counties, VA (prior to 6/30/93)

Appendix C

Chambers of Commerce and Economic Development Organizations

Akron

Akron Chamber of Commerce
1 Cascade Plaza
8th Floor
Akron, OH 44308
Phone: (330) 376-5550
Fax: (33) 379-3164

Akron Economic Development Department
166 South High Street
Room 202
Akron, OH 44308
Phone: (330) 375-2133
Fax: (330) 375-2335

Baltimore

Baltimore City Chamber of Commerce
3 West Baltimore Street
Baltimore, MD 21202
Phone: (410) 837-7101
Fax: (410) 837-7104

City of Baltimore
Development Corporation
36 South Charles Street
Suite 1600
Baltimore, MD 21202
Phone: (410) 837-9305
Fax: (410) 837-6363

Boston

Greater Boston Chamber of Commerce
One Beacon Street
Boston, MA 02108
Phone: (617) 227-4500
Fax: (617) 227-7505

Charlotte

Charlotte Chamber of Commerce
P.O. Box 32785
Charlotte, NC 28232
Phone: (704) 378-1300
Fax: (704) 374-1903

Charlotte Region
Carolinas Partnership
112 South Tryon Street
Suite 900
Charlotte, NC 28284
Phone: (704) 347-8942
Fax: (704) 347-8981

Cincinnati

Department of Economic Development
Two Centennial Plaza
805 Central Avenue
Suite 710
Cincinnati, OH 45202
Phone: (513) 352-3950
Fax: (513) 352-6257

Greater Cincinnati Chamber of Commerce
Suite 300
441 Vine Street
Cincinnati, OH 45202
Phone: (513) 579-3100
Fax: (513) 579-3101

Greensboro

Greensboro Area Chamber of Commerce
P.O. Box 3246
Greensboro, NC 27402
Phone: (336) 275-8675
Fax: (910) 230-1867

Cleveland

Cleveland Department of Economic
Development
601 Lakeside Avenue
Cleveland, OH 44114-1015
Phone: (216) 664-2406
Fax: (216) 664-3681

Greater Cleveland Growth Association
200 Tower City Center
Cleveland, OH 44113
Phone: (216) 621-3300
Fax: (216) 621-6013

Lexington

City of Lexington
Mayor's Office of Economic Development
200 East Main Street
Lexington, KY 40507
Phone: (606) 258-3131
Fax: (606) 258-3194

Greater Lexington Chamber of Commerce
P.O. Box 1968
Lexington, KY 40588
Phone: (606) 254-4447
Fax: (606) 233-3304

Louisville

Louisville Chamber of Commerce
600 West Main Street
Louisville, KY 40202
Phone: (502) 625-0000
Fax: (502) 625-0010

Manchester

Manchester Chamber of Commerce
889 Elm Street
Manchester, NH 02101
Phone: (603) 666-6600
Fax: (603) 626-0910

Manchester Economice Development
Department Office
1 City Hall Plaza
Suite 110
Manchester, NH 03101
Phone: (603) 624-6505
Fax: (603) 624-6308

New York

New York City Chamber of Commerce
One Battery Park Plaza
New York, NY 10004-1479
Phone: (212) 493-7500
Fax: (212) 344-3344

New York City Economic Development
Corporation
110 William Street
New York, NY 10038
Phone: (212) 619-5009
Fax: (212) 312-3990

Norfolk

Hampton Roads Chamber of Commerce
420 Bank Street
P.O. Box 327
Norfolk, VA 23501
Phone: (757) 622-2312
Fax: (804) 622-5563

Philadelphia

Greater Philadelphia Chamber of Commerce
200 South Broad Street
Philadelphia, PA 19102-3896
Phone: (215) 545-1234
Fax: (215) 790-3600

Greater Philadelphia First
1818 Market Street
Suite 3150
Philadelphia, PA 19103-3681
Phone: (215) 565-2230
Fax: (215) 575-2222

Pittsburgh

Allegheny County Industrial Development
Authority
425 6th Avenue
Suite 800
Pittsburgh, PA 15219
Phone: (412) 350-1067
Fax: (412) 642-2217

Greater Pittsburgh Chamber of Commerce
Pittsburgh, PA 15210
Phone: (412) 392-4500
Fax: (412) 392-4520

Providence

Providence Chamber of Commerce
30 Exchange Terrace
Providence, RI
Phone: (401) 521-5000
Fax: (401) 751-2434

Providence Economic Development Department
City Hall
400 West Minister Street
Providence, RI 02902
Phone: (401) 421-7740
Fax: (401) 351-9533

Raleigh

Wake County Economic Development
P.O. Box 2978
800 South Salisbury Street
Raleigh, NC 27601-2978
Phone: (919) 856-6320

Richmond

Greater Richmond Chamber of Commerce
P.O. Box 12280
Richmond, VA 23241-2280
Phone: (804) 648-1234
Fax: (804) 780-0344

Greater Richmond Partnership
901 East Byrd Street
Suite 801
Richmond, VA 23219-4070
Phone: (804) 643-3227
Fax: (804) 343-7167

Rochester

Rochester Chamber of Commerce
55 St. Paul Street
Rochester, NY 14601
Phone: (716) 454-2220
Fax: (716) 263-3679

Rochester Economic Development Department
City of Rochester
30 Church Street
Room 005A
Rochester, NY 14614
Phone: (716) 428-6808
Fax: (716) 428-6042

Washington

District of Columbia Chamber of Commerce
1301 Pennsylvania Avenue Northwest
Suite 309
Washington, DC 20004
Phone: (202) 347-7201
Fax: (202) 638-6764

District of Columbia Office of Business &
Economic Development
441 4th Street Northwest
Washington, DC 20001
Phone: (202) 727-6365
Fax: (202) 757-6703

Appendix D

State Departments of Labor and Employment

District of Columbia

District of Columbia
Department of Employment Services
500 C Street Northwest
Washington, DC 20210
Phone: (202) 219-5257

Kentucky

Kentucky Department for Employment Services
Research & Statistics
P.O. Box 592
275 East Main Street
Frankfort, KY 40602
Phone: (502) 564-7046

Maryland

Maryland Department of Employment &
Training
Research & Analysis Division
1100 North Eutaw Street
Baltimore, MD 21201
Phone: (410) 767-2000

Massachusetts

Massachusetts Department of Employment &
Training
Hurley Building
19 Staniford Street
Boston, MA 02114
Phone: (617) 727-6560

New York

New York State Department of Labor
Division of Research & Statistics
State Office Campus
Building 12
Room 480
Albany, NY 12240
Phone: (518) 457-1130

North Carolina

Employment Security Commission
Labor Market
Information Division
P.O. Box 25903
Raleigh, NC 27611-5903
Phone: (919) 733-3098

Ohio

Ohio Bureau of Employment Services
Labor Market
Information Division
145 South Front Street
P.O. Box 1618
Columbus, OH 43216-1618
Phone: (614) 466-2100

Pennsylvania

Pennsylvania Department of Labor & Industry
102 Capital Associates Building
901 North 7th Street
Harrisburg, PA 17102
Phone: (717) 787-4895

Rhode Island

Rhode Island Department of Labor
Labor and Training
275 West Minister Street
Third Floor
Providence, RI 02903
Phone: (401) 222-3533

Vermont

Vermont Department of Labor
Labor Market Information
P.O. Box 488
Montpelier, VT 05602
Phone: (802) 828-4202

Virginia

Virginia Employment Commission
Economic Information Services
P.O. Box 1358
Richmond, VA 23218
Phone: (804) 786-1485